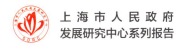

上海市人民政府
发展研究中心系列报告

VALUING OUR COMMUNITIES AND CITIES

提升社区和城市品质

联合国第七届世界城市日全球城市论坛实录

The Record of Global Cities Forum
on the Seventh UN World Cities Day

上海市人民政府发展研究中心 编

EDITOR
The Development Research Center
of Shanghai Municipal People's Government

格致出版社　上海人民出版社

主　编　　　Chief Editor
祁　彦　　　　Qi Yan

副主编　　　Subeditor
周国平　　　　Zhou Guoping
严　军　　　　Yan Jun
徐　净　　　　Xu Zheng

编　辑　　　Editing Team
（按姓氏拼音排列）　(in alphabetical order)

柴　慧	Chai Hui	吴苏贵	Wu Sugui
陈　畅	Chen Chang	吴也白	Wu Yebai
陈群民	Chen Qunmin	徐　婷	Xu Ting
陈　蓉	Chen Rong	向明勋	Xiang Mingxun
陈伟青	Chen Weiqing	姚　治	Yao Zhi
樊　星	Fan Xing	余艺贝	Yu Yibei
高　骞	Gao Qian	张黄付	Zhang Huangfu
高炜宇	Gao Weiyu	张明海	Zhang Minghai
高　瑛	Gao Ying	张义春	Zhang Yichun
谷　金	Gu Jin	赵露露	Zhao Lulu
黄佳金	Huang Jiajin	赵欣冉	Zhao Xinran
黄玉抒	Huang Yushu	钟灵啸	Zhong Lingxiao
江海苗	Jiang Haimiao	周师迅	Zhou Shixun
李敏乐	Li Minle	朱惠涵	Zhu Huihan
李司东	Li Sidong	朱　咏	Zhu Yong
李银雪	Li Yinxue		
梁绍连	Liang Shaolian		
刘　钢	Liu Gang		
娄蓉媛	Lou Rongyuan		
陆丽萍	Lu Liping		
吕　朋	Lv Peng		
倪颖越	Ni Yingyue		
潘春来	Pan Chunlai		
彭　颖	Peng Ying		
钱　洁	Qian Jie		
钱　智	Qian Zhi		
邱鸣华	Qiu Minghua		
史晓琛	Shi Xiaochen		
宋　奇	Song Qi		
宋　清	Song Qing		
宋　珊	Song Shan		
谭　旻	Tan Min		
王　丹	Wang Dan		
王　帆	Wang Fan		
王斐然	Wang Feiran		
王培力	Wang Peili		

PREFACE I

序一

2020年以来，新冠肺炎疫情与百年变局交织。各国城市和社区也遭遇了疫情的巨大挑战。众所周知，城市是让生活更美好的重要空间，而能够满足人民群众日益增长的美好生活需要的一定是高品质的城市和社区，它们能够提供丰富优质的公共服务、宜居宜业的城市环境，健康安全的社区空间。上海在"人民城市"重要理念指导下，持续推动精细化管理、基层治理创新、生活垃圾分类等工作，正朝着建设高品质宜居、宜业社区环境的目标而努力。

2020年10月31日至11月1日，以"提升社区和城市品质"为主题的2020全球城市论坛在上海交通大学举行，上海市人民政府发展研究中心、上海市住房和城乡建设管理委员会、上海市应急管理局、上海交通大学、联合国人居署和世界银行等机构的领导，以及来自全球20余个国家和地区的著名高校和学术研究院机构的专家学者、媒体代表和高校师生等400余人，通过线上、线下相结合的形式参会。论坛上，世界各地的专家学者重点围绕新兴技术与协同治理、宜居城市、未来社区、城市应急管理、经济内循环背景下的城市文旅融合与发展、长三角公园城市发展、生态园林城区等议题，讨论交流提升社区和城市品质的相关研究。

为了让本次论坛众多宏大主题的深邃洞见和由己而发的现实思索流传开来，上海市人民政府发展研究中心将参会嘉宾的演讲内容整理成文，由格致出版社结集出版，《提升社区和城市品质——联合国第七届世界城市日全球城市论坛实录》一书的框架结构大致遵循论坛的议程安排，内容方面基本上以与会嘉宾的发言内容为准。相信本书的出版能够让读者感受到世界各地专家学者在论坛上思想的碰撞、智慧的交流和情谊的结识，群策群力，进一步推动互利合作，一起努力创造一个更加美好的未来。

是为序。

上海交通大学中国城市治理研究院院务委员会主任、院长

Since 2020, the world has faced the pandemic outbreak of a century and changes in the global development unseen in a century. Cities and communities in various countries have been hit by COVID-19. As we all know, a city is a desired space for a better life, so urban communities must meet the growing needs of their citizens and be able to provide wide-ranging and high-quality public services and a resident and business-friendly urban environment which is safe and healthy. Following the concept that cities should serve the people well, Shanghai continues to refine its urban management, encourage innovations in community governance, and promote household waste sorting, and is working towards the goal of building high-quality livable and business-friendly communities.

From October 31 to November 1, 2020, the 2020 Global Cities Forum "Valuing Our Communities and Cities" was held at Shanghai Jiao Tong University. Over 400 people participated in the Forum online and online, including officals, experts and scholars from the Development Research Center of Shanghai Municipal People's Government, Shanghai Municipal Commission of Housing and Urban-Rural Development, Shanghai Emergency Management Bureau, Shanghai Jiao Tong University, UN-Habitat and the World Bank, as well as media representatives and teachers and students from well-known universities and academic institutes of more than 20 countries and regions around the world. At the forum and its panel sessions and workshops, their discussions focused on emerging technologies and coordinated governance, livable cities, future communities, urban emergency management, the integration of urban tourism and culture, especially when China drives domestic economic circulation, and development of garden cities and garden districts in the

Yangtze River Delta, which all bear on the improvement of the living space for people.

In order to spread the profound insights of this forum and the practical innovations it has triggered, the Development Research Center of Shanghai Municipal People's Government has recorded the speeches of the participants and transformed them into bilingual texts which have been compiled and published in a book Global Cities: Enhancing Communities and Cities — A Collection of Presentations at the Global Cities Forum on the 7th World City Day. The structure of this book is based on the agenda of the Forum, reflecting the speeches of participants. It is hoped that this book will allow more people to experience the exchange of innovative ideas as well as friendship between experts and scholars from all over the world at the Forum.

Jiang Sixian

Dean, Shanghai Jiao Tong University China Institute for Urban Governance

PREFACE II

序二

    城市是人类生活的重要空间，城市治理的水平关乎人民群众的生活品质。社区连着千家万户，是社会的基本单元，也是城市治理的"最后一公里"，对于提高城市治理现代化水平具有基础性、决定性作用。进入新时代以来，人民对美好生活的需要不断增长，对物质文化、民主法治、安全环境等方面提出了更高期待，对城市品质提出了更高要求，并不断投射到社区层面。为此，以习近平同志为核心的党中央以最广大人民根本利益为根本坐标，不断创新社会治理理念思路、体制机制、方法手段，明确提出要打造共建共治共享的社会治理格局，并强调夯实基层基础，加强社区体系建设，推动社会治理重心向基层下移。从全球范围来看，全球城市治理也日趋呈现出回归"以人为本"、强调社区治理、以数字技术驱动创新的新趋势。特别在全球疫情蔓延的背景下，如何保障城市安全，如何更好地发挥社区的作用与价值更是成为全球共同关注的焦点。全球城市是人流、物流、信息流和资本流交互最密集、最核心的枢纽节点，具有丰富的治理场景、社区和城市品质提升经验，同时也首当其冲地面临新形势、新技术等对传统社区治理模式的挑战，亟待进一步完善交流合作平台，分享治理经验和创新做法，为城市发展与治理提供新思路、新方案。

    2020 年 11 月 1 日，以"提升社区和城市品质"为主题的 2020 全球城市论坛在上海交通大学徐汇校区隆重举行。作为"世界城市日"的主题活动之一，本届全球城市论坛是自 2014 年联合国首届"世界城市日"活动举办以来的第七届，由上海市人民政府发展研究中心、上海市住房和城乡建设管理委员会、上海市应急管理局、上海交通大学、联合国人居署和世界银行共同主办，上海交通大学中国城市治理研究院、上海交通大学国际与公共事务学院、上海世界城市日事务协调中心、上海交通大学应急管理学院、上海交通大学国际应急治理研究院共同承办。本届全球城市论坛邀请了来自中国、美国、法国、英国、日本、韩国、澳大利亚、新加坡、加拿大、丹麦和中国香港等国家和地区社区发展相关领域的学界、政界和业界嘉宾，聚焦新兴技术、宜居城市、未来社区、文化形象等领域，共同探讨城市发展的新机遇、新挑战、新样态，社区治理的新思维、新方案和新举措，为全球城市的持续发展提供新洞见。

展现在读者面前的这本《提升社区和城市品质——联合国第七届世界城市日全球城市论坛实录》，生动再现了该届论坛现场的交流盛况，翔实记录了与会嘉宾的演讲内容，详细总结了全球城市社区发展与治理的先进经验，对上海、中国乃至世界的社区治理与发展具有重要的借鉴意义。

2020年是新中国历史上极不平凡的一年。面对极其艰难的国内外各种挑战，中国在全球率先控制住疫情，率先恢复经济社会发展，有力彰显了中国国家制度和国家治理体系的优越性，充分展现了中国的现代化治理水平。近年来，上海按照习近平总书记"城市管理应该像绣花一样精细"的要求，对标最高标准、最好水平，在推进超大城市精细化治理、完善共建共治共享社区治理格局方面积累了一系列有益经验。未来，在"人民城市人民建，人民城市为人民"重要理念的引领下，上海应在总结以往经验的基础上，进一步加大创新力度，充分汲取全球城市先进经验，特别是在强化社区治理、提升城市品质、依托数字化手段创新治理方式上的智慧，在细微处下功夫、见成效，进一步提升社区治理规范化、精细化、现代化水平。让我们共同期待上海持之以恒、精益求精，在汇集全球经验、凝聚共同智慧的基础上，探索提升社区和城市品质的创新之路，推进全球城市可持续发展，使"城市，让生活更美好"的共同愿景变为现实！

是为序。

上海市人民政府发展研究中心主任

The city is a major living space for human beings, so urban governance is crucial to the quality of people's lives. The governance of communities, which are the primary level of our society, is a key link of urban governance, and good community governance plays fundamental and decisive role in optimizing urban governance. In the new era, people have a stronger desire for a better life and their needs for material abundance, democracy, rule of law, security, and a better environment are growing, which can be always seen at the community level. Therefore, the CPC Central Committee with Comrade Xi Jinping at the core welcomes and embraces innovative ideas, systems, mechanisms, methods and tools to improve social governance and meet people's needs. It has been made clear that a social governance system based on collaboration, participation and common interests will be established, with priority given to improving primary-level governance and shifting the focus of social governance to communities. Globally, urban governance is showing a tendency toward people-centered and digitalized community management. When COVID-19 is still ravaging the world, it has become an issue of common concern to all people around the world how the safety of cities can be ensured and communities can play a bigger role.

Cities are hubs where logistics, information and capital come together to support people's wellbeing. Their interactions create urban governance scenarios and bear on then improvement of communities and cities. At the same time, cities would witness challenges posed by new developments and technologies to traditional community governance models. They will upgrade the platforms for exchanges and cooperation through which best and innovative governance practices will be shared and new ideas and schemes for urban development and governance generated.

On November 1, 2020, the 2020 Global Cities Forum themed on "Valuing our Communities and Cities" was held at the Xuhui Campus of Shanghai Jiao Tong University. As a theme event of World Cities Day, this annual Forum has been held eight years since the first World Cities Day was announced in 2014 by the United Nations. It was jointly hosted by the Development Research Center of Shanghai Municipal People's Government, Shanghai Municipal Commission of Housing and Urban-Rural Development, Shanghai Emergency Management Bureau, Shanghai Jiao Tong University, UN-Habitat and the World Bank, implemented by China Institute for Urban Governance and School of International and Public Affairs of Shanghai Jiao

Tong University, Shanghai Focal Point for World Cities Day, School of Emergency Management, and Emergency Management Research Instituteof Shanghai Jiao Tong University. At this Forum, we had the privilege of the presence of distinguished experts and scholars from the academia, governments and industry from various countries and regions like China, the United States, France, Britain, Japan, Korea, Australia, Singapore, Canada, Denmark, and Hong Kong Special Administrative Region of China. Focusing on emerging technologies, livable cities, future communities, and cultural images, the participants discussed opportunities, challenges and new forms of urban development. They also shared new ideas, schemes and measures of community governance to improve the sustainable development of cities across the world.

This *Valuing our Communities and Cities—The Record of the Global Cities Forum on the Seventh UN World Cities Day* reproduces vividly the pageant of ideas at the forum, documents the speeches delivered by the participants, and presents the best practices of development and governance of urban communities around the world. It is a hallmark of community governance and development for Shanghai, China, and even the whole world.

The year 2020 was an extraordinary year in the history of the People's Republic of China. Facing the major domestic and international challenges, China managed to recover from the COVID-19 pandemic ahead of the world, which demonstrates the merits of China's governance system, and fully displays China's governance capability. In recent years, in accordance with General Secretary Xi Jinping's requirement that urban management should be as careful as making embroidery, Shanghai has developed and implemented high-standard initiatives and has gained useful experience in improving the governance of a megacity and improving community governance based on collaboration, participation, and common interests. In the future, under the guidance of the concept of "cities built by the people and for the people", Shanghai will further innovations by learning from past lessons and successes of other cities in the world, especially the wisdom of other cities in enhancing community governance, boosting urban development, promoting governance innovations with the help of digital tools. We will focus on details and try to further standardize, refine and modernize our community governance. Let's look forward to Shanghai's action to improve and excellence in community and urban governance, and let's contribute to the sustainable development of cities by pooling global experience and collective wisdom. Shanghai will make the common dream of "Better City, Better Life" come true.

Qi Yan

Director, Development Research Center of

Shanghai Municipal People's Government

出席联合国第七届世界城市日全球城市论坛的中外嘉宾合影

The group photo of domestic and foreign guests attending 2020 Global Cities Forum on the Seventh UN World Cities Day

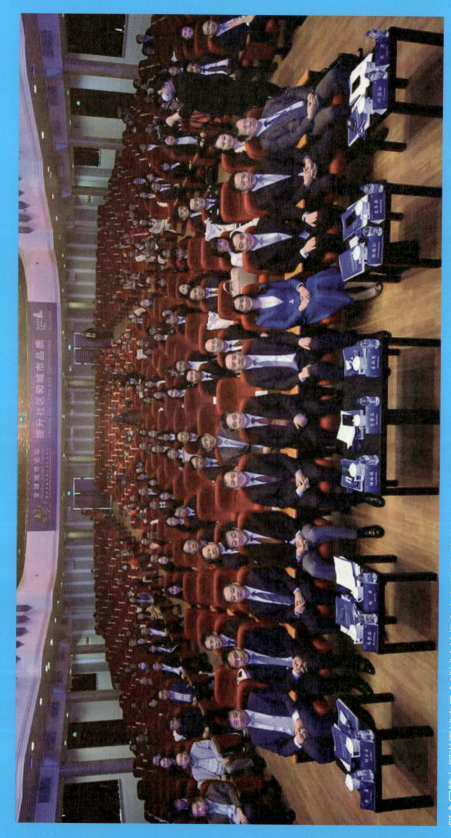

联合国第七届世界城市日全球城市论坛在上海交通大学徐汇校区（上海）隆重举行

2020 Global Cities Forum on the Seventh UN World Cities Day is solemnly held in Shanghai Jiao Tong University Xuhui Campus

首届 "上海城市治理最佳实践案例评选" 最佳案例

上海交通大学中国城市治理研究院院长姜斯宪、上海市住建委副主任金晨，上海市人民政府发展研究中心党组成员、二级巡视员徐净，人民日报社上海分社社长刘士安、上海交通大学党委副书记周承为首届"上海城市治理最佳实践案例"最佳案例颁奖

Jiang Sixian, President of China Institute for Urban Governance, SJTU, Jin Chen, Vice Director of Shanghai Municipal People's Commission of Housing and Urban-rural Development and Management, Xu Zheng, Member of the Party group and second level inspector of the development research center of Shanghai Municipal People's Government, Liu Shian, President of Shanghai Branch of People's Daily and Zhou Cheng, Deputy Secretary of the Party committee of Shanghai Jiaotong University present awards to winners of best cases of the first "Best practice case of urban governance in Shanghai"

上海交通大学国际与公共事务学院代理院长胡近、上海交通大学中国城市治理研究院常务副院长吴建南、上海交通大学中国城市治理研究院副院长徐剑、人民网上海频道总经理金煜纯为首届"上海城市治理最佳实践案例"优秀案例颁奖

Hu Jin, Acting Dean, School of international and public affairs, Shanghai Jiaotong University, Wu Jiannan, Executive vice president of China Urban Governance Research Institute, Shanghai Jiaotong University, Xu Jian, Vice president of China Urban Governance Research Institute, Shanghai Jiaotong University and Jin Yuchun, General manager of Shanghai channel of people's network present awards to winners of excellent cases of the first "Best practice case of urban governance in Shanghai"

上海交通大学党委书记杨振斌为第六届全国大学生城市治理案例挑战大赛（2020）获得一等奖团队颁奖

Yang Zhenbin, Secretary, The CPC Committee, SJTU present awards to the first prize winners of the sixth Collegiate Urban Governance Case Challenge Competition (2020)

上海市住建委副主任金晨、上海交通大学中国城市治理研究院副院长陈际宏、上海交通大学中国城市治理研究院院长张录法共同发布新书《世界城市日活动成果精粹·2019》《中英文版》、《探索城市善治：城市治理的徐汇实践》《像绣花一样精细》《探索城市善治：理论反思与国际实践》

Jin Chen, Vice Director of Shanghai Municipal People's Commission of Housing and Urban-rural Development and Management, Chen Gaohong, Vice president of China Urban Governance Research Institute, Shanghai Jiaotong University and Zhang Lufa, Vice president of China Urban Governance Research Institute, Shanghai Jiaotong University jointly release new books *Selected Speeches of 2019 World Cities Day Events* (Chinese and English versions), *Urban Practices from Delicacy Management to Governance in Contemporary China: The Case of Xuhui District, Shanghai* (English versions), *The Quest for Good Urban Governance: Theoretical Reflections and International Practices*

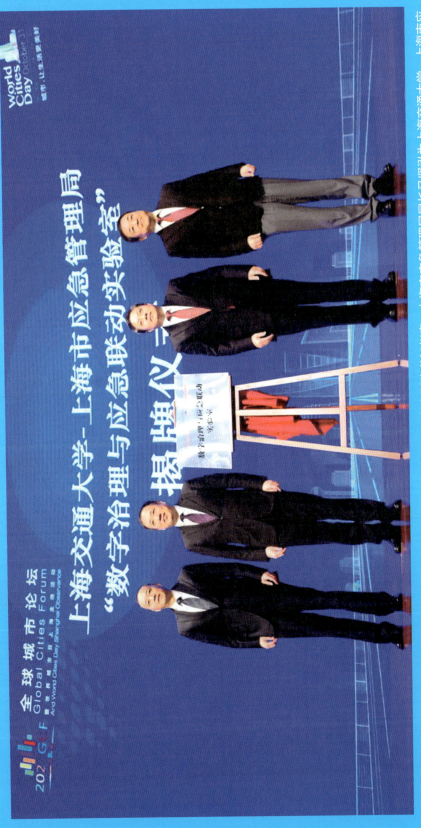

上海市人大常委会副主任肖贵玉、上海交通大学党委书记杨振斌、上海市委市府副秘书长赵奇、上海市应急管理局局长马坚泓为上海交通大学—上海市应急管理局"数字治理与应急联动实验室"揭牌

Xiao Guiyu, Vice Director, The Standing Committee of Shanghai Municipal People's Congress, Yang Zhenbin, Secretary, The CPC Committee, SJTU, Zhao Qi, Vice Secretary, Shanghai Municipal People's Government and Ma Jianhong, Director of Shanghai Emergency Management Bureau unveil Shanghai Jiao Tong University — Shanghai Emergency Management Bureau Joint Laboratory in Digital Governance and Emergency Collaboration

CONTENTS
目 录

OPENING ADDRESSES

KEYNOTE SPEECHES

PARALLEL FORUMS

FORUM   New Technologies and Coordinative Governance

FORUM Liveable Cities

FORUM Future Communities

POSTSCRIPT

OPENING ADDRESSES

开幕致辞

上海市人大常委会副主任肖贵玉在 2020 全球城市论坛开幕式上致辞

Xiao Guiyu, Vice Director, The Standing Committee of Shanghai Municipal People's Congress addresses at the opening ceremony of 2020 Global Cities Forum

上海交通大学党委书记杨振斌在 2020 全球城市论坛开幕式上致辞

Yang Zhenbin, Secretary, The CPC Committee, SJTU addresses at
the opening ceremony of 2020 Global Cities Forum

上海市委副秘书长、市政府副秘书长、市委政法委副书记、市城市运行管理中心主任
赵奇在 2020 全球城市论坛开幕式上致辞

Zhao Qi, Vice Secretary, Shanghai Municipal People's Government
addresses at the opening ceremony of 2020 Global Cities Forum

上海交通大学国际与公共事务学院党委书记、中国城市治理研究院党支部书记
姜文宁主持 2020 全球城市论坛开幕式

Jiang Wenning, Secretary, The CPC Committee, School of
International and Public Affairs; Secretary, The CPC Committee,
China Institute for Urban Governance, SJTU hosts the opening
ceremony of 2020 Global Cities Forum

致辞——

肖贵玉

上海市人大常委会副主任

1. 全球城市论坛与中国城市治理研究院之间的紧密联系

今年是我第二次参加全球城市论坛，第一次是在 2016 年上海交通大学首次承办全球城市论坛时，担任开幕式主持人，并参与上海交通大学中国城市治理研究院揭牌仪式。上海交通大学是一所历史悠久的著名学府，具有雄厚的多学科研究优势并拥有一批具有国际声望的专家学者，多项研究成果位居世界前列。上海交通大学在服务上海经济社会发展中与上海市政府各部门紧密合作，形成了一批极具价值的科研成果，为上海发展提供了有力的支持。在上海市政府的支持下，在学校的积极推动下，在姜斯宪院长的带领下，中国城市治理研究院充分发挥高校学者专业智慧，充分对接政府城市治理实际需求，成立四年来取得了丰硕的成果。研究院主编的《决策参考》为城市治理提供了许多真知灼见。同时，学院专家学者们提出的政策建议也在城市治理中发挥着越来越大的作用和影响。

2. 新冠肺炎疫情下的全球城市论坛

新冠肺炎疫情的发生一定程度上阻碍了全球的国际交往，但人类永远是一个休戚与共的命运共同体。在当前的特殊环境下，本届全球城市论坛通过线上线下互动，集聚了来自中国、美国、法国、英国、日本、韩国、澳大利亚、新加坡、加拿大、丹麦和中国香港等国家和地区，以及联合国、世界银行等国际组织的学界、政界、业界的嘉宾，参会人数远超往届，充分彰显了全球城市加强合作、携手攻克疫情难关的强烈愿望。

2020 年世界城市日的主题是"提升社区和城市品质"。众所周知，城市是让生活更美好的重要空间。要满足人民日益增长的美好生活需要，就必须建设高品质的城市和社区，提供优质的公共服务、宜居的生活环境、健康安全的生活空间等等。上海作为超大型城市，在"人民城市人民建，人民城市为人民"的重要理念指导下，一直在城市发展的治理中追求高品质。

近年来全市上下持续推动的生活垃圾分类、精细化管理、基层治理创新等都是在朝着建设高品质、宜居、宜业社区环境的目标而努力。

3. 结语

当前，面对百年未有之大变局，面对全球治理难题和城市发展困境，更需要全体国际和国内同仁充分沟通、密切合作、共克时艰。这次论坛充分证明疫情阻隔不了思想的碰撞、智慧的交流和情谊的结识，希望各位与会嘉宾能借助此次全球城市论坛，围绕提升社区和城市品质这一主题畅所欲言，献计献策，进一步推动互利合作，一起努力创造一个更加美好的未来。

致辞二

杨振斌

上海交通大学党委书记

全球城市论坛由上海市人民政府发展研究中心、上海市住房和城乡建设管理委员会、上海交通大学、联合国人居署和世界银行共同主办，在各方支持下已经连续举办了七届。本届又有上海市应急管理局共襄盛会，可见全球城市论坛共同体每年都在壮大发展。上海交通大学中国城市治理研究院自 2016 年承办全球城市论坛以来，一直在思考谋划，如何将全球城市论坛打造成"世界城市日"系列主题活动中的品牌活动，使之得到更多关注。从新华网相关报道的浏览量累计过千万来看，全球城市论坛的影响力已越来越大。在 2020 年全球遭遇新冠肺炎疫情挑战的特殊时期，如何适配特殊背景和特殊困难，使论坛常办常新，是 2020 年论坛的一大挑战。通过与上海市人民政府发展研究中心、上海市住房和城乡建设管理委员会等主办方密切沟通和协商，本届论坛采取线上线下相结合的方式，共同探讨世界各国城市面临的共同议题，分享关于社区和城市的思考。

1. 上海交通大学的历史沿革

本次主论坛会场位于上海交通大学徐汇校区的文治讲堂，我简单介绍一下上海交通大学。上海交通大学历史悠久，是中国官方定义上最早成立的现代高校之一。1896 年，盛宣怀先生奏请清政府创建了南洋公学，即后来的交通大学。在 124 年发展历程中，上海交通大学为国家发展做出了巨大贡献。上海交通大学原是一所综合性学校，1952 年院系调整后，上海交通大学将很多专业分出，帮助兄弟高校恢复学科，创办了专门的工科性大学。尤其在 1956 年，上海交通大学将相当一部分院系西迁到西安，形成了现在的西安交通大学，体现了习近平总书记前几个月表彰的"西迁精神"。可以说，上海交通大学、西安交通大学、台湾新竹交通大学都是从徐汇校区走出来的，只不过西安交通大学和上海交通大学是一棵树上分出的两条枝，新竹交通大学则是一批交通大学校友到台湾后创办的，三所学校都同根同源。

进入改革开放时代，早在中美尚未建交时，上海交通大学便派出了第一个赴美代表团。

代表团在美国进行了长时间的参观、学习、考察，对上海交通大学的发展，乃至中国高等教育的发展发挥了重要的作用。整个 80 年代，上海交通大学一直引领中国高等教育的改革和发展，多项改革措施曾被写入国务院政府工作报告当中。经过几十年的发展，上海交通大学成为一所国内学科排名比较靠前、成长比较迅速的高校。相信有在座各位专家的支持，上海交通大学在未来将取得更好更快的发展。

2. 上海交通大学与城市治理

我曾在北京、厦门、长春等地工作学习过，深刻感受到了中国城市化的高速发展。特别是改革开放 40 多年以来，中国步入大转折时期，人口和经济向大城市群集聚的程度越来越高，创新引领产业结构调整和经济转型，空间均衡理念逐渐成为城市发展的主线，高质量发展为本的主流观念不断充实城市发展的内涵。来到上海交通大学工作后，我深刻体会到上海作为中国，乃至世界各大城市的典型代表，拥有先进的城市治理经验。上海交通大学如何落实体现习近平总书记提出的"人民城市人民建"精神，发挥综合性高校的文、理、医、工、农多学科优势，进而辅助城市治理，是需要一直思考并努力解决的问题。

在上海市政府的大力支持下，中国城市治理研究院在上海交通大学诞生，成为研究城市治理问题的平台。成立四年来，研究院在上海市各级领导的关心支持下，在咨政建言、学术期刊、数据中心、课题研究、跨学科平台等方面取得了卓越的成绩和进展，先后入选中国智库索引、全国高校智库百强榜、上海高校重点智库等榜单。研究院打破了学校围墙内外的知识壁垒，协调了象牙塔和大熔炉之间的步调。未来，研究院将继续系统挖掘、总结上海的城市治理经验，将健康、生态、应急管理等方面融入城市全生命周期管理，强化校企合作、理论研究和咨政启民，努力使理论和政策创新符合中国实际、具有中国特色、形成上海品牌。

3. 结语

全球城市论坛长期由上海交通大学承办，希望能借此平台对外进 步推动国际学术交流，讲好中国城市治理的故事，唱响中国城市治理的声音；对内引进国际城市治理的先进经验，吸引国际一流城市的治理人才、机构和组织汇聚上海，让全球城市论坛发挥新的作用、做出更大贡献。

致辞三

赵 奇

上海市委副秘书长、市政府副秘书长、市委政法委副书记、市城市运行管理中心主任

21 世纪是城市的世纪，随着城镇化的发展，城市治理问题日益凸显。城市治理中的焦点和难点严重影响了人民生活质量和政府公信力，引起了国内外各界人士的高度关注。结合本次论坛的主题"提升城市和社区品质"，我将简要介绍上海近年来围绕新技术赋能城市和社区所做的工作和对未来的思考。

随着城市发展规模越来越大、人口越来越多、经济社会的活动越来越复杂，城市在创造效率、创造财富的同时，也产生了诸多不均衡、不协调的问题。中国在历经 40 多年高速城镇化后，正在进入一个迫切需要城市治理的新时代。而增强城市治理能力，必须从创新技术手段上下功夫，这也是实现城市治理现代化的牛鼻子。

1. 上海依托创新技术手段，实现城市治理现代化

近年来，上海认真学习贯彻习近平总书记重要讲话精神，抓好政务服务"一网通办"，城市运行"一网统管"，坚持从群众需求和城市治理突出问题出发，采用更多先进技术把人从繁杂的基础工作当中解放出来，把分散型的信息系统进行有机的梳理整合，做到实战中管用、基层干部爱用、群众感到受用。经过两年多时间的推进，政府部门通过数据多跑路、百姓少跑腿，把困难留在后台、便利留在平台，把复杂留在后台、简单留在前台，大大提升了群众和企业的满意度。老百姓和企业到政府部门办事更加方便快捷，切实感受到线下窗口有温度、线上"一网"有速度。据统计，上海实行"一网通办"以来，办事时间总体减少了60%，材料总体减少了52.9%，好评率达到了99.7%。这些城市治理现代化的探索是新时代上海"互联网＋政务服务"改革的新名片，跑出了优化营商环境的加速度。

2. 上海打造智能社区，实现城市治理现代化

社区是城市运行的底盘，也是城市治理的基本单元，然而传统的社区管理难以顺应超大城市日益复杂、高速流动、多元意志的发展态势。上海在全国率先推进城市精细化管理，将新技术应用深入到社区，通过智能社区建设提升社会管理精细化水平和智能化水平。在这次抗击新冠肺炎疫情的过程中，全市 6 000 多个村、居委会，1.3 万个住宅小区，20 多万基层一线工作人员借助信息网络服务、AI 语音外呼系统等新技术新手段各司其职、同向发力，根据不同居住特点分类加强疫情防控，切实担负起管好门、看好人的重任。我们要及时总结经验，不断提高城市治理现代化水平，让市民过上更好的日子，增进居民对社区的认同感与归属感，进而提升城市向心力与凝聚力。

3. 上海交通大学为城市治理现代化贡献力量

上海交通大学是中国顶尖高校之一，为上海的经济社会发展做出了重要贡献。中国城市治理研究院近年来在超大城市治理领域开展了诸多研究和探索，相关的咨政建言成果得到了国家和市领导的高度肯定。2020 年，上海市应急管理局与上海交通大学共建了应急管理学院，双方将为联合建设的数字治理与应急联动实验室举行揭牌仪式。这些新的平台、新的机构一定能创造出更多政、产、学、研、用紧密结合的城市治理创新成果，为上海、中国乃至全球的城市治理现代化提供更多智慧和力量。

Address I

Xiao Guiyu

Vice Director of the Standing Committee of Shanghai Municipal People's Congress

1. Close relations between the Global Cities Forum and China Institute for Urban Governance (CIUG)

It is the second time for me to attend the Global Cities Forum. The first time was in 2016 when Shanghai Jiao Tong University (SJTU) hosted the Forum for the first time in its history. I was the host of that opening ceremony and a witness of the inauguration ceremony of China Institute for Urban Governance (CIUG). SJTU is a prestigious university with a long history. It is known for its advantages in multidisciplinary research and the excellence of its world-renowned experts and scholars. Many of its research achievements rank top in the world. In serving the economic and social development of Shanghai, SJTU has been working closely with Shanghai Municipal People's Government agencies and has produced a number of valuable scientific research in strong support of the development of Shanghai. With full backing from the Shanghai Municipal People's Government and from SJTU, and led by the Dean Jiang Sixian, CIUG has given full play to the professional wisdom of its scholars and has worked hard to meet the actual needs of the government in terms of urban governance. A number of achievements have been made. For instance, *Decision-making Reference*, a journal edited by CIUG, has provided invaluable insights for urban governance. At the same time, policy proposals made by the experts and scholars of CIUG have also played an increasingly important role in Shanghai's urban governance.

2. Global Cities Forum under the COVID-19

The outbreak of COVID-19 has, to some extent, hindered international exchanges, but mankind will always be a community with a shared future. At this unique time, this year's Forum has drawn people from many countries and regions including China, America, France, Britain, Japan, Korea, Australia, Singapore, Canada, Denmark and Hong Kong, China, and from international organizations including the United Nations and the World Bank to participate, either in person or via remote meetings. The number of participants far exceeds that of previous sessions, which demonstrates the strong aspirations of cities worldwide to strengthen cooperation and to work together to overcome the pandemic.

The theme of this year's World Cities Day is "Valuing Our Communities and Cities". As we all know, cities play a vital role in making people's lives better. To meet people's ever-growing needs for a better life, we must build high-quality cities and communities, provide quality public services, livable environment, and healthy and safe living space. Shanghai, as a megacity, has been continuously improving urban governance, guided by the idea of "building the city by its people and for its people". In recent years, Shanghai has been working hard to meet the goal of building high quality communities for people to live and work in, through the initiatives such as waste sorting, targeted management reform, and primary-level governance innovation.

3. Conclusion

At present, in the face of profound changes unseen in a century, and confronted by the problems in global governance and urban development, it is all the more important for us all to fully communicate and cooperate with each other to overcome the difficulties together. This Forum has fully proved that the pandemic cannot prevent the exchanges of ideas and wisdom and friendship building. I hope all participants can use this Forum to contribute their opinions and advice on how to improve the quality of communities and cities, so as to further promote mutually beneficial cooperation and work together to create a better future.

Address II

Yang Zhenbin

CPC Committee Secretary of Shanghai Jiao Tong University

The Global Cities Forum is jointly hosted by the Development Research Center of Shanghai Municipal People's Government, Shanghai Municipal Commission of Housing and Urban-Rural Development, Shanghai Jiao Tong University, the United Nations Human Settlements Programme (UN-Habitat), and the World Bank. It has been held for seven consecutive sessions, thanks to the support of all parties. This year, we were joined by a new host, the Shanghai Emergency Management Bureau. This is evidence of the growing influence of the community represented by the Forum. As the organizer of the Global Cities Forum since 2016, China Institute for Urban Governance (CIUG) at Shanghai Jiao Tong University has been working to make this Forum a hallmark among the series of events of the World Cities Day, and has managed to garner increasing attention. According to Xinhuanet, the Global Cities Forum has accumulated more than 10 million page views, showing the Forum's increasing influence. The world has been in tight grip of the COVID-19 pandemic since 2020. At this unique time, how to rise up to the challenge of the day and keep the Forum up to date has become a major challenge for the organizers. After communication and consultation with the Development Research Center of Shanghai Municipal People's Government, Shanghai Municipal Commission of Housing and Urban-Rural Development and other organizers, CIUG decided to hold this year's Forum both online and offline, to facilitate the discussions of issues shared by cities around the world and the exchange of ideas about communities and cities.

1. The history of Shanghai Jiao Tong University

The main forum venue is located within the Wenzhi Hall of Xuhui Campus of Shanghai Jiao Tong University (SJTU). Please allow me to give you a brief introduction of this university. SJTU has a long history and is officially described as one of the oldest modern universities in China. In 1896,

Mr. Sheng Xuanhuai, after gaining the approval from the Qing imperial government, established the Nanyang Public School, which later evolved into Jiao Tong University. Over the past 124 years, SJTU has made great contributions to China's development. SJTU was originally a comprehensive university. In 1952, as China's higher education system went through restructuring, many SJTU departments were relocated to other universities to help them restore their disciplines and establish specialized universities for engineering. In 1956, SJTU relocated a large number of departments to Xi'an, which formed into what is the present-day Xi'an Jiaotong University (XJTU). President Xi Jinping spoke highly of the spirit of westward academic migration represented by SJTU faculty a few months ago. It is fair to say that Shanghai Jiao Tong University, Xi'an Jiao Tong University and National Chiao Tung University are all derived from the Xuhui campus. The only difference is that XJTU and SJTU are like two branches growing on the same tree, whereas NCTU was founded by a group of alumni of Jiao Tong University after they moved to Taiwan. The three universities essentially share the same genes.

When China entered the new era of reform and opening up, SJTU sent its first Chinese delegation to the United States even before the diplomatic relations between China and the U.S. were established. The delegation spent a long time visiting, studying and learning from America's education system, which contributed tremendously to the development of SJTU and even that of China's higher education. Throughout the 1980s, SJTU led China's reform and development of higher education. Many of its reform measures were written into the Reports on the Work of the Government of the State Council. After decades of development, SJTU has become one of China's top universities with remarkable discipline ranking and rapid growth. I believe that with your support, SJTU will achieve better and faster development in the future.

2. Shanghai Jiao Tong University and urban governance

I worked and studied in Beijing, Xiamen, and Changchun before. This experience enabled me to feel the pulse of China's rapid urbanization. After four decades of reform and opening up, China has now reached a key turning point of urbanization. Its population and economic activities are more concentrated in city clusters. The industrial restructuring and economic transformation have become more innovation-driven. China's urban development is guided more by the philosophy of balanced space development, and quality development. Since working at SJTU, I have recognized that Shanghai, as a typical Chinese and world megacity, has accumulated advanced experience in urban governance. Therefore, one thing that SJTU needs to consistently work on is to tap into its multidisciplinary strengths in liberal arts, science, medicine, engineering and agriculture, and to assist urban governance in accordance with the idea of building the city by its people, as is proposed by President Xi Jinping.

Supported by the Shanghai Municipal People's Government, SJTU set up the China Institute for Urban Governance (CIUG), as a dedicated platform to study urban governance issues. Since its establishment four years ago, the institute has received much support from the government and has made remarkable progress by providing policy proposals for better governance, publishing academic journals, implementing research projects, and establishing data centers as well as interdisciplinary platforms. CIUG has found its way in China Think Tank Index, Top 100 Chinese University Think Tanks, and Influential Think Tank of Shanghai Universities. CIUG works to break down barriers of knowledge and to bridge the gap between the ivory tower and the real world. In the future, CIUG will continue to discover and reflect on Shanghai's experience in urban governance. It will incorporate health, ecology, and emergency management into every aspect of urban management. It will enhance its school-business partnership and theoretical research while offering intellectual support for better governance. By doing so, CUIG hopes to align its theoretical and policy innovations with China's situation, imbue them with Chinese characteristics, and help set up a Shanghai model of urban governance.

3. Conclusion

As the long-time organizer of the Global Cities Forum, we hope that this platform can further promote international academic communications, and let the world hear China's stories and lessons learned in urban governance. We are also ready to learn from other countries' advanced experience in urban governance, and draw minds, institutions, and organizations from world-class cities to Shanghai, so that the Forum can play a new role and make more contributions to urban governance.

Address III

Zhao Qi

Deputy Secretary-General of CPC Shanghai Municipal Committee, Deputy Secretary-General of Shanghai Municipal People's Government, Deputy Party Secretary of Subcommittee for Political and Legislative Affairs of CPC Shanghai Municipal Committee, Director of Shanghai Urban Operations Management Center

The 21st century is a century of cities. With the development of urbanization, problems relating to urban governance are emerging and becoming increasingly prominent. The critical and difficult problems in urban governance have seriously affected the quality of people's lives and the credibility of the government, which has aroused great attention of people from all walks of life around the world. Echoing the theme of the forum, "Valuing Our Communities and Cities", I would like to briefly introduce the achievements Shanghai has made in recent years on using new technologies for city and community management, as well as some thoughts towards the future.

With the scale of urban development and population getting larger, and economic and social activities more complex, cities have been constantly improving efficiency and creating wealth. But at the same time, they have also created many problems. After more than 40 years of high-speed urbanization, China is entering a new era in which there is an urgent need for better urban governance. To enhance the urban governance, more efforts must be made in technology innovation, which is also the key to realizing the modernization of urban governance.

1. By leveraging innovative technological means, Shanghai has modernized urban governance

In recent years, Shanghai has been earnestly studying and implementing the Spirit of the Series of Important Speeches by President Xi Jinping, advancing the access of citizens to government services via one website, optimizing the conduction of urban management via a single website. With the focus on the needs of the masses and the prominent problems in urban governance, Shanghai has adopted more advanced technologies such as reorganizing and integrating the information system to free its citizens from cumbersome procedures when accessing government services, so as to make the whole system more practical, benefiting both civil servants and citizens. After more than two years of efforts, the Shanghai government has successfully saved people's time and energy in the access to government services by reducing the cumbersome procedures through technology and network platform. The government will handle the difficult and complex parts, while the people can enjoy the convenience, which makes both people and businesses much more satisfied. It has become more convenient for citizens and businesses to access government services. In front of the offline windows of government departments, they can feel the warmth of government staff, and on the government website they can enjoy higher efficiency. According to statistics, since Shanghai enabled people to access government services via one website, the amount of time people spent on them has decreased by 60%. Paper documents have decreased by 52.9%, and 99.7% of people have rated the services as excellent. These efforts to modernize urban governance reflect Shanghai's commitments to the "Internet + Government Services" reform in the new era. Moreover, Shanghai's business environment has also been optimized.

2. Shanghai is building smart communities and modernizing urban governance

Communities are the foundation of city operations. It is also the basic unit of urban governance. However, the traditional community management fails to keep up with megacities' development, which is getting increasingly complex, mobile and diverse. Shanghai takes the lead in refining urban governance, applying new technologies to community management, and making social management more meticulous and smarter through building intelligent communities. In Shanghai's fight against COVID-19 pandemic, more than 6 000 village and residents' committees, 13 000 residential quarters, and more than 200 000 grass-roots staff have taken advantage of new technologies and means such as Network Information Service and AI-powered Voice Call System to perform their duties and work together. They adjusted protective measures to local conditions, strengthened the prevention and control of COVID-19, successfully blocked the further spread of the pandemic and safeguarded the people's health. We will sum up the experience in time to improve people's life, enhance their sense of identity and belonging to the community, and constantly promote the modernization of urban governance, so as to enhance the cohesion of the city.

3. Shanghai Jiao Tong University has been contributing to the modernization of urban governance

As one of the top universities in China, Shanghai Jiao Tong University (SJTU) has made important contributions to the economic and social development of Shanghai. In 2020, China Institute for Urban Governance has carried out a series of research and trials in the governance of megacities, and the relevant achievements have been highly recognized by the municipal and national governments. This year, Shanghai Emergency Management Bureau and SJTU have jointly established School of Emergency Management, and both parties will hold the opening ceremony for the co-constructed Digital Governance and Emergency Network Laboratory. These new platforms and institutions will surely create more innovative achievements in urban governance that closely integrate government, industry, education, research and application, providing more wisdom and strength for the modernization of urban governance in Shanghai, China and even the world.

KEYNOTE SPEECHES

主旨演讲

数字经济时代下的绿色智慧城市治理现代化战略

陈晓红

中国工程院院士，湖南工商大学校长

1. 智慧城市治理现代化研究背景及意义

（1）研究背景。

一是治理体系和治理能力现代化是实现中国"两个一百年"奋斗目标的根本保障。党的十九届四中全会提出要坚持和完善中国特色社会主义制度，推进国家治理体系和治理能力现代化，明确了"构建基层社会治理新格局"的战略目标及"加快推进市域社会治理现代化"的行动目标。

二是城市治理是推进国家治理体系和治理能力现代化的重要内容。习近平总书记指出，"推进国家治理体系和治理能力现代化，必须抓好城市治理体系和治理能力现代化"。在深圳经济特区建立 40 周年庆祝大会的讲话中，习近平总书记又指出："要树立全周期管理意识，加快推动城市治理体系和治理能力现代化，努力走出一条符合超大型城市特点和规律的治理新路子。"

三是随着中国城镇化进程不断加快，城市治理议题日趋复杂多元，城市的高速发展引发了一系列的治理难题。诸如人口激增、交通拥堵、能源紧张、水气污染、土壤污染等问题每一个城市都会遇到，对于大城市、特大型城市尤其如此，这就导致城市的生态环境和可持续发展面临着巨大的挑战。根据世界银行和联合国的报告，中国城镇化将会保持高速增长的态势，到 2050 年中国城镇化率将达到 80%。这就要求国内的城市建设以资源环境承载力为基础，进一步加大自然生态系统和环境保护力度，优化国土空间开发格局。

四是智慧城市的建设为推进城市治理能力现代化带来了新的契机。智慧城市建设的加快推进，特别是数字经济方面，为智慧城市治理创新和治理能力现代化提供了重大的技术支撑，人工智能、区块链技术、物联网、云计算平台、大数据、5G 通信等新一代信息技术为绿色智慧城市治理创新提供新的有效手段，在生态城市、智慧领域、环保、出行等应用领域都发挥了积极作用。

五是国家治理现代化的迫切需求进一步促进了智慧城市的转型升级。传统智慧城市建设中，由于细分应用领域众多，建设内容广，城市在规划发展建设中容易失焦，地区行业发展水平和资源禀赋不同也限制了智慧城市整体建设落地。国家提出的"新型智慧城市"，要求将城市发展需求与新一代信息通信技术应用深度融合，实现城市末端互联互通，通过数字信息技术，推动城市运行管理向人本化、生态化、智能化、系统化发展。

如今，我们的智慧城市建设正在加速向新型绿色智慧城市演进和发展，绿色智慧城市更加强调绿色生态的发展理念、无处不在的惠民服务、透明高效的在线政府、融合创新的信息经济、精准精细的城市治理和安全可靠的运行体系，以及其他新的要求和新的变革。然而当前的绿色智慧城市仍然面临巨大的挑战，如顶层设计不系统、大数据难以共享、缺乏标准化引领等问题，所以城市治理体系和治理能力现代化的战略设计至关重要。数据作为一个最重要的生产要素核心资源，正成为科技创新的突破口。在统筹规划、决策智慧、实施执行、监控预警和应急处理等方面切实提升市域治理能力，是有效解决目前市域治理面临的一系列问题的关键途径。在此次新冠肺炎疫情中，也凸显出社会应急反应滞后、数据信息共享受阻、人们观念认知变化等问题，中国城市治理体系亟待完善。

（2）研究意义。

开展数字经济时代绿色智慧城市治理现代化战略研究具有重大意义。首先，它是推进国家治理体系和治理能力现代化的有力探索；其次，它是完善应急管理体系，提高城市治理能力的重要保障；再次，它是维护社会稳定，提升人民群众获得感、幸福感、安全感的必要手段；最后，它为全球绿色智慧城市治理现代化提供中国方案，贡献中国智慧，探索出一条具有中国特色的城市治理体系和治理能力现代化的道路。

2. 智慧城市治理现代化的治理路径

（1）研究框架。

我们团队最近承担了中国工程院重大咨询项目"面向新型城市治理体系市域治理体系和治理能力的战略研究"，其中提出了关于新型智慧城市治理的总体战略框架和目标，体现了高度的学科交叉和融合，用先进技术和前沿理论作为战略设计和政策设计，进行典型的应用示范。我们开展的研究主要包括总体战略、体系结构现代化、治理手段和融合创新，以及典型经验和应用示范等；取得的目标成果主要包括理论体系、体系结构的优化策略、创新的技术手段、政策措施，以及示范应用和经验推广。

（2）智慧城市治理现代化总体战略。

智慧城市治理现代化的总体战略框架，包括基础理论、战略目标、战略路径及战略重点。

一是面向智慧城市治理现代化的总体战略理论基础。我们对它的制度进行了溯源及归纳，包括参与治理的各种主体力量、治理的机制和规则、治理的方式方法等。

二是面向智慧城市治理现代化的科学理念，这个理念包括几个导向：目标导向、政治导向、问题导向、为民导向和效果导向。

三是面向智慧城市治理现代化的总体目标，包括结构维度、技术维度、机制维度。结构维度旨在构建一个泛在化、融合化、智敏化的绿色智慧城市治理结构框架。技术维度是为了构建新一代信息技术和绿色智慧城市市域治理融合发展新体系。机制维度是建立完善财政资金向智慧城市建设、应用和推广的财政资金保障和分级投入机制。

四是面向智慧城市治理现代化的阶段目标。阶段性目标分为两个阶段：一个是短期到2025年，科学集约的"城市大脑"基本建成，全量汇聚的数据中枢高效运行；新一代信息基础设施全面优化，网络安全坚韧可靠，制度供给更加有效；市域治理制度创新、模式创新、手段创新有序推进，城市科学化、精细化、智能化管理体系基本形成。中长期是到2035年，反应快速、预测预判、综合协调的一体化智慧城市治理管理体系建成；共建共治共享的管理制度逐步完善，具有中国特色、时代特征的治理新模式基本形成；智慧城市治理体制现代化、治理工作布局现代化、治理方式现代化基本形成，社会治理能力达到世界领先水平。

五是面向智慧城市治理现代化的总体战略路径和目标，包括第一阶段（2020—2022年）：顶层设计，总体布局；第二阶段（2023—2025年）：试点示范，初见成效；第三阶段（2026—2035年）：纵深推进，全面建成。

六是面向智慧城市治理现代化的总体战略重点，包括智慧应急管理与应急治理体系，切实增强城市规划的科学性、前瞻性和连续性，着力破解城乡居民养老问题，加速建设智慧教育系统，加速推进城市智慧交通一张网建设，积极开展全民智慧医疗＋康养新模式，完善生态环境全要素监控体系和全面提升政府现代化治理能力。

（3）推进智慧城市治理现代化战略的重点方向。

注重以人为本的"智慧社会"，也会成为中国新型智慧城市建设和发展的未来愿景。相比智慧城市，"智慧社会"让智慧城市真正为民所用，实现"城市即服务"的愿景。智慧社会是对新型智慧城市理念的规划和范围的拓展，使市民拥有更多的获得感和幸福感，更加注重以人为本。中国的"新型智慧城市"建设将以"人、服务、管理"为重心，逐步实现从智慧城市向智慧社会转变。具体的重点方向包括：

一是智慧医疗与公共卫生。综合运用大数据、5G、人工智能等技术，通过监测、整合、分析、智能响应，实现跨机构互联互通、自动化高效运营、全流程重塑体验、大数据驱动优化、持续性创新机制，全面提升医院系统和公共卫生系统的智慧化水平。

二是智慧政务。综合运用云计算、大数据、物联网、人工智能等技术，实现各职能部门的各种资源的高度整合，提高政府的业务办理和管理效率，同时加强职能监督，使政府更加廉洁、勤政、务实，提高政府的透明度，并形成高效、敏捷、便民的新型政府，保持城市可持续发展，为企业和公众建立一个良好的城市生活环境。

三是智慧交通出行。利用卫星定位、移动通信、高性能计算、地理信息系统等技术实现城市、城际道路交通系统状态的实时感知，准确、全面地将交通情况，通过手机导航等途径提供给公众，提高出行效率和减少污染排放，推进城市交通智能化、数字化、标准化发展，全面提高社会的出行质量。

四是智慧教育。依托5G、人工智能、物联网等信息技术所打造的智能化教育信息生态系统，提升现有数字教育系统的智慧化水平，实现信息技术与教育主流业务深度融合，促使教育领域利益相关者的智慧养成与可持续发展。

五是智慧社区。综合运用新一代信息技术，系统研究智慧社区管理的智慧网格关键技术、智慧社区共治关键技术和社区多领域多场景智慧服务技术等，支撑一核多元共治共享的社区治理创新体系构建，推进社区公共服务功能完善和优化，实现社区管理与服务网格化、精细化和智能化。

六是智慧康养。依托新技术，建设医疗和健康云数据库，开放健康大数据共享智慧服务平台，推动医疗服务智能化，实现信息与资源的共享，跨越时间、空间、人群边界，打造覆盖社区、医疗机构、政府、服务机构等元素的综合一体的大型智慧康养有机体系，为老年人提供更便捷多样、更契合需求的服务，从身心层面满足老年人需求，实现老年人客观物质与主观精神双重满足的目标。

七是智慧物流。运用新一代信息技术，建立布局合理、技术先进、便捷高效、绿色环保、安全有序的现代智慧物流服务体系，提升物流企业数字化、一体化运作和网络化经营能力，提高城市供应链管理的智慧化水平。

八是智慧监督。综合运用先进新技术，推动国内跨部门跨层级多业务市场、多金融机构和多层级海关监管协同关键技术达到国际领跑水平，打造国家智慧市场监管、互联网金融风险防范和海关进出口业务智慧监督运行支撑体系，为市场公平竞争、金融环境优化和海关监控智能化等提供科技支撑。

（4）推进智慧城市治理现代化的对策和举措。

一是分层次制定政策规划，因地制宜设立市域治理方案。从国家层面、地方层面升级治理方案，通过行政基础手段，切实加强数据共享。

二是通过行政与技术手段加强数据共享。通过行政手段分享政务数据，解决政府管理部门公共数据的共享与融合问题，通过技术手段解决敏感数据与私有数据的共享问题。如以法规突破公共数据共享壁垒，对敏感数据进行脱敏处理，利用区块链分离数据拥有权与使用权。

三是设计标准总体框架，分阶段推进标准制定。建立中国市域治理标准化总体推进组织和机制，以目标为引领，设计标准总体框架，注重既有标准的选择，分阶段推进标准的制定，注重系统集成、行业交叉融合的相关标准。

四是加强纵向、横向的协同，健全社会多元治理体系。改善基层社会治理的组织架构，发挥纵向秩序的整合作用。完善横向业务架构，建立部门协作的社会治理体系。丰富基层社会治理的主体，建立横向秩序的扩展机制，形成"强国家—强社会"的社会治理模式。

3. 智慧城市治理的实践探索及应用示范

最近中南大学和上海交大、中国地质科学院共同获批了"数字经济时代的资源环境管理理论与应用"基础科学中心项目。研究团队围绕智慧城市治理的重点领域和关键问题，进行了一系列实践探索与应用示范，取得了较为丰硕的前期研究成果。围绕国家基础科学中心，我们组建了系统化的研究机构和人才团队，通过人工智能、区块链、物联网、大数据、智慧物流的平台，做了相关的研究。一是智慧城市治理的基础信息共享平台建设，二是智慧城市的泛应用的服务支撑平台建设，并对相关数据进行采集管理，包括资源环境、公共医疗、政府治理、交通出行、智慧交通等。

此外，中心还构建了关于智慧城市治理技术及能力现代化的评估体系，选取国内 11 个典型城市作为评价对象，采用大数据分析、AI 技术和改进熵权法等方法从城市协调联动能力、决策指挥能力、监控预警能力、资源共享、应急处置等方面开展多维评估，为中国智慧城市治理技术及能力评估提供数据支撑、科学方法及决策建议。

从 2020 年 2 月初以来，我们根据国家疫情防控的需要，进行了一系列风险评估、可视分析和风险监控工作。基于手机人口定位大数据，提取人口驻留位置和出行轨迹，运用统计分析和机器学习方法评估新型冠状病毒在全国不同地区的传播风险，建立风险源模型，评估流行病从源头向各地传播的风险。研究表明，准确掌握人口流动性是预测疫情早中期发展的最有效的大数据手段之一，该研究成果也于 2020 年 4 月以长文形式发表在《自然》（*Nature*）杂志。研究团队也制作了城市级新冠肺炎疫情区域风险可视分析系统，旨在为居民提供参考，为政府精准落实分区分级防控措施提供决策依据。另外，我们还构建了公共卫生疫情警报和管控系统，对国内外疫情进行实时监测，并对新冠肺炎疫情区域风险评估、突发公共卫生疫情进行预警，分析疫情舆情和传染病区域分布状况。中心也研发了在线医疗大数据监控和分析平台，构建了医疗大数据智能分析方法，在民生保障和企业复工复产方面也提供了很多决策建议。

研究团队还在数据驱动的生态环境集成管控、公共安全治理应用示范、智慧出行大数据分析管理、智慧教育、区块链等领域做了大量工作。尤其是区块链领域，研究团队围绕探索区块链技术在智慧政务、数字征信、电子商务、教育等领域的应用，专注于区块链与 AI、大数据及多方安全计算技术的融合创新研究，构建了自主产权的区块链技术体系，并开放了HOPE 数据共享安全平台以及区块链浏览器，具备完整的安全特性支持、增强的安全计算环境、强大的数据聚合和计算能力，以及高级语言支持等优势，为区块链技术在电子商务、企业信用、教育等领域的应用推广提供了良好基础。

2020年1月以来，团队围绕智慧城市治理中的公共卫生安全、疫情防控措施、城市应急管理等方面，为党中央、国务院、科技部等提供分析报告和决策建议30份，其中有8份报告被采纳，得到了国家领导人的重要批示。

总体来说，数字经济时代下智慧城市治理应用示范及经验总体框架，就是通过数字新技术提升智慧城市供给能力，包括精准感知、集约融合、聚焦民生、开放动员、虚实互动。

第一，用数字技术驱动智慧城市，构建数字孪生城市。数字孪生技术应用于智慧城市的城市建设，通过构建城市物理世界、网络虚拟空间"一一对应、相互映射、协同交互"的复杂巨系统，在网络空间再造一个与之匹配、对应的"孪生城市"，实现城市全要素数字化和虚拟化，城市全状态实时化和可视化，城市管理决策协同化和智能化。数字孪生赋予城市实现智慧化的重要设施和基础能力，基于数字的标识、自动化感知、网络智能化控制、平台化服务等强大的技术能力，实现数字技术驱动下城市信息化从量变走向质变的里程，由点到线、由线到面的精准管控。BIM技术对智慧城市信息化建设也有助力，其贯穿了智慧城市建设的全过程，实现全程自动化和全程信息化协同，实现对建设全过程"可知、可测、可控"，提升社会治理的数字化智慧水平。另外还有AR和VR的结合，助力全景智慧城市的规划。

以上海临港的"虚拟城市"为例，临港利用数字孪生技术，通过BIM+GIS构建精细化的"虚拟临港"，原样复制整个临港315平方公里城市空间，实时感知城市人口热力图、实时交通车流、停车库状态、视频实时监控等城市运行态势，通过无人机采集回传到中心的数据进行图像自动识别分析，并对未来发展进行推演和预测。此外，天津滨海新区也成立了数字孪生城市运营中心。

第二，物联网自动获取城市数据资源，推动社会智能感知泛在升级。物联网泛在智能感知系统，采集"视觉、听觉、嗅觉、触觉"等城市感知数据，整合城市的"眼、耳、鼻"，不断突破城市管理不同部门之间的数据壁垒和"孤岛"状态，提升城市管理和服务水平。城市的"眼睛"就是5G+AI打造超高清视频监控，城市的"鼻耳"就是智能监测传感器。此外，边缘计算也是需要我们高度关注的，在推动智慧城市网络架构、算力模式和业务模式的变革方面发挥着重要作用。

第三，区块链赋能重塑城市治理结构、构建分布式信任社会体系。2020年4月20日，国家发改委首次明确"新基建"范围，正式将区块链纳入"新基建"，区块链在新基建中主要发挥的是信任工具的作用，具有巨大的发展潜力。区块链拥有"五全基因"，即全空域、全流程、全场景、全解析、全价值，它能够重塑社会治理结构，助力智慧城市治理过程的数据共治、共享、共用，构建一个无形的信任框架，提升社会治理的智能化、精细化、法制化，促进能源的利用和能源行业的变革，构建智慧城市的绿色能源岛，营造协同、协作型的生产环境。

第四，人工智能深度渗透，赋能城市的高效协同，推动智慧民生服务的升级。在智慧城市建设中，民生服务智慧化是重点，惠民服务是绿色智慧城市建设的主要风向标。交通、医疗、安防、教育等领域与 AI 技术结合能不断提升民生服务智能化的水平，提高服务民生的效率。赋能智慧交通可以有效提高生产和交通效率，整合交通数据强化数据应用价值，提升交通运输效率支撑城市发展。赋能智慧医疗可以推动精准医疗、提高医务工作效率，并催生新型诊疗体系。

绿色智慧城市为人们描绘了美好城市生活的蓝图，但其目标的实现却任重道远，需要我们抓住新一代信息技术的机遇，通过赋能于人、赋能于城市、赋能于社会，用新型绿色智慧城市建设引领市域治理现代化，构建并推进市域治理现代化总体战略，最终实现"智慧城市带动市域治理、市域治理创造社会新价值"的智慧城市愿景。

智能技术和智慧政府：提升社区和城市品质

叶嘉安

中国科学院院士，城市规划及设计学系讲座教授

我们已经进入了智慧城市的时代。20世纪90年代，关于可持续发展的讨论十分频繁，它有多种定义。目前智慧城市同样也有很多不同的定义。我主要使用欧盟的定义：智慧城市由智慧人民、智能交通、智能经济、智能环境、智能生活和智能治理组成。[①]该定义涵盖了现代城市的大部分元素。

1. 从数字城市到智慧城市

我常把智慧城市的概念描述为"新瓶装旧酒"，因为大多数关于智慧城市的讨论和使用日益频繁的信息和通信技术（ICT）有关，但这并不是一项新技术。1985年至1995年间，人们开始使用小型电脑，以及与大型计算机不同的工作站。更重要的是，此时出现了一种名为局域网（LAN）的颠覆性技术，用以连接楼房或办公室内所有的电脑。许多政府都试图将地图数字化，并将其放入局域网，以便在不同办公室间共享信息，这标志着数字城市的出现。然而当时只有政府和公司配备了局域网，所以只有他们能使用这项技术。1995年，互联网和传感器的普及引发了关于智能城市的讨论，因为人们在办公室和家里都可以使用电脑。也就是说，政府、公司和人民都从智能城市中受益。智慧城市的概念在2010年后出现，人们借助带有传感器的手机、无线网络（Wi-Fi）和物联网可以随时随地地使用局域网。人们基本上可以通过手机获取所有信息，而这仅仅是个开始。智慧城市的基础结构包含地理信息系统（GIS）、传感器、ICT和Wi-Fi，未来或将出现第五代智慧城市。目前，智慧城市得到了5G、物联网、人工智能（AI）和自动驾驶汽车的技术支持。

---

① Rudolf Gifinger, 2007, "Smart Cities—Ranking of European Medium-sized Cities".

图1
1985 年以来的技术
发展

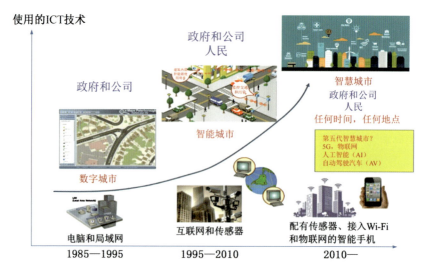

2. 智能技术

（1）智能技术的三种类型。

智慧城市依赖于三种智能技术：第一，数据收集技术。我们如何收集数据？我们如何感知环境？GIS、全球卫星定位系统（GPS）、遥感、传感器技术、物联网和大数据可以帮我们完成这些任务。第二，信息处理技术。我们通过云计算、机器学习和数据挖掘处理收集到的数据信息。第三，服务提供技术。我们在收集数据和处理信息后，可以向公众、政府和行业提供信息服务。

（2）智能技术的定义。

智能技术是一种易于使用的自动化技术，可以进行实时数据挖掘和自我学习。然而人们经常忽略这些技术的定价，因为如果价格太高，没有人买得起，智能技术就不会存在。

3. 传感器的应用

传感器、信息、相关的信息技术和应用是智慧城市的核心。

图2
传感器的应用及其
用途

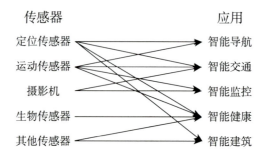

（1）智能交通中的传感器。最常用的传感器在智能交通领域应用了超过 15 年。导航仪曾被广泛使用，但现在被 GPS 导航取代，如中国的北斗卫星导航系统。目前，几乎所有人都在手机上安装了导航应用，中国国内主要使用高德地图导航，其他地区则倾向于使用谷歌地图。

（2）智能灯柱。另一种传感器是智能灯柱，它能感知整条街道的车和人。

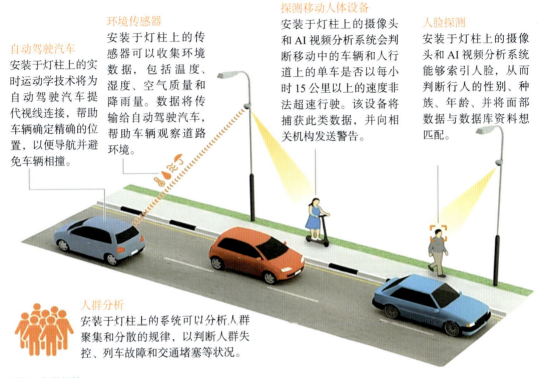

自动驾驶汽车
安装于灯柱上的实时运动学技术将为自动驾驶汽车提代视线连接，帮助车辆确定精确的位置，以便导航并避免车辆相撞。

环境传感器
安装于灯柱上的传感器可以收集环境数据，包括温度、湿度、空气质量和降雨量。数据将传输给自动驾驶汽车，帮助车辆观察道路环境。

探测移动人体设备
安装于灯柱上的摄像头和 AI 视频分析系统会判断移动中的车辆和人行道上的单车是否以每小时 15 公里以上的速度非法超速行驶。该设备将捕获此类数据，并向相关机构发送警告。

人脸探测
安装于灯柱上的摄像头和 AI 视频分析系统能够索引人脸，从而判断行人的性别、种族、年龄，并将面部数据与数据库资料想匹配。

人群分析
安装于灯柱上的系统可以分析人群聚集和分散的规律，以判断人群失控、列车故障和交通堵塞等状况。

图 3　智能灯柱
资料来源：GOVTECH SUNDAY TIMES GRAPHICS.

（3）众包传感器。众包是最近出现的技术创新。人们不仅使用高德地图或谷歌地图的服务，还向这些应用程序提供信息。这实际上是传感器的主要发展趋势之一。这项技术之所以名为"众包"，是因为它并非依靠物理设备搜集信息，而是依靠大众。在未来，汽车摄像头可能会成为另一种众包传感器。司机可以通过摄像头了解路况。

（4）自动驾驶汽车中的传感器。自动驾驶汽车和机器人也属于传感器，它们将在未来得到广泛应用。自动驾驶汽车配备许多传感器，包括 GPS、摄像头和激光探测及测距系统（激光雷达）。

（5）室内导航传感器。iBeacon 是一种室内传感器。苹果公司于 2013 年推出这款应用，它通过低功耗蓝牙（BLE），又名智能蓝牙，向周围发送位置信息，可以在支持双模式的蓝牙 4.0 设备上使用，如安卓设备和 Windows 设备。

香港大学为学生和教师提供类似的服务。学生可以通过香港大学智能导航系统找到教室，

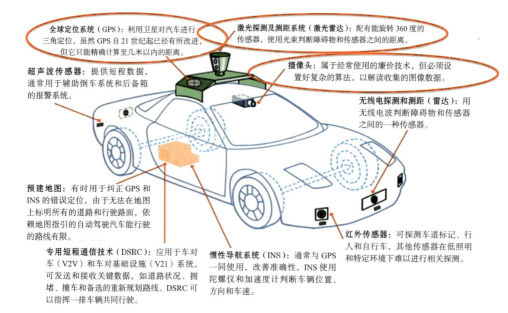

全球定位系统（GPS）：利用卫星对汽车进行三角定位，虽然 GPS 自 21 世纪起已经有所改进，但它只能精确计算至几米以内的距离。

激光探测及测距系统（激光雷达）：配有能旋转 360 度的传感器，使用光束判断障碍物和传感器之间的距离。

超声波传感器：提供短程数据，通常用于辅助倒车系统和后备箱的报警系统。

摄像头：属于经常使用的廉价技术，但必须设置好复杂的算法，以解读收集的图像数据。

无线电探测和测距（雷达）：用无线电波判断障碍物和传感器之间的一种传感器。

预建地图：有时用于纠正 GPS 和 INS 的错误定位，由于无法在地图上标明所有的道路和行驶路面，依赖地图指引的自动驾驶汽车能行驶的路线有限。

专用短程通信技术（DSRC）：应用于车对车（V2V）和车对基础设施（V21）系统，可发送和接收关键数据，如道路状况、拥堵、撞车和备选的重新规划路线。DSRC 可以指挥一排车辆共同行驶。

惯性导航系统（INS）：通常与 GPS 一同使用，改善准确性，INS 使用陀螺仪和加速度计判断车辆位置、方向和车速。

红外传感器：可探测车道标记、行人和自行车，其他传感器在低照明和特定环境下难以进行相关探测。

图 4　自动驾驶汽车中的传感器

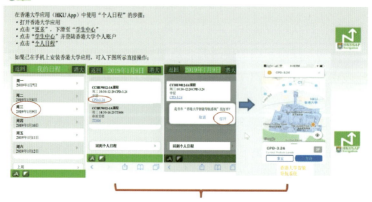

图 5
香港大学智能导航系统

香港大学学生信息系统应用

也可以将课程表上传至该应用，由此得知授课的地点和时间。

另一种发展迅猛的室内导航技术是超宽带（UWB）。这是一种标签，其成本已从人民币3 000 元降至人民币 400 元。最新的苹果手机和华为手机都内置了超宽带接收器。

（6）5G 定位技术。5G 定位技术提供了很多信息，但和超宽带相同，它的发展很大程度上受成本制约。

（7）智能健康。无线身体区域网络（WBAN）探查人们的行动状况，在有人摔倒时迅速提供帮助。

（8）智能家居。智能家居和智能生活不是一个新概念，最早于 2010 年上海世界博览会首次提出，在今天依然受到广泛关注。在众多传感器的辅助下，智能家居技术几乎能帮人们控制家中的方方面面。

（9）智能建筑。配有不同传感器的智能建筑可以减少碳排放，节约能源。

图 6
绿色智能建筑降低能源消耗

（10）智能社区。在智能社区方面，人们可以借助互联网和传感器监控社区的状况。智能社区为居民提供更好的服务。

（11）智能环境。许多使用物联网的设备被用于监测空气和水质，以构建智能环境。

（12）电子支付。如今，电子支付已非常普遍，中国尤为如此。人们在扫描二维码后可以不用现金直接支付。同样，网上购物也不是什么新鲜事。

4. 大数据

传感器最重要的输出之一就是大数据，例如 GPS 轨迹数据、移动数据和智能卡数据。它包含的数据集大小超过了常用软件工具捕捉、组织、管理和处理的范畴。大数据是用于城市规划和管理的丰富信息数据源。

（1）大数据应用。

① GPS 轨迹数据。人们用了 15 年以上的 GPS 就是一个范例。GPS 轨迹数据通常应用于交通领域，对城市、商业和人类行为分析等领域的应用都有重要的价值。

② 智能卡数据。智能卡追踪用户的信息，包括用户位置和消费行为。智能卡数据已被用于判断通勤模式以及研究城市空间结构。

③ 手机数据。手机数据是最准确、信息量最大的数据类型之一。它已被广泛应用于人类移动规律和行为的研究。

④ 传感器数据。这类数据来自环境传感器和物联网。

⑤ 空间时间数据。典型的例子是 GPS 和移动电话数据。

⑥ 社交媒体数据。这类数据收集自 Facebook、Twitter、Instagram 和微信等社交媒体网络。

⑦ 网络数据。这些数据包括页面浏览量、检索和消费信息。

⑧ 文本数据。这些数据收集自电子邮件和新闻。

（2）大数据分析。

大数据可以服务于以下场景：第一，目标市场营销，如数据挖掘、消费者画像和消费者行为分析；第二，提供基于位置的服务（LBS），即实时、实地的服务；第三，提高政商服务效率，改善反馈环节。

例如，当人们去购物中心时，大数据会根据他们过去的消费偏好，提供个性化的餐饮推荐。这种大数据分析可以被称为"AI 万物"，自动 AI 系统不计其数。

（3）将大数据应用于交通运输规划与管理。

我们在过去很难获取出行生成、出行分布、交通方式划分和交通分配等信息。现在我们能通过手机数据，准确便捷地计算出行生成，也可以进行始发地—目的地的行程估算。同样，在获得出租车数据和公交智能卡数据后，我们可以对交通方式进行划分。因此，我们每天都能进行交通规划和管理，可见大数据让人人受益。

5. 大数据和智能治理

迈克尔·巴蒂教授和他的同事已在 2012 年讨论过未来的智能城市。他们表示，ICT 技术将帮助城市节约能源，实现更好的城市管理，并提供许多过去无法提供的信息。

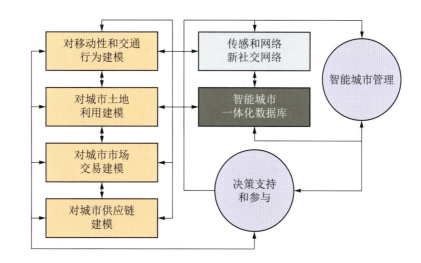

图 7　未来使用 ICT
的智能城市结构
资料来源：Batty, M.,
Axhausen, K., Giannotti,
F., Pozdnoukhov,
A., Bazzani, A.,
Wachowicz, M.,
Ouzounis, G. and
Portugali, Y., 2012,
"Smart Cities of the
Future", *The European
Physical Journal
Special Topics*, Vol.
214, No. 1, pp. 481-518.

（1）公众参与智慧规划。

ICT 技术可用于智能规划，也可以让公众在线上参与城市治理。例如，武汉居民通过名为"众规武汉"的线上平台提交对城市规划的建议。

（2）智能治理。

2005 年，北京市民只能通过手机向政府报告问题。图 9 是"移动政务"的一个例子。移动政务指政府利用智能手机、个人数字助理和无线网络等移动技术提供服务，促进不同市辖区的城市管理。

（3）众包技术支持的智慧政府。

众包技术和智能手机出现后，每个携带手机的人都有更多的方式来报告城市中的问题，他们实际上成了一个个传感器。看到城市设施损坏时，市民可以发送一张带有位置信息的照片，报告他们发现的状况，政府会派负责小组修复设施，并告知市民问题的处理结果。毫无疑问，新的智慧政府形式正在出现，即众包技术支持的智慧政府。

图 8
武汉市政府推出的
"众规武汉"线上平台

图 9
2005 年北京不同市
辖区的移动政务平台

（4）新冠肺炎疫情与智能治理。

自疫情爆发以来，人们一直深受其冲击影响。幸运的是，健康码有助于追踪确诊病例、病毒类型和病情传播的状况，从而控制疫情。新冠肺炎疫情爆发后，中国政府采取使用健康码等措施，在两个月内成功遏制住疫情。这是政府使用智能技术辅助治理的一个例子。

（5）数字孪生城市和智能治理。

我们过去在研究城市相关话题时，倾向于关注现实中的城市。然而，我们现在能借助智能城市管理和维护系统，使用 GIS、建筑信息模型（BIM）以及连接万物的传感器创建数字网络城市。例如，AI 运营管理系统会在获取交通和环境、建筑和设施的信息和预测后，建立一个反馈回路，以模拟现实世界的城市。网络城市的信息帮助 AI 系统控制现实城市的设备，从而构建效率更高、运营与维护更好的城市管理体系。

图 10
珠海居民报告下水道
堵塞的问题

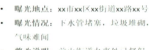

报告前

报告后

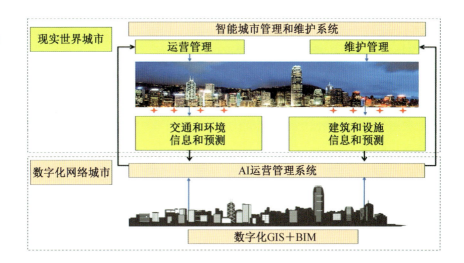

许多城市和建筑建立的 BIM 可以用于城市管理。BIM 技术正演变为区域信息建模
（DIM），之后或将进一步发展为城市信息建模（CIM）。构建 DIM 和 CIM 的方法与 BIM 的建
模过程类似。建筑师和规划者可以通过 CIM 模拟城市的诸多情况，如交通、拥堵、能源、地
震和飓风等自然灾害的影响。

6. 智能技术对智能社会的影响

1938 年，当城市化即将来临时，路易斯·沃斯（Louis Wirth）发表了一篇著名的论文
《作为一种生活方式的城市化》（Urbanism as a Way of Life）。该论文指出，以前的时代是农村
社会，而城市化带来了匿名化和大量的社会控制，导致人们的行为方式发生变化。同样，如
果今天沃斯要写另一篇论文，这篇论文的主题可能是"作为一种新生活方式的智慧城市"。

曼纽尔·卡斯特尔（Manuel Castells）于 1989 年写了一本关于信息社会的书，《信息城

市》(*The Informational City*)；于 1996 年互联网普及的时候写了另一本关于网络社会的书，《网络社会的兴起》(*The Rise of the Network Society*)。今天，如果他要再写一本新书，我想他一定会提到智能社会的兴起。智能社会将影响经济、环境、政府治理和各行各业。

在新冠肺炎疫情期间，许多人借助智能技术在家购物和办公，这将影响人们对购物空间和办公室的需求。由此可见，智能技术为我们带来了诸多好处，让我们的生活在疫情期间仍能步入正轨。

如果不是因为新冠肺炎疫情，智能技术已经可以让我们的旅行和生活变得更加便利。智能技术也使环境更可持续、商业机会更丰富、政府办公更高效、经济和旅游共享程度更高。但这些技术也有缺点。拥有智能技术的人和没有智能技术的人之间的社会差距会有所增加；从事智能技术相关职业的人会比其他人赚更多钱，所以收入差距将进一步扩大；智能技术可能会取代一些工作岗位，更多人将会因此失业；最重要的是，未来会出现更多的数据隐私问题。

7. 政治在智能技术中的作用

在智慧城市的智能技术方面，我们需要关注传感层部分。如图 13 所示，最上面的应用层与用户直接相关，但我们需要先研究感知层，再依次研究传输层、处理层、应用层。通常情

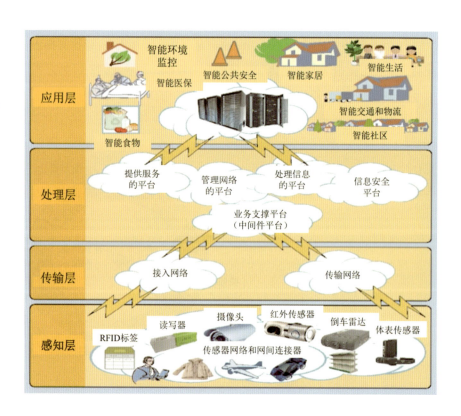

图 13
智慧城市的结构
资料来源：刘璨、彭正洪，《中国智慧城市试点：进展报告》，《计算机》2014 年第 47 卷，第 72—81 页

况下，4 个 P 为我们提供传感器：公众（Public）、私营公司（Private）、人员（People）、伙伴关系（Partnership）。例如，公众向高德地图或谷歌地图提供数据；高德或谷歌等私营公司处理接收的数据，而人员则在这些公司里负责处理数据。上述三者形成了伙伴关系。然而，如今代表政治（Politics）的另一个 P 已经出现，这意味着我们要讨论的不再是 4 个 P，而是 5 个 P。以美国为例。政界可能会提议暂缓新技术的推广。社会和公众对某些技术的接受程度较低，这为它们的发展带来诸多挑战。例如一种奇怪的现象：人们允许移动电话公司获取所有的个人信息，却反对政府采集他们的数据。这就是现在的困境。

新冠肺炎疫情背景下全球城市治理走向

郑永年

上海交通大学政治经济研究院名誉院长

1. 新冠肺炎疫情暴露全球城市治理问题

在新冠肺炎疫情背景下，中国、北美和欧洲的诸多城市都面临着前所未有的挑战。更确切一点，由于毫无准备，新冠肺炎疫情暴露了这些城市一直存在的短板。总体而言，城市所面临的问题来自两方面：自然因素和人为因素。

自然因素不胜枚举。例如，气候变化导致环境变化，包括水资源匮乏、干旱、超强寒流、极端高温等。一些城市气温升高、越发炎热，另一些城市则一到冬天，甚至还未入冬就遭遇超强寒流。因此，现在的城市生态和以前大相径庭。人为因素是指由于城市化，人类的生存空间扩大，与自然的边界模糊化。人类挤压大自然，大自然便进行反抗。尽管新冠病毒的确切来源还未查清，但我个人认为，从前的 SARS（非典型肺炎）和现在的新冠病毒本质上都是城市化导致的。科学家已经发现 100 多万种冠状病毒，人类随时都可能受到感染。从历史上看，病毒流传与城市化相关。但是城市化不可避免，因此，必须将针对冠状病毒等的病毒防护纳入城市治理。

2. 社会不公平阻碍可持续城市发展

人类在发展的同时也面临十分严峻的挑战。从 20 世纪 80 年代到 2008 年，人类经历了一波超级全球化，资本、技术、人才自由流动，生产要素在全球范围内进行配置，生产效率大大提高，技术不断进步。一方面，超级全球化带来了海量财富，美国、中国等国家均从中获益获利。另一方面，社会不公平、不平等加剧，财富流向极少数人的手里。二战到 20 世纪 80 年代期间，美国的中产阶层占 70%，但是 80 年代以后，由于超级全球化，美国的中产阶层占比便不断下降。西方其他国家均呈现相似趋势。由于财富过于集中，美国从中产社会转变为如今的富豪社会，引发社会不公平问题，导致社会很难治理。

美国和欧洲现在爆发的民粹主义运动和种族运动，如美国的"黑命贵"运动，实际上是结构性问题的反映，是城市治理、国家治理的问题。因为收入分配不公平，人们借助这些运动表达愤怒与不满。如果收入分配不公平不能得到有效解决，社会城市发展的可持续性必然会出现问题。

3. 改善城市治理涉及三大结构性平衡问题

第一，大城市和中小城市之间的发展必须达到平衡。从中国武汉到意大利、法国、德国、英国等欧洲国家的大规模封城可以看出，封锁大城市不仅十分困难，还会造成巨大的损失。中国执政党出于人道主义精神，将人民的生命放在第一位，决定封锁武汉，但也承受了巨大的经济损失。

城市的治理与城市规模有关。从经济学上来看，大城市化不可避免，很多经济学家也在提倡大城市化。日本 1/3 左右的人口集中在东京周边，韩国的人口主要集中在首尔，中国的人口则向北京、上海、广州、深圳等一线城市集中。这是因为大城市化与经济效率呈正相关，城市越大，人与人的交流就越多，越能创造 GDP。另一方面，大城市化带来了巨大的风险。除了上面提到的气候变化、新冠病毒大流行等，还包括战争、社会动荡等风险。现在是和平时代，因此大多数人对于战争冲突的风险意识比较薄弱。实际上，许多欧洲城市在一战、二战中被毁灭。城市越大，风险越大，城市治理必须将战争风险等问题纳入考量。

很多发达国家的城市规划注重均衡发展，意在遏制超大城市，实现超大城市和大城市，大城市和中小城市的均衡发展。我认为城市规划不仅要考虑经济效益，还要考虑城市安全。尽管超大城市化不可避免，但这一趋势不应由人推动。政府要想发挥更好的作用，应当注重城市的平稳发展，尤其是要筛选、发展三、四线的城市，避免将所有的优质资源都集中在一线城市。否则大城市和中小城市发展一旦失去均衡，一线城市以后的治理会变得越来越困难。

第二，经济增长与社会发展和社会安全之间必须达到平衡。根据经济增长和社会稳定之间的关系，全球城市可分为三类：

一是经济发展良好但社会不稳定的城市，比如一些美国和亚洲城市。社会不稳定是因为经济增长方式有问题，也即城市治理存在问题。经济的高速增长往往会带来收入、财富、环保等问题，进而影响到城市的稳定。

二是经济发展停滞、长期陷入中等收入陷阱的城市。经济发展停滞导致社会死气沉沉，或者街头运动经常爆发，社会无法稳定。我担忧一些城市经济发展后会变得高度政治化，致使街头运动频发。社会环境不稳定，经济便无法发展，就业和税收将成为难题。城市进步很困难，衰落却很容易。社会抗议造成社会不稳定，经济无法发展，如此陷入恶性循环，必将麻烦重重。

三是经济发展与社会稳定均实现可持续的城市，这些城市数量较少。

无论从理论还是实践上来看，经济的根本问题在于政府和市场之间的关系。资本过于强势的城市会引发问题。美国"铁锈带"（Rust Belt）等西方城市之所以衰落，是因为这些城市的资本处于主导地位。正如马克思所说，资本是不断流动的，从获利少的地方流向获利多的地方。资本来，城市就会发展，资本走，城市就会衰落。与之相反，一些发展中国家的城市中，政府起主导作用。但是政府趋于保守，导致市场不发达，经济也无法发展。

不管是资本主导还是政府主导，城市都无法发展起来。在发展良好的城市群中，政府和市场两个角色都充分发挥作用。正如中共十八届三中全会所提到的，要让市场在资源配置过程中起主导作用，更好地发挥政府作用。我认为这不仅适用于国家发展，也适用于城市发展，因为城市发展同样需要市场和政府。两条腿走路，城市才能更好地进行发展。在这方面，西方和中国都有很多的经验可供参考和学习。

第三，国际化和地方化必须达到平衡。一方面，国际化对于城市的发展非常重要。越是国际化的城市，开放度就越高，发展动力就越强，发展水平就越高。一个高度开放的城市，能从国内和国际两方面输入需要的生产要素并进行优化配置。如果深圳不开放，那么深圳市发展所需要的生产要素和人才就无法进入。因此国际化非常重要，不管是西方还是中国的城市，想要发展就一定要国际化。

另一方面，城市在发展的同时要照顾到地方居民的需求。城市是人居住的地方，所以城市的发展要和城市居民的需求结合起来。如果一个城市只顾发展，忽略居民的需求，社会稳定就会出现问题。城市的经济和社会是一体的，要发展经济，就要解决就业和税收问题。20世纪80年代至2008年是超级全球化时期，劳动分工在国际层面进行，经济和社会互相脱节。尽管城市经济突飞猛进，但城市居民的需求却遭到忽视。这次新冠肺炎疫情在英国和美国扩散迅猛就是一个例证。英国和美国均为西方发达经济体，却无法有效地应对、遏制疫情扩散。除去制度因素，早期一个被忽视的因素非常重要，就是国际劳动分工导致的医疗物资的短缺。

美国总统唐纳德·特朗普曾在电视上发表讲话，表示美国人民无需害怕，因为美国是世界上最强的经济体，拥有最先进的医疗体制。但由于缺少口罩、洗手液、防护服、呼吸机等防疫物资，美国人民并不能感觉到安全。美国并非没有能力生产这些防疫物资，只是由于附加值较低，美国早已把大量的医疗物资生产线转移到了中国以及其他发展中国家。从经济上说，这是国际劳动分工，美国掌控高附加值产品的生产，把低附加值产品的生产都转移到了其他国家。这种国际劳动分工不仅出现在美国，欧洲也不例外，中国未来也会发生。但是，国际劳动分工发展的同时也要考虑到社会的需要和人民生命安全的需要。如果劳动分工过于为国际资本主导，社会需要便会遭到忽视，一旦危机来临，资本就会与社会需要产生矛盾。因此，美国虽然是发达经济体，却缺少医疗物资，无法为人民带来安全感。今天城市治理中的很多问题其实都和结构性问题有关系。城市发展一方面要国际化，另一方面也要考虑到地方居民的需求。

4. 结语

综观全世界，机会都是均等的。20世纪80年代以来，有些城市发展成功，有些城市发展失败，有些城市停滞不前。这些城市成功和失败的原因各不相同，全球城市论坛的目的之一就是让各国互相学习成功的经验和失败的教训，避免重复悲惨历史，共同追求更加美好的城市生活。

城市乡村空间蝶化，国际化大都市背景下的乡村振兴

庄木弟

上海市奉贤区委书记

1. 城市发展的四大规律

事实上，城市就是从农村而来的，从农耕文明到工业文明再到城市文明，农村和城市的互相蝶化一定会给城市增加新的生命的力量。而针对城市发展，我总结有四条规律：

第一，企业让城市强大，企业越多，产业越发展，城市越强大。

第二，人民让城市伟大。英雄的人民，像新冠肺炎疫情时的武汉，让这个城市伟大。

第三，文化让城市高大。这个城市的文化发展越好，品牌越好，那这个城市形象就会越好。

此外，国际化大都市旁边的乡村是美丽乡村，这是一座城市的标配。

全世界所有优秀的城市都有美丽乡村，上海市委书记李强也提出要做好国际化大都市背景下的乡村建设。奉贤区作为国际化大都市的乡村，其乡村建设对于城市发展尤为重要。站在这样的角度来看，乡村振兴、"三农"问题、城市发展，需要各级政府的重视和作为。

中共十九届五中全会精神讲了要继续全力推动乡村振兴战略，而乡村振兴不是一个简单的拼凑，它是城乡空间的再造、优化，也是发展方式的自觉转变，它的最终形态是可以被期

图1
全国第一个森林剧
场——奉贤区九棵
树未来艺术中心

待的。我们期待乡村建设更科学、更迅速、更高效，农村更有活力，农民更富，农业更强。

2. 乡村振兴存在的问题

第一，宅基地的动迁。在农村家家户户都有一块宅基地，都有两个 60 岁以上的老人，他们的梦想就是动迁，即农民变成市民，向城市化的进程推进，这是一种消极的等待与期望。

第二，"被规划"的限制。"被规划"的意思就是该地成为国家或者地方规划区，那么在未来几年将无法进行生产作业，限制了该地现阶段的发展。现在农民看似人均收入很高，但主要依靠的还是工资性收入和经营性收入，而资产性收入比重较低。那么"被规划"区的农民的收入如何保障，是一个很重要的问题。

第三，城乡发展不同步，信息、产业不对称。现在的城乡互补在有的情况下变成了以乡补城，如土地指标、开发空间、资源要素，都存在不平衡的问题。要解决这个问题，不仅需要体制机制的改变，关键还是要依靠农民的自觉性。

第四，乡村振兴发展的思路和模式较为单一。现在美丽乡村的发展思路和结果都是千村一面、千镇一貌，因为政策没有针对性。现在农村只搞刷墙、绿化，最后只会是越刷越穷；挨家挨户的农家乐，结果是农家乐"只乐一家"，不能变成"家家乐"。从这一角度来看，农村发展还是不平衡、不可持续的。

3. 乡村振兴发展的新路径

针对这些问题，站在新的起点，我们要探求乡村振兴的新思路。农村现在有大量的资源如土地资源还有待开发，以奉贤区为例，宅基地就 10 万亩，农民在银行中有大量的存款，要素市场流动极其不充沛。用一句话概括，现在的"三农"工作是"捧着金饭碗要饭"，只是消极地等待政策的倾斜，而不是主动出击、主动作为。现在奉贤区推进的方式，用八个字总结就是："我看世界，世界看我"。现在奉贤区对标全球所有的乡村振兴先进的模式、方案、路径，未来通过努力创造出具有中国特色的乡村振兴思路和模式，这是奉贤区对乡村振兴的追求。

要实现这些追求，仍需要解决几大问题：一是空间固化。农村土地控制相对严格，"三线"的边界直接限制了农村未来的发展。二是产业壁垒。第一、第二、第三产业联动不足。尽管农产品品质优良，但是没有形成品牌，与工业文明、农耕文明、城市文明的融合不充分、不完全。三是农民身份。城市化的进程就是农民不断进城的过程，就是农民变成职业农民、产业工人、城市市民的过程。但在现实中，农民仍存在"被农民"、"被固化"的现象。

那么如何激发城市乡村的资源，整合稀缺资源、优质资源，将其作为乡村振兴重要的内容去推进？奉贤区做了一些探索：

第一，着力推进城镇化的过程。城市化是人的城市化，这个过程当中，需要按照党的十九届五中全会的要求系统化推进，而系统化推进首先要构建城镇发展体系，也就是"新城—新市镇"体系。只有纳入这个体系，让它和城乡互动联动，未来乡村才会产生蝶化。而这个过程中我们强调，先策划、再规划，不规划、不建设，从顶层设计上考虑如何实现蝶化。

按照这样的指引，奉贤区围绕以下两个方面做工作。一是进行有机更新，让人民记得住乡愁，通过打造城市乡村印象，唤醒人民记忆中的家园。奉贤区的城市印象，可总结为"十字水街，田字绿廊，九宫格里看天下，一朝梦回五千年"，让来奉贤的外地人打破千村一面、千镇一貌的固有观念，让住在奉贤的本地人有认同感和归属感。二是注重城市的色彩和空间。通过营造"小桥流水人家"的空间以及"三灰七白"的建筑重现江南水乡的韵味，从传统与现代入手，让古朴与时尚对话，实现科技与艺术的融合，集高雅与通俗于一体。

这些最关键的是要以人为核心推动城市化建设，通过机制和体制的引领，改变农民的生活方式和生产方式。城市更新就是这种方式，避免大拆大建、人口大量流动迁徙。以浦南运

图2
有机更新后的庄行港

图3
有机更新后的古华港

河为例，浦南运河东西长100里，被称为"百里运河，千年古镇，一川烟雨，万家灯火"。运河串联起五个古镇，规划以"一河二十四湖，五港十六渡，两路一百零八桥，六十六里樱花径，三十三片银杏林，四片二十七处枕河而居的乡间庄园"为重点，以古镇复兴、乡村振兴、园区更新、田园总部、环境美化为建设方式，打造城镇岸线、村庄岸线、农田岸线、园区岸线四类特色岸线，力求做到花钱少、效果好、受老百姓欢迎、成为记得住的乡愁。

规划之后要实现经济的发展。如何让人民看得见经济的发展，主要依靠的是生产方式的改变。奉贤提出的"三园一总部"，可能是全国唯一的模式，即"一个庭园一个总部""一个庄园一个总部""一个公园一个总部"，实现了一、二、三产业融合，其底色就是大地公园、田园综合体和城市综合体的复合体，从而实现新的乡村振兴生产方式。希望这种模式能成为国际化大都市背景下乡村振兴的新样式。在"三园一总部"里面，我们又推动让农民"既要富口袋，还要富脑袋"，这样一来，青年人多了，产业发展了，生态更好了，荒芜乡村不见了，"一个宅基地两个老人"的模样不见了，繁荣乡村出现了，这就是乡村振兴的实现。

第二，处理好城市化和逆城市化的关系。逆城市化是城市化更高阶段，要找到城市化和逆城市化的最佳结合点，农村不断进城、市民不断下乡，这是文明的进程。奉贤建立了一个关于"绿水青山就是金山银山"的转化指标体系，叫奉贤指数。奉贤指数根据五大理念，建立起关于空间保护情况、农民收入水平、生态环境现状的标准衡量体系，真正做到回归自然，自然而然，同时让农民能够得到很大的发展。所以城市化和逆城市化当中找到最佳结合点，就在于农民能变成职业农民、技术工人或者市民，农业能变成发展的底色和亮色，农村能成为乡村里的都市、都市里的乡村。

第三，乡村振兴必须有创新的手段。党的十九届五中全会中提出，坚持创新在我国现代化建设全局中的核心地位。乡村振兴的创新点就在于如何将之前所说的"金饭碗"变成进入市场的催化剂，如宅基地、承包地、建设用地等三块地的改革，奉贤区在"农民离地不失地、离房不失房"理念的基础上，为农民提供变现、置换等多样化选择，充分发挥农民的主观能动性和积极性，让他们主动地投入到乡村振兴的事业中来。另一个例子是农产品品牌的打造。奉贤农产品绿色无公害，但由于缺乏品牌建设，不受市场欢迎。目前要做的就是将生态农业、绿色农业、科技农业融入农产品品牌打造之中，大大增加农产品附加值。

这样一来，我们就可以实现乡村振兴的三级跳，从自然村落跳到新市镇，从新市镇跳到新城，把国际化大都市和城市文明植入新市镇和乡村，打破乡村振兴的固有模式，走出一条新路。

4. 奉贤区的改革措施

第一，农村宅基地确权。宅基地确权到个人，通过房产的股权证进行上市交易。

第二，宅基地可以流转。流转期限可达二十年或三十年，宅基地成为农民重要的生产资料和生产资源。

第三，加强现代化的社会治理。充分调动农民的创造性和主动性，让农民有自我管理的能力。构建农村乡村振兴现代化的治理体系，简而言之就是"美丽乡村，美丽约定"，通过公序良俗对农民的行为进行规范，并通过一定的激励手段鼓励农民自我管理。

包容性城市：高品质社区的必要先决条件

梅柏杰

世界银行东亚城市与灾害风险管理团队首席城市发展专家

论坛召开之际，世界各国都在应对新冠病毒引起的前所未有的公共卫生危机。纵观历史，乃至疫情爆发的当下，人们都一直倾向于定居城市，希望获得更高的薪水、更好的工作机会，以及更优质的医疗条件、教育资源和文化设施。中国将城市化作为大力扶贫的重要手段，可谓是世界范围内推进城市化的典范。因此，至关重要的是，中国还应继续努力，在未来创建真正的包容性城市，容纳所有希望住进城市、把握各种机会的家庭。

中国于 2014 年开始实施《国家新型城镇化规划》，并将于 2020 年完成该规划。此规划提供了城市化进程所需要的指导和支持。鉴于中国是全球人口最多的国家，世界银行对此规划的进程非常感兴趣，并于 2018 年进行了相关考察。2020 年全球城市论坛的主题是"提升社区和城市品质"，同时考虑到 2020 年也是中国《国家新型城镇化规划》的收官之年，我认为有必要在此讨论"城市应如何更具包容性并接纳所有社区"这个话题。

1. 影响城市包容性的六大方面

（1）农民工与城镇职工收入差距扩大。农民工与城镇职工之间的收入差距在疫情爆发前便已持续扩大。2014 年之前，农民工与城镇居民间的收入差距持续缩小，但这种趋势在 2014 年后未能维持下去。相较于有资历的城镇职工，农民工的平均月薪已处于较低水平，且涨薪速度更慢。城乡间日益扩大的收入差距关乎城市的社会包容性，应引起较高关注。

（2）农民工年龄上涨，需求增加。我们发现农民工的平均年龄在不断上涨。2010 年至 2016 年间，30 岁以下的农民工人数减少，而 40 岁以上的农民工人数却有所增加。农民工的平均年龄也有所上升。他们对医疗服务和社会保障的需求也随年龄增长而增加。我们需要特别关注这些需求，包括医疗保险的可转移性以及覆盖范围等。

（3）人口集中向大中型城市流动。就空间流动方式而言，农村人口持续向大中型城市聚集。这一趋势未来十年将继续存在。尽管政府努力遏制流动人口，但北京、上海、天津和重庆等一线城市的农民工总数一直十分庞大，未来也不会有所下降。与此同时，流入小城镇的农民工比例略有下降。面对这样的变化，我们需要继续努力，进一步改革相关制度，以接纳农民工并帮助他们成为真正的城市居民。

（4）不当的资源再分配和人口政策。中国的主流观点认为国内特大城市的规模过大，而现在决策者应该重新审视这一观点。与现行政策的观点相反，研究表明，中国的城市规模现在还不算特别大。而受"城市过大"论影响的政策可能会损害中国长期的经济发展，因为若将资源或人口从生产力最高的地区转移到其他地区，可能导致总生产率降低。

（5）留守儿童获得社会服务的机会。公众广泛讨论的一个议题是留守儿童的问题，该问题严重阻碍了城市包容性建设的进程。截至 2018 年底，中国仍有约 700 万名留守儿童。能否为所有儿童提供良好的教育，将对中国的社会包容性以及国家未来的劳动力素质产生巨大深远的影响。因此，各城市应接纳所有希望移居进城的家庭，并为所有居民提供医保和教育等各类社会服务。请记住，对国家而言，每多一个留守儿童，都意味着未来会流失一次机会。

（6）中国城市人口下降。一个令人惊讶的现象是中国部分城市规模在不断缩小。我们没有预料到会发生这种状况。中国的经济蓬勃发展，城市化战略一直强调适应性增长，特别要适应人口增长，但很少有人关注某些城市人口下降的问题。通过比较 2013 年和 2016 年中心城区的城市人口，我们发现 661 个城市中至少有 115 个城市在这三年里出现了不同程度的人口流失。国际经验表明，相较于将更多新投资引向这类城市，采用"合理规制或适当缩减城市规模"的政策规划可能更为合理。

2. 如何构建真正的包容性城市

第一，努力缩小农民工与城镇职工间的收入差距；第二，更加重视城市的老年群体，因为他们需要新型的城市服务、社区设施和合适的住房；第三，接纳所有社区，欢迎并接纳移居人口；第四，更具创造性地解决城市规模日益缩减的问题，这些城市的社区需要的可能不是更多的公共投资，而是因地制宜、能解决当地问题的灵活方案。

世界银行重视与中国的长久关系，特别是与上海这个大城市的关系。我们希望通过学习上海和中国其他城市的发展经验持续深化此种关系。我们将继续提供国际经验和知识，打造更美好的未来。

提升社区和城市品质：以人民为中心的数字治理

吴建南

上海交通大学中国城市治理研究院常务副院长

2020 年全球城市日的主题是"提升社区和城市品质"，核心是通过大家的共同努力来创造人人共享的城市。这种创造很大程度上在于是不是能够给市民提供更好的服务，而根据以往的研究可以发现，服务水平的提升，与技术水平的提升有很大关系。原因就在于技术的存在和使用，给它的服务对象和服务提供者带来明显的互动，进而促进更多的交流。在这个基础上，最终形成了转型，这种转型很大程度上就是数字治理技术所带来的。联合国对数字技术的定义，就在于随着信息沟通技术的进一步拓展，我们可以更快地访问网络，更多地使用移动服务，更多地采用信息技术，从而能够进行更多的交流沟通，这也使得政府之间的联系更加紧密。这种技术的使用，改变了政府和公务员、政府和政府、政府和公众、政府和企业之间的关系。

图1
数字治理

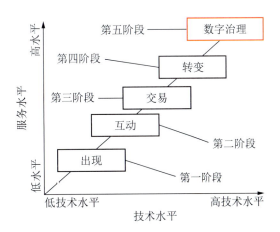

1. 数字治理的全球趋势

从 2011 年到现在，有越来越多的国家开始开放数据，开始让数字治理成为全球的趋势。2011 年 9 月 20 日，美国、英国、挪威、墨西哥、印度尼西亚、菲律宾、巴西、南非等八个国家联合签署《开放数据声明》，成立开放政府合作伙伴组织。在中国，2017 年习近平总书记特别强调要推动实施国家大数据战略，加快完善数字基础设施，推进数字资源整合和开放共享，加快建设数字中国。李克强总理在 2019 年的政府工作报告中也特别强调深化大数据、人工智能等技术的应用。

上海 2018 年提出了"一网通办"的概念，并于 2018 年 3 月付诸实施。一方面，我们可以看到在《全面推进"一网通办"加快建设智慧政府工作方案》和《上海市公共数据和一网通办管理办法》等文件的指引下，"一网通办"从线下服务中心到手机应用，已经得到了极大的推广。而"一网通办"的概念就是依托全流程一体化在线政务平台和线下办事窗口整合公共资源，加强业务协同办理，优化政务服务流程，推动群众和企业办事线上一个总门户、一次登录、全网通办，线下只进一扇门、最多跑一次。现在"一网通办"已经融入城市的社区和人们的生活，截至 2020 年 9 月 25 日，已经有 2 500 多项服务事项接入到"一网通办"之中，84% 是全程网上办理，95% 可以实现最多跑一次。目前实名的注册用户已经有 3 100 多万，超出了上海 2 400 万的常住人口，法人用户已有 210 多万。

我今天和各位分享的是两个研究问题：第一，"一网通办"到底是怎么实现的。第二，"一网通办"如何实现城市的善治。

2. 数字治理的"一网通办"如何实现

第一个问题，作为数字治理"一网通办"，要如何实现。

在图 2 中，左边的图是原来没有实现"一网通办"的政府形态，右边的图是现在的政府形态，一方面是行政服务中心，在其中设立各办事部门的窗口，另一方面是"一网通办"的

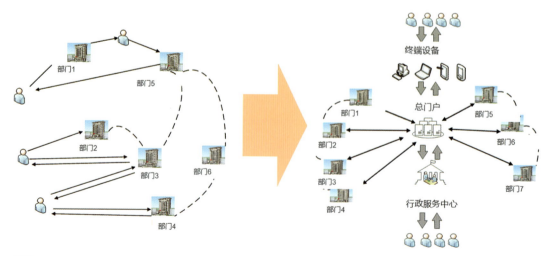

图 2
数字转型的结果

总门户，用户通过终端来获取信息。这种形态的变化就是数字转型的结果。如果我们梳理过去大数据中心为代表的一批相关政府所做的工作，大致是两个层面，一方面面向政府自身，另一方面面向政府外部。

上海实施"一网通办"三年来，在 2018 年率先成立了上海大数据中心，对各类服务进行集成化、标准化，与此同时，又强化了原有的"12345"的服务热线，另一方面建立了"一网通办"的总门户和相关的 App。在这个基础上，2019 年成立了相关的领导小组，在小组的带领下，各部门的专题推进会不断进行，面对用户实施"好差评"以及"我要找茬"的模式。2020 年进一步强调专题推进会，构建大数据资源平台，以及推出微信、支付宝小程序。事实上，这一系列改革就是一个从技术到治理的过程，我们称之为政府的组合式创新。中国地方政府的组合式创新可以分成五类，首先就是技术创新，如互联网、云计算、5G、人工智能、大数据技术的应用。然而在这个过程当中，仅有技术应用是远远不够的，特别重要的是以新架构、新流程为代表的管理创新。从领导小组的成立到大数据中心的建立，再到行政服务中心的建立，再到线上线下的融合，充分体现了架构和流程等的管理创新。之后基于管理创新，进行服务创新，包括一站式不见面服务，线上线下的整合得到了推动。在这一过程中也特别展现了跨部门协作网的合作创新以及政府社会互动方式变革的治理创新。简而言之，新技术应用实现了新政府形态的转化，新政府形态的转化实现了新治理模式。

3. 数字治理的"一网通办"如何走向善治

第二个问题，关于数字治理的"一网通办"如何走向善治。善治就是一种参与式的治理体制，在这种体制下，代表人民的政府，以人民的愿望为动力，为人民服务，为人民做好事，解决人民的问题，使人民生活更加宜居、更加满意、更加愉快，核心就是以人民为中心。

上海"一网通办"以人民为中心的出发点就是让政务服务像网购一样方便。人们可以通过手机 App 或者支付宝和微信的小程序，随时随地获得政府服务，接触到政府。以人的出生

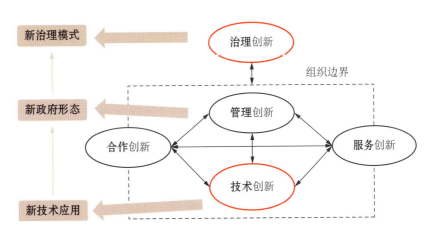

图 3
"一网通办"的组合式
创新：从技术到治理

为例，原来新生儿出生后父母需要办理十件事，如出生证明、身份证明、生育保险申请等，"一网通办"的实施之后，多个部门彼此之间协同整合了信息系统，共享了数据，并且使用电子证书和电子签名，这使得原来分开办理的 100 天缩短到现在的 25 天，原来跑动次数 14 次，现在最多 1 次，原来递交 26 份材料，现在只要 5 份，原来办理环节是 22 个环节，现在只需要 2 个环节。

再以一个企业的出生为例。2018 年，在上海创业需要 22 天、7 个步骤，通过一系列新技术的应用整合，包括实施数据的传输、存储和利用、无纸化服务、电子证照等等，现在在上海办一家企业只需要两天时间。

刚才提到的政务服务"好差评""我要找茬"活动也是以人民为中心的重要体现。政务服务实施"好差评"以来，9 个月收到了近 130 万条建议，其中 5 000 条是负面的评价，这里面的每一条负面评价都会被分析并作反馈。在此基础上，上海还实施了"我要找茬"的活动，在一个月内收到 4 000 多条市民建议，并且在一个工作日接收并予以回复，一半以上的建议在一个月内得到采纳。正是在新技术的使用过程当中，"一网通办"把以人民为中心的理念践行到新政府形态当中，进而实现了以人民为中心的善治。

4. 以数字善治让城市和世界更美好

最后，我们来谈一谈如何通过数字善治让城市和世界更美好。首先需要考虑的是将以"一网通办"为代表的数字治理转型成为数字善治。

图 4 中左边是原来的政府形态，有政府间不同的部门，也有政府的公务员和政府体系，当我们把以人民为中心的理念连同技术赋能引入政府体系之后，并且通过结构优化，以及流程再造，形成新的政府形态。在政府体系内部，政府部门之间，尽管有职能的划分，但是也有更多的数据共享、更多的数据交换、更多的部门协同。在这个基础上，我们的政府和企业、和公众的关系也发生了明显的变化。所谓政府改革的刀刃向内，其目的很大程度上就是让老百姓从政府那里获取的服务更加便利、更加舒心，其中的核心就是人民导向。

图 4
"一网通办"前后政府形态变化

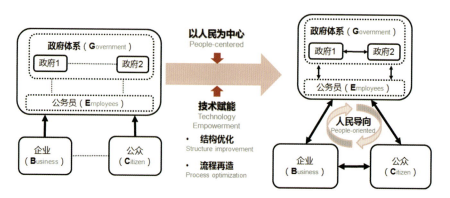

现如今，在全中国乃至全世界，数字治理已经成为一个非常重要的新趋势，在这个新趋势下，上海以"一网通办"为代表，在以人民为中心的数字治理方面发挥了重要的作用。最大的经验就是通过新技术的使用，赋予政府和政府工作人员新的能力，在这个过程当中，政府不同部门之间不断地合作交流、分享数据、分享信息。在这个基础上，以人民为导向的理念得到了充分的利用，并向善治——包括城市的善治和世界的善治——不断前进。

Green and Smart City Governance Modernization Strategy in the Digital Economy Era

Chen Xiaohong

Member of Chinese Academy of Engineering, President of Hunan University of Technology and Business

1. Research background and significance of smart city governance modernization

(1) Research background.

First, modernization of China's system and capacity for governance provides basic assurance for China to achieve its two "centenary goals". According to the Fourth Plenary Session of the 19th CPC Central Committee, we need to adhere to and improve socialism with Chinese characteristics and promote the modernization of China's system and capacity for governance. The meeting made "building a new pattern of primary-level social governance" the strategic goal and "to accelerate the modernization of social governance in urban areas" the action plan for China.

Second, urban governance is an important part of the modernization of China's system and capacity for governance. President Xi Jinping pointed out that "to promote the modernization of China's system and capacity for governance, we must focus on the modernization of urban governance system and capacity." In his speech at the celebration of the 40th Anniversary of the Establishment of the Shenzhen Special Economic Zone, President Xi again pointed out that: "We should develop a sense of full-cycle management, accelerate the modernization of urban governance system and capacity, and strive to find a new path of governance in line with the characteristics and rules of mega-cities."

Third, with the accelerating urbanization in China, urban governance has become increasingly complex and diversified. The rapid development has brought forth a slew of governance challenges. Problems such as population surge, traffic congestion, energy shortage, water and gas pollution, soil pollution can happen in any city, especially in big cities and megacities, thus putting the urban ecological environment and sustainable development under great strain. According to a report made by the World Bank and the United Nations, the speed of urbanization in China will maintain at a high speed. By 2050, 80% of China's towns will be urbanized. This means China must promote urbanization within the carrying capacity of its resources and environment, further protect its natural ecosystem and environment, and optimize the pattern of land space development.

Fourth, the development of smart cities has brought new opportunities for the modernization of urban governance capacity. The acceleration of smart city development, especially the development of the digital economy, has provided important technical support for China to innovate its smart city governance system and capacity. A new generation of information technologies, such as artificial intelligence, blockchain, the Internet of things, cloud computing, big data, 5G communication, has offered new effective ways for us to achieve innovations in green and smart city governance. They have played a positive role in fields such as eco-city construction, Intelligent Field, environmental protection, and mobility.

Fifth, the need to modernize China's governance system further promotes the transformation and upgrading of smart cities. In the traditional development of smart cities, given the sheer number of niche applications involved and the scope of tasks, it is easy for a city to lose focus in planning and development. The differences in regional development and resource constraints also limit the overall construction of smart cities. A new type of Smart City, which is proposed by China, integrates urban development needs and the application of the new generation of information and communication technologies to achieve urban connectivity. The use of digital technology will promote human-oriented, ecological, intelligent, and systematic development of urban operation and management.

Today, building a smart city means we also need to build a green city. A green smart city sets great store by the concept of green ecological development, ubiquitous people-oriented services, transparent and efficient online government, innovative information economy, precise urban governance, and safe and reliable operation system, and is responsive to new requirements and new changes. But a green city also faces many challenges, such as insufficient top-down design, difficulties in big data sharing, and lack of standardization. It is critically important to have a strategic design in place before we modernize our urban governance system and capacity. As a key factor of production, data has become the breakthrough for scientific and technological innovation. The key to effectively solve problems in the current urban governance is to improve overall planning, decision-making, implementation, monitoring, and early warning and emergency response. The COVID-19 pandemic has exposed weaknesses in China's urban governance system. We need to address the slow social emergency response systems, lift barriers in data and information sharing, and change old ideas and conceptions.

(2) Research implications.

Research on the strategic modernization of green and smart city governance in the era of digital economy is of great significance. First of all, it advances the modernization of China's system and capacity for governance. Secondly it improves the emergency management system and the urban governance capacity. Thirdly, it provides a means for us to maintain social stability and promote people's sense of achievement, happiness and safety. Lastly, by finding a path towards governance of green and smart cities with China's characteristics, we hope to contribute China's solution and wisdom to the world.

2. Ways to promote modernization of smart city governance

(1) Research framework.

"Strategic Research on New Urban Governance System and Capacity" is the name of a big consulting project we were recently commissioned by the Chinese Academy of Engineering. The project puts forward an overall strategic framework and objectives of new smart urban governance. It aims to cross disciplinary boundaries and apply advanced technologies and cutting-edge theories in strategy and policy design and put them into real usage. The work we intend to carry out include overall strategy, modernization of urban governance system and structure, integration and innovation of governance measures, and typical experience and application demonstration. The goals we aim to achieve include strategies to optimize the system structure and theoretical system of urban governance, innovations in technologies and policy measures, and demonstrations and promotions of our experience.

(2) Overall strategy of the modernization of smart city governance.

The framework of the overall modernization strategy of smart city governance encompasses theoretical foundations, strategic goals, strategic approaches and strategic priorities.

First, we must solidify the theoretical foundations of modernization of smart city governance. We have traced the origins of this system and built a basic idea of the various major entities engaged in governance, the mechanisms, rules and methods of governance.

Second, the scientific concept used in the modernization of smart city governance should be goal-driven, policy-oriented, problem-oriented, people-oriented, and result-driven.

Third, the arch-goal of smart city governance modernization is marked by its structural dimension, technical dimension and mechanic dimension. Structural dimension aims to build a general, integrated and agile structure framework for green and smart urban governance. Technical dimension is about building a new system integrating information technology and green and smart urban governance. Mechanic dimension is about establishing and improving the funding and hierarchical investment mechanism in order to direct funds to the construction, application, and promotion of a smart city.

Fourth, we have divided the modernization of smart city governance into two stages and set up the goal for each stage. The immediate stage ends in 2025. By then, we will build a fully aggregated data center which functions like a "city brain"; we will optimize the new generation of information infrastructure to ensure cybersecurity and effective institutional supply; we will also innovate urban governance system, models, and means so that a scientific, refined, and intelligent urban management system will take shape. The mid-long stage ends in 2035. By then, we will form an integrated smart city governance and management system with quick response, acute prediction and comprehensive coordination; we will put in place a social governance system based on collaboration, participation, and common interest and form a new governance model with Chinese characteristics and marks of the time. We will achieve modernization of a smart city governance system, modernization of its work distribution system and modernization of its governance approaches and our social governance capability will be at world-class level.

Fifth, the overall strategic path of the modernization of smart city governance includes three phases. The first is to complete the top-down design of the strategy from 2020 to 2022, the second is to pilot our model from 2023 to 2025, and the third phase, which lasts from 2026 to 2035, is to comprehensively promote our achievements and achieve the full modernization of smart city governance.

Sixth, the overall strategic priorities of the modernization of smart city governance include establishing a smart emergency management and governance system that can make urban planning more scientific, forward-looking, and continuous, improving the pension system for both urban and rural old people, speeding up the development of smart education system, accelerating the construction of urban smart transportation network, implementing the new smart medical plus health care services, improving the monitoring system of the ecological environment and comprehensively promoting the modernization of government governance.

(3) Priorities of the modernization strategy of smart city governance.

A "smart society" that puts people at its center is also China's vision for its new smart cities. Compared with smart cities, a "smart society" makes smart cities truly people-oriented and can turn the vision of "city is service" into reality. A smart society expands and builds on the concept of new smart city. A smart society can give its residents a higher sense of achievement and happiness. It focuses more on people. The development of China's "new smart city" will focus on "people, service and management", and will transform a smart city into a smart society. The priorities of a smart society include:

First, smart medical and public health systems. We will use technologies such as big data, 5G, and artificial intelligence to monitor, integrate, analyze, and respond to emergencies so as to achieve inter-institutional connectivity, automated and efficient operation, remodeling experience throughout procedures, big-data-driven optimization, and continuous innovation mechanism and comprehensively improve the level of smart hospital system and public health system.

Second, smart government. By using cloud computing, big data, internet of things artificial intelligence and other technologies, we can re-organize resources across different departments to improve the efficiency of government operation and to strengthen supervision. We want to have a clean, efficient and pragmatic government, increase its transparency, and make sure the services offered are efficient, convenient and accessible. We want our city to develop sustainably and create a better living environment for its businesses and people.

Third, smart transportation. With satellite positioning, mobile communications, high-performance computing, geographical information system and other technologies, we will know urban and inter-city road traffic conditions in real-time and feed such information to our people through mobile phone navigation apps. We will improve the efficiency of mobility, reduce pollution, promote the development of smart, digital and standard urban traffic systems and enhance mobility quality.

Fourth, smart education. By building a smart education information ecosystem based on 5G, artificial intelligence, internet of things and other technologies, we will improve the level of the existing smart digital education system, make information technology more integrated in mainstream education, and promote the smart and sustainable development of education stakeholders.

Fifth, smart communities. By comprehensively using a new generation of information technologies, systematically studying key smart community grid technologies, key community joint governance technologies and multi-field and multi-context smart services technologies, we can build an innovative community governance system based on diversity, participation and common interest. We will improve the public services offered by our communities, and make community management and service systems more organized, targeted and smart.

Sixth, smart health care. With the help of new technologies, we want to build a medical and health cloud database, and a data sharing and smart service platform that can promote smart medical services, share information and resources, and break the boundary of time, space, communities. We want to build a large and integrated smart health care system that brings the communities, medical institutions, government and service institutions on board. We will provide the elderly with more convenient and diverse services and provide care for their physical and mental needs.

Seventh, smart logistics. By using a new generation of information technologies, we want to establish a modern smart logistics service system that are well distributed and equipped with advanced technology, convenient and efficient, environmental-friendly and safe and in order. We want to make the operation of logistics businesses more digital, integrated and networked to promote the city's intelligence level of supply chain.

Eighth, smart supervision. With the comprehensive application of advanced technologies, we will raise the coordination capacity of our market regulators, financial institutions and customs offices to international levels. We want to build a smart supervision, operation and supporting system for smart market supervision, internet financial risk prevention and import and export businesses and provide technological support for fair market competition, financial environment optimization and smart customs supervision.

(4) Measures to promote the modernization of smart urban governance.

First, we need to set up policy plans at different levels and make urban governance plans in considerations of local conditions. We want to upgrade governance plans not only at national level but also at local level and use all necessary administrative means to strengthen data sharing.

Second, we intend to strengthen data sharing through administrative and technical means. Through administrative means, we can promote government open data sharing and integration, and through technical means, solve issues related to sensitive and private data sharing. For example, we need to set up specific laws and regulations to break public data sharing barriers and desensitize sensitive data. We can also separate data ownership and usage right using blockchain technology.

Third, we will design an overall framework of standards and make specific standards in each stage. We will set up a macro mechanism to push for regional governance standardization and use our arch goal to set up the overall framework of standards. In doing so, we must be careful regarding which prevailing standards to use as reference and push for its formulation in stages. We need to make sure this framework is not only compatible with system integration but also with cross-industry integration.

Fourth, we need to achieve the synergy of vertical and horizontal coordination and bring in more actors in social governance. We should improve the organizational structure of primary-level social governance and make multi-level government agencies fully integrated. We need to improve the horizontal structure of social governance system to have more inter-departmental collaboration. We should bring more actors on board at the grassroots level, establish an horizontal extension mechanism, and form a model of "strong state-strong society".

3. Practices and applications of smart urban governance

Central South University, Shanghai Jiao Tong University and Chinese Academy of Geological Sciences have recently obtained government approval to jointly establish "Resources and Environment Management Theory and Applications in the Digital Era" National Basic Research Center. The research team has carried out a series of practical work and demonstrations on the key areas and key issues of smart city governance and has achieved fruitful preliminary results. We have set up a research institution and a team and carried out research through artificial intelligence, blockchain, Internet of Things, big data and smart logistics platforms. we have explored the possibilities of establishing a basic information sharing platform for smart urban governance. we have also tried to construct a universal application service support platform for smart cities and have collected relevant data on resources and environment, public health care, government governance, smart transportation, etc.

In addition, we have also built an evaluation system to measure the technologies and capacities of urban governance system. We selected 11 Chinese cities and applied methods used in big data analytics, artificial intelligence technologies and improved entropy weight method to evaluate their urban coordination capacity, decision making and leadership capacity, monitoring and early warning capacity, resource sharing, emergency response. We hope this initiative could provide data support, scientific methods and decision-making suggestions for Chain's smart city governance technology and capacity evaluation .

During the COVID-19 pandemic, we have conducted a lot of risk assessment, visual analysis and risk monitoring work since early February, 2020. We used smartphone-generated big data to track the location and movements of its user and evaluated how likely COVID-19 was to spread in China's different areas by means of statistical analysis and machine learning. We designed a model to evaluate the risk of COVID-19 transmission from its origin to other areas. One research, which was published by Nature in April 2020, shows that human mobility plays an important role in effectively predicting the spread and size of COVID-19 in its early and middle stages. Our research team has developed a visual analytics system for COVID-19 regional risk assessment. This system provides information for the residents and helps the local governments make decisions in the implementation of prevention and control measures. We have also established a COVID-19 early warning and control system, which provides real-time monitoring of the pandemic both in China and at global level, COVID-19 regional risk assessment, early warnings of public health emergencies, and analysis of the public opinion of the epidemic and regional distribution of infectious diseases. In addition, our center has developed an online monitoring and analytics platform of healthcare big data, and built data-based intelligent analytics to provide policy proposals on protecting people's livelihood and promoting work resumption.

The research team has done a lot of work in areas of data-driven, integrated ecosystem management, demonstrations of public security governance, big data and public transportation, smart education and blockchain technologies. The team focused in particular on the application of blockchain technologies in smart government services, digital credit score systems, e-commerce, education. By combining blockchain technologies with AI, and big data with secure multiparty computation, we established our own system of blockchain technologies and launched a HOPE secure data sharing platform and a blockchain browser that comes with advanced security features, secure computing environment, strong data collection and computing capabilities and high-level programming language support. These efforts have provided strong impetus to the development of blockchain technologies in e-commerce, enterprise credit evaluation and educational services.

Since January 2020, the team has prepared for the CPC Central Committee, the State Council, and the Ministry of Science and Technology a total of 30 reports and policy proposals on public health, pandemic prevention and control measures and urban emergency management. 8 of them have been adopted and received a response from national leadership.

In summary, in the era of digital economy, the overall framework of smart city governance demonstration and experience is about using digital technologies to improve the capabilities of smart city, to achieve accurate perception, data sharing and integration, to focus on people's livelihood issues, to mobilize everyone in the cause, and to achieve interaction between VR and AR.

First, we need to use digital technologies to empower a smart city and use digital twin technologies to build its digital twin city. We need to create a nearly complete digital replica of a physical city so that all of a city's factors of production can be digitalized and visualized in real time and the decision-making of urban planning can become better coordinated and intelligent. The strength of digital twin technologies in digital signage, automatic perception, intelligent network control and platform-based services can substantially raise the amount of accessible information and increase precision of management. BIM also has a role to play in information construction. It is such an enabler in the construction of a smart city. It facilitates information collaboration and management of information and increases accuracy and measurement and management predictability. In addition, the combination of AR and VR technologies can also help with the planning of smart cities in a panoramic way.

Take the digital city of Lin-gang Special Area in Shanghai as an example. The area uses digital twin technologies and combines BIM and GIS to build a virtual Lin-gang, an exact digital copy of this 315 square kilometer area, so that we can obtain instant information in term of the real-time thermodynamic diagrams of urban population, traffic flows, parking conditions and can monitor the area in real-time. The data collected by drones will be automatically identified and analyzed to make estimations and predictions. Tianjin Binhai New Area has been making similar efforts to set up a digital twin city operation center.

Second, the Internet of Things (IoT) can automatically obtain data to increase a city's intelligent perception capability. The IoT-based intelligent perception system collects data from devices that serve as a city's eyes, ears and nose and bridge data silos of different urban management departments to improve urban management and services. The smart HD video monitoring system, which is based on 5G and AI, serves as the eyes of a city, and the intelligent monitoring sensors serve as the nose and ears of a city. Moreover, we also need to pay attention to edge computing, so that we can push for the revolutionizing change of a smart city's network architecture, computing power models and business models.

Third, blockchains can reshape urban governance structure and build a distributed trust social system. On April 20, 2020, for the first time in its history, the National Development and Reform Commission defined the scope of New Infrastructure plan and officially incorporated blockchain technologies into the plan. Blockchains mainly serve as a trusted tool and are of huge application potential. The technology is marked by its massive connectivity, integrated network, ubiquitous connections among people and the things, large-scale data collection and a strong value chain. It helps reshape the structure of social governance; facilitate data governance and sharing, build invisible trust framework; make social governance smarter and more precise, and strengthen rule of law in social governance; promote energy use and energy industry reform to build clean energy islands in smart cities, and create a coordinated production environment.

Fourth, the integration of AI in urban services can empower coordination among different parts of cities and better serve people's livelihood. A key area in building a smart city is to provide intelligent services for people. The combination of AI with transportation, medical care, security, education and other fields will make services smarter and more efficient. An AI-empowered intelligent transportation system can effectively improve transportation efficiency to support urban development. Meanwhile, an AI-empowered intelligent healthcare system can promote the development of precision medicine, improve the efficiency of medical work, and build a new medical system.

A green smart city embodies a blueprint of ideal city life for everyone, but we have to make real efforts to make it a reality. We need to take advantage of new information technologies. We need to empower people, cities and societies and use new green smart city construction to improve the pattern of modern urban governance and push the overall strategy of modernization of urban governance. We hope the development of smart cities will eventually bring exhilarating changes to urban governance and create new social values.

Smart Technologies and Government for Better Communities and Cities

Anthony G.O. Yeh

Academician of the Chinese Academy of Sciences, Chair Professor in the Department of Urban Planning and Design

We have already entered the era of smart cities. The term *smart city* has many different definitions, the same way as sustainable development did when it was intensely discussed in the 1990s. I mostly use the definition given by the European Union in which a smart city features smart people, smart mobility, smart economy, smart environment, smart living and smart governance.[①] This definition covers most of what happens in modern cities.

1. Evolution from digital cities to smart cities

I would describe the idea of smart cities as putting old wine into new bottles, because most discussions regarding smart cities revolve around the increased use of information and communications technology (ICT), which is not that new. Smaller computers and workstations which are different from mainframe computers emerged between 1985 to 1995. More importantly, a disruptive technology called the local area network (LAN) was invented to link up computers within a building or an office. Many governments were trying to digitize maps and put them into LANs so that the information could be shared among different offices, which signaled the start of digital cities. However, back then, only governments and firms could use this technology because they were the only ones who had LANs. In 1995, the widespread of the internet and sensors led to discussions about intelligent cities, because computers became available both in offices and at home. That is to say, governments, companies and people all benefited from intelligent cities. The concept of smart cities appeared after 2010 when smart phones with sensors, Wi-Fi and the Internet of Things (IoT) enabled people to use LANs anytime anywhere. Basically, all information became accessible to

---

① Rudolf Giffinger et al, 2007, Smart Cities — Ranking of European Medium-Sized Cities.

people via mobile phones, and this was only the beginning. The backbone of smart cities consists of GIS, sensors, ICT and Wi-Fi, and Smart City V may appear in the future. Currently, smart cities are supported by 5G, IoT, artificial intelligence (AI) and autonomous vehicles.

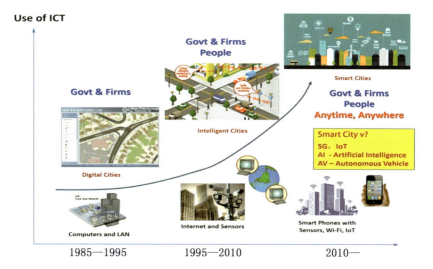

Fig. 1
Technology
developments
since 1985

2. Smart technologies

(1) Three types of smart technologies.

Smart cities depend on three types of smart technologies.First, data collection technologies. How do we collect data? How do we sense an environment? Examples are GIS, GPS, remote sensing, sensor technology, IoT and big data. Second, information processing technologies. The information of the collected data is processed using cloud computing, machine learning and data mining. Third, service providing technologies. After data collection and information processing, services will be provided to the general public, governments and industries.

(2) Definition of smart technologies.

Smart technologies are easy-to-use, automatic technologies that employ real-time data mining and are capable of self learning. One thing people often ignore, however, is that these technologies should be affordable, because smart technologies will not exist if nobody can afford them.

3. Application of sensors

Sensors, information, and related IT and applications are the heart of smart cities.

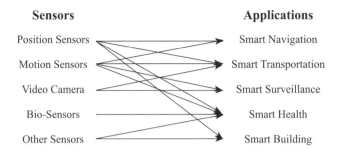

Fig. 2
Application of
sensors and its
uses

Sensors

Position Sensors
Motion Sensors
Video Camera
Bio-Sensors
Other Sensors

Applications

Smart Navigation
Smart Transportation
Smart Surveillance
Smart Health
Smart Building

(1) Sensors in smart mobility. One of the most commonly used sensors are those in smart mobility that have been in service for over 15 years. Navigators were once widely used, but now they are replaced by GPS navigation, for example, the BeiDou Navigation Satellite System in China. Currently, almost everyone installs navigating apps on mobile phones, such as Gaode Map in China and Google Maps outside of China.

(2) Smart lamp posts. Another type of sensors are smart lamp posts that sense cars and people of the entire street.

(3) Crowd-sourcing sensors. A latest technology development is crowd sourcing. People are not just using the services of Gaode Map or Google Maps, but also providing the information to these apps. This is in fact one of the major trends of sensors. Instead of physical devices, this technology depends on human beings, which is why it is called crowd sourcing.

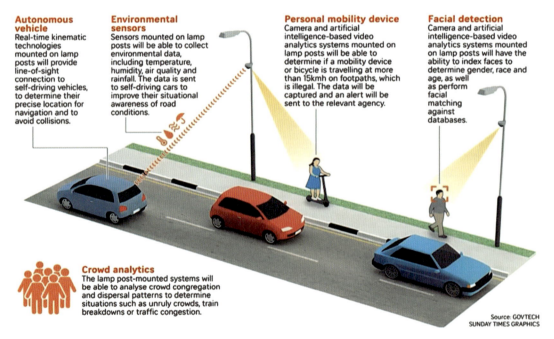

Autonomous vehicle
Real-time kinematic technologies mounted on lamp posts will provide line-of-sight connection to self-driving vehicles, to determine their precise location for navigation and to avoid collisions.

Environmental sensors
Sensors mounted on lamp posts will be able to collect environmental data, including temperature, humidity, air quality and rainfall. The data is sent to self-driving cars to improve their situational awareness of road conditions.

Personal mobility device
Camera and artificial intelligence-based video analytics systems mounted on lamp posts will be able to determine if a mobility device or bicycle is travelling at more than 15kmh on footpaths, which is illegal. The data will be captured and an alert will be sent to the relevant agency.

Facial detection
Camera and artificial intelligence-based video analytics systems mounted on lamp posts will have the ability to index faces to determine gender, race and age, as well as perform facial matching against databases.

Crowd analytics
The lamp post-mounted systems will be able to analyse crowd congregation and dispersal patterns to determine situations such as unruly crowds, train breakdowns or traffic congestion.

Source: GOVTECH
SUNDAY TIMES GRAPHICS

Fig. 3
Smart lamp post

In the future, car cameras may become another kind of crowd-sourcing sensors. Drivers will know what is happening on the road with the help of the camera.

(4) Sensors in autonomous vehicles. Autonomous vehicles and robots which will become widely available in the future are also sensors.

Autonomous vehicles are equipped with many sensors including GPS, cameras and Light Detection and Ranging (LIDAR).

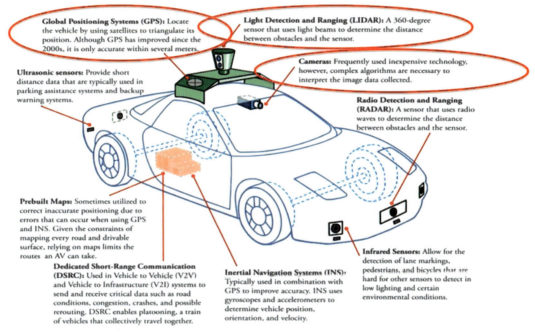

Fig. 4
Sensors in autonomous vehicles

(5) Indoor navigation sensors. A type of indoor sensors is iBeacon. Launched by Apple in 2013, it works on Bluetooth Low Energy (BLE), also known as Bluetooth Smart, with Bluetooth 4.0 devices that support dual mode such as Android and Windows devices.

The University of Hong Kong provides similar services for students and teachers. Students are able to locate classrooms via the HKU Smart Address Plate system, and they can link their timetables to the app to know where to go next and what time to attend lectures.

Another indoor navigation technology that is growing fast is the Ultra WideBand (UWB). It is a type of tags and its cost has been reduced from RMB3 000 to RMB400. The latest iPhone and Huawei phones both have built-in UWB receivers.

(6) 5G positioning. 5G positioning provides a lot of information, but its development largely depends on its cost, as is the case with UWB.

Fig. 5
Hong Kong
University Smart
Address Plate

Fig. 6
Smart green
buildings
reduce energy
consumption

(7) Smart health. The smart health that contains the Wireless Body Area Network (WBAN) monitors people's movements and offers instant help if someone falls down.

(8) Smart home. Smart home and living as a current subject of broad interest was first introduced in the Shanghai Expo in 2010 and is no longer a new concept. Assisted by many sensors, the smart home technology helps people control almost everything inside their houses.

(9) Smart buildings. Smart buildings with different sensors can decrease carbon emission and save energy.

(10) Smart community. As for smart community, people can monitor neighborhoods with the help of the internet and sensors. Smart communities provide residents with better services.

(11) Smart environment. A lot of devices that involve IoT are used in monitoring the air and water quality to build a smart environment.

(12) E-Pay. Today E-Pay is commonplace, especially in mainland China. After scanning a QR code, people can pay without using any cash. Likewise, e-shopping is nothing new either.

4. Big data

One of the most important output of sensors is big data, for example, GPS trajectory data, mobile data and smart card data. It includes data sets with sizes beyond the ability of commonly used software tools to capture, curate, manage and process, and is a rich informative data source for urban planning and management.

(1) Big data applications.

① GPS trajectories data. The GPS that has been used for over 15 years is a typical example. GPS trajectories data, usually used in transportation field, is valuable for many applications including urban, business and human behavior analyses.

② Smart card data. Smart cards trace users' information, including their locations and spending behaviors. Smart card data has been used to identify commuting patterns and study city spatial structures.

③ Mobile phone data. Mobile phone data is one of the most accurate and informative type of data. It has been widely used in human mobility patterns and behavioral research.

④ Sensor data. This type of data is from environment sensors and the IoT.

⑤ Spatial temporal data. Typical examples are GPS and mobile phone data.

⑥ Social media data. This kind of data is collected from Facebook, Twitter, Instagram, WeChat and other social media networks.

⑦ Web data. These data include information regarding page views, searches and purchasing.

⑧ Text data. These data are collected from emails and news.

(2) Big data analytics.

Big data can be used for the following purposes. First, target marketing, such as data mining, consumer profiling and consumer behavior. Second, provision of location-based services (LBS), that is, just-in-time, just-in-location services. Third, provision of government and business services with increased efficiency and improved feedback.

For instance, when people go to shopping malls, they will be offered personalized dining recommendations based on their past preferences analyzed from big data. These big data analytics can be seen as the AiE (AI in Everything) or AoE, and automatic AI systems are numerous.

(3) Using big data in transport planning and management.

In the past, it was difficult to get information about trip generation, trip distribution, mode split and trip assignment. With mobile phone data, trip generations can be calculated accurately and conveniently, and origin-destination trip estimation is made possible. Similarly, mode split is formed when taxi data and transit smart card data are provided. Therefore, transport planning and management can be done every day, and big data benefits everyone.

5. Big data and smart governance

Professor Michael Batty and his colleagues already discussed future smart cities in 2012, saying that the ICT will help cities save energy, achieve better city governance, and provide a lot of information that could not be offered in the past.

Fig. 7
Structure of future
ICTs smart cities
Source: Batty,
M., Axhausen,
K., Giannotti, F.,
Pozdnoukhov,
A., Bazzani, A.,
Wachowicz, M.,
Ouzounis, G. and
Portugali, Y.(2012),
"Smart Cities of
the Future", *The
European Physical
Journal Special
Topics,* Vol. 214, No. 1,
pp. 481-518.

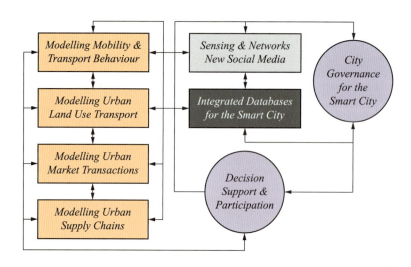

(1) Public participation in smart planning.

The ICT can be used for web-based citizen participation and smart planning. For instance, Wuhan residents submit their suggestions about the planning of the city on an online platform named Zhonggui Wuhan.

(2) Smart governance.

In 2005, people in Beijing could only report problems to the government using their mobile phones. Fig. 9 is an instance of m-governance, which refers to the delivery of government services by mobile technologies such as smart phones, PDA and wireless networks which facilitates urban management of different districts in a city.

(3) Crowd sourcing-backed smart government.

With the advent of crowd sourcing technology and smart phones, every individual carrying a phone has more ways to report problems in cities and is in effect a sensor. They can send a photo with location information to report damages they spotted, and a team will be sent to repair the damages

Fig. 8
Zhonggui Wuhan
platform launched
by the Wuhan
government

Fig. 9
M-governance
platform for
different districts
in Beijing in 2005

Fig. 10
A resident in Zhuhai reported a clogged sewer

Before Reporting

After Reporting

and inform them of the results. Undoubtedly, a new form of smart government, the crowd sourcing-backed smart government, is coming up.

(4) COVID-19 and smart governance.

People have been all suffering from the COVID-19. Fortunately, a health code helps track confirmed cases, the type of virus and the spread of the disease, thus containing the epidemic. The Chinese government managed to contain the COVID-19 epidemic within two months after the outbreak in January using health codes and other measures. This is an example of employing smart technologies in governance.

(5) Digital twin cities and smart governance.

We tended to focus on the actual cities when talking about the physical real cities in the past. Nevertheless, current intelligent urban management and maintenance system enable us to create digital cyber cities using GIS and the Building Information Modeling (BIM) along with sensors that link everything up. For example, after the information and predictions of traffic and environment as well as building and facility are provided, an AI operation and management system will build a feedback loop so as to simulate the real city. The information about cyber cities helps the AI system control devices in the real city, creating more efficient city management that offers better operation and maintenance.

The building information model(BIM) that is created by many cities and buildings can be used in management.BIM technology is evolving to district information modeling (DIM) and then to city information modeling (CIM), which are similar in how people build models for buildings and infrastructures. A CIM model enables city-wide simulation for architects and planners of

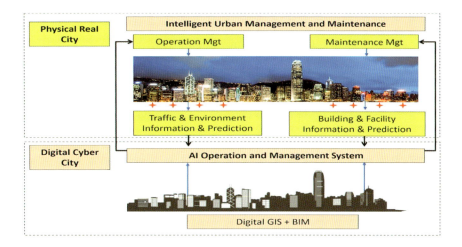

various aspects such as traffic, congestion, energy, impacts of natural disasters like earthquakes and hurricanes.

6. Impacts of smart technologies on smart societies

In 1938, when the urbanization was around the corner, a famous paper, "Urbanism as a Way of Life," by Louis Wirth was published.[①] It suggested that there had been rural societies in the past, and that urbanization made people anonymous and resulted in a lot of social control, which caused people

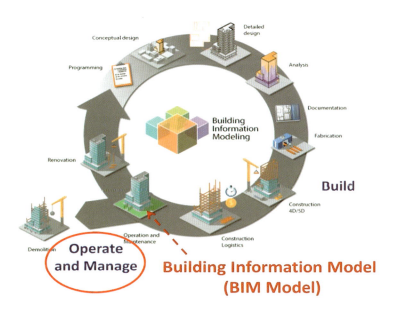

---

① Louis Wirth, 1938, "Urbanism as a Way of Life", *American Journal of Sociology*, Vol.44, No.1, pp.1—24.

to behave differently. Likewise, today if Wirth were to write another paper, he would probably write a paper entitled "Smart City as a New Way of Life."

Manuel Castells wrote a book discussing the information society in 1989, The Informational City, and another about the network society in 1996, The Rise of Network Society, when the internet became widely available. Today, if he were to write another new book, I think he would definitely reference the rise of the smart society. The smart society will affect the economy, the environment, the governance and all walks of life.

During the COVID-19 lockdown, many people use smart technologies to shop and work at home, which will affect the demand for shopping space and offices. Therefore, we are enjoying the fruits of smart technologies that can keep our life on track during the pandemic.

Smart technologies would have already made traveling and living more convenient, if it were not for the COVID-19. They also bring a more sustainable environment, more business opportunities, more efficient governments, and more shared economy and travel. But smart technologies also have their downsides. They will cause more social divides between those who have technologies and those who have not; widened income inequality since people engaging in smart technologies will earn more than other professions do; more unemployment problems because smart technologies may replace some jobs; and most importantly, more data privacy issues.

7. The role of politics in smart technologies

In terms of smart technologies in smart cities, attention needs to be drawn to the sensing layer. As is shown in Fig. 13, the application layer on the top is directly related to users, but we need to first study the sensing layer before moving on from the transmission layer to the processing layer, and at the end to the application layer. Normally the four Ps provide sensors: Public-Private-People partnership. For instance, the public provides data to Gaode Map or Google Maps; private businesses like Gaode or Google process these data, and people are the ones who do the processing. These three form a partnership. However, another P that represents politics has emerged, meaning that five Ps have replaced the four Ps. Take the U.S. as an example. When new technologies are invented, the politics may suggest to suspend them for the time being. There are many challenges in terms of the society and the public's acceptance of certain technologies. For instance, a strange thing is that people allow mobile phone companies to get all their data while opposing governments' collection of data. This is a kind of dilemma.

Fig. 13
Structure of smart cities

Source: Liu, Pu and Peng, 2014, "China's Smart City Pilots: A Progress Report", *Computer*, Vol. 47, pp. 72—81.

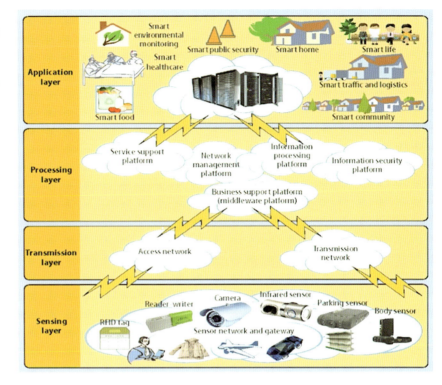

How to Improve Global Urban Governance in the Context of COVID-19

Zheng Yongnian

Honourary Director of Institution of Politics and Economics, Shanghai Jiao Tong University

1. Global urban governance problems exposed by COVID-19

In the context of the COVID-19 pandemic, many cities in China, North America and Europe are facing unprecedented challenges. More specifically, being caught off guard by COVID-19, these cities have exposed some deep-rooted problems. Generally speaking, the problems faced by cities come from two aspects: natural factors and human factors.

There are too many natural factors. For example, climate change has caused many environmental changes, including water scarcity, drought, cold air outbreaks, and extreme temperatures. Some cities are getting hotter and hotter, while others are suffering from cold snaps in early winter, even before winter arrives. As a result, today's urban ecology is very different from that of the past. Human factors mainly refer to the expansion of living space and the blurring of the boundary between mankind and nature due to urbanization. And when the space of nature gets further occupied by human beings, nature will also take revenge. Although the origin of the novel coronavirus has not been identified, I hold that both SARS (severe acute respiratory syndrome) and COVID-19 are essentially caused by urbanization. Scientists have identified more than a million types of coronaviruses that can infect humans at any time. Historically, the spread of the virus is related to urbanization. However, urbanization is inevitable. Therefore, prevention against coronavirus and other diseases must be taken into consideration in urban governance.

2. Social inequality impedes sustainable urban development

At the same time, human development has faced serious challenges. From the 1980s to 2008, mankind experienced a wave of hyper-globalization. With the free flow of capital, technology and

提升社区和城市品质

talent, factors of production got allocated on a global scale, and productivity and technology got improved greatly. On the one hand, hyper-globalization has generated huge wealth for countries such as the United States and China. On the other hand, social injustice and inequality have become worse, and a large amount of wealth has been controlled by a few people. From World War II to the 1980s, the middle class accounted for 70% of the total population of the United States, but after the 1980s, due to hyper-globalization, that figure continued to decline. Similar situations have also emerged in other western countries. Because of the excessive concentration of wealth, the United States has changed from a middle-class society to a rich-class society, leading to social inequality and thorny social governance problems.

The populist and racial movements that happened in the United States and Europe, such as the Black Lives Matter movement in the United States, are a reflection of structural problems, as well as urban and national governance problems. People participated in these movements to express their anger and dissatisfaction with the unfair distribution of wealth. If the inequality of income distribution cannot be effectively addressed, the sustainability of social urban development will inevitably get obstructed.

3. Improving urban governance calls for structural balance regarding three aspects

Firstly, development must be balanced between big cities and small- and medium-sized cities. The large-scale lockdowns of cities such as Wuhan in China, and many others in Italy, France, Germany, Britain and other European countries show that locking down large cities is not only difficult, but also causes great losses. Out of the humanitarian spirit and the principle of putting life first, the Communist Party of China decided to lock down Wuhan, which at the same time, has caused huge economic losses.

City governance is closely related to the size of the city. Economically speaking, metropolitanization is inevitable, and many economists are also advocating it. About one third of Japan's population is concentrated around Tokyo, and South Korea's population is mainly concentrated in Seoul. China's population is concentrated in first-tier cities such as Beijing, Shanghai, Guangzhou and Shenzhen. This is because there is a positive correlation between metropolitanization and economic efficiency. The bigger the city is, the more people interact with each other, and the more GDP can be created. On the other hand, metropolitanization brings great risks. In addition to climate change, plague, coronavirus, SARS, etc., as mentioned above, there are also risks such as war, social unrest and so on. Most people today are less aware of the risks of war and conflict as we are living in a peaceful time now. In fact, many European cities were once destroyed during World War I and World War II. The bigger the city is, the greater the risk is. Urban governance must take into account issues such as the risk of wars.

Many developed countries attach great importance to balanced development in urban planning, trying to curb the development of megacities, and realize the balanced development between megacities and big cities, between big cities and small- and medium-sized cities. I think when making urban planning, we should consider not only economic benefits, but also urban safety. While metropolitanization is inevitable, it should not be driven only by people. If the government wants to play a better role, it should pay attention to the balanced development among various cities, especially to select and develop third-and fourth-tier cities, avoiding concentrating all high-quality resources in the first-tier cities. Otherwise, once cities' development gets out of balance, the governance of the first-tier cities will become more and more difficult.

Secondly, a balance must be stricken among economic growth, social development and social security. According to the relationship between economic growth and social stability, global cities can be divided into three categories:

First, cities with good economic development but unstable in society, such as some cities in the United States and Asia. The social instability is due to these cities' problematic economic growth mode, that is, there are problems in their urban governance. Rapid economic growth will often bring challenges like income inequality, wealth gap, and environmental problems, which will further affect the stability of the city.

Second, cities with stagnant economies and those that have long been stuck in the middle-income trap. Economic stagnation may lead to a stagnant society, or an unstable society where street movements are very common. I am worried that some cities will become highly politicized as their economies develop, resulting in frequent street movements. The economy cannot develop in an unstable society, which will cause tough issues in terms of employment and tax revenues. It's hard for cities to progress, but it's easy for them to decline. Social protests will result in social instability, which will bring the economy to stagnation, and stagnation will lead to a new round of social protests, and the vicious cycle goes on and on and on, getting worse every single time.

Third, cities with sustainable economic development and social stability. The number of these kinds of cities is relatively small.

Theoretically or practically speaking, the foundation of the economy relies on the relationship between the government and the market. When the capital of a city is too powerful, problems will arise. The reason why some western cities such as Rust Belt cities in the U.S. are declining is because capital occupies a dominant position in these places. Just as Marx's theory mentioned, capital is constantly flowing, and it will flow from the place with less profit to the place with more profit. Capital comes, and cities will develop. Capital leaves, cities will decline. In contrast, in some cities in the developing world, governments play a leading role. But because governments tend to be conservative, markets are underdeveloped so the economy cannot develop.

Neither the capital nor the government alone can help cities develop. In a well-developed city cluster, both the government and the market play a full role. As mentioned at the Third Plenary Session of the 18th CPC Central Committee, we should let the market play a decisive role in the allocation of resources and giving better play to the role of the government. I think this is true not only for national development, but also for urban development, because urban development also needs markets and governments. Only when the two work together can cities develop better. In this respect, both the West and China have a lot of experience for reference and learning.

Thirdly, a balance must be stricken between internationalization and localization. On one hand, internationalization is very important for the development of cities. The more internationalized a city is, the higher its openness and development level can achieve, and the stronger its development momentum will be. A highly open city can input and optimize factors of production from both domestic and international aspects. If Shenzhen were not open to foreign investments, it would not enjoy the factors of production and talents it needed for its development. Therefore, internationalization is very important. Whether in the West or in China, cities must be internationalized if they want to develop.

On the other hand, cities should take into accounts the needs of residents while developing. Cities are places where people live, so the development of cities should also meet the needs of their residents. If a city only focuses on development and ignores the needs of its residents, its social stability will be in trouble. There is a strong correlation between economic and social conditions of a city. To develop the economy, it is necessary to solve the problems of employment and taxation. In the period of hyper-globalization, that is from the 1980s to 2008, the division of labor was carried out at the international level, and the national economy and society began to decouple from each other. The economies of many cities had been booming, but the needs of its residents had been ignored. The rapid spread of the COVID-19 in the UK and the U.S. is a case in point. The UK and the U.S., both are Western developed economies, have been unable to effectively respond to and contain the spread of the pandemic. Apart from institutional factors, a once overlooked factor is very important, that is, the shortage of medical supplies caused by the international division of labor.

The U.S. President Donald Trump once made a speech on TV, saying that the American people needed not be afraid because the United States was the strongest economy in the world and had the most advanced medical system. But due to the lack of COVID-19-related medical supplies such as masks, hand sanitizers, protective suits, and ventilators, Americans could not have a sense of security. It is not that the United States cannot produce these supplies, but it has already transferred a large number of related production lines to China and other developing countries because of the low added value of these products. Economically, this is a result of the international division of labor, in which the U.S. controls the production of high value-added products while transferring the production of low value-added ones to other countries. In addition to the U.S., this kind of division of labor has also appeared in Europe, and it will happen in China in the future. However, while developing the international division of labor, the needs of local society and residents' life safety should also be taken into account. If the division of labor is over dominated by international capital, social needs will get ignored. Once the crisis comes, there will be a conflict between capital and social needs. As a result, the U.S., despite being a developed economy, lacks the medical supplies to provide people with a sense of security. Many of the problems in urban governance today are related to structural problems. When developing a city, we should consider not only the internationalization but also the needs of local residents.

4. Conclusion

Throughout the world, opportunities for urban development are equal. Since the 1980s, some cities have developed successfully, some have failed, and some have stagnated. The reasons for the success and failure of these cities are different. And one of the purposes of the Global Cities Forum is to help countries learn from each other's experiences, avoid repeating similar failures, and jointly build a better urban life.

How to Achieve Rural Vitalization in the Context of Building a Global Megacity

Zhuang Mudi

Secretary of CPC Shanghai Fengxian District Committee

1. Four principles guiding urban development

I believe all cities evolve from rural villages. As we move from farming civilization to industrial civilization and to urban civilization, a village turns into a city and picks up new strength. I have identified four principles that drive urban development: First, a city is made strong by its business. The more businesses a city has, the more developed its industries are, the stronger a city will be. Second, a city is made great by its people. The heroism of the Wuhan people has made the city great during the COVID-19 pandemic. Third, a city is made unique by its culture. The better-developed a culture is, the more famous brands a city has, the better image a city will have.

Moreover, a city is made beautiful by its surrounding countryside. Having beautiful villages on its side is an essential part of a city.

All international megacities have beautiful villages. Li Qiang, the secretary of the CPC Shanghai Municipal Committee has pointed out, it is important to do a good job in rural construction in the context of making Shanghai an international megacity. Fengxian is one of the surrounding villages

Fig. 1
The first forest theater in China: Nine Trees Shanghai Future Art Centre in Fengxian District

of Shanghai, and its rural construction is particularly important for urban development. It is therefore important for the governments at all levels to work on rural vitalization and address the issues related to the agriculture, rural areas and farmers and urban development.

One of the key messages from the fifth plenary session of the 19th Central Committee of the Party of China is that China needs to continue to promote rural strategy. But rural vitalization is not about piecing each individual achievement together. Rather, it is about reshaping and optimizing the space between urban and rural areas. It involves transforming the development patterns of a village in a way that makes its functioning more scientific, faster and more efficient so eventually, the rural villages will become more dynamic, the people living there will get richer and the local agriculture will be stronger.

2. Problems that exist in rural vitalization

The first, the relocation of homestead. It is common for a household in a rural village to have an ancestral homestead and at least two elderly people that are aged 60 years old and above. Rural folks want to move from their old houses to new houses and become urban residents. But sometimes, they just wait for this to happen.

Second, we must deal with challenges brought by the designation of "planned area". If an area a family owns is designated as a national or regional "planned area", then they cannot use the land for agricultural purposes in the next few years, which might limit the development of these places. Although most farmers can now make a respectable living judged by the per capita income, they mainly rely on their labor and services, incomes that are generated from their fixed asset remains low. We must figure out a way to protect the livelihoods of the families whose land has been included in "planned" areas.

The third problem has to do with the asynchronized development of urban and rural areas, and the asymmetry of information and industries. While the policies are designed to achieve the complementarity between urban and rural areas, in reality, sometimes, the urban areas are developed at the expense of the development of rural areas, leading to the imbalanced allocation of land quotas, space and resources. To solve this problem, we should not only reform the design of these mechanisms, but also raise farmers' initiative.

Finally, the development patterns of rural areas are not flexible and varied enough. Under the current model, which only focuses on the outside visual aspects of a village, most villages may end up looking as the same, because we do not have any tailored made development policies. If all the people in rural areas are engaged in wall painting and planting, they will only get poorer. If every household opens a farmhouse restaurant, only "one family", rather than "all families", will get businesses. Seen in this way, the development of the rural areas is still lopsided and lacks substance.

3. Approaches in achieving rural vitalization and development

The emergence of these problems requires us to seek new approaches in achieving rural vitalization. There are so many resources, such as land resources, waiting to be tapped in rural areas. In Fengxian District, the total area of the homestead now stands at 100 000 mu (about 66.67 square kilometers). Farmers save plenty of money in banks, leaving little to spend in the market. To use an analogy, it is as if they hold a golden rice bowl, but still begs for money. They wait passively for policy support, rather than taking the initiative to change their circumstances. What we are now trying to do in Fengxian is to open their eyes to the world. By benchmarking all the advanced models, plans and approaches of rural vitalization in the world, we hope to find a path that comes with Chinese characteristics and works best for our case. This is how we intend to achieve rural vitalization in Fengxian.

To achieve this goal, we need to tackle several immediate problems:

First, rigid space control. The rural land control on distribution of infrastructure construction has restrained the future development of rural areas.

Second, industrial barriers. We need to make the primary, secondary and tertiary industries more interconnected. Although the quality of our agricultural products is good, we have little branded products. We are still not fully integrated with industrial civilization, farming civilization and urban civilization.

The third is the identity of farmers. Urbanization is a process for the farmers to move from the countryside to the cities. It is a process in which they change from being a farmer to a worker and finally to an urban resident. In this process, they might label as farmers for life and face the associated stigma.

How to make good use of urban and rural resources? And how to make the scarce resources and high-quality resources better integrated in order to promote rural vitalization? Here are some of the practices we have adopted in Fengxian district:

First, to promote urbanization. Urbanization is about urbanization of humans. We need to systematically promote urbanization in accordance with the requirements made by the fifth plenary session of the 19th Central Committee of the Communist Party of China. It starts with the construction of an urban development system, that is, the system of "new town — new city". We want to make the two interact with each other. Only in this way will the countryside be vitalized in the future. In this process, we must make sound plans and strategies, and never go ahead without planning in advance, and use top-down approach.

Guided by this approach, our work is focused on two aspects. Firstly, we need to revitalize a rural area organically. We aim to provoke a sense of nostalgia and awaken residents' memories of their hometown. In many people's minds, Fengxian is known for it crossed waterways and green farmlands. People who first come to Fengxian should be able to immediately recognize these features and those longtime residents of Fenxian should also be proud of this heritage and can find a sense of identity and belonging here. Secondly, we need to pay attention to the color and space of the area. We hope to restore the traditional water town architectural style by rebuilding all the white walls, gray tiles, tiny bridges and hamlet houses. In this way, we aim to fuse its rustic charm with the fashion elements, and by using scientific technology and art, combine tradition with popular culture, and

Fig. 2
Zhuanghang
Bay after
sustainable urban
regeneration

Fig. 3
Guhua Bay after
sustainable urban
regeneration

modernity with elegance.

The most important thing is to promote urbanization with human beings at the core, and to change farmers' lifestyles and production methods through the guidance of mechanisms and systems. To help with the urban renewal, we need to avoid massive demolition and construction and mass migration of people. Take Punan Canal as an example. The 100 li (about 50km) long Canal flows

from east to west and links five ancient towns. Based on our reform plan, we hope to restore its river and lake system, the bays, ferries, roads, bridges, cherry blossom paths, gingko woods and riverside houses. These landscaping efforts will help us rebuild distinct old farmhouses, parks, rural villages, and riverside sceneries in a way that reduces the overall cost and achieves the best results.

The purpose of planning is to achieve economic development. To make the results of economic development visible and tangible to everyone, we need to change the mode of production. Fengxian is probably the first in China to adopt a "three complexes/one headquarter" model. To describe the model in succinct terms entails efforts to combine a garden complex, a farm complex and a park complex. It also seeks to foster links between the primary, secondary and tertiary industries. We hope this model can become the new pattern for rural vitalization in our drive to build international megacities. Under this model, we expect the farmers to become rich not only financially but also knowledge-wise. We hope to bring in more and more young people to develop industries and improve the environment. We hope that people no longer have to worry about the well-being of their elderly parents and the future of their family homestead. This is the way to achieve the prosperity of the rural areas and achieve rural vitalization.

Second, we need to strike a balance between urbanization and counter urbanization. Counter urbanization is a higher stage of urbanization. As human society evolves, it is natural for rural people to move into cities, and for urban folks to settle in the countryside. Fengxian has taken the lead to set up a transformation index system called Fengxian Index. It is a product we made based on President Xi's call to "turn lucid waters and lush mountains into invaluable assets". The Index seeks to gauge how innovative, coordinated, green, open and inclusive the rural development is and can be used to measure space protection, farmers' income and the status of the ecological environment. It enables farmers to develop in a sustainable way. We hope to find a way that can merge urbanization and counter urbanization in a coherent way and help farmers transition from being professional farmers, to skilled workers and to urban residents. We will make the agriculture the basis of everything and the countryside a home for both urban and rural folks.

Third, innovation is essential for rural vitalization. According to the fifth plenary session of the 19th Central Committee of the Communist Party of China, Innovation is the core of the overall situation of my country's modernization. Being innovative in rural vitalization means we need to turn the so-called "golden rice bowl" into market drivers. We need to reform the current schemes governing the use of the homestead, contracted land and construction land. Farmers should know that if they live in cities, they will not lose ownership of the homestead and houses. But we also give them options to cash out or replace their land. Doing this will raise farmers' motivation and initiative in revitalizing their rural homes. Another way to innovate is to raise the profile of Fengxian's agricultural products. Our agricultural products are green and pollution-free, but the lack of branding means they are not popular on the market. we need to create more branded names of our ecological agriculture, green agriculture and sci-tech agriculture and increase the added value of our agricultural products.

In this way, we hope to achieve three leaps of development in rural revitalization: a natural rural village changing into a new town and finally changing into a new city. We hope to bring in urban culture and practices of international megacities into these new towns and blaze a new trail of rural vitalization.

4. Reform measures taken by Fengxian District

First, establishing the ownership of rural homesteads. We need to establish people's ownership of their homestead so that they can sell and buy such land in a legitimate way.

Second, we must make sure the ownership of homestead can be transferred up to a period of 20 to 30 years, so that such land can become a source of productive resource for rural residents.

Third, we need to strengthen modern social governance. We should give full play to the creativity and initiative of farmers and let them manage their own affairs. In short, the key to a modern governance system is to ask the rural residents to observe their own set of codes of conduct, and encourages them to take ownership of their own affairs through incentives.

Inclusive Cities: Necessary Preconditions for High-Value Communities

Barjor Mehta

Lead Urban Specialist in the East Asia Urban and Disaster Risk Management team of the World Bank

This event is taking place as countries around the world are dealing with an unprecedented public health crisis caused by the COVID-19 pandemic. Historically and even before the current crisis, cities have been people's favored locations where they have moved to seek better and well-paying jobs, health, education and cultural amenities. In that respect, China is an example to the world in embracing urbanization as a means towards spectacular reductions in poverty. It is therefore important that China itself makes further strides towards creating truly inclusive cities that welcome all families who wish to move and take advantage of the opportunities that are available in cities.

China's National New Urbanization Plan, which started implementation in 2014 and will end this year in 2020, has provided much needed guidance and support to the country's urbanization process. Given the plan's coverage in a country with the world's largest urban population, we at the World Bank examined the plan's progress with great interest in 2018. As we participate in today's 2020 World Cities Forum with the theme of "Valuing Our Communities and Cities" and considering that China's National New Urbanization Plan will conclude this year, it is pertinent to highlight how cities can become more inclusive and welcoming of all communities.

1. Six highlighted areas with implications for achieving inclusive cities

(1) Widening income gap between migrant workers and urban employees.

Even before the current crisis, the income gap between migrant workers and urban employees has continued to widen. Before 2014, the income gap between migrant workers and urban residents had been narrowing, but this trend was not sustained after 2014. Monthly salaries of migrant workers, despite already at lower levels, grew even slower than that of the established urban employees. This increasing gap should be a matter of great concern with respect to social inclusion in cities.

(2) Added needs from aging migrant workers.

We found that migrant workers are becoming older. From 2010 to 2016, the number of migrant workers below 30 had decreased while the number of migrant workers above 40 had increased. The average age of migrant workers also increased. As migrant workers grow older, their needs for medical services and social security also increase. This added demand will require specific attention and issues such as the portability and the coverage of healthcare insurance.

(3) Concentrated migration flows to large- and mid-sized cities.

In terms of spatial movement patterns, rural to urban migration has continued to concentrate in large- and medium-sized cities. This trend is expected to continue over the coming decade. Despite official efforts to stem the flow, the total number of migrants in top-tier cities such as Beijing, Shanghai, Tianjin and Chongqing has been and will remain large. At the same time, the proportion of migrant workers flowing into small towns and cities have slightly declined. These changes require continued efforts to further reform the system of accepting and supporting rural migrants to become truly urban residents.

(4) Erroneous policies on reallocating resources and populations.

It is time for policy makers to re-examine and reconsider the prevailing thinking that China's megacities are too large. Contrary to current policies, research indicates that China's cities could easily be much larger than what they are today. Policies induced by such thinking may be harming China's long-term economic development because when resources or population are reallocated away from the most productive areas, aggregate productivity may be lowered.

(5) Access for left-behind children to social services.

A much-discussed area that severely impacts inclusion in cities is the continuing situation of left-behind children. As of the end of 2018, there were still around 7 million left-behind children across China. Providing all children with access to decent education will have a big and long-lasting impact on China's social inclusion as well as the future quality of human resources in the country. It is therefore time to accept all families who want to move to cities and provide access to all social services such as health and education for all their family members. Please remember that every child left behind today is one more lost opportunity in the future.

(6) Declining populations in Chinese cities.

A surprising observation was the phenomenon of shrinking cities in China. We did not expect to find this. As a booming economy, China's urbanization strategy has always put an emphasis on accommodating growth, particularly population growth, but little attention has been drawn to population decline in some cities. By comparing urban populations in central urban districts in the years of 2013 and 2016, we found that at least 115 cities out of 661 had been losing population to different degrees during those three years. Rather than directing new and larger investment towards such cities, international experience suggests that right-sizing-urban-scale or smart-shrinking policies and programs may be more appropriate.

2. How to achieve truly inclusive cities

First, strive towards reducing the income gap between migrant workers and urban employees; Second, pay greater attention to the aging population of cities as they require new forms of urban services, community facilities and appropriate housing; Third, welcome all communities to the cities of their choice, including those who wish to move to larger cities; and Fourth, be more creative in dealing with the shrinking cities because communities of such cities may not require increased public investment but locally identified solutions that address localized challenges.

We at the World Bank value our long-standing relationship with China and particularly with the great city of Shanghai. We look forward to continuing the relationship by learning from the development path of Shanghai and other cities in China. We remain available to bring international experience and knowledge to inform the future.

Valuing Our Communities and Cities: People-centered Digital Governance

Wu Jiannan

Executive Vice President of China Academy of Urban Governance,

Shanghai Jiao Tong University

The theme of this year's Global Cities Day is "Valuing Our Communities and Cities", which focuses on building cities through joint efforts. Whether we can turn this vision into reality largely depends on whether cities can provide better services to the public. According to previous studies, the improvement of services is closely correlated with technological advancement. This is because technology provides conditions for the users and the service providers to interact with each other, and enable more communication between the two. This further contributes to the transformation of the digital governance technology. The United Nations defines digital technology as the expansion of information and communication technology that enables people to have access to the Internet, the mobile services, and the information technology in a faster and convenient way. The resulting closer communication will in turn leads to closer ties between governments. The use of such technology can change the dynamics between the governments and the civil servants, between governments, between governments and their citizens, and between the governments and the businesses.

Fig. 1
Digital governance

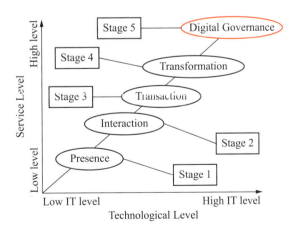

1. Global trends of digital governance

Since 2011, more and more countries have started to open up their data, making digital governance a global trend. On September 20, 2011, the United States, the United Kingdom, Norway, Mexico, Indonesia, the Philippines, Brazil and South Africa signed the "Open Government Declaration" and established the Open Government Partnership Group. In China, President Xi Jinping emphasized the need to promote the implementation of the national big data strategy in 2017, in order to accelerate the improvement of digital infrastructure, promote the integration and opening-up sharing of digital resources, and promote the construction of a digital China. In government report of 2019, Premier Li Keqiang also emphasized the importance of the application of technologies like big data and artificial intelligence.

Shanghai put forward the concept of "One-stop government services" in 2018. The scheme was officially launched in March 2018 with the promulgation of a series of official documents. Today, the One-stop government services not only provide one-stop services offline but also moved online as a one-stop mobile service app. It is designed to integrate public resources based on the all-process integration of online and offline services, to strengthen business coordination, to streamline government services, and to enable the public and enterprises to have access to all the government affairs via an integrated portal, and one-time application for all services. Now One-stop government services have literally become an essential part of urban communities. As of September 25, 2020, more than 2 500 types of services are offered on the platform, 84% of which are processed entirely online, and 95% of them only require only one visit to the offline center. So far, the total number of real-name registered users has reached more than 31 million, higher than Shanghai's 24 million permanent residents, more than 2.1 million of them are corporate users.

I'm going to discuss two questions today: First, how is the scheme of "One-stop government services" implemented? Second, how to achieve the good governance of cities through the scheme?

2. How can "One-stop government services" achieve digital governance?

The first question is how we have used "One-stop government services" in digital governance?

In Fig. 2, the picture on the left is the government structure before One-stop government services, and the picture on the right shows its current structure. The administrative center is where various service departments are set up, and above the center is the general portal of "One-stop

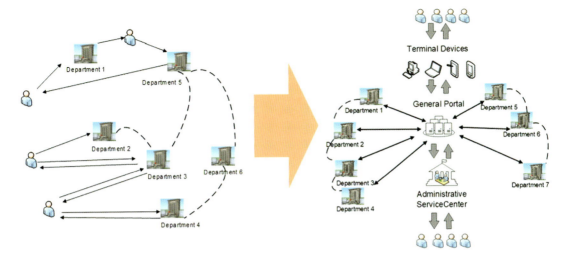

Fig. 2
Results of the Digital Transformation

government services", through which users can access information. This change of structure is the result of digital transformation. The work done by the government on big data centers in the past can be divided in two types: one is for the government and the other is for the public.

In 2018, Shanghai took the lead to set up the Shanghai Municipal Big Data Center in order to integrate and standardize all the services offered. At the same time, we started to upgrade the original service hotline "12345" and set about setting up the central portal and apps of "One-stop government services". In 2019, a special task force was set up, to oversee the implementation of the "good and bad comments" and "I need to find fault" campaigns. In 2020, a special working conference was organized to discuss ways in setting up a big data resource platform and mini programs on WeChat and Alipay. These efforts are making the governance more technology driven. We would like to describe them as integrated innovations, which can be divided into five categories. The first type consists of technological innovations, such as the application of the Internet, cloud computing, 5G, artificial intelligence, and big data technology. But application of technology is far from enough. We also need management innovation represented by new structure and new process. Examples of management innovation include putting in place a special task force, a big data center, an administrative service center, and the integration of online and offline services. Building on the success of management and service innovation such as one-stop online services, the online and offline services have been closely integrated. We have been able to push for innovation that promotes inter-departmental collaboration and governance innovation that changes the way of government-public interaction. In short, the application of new technology has pushed the transformation of the new government structure, which in turn has brought about a new governance model.

Fig. 3
Innovation
of "One-stop
government
services": from
Technology to
Governance

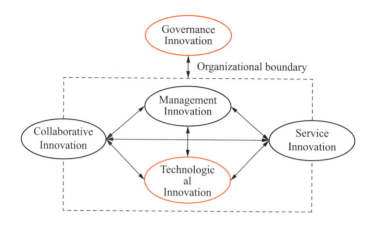

3. The digital governance of "One-stop government services" toward good governance

The second question is how the digital governance of "One-stop government services" has helped us achieve better governance. Good governance is a participatory system of governance in which the government, representing the people, is driven by the people's aspirations, serves the people, does good work for the people, solves the people's problems, and makes the people's lives more livable, satisfying, and enjoyable. To put it simply, good governance is about putting people at the center.

The goal of "One-stop government services" is to make government services as convenient as online shopping, so that people can access government services and reach out to the government anytime, anywhere through mobile apps or mini-programs of Alipay and WeChat. For instance, if a couple has a new child, in the past, they had to apply for up to ten types of documents for their baby, including birth certificates, identity certificates, maternity insurance applications, etc. Now with the implementation of the scheme, different government organizations started to integrate their information systems, shared data, and used electronic certificates and electronic signatures. In this way, the same process was cut from 100 days to 25 days. The couple now only need to visit the application center once instead of the original 14 times, and submit 5 documents instead of 26, and go through 2 processes instead of 22.

Take setting up of a business as another example. In 2018, it took 22 days and 7 steps to start a business in Shanghai. Now with the integration of new technology applications, including the implementation of data transmission, storage and utilization, paperless services and electronic licenses, it only takes only two days to complete the same process.

The "good and bad comments" and "I want to find fault" campaigns that I briefly mentioned a moment ago are also manifestations of a people-centered approach. Since the implementation of the "good and bad comments" campaign, we have received a total of 1.3 million suggestions in 9 months, of which 5 000 were negative. Each of these comments has been analyzed and given feedback. We also launched the "I want to find fault" campaign. More than 4 000 suggestions were submitted from the public within a month. We managed to respond to each suggestion within one working day, and in the end adopted more than half of the suggestions within a month. By implementing new technologies, "One-stop government services" put people-centered concept into practice and has helped us achieve people-centered good governance.

4. Digital governance: make the city and the world a better place

Finally, I'd like to address how good digital governance can make cities and the world a better place. We need to first think about how to transform the digital governance represented by "One-stop government services" into good digital governance.

On the left in Fig. 4 is the old form of government before the introduction of "One-stop government services", under which we see different government departments, civil servants and government systems existing as distinct entities. After we introduced the people-centered concept and applied technology into the government system, and through structural optimization, as well as process re-engineering, a new form of government has taken shape. Although each department still assumes different functions, we see more data sharing, data exchange, and more departmental collaboration taking place. As the result, the relationship between our government and enterprises and the public has shown significant new changes. The reform of government should start from within. Such reform is people-oriented because it can give the public more convenient access to the

Fig. 4
Government form before and after the implementation of "One-stop government services"

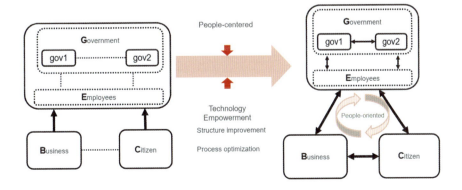

government services.

At the moment, digital governance has become an important new trend not only in China but also the whole world. By implementing "One-stop government services", Shanghai has made good progress in achieving people-centered digital governance. In terms of any lessons gained from the experience, the first is to empower the government and government staff through the use of new technologies, so that they could collaborate across different departments, share data and information. We should make people-oriented concept a guiding principle of all efforts, and make continued progress toward good governance, not only at the city level but also at the world level.

PARALLEL FORUMS

平行分论坛

FORUM

分论坛

New Technologies and Coordinative Governance
新兴技术与协同治理

主持人·HOST

崔兴硕·Heungsuk Choi

韩国高丽大学教授，亚洲公共管理学会副主席

Professor of Korea University, Vice Chairman of AAPA

亚历山大·科切古拉·Alexander Kochegura

俄罗斯总统国民经济和公共管理学院教授，亚洲公共管理学会副主席

Professor of The Russian Presidential Academy of National Economy and Public Administration, Vice Chairman of AAPA

Masao Kikuchi·菊池端夫

日本明治大学教授，亚洲公共管理学会执行理事

Professor of Meiji University, Executive Board of AAPA

韩国首尔的电子政务经验

崔兴硕

高丽大学教授，亚洲公共管理协会副会长

我将介绍首尔的电子政务，重点介绍智慧城市建设。

1. 城市衰落的情况和标准

韩国的人口正在消亡。预计约 37% 的地方政府，或者说 1 383 个由地方政府管辖的地区单位将永远消失。

2. 哪些区域会消失？

我们采取 5 个等级标准来评定即将消失的区域，比如某个区域问题的严重程度可能是二级或三级。在首尔，68% 的家庭单位陷入困境。所以，这个地区的所有人都面临着城市衰落的问题。

3. 城市振兴项目

按照上文的标准，首尔的评级是 3+，衰落和逐渐消失的可能性更大。韩国政府一直在尝试解决问题。他们正在推动更加平衡的发展。

60 个振兴项目分为 5 个不同类型，分别是降低失业率、创造就业、复苏、社区和社会融合。第一个是劳动社区振兴，更多关注社区中的人类发展。第二个是振兴城市设施衰败的地区。第三个是创造、重塑或恢复商业区域。第四个是 CBD（中央商务区）。第五个是最大的项目，即恢复经济基础。

2018 年共有 90 个区域被划入项目。其中一个是统营市。这座城市因造船业而繁荣。通过这种方式，他们正在重塑当地工业。这些地区中几乎有一半将由财政部门直接管理。其余 3

个较小的将由区政府管理或负责实施项目。首尔有 25 个区政府。

4. 智慧城市和电子政务

综合智慧城市平台由中央政府打造，并向地方政府推广。美国有一个移动平台，其中包括各种资源，如社区参与、安全保障、公共交通等。

作为国家智慧城市建设的两个基地之一，釜山生态三角洲智慧城为基层地方政府提供了相应的模式。韩国正大规模建设由国土交通部和中央政府负责的两座智慧城市。这一宏大目标包括计划增加 20% 的可再生能源，100% 的废物回收，创造 2.8 万个新工作岗位等。这些不是地方层面的目标，而是国家层面的目标。

5. 增强城市平台

增强城市平台有三个部分，通过这个平台，即使是在农村，人们也能轻松申请公共服务。基础服务的应用是在增强城市平台的第二层。

我们将继续向地方政府提供综合平台。2015 年，综合平台开始开发并投入使用。该平台已有数十个地方政府使用。

6. 平台的问题

有些平台在可持续性方面的理论基础不扎实。一些智慧城市服务是有针对性的。其中一些是常见的，还有一些具有连接性。由于政府可以参与并建立一些服务，然后将它们合并，可持续性问题就出现了。

新冠肺炎疫情与特大城市数字化治理的发展：日本东京的经验与启示

菊地端夫

明治大学公共管理系公共政策与管理教授

日本首都圈包括东京都和横滨市等地区，人口超过 3 800 万。我将快速介绍日本的疫情状况、电子政务举措及数字化转型问题。

1. 日本当前的疫情形势

2020 年 4 月初，日本出现了第一波疫情。在之后的第二波疫情中，死亡率远低于前一波。许多欧洲国家目前正经历第二或第三波疫情。日本将进入冬季，因此可能会出现第三波疫情。

日本是一个超级老龄化社会。按人均计算，日本的老年人口比其他任何国家都多。65 岁

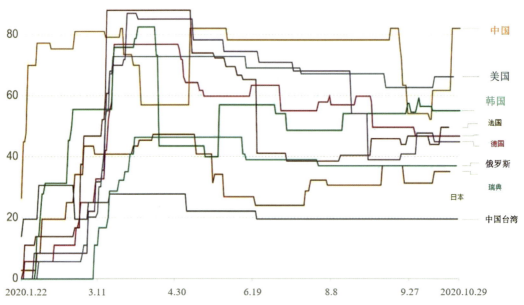

图 1　新冠肺炎疫情政府响应严厉指数

资料来源：Hale, Webster, Phillips, and Kira(2020)，牛津大学新冠疫情政府响应追踪系统，更新时间 2020 年 10 月 31 日 23:21（伦敦时间）。

及以上的老年人占到日本总人口的28%。然而，日本的新冠肺炎死亡率不高。据英国广播公司报道，日本每10万人中与新冠肺炎相关的死亡人数低于菲律宾等其他一些国家。尽管就目前的人口结构而言，日本是老龄化程度最高的国家。

尽管新冠肺炎检测能力有限，但是日本没有出现超额死亡。与美国等其他国家相比，日本政府采用了一种强制程度更低的模式。日本的国家紧急状态持续了两个月，从4月7日持续到5月底。国家紧急状态非常需要公民配合并遵循相关建议。牛津大学的研究显示，日本和瑞典的政府响应严厉指数低于其他国家和地区。

2. 数字治理发展

表1是最新发布的2020年版《联合国电子政务调查》。丹麦和韩国位列前两名，日本排在第14位。但是，作为提供电子政务服务的硬件和软件平台，社会保障与纳税人识别号制度于2016年启动，用途仅限于社会保障、税收和灾害管理。

表1
2020 年电子政务发展领先的国家

国家	EGDI 等级（子组）	区域	在线发展指数	人力资本指数	通信基础设施指数	EGDI 指数（2020）	EGDI 指数（2018）
丹麦	VH	欧洲	0.970 6	0.958 8	0.99/ 9	0.975 8	0.915 0
韩国	VH	亚洲	1.000 0	0.899 7	0.968 4	0.956 0	0.901 0
爱沙尼亚	VH	欧洲	0.994 1	0.926 6	0.921 2	0.947 3	0.848 6
芬兰	VH	欧洲	0.970 6	0.954 9	0.910 1	0.945 2	0.881 5
澳大利亚	VH	大洋洲	0.947 1	1.000 0	0.882 5	0.943 2	0.905 3
瑞典	VH	欧洲	0.900 0	0.947 1	0.962 5	0.936 5	0.888 2
英国	VH	欧洲	0.958 8	0.929 2	0.919 5	0.935 8	0.899 9
新西兰	VH	大洋洲	0.929 4	0.951 6	0.920 7	0.933 9	0.880 6
美国	VH	美洲	0.947 1	0.923 9	0.918 2	0.929 7	0.876 0
荷兰	VH	欧洲	0.905 9	0.934 9	0.927 6	0.922 8	0.875 7
新加坡	VH	亚洲	0.964 7	0.890 4	0.889 9	0.915 0	0.881 2
冰岛	VH	欧洲	0.794 1	0.952 5	0.983 8	0.910 1	0.831 6
挪威	VH	欧洲	0.876 5	0.939 2	0.903 4	0.906 4	0.855 7
日本	VH	亚洲	0.905 9	0.868 4	0.922 3	0.898 9	0.878 3

资料来源：2020 年《联合国电子政府调查》"EGDI 指数"即"电子政务发展指数"。

表 2 是日本、美国和韩国的社会保障与纳税人识别号制度的比较。在日本，允许使用的范围仅限于社会保障、税收和灾难应对，而在韩国和美国，该系统被广泛用于公共和私营部门。

表2
日、美、韩三国社会保障与纳税人识别号制度的比较

	日　　本	美　　国	韩　　国
编号系统	个人编号系统（My Number）	社会安全号码（SSN）	居民注册号
编号组成	12 位数字	9 位数字	13 位数字
数字含义	无	无	前六位代表出生日期
适用范围	仅限于社会安全、纳税和灾害响应	广泛应用于公共和私营部门	广泛应用于公共和私营部门
私企的运用	除非《个人编号法案》中规定，否则禁止使用	无限制	无限制（从 2012 年开始设置限制）
身份认证	使用带有个人编号图片的身份证	只能使用编号认证	只能使用编号认证
个人信息共享	去中心化管理（通过代码共享，而非直接使用编号）	只能使用编号共享（个人信息也存储在各个机构）	只能使用编号共享

资料来源：日本内阁官房个人编号推广办公室。

3. 新冠肺炎疫情与数字化治理

政府需要什么来应对新冠疫情？M. Jae Moon 指出了应对疫情的三个关键：敏捷性、透明度和公众参与。克里斯藤森（Christensen）和莱格雷德（Laegreid）提出了治理能力和合法性及两者间的平衡。戴必兵等人指出了风险沟通、信息和辟谣等问题。这些都与数字化治理有关，且未来有很大的研究与行动空间。

负责经济和社会事务的联合国副秘书长刘振民指出，新型冠状病毒大流行更新并巩固了电子政务的作用。这既体现在传统的数字服务提供方面，也体现在危机管理的创新实践之中。

疫情期间，日本在数字化治理或电子政府方面采取了怎样的行动？事实上，此次疫情揭示了日本电子政务工作的滞后。例如，用于接触者追踪的"疫情接触追踪应用（COCOA）"于 2020 年 6 月 19 日发布。虽然下载量超过 1 900 万次，但只覆盖了 20% 的人口。4 月，所有在日居民均可获得金额为 10 万日元（相当于 955 美元）的"特别定额给付金"。人们可以通过邮寄申请或在线上注册，但邮寄申请比线上申请更快。

在日本，政府机构喜欢使用传真。鉴于政府机构喜欢使用传真，在疫情初期，医院和诊

所都被要求使用传真报告病例，现在已经改成了线上报告。

东京都政府 2020 年 9 月刚刚发布了数字化转型策略，并宣布了"五个无"策略，即无纸化、无传真、无接触、无印章和无现金。这意味着将不再使用纸质、传真和印章且避免接触。

4. 总结

尽管有技术进步，但是数字化转型和电子政务的发展很大程度上还没有受到影响。尽管没有数字化转型措施，疫情却得到相对的控制。这是我们需要进一步探索的问题。日本的电子政务、电子配送和数字化转型都不尽如人意。然而，大流行病已得到控制。我并不是说数字化转型在应对疫情上不重要。在 2020 年的疫情或之后的后疫情时代，数字化服务对易感人群及老年人至关重要。

包括东京都政府在内的中央和地方政府都启动了智慧城市项目、数字办公室培育民用科技、5G 数据高速公路、人工智能、物联网和其他用于实现社会 5.0 的项目。然而，由于大流行以及随之而来的经济和财政停滞，它的未来并不明朗。对日本政府和社会来说，追求数字化转型既是机遇，又是挑战。

数字技术在城市居民就业中的生态系统分析：以澳大利亚的经验为例

李秉勤

新南威尔士大学

1. 数字化转型与电子政务——以澳大利亚为例

数字化转型有三个层次：数据化——数字数据；数字化——使用数字工具；数字化转型——改变行业的运作方式。由此我们可以看出，数字化转型不仅是指数字数据或使用数字工具，而且旨在改变行业的运作方式。

2014 年，澳大利亚政府决定开展一项审计工作，以探讨如何实现数字化转型。从 2015 年到 2018 年，澳大利亚政府逐步制定了数字化转型议程。议程分为三个方面：易于处理的政府，由民众提供信息的政府，以及适应数字时代的政府。前两个较为直观。为了实现最后一个目标，政府需要建设相关的基础设施，政府员工需要具备数字知识，以应对数字时代的挑战。

2. 数字化转型的生态系统方法

政府的职责是发布政策还是提供服务？在过去几十年里，政府提供的服务越来越少，但在制定政策和赋能方面做了更多的工作。面对数字化转型的挑战，政府不能只关注政策，因为制定政策和提供服务之间的关系在某种程度上发生了变化。例如，议程的三个方面是关于政府如何努力平衡以人为中心的服务和以企业为中心的服务之间的关系。人们逐渐意识到，政府、企业和民众必须联系在一起，联合行动，实现转型。

3. 以残障者数字化就业为例

如何进行联合行动或者说开展联合行动意味着什么？我将以一项政策为例。澳大利亚政府将儿童保育、老年护理、就业服务和残障者数字化就业等列为重点工作。残障者数字化就业对澳大利亚来说是最具挑战性的领域之一。尽管澳大利亚在促进残障者在数字化时代的就业方面做了很多努力，但成效并不显著。

根据数字化转型议程，澳大利亚的目标是在 2018 年新增 10 000 个岗位。但是受新冠肺炎疫情影响，这一目标的实现将会更加艰巨。残障者就业率已经非常低，而且会逐渐变得更加不容乐观。

（1）促进残障者就业的生态系统方法。政府需要运用生态系统方法来解决残障人士的就业问题。生态系统方法就是给予残障者不同类型的就业机会。人们需要一个无障碍的"环境"，包括物质环境（工作场所、通勤、技术、教育）和支持性的社会环境（员工、家庭、同事、客户），这对残障者来说更是如此。所有利益相关者都需要适应残障者就业生态系统的变化。

（2）数字时代残障者就业的政策体系。针对数字经济，政府出台了一些国家战略，以帮助雇主和职员并为他们提供培训。这些战略也适用于残障者。初创公司较为关注数字包容性和残障者就业，帮助残障者进入就业市场。一些公司已经开发了帮助残障者进入劳动力市场的软件。在数字技术方面，澳大利亚建立了一个全国宽带网络，让更多偏远地区的残障人士能够使用数字技术。此外，国家残障者战略旨在帮助更多的人找到工作。政府还鼓励非政府组织参与残障者创新就业计划。

幸运的是，在过去的几十年里，澳大利亚已经做出了巨大的努力，以提高残障者对物理环境的可及性，并将数字技术政策应用于目前的物质环境中。

4. 小结：数字化转型存在的问题

澳大利亚政府并没有将数字经济作为一种战略，这让数字化政策有了一个更好的未来。综上所述，数字化转型要求缩短政策与服务之间的距离；有了数字化转型，政府依然需要为残障人士改变社会环境，消除社会上对残障者的歧视；电子政务需要嵌入电子服务体系这一更广阔的市场和服务体系中。

当这一数字体系运转不畅，或试图控制政府和服务提供商的日常运营时，它会给人们，特别是残障人士带来更多的障碍，使他们无法很好地参与到这个系统中。

法国巴黎数字化转型的实践

丹尼尔·舍尔茨

法国国立路桥大学水文气象与复杂性实验室

1. 大巴黎地区的治理

大巴黎地区的多层次治理相当复杂。它是法国 18 个大区之一，由 8 个省和 1 268 个城市组成。

大巴黎快线就是一个例子。这是一条新的超级地铁。它将新增 200 公里的新铁路和 68 个新车站，使现有的地铁网络规模扩大一倍。它还需要 350 亿欧元的巨额投资。大巴黎快线计划每天运送 200 万名乘客，每 1—2 分钟发出一辆列车。

图 1
大巴黎快线

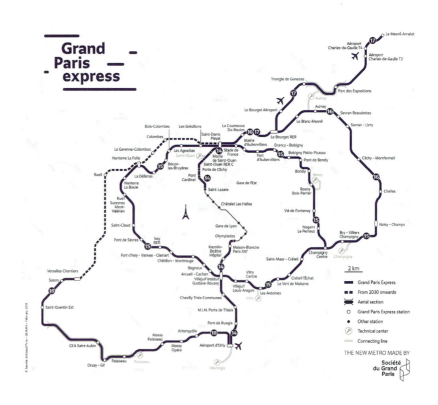

图 2
大巴黎快线站的多种
功能

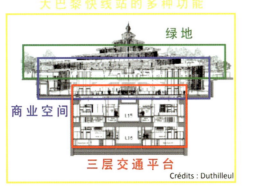

大巴黎地区情况非常复杂，意味着创新概念的实现不仅需要完善的基础设施网络，还需要参与者、观察和模型化的相互作用。

以车站为例。图 2 中的车站包括三层交通平台、商业空间和绿地。这个车站的设计理念是，利用不同的空间在此区域打造一个让人神清气爽的休闲平台。但是，这个车站的复杂之处在于，我们必须处理很多不同的物理问题，比如行人和规划。不同的平台组成了这个系统。我们需要让不同的空间一起作用，让这个车站变得更好。

目前需要建造 68 个站点。图 3 是 15 号线南行。乘坐大巴黎快线，你会发现城市中不同的主题地图，从地热能到城市改造、生物多样性、生态区等。真正的困难在于我们必须解决这些问题。

图 3
大巴黎快线 15 号线南行

2. 数字化治理原则

基于对 100 多家公司的数字挑战的研究和对 55 名数字高管的采访，flevypro 提炼出了将数字转型与有效成功联系起来的 7 个关键管理原则。第一点是如何理解所有信息，并从数字平台上连接起来。五年前提出的主要想法是集中共享信息，相反，随着时间的推移，如今的大势则是分散管理数字项目。

3. 威立雅的 2020—2023 战略规划

像威立雅这样的许多大企业在发展过程中会将联合国可持续发展目标纳入考虑，以便解决这些问题。威立雅试图在地球、社会、员工、股东和客户等各个层面上与联合国的可持续发展目标建立联系。

图 4
威立雅公司用于跟踪和报告其多方面业绩的仪表盘

4. 经验教训

我们获得了很多经验教训。首先，手机、互联网和社交媒体的用户群体庞大，约有 500 万。因此，与终端建立连接更可取。此外，新技术使我们能够快速处理大容量的、多类型的数据。但也存在一种信息过载，信息经历了由缺乏到过剩的过程。好在各国政府如今可以通过数字化手段来制定政策，满足公众需求。此外，政府还能提供个性化服务，增加决策透明度。数字化治理也为政府提供了一种更间接有效的干预自由市场的新途径，而不是集中规划。通过数字化治理，各国政府可以就新冠肺炎疫情期间的数字化等议题采取政策措施。除此之外，数字化可以帮助企业家建立和经营企业，极大程度减少繁杂手续，基本实现无纸化办公。但是现存的主要问题是我们对数字化不够熟悉，或者更确切地说，是假装非常了解它。虽然不了解人类的喜好，我们却可以轻易地装出了解的样子。现在的主要问题是，数字化治理这个复杂的系统能够帮助我们打破这个僵局吗？

5. 法国数字与生态转型中心

以法国数字和生态转型中心 Cap·digital 为例。它聚焦于巴黎地区，拥有 1 000 多名会员和擅长不同领域的律师，并承接了很多项目。它自称是欧洲范围内第一个关注数字和生态转型的机构。

Cap·digital 与巴黎地区的机构人员合作紧密，主要研究未来的建筑和生活。它获得了国家和法国地区一项特别投资计划的协助和支持，并得到许多人的声援。

这个大型项目有 120 个合作伙伴，包括经济学家、地方团体、机构、大学和学校，旨在利用人工智能让市民更多地参与该地区的发展。一项有关人们对现在数字化发展的态度的调查显示，人们对数字化发展的看法普遍比较负面，认为市民在城市建设中没有足够的话语权。Cap·digital 的目标是让 100 万法国居民能够在当地使用数字支付消费，并在 85% 的新建筑建设过程中使用 BIM 模型。这只是数字服务革新的一个例子，Cap·digital 的总体构想是为整个巴黎地区开发一个智能平台。

6. 展望未来

一个需要回答的问题是，谁将决定未来的城市？资金从何而来？对法国而言，这个问题的答案与国家、城市、私营部门都有关联。我们还必须搞清楚，科技的哪些新运用会改变城市生活？新的发展提案是什么？公众应该主动了解，而不是被动接受。我们要克服疑虑，实现可持续发展。大数据和人工智能是巨大的挑战，它们可能会改变观测和建模之间的界限。

7. 数据革命

有两个数据很重要。一是世界范围内 90% 的数据是在过去两年中收集的；二是其中 80% 的数据尚未整合或格式化，因此还未使用。那么，在数据时代，我们将引领怎样的革命？

克服政府数字化转型的系统性失败：对英国当前实践和未来方向的再思考

维尚·韦拉科迪

管理、法律与社会科学学院

数字化转型对政府意味着什么？我们应如何避免公共行政中出现的一些重大失误？在英国、欧洲、北美的部分地区，很多纳税人的钱被虚掷在耗资巨大的数字化转型项目中。对于这些未能达到预期效果的政府项目，我将总结其失败的原因。我会以英国政府的数字化转型项目为主要案例，并阐述我在过去20年中对电子政务的研究。

过去的20年里，我一直在研究电子政务这一概念，发现人们对其认识并未取得真正意义上的进步，我们也未能从失败中汲取经验。在过去的两三年里，我对那些未能按计划执行的项目一直抱以批评的态度。2018年12月，英国政府邀请我到下议院，面向科技界人士总结相关项目失败的原因。我今天的演讲将基于我此前在英国下议院所做的汇报工作展开。

1. 背景：反思英国数字化转型项目的失败实践

英国政府的国家IT发展计划主要的大型项目，均在2002年启动。英国的国民医疗服务体系（NHS）是全球最大的公共政府机构，数十万雇员遍布于全英各地的医院和基层医疗机构。项目的设想非常宏伟，它试图将整个英国的初级和二级医疗机构数字化，推出患者能随时随地通过电脑或移动设备访问的电子病历。医院和全科医生也将共享患者病历，服务过程将会更加顺畅和高效。然而，这个项目最后以失败告终，纳税人数十亿英镑打了水漂。在2012、2013年左右，该项目被叫停。

另一个失败案例是欧盟于2015年发起的面向农民的数字化支付项目。当农民从欧洲联盟委员会获得补贴时，整个过程主要是半人工操作或全数字化的。但是由于各种各样的问题，该项目陷入了停滞。例如，缺乏宽带接入、农民缺乏数字化技能、与各种系统的整合问题等等。

第三个案例是目前仍在进行的"统一福利救济金"项目，但实际的项目花费已经超过了预期。尤其是在疫情期间，封锁令使得许多人找不到工作或处于失业状态，人们不得不申请各种救济。由于该项目将原本半自动化的付款流程完全数字化，导致大量的付款延迟的情况发生。目前这个项目还在进行中，但由于太过复杂、庞大，还需要各个公共行政部门进行资源整合，该项目面临着许多问题与挑战。

英国政府数字化转型项目的其他失败案例如图 1 所示。通过比较初始成本、最终成本和纳税人成本，我们可以看到这些项目和预期的差距。英国运输部共享服务中心项目使纳税人多花了 2 800 万英镑；共同农业政策交付计划则额外花费 6 000 万英镑；裁判员天秤法项目额外花费 2.46 亿英镑；国防基建项目额外花费 480 万英镑；英国国家 IT 发展计划花费 4.04 亿英镑，但最终仍被叫停；苏格兰议会大楼项目额外花费 4.04 亿英镑。通过这些数据，我们可以看到，这些项目似乎从来没有按照计划、预算和时间表进行。

图 1
英国政府数字化转型
项目的失败案例

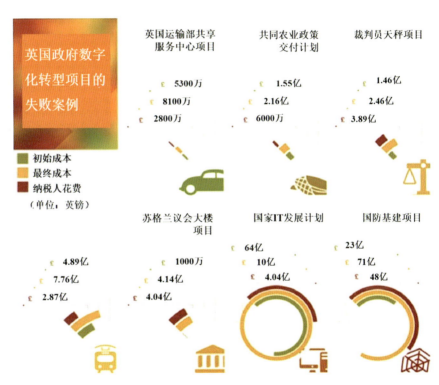

在韩国和中国等国家，这种情况同样存在。一些项目总是超出预算，纳税人的钱有去无回。导致这一现象的原因是什么？作为电子政务方面的研究者，在过去的 20 多年间，这个问题一直困扰着我。

2. 数字化转型中的问题

在数字化时代背景下，技术在政府和公共行政中应当处于什么样的位置？我们如何利用技术推动政府转型？在讨论数字化转型和政府服务转型之前，我们需要思考数字化在公共行政部门和数字化时代中的作用。我希望我今天的演讲，能提供一种新的思考、讨论数字政府的方式，抑或提供一个新的参考框架，而并非重新定义数字政府或电子政务。转型不依赖于技术，而是根植于政府作为一种社会和法律现象的本质。我们如何变革公共行政的现状，未来的公共行政又会是什么样的？我们又能否在政府数字化转型中实现破茧成蝶的故事？

3. 数字化转型的历史

自 20 世纪 90 年代末以来，我一直在研究电子政务领域。从 20 世纪 90 年代到 2000 年年中，我们的研究处于第一阶段。这一阶段的学者和研究人员非常关注电子政务的执行问题，包括发展支持、技术解决方案、执行问题和制度问题。

就商业和管理文献、科技文献和组织文献而言，我们已做了大量研究，但却鲜有学者关注公共行政和政策制定的相关文献。这是因为在研究电子政务的学者中，有超过 75% 的研究人员来自信息系统、信息技术、商业和管理背景，他们对于公众行政领域的了解并不深入。

进入 21 世纪头十年的后期，政府开始寻求打造智慧城市，但年轻人对政府引进的新技术并不买单。智慧城市的概念已经存在了 15、20 年，但它经过了很长时间才被人们所接受并成为城市生活的主流形式。过去人们所研究的理论和模型，都是围绕以技术为中心的概念所得出的，如统一使用技术模型、技术接受模型和创新扩散模型。一些已发表的论文，即使是基于不同的研究背景，采用的理论模型却千篇一律，几乎都是来自商业和管理文献以及技术应用文献。因此，智慧城市概念的应用和执行一直以来都是朝着一个方向发展。人们对电子政务没有产生新的思考，这很令人失望。

但目前这个领域已经开始朝着新的方向发展。20 世纪 90 年代以来，影响数字政府和公共行政领域的各种概念相继出现，包括合作、开放政府、大开放数据、去中心化区块链技术和政府物联网。科技的快速发展为人类带来诸多好处，然而研究人员并未对这些技术在公共行政背景下可发挥的作用及潜力引起重视。

我编辑过很多关于数字政府和电子政府领域的学术文献和期刊，但这些论文总是重复着老一套的研究理论和方法。我们需要做出改变。技术日新月异，但我们却对一些概念的理解产生了偏差，甚至应用了错误的研究理论和工具。

4. 重新思考电子政务的本质

自 20 世纪 90 年代至今涌现了许多电子政府的定义，大多都围绕着一个以网络为中心的子集。互联网和数字技术将会推动政府转型的观念目前仍深入人心，但我们要做的是探知未来。我并不是要提出一个新的定义，而是希望提供一种新的思维方式，一种基于政府本质角色的参考框架。

包括我们的同行以及从业者在内的人们，对电子政务的理念都非常熟悉，例如为民众提供信息、推行电子民主等等。但是，这是否意味着我们已经实现了电子民主呢？我们甚至还没有推行电子投票，至少在一些大的民主国家是如此。以技术为中心的电子政务进程是联合国最新采用的一种模式。通过门户网站这一以网络为中心的方法来推动政府转型，衡量的标准是基于政府在网站上的形象展示以及网站的交互性和交易性。按照政府的交易能力和信息能力，联合国电子政务服务机构对各国进行了排名。

不可否认电子政务有其好的一面。在过去的 20 年里，电子政务在接触渠道、透明度以及可及性等方面做出了许多努力，使民众的生活获得了极大改善。同时它也提高了政府的行政和运营效率。然而另一方面，它直接在现有流程上实施自动化，没有考虑这些流程本身是否高效。尤其要指出的是，有些公共行政部门成立已久，有很多历史遗留问题。电子政务也将这些部门中的流程自动化。在对现有流程进行调整之前就将现有业务流程自动化。

5. 电子政务现状：过去成绩优异但止步不前

从 20 世纪 90 年代至今，停滞的情况仍未改变：因为政府只注重电子政务的"电子化"，而忽视了背后庞大的"政务"系统。这个想法看似双管齐下：在政府前端对服务设计进行创新性改变，现有的服务衔接看似更加紧密，以此为庞大后端的转型争取时间。但是，这就像给猪涂口红一样——只能粉饰门脸，却无法改变事物的本质。但"让我们给猪涂上口红让它更加好看"的理念似乎已经变得有些根深蒂固。我认为这就是数字化转型和"转型"这个词的由来。在电子政务出现 15 到 20 年后，许多民主国家政府意识到自己并没有真正做到职能转型以及一些复杂操作。我们所做的仅仅只是将它们中的大部分数字化，使其更为便捷和可及，但这同时也是一个大问题。如今情况开始有所改变。但技术发展速度过快，以致我们难以掌握全局，因此导致了一些项目的重大失败。

在欧洲和北美，公共行政存在的一大问题在于，政府像是个服务行业，公民则作为客户，购买政府提供的服务和产品。那么，当你在申请护照时，你是客户还是公民？公民有纳税的义务。如果一个人不纳税或不持护照旅行，他将被起诉。因此，理解并厘清客户和服务、公民和公共行政的概念是非常重要的。在英国，公共行政意味着要么公民为其买单，要么公民为政府工作。

纳税人为医疗、警察、军队和教育买单。这些都服务于大众。公务员为政府工作。"公共"还意味着它为每个人所有，对所有公众开放而不是仅受限于私人。在政府语境中，我们常常将一切东西都囊括到"公共"的尺度下。

另一个有趣的词汇是"服务"。在字典中，"服务"可以指国家层级的工作，例如王室、军队等。它也可以指服务于国家的相关机构，提供如医疗、治安、消防、公务员、监狱、法院等服务。但在电子政务的语境中，"服务"指的是一个过程、一笔交易还是一段计算机代码？

电子政务服务有很多种含义，如数字化服务或在线公共服务、以民为本的服务、开放政府服务、组合服务和综合服务等。当我们在公共行政中使用"服务"这一概念时，我们需要格外注意其真正含义。

政府信息非常独特，因为它使公民了解国家和公共行政的政策及法律。政府信息对于民众的可及性至关重要，每一个人都应平等获得接触政府信息的渠道，并且政府信息必须是全面、最新的和准确的。

6. 关于政府与转型的基本问题

首先我们来看看以下几个基本问题。

政府是什么？政府是一个社会的决策机构。

政府的职能是什么？其职能是就有争议的社会事务给出解决方案并采取行动，即政府决策。

政府如何做到这一点？通过政策设计、实施和管理，对社会、经济和环境采取行动。至少，这个概念是基于已有的公共行政设置的意义上的。

政府如何转型？这是一个很宽泛的问题。如何真正做到政策设计、执行和管理层面的真正转型，从而促进社会和经济环境的发展？上述这些都是政府转型过程当中需要回答的基本问题。它们与技术的应用无关，政府需要回答的问题还包括：这一技术将如何影响某些政策决定，在技术实施的背后政府想要达到的政策成果是什么，政府想要实现什么效益，它们会对民众产生什么影响，如何开始转型等等。本人的研究表明，政策工具是实现转型目标的关键。

7. 政策工具是解决问题的关键

政策工具是政府用以改变社会、经济或环境来实现其政策目标的工具。它由政府内部的不同公共行政机构执行，以在政策的设计、实施和管理中实现政府目标。例如税收、法律、医疗和保险等皆为政策工具。

在新冠肺炎疫情的大环境下，我们应使用何种政策工具以确保教育继续发展同时又不妨碍医疗服务？这一思考是非常重要的。

表1
胡德对政策工具的分类

政府工具	意义解释	工具的例子
信息型工具	收集和传播信息的能力	安全项目，公共及公司档案
权威型工具	规范公众行为的能力	法律、税收、许可证、法规
财政型工具	提供资金的能力	福利、补助金、贷款、补贴
组织型工具	直接作用于人或环境的物理能力	基础设施、医疗服务（公共产品和服务）

资料来源：Hood, C., and Margetts, H. Z., 2007, *The Tools of Government in the Digital Age,* Basingstoke: Palgrave Macmillan.

大多数的转型都发生在这个框架内：信息型工具、权威型工具、财政型和组织型工具。若政府想要在应用型数字化转型中取得成功，就需要重视这一点。

疫情期间，英国政府为疫情导致的无法工作的民众支付了 80% 的工资。这一计划原本即将暂停，但由于另一轮封锁即将到来，该计划在本月底被延长实施一个月。

政府所使用的政策工具对公共行政、公共服务和公共产品都会产生影响。政府制定政策目标，并通过与公民、企业和社区密切相关的公共行政机构、公共服务和商品来实施政策。

表2
政策子工具的分类

资源类型	政策子工具	例子
信息型工具	信息提供	公共医疗项目，健康咨询网站
	数据发布	国家统计数据，普查数据，绩效数据
	自助服务信息	国家档案，法律数据库，公司信息
权威型工具	国家特权	刑法，外交关系，军事行动，边境管制，货币管制
	税收和关税	个人所得税，公司税，营业税，进口税，燃油税，酒税
	登记，许可和标准	护照 / 身份证，驾驶执照，出生登记，贸易许可证，停车许可证
财政型工具	津贴，拨款，补贴，贷款	失业救济金，养老金，住房 / 护理津贴，研究补助金，学生资助金
组织型工具	公共服务	公用事业，邮件，卫生，教育，福利，交通，应急，废物处理，住宿
	公共产品	公路，铁路，机场，公园，广播，博物馆，图书馆，公共住房
元类		
政策工具信息		

图 2
数字化转型

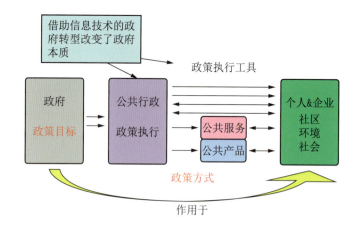

如今，英国应用的新技术包括默认数字化、设计数字化、政策设计数字化以及政策设计转型。

语言非常重要，因此政府应当注意语言的使用。公民不是"客户"，政府也不提供"服务"。政策设计是实现转型的途径，政策工具是政策设计的手段。技术只是对政策工具起到辅助的作用。治理国家是一项艰巨的任务，现有的官僚公共行政因此变得复杂。

8. 政府数字化转型的未来努力方向：政府应将精力放在公共服务和公共产品上

政府应将精力放在公共服务和公共产品上。应当以人为本，切实考虑民众真正的需求，关注复杂的、不断演变的、多机构系统，关注信息与通信技术（ICT）的潜力之有限性。

政府应当注重需求管理：更好地利用自身能力；有针对性地满足不同需求，优化服务；采取新措施以未雨绸缪。当新需求出现而政府又未能管理需求时，更大的问题就会出现。

如果政府想要从发展的早期阶段最终实现破茧成蝶，应重点关注政策方面的转变。

一网通办：线上线下融合的政务服务

郑　磊

复旦大学教授

我想谈谈上海的"一网通办"，这是一个为所有市民提供线上线下一体化服务的中心，这一案例被列入了《2020 年联合国电子政府调查》。在上海，"一网通办"被称为以数据为中心的数字政府线上线下一体化。

1. "一网通办"的建设

在"一网通办"项目出现之前，政务服务存在一些问题。市民如果想要办一个业务，必须跑很多不同的机构。比如说，如果我想成立一家新公司或买一套房子，我必须去 A 机构提交申请和其他必要文件。一周后，A 机构会将之前提交的资料还给我，并给我一张证明。然后，我要带着我从 A 机构收到的证明去 B 机构或 B 部门，提交新的申请，然后去 D 机构……我只需要办一个业务，却要在不同的机构或部门之间来回奔波。这是市民与政府互动的传统业务模式。这一模式的问题是，每个服务机构都需要确定它负责哪种服务，并向市民颁发特定证明。但从市民的角度来看，所有这些服务都只为办一个业务。这样很浪费时间。因此，上海市政府决定建造一个中心，让市民可以一次性办完业务。

为此，政府必须重新命名每个业务。不管市民是想要开餐馆、买房子、申请入学、升学，还是想办理其他业务，他们只需要提交一次申请。一个业务的所有相关机构或部门都在一个系统里，共享相关文件和信息。这就是"一网通办"的理念。此外，为了整合数据，上海市政府决定成立一个新的机构——上海市大数据中心。它将整合所有机构的数据，从而使这种"一站式"服务成为可能。基于数据流和跨部门信息共享，政府将分散的机构服务整合为一站式流程。

"一网通办"服务在线上线下均可使用。所有公民均可享受这项服务。如果市民不知道如何使用手机应用程序或电脑网站，可以去线下服务中心。全上海共有 200 个服务中心，分布在各个社区。线上网站和线下中心共享信息，使得线上和线下服务更加便利。如今，大多数市民更喜欢使用手机而不是电脑，因此政府推出了手机应用，可以通过微信和支付宝小程序使用，也可以在安卓或苹果商店下载使用。不过，办理公司业务必须在电脑网站上进行，因为公司业务的流程较复杂，难以在较小的手机屏幕上操作。此外，市民也可以拨打"12345"热线，咨询提交申请和准备材料等相关事宜。

2."一网通办"面临的挑战

上海市政府在推行"一网通办"时面临着许多挑战。首先，如何为游客或外商服务？其次，如何提高线上服务的比例？

市民可以到上海的任何一个服务中心获取所需服务。例如，如果市民想要创业，他们可以去 200 个服务中心中的任何一个来完成相关流程，因为所有服务中心都连接着同一个大数据中心。所以他们可以"随地"获取服务。市民也可以"随时"获取服务，也就是说，市民可以全年 24 小时获取服务。如果市民使用线上服务，可以随时收到业务证明。在线下服务中心，有类似自助取款机的自助服务机器，所以在线下服务中心的非营业时间，市民也能够自助获取服务。

3. 城市服务与管理的未来

"一网通办"项目启动至今已有两年。项目中存在一些错误或漏洞，市民可能对此也有不满意的地方。在接下来的五年里，我们将从市民的角度出发，而不是只局限在政府的视角，努力把"一网通办"做得更好。政府需要收集每次服务后市民的反馈，并改进项目。基于这些反馈，政府将进一步提升服务。

接下来的五年里，政府也会尝试整合城市的服务与管理。除了"一网通办"服务体系，还有另一个旨在通过一个平台管理全市的系统。该系统借助一个平台，对城市交通、环境保护、食品安全进行管理，推动智慧城市、智慧政府和智慧治理项目的建设。如果城市的服务和管理可以共享数据，这两个系统就可以在社会中融为一体。现在，我们仍在为此而努力。

公众投诉与政府回应：以北京为例

马　亮

中国人民大学教授

我将以北京市"12345"政府服务热线为例，谈谈它为中国其他城市和其他国家带来的启示。我将提到目前我们对政府服务热线的认识，北京热线的快速发展，以及在发展过程中出现的问题。

1. 政府服务热线与城市治

政府要切实有效地回应市民诉求，这点非常重要。中国的地方政府被划分为市、区、乡镇、街道等层级，每一层级都设有各类政府部门，提高政府效率和效力的关键是提高其对市民需求的响应能力。

目前有很多关于非紧急热线使用的研究。例如，在美国，"311"非紧急服务热线被广泛使用。这不仅能够提升政府服务，而且能够管理绩效。将热线数据分派至各政府部门，每周或每月监测进展情况，可以实现热线与政府机构的紧密结合，使战略管理更具可行性。

2. 中国的城市热线

在中国，政府服务热线的使用存在一些问题。例如，由于领导层更替或文化因素，热线在有的市、县被叫停。近年来，许多学者开始关注政府服务热线的可持续性问题。辽宁省沈阳市在 1983 年开通了中国第一条城市热线，此后，越来越多的城市开通了市级热线。除此之外，一些政府机构也开通了热线，来满足特定的需要。部分城市有近 60 条甚至更多的政府服务热线。这种情况下，市民和企业不知道该拨打哪一个号码。之后，这些热线被整合为一个统一的热线号码"12345"。社交媒体也为市民向政府反映诉求或提建议提供了更多元化的渠道。

3. 北京的政府服务热线及反馈机制

2008 年北京奥运会期间，热线"12345"得到了整合和完善。但直到 2019 年，该热线才得到了实质性改进，得以高效运行，北京政府提出了"接诉即办"的群众诉求快速响应机制。仅一年时间内，服务效果就有了明显的改善。首先，响应率提高至 100%，这意味着市民反映的每一个诉求都能得到回应；其次，解决率提高至 75% 左右，即市民诉求已经被提交和处理的比例；最后，群众满意率高达 87% 左右。目前，北京已经建立了"双循环反馈机制"，这意味着市民可通过热线反映诉求，热线服务与政府沟通和合作，解决市民的关切并作出回应。这种反馈机制有助于使市民诉求更方便更直接地得到政府的回应。

4. 北京政府服务热线的激励机制

北京市政府在市、区、街道三个层面推行高效激励制度。该制度覆盖所有政府机构、地区和城镇。每月举行考核会议，审查各政府机构办理市民诉求的情况，进行"响应率、解决率和满意率"的"三率"考核排名，并将结果对外公布。市委书记也会对每名干部的表现进行考评，使各政府机构了解彼此的表现。北京市政府以人为本，对所有市民和企业的反馈意见进行多轮审查。

自上而下的排名和评级能有效地鼓励地方政府回应市民的关切，对地方政府的表现评估取决于其管理和回应市民关切的质量。此外，由于表现的评价是相对的，各地方政府都积极地与兄弟单位交流学习。北京推行的高效激励制度的特点，主要体现在社区层面。北京在社区设立了回应市民关切的机构，反馈途径更为直接。

5. 北京政府服务热线存在的问题

然而，北京政府服务热线的运作也存在一些问题。第一，商业成本高昂。目前，北京的呼叫中心有近 1 500 名话务员，且计划继续扩大员工队伍。但由于预算削减，这将很难实现。因此，如何维护系统和降低成本是重要问题。第二，北京的热线运行机制是事后响应模式，而不是事先预测。市民诉求可能是周期性的，或者最初就会通过某些信号表现出来。大数据分析等技术可以帮助政府提前加以干预解决，而不是被动回应。第三，有一定的暗箱操作可能。由于高效激励制度，地方政府为实现目标可能会采取不合理的方式方法。第四，在主要领导卸任后很难维持制度运转。

6. 北京政府服务热线的成功转型

目前，北京"12345"热线正向 2.0 版升级转型。转型成功的关键在于以下四点。第一，通过立法或文化变革使政府制度化；第二，开发更多基于人工智能（AI）的应用，减少话务员的工作；第三，将数据在政府内部、各部门间、甚至全社会共享；第四，通过对案例的归纳和与其他案例的比较，完善治理模式的运作。

智慧城市与智能汽车：整合协同视角

西蒙·马文
英国谢菲尔德大学城市研究所教授

艾丹·怀尔德
英国谢菲尔德大学城市研究所教授

1. 背景

西蒙·马文：我们今天演讲的主题是"智慧城市与智能汽车"。智能汽车通常被称为"自动驾驶汽车"，所以在接下来的演讲中我会使用这个词。我们要思考的是有关智慧城市和自动驾驶汽车之间的关系。

艾丹和我来自谢菲尔德大学城市研究所，我们组成了一个跨学科的研究小组，已经做了很多研究来探索技术变革、低碳转型、智慧城市、机器人和自动化之间的相互关系，以及它们在城市背景下是如何相互作用的。我们工作的一部分就是厘清一些夸大技术好处和变革潜力的说法。我们也想看看城市生活通常如何影响这些技术的使用和实施（这些技术的使用和实施方式有时不同寻常），还想看看过分夸大新技术的变革性影响所带来的问题。

针对技术变革和城市生活之间的相互关系，以及这些关系互动的方式，我们希望观点更加中立和有批判性，特别是我们在自动化和机器人领域所做的工作。在过去的五年里，我们做了大量关于智慧城市的工作，对一系列新技术的出现尤为感兴趣，也就是第四次工业革命，包括人工智能、自动化和机器人。某种转变可能正在发生，城市环境被用作展示一些技术的平台。然而，这些技术不一定会受到智慧城市的青睐，因为智慧城市更注重软件开发。

因此，我们一直在试图理解城市环境如何成为人工智能、无人机、送货机器人和自动驾驶汽车的科学实验场。我们在问自己一个目前还没有答案的问题：这与智慧城市相比有什么异同点？几年前，我们为英国机器人和自动系统网络做了一项工作，其中提到了人工智能、机器人和自动驾驶汽车实验的出现。尽管这种城市实验的情况与智慧城市有时存在部分重叠，但通常在实验的总体优先级和参与者方面会有很大的差异。这似乎表明这种新的技术变革可能会有一些不同之处。

2. 观点一

西蒙·马文：我们需要了解这种新的技术变革。正如论坛组织者所问的，智慧城市和自动驾驶汽车之间的关系是什么？为什么关于智慧城市和自动驾驶汽车会存在争论？为什么它们被分开研究并一直处于分隔状态？我们应该如何思考这种关系？这种分割的原因是什么？我们该如何把它们完美地结合在一起呢？在我们看来，存在三大挑战。关于智慧城市的辩论主要围绕计算逻辑、二元决策和二元逻辑的应用、数据的利用及其在城市生活中不同领域的应用。

我们已经听到很多关于国家技术项目的警告，称其中存在一些问题。机器人和自动驾驶汽车有着不同的内在逻辑。机器人和自动驾驶汽车更多的是关于物流、效率和时空运动的优化，关注城市的物质性。

有人提到了数字化在实际应用方面的困难，这些困难造成了一些障碍。我认为这是一个非常有趣的见解，因为我们还没有真正理解关于软件和硬件之间的相互关系。问题是我们如何开始将有关软件和硬件的讨论放在自动化城市重组这一概念中，而且我们也在努力设想一种语言，通过这种语言，我们可以描述社会和物理过程的自动化过程，该过程将以新的方式重新平衡人类和机器之间的关系。

在这些技术系统中，思考城市和机器人之间的关系至关重要。很明显，城市环境并不是一张空白的纸，因为这些技术已在城市中得到应用，但并不彻底。过程中有阻力和成本问题，也存在争议。技术项目因其所处的城市不同，可能会失败或者以不同的方式被重塑。但即便没有这一问题，我们也一直在努力解决并思考智慧城市和自动驾驶汽车之间的关系。我们将在接下来的演讲中简要地讨论这个问题。我们认为我们需要从单纯的技术和经济重心中走出来。我们需要设想建立一个更具混杂性的城市环境。在城市环境中，我们思考在决策过程中人类和机器的相互作用。而混杂性的概念可能提供了一种更富有成效和不那么绝对的方式来帮助我们思考这些关系。

为什么会有关于智慧城市的争论和关于自动驾驶车辆的争论？你可能认为两者是高度关联的，因为它们都关心数字和统计技术的应用，应该能很好地结合在一起。但当我们真正开始研究有关这些实验和应用的文献时，我们发现它们之间有很多脱节之处。

这不同于我们今天上午听到的有关智慧城市的应用，这些应用主要围绕着效率、合理化和提高政府服务的有效性和响应速度。自动驾驶汽车、无人机和机器人如何才能符合这种逻辑？这是一个完全不同的逻辑吗？它是否涉及完全不同的领域？它能否更广泛地与城市管理和城市服务有关的问题联系起来？我认为在回答这些重要的问题时，我们首先要尝试和理解的是智慧城市和自动驾驶汽车有非常不同的历史轨迹。我们认为，与城市生活和城市的未来相关的智慧城市和自动化驾驶汽车应成为两个独立的议题。

我们今天上午听到的关于智慧城市的讨论就是利用数据和软件在城市生活诸多不同领域之间实现某种形式的联系，特别是关于这些综合系统在地方政府中的应用，以及它们连接目前城市服务中不相连的领域的能力。这主要是一种基于软件系统的组织逻辑。这些软件系统在企业环境中的应用有特定的历史。我们开发这些智慧城市的技术和产品来整合企业商业实体，在城市管理中这些技术和产品得到了应用。最初的想法是它们可以串联起基础设施、住房和建筑环境，并可以提供能源管理和交通管理。

人们对智慧城市总的设想上问题更大。就自动驾驶汽车的争论而言，实际上有一个完全不同的逻辑，即把自动驾驶汽车而非综合系统的概念放在首位，因此它的关注范围要小得多，集中在尝试生产一辆自动驾驶或更自动、更智能的汽车上。争论点并没有关注整个城市系统，也没有试图去理解城市一体化。这是一个完全不同的出发点。我们可以看到，不管是无人机送货还是社交机器人的使用都围绕着交通工具本身，而不是考虑工具在城市环境下的作用。这意味着，一方非常关注软件和组织变革，而另一方则关注硬件和移动性。

当我们审视这些发展史，并且将发展置于城市发展的背景下时，我们将会看到有关智慧城市的各种争论可追溯到 20 世纪二三十年代。那时，争论涉及电话，电话的发明使得家庭和企业分隔，与此同时高速公路、州际公路和其他提升交通运力的设施的发展，共同助力郊区化的发展。20 世纪八九十年代出现了更多关于电信的争论，比如网络城市和数字城市。因此，智慧城市中关于数字技术应用的想法由来已久。其中涉及的组织机构主要是软件公司和科技公司。由于市场已经饱和，加之互联互通城市系统愿景，人们正开发产品并开拓智慧城市市场。因此，有一种说法是，出于一些合理的原因，互不相关的事务通常可以重新连接。

例如，数字化的企业实体不仅利用以企业经营为基础的软件系统，而且整合了公司的生产、物流、人力资源等方方面面。这种理念可应用于城市环境中。城市场景的应用更加急迫。这反映了政府所面临的一些问题。这一观点背后的原因主要是围绕计算逻辑和二进制数据的首要地位，以及将其作为首选的决策模式纳入软件系统。

相比之下，在自动驾驶领域，如自动飞机、交通通信技术、仓库和封闭空间内研发的自动驾驶汽车，特别是军事活动，对促进自主技术的发展起到了至关重要的刺激作用。即便如此，这些技术实际上是在一个封闭的军事环境中发展起来的，应用于城市时，仍然需要关注安全性和可控性。这涉及智慧城市中不同的参与者，包括汽车和自动化汽车技术的专家、汽车制造商、高度数字化的科技公司以及地理信息系统绘图体系和中心。这是一个全新的视角，让我们得以了解那些可能从未将自动驾驶技术和城市政策、战略及政治联系起来的研究者现在如何开发系统，以便在城市环境中加以利用。

上述所谈到的互联互通的愿景和案例涉及高效的物流产业。因此，我们需要重点关注物流产业开发的软件，比如货运、航空、配送和仓储，能够可以被应用于城市生活中。上述提到的愿景围绕自动移动的概念，克服交通拥堵的问题，超越时间和空间限制，改善城市内的交通运输。该愿景合乎情理，符合物流逻辑。它依赖于竞争，但更多的是围绕着城市内的硬件、移动、人、货物和服务。

我们正在处理两种完全不同的逻辑。接下来由我的同事艾丹·怀尔德做第二部分的演讲。

3. 观点二

艾丹·怀尔德：我们的第二个观点是，思考数字营销的软件和源自机器人和自动化系统应用的硬件之间的关系。这些应用包括自动驾驶汽车、服务机器人、各类无人机等。自从我们围绕城市机器人和自动化展开讨论以来，这个问题就一直困扰着我们，它也是我们在思考硬件问题上的一个显著的转变。而这个问题所探究的关系不同于以往人和机器之间的关系，特别是人类和机器人的互动。这对城市建设意味着什么？它是如何将基础设施的硬件与数字和非数字形式的城市管理连接起来的呢？我们认为，一直令我们心驰神往的城市机器人就是交通工具方面硬件的开发。

我们都是城市人，都对城市很感兴趣。我作为一名城市设计师，十分关注城市规划。我们致力于社会和技术的发展以及城市的未来。硬件的吸引力在于它事关城市的物理变化，它深刻影响着我们如何设计城市、规划城市，影响着人们的出行和生活方式。

硬件的早期开发至关重要，因为它奠定了未来的发展方向。我们的每一项实验都集中研究这些道路是如何发展的，我们如何思考这些新的关系，什么样的模式和方法变得更具主导地位，其中涉及哪些因素，以及什么样的场景更为重要。我们认为，尽管智慧城市的有关讨论早于机器人，但目前的发展却处于落后阶段。

有个问题是，为什么我们会有后智慧城市、"智慧城市+"和一般意义上的智慧城市，还是说我们用的是不同的指称。之前的一个演讲强调了语言描述的重要性，并仔细思考了我们目前使用的语言以及不同的参与者使用的语言。机器人领域是否正在使用与智慧城市领域相同的语言？还是针对不同的逻辑有不同的语言？就是否容易受影响来讲，软件、数据和硬件变化之间确实存在着脱节。我们已经在世界各地的不同环境中做了很多工作。

我们正以试验、生活实验室等方式对机器人基础设施采取实地研究，进行前沿探索。但是，要将数字技术与硬件结合，还存在很多困难。我将在后续演讲中阐述其中的一些挑战。

目前机器人处于研发阶段。数字领域和智慧城市都不是固定不变的。就可能性而言，未来能做些什么呢？随着人工智能不断发展，我们对人类、智慧城市以及机器人两个领域的变化有了有趣的认识。但关键在于我们该如何看待智慧城市的软硬件之间的相互关系。智慧城市的框架、软件和平台之间总是相互割裂。英国的例子就清楚地反映了这一点，特别是不同公共政策领域的不同平台。但在世界各地，你可以在不同的地方看到不同的方法来实现智慧城市。在某些领域，它们或多或少相互连通。

我一直在关注数字化方面的动态，关注数字化如何扩展硬件功能并促使某些领域相互连通。我们在里约热内卢进行了一些其他的研究，那是一种割裂——另一种城市管理形式。但这并不是智慧城市问题的必要部分。在最新的智慧城市管理的案例中，这一形式十分常见，并开始影响硬件管理层面。

无论是自动驾驶汽车，还是各种形式的服务机器人，如送货机器人、安防机器人和无人机等，甚至包括外骨骼等增强个人能力的机器人，这些机器人和自主系统的硬件可能采取不同管理形式。在早期阶段，我们的城市可能会被不同类型的机器人和自动驾驶汽车以不同的方式重塑。它们会如何运作？它们的经营模式可能是什么？对于集体管理系统中的每个选择，这些技术是否会均匀分布在城市各处？出于资金和投资考虑，一些更具变革性的技术或者对社会有益的技术能否被用于人口较少的自然场所？

机器人和自动驾驶汽车的未来并不是单一的。我们研究的益处之一是思考政府机构、私有企业和竞争对手如何通过研发和实施技术来塑造未来。现在正是思考智慧城市和机器人之间可能的互动领域的好时机。自动驾驶汽车领域凸显了一系列更广泛的问题。这些问题必须被放置在一个更大的框架（城市机器人结构或重建城市自动化）中加以研究。

4. 观点三

艾丹·怀尔德：我们现有关于智慧城市的设想中，部分是智慧城市领域中的原创，但部分是由希望通过提供整套方案来获得商业利益的公司所推动的。我们认为，完全一体化和无限制自主权是不可能实现的。因此，我们如何按照另外一个理念来实现？这个理念使我们摆脱所谓的智慧城市融合的观念，转而认为有必要形成不同种类的混合解决方案。实际上，从智慧城市和机器人及自动化系统之间的关系看，我们对混合解决方案的需求将更为迫切。

尽管愿景雄心勃勃，但是智慧城市常被切分为不同的平台和应用。我们已在智慧城市标准方面开展了一些研究，发现推行标准化存在困难，将特定的领域整合或实施跨地区的共同标准更是难上加难。其中涉及多类产品、服务和供应商。之前演讲中的英国案例清楚地表明，这些标准在多数情况下是碎片化的。就智慧城市的协调发展或碎片化程度方面来看，一些国家则相对较好，比如中国和韩国。碎片化问题已经成为智慧城市讨论的一部分。智慧城市目前存在困惑和不适。所以，单一的项目永远无法处理城市的复杂性，我们还需解决许多不同的问题。

就自动驾驶汽车而言，我们希望它最终能实现完全自动化，希望这一理想化的愿景能成为常态。自动驾驶汽车在工程层面来讲有一个目标，也可以说有一个挑战。同一体化概念一样，自动驾驶汽车同样问题重重。一些人表示，机器人和自动驾驶汽车将受到质疑和抵制，他们需要在复杂、混乱和困难的城市中运行，而且需要和人打交道——所有汽车自动化问题的解决都耗资巨大。这并不是我们研究的重点。我们想要找到一种方法来融合"非人"因素，而这离不开全新的、改造过的基础设施。

如今，我们正处在过渡期，想要将自动驾驶汽车融入城市，我们必须开发能解决各类复杂问题的自动系统。除此之外，非自动驾驶汽车必须由人类驾驶。目前基础设施并不完全适合自动驾驶汽车。无论自动驾驶汽车是否能满足工程和物流需求，我们都需重点关注智慧城市和自动驾驶汽车之间的复杂关系。

其中主要挑战在于已经融入城市发展中的治理、政策和技术。这需要制定满足不同地区的混合解决方案。那么，混合解决方案到底是什么？它要求所有自动驾驶汽车都必须融入城市，能应对各类复杂问题，包括城市治理、提高公众参与度、保持公众信任；还包括如何规划以实现空间自动化以及调整各地立法，如何应对所有新的基础设施，如何将自动驾驶汽车和其他形式的自动化系统和机器人融入城市的发展中；还涉及商业模式、投资，如何思考移动性的问题，个人和集体移动形式，以及公共交通等。就混合式解决方案来讲，没有单一的模型或蓝图，这需要考虑不同的城市各自的特点（不同的政府各有其优先事项）、不同资源的获取途径以及与一系列私营企业、咨询企业的合作事项。

我们已在无人机基础设施方面做了很多研究。我们一直在思考如何在不同地区为无人机创造空间以及规划合理的无人机配送路线。但无人机融入城市还有其他模式，需要进行试验。机器人企业有时会受挫，因为他们无法在实际场景中来进行试验。

我们对自动驾驶汽车的研究不仅仅局限于自动驾驶汽车本身，还包括城市机器人管理和智慧城市管理的方法。我们将城市视为一个管理实体，因为城市需要通过不同的方式被管理，如数字手段、增加人工智能应用和城市中的人类决策。就国际社会、不同国家、不同城市和城市内部的事务而言，地理是一个重要的影响因素，不同场景的试验十分重要。各国政府以不同的方式来处理这个问题，治理逻辑也各不相同。关于机器人和各种其他方式，还有围绕风险信任的问题，可以通过公共优先事项和人的作用等不同的方法思考解决方案。这是一组混合的问题。

5. 结论

艾丹·怀尔德：我们发现智慧城市和自动驾驶汽车在我们的研究中具有重要的价值。这一点在上述演讲中尚未详细说明。以英国为例，研究过程中，我们确实为智慧城市和自动驾驶汽车之间的关系感到困惑，但也发现这方面研究有巨大的成效。我们在实际场景中对自动驾驶汽车进行了试验和应用研究，希望这能为本次论坛提供一些参考。

目前，自动驾驶汽车被期待在更广泛的领域得到应用，成为城市管理系统的一部分。它们可以取得何种发展，我们可以从中学到什么，如何通过规范化治理解决技术管理问题，这不仅仅是在工程上的挑战，还面临治理、政策和法规问题。不同的区域、国家和利益方应该相互借鉴。至于智慧城市和自动驾驶汽车使用何种语言，则需要国际上共同的经验帮助我们在真实的场景中进行思考。

最后一个问题是如何将自动驾驶汽车整合到更广泛的城市自动化系统中。这实际上已经取得了进展。我们在世界各地的城市，比如广州，做过研究，我们还和阿里巴巴探讨过"城市大脑"。我们的项目为不同方式下自动化的推进提供了平台，部分正在试验中，部分已经成功推进智慧城市和机器人的融合。这似乎并不是直接针对自动驾驶汽车。一些新的框架已经以不同的方式付诸实践，但并没有使用我们期待可能会使用的语言。

总而言之，当你在思考智慧城市、自动驾驶汽车和机器人自动化的不同逻辑时，认识到它们之间的区别和差异非常重要，尽管其中还存在局限性。我们正在重塑这一关系并为此制定了框架。

"新基建"如何驱动智慧城市建设

刘志毅

商汤智能产业研究院主任

我的演讲主题是"新基建"如何驱动智慧城市建设。在这一主题下，我想谈谈如何理解"新基建"政策推动的智慧城市建设，以及如何看待以人工智能为代表的新技术与社会治理的关系。

1. 背景：随着城市化进程加快，城市问题需要解决

总体来说，全球城市化进程势不可挡。预计到 2050 年，世界上将有近 70% 的人口居住在城市。

中国的城市化也在快速推进。然而，中国的城镇化率与发达国家相比仍有近 20% 的差距（见图 2）。中国的城市人口基数超过 8 亿，而这一数字仍在以每年 2%—3% 的速度增长（见图 3）。

城市人口密度不断增加。预计到 2020 年底，中国的城市人口密度将达到每平方公里 2 600 人左右。

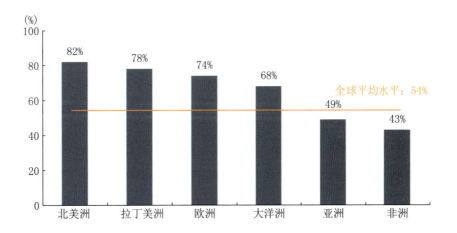

图1
2019 年全球城市化
进程
资料来源：Statista.

图 2
中国与发达国家城市
化率对比
资料来源：联合国

图 3
中国城市人口及增
长率
资料来源：德勤。

图 4
中国城市人口密度
资料来源：德勤
（含预测）

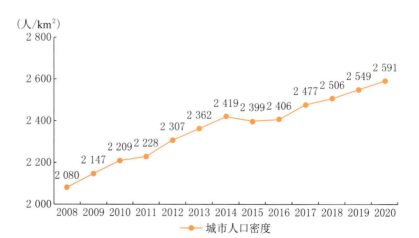

2. 现状：政府大力推进智慧城市试点项目建设

城市化促进了城市的扩张和相关设施的建设。在城市化的过程中，机遇和挑战并存。为应对城市化带来的挑战，中国从 2012 年起启动了大规模的智慧城市试点项目。中国不断扩大智慧城市试点项目的覆盖范围，并将这些项目纳入国家战略。2018 年，中国政府提出在各级建设 100 个新型智慧城市的目标。相关战略和政策见表 1 和表 2。

表 1
中国的顶层战略

2012	2013	2014	2015	2018
综合运用现代科学技术、整合信息资源、统筹业务应用系统，加强城市规划、建设和管理。 ——住房和城乡建设部	推动集约、智能、绿色、低碳的新型城镇化发展将拉动内需，带动产业转型升级。 ——住房和城乡建设部	运用物联网、云计算、大数据、空间地理信息集成等新一代信息技术。 ——国家发展和改革委员会	推动新一代信息技术与城市现代化深度融合和迭代演进，实现国家与城市协调发展的新生态。 ——国家互联网信息办公室	形成无处不在的惠民服务、透明高效的在线政府、融合创新的信息经济、精准精细的城市治理、安全可靠的运行体系。 ——国务院

表 2
中国的政策支持

出台时间	政策	出台时间	政策
2012.11	《国家智慧城市试点项目暂行管理办法》	2016.11	《关于组织开展新型智慧城市评价工作务实推动新型智慧城市健康快速发展的通知》
2012.11	《国家智慧城市（区、镇）试点指标体系（试行）》	2016.12	《新型智慧城市评价指标（2016年）》
2013.08	《国务院关于促进信息消费扩大内需的若干意见》	2017.01	《推进智慧交通发展行动计划（2017—2020 年）》
2014.03	《国家新型城镇化规划（2014—2020 年）》	2017.07	《新一代人工智能发展规划》
2014.08	《关于促进智慧城市健康发展的指导意见》	2017.09	《智慧城市时空大数据与云平台建设技术大纲（2017 版）》
2015.01	《关于促进智慧旅游发展的指导意见》	2017.09	《智慧交通让出行更便捷行动方案（2017—2020 年）》

3. "新基建"简介

智慧城市建设面临着持续不断的挑战，引起了政府的关注。从 2018 年初开始，中国政府就在不断落实"新基建"政策。所谓"新基建"，是指建设一种全新的基础设施。不同于道路、桥梁、房屋等传统基础设施建设，"新基建"主要侧重于技术层面的基础设施建设。根据官方定义，"新基建"涵盖 5G 网络、工业互联网、城际高速铁路和城际轨道交通、大数据中心、人工智能、特高压、新能源汽车充电桩共七大领域，涉及今后通信、交通、生活和产业的方方面面。我们的研究显示，"新基建"是未来两年最重要的发展领域之一。

4. "新基建"的作用：加快智慧城市建设进程

第一，"新基建"能够推动社会治理智能化，加快智慧社会建设。城市治理体系和治理能力的现代化需要"新基建"。特别是在疫情防控进入新常态的情况下，这也为推动智慧城市项目、整合高效智慧的城市管理带来了机遇。

第二，"新基建"能够加快智能生产进程，推动数字经济发展。"新基建"让生产决策更加智能化。企业可以低成本使用先进的云计算、人工智能和大数据等新型基础设施，解决信息技术资源的短缺问题，专注于自身业务和市场开发。

第三，"新基建"能够让人民生活更加便利。2020 年初，"新基建"在抗击疫情、促进经济迅速复苏方面发挥了不可替代的作用。疫情期间，"5G+ 教育"广为流行起来。"新基建"也打破了医疗资源配置的空间限制。此外，复工复产等各类活动都在一定程度上依赖"新基建"，尤其是电子商务。

5. 人工智能智慧城市落地方案分类

人工智能智慧城市落地方案共同形成了"一个核心、三方应用"的产业发展框架。一个核心指人工智能，包括人工智能算法、人工智能产品、人工智能服务和人工智能系统。三方应用指"人工智能 + 管理""人工智能 + 生态"和"人工智能 + 生活"。"智慧产业"规划由政府主导，以智能产业链模式为导向。该规划致力于构建促进城市发展的人工智能产业模式，大力发展人工智能科技产业，通过智能管理、智能生态和智能生活提升城市建设水平。

6. 应用领域：国家和市场需求

智慧城市结构模型由基础设施、智慧中心和应用服务三部分构成。

图 5
智慧城市结构模型

7. 智能建筑：以上海"虚拟临港"为例

商汤正在参与上海"虚拟临港"的建设。该项目于 2019 年正式启动，具有重要意义，目前投入超过 56 亿元人民币。2017 年，上海临港启动"智慧临港 BIM+GIS 城市大数据平台"建设，借助 BIM（建筑信息模型）+GIS（地理信息系统）技术，旨在打造一个完善的"虚拟临港"。该平台是国内外首个集成城市级地埋建筑设施的数据平台，覆盖临港 315 平方公里的城市空间，原样复制了城市的建筑地理构造。该平台能够感知城市人口热力图、实时交通车流、停车场状态、视频实时监控等城市运行态势。还能利用无人机进行自动图像识别和分析，智能发现城市异常问题，推演预测未来发展。

图 6
上海"虚拟临港"

8. 商汤产品图的变化

作为全球领先的人工智能科技公司，商汤科技面向全球，致力于推动经济、社会和人类的发展，建设更美好的未来。商汤实现了多项技术突破，坚持在基础研究领域投资，进一步认识和推进领先的人工智能技术。商汤拥有国际化的研发团队。自 2015 年以来，虽然我们的产品图不断演变，但我们始终致力于通过智慧城市建设改善城市治理，助力零售、金融、旅游、制造和自动驾驶等行业，并借助发展智能硬件和互联网金融等方式让人民受益。我们一直努力坚持原创，让人工智能引领人类进步，希望人工智能技术能够推动社会的可持续发展，革新世界。

移动互联和智慧交通

徐守龙

上汽大众移动互联运营总监

在上汽大众，我的工作包括如何让汽车通过通信提供娱乐，以及推动车联网和汽车自动驾驶在中国的发展。此外，我现在是一名博士生，正在从事一些关于智慧交通的研究。我想和大家分享一下我对于移动互联和智慧交通之间相互关系的思考。

1. 移动互联赋能智慧交通

第一，我想阐述一下我对汽车、互联网、道路、云和智能大脑之间关系的看法（见图1）。在汽车行业，我们一直关注汽车本身，并一直在思考我们能否将汽车与司机联系起来，我们是否能拥有这样一辆汽车，它能实现完全自主思考，拥有一些感官并借助人工智能自动驾驶。我们要做的是让车辆从实验室中脱离出来，利用车载信息服务将汽车的智能与基础设施、其

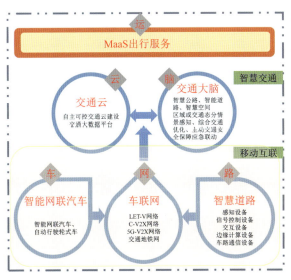

移动互联连接人车路，为交通和出行提供能力

- **车**：以智能网联汽车为代表的智慧交通时代的自动化运载工具
- **路**：数字化、网联化、智能化、集感知、计算、控制、通信、交互、管理、服务于一体的智慧交通基础设施
- **网**：以5G车联网、物联网为代表的信息通信网络建设
- **云**：分布式、多层级、智能化的交通云，以及端、边、云协同的数据计算式服务
- **脑**：在交通大数据基础上，实现全局最优调度、系统协同运行、出行智能服务的智慧决策大脑、智慧监督大脑和智慧运营大脑
- **运**：便捷、以人为本、愉悦、实时、应需的MaaS交通运输服务，以及全新智慧交通运营

图1

移动互联与智慧交通的关系

他车辆、车联网以及道路或驾驶环境中的其他物体结合起来，从而让汽车在交通中更加智能，而非仅在实验室层面进行研发。借此，我们希望将智能大脑或交通云运用于道路，从而为汽车出行提供便利。

2. 车网路的分级发展

第二，我想分享一下我对当前汽车行业结构的一些想法。正如我们现在看到的，技术进步提高了我们使用车载信息服务和实现互联的效率。然而，我认为这还不够，因为如果不改变发展交通的根本方式，就不可能取得成功。前面的演讲者也提到了，在这方面存在着诸多限制。到目前为止，实现完全自动驾驶并不容易。在这个行业有一个关于混杂性的想法，其中涉及汽车、司机和其他因素。这种混杂性该如何处理呢？因此，我想谈谈移动互联与智慧交通的关系。在图 2 中有三个不同的标准，分别针对的是汽车、互联网和道路，中国、日本、欧洲和美国在不同的领域有着不同的标准。从图 2 中，按照 SAE 的标准，目前有 5 个级别。一些商业广告、不同的原始设备制造商或不同的汽车制造商都声称他们已经达到了第 4 级或第 5 级。特斯拉可能就是其中之一。但实际上，在这个行业中，经常谈论的是 2 级、2 级 + 或 2.5 级。

按照美国汽车工程师学会分级标准：
L3：限定的条件下的自动驾驶，驾驶者需要随时接管。
L4：限定的条件下的完全自动驾驶。
L5：所有条件下的完全自动驾驶。

按照国际电信联盟分级标准：
LTE-V2X 支持向 5G-V2X 的平滑演进。
都支持车路之间的短距离直连通信（PC5）和终端、基站之间的长距离空口通信（Uu）。

按照欧洲道路交通研究咨询委员会分级标准：
按照道路基础设置智能化程度，由低到高分为 E 到 A 五个级别。

图 2
车网路的分级发展

如果达到第 3 级，这意味着在某些情况下，汽车可以实现自动驾驶。但当驾驶情况超出汽车的控制能力时，它就会把控制权交还给人类。但汽车如何识别何时应对这种情况呢？实际上，这一问题仍在讨论中，因为我们可以为人工智能设定自我引导的规则，但对于人类来说，情况会更加复杂：如果驾驶员没有准备好、分心或者根本没有能力处理如此复杂的情况，会发生什么？这个问题的答案有待讨论。目前我们还处在努力达到第3级的过程中。一些新兴的原始设备制造商正在讨论从第3级升级到第4级，但企业仍然需要考虑如何以更合理的方式达到第3级。这就是汽车目前发展的情况。

在通信方面，有很多关于5G及其优势的讨论。如何才能真正利用好5G既是一个行业问题，也是一个学术问题。我曾在中国移动等知名公司做过调研，他们现在正在做的是尝试实现远程控制，让一名操作员坐在一个遥远地点的屏幕后面远程操控车辆，而不是完全依赖5G在特定场景下来完成驾驶工作。

在道路方面，欧洲道路交通研究咨询委员会（ERTRAC）制定了一些标准。他们把道路分为A、B、C、D和E五个等级。而中国在道路和基础设施的发展上仍然处于落后地位。要解决这个问题需要大量资金，特别是政府投资。至于政府应该做些什么才能采取一个全面的策略来确保司机和其他行人的利益，目前还有待研究。

3. 车网路的协同发展

第三，我想谈谈这三个领域是如何相互联系的，以及汽车、互联网和道路的相关标准。如图3所示，我们目前处于从信息化走向智能化的中间阶段；自动驾驶汽车可以实现"部分自动驾驶"，或者说介于"部分自动驾驶"和"有条件自动驾驶"之间；移动通信网络发展处于第二阶段；智能道路达到了C级。我们还有很多工作要做。

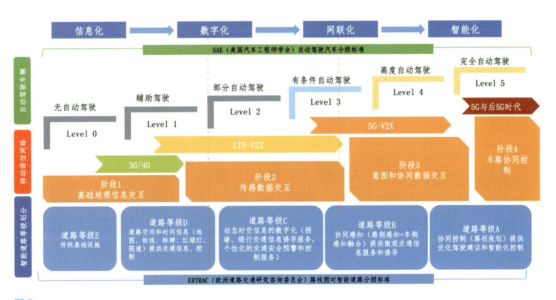

图3
车网路的协同发展

4. 聪明的车，智慧的路

第四，我想探讨"聪明的车"和"智慧的路"。现在，自动驾驶汽车可以实现半自动化，但是智能道路发展相对缓慢，相关投资还不足够。此外，互联网无处不在，具有高速率、低延时和大容量的特点。具体信息如图4所示。但是，我们仍然需要更完善的基础设施来发展智慧道路，应当系统看待车网路的协同发展。

图 4
聪明的车、智慧的路、泛在的网、云脑结合

5. 目前待解决的问题

最后，基于上述内容，图5展示了目前待解决的问题。各汽车制造商已经收集了不少数

图 5
目前待解决的问题

路侧&车侧&管理侧的标准不完备
- 通信标准在逐步建立，但是车侧，路侧和管理侧的标准空缺，导致规模效应不明显

缺乏协同应用的场景
- 各领域独立发展，缺乏车网路云的协同应用场景
- 联合才有应用，没有应用无法联合(鸡生蛋，蛋生鸡)

缺乏可行的商业运行模式
- 有利可图的商业模式和运营模式才能促进多方对移动互联的投入

据，但是事实上，我们正在建构的体系是彼此隔绝的孤岛，彼此之间并没有合作。我们需要加强合作，共同解决问题。目前待解决的问题主要有三：第一个问题是路侧、车侧、管理侧的标准不完备。第二个问题是如何创建应用场景和融合不同的因素。第三个问题是缺乏可行的商业运行模式。当然，政府可以在这方面进行投资，但这并不是最好的解决方案，只有有利可图的商业模式和运营模式才能真正吸引企业投资、吸引资金，促进多方对移动互联的投入，创造营商的生态系统。根据我个人的研究和实验，很多公司都愿意投资自动驾驶汽车和智慧城市，不过他们投资的兴趣点在于如何从中获得利益。但如今的商业模式尚不清晰，盈利能力有待提高。

我们该如何解决这些挑战并继续前进？这需要不同领域的人才共同努力。我期待在未来能生活在拥有移动互联和智慧交通的智慧城市之中。

智慧城市及智能交通下的城市空间与产业规划

胡楚焱

Urban Space 技术总监

1. 智慧城市的发展历程

全球智慧城市市场广阔，公共安全需求、智慧政务及智能交通将成为市场增长的主要驱动力。目前，全球多数国家都积极投身于智慧城市的建设与发展。中国是全球智慧城市建设最为火热的国家，试点项目数量占比达到了 48%（见图 1）。根据市场研究机构 Markets and Markets 最新发布的研究报告统计，2018 年全球智慧城市市场规模为 3 080 亿美元，预计到 2023 年，这一数字将增长至 7 172 亿美元，年均复合增长率为 18.4%。

图 1
全球在建智慧城市数
量分区域占比

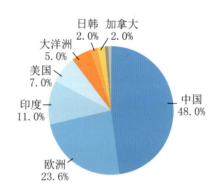

中国智慧城市建设历经三个发展阶段：从智慧城市概念导入的分散建设阶段，到智慧城市试点探索的规范发展阶段，再到 2016 年正式进入以人为本、成效导向、统筹集约、协同创新的新型智慧城市发展阶段。如今，中国智慧城市建设已进入第三阶段，致力于构建一体化运行格局。

2. 智慧城市和国土空间规划

新时代要求下，中国城市规划进行了从体制到内容的整体改革，国土空间规划应运而生。

自 2010 年起，空间规划体系逐渐形成，"多规合一"常被提及。随着时间的推移，我们确立了讲求生产、生活、生态的"三生融合"目标，空间规划体系得到完善。2017 年发生了翻天覆地的变化。自然资源部启动了新的机构改革方案。自此，我们有了一套新的规划体系。该体系以空间规划为基础，以国家发展规划为主导。但是，同时也要认识到，空间规划应考虑更多的因素，不仅包含当前的需求，还应囊括未来人与智慧城市的关系。

在这一背景下，大数据平台对国土空间规划中决策的影响愈加显著，为智慧城市建设奠定了坚实的基础。国土空间规划与城市运营大数据平台结合，是建设智慧城市的重要保障。利用成熟的分析模型，我们可以通过平台，为人们提供个性化服务。通过大数据平台，我们还能制定土地利用总体规划和城市总体规划。

3. 智能网联汽车的发展前景

智能交通是智慧城市的一个重要应用。智能应用可分为四个阶段，智能网联汽车目前处于 L1-L2 产业化阶段，L3 尚处于研发阶段。但我们很高兴地看到，智能汽车已经进入了上海和北京等城市的市场。一项行业研究表明，智能网联汽车仍处于研发阶段，关键技术在未来将不断进步。

中国智能网联汽车新车市场规模及增长状况，万辆

图 2
中国智能网联汽车新车市场规模及增长情况
资料来源：蔚来资本、罗兰贝格、国家发改委《智能汽车创新发展战略》（征求意见稿）、《节能与新能源汽车技术路线图》、《汽车产业中长期发展规划》。

智能汽车不仅仅是一种交通工具。我们在距离上海不远的工业城市嘉兴搭建了平台，研究智能汽车的应用。在整个过程中，我们发现，对于智慧城市来说，智能汽车不仅仅是一种

交通工具，而且是关联其他设施的纽带。智能汽车可以解决旅途中所有的需要，而大多数需求不单和旅途有关。我们应该不断思考，推动市场取得更佳的成果，促使智能汽车项目取得成功。车辆的行驶数据还可以反映城市道路管理状况，从而推动我们进行更多适合智能汽车的道路设计。在规划方面，我们应该加大力度，推进基础设施的建设。

4. 智慧城市，智能交通

车路协同（V2X）建设已成为城市智能道路交通建设的起点。我们要根据实际情况调整、制定具体的规划。规划需要考量车路协同应用，包括危险路况预警、交通信号播报和协同控制等布置。更重要的是，为了使新型智慧城市基础设施适用于自动驾驶汽车，我们需要改进车道标记、路边传感器、智能标牌并加强 5G 建设。

我们相信，新型城市空间建设能够推动智能汽车和智慧城市的协同发展。我们需要探索城市智能基础设施建设的发展趋势，努力探索智能汽车和智能交通的应用场景，思考多主题的建设模式和技术创新的前景。我希望我们可以勇于尝试，这样我们可能会得到更多的资源，共同开展研究。

推进"未来空间"建设，构建智能车路网络创新生态链

张　希

上海交通大学教授

今天我想谈谈我们如何在上海奉贤区推进了"未来空间"建设，构建起了智能车路网络创新生态链。

1. 智慧城市——"未来空间"

我们希望在上海市奉贤区打造一个"集居住、生活、生产和生态为一体"的"未来空间"。在奉贤，我们推出了以下方针：开放创新、智慧生态、产城融合以及适商宜居。"未来空间"的最终目标是实现智能、电气化、高效、安全的绿色出行。其内涵可以总结为"4+2+1"的一体化模式（图1）。

我们与上海交通大学的研究人员开展合作，专注网络安全，并已经在智能汽车上实现了网络安全。

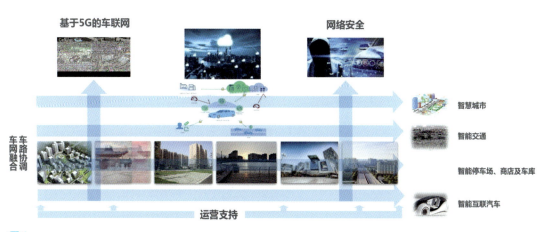

图1
"4+2+1"一体化模式

2. "未来空间"的意义

通过"未来空间"的建设，我们在奉贤区打造出新的经济形态，并有望拓展至整个上海。如研发智能汽车和核心部件，生产集驾驶、商务和娱乐功能于一身的汽车；通过软件、服务和车联网的应用，在车载软件中载入了算法；开发配套道路系统，建设 5G 基站，识别行人、电动自行车和行驶的车辆，并向汽车发送信息，打造相关生态系统；通过车载 T-Box 转换车内信号，将其发送至路边的道路系统；从云端获取汽车上的大数据，为政府、汽车制造商提供服务。

最重要的不仅仅是基础设施，除了硬件，我们还关注软件和信号。我们为车辆制定了统一标准，这样所有相关公司就可以共享信号，实行相同的标准。

3. 上海交大的实践

参考"斯坦福大学—硅谷"的模式，我们在上海交大周边也建立起了产业集群。交大位于闵行区，与奉贤区隔黄浦江相望。交大周边地区和斯坦福大学-硅谷地区在一些方面很相似。最终我们的方案成功在交大校园周边落地。在此过程中，许多研究人员也共同参与其中。

我们还在交大校园周边建立了一个全链条出行示范区。该示范区内有高速公路、快速公交系统、地下车库和一个工业园区。

这个示范区内还有六种相互作用的典型场景：社区、工业园区、校园、景区、商业区和

图 2
上海交大周边的出行全链条

图 3
六种典型场景的相互作用

城区。这些场景可以通过自动驾驶串联起来，它们共同构成了交大周边的产业基地。

此外，我想介绍一些有趣的技术。行人和电动自行车使得中国的路况很复杂。因此，自动驾驶需要关注行人。中国相关法律的缺失也使自动驾驶面临的情况更加复杂。2018 年，我们首次将关注点放到行人身上，对行人过马路的过程进行了识别，将这些过程划分为 20 多个点，并开发出相应算法来判断行人是否要过马路。

此外，我们还利用了社会科学，对决策控制器进行完善。有时候，心理状态会决定行人是要前进还是后退。我们设想了两种情况。第一种情况，一个孩子在过马路时突然停下来，他/她不确定车辆什么时候会开到跟前。如果发生这种情况，车辆就必须避开孩子。第二种情况，如果孩子在追一个足球，他/她的心思就都在足球上，不会注意到驶来的汽车。这种情况下，车辆需要做出判断，是继续行驶还是停下。

我们还意识到自动驾驶需要融入环境。汽车给交通带来了一定的耦合效应，交通也影响着汽车的决策。我们需要打造配套的环境，不仅为了发展自动驾驶技术，也是为了建设智慧城市。为此，我们已经建成许多大楼和高速公路，也确定了智能交通系统的出口位置，可以作为建造的基准或参考标准。

最后，我们还在智能交通系统中录入了全北京的城市场景，包括成千上万的道路和十字路口，还录入了城市的夜间场景。我们还将在该系统中录入电动汽车或燃油汽车的类型以及人口数据，以达到尽可能高的还原度。

智慧城市中的智能交通协同发展

俞俊利

中国城市治理研究所研究助理教授

今天，我们了解了有关人工智能技术的知识，现在我还想讨论另一个话题。

1. 索洛内生增长模型

首先，请允许我介绍这个经济模型。这个模型名为索洛内生增长模型，等式左边是产出，即国内生产总值和生产力。而等式右边的 a 指生产力，函数包括资本、劳动力和土地等因素。这是一种基础的经济增长模型。

图 1
索洛内生增长模型

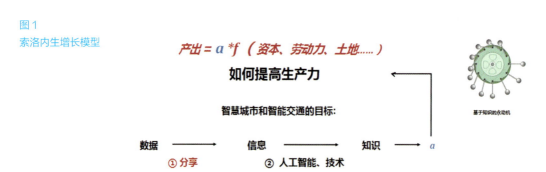

在智慧城市的交通布局中，我们有海量数据，以此共享并形成信息。我们使用人工智能技术来促进信息流动。知识是一种新的生产力。如果"函数"不变，而在最后一步引入"知识"，就能够带来发展，提高城市的福利。可以说，知识是一种新的生产力，是推动城市经济和福利发展的因素。

2. 智能交通和智慧城市的主体

智能交通和智慧城市有三种类型的主体：企业、消费者（用户、司机等）和政府。然而，三者间的供需并不平衡。例如，企业 A 向企业 B 提供数据，双方就会拥有一个共享平台。企业 B 可以利用这些数据提高交通质量。但是，企业一般不愿意培养潜在的竞争对手，所以缺乏共享的动力。而消费者作为另一个主体，他们可以得到这些数据信息，但不愿意为信息付费，而且他们并没有建立数据的能力。第三个主体是政府。政府拥有资金、能力和其他因素，但政府具有多重身份，可能是监管者，也可能是构建者等等。因此，三类主体都缺乏建设数据共享平台的动力。

这一困境应该如何解决？首先，我们必须对三方进行区分，明确谁建立平台，谁分享或学习智能交通使用数据，谁监督或监管这个平台。其次，我们要明确产权的归属者是用户、企业还是政府？

3. 案例参考

我们来看一个欧盟的例子。2018 年，欧盟推出了《通用数据保护条例》。该条例声称，智能交通用户作为主体，享有信息自决权。汽车制造商或公司和软件开发商负责控制，政府机构负责监督。如你所见，政府机构、利益相关者和欧洲委员会成立了一个工作组，来讨论数据保护问题。

回到国内，每个人都有银行卡，我们的银行卡联盟叫做银联，此外还有中国银行保险监督管理委员会，这是一个负责监管的政府机构。在这一框架模型下，用户将数据分享给银联，银联可以提供持卡人身份、品德等信息，政府则负责监管，形成支付产业完整的生态。

4. 可能的解决方案

我们认为，这一案例有望为智能交通产业协同模型提供解决方案。或许，可以由产业联盟来搭建共享平台，信息共享方为公司和司机，监管方为政府。

为此，我们要制定相应的法律法规，明确产权界限，明确各主体的责任。同时也需要更多的公众参与，拓宽公众监管和问询的渠道。

E-government in Seoul, South Korea

Heungsuk Choi

Professor of Korea University, Vice President of Asian Association for Public Administration

I will be talking about the e-government in Seoul, focusing on the smart city concept.

1. The situation and criteria of urban decay

The citizens of South Korea are disappearing. It is expected that about 37% of local government, or 1 383 domestic units below local government will be disappearing forever.

2. Where is it to disappear?

There are 5 criteria to designate the areas to disappear, so that the certain area is the phase of two or three out of the problems. In Seoul, 68% of the domestic unit are in trouble. So, all the people in this area have the problem with urban decay.

3. Revitalizing projects

Seoul is an area with the 3+ criteria, which has higher possibility of disappearing with decay. The South Korea government has been tried to do something. They are investing on more balanced development.

Unemployment decline, job creation, recovery, community and social integration are the 5 different types of 60 revitalizing projects. The first one is a labor community revitalization. There's more focus on the human site of the community. The second one is in the area where they have certain urban facilities which are in decay. The third is the general invention of commercial areas and a regeneration or recovering of commercial area. The fourth one is CBD (Central Business District).

And the largest project is recovery of economy basis.

In 2018, 90 areas were designated. One of them is Tongyeong city. This city is flourishing with the ship building industry. In this way, they are rebuilding the local industry. Almost half of those areas would be directly administered by the financial government. The other 3 smaller ones will be conducted or carried down by district government. Seoul has 25 district governments.

4. Smart city and e-government

The integrated smart city platform has been created by the central government and introduced and distributed to local government. The United States has a mobile platform, which includes all kinds of resources, such as community participation, the security and safety, public transportation, and so on.

There is a relevant model developed for basic level of local government, which comes from Busan eco delta city, one of the two sites of national smart city establishment. Korea are building two smart cities in a very large scale, which are conducted by the Ministry of Land, Infrastructure and Transport and central government. The ambitious targets were to add renewable energy by 20%, waste recycle by 100%, create 28 000 new jobs, and so on. Those are not local level targets but at national level.

5. The augmented city platform

The augmented city platform has three players, through which people can build up an easily application for public service even in villages. The application of basic service is on the second layer of augmented city platform.

Integrated platform for local government is the area where we are continuing distributing. In 2015, the integrated platform started to develop and distribute. The platform has been distributed to dozens of local governments.

6. The problems of the platform

Some platforms have a very bad experience of theories, in terms of lack of sustainability. Some of smart city services are targeted. Some of them are common ones. Some of them are pooled connectiveness. As the government can engage and build some services and then they pooled up, the sustainability problem came up.

COVID-19 and Digital Governance Development in Megacities: Experiences and Insights from Tokyo, Japan

Masao Kikuchi

Professor of Public Policy and Management, Department of Public Management, Meiji University

The Greater Tokyo area includes Tokyo and Yokohama area with more than 38 million population. I will make a quick assessment of what is happening during COVID-19 and the measures related to the e-government and issues related to the digital transformation.

1. The current situation of COVID-19 in Japan

The first wave occurred in early April and in the second wave, the death rate was much lower than that in the first one. Many European countries are under the second or third wave now. Japan

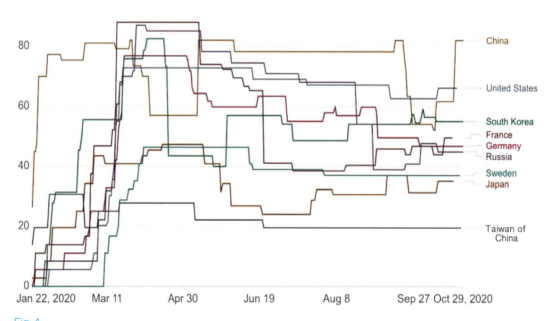

Fig. 1

COVID-19: Government Response Stringency Index

Source: Hale, Webster, Phillips, and Kira (2020), Oxford COVID-19 Government Response Tracker, Last Updated 31 October, 23:21 (London Time).

will step into the winter season so there could be a third wave sooner or later.

Japan is a super-aging society. Per capita, Japan has more elderly people than any other country. 28% of Japanese citizens are or are over 65 years old. However, Japan has a low virus death rate basically. According to BBC, the number of coronavirus-related deaths per 100 000 population in Japan is smaller than that in Philippine and some other countries. Though Japan is the most elderly country in terms of the current population structure.

There is no excess mortality in Japan albite the low capacity of COVID-19 test. Compared to other countries like United States, Japan's government used a less coercive model. Japan had a state of emergency for two months, from April 7th to the end of May. The state of emergency had strongly request for the cooperation of citizens and urged them to follow the recommendations. According to Oxford University, Japan and Sweden have lower government response stringency index than other countries.

Table 1

Leading countries in E-government development in 2020

Country	Rating class	Region	OSI value	HCI value	TH value	EGDI value (2020)	EGDI value (2018)
Denmark	VH	Europe	0.970 6	0.958 8	0.997 9	0.975 8	0.915 0
Republic of Korea	VH	Asia	1.000 0	0.899 7	0.968 4	0.956 0	0.901 0
Estonia	VH	Europe	0.994 1	0.926 6	0.921 2	0.947 3	0.848 6
Finland	VH	Europe	0.970 6	0.954 9	0.910 1	0.945 2	0.881 5
Australia	VH	Oceania	0.947 1	1.000 0	0.882 5	0.943 2	0.905 3
Sweden	VH	Europe	0.900 0	0.947 1	0.962 5	0.936 5	0.888 2
United Kingdom of Great Britain and Northern Ireland	VH	Europe	0.958 8	0.929 2	0.919 5	0.935 8	0.899 9
New Zealand	VH	Oceania	0.929 4	0.951 6	0.920 7	0.933 9	0.880 6
United States of America	VH	Americas	0.947 1	0.923 9	0.918 2	0.929 7	0.876 9
Netherlands	VH	Europe	0.905 9	0.934 9	0.927 6	0.922 8	0.875 7
Singapore	VH	Asia	0.964 7	0.890 4	0.889 9	0.915 0	0.881 2
Keland	VH	Europe	0.794 1	0.952 5	0.983 8	0.910 1	0.831 6
Norway	VH	Europe	0.876 5	0.939 2	0.903 4	0.906 4	0.855 7
Japan	VH	Asia	0.905 9	0.868 4	0.922 3	0.898 9	0.878 3

Source: 2020 United Nations E-Government Survey.

2. Digital governance development

Table 1 is the United Nations E-government survey 2020, which is the latest version. Denmark and the Republic of Korea are the top two and Japan ranks 14th. Yet the Social Security and Tax Number Systems, which are regarded as both hardware and software platform for e-government services delivery, started in 2016, and its usage is limited to social security, taxation and disaster management.

Table 2 is a comparison of social security and tax number systems among Japan, United States and South Korea. The range of the allowed use in Japan is limited to social security, taxation and disaster response while in South Korea and the United States, the system is widely used by both public and private sectors.

Table 2

Comparison of social security and tax number system among Japan, U.S. and South Korea

	Japan	U.S.	South Korea
Numbers system	Individual Number (My Number system)	SSN (Social Security Number)	Resident registration number
Number composition	12-digit number	9-digit number	13-digit number
Meaning of numbers	None	None	The first 6 digits represent the date of birth
The range of allowed use	Limited to social security, taxation and disaster response	Widely used by both public and private sectors	Widely used by both public and private sectors
Usage by private business operators	Prohibited except in cases stipulated by the My Number Act	No restrictions	No restrictions (Restrictions imposed in stages starting in 2012)
Identify verification	By an ID card showing the Individual Number with photo	Can be done only with the numbers	Can be done only with the numbers
Personal information sharing	Decentralized management (Sharing by using codes instead of directly using the numbers)	Can be done only with the numbers (personal information is also stored by each organization)	Can be done only with the numbers

Source: My Number Promotion Office, Cabinet Secretariat, Japan.

3. COVID-19 and digital governance

What is needed for Government Response to COVID-19? M. Jae Moon identifies three key issues to deal with COVID-19, which are agility, transparency, and citizens participation. Christensen and Laegreid proposed the governance capacity and legitimacy and its balance. Bibing Dai and others identified risk communication, information and rumor refutation. These are all related to digital governance and there's a huge room for future research as well as actions.

Liu Zhenmin, the UN under-secretary-general for economic and social affairs, pointed out that the pandemic has renewed and anchored the role of digital government, both in its conventional delivery of digital services as well as new innovative efforts in managing the crisis.

What is happening during the COVID-19 in Japan in terms of the digital governance or e-government? Actually, coronavirus revealed lagging e-government efforts in Japan. For instance, the contact tracing app, COVID-19 tracing app (COCOA) was released on June 19th of 2020. It had more than 19 million downloads, yet covered only 20% of the whole population. In April, all the citizens in Japan could receive Corona Relief Special Cash Payment, which is JPY 100 000, equal to USD 955. People could register both by mail or online, and mail application was sooner than online application

Japan has fax-loving culture in the government agencies. In terms of the fax-loving culture in the government agencies, hospitals and clinics were required to report the cases via fax in the beginning, but now online.

The Tokyo metropolitan government just released the DX transformation strategies in September of 2020 and announced "5 less" which are paperless, faxless, touchless, hanko (shield)less and cashless. This means, paper form, fax form, touch form and hanko is no longer needed.

4. Concluding remarks

Though technical advancement, both DX and e-government development were largely untouched. The pandemic is relatively controlled without DX efforts. This is the puzzle or enigma we need to explore more. Japan didn't have an e-government, a nice e-delivery or a nice digital transformation. Yet, the pandemic is under control. I don't say digital transformation is not important to deal with the COVID-19. Concerning "post" or "with" corona period, in 2020 and beyond, digital service is essential to those who are vulnerable to the virus and the senior.

Both central and local governments, including the Tokyo metropolitan government, initiated smart city projects, digital office, fostering civic tech, 5G data highway, AI, IOT and others for perusing Society 5.0. Yet, its future is less clear due to the pandemic and following economic and fiscal stagnation. There are both opportunities and threats to pursue the digital transformation in both the Japanese governments and the society.

Digital Technology and the Eco-system of Employment: Experience of Australia

Bingqin Li

University of New South Wales

1. Digital transformation and E-government—Australia

There are three levels about digital transformation: digitization — digital data; digitalization — using digital tools; and digital transformation — change the way the sector works. From this, we can see digital transformation does not just refer to digital data or using digital tools, but aims to change the way the sector works.

In 2014, Australian government decided to do an auditing to figure out how to achieve the digital transformation. From 2015 to 2018, the Australian Government's Digital Transformation Agenda was gradually developed. The Agenda is divided into three perspectives: the government that is easy to deal with; the government that is informed by you; and the government that is fit for the digital age. The first two are very intuitive. To achieve the last one, the government needs to build relevant infrastructure, and the government staff need to have the digital knowledge to be able to deal with the challenges in the digital age.

2. Ecosystem approach for transformation

Is the government for policy or for service delivery? In the last several decades, the government has provided less and less service but done more on policy making and enabling roles. Facing the challenge of digital transformation, the government cannot just focus on policies, because the relationship between the policy making and the service delivery has also somehow changed. For example, the three perspectives of the Agenda are about how the government is trying to balance the relationship between people-centered services and business-centered services. It has been gradually realized that the government, the businesses and the people must be linked together to make joint actions to achieve transformations.

3. Digital employment for people with disability as an example

How to make joint actions or what does it mean to have joint actions? I will use one policy as an example. Australian government has several priorities such as childcare, old age care, employment services, and digital employment for people with disabilities. The last one is one of the most challenging fields for Australia, because Australia has been one of the countries that have tried very hard to get people with disabilities into employment during the digital age, but somehow it wasn't very successful.

According to Australian's Digital Transformation Agenda, Australia is trying to create 10 000 jobs in 2018. Probably after COVID-19, the goal will be even more demanding. The disability employment rate is low and gets worse over time.

(1) Ecosystem approach to disability employment. To deal with employment problem, there needs to be an ecosystem approach, which means that different types of employment can be available to people with disability. People, particularly people with physical disabilities, need an accessible "environment", including physical environment (workspace, commuting, technology, education) and a supportive social environment (employees, families, co-workers, customers). All stakeholders need to adapt as the ecosystem faces changes.

(2) Policy system for disability employment in digital age. There are some national strategies for the digital economy, trying to help employers and employees and to offer them trainings. These strategies are also used for people with disabilities. Digital inclusivity and disability employment are stressed on startups for accessibility. Companies have developed software for people to gain access to the labor market. In terms of digital technology, there is also a national broadband network to make more remote areas to be able to access the digital technology. In addition, the national disability strategy aims to help more people to get employed. The government also encourage NGOs to participate in innovative employment initiatives.

Luckily, in the past several decades, Australia has made a big effort to improve the physical environmental access and apply the digital technology policy to the existing physical environment.

4. Conclusion: problems of digital transformation

In Australian, the government does not actively use the digital economy as a strategy, which brings an advantage: it allows the policy to have a better future. In a word, the digital transformation demands shortened distance between policy and service delivery; the digital transformation cannot replace the need for adaptation of physical environment and elimination of discrimination; e-government needs to be embedded in e-service system, a broader market and service systems.

When there's a disconnection or this kind of digital system is trying to take over the daily operation of the government and service providers, it will create greater barrier for people, particularly the people with disabilities, to get involved in the system.

Digital Transformations and Governance Innovations in The Greater Paris Area

Daniel Schertzer

Ecole des Ponts Paris Tech Hydrology Meteorology and Complexity lab (HM&Co)

1. Governance of the Greater Paris area

The Greater Paris area is rather complex with the multi-level governance. It corresponds to one of the 18 regions of France. It is comprised of 8 counties, and 1 268 cities.

A challenging example is Grand Paris Express. It's a new Super-Metro. It will start 200 kilometers of new rails, doubling the presumed size of the metro network with 68 new stations. It also needs large investment of 35 billion euros. It aims to transport 2 million passengers per day and one train every 1-2 minutes.

Fig. 1
Grand Paris
express

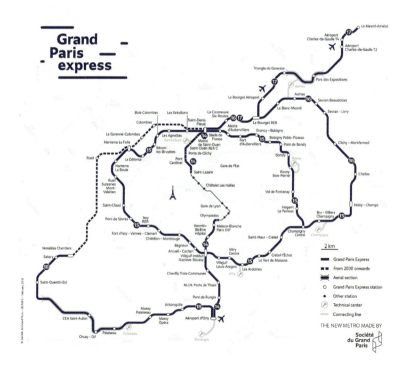

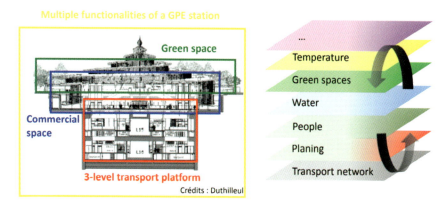

Fig. 2
Multiple
functionalities of a
GPE (Grand Paris
Express) station

Such complexity means that, innovative concepts aren't just about the infrastructure network, but the question of the interplay of actors, observation and modelisation.

This is an example about the station. The presented station includes 3-level transportation platform, commercial space and green space. The idea is to create a refreshing island in the area with the use of different spaces like that. But the complexity of such station is that we have to deal with a lot of different physical problems, such as people and planning. Those different platforms represent this system and we need to make different spaces work together to make this station better.

There are 68 stations to deal with. Fig. 3 is the line 15 south. When traveling with it, you are discovering different types of urban thematic maps going from geothermal energy to urban retrofitting, biodiversity, eco-district and so on. It's a real trouble that we have to overcome all these problems.

Fig. 3
GPE line 15 south

2. Digital governance principles

Based on a study of more than 100 companies on their digital challenges and interviews with 55 digital executives, flevypro has distilled out 7 key governing principles that link Digital Transformationto impactful success. The first point is how to understand all the information, how to connect it from the digital platform and so on. The main idea, which is put forward five years ago, is to centralize shared information, and on the contrary, to decentralize governance of digital initiatives over time.

3. 2020—2023 strategic plan of Veolia

Big enterpriseslike Veolia, are taking into account the UNSDGs in order to make a battle with these problems. There are levels of planet, society, employees, shareholders and clients. Veolia tries to connect with the SDGs of UN at each level.

Fig. 4
A dashboard to track and report its multifaceted performance by Veolia

4. Learnt lessons

We have learned a lot of lessons. First, the number of users, for example, of mobile, internet, and social media, are about 5 million. Therefore, the connection with the end is better. Also, new technologies enable us to process data in big volumes, varieties, and velocities. But there is a kind of information overload, a shift from lack of information to a plethora of information. Nevertheless,

提升社区和城市品质

governments now have a new instrument to formulate their policies and address its citizens' needs. In addition, they are able to personalize services and increase transparency and so on. They also have a new way to intervene in the free market. Instead of a centralized planning situation, they could determine in a more indirect and impressive manner in the market. Through the new instrument, governments take policy measures on topics such as the digitalization during COVID-19 epidemic. Digitalization can help entrepreneurs establish and run a business with much less bureaucracy and practically no paper work. The main problem is the knowledge problem, or more precisely, a pretense of knowledge of it. We can easily pretend to have acknowledge on the preferences of human beings without actually having it. The main question now is, does the complex systems approach overcome this deadlock?

5. The French Hub for Digital & Ecological Transformation

There is the example of the French Hub for digital and ecological transformation, which is called Cap·digital. It focuses on the Paris region and considers itself as the first European cluster, with more than 1 000 of member, a lot of lawyers of different challenges, and many projects.

Cap·digital is in particular working with the Paris region on the question of buildings in the future and life in the future, which is a mega project. It is assisted and supported by a special investment plan of the state and the region of France called ile-de-France, and supported by many people.

This mega project has 120 partners, including economic collectors, local collectivities, agencies and universities and schools. The big idea is indeed to use artificial intelligence to enable citizens to be more involved in the development of the region. A survey about how people are feeling of present development of digitalization showed the general feeling was very negative. Like Francis said, "I live in a city where infrastructure is built without me. I would like to have a vision of my territory and give my opinion." The objectives are now to enable 1 million lle-de-France residents to consume locally thanks to digital technology, and also to have 85% new buildings in the BIM models. This is just one example of digital service to support renovation. Its general idea is to develop a smart platform for the full area of the region of Paris.

6. Towards new postures

One question is that who will decide the city of tomorrow? Who will finance it? As a question of lle-de-France, it is all about the state and cities and private sectors and so on. We have also to be clear about what new uses will transform urban life? And what would be the new offers? And citizens should be engaged in knowledge, rather than just be passive. We should achieve sustainable development and overcome doubts. The big challenges are big data and artificial intelligence, which may shift the borderline between observation and modelling.

7. Data revolution

Two figures are important about that. One is that 90% of the world data were collected during the last 2 years, and 80% of the data are not yet gathered or formatted, and therefore not used. Finally, what kind of revolution are we leading in the time of data?

Combating Systematic Failures in Governmental Digital Transformation: Rethinking Current Practise and Future Directions

Vishanth Weerakkody

Faculty of Managements, Law and Social Sciences

What does digital transformation mean for the government? How do we avoid some of the big failures happening in public administrations? In the UK, some parts of Europe, North America and the US, a lot of taxpayers' money was vainly invested in very large, ambitious digital transformation projects. I'm going to draw reasons for failures from the projects that have not delivered the desired results.

I will be drawing mainly from projects in the UK and my research over the last 20 years into the concept of e-government. In the last 20 years I have been looking at this concept, finding that the concept hasn't really moved forward enough and we haven't learned lessons from some failures. I have been quite critical in the last 2 and 3 years of the projects that have not gone according to plan. In December, 2018, I was called to the parliament to give evidence to a science and technology community on why some projects had not gone according to plan. My presentation will be based on the work I did for the House of Commons in 2018.

1. Context: reflections on failed digital transformation projects in UK

In the UK, there are some huge projects starting in 2002 with the National Program for Information Technology. NHS (National Health Service) in the UK is the biggest public organization across the entire planet. It employs hundreds of thousands of people across different hospitals and primary care settings in the UK. The NHS National Program for Information Technology was an ambitious project that started in 2002, which tried to digitize the entire primary and secondary care setting and develop electronic patient records that can be accessed by patients anywhere and anytime, with a computer or a mobile device. Hospitals and GP surgeries of primary and secondary care would share patient records to make things smoother and more efficient. This project, however, crashed, costing billions of pounds for the taxpayer. It had to be abandoned around 2012 and 2013.

Another project which did not go according to plan in 2015 was a project initiated by EU that was trying to to digitize payments to farmers. When farmers get subsidies from the European Commission, the process was mainly semi-manual and automated. But the project did not go according to the plan because of various issues, such as a lack of access to broadband, farmers not having the digital skills, integration problems with various systems, etc.

Another example is the Universal Credit Project which is currently ongoing but costing more money than ordinarily anticipated. Particularly during the pandemic when cities went lockdown, people have to claim various benefits because many people were unemployed or lost their jobs. There were lots of delays in payments because a semi-automated process has been fully digitized through the Universal. But it's an ongoing project at the moment, facing lots of challenges and issues due to the complexity and the size of the project and the different public administration settings that need to be integrated in the project.

There are few more examples of UK government project failures as Fig. 1 Shows. By comparing the initial cost, the final cost, and the cost to the taxpayer, we can see the difference in those projects. The Department for Transport Shared Services Centre Project cost an extra £28 million to the

Fig. 1
UK government
project failures

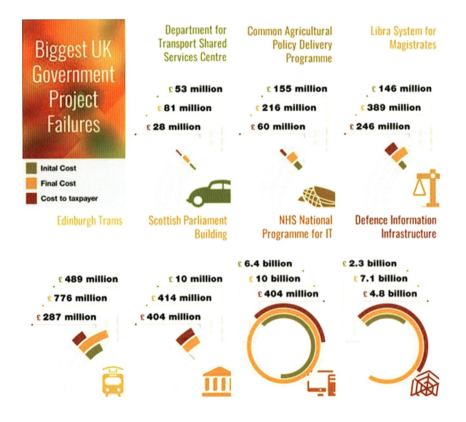

taxpayer; Common Agricultural Policy Delivery Programme £60 million extra; Libra System for Magistrates, a digitalization project, £246 million extra; Defense Infrastructure System £4.8 million extra; NHS program for IT cost £404 million, and it was abandoned in the end; Scottish Parliament Building project £404 million extra. Through these data we see the trajectory of these projects that never seems to be going according to plan, budget and time.

There are also cases in countries like South Korea and China where some projects always go over budget, costing money to the taxpayer. Why is this? The answer to the question is something that has been bugging me being an e-government researchers for more than two decades.

2. Questions for digital transformation

Where does technology fit into government and public administration in the digital era? How might we transform government using technology. Before we talk about digital transformation and government transformation of services, we need to think about the role of digital in public administration setting and the digital era. The aim of my today's lecture is to provide a new way of thinking and talking about digital government, not to redefine the digital government or e-government but to provide a new frame of reference. Transformation is free from technology and rooted in the nature of government as a social and legal phenomenon (Hood, 2007). How do we transform the current state of the public administration and what is the future state? Can we actually achieve that butterfly story in governmental digital transformation?

3. History of digital transformation

I've been looking at the e-government field since the late 1990s. We've been in the first stage from1990s to the mid-2000s. Academics and researchers in this stage look very much at the implementation side, including development champions, technology solutions, the implementation issues and the institutional issues.

We have done very much research on business and management literature, technologically literature, organizational literature, but very few onthe public administration and policy making literature, because over 75% of the researchers that are looking at the concept of the e-government are people coming from information systems, information technology, and business and management backgrounds, who do not understand public administration settings.

When we moved into the late 2000s, we started looking at adoption such as smart cities. Young people did not adopt the technology that government are introducing. The concept of smart cities has been around for the last 15 to 20 years, but it has taken so long for this smart concept to be adopted and become mainstay in citizens' lives. We were looking at theories and models that were drawn from technology-centric concepts, such as the unified use of technology model, the technology acceptance model and the diffusion of innovation model. I find that some of the published paper, though being different contexts, use the same theoretical models that are drawn from business and management literature and technology adoption literature. Therefore, the implementation and the adoption has been progressing on the same direction. There is no change of thinking around digital government, which is quite disappointing.

But the field has moved on. Since 1990s, various concepts that influenced the field of digital government and public administration have appeared, including cooperation, open government, big openly data, decentralized block chain technologies and IOT in government. Technology is moving so fast and offers so many benefits. However, researchers are not actually paying attention to what these technologies can do and their capability within the context of public administration.

There are many academic literature and journals dedicated to the field of digital government and e-government edited by me. The papers I have seen are the same old papers with the same old theories and methods, and that needs to change. Technology has moved fast, but we are latching on the wrong concepts or we are using the wrong theory and tools.

4. Rethinking the essence of e-government

There are many definitions of e-government from the 1990s up to now and mostly revolves a common web-centric subset. The notion that the internet and digital will transform government is still held quite high. But what we want to do is to make sense of the future. I am not going to develop a new definition, but to put forward a new way of thinking, a frame of reference based on what governments actually do.

People including our colleagues and practitioners are always very familiar with the whole idea of e-government, from providing information to the electronic democracy. However, how many can say that we really have electronic democracy? We even don't have electronic voting yet, at least in some of the big democracies. Technology-centric progression of e-government is a more recent model adopted by united nations. The web-centric method and the web portal which the transformation is using and the measures are based on how you are presented on your websites and how interactive and transactional you are. UN e-government service actually places the countries in the league tables based on the transaction capability and information capability of governments.

Undeniably, e-government has its good side. It has done lots of things in the last 20 years that has made citizens' lives so much better in terms of access, transparency and availability, and it has created administrative and operational efficiencies for many governments. But it has also paved cow paths that is automated existing processes, particularly in established public administrations with a lot of legacy, and complex public administrations have actually automated existing processes without transforming them first.

5. E-government: it is good but not progressing

It is still happening from 1990s to now, putting the E in front and not lifting the heavy machinery at the back. The idea was two-pronged: deliver innovative changes to service design at the front-end of government to make existing services appear more joined-up (involving the application of generous amounts of lipstick) in order to buy time to enable the heavy lifting changes required at the back-end (the pig). it's like putting a lipstick on a heavy pig, which is difficult to move. Therefore, "let's put some lipstick on the pig to make it more attractive" has been the concept for a very long time. That's where I think the digital transformation and the word "transformation" came. 15-20 years after the E-government occurred, many established democracies realized that we haven't really changed its functions and some of the complex operations. What we have done is to digitize most of them to make it easier and accessible, which is a big problem. It is beginning to change now, but technology is moving so fast that we are getting carried away, resulting in some big failures along the way.

One of the big problems is that government is like a service industry in Europe and North America. We pay for services and goods. If you are applying for a passport, are you a customer or a citizen? It's an obligatory requirement for a citizen to pay his/her taxes. One will be prosecuted if one does not pay taxes or travel without a passport. So, it's really important to understand and make that difference between the concept of customer and services, and citizens and public administration. The actual definition of public administration, from UK's concept, is either paid for or working for a government.

The taxpayers paid for health care, police, the military, school's education, which belongs to the public. The public servant works for a government. Public is able to be used by anyone and accessible to people in general rather than restricted or private. We tend to use the notion of public for everything within the context of government.

Service is another interesting word that is strategically used. In the dictionary, service means state employment, e.g., crown, military. It can also be defined as an organization supporting the state, such as health, police, fire, civil services, prison, courts, probation. But even in the e-government, service refers to a process or a transaction or a piece of computer code in the context of digital government.

There are definitions of e-government services that we use, like digital service or online public service, citizen-centric service, open government service, composable service and integrated service. We need to be really paying attention when we bring in the concept of service in the context of public administration.

Government information is very unique. It explains policy and law when it comes to information for citizens and in public administration. Availability is critical to information in the government context. Information has to be accessible to all people of all abilities, to be channeled to reach all its audiences and to be comprehensive, up to date and accurate.

6. Basic questions about government and transform

Here are basic answers to basic questions.

What is government? Government is a decision-making body for a community.

What does it do? It decides and acts on common answers to contested community issues, which is policy.

How does it do it? Through policy design, implementation and administration, to act on society, economy, and the environment. At least, this is the notion in the sense of established public administration settings.

How do you transform that? It's a massive question. How do you actually transform policy design, implementation and administration that act for society and economic environment? These are the fundamental questions about transform that needs to be answered. It's not about the technology that is going to be implemented. Questions need to answer include: How is that technology going to influence certain policy decisions? What is the policy outcome behind the technological implementation that you're trying to achieve? What benefits are you trying to realize? What impact would them have on citizens? How do you begin to transform all of these? My research indicates that policy instruments are the key to transform it.

7. Policy instruments are the key to the answer

Policies instruments are tools that government used to make a change to society, the economy, or

Table 1

Hood's classification of instruments

Instrument Resource	Interpretation	Examples of Instruments
Nodality	The ability to collect and disseminate information	Safety campaigns, public & company records
Authority	The ability to determine how people must act	Laws, taxes, permits, regulation
Treasure	The ability to provide money	Benefits, grants, loans, subsidies
Organisation	The Physical ability to act directly on people or the environment	Infrastructure, health service (public goods & services)

Source: Hood, C., and Margetts, H. Z., 2007, *The Tools of Government in the Digital Age*. Basingstoke: Palgrave Macmillan.

Table 2

The sub-classification of instruments

Resource Type	Instrument sub-class	Examples
Nodality	Information Provision	Public health campaigns, health advice website
	Data Publication	National statistics, census data, performance data
	Self-service Information	National archives, law databases, company information
Authority	State Prerogatives	Criminal law, diplomatic relations, militaryaction, border control, currency control
	Taxes and Duties	Personal tax, corporate tax, sales tax, import duty, fuel duty, alcohol duty
	Registration, Permits and Standards	Passport/ID card, driving license, birthregistration, trading permit, parking permit
Treasure	Entitlements, Grants, Subsidies, Loans	Unemployment benefit, pensions, housing/care allowance, research grants, student support
Organization	Public Services	Utilities, mail, health, education, welfare, transport, emergency, waste, accommodation
	Public Goods	Roads, railways, airports, parks, broadcasting, museums, libraries, public housing
Meta-class		
Information about Instruments		

the environment to achieve their policy goals through introducing and implementing various policy instruments. Policy instruments are implemented by different public administration institutions within the government to achieve the policy goals we design, implement, and administer. Some examples of policy instruments are taxes, laws, health care and insurance.

In the COVID-19 context, what is the policy instrument we need to use to ensure that education continues without having negative implications on health care? That's really important.

Most of the transformation happens within this framework: nodality, authority, treasure and organization. We need to pay attention to that if we want to succeed in applied digital transformation.

In the context of COVID-19, we have the follow scheme where the government is paying 80% of the salaries for people who have been unable to work due to COVID-19. This scheme was going to stop, but at the end of this month it has been extended for a further month because another upcoming lockdown.

The instruments that government applies has an implication on the public administration setting, public services and goods. Governments make policy goals, and they implementthe policies through a public administration institutions, public services and goods that impact citizens, businesses and communities.

Digital by default, digital by design, digital by policy design and transformation by policy design are the new technologies in the UK.

Language matters a lot. Be careful when we use language. Citizens are not customers. Government does not deliver services. Policy design is where transformation happens. Policy instruments are the tools of policy design. Technology is a modifier of policy instruments. Statecraft is very difficult as it is. It makes established bureaucratic public administration settings complex.

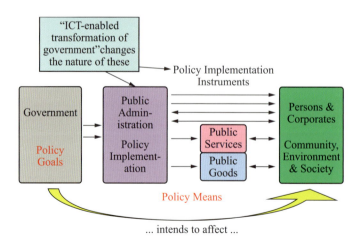

Fig. 2
Digital
transformation

8. Future directions for digital transformation efforts in government

We should focus on public services & goods: We should focus on real people, real-life activities, real demand, complex, evolving, multi-agency systems, limited potential for ICT.

We should focus on demand management: We should better use current capacity; meet demand differently and reform services; take new measures to reduce future demand. When there is demand, if you don't manage the demand, that's where the big problems happen.

If we wish to change from an early state into a butterfly, focus on the policy aspect of transformation.

"One-stop Government Services" in Shanghai

Zheng Lei

Professor of Fudan University

I'd like to share a case from Shanghai called "one-stop government services", which refers to a service center providing online and offline integrated services for all citizens. This case is listed in the UN E-government Survey at 2020. It is called the data centric online and offline integration of digital government in Shanghai.

1. "One-stop government services" building

There are some problems before this project. Citizens have to go to many specific individual agencies to start business. For example, if I want to establish a new company or buy a house, I have to visit agency A and submit my applications and other documents requested. After one week, agency A will return my materials and issue me with a certificate. Then, I have to go to agency B or department B to submit new applications together with the certificate I received from agency A. Then go to agency C, agency D… I just go back and forth between different agencies or departments to finish one business. This is the traditional business model that the citizens interact with governments. The problem of this model is that every service agency needs to identify which kind of service it is responsible for and issue citizens with a specific certificate. But from citizens' perspective, all of these are served for one business. It wastes time. In this case, Shanghai government decided to build a stop that citizens can finish their business at a time.

To this end, the government have to rename each business. When citizens want to open a restaurant, buy a house, apply for education, enter a school or do any other business, they just need to submit their application once. All agencies or departments concerned will get involved in one system for one business and share related documents and information. That's the whole idea of "one-stop government services". In addition, in order to consolidate all these data, Shanghai government decided to set up a new organization — Shanghai Municipal Big Data Center. It will consolidate data from all agencies and thus make this "one stop" service possible. Based on data flew and cross-boundary information sharing, the government integrated separated agencies into one stop process.

The "one-stop government services" service is applied both online and offline and is available for all citizens, either they are digitally disadvantaged or advantaged, elderly or young, rich or poor. For citizens who do not know how to use mobile applications or PC websites, they can visit offline service centers. There are 200 service centers scattered in various communities in the city. Both online website and offline centers share the same information, which facilitates both offline and online services. Since most citizens now prefer mobile applications rather than a PC website, the government launched the mobile application that can be used through WeChat and Alipay, or be downloaded from an Android or an Apple Store. However, companies have to go to website for services, because the process for them is too complicated to operate on a small mobile screen. Besides, citizens can also choose to call the hotline — "12345", for consulting or asking questions about how to submit their applications or what kind of documents they need to prepare.

2. Challenges of "one-stop government services"

There are many challenges the government is faced with. First is how to serve visitors or foreign businessmen in Shanghai. Second is how to increase the percentage of online services.

In fact, citizens can visit any service center in Shanghai to get the services you need. For example, if citizens want to start a business, they can visit any of the 200 service centers to finish the relevant process, because all these 200 service centers are connected to the same big data center. That is what "anywhere" means. In terms of "any time", it means that citizens can get services 24 hours the whole year. If citizens get service online, they can receive their certificates any time. Even in the offline service center, there are some self-service machines, like ATM, so after office hour, citizens can receive services from self-service machine in offline centers.

3. The future of city service and management

It has been 2 years since the "one-stop government services" project was launched. There are some bugs or gaps in this project. Citizens may not be very satisfied with it. In the next 5 years, we will try to make it better from citizens' perspective rather than government's perspective. The government needs to conduct some surveys and to collect the feedback from citizens after each service. Based on these feedbacks, the government will make some improvements on the project.

In the next 5 years, the government will also try to integrate service and city management. In addition to this "one-stop government services" service system, there is another system that aims to use one platform for managing the whole city. This management system manages city transportation, environmental protection, and food safety through one platform and facilitate the achievements of a smart city, a smart government or smart governance projects. If the data can be used both for service and management of the city, these two systems can be integrated together in the society. Now, we are still working on it.

Public Complaints and Government Responses: A Case Study of Beijing

Ma Liang

Professor of Renmin University of China

I will talk about the city hotline, "12345", in Beijing, and its implications for other cities in China and other countries. I will briefly talk about what we've learned about the government hotline, the hotline's rapid development in Beijing and the problems that have arisen during its development.

1. Government hotline and urban governance

It's important for the government to respond to citizens' demands efficiently and effectively. There are governments at different levels (municipal, district, township, and community levels) and governments in different agencies.

The key to improve the efficiency and effectiveness of the government is to improve the responsiveness to citizens' demands. Lots of studies have been focused on the use of non-emergency hotline. For example, in the US, "311" has been used widely. Such kind of use is not only in the area of service improvement, but also in performance management or performance leadership. We disaggregate the hotline data into different agencies, and monitor the progress weekly or monthly. By doing so, we can combine the hotline with agencies to make the strategic management more doable.

2. The city hotline in China

There are some problems with the use of government hotline in China. For example, at the city and state levels, the hotline was suspended, partially because of the succession of the leaders or culture. In recent years, many scholars are concerned about the sustainability of government hotline. China has the first city hotline in 1983 in Shenyang, Liaoning province. Later, more cities have introduced their city level hotline. Apart from that, some agencies have their specific outlines.

Some cities have almost 60 or even more hotlines. Therefore, for citizens and enterprises, it's quite a problem for them to know which number they should call.

Then all these hotlines have been integrated into one, which is "12345". In social media, more channels have been used for citizens to file their complaints or suggestions to the government.

3. Beijing government hotline and its feedback mechanism

Last year in Beijing, the government introduced what we call the " 接诉即办 " in Chinese, which is "public complaints processed without delay" or "swift response to public complaints". In 2008, during the Beijing Olympic Games, this hotline was integrated and improved. Not until 2019 was it substantially improved to make sure it can be run very efficiently. It was improved significantly in only one year.

First, the response rate increased to 100%, which means every call received will be responded.

Second, the resolution rate, which means your request has been filed and addressed, was improved to around the 75%, which was quite high.

Third, the satisfaction rate of citizens was around 87%, which was also very high.

It's quite an amazing achievement. Beijing have developed "the double-loop feedback mechanism", which means citizens can file their complaints to the hotline, which communicates and works together with the government to address citizens' concerns and respond to them. This kind of feedback helps to integrate citizens' demands and government responses in a smooth way.

4. The incentive system of Beijing government hotline

There is a kind of high-power incentive system that works for the government at city, district and sub-district levels. The system covers all agencies, all districts and all towns. Every month, there will be communication meetings to review the performance of all the agencies. They will be ranked quantitatively and clearly with three KPIs, which are response rate, resolution rate, and satisfaction rate. All the results will be publicly released. In this way, the government can know their relative performance to peers.

Such kind of high-power incentive system is quite useful because the local cadres are quite concerned about their career future and their reputation. At the monthly meeting, the municipal party secretary will evaluate everyone's performance. If the local cadres don't perform as well as expected, they will feel embarrassed at the meeting. Therefore, Beijing has established a kind of people-centered government, which means that all citizens' and enterprises' feedback will be reviewed back and forth.

To encourage a local government to respond to citizens' concerns, the top-down rankings and ratings work well. All the local governments will be evaluated by their performance, which is linked to their management and responding to citizens' concerns. What's more, as one's performance is relative to others, the local governments are quite active in learning from their peers. What this system features lies in the community. At the community level, Beijing has organs which can be used to respond to citizen's concerns, which is a more direct approach.

5. The problems of Beijing government hotline

However, there are many problems with the operations of Beijing Government Hotline.

First, the high business cost. So far in Beijing, there have been almost 1 500 operators working at the call centers which are going to expand the workforce. Given the budget cut back, it's not easy to do so. Therefore, how to maintain and reduce the cost is a big concern.

Second, this kind of operation is still a reactive one, which is quite different from a predictive operation. Citizens' concerns might be seasonally or originally linked with some signals, which can be analyzed by big data or other technologies to help the government to respond in advance, instead of responding passively.

Third, there are some gaming and manipulations. Because of this kind of high-power incentives, the local governments are incentivized to game the system. How to address it is a big concern.

Fourth, how to sustain the system is a big problem after the leading cadre leaves. As the cadres at the community level are quite busy with the daily operation of the system, they are burnt-out at work. Such kind of system is mainly driven by the leading congress and the party secretary. However, next year or the year after next year, there will be changes in leadership.

6. The successful transformation of Beijing government hotline

Right now, the system is transforming from 1.0 to 2.0 version. How to successfully transform it depends on the following points.

First, we should institutionalize government either by legislation or by cultural change.

Secondly, we should develop more artificial-intelligence (AI)-based applications, to reduce the use of operators.

Thirdly, the data can be shared both within the government and across agencies and even in the whole society. In this way, both enterprises and academia can use the data for a better future.

Finally, we should improve the operation of this kind of governance models by generalizing this case and comparing it with other cases.

Smart Cities and Intelligent Vehicles: Integrated Collaborative Perspective

Simon Marvin

Professor of the Urban Institute, the University of Sheffield, UK

Aidan Wilde

Professor of the Urban Institute, the University of Sheffield, UK

1. Background

Simon Marvin: Our topic is "Smart Cities and Intelligent Vehicles". We usually call them "autonomous vehicles", so I'll use that language. The question we've been asked to think about is the interrelationship between smart cities debate and autonomous vehicle debate.

Aidan and I are from the Urban Institute of the University of Sheffield, and we are an interdisciplinary group of researchers. We have done a lot to understand the interrelationship between technical change, low carbon transitions, smart cities, robotics and automation, and how they interrelate within the urban context. And part of our work is to disentangle some of the claims that are overstated about the benefits and transformative potentials of the technologies. We also want to look at the way in which urban life often shapes how these technologies are used and implemented in sometimes unusual and odd ways and the challenges from the rather overstated transformative effects of new technology.

We want to develop a more balanced and critical view of the interrelationship between technical change and urban life, and the ways in which the relationships are mutually shaping and defining each other. And in particular, we want to reflect on work we've been doing in the theme of automation and robotics. We've done a lot of work on the smart city over the last five years. And one of the things we are interested in is the emergence of a new set of technological capabilities and sometimes it's called the fourth industrial revolution, including artificial intelligence, automation and robotics. There seems to be potentially a shift taking place and the urban context is used as a site of demonstration with other sorts of technologies that can't necessarily be captured by the focus on the smart city which is primarily concerned with software.

So, we've been trying to understand the ways in which the urban context is becoming a science experimentation with AI, the drones, delivery robots and autonomous vehicles. We're asking ourselves the question to which we don't have the answers yet. Is this something that's different from the smart city or is it consistent to the smart city? A couple of years ago, we did a piece of work for the UK robotics and autonomous systems network, mapping the emergence of experimentation around AI, robotics and autonomous vehicles. This landscape of urban experimentation is different to the smart city. Sometimes they overlap in the same places, but often there seems to be quite distinctiveness in terms of the overall priorities of experimentation and who's involved in them, which seemed to indicate that there might be something different about this new logical technological change.

2. The First Proposition

Simon Marvin: We need to understand the new logical technological change and, as what the organizers of the forum have asked, what's the relationship between smart cities and autonomous vehicles? Why are there debates around smart cities and intelligent or autonomous vehicles? Why have they been disconnected and kept separate? And how might we productively think about this relationship? What are the reasons for that separation? And how may we think about how we bring them together perfectly? It seems to us that there was a set of three challenges and the smart cities debate is primarily around the application of computational logic, binary decision making and binary logic, the utilization of data and its applications in different domains of urban life.

And we've heard a lot about that warning in relation to national technology projects, saying that there are problems. Robotics and autonomous vehicles have a different underlying logic. It's more about logistics, efficiency and optimization of movement in time and space, which is a focus on the material nature of the city.

Somebody mentioned the difficulty that the digitalization has in dealing with the material world, causing some disability. I think that's a very interesting insight because there's something happening here about the interrelationship between software and hardware which we don't really understand. The question is how do we start to entwine debates about software and hardware in some notion of automated urban restructuring and we're trying to think of a language by which we might capture the way in which social and physical processes are being automated in new ways of rebalancing the relationship between human and machinery.

It is important to think about the relationship between cities and robotics in these technological systems. It's clear that the context isn't a blank sheet on which these technologies are incomprehensively implemented. There's resistance, cost, and contestation. And the nature of the technological project could fail or be reshaped in quite different ways because of the context that it's located in. But without the sort of question, we've really been trying to grapple with and think about the relationship between smart cities and autonomous vehicles through the work in this theme and we're going to reflect on that briefly in the rest of the talk. And our argument is that we need to shift away from a purely technological and economic focus. We need to develop a vision of a more hybridized urban context in which we think about the intertwining of human and machining capacities in decision making. The notion of hybridity might provide a way of thinking about those relations in a more productive and less deterministic manner.

Why are there smart cities debates and automated vehicles debates? You may think they are highly interconnected because they're both concerned about the application of digital and statistical technologies and they would fit together quite neatly and nicely. But when we actually start to look at the literature of the experience of these experimentation and application, we see that there are a lot of disconnections between them.

It's not what we've heard this morning about smart cities applications that are very much around the efficiency, rationalization and improving the effectiveness and responsiveness of government services. How do automated vehicles, drones, and robots fit in with that logic? Is it an entirely different logic? Does it deal with entirely different domains? Can it be connected more broadly with questions around urban management and urban service delivery? I think the first thing that we wanted to try and understand in answering these important questions is that smart cities and automated vehicles have very distinctive historical trajectories and we would argue to keep them largely disconnected debates about the future of urban life and the future of cities.

So, the smart cities debate as we heard this morning has the idea around using data and software to affect a form of interconnection between many different domains of urban life. Particularly, the examples we have this morning were about the application of those sorts of integrative systems in local governments and their ability to connect together currently disconnected domains of urban service delivery. Now this is primarily an organizational logic rooted in software systems that have a particular history in their application in corporate context. Around these smart cities' technologies and products, we develop to enable the integration of corporate commercial entities and have been applied particularly in urban and municipal governments. The claim initially was that they could connect infrastructures, housing and building environment, and could provide energy management and traffic demand management.

That's been a bit more problematic in terms of that total level of inspiration. As for the autonomous vehicles debate, actually it has quite a different logic. Rather than the notion of the integrated system, it puts the primacy on the notion of an autonomous vehicle, so it has a much narrower focus around the attempt to mobilize an autonomous or more autonomous and intelligent vehicle. It tends not to try and look at the whole of the urban system or make claims about urban integration. That's quite a different origin. If we look at drone delivery, the use of social robots, it's very much around the vehicle itself rather than thinking about the vehicle itself in its urban context. Now this means one is very much concerned around software and organizational change while the other is concerned about hardware and mobility.

When we look at the history of these developments and place them in that context, which we often don't do, we will see the smart city has all sorts of entities in debates going back to the 1920s and 1930s around the introduction of telephony and telephones which allow separation of the domestic home and businesses to enable sub-urbanization with the development of motorway, interstate and extra boosted mobility. There's much more tendency in debates of telecommunications in the 1980s and 1990s, the cyber city and the digital city. The smart city has a much longer antecedent in thinking about the application of digital technologies. The organizations involved primarily tend to be software companies and tech companies who are developing products and sell them in smart cities market partly, because of the saturated corporate market and the vision of inter-connectivity of urban systems. Therefore, the claim is that what's disconnected often can be reconnected for very good reasons.

The analog is the digitally enabled corporate entities which use these enterprise-based software systems, but integrate every aspect of the corporate entity from production, logistics, human resources could be applied to the urban context. The city almost became scenes additionally enable for intensity which explains some of the problems around the government. The rationality that underpinned this was largely around the primacy of computational logic and binary data and its incorporation into software systems as a preferred mode of decision-making.

Whereas in contrast, the autonomous vehicles sector, like automated aircraft and transportation telematics, automated vehicles within warehouses and closed spaces. In particular, the military mobility has played a critical role in stimulating the development of autonomous technologies. Even so, such technologies are actually developed in an enclosed world of the military and particularly remain secure and controlled concepts. It involves different types of actors to the smart city, including specialists in vehicles, automated vehicle technologies, vehicle manufacturers, the tech companies developing highly specific digitized and GIS mapping systems and centers. It's a whole new entrance to how actors who have never perhaps been concerned with urban policy, urban strategy and urban politics are now developing systems so as to be utilized in the urban context.

The vision and the analog that have been talked about here are the efficient logistical entity. So, it's very much focused around the idea that the applications developed in logistical context, like freight delivery, aviation, the distribution sector and the warehouse sector, can be applied in urban life. The vision is very much around the notion of automated mobility, transcending the limits of congestion and overcoming problems of time and space in enabling urban circulation. This has a rationality and logistical logic and it relies on competition, but rather it's very much around the hardware and movement, the people goods and services in the urban domain.

So, we're dealing with two quite different logics there. I just like to pass over to my colleague Aidan Wilde for the second part of the talk.

3. The second proposition

Aidan Wilde: Our second proposition it's to think through a sign as indicated in the relationship between software of the digitally based marketing and the hardware that comes from extended robotic and autonomous system application whether autonomous vehicles, service robots, or drones in the various forms. And this has really preoccupied us since the start of setting up themes around urban robotics and automation and it is a distinctive shift around how we think about that hardware. And it's different sets of relationships around human and machinery, specifically human robotic interactions. What does that mean for the city? How does that link up that interface around the hardware of an infrastructure with the underlying digitally based and non-digitally based forms of urban management? So, we would argue that urban robotics that fascinates us in terms of vehicles is about the development of hardware in vehicle expansion.

We're urbanists and we are interested in cities. I'm an urban designer, and I'm interested in urban planning. We work on social and technical development and the future of cities. And hardware dimension really interested us because it is about a physical change in the city which influences how we design the cities, plan the cities, how people move around, and what they do in all kinds of profound ways.

This early phase of development matters, because it sets in train some of the future pathways. Our answers on every experimentation are focused on how those pathways are being developed, how we think through this new set of relationships, what sort of models and approaches become more dominant, what factors are involved in that and what sort of places are important. So, we would argue that the smart cities debate which precedes the robotics debate is not yet caught up with it.

There's a question about why we call that the post smart city, the smart city plus, smart city in general or whether we have a different sort of language. One of the presentations early emphasized the importance of language and thinking through what language we use for this and what language that different actors use. Is the robotics community using the same sort of language reflecting as smart cities or is it a different language available for different logic instead of rationality as explained in Proposition One? There's a real disconnection between the relative malleability of software, data and hardware changes. We've done quite a lot of work on this in various contexts around the world.

We're looking at the cutting edge of thinking through robotic infrastructure on the ground to leave it through experiments and living labs and that sort of initiatives. But there are difficulties in bringing together the digital and the hardware. The whole set of challenges will be talked about later.

Robotics is under development. The digital field is not fixed, nor are the smart cities. In terms of the possibilities, what could be done? AI is constantly evolving, so we've got a very interesting picture of people and changes on both smart cities side and on the robotics side. But the key issue is how do we think about the interrelationship between the software and hardware of smart cities. What is that relationship?

The framework of the smart city, software and platforms are always fragmented. And it was clearly reflected by the UK experience, particularly different platforms for different areas of public policy. But around the world, you can see a different set of smart city approaches in different places. And it's more or less integrated in some places than others.

I've been looking at what's happening around the digital issue, how that's been extending hardware and been more integrated as a set of processes in some places. We've been looking at some of the other things in our research based in Rio de Janeiro. It's a sort of separation, other form of urban management. It's not a necessary part of the smart cities issue. It becomes common when we look at cutting edge examples of interesting approaches to smart city management, which begins to get into the hardware dimension.

The hardware of robotics and autonomous systems might take different forms, whether it's autonomous vehicles, or various forms of services, delivery robots and security robotics on the streets, underground and flying vehicles. Perhaps we haven't even thought of some of the applications of robotics yet, for example, exoskeletons and the augmentation of individual capacity. At the early stage, our city might be remade in different ways by different types of robotics and autonomous vehicles. How they might operate? How they might run the business models? For individual choices within a collective management system, whether those technologies will be evenly distributed around the city, whether some of the more transformative, or whether socially beneficial technologies will be available to the natural places with less populations because they cost money and need investment.

Where we're going with the robotics and autonomous vehicles is not a singular future. One of the strengths of our researches is to think about how that future is being made through imagining the visions: governance structures, the nature of private sectors, firms of the competition within the sector to develop technologies and get them implemented. It's a really good time to be thinking about possible smart cities and robotic interactions. Autonomous vehicles highlight a wider set of issues. And they have to be placed in wider frame called an urban robotic structure or a restructuring of the urban automation.

4. The third proposition

Aidan Wilde: Some of the visions we are now putting forward are original ones of the smart cities and some of those are promoted by firms that had a commercial interest in presenting an overall solution. We think that imaginary of total integration and unrestricted autonomy are just impossible to achieve. Therefore, how do we work with a different conception that moves away from what we call the integrated idea of the smart city to a recognition of the need for different hybrids? The need for hybrids becomes actually enhanced when we think about the relationship between smart city and the machine dimensions of robotic and autonomous systems.

The smart city is segmented into different platforms and applications despite the wider vision. We've done some work on smart city standards, finding difficulty in standardizing, let alone trying to integrate with particular places or even commonality across places. There are multiple products, services and providers. The UK example from the first session demonstrated clearly how fragmented those standards are in many contexts, not in all context, like China and Korea in terms of relative coordination or fragmentation in the approach to smart city. The fragmentation has been part of the smart city debate, and there is some frustration and uncomfortableness about the smart city. So never can a single project deal with the complexity of cities and the different issues need to be dealt with.

In terms of autonomous vehicles, our ideal is about the whole autonomous system. It has its own normality and idealized vision of the final version of autonomous vehicles. There is an engineering goal or engineering challenge of autonomous vehicles. But the idea of autonomous vehicles is just as problematic as the idea of integration. Some people say robotics and autonomous vehicles will be contested and resisted. They need to be worked within the complexity, unruliness and difficulties of different cities and they have to deal with people — it's extremely expensive to automate vehicles. That's not what we want to do. We want to find ways of blending the best of the non-human, which needs a new and retrofitted infrastructure.

In this moment of transition, integrating autonomous vehicles into the city means that the autonomous elements which have to be developed by ourselves need to deal with the messy complexity. What else is there? Vehicles that aren't automated have to be driven by humans. Infrastructure is not entirely suited to the operation of autonomous vehicles. As for the nature of this imaginary ideal of autonomous vehicles, whether it is possible or not to catch up with engineering and logistical rationality, it's really important to think about the existing complexities of the relationship between smart cities and autonomous vehicles.

The challenges lie in governance, policy and technologies that have been integrated into the city. It's about developing blended hybrid solutions in response to the geographical variables. How do we think about the nature of blended hybrid system? All autonomous vehicles have to be integrated within urban complexity. It's the complexity about governance and building trust among humans. It's the issue of public engagement. It's about how we regulate and re-regulate the environment to make space automation, about the legal systems in different places, about how we deal with all the new infrastructure and how we blend autonomous vehicles and other forms of autonomous systems and robotics into the city. It's about business models. It's about investment. It's about how we think about mobility and its individual and collective forms and public transport. And there is no singular model or blueprint to deal with that. It will be made on the ground in different cities as different governments with different priorities, different access to resources and will engage with a range of private sector companies, consultancies, and so on.

We've been doing quite a bit of work of drone infrastructure. We've been thinking about how we create space for drones in different places and logical corridors around drone delivery. But there are other models for integrating drones into cities, which need experimentation. Robotic companies are frustrated at times that they don't have real world context to do this form of experimentation.

The way we think about autonomous vehicles is not just about autonomous vehicles. It's about a wider approach to those urban robotic management and smart city management. We see the city as a management entity because it needs to be managed in different ways including the digital field, the increase application of AI and the human decision making within that context. Geography is an important factor in terms of what is happening internationally, what is happening in different countries, what is happening in different cities, as well as what is happening within cities. The role of experiments is of enormously importance to reflect on different contexts. Governments approach to this issue in different ways. There are different logics of governance. There are different ways of thinking through public priorities and the role of the human, with regard to robotics and various ways and also around issues of risk trust. This is a blended or hybrid set of issues.

5. Conclusions

Aidan Wilde: We found the smart cities and autonomous vehicles are enormously valuable in our research. We've not been explicit about it. Take UK as an example. When we studied the relationship between smart cities and autonomous vehicles, we were really puzzled and it was difficult for us to think through such a relationship, but we've found it enormously productive. We did research on autonomous vehicles in real world experiments and applications. Hopefully, it will provide a bit of a framework for what will come in the session.

What is going on at the moment is a vision of autonomous vehicles in the wider area as a part of wider urban management system. Where are those being developed? What might we learn from them? With a regulatory governance, technical management issues have been addressed. This isn't simply an engineering challenge. Rather, it's moving from an engineering challenge into a wider issue of governance, policy and regulation. Different places and countries, different types of interests should learn from each other. What language is being used for smart cities and autonomous vehicles? It's bringing an international experience to help us think about these things in the real context.

The final question is how autonomous vehicles can be integrated to wider urban automation systems. And all these things are happening already. We've done research in various cities around the world, like Guangzhou, and talked with Alibaba about the City Brain. And our project is a platform that can be used to facilitate automation in various ways. Some of this might be happening or some of the platforms have been moving forward on the integration of smart cities and robotics in various ways. It might not appear to be direct about autonomous vehicles. Some of the new frameworks have already been put into practice in different ways but not actually using some of the language we might expect to use.

To summarize, if you're thinking through the different logics of the smart city, autonomous vehicles and robotic automation, it's really important to recognize the distinctions and differences in their relationships despite the limitations. We are in the stage of remaking this relationship and we've set out a framework to do so.

How "New Infrastructure" Drives the Construction of Smart City

Liu Zhiyi

Director of SenseTime Intelligent Industry Research Institute

Under My topic How "New Infrastructure" Drives the Construction of Smart City, I will discuss how we understand the construction of smart city is driven by new infrastructure policies and how to treat the relationship between new technologies represented by AI and social governance.

1. Background: urban problems need to be solved with the acceleration of urbanization

On the whole, the process of global urbanization is advancing with an unstoppable trend. Nearly 70% of the world's population is expected to live in cities by 2050.

Fig. 1
Global urbanization process in 2019
Source: Statista.

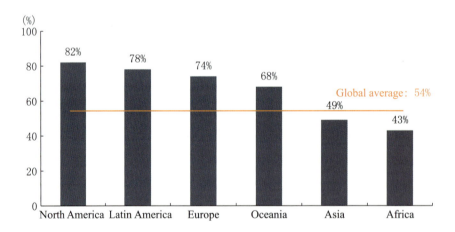

China is also in the process of rapid urbanization. However, there is still a gap of nearly 20% in the urbanization rate between China and developed countries (Fig. 2), and the urban population of China is still growing at a rate of 2—3% per year (the urban population base is over 800 million) (Fig. 3).

提升社区和城市品质

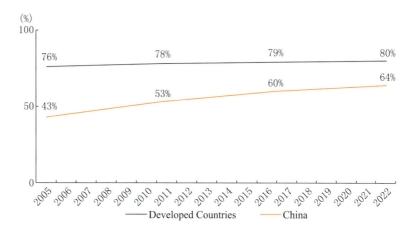

Fig. 2
Comparison of
urbanization ratio
between China
and developed
countries
Source: United
Nations.

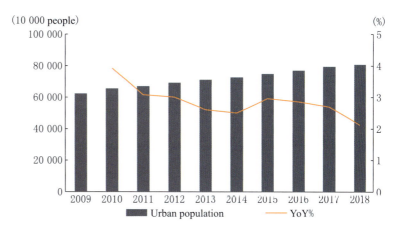

Fig. 3
China's urban
population and
growth rate
Source: Deloitte.

The urban population density is increasing. It is estimated the urban density in China will reach approximately 2 600 people per square kilometer by the end of 2020.

1. Current situation: the government vigorously promotes the construction of smart city pilot projects

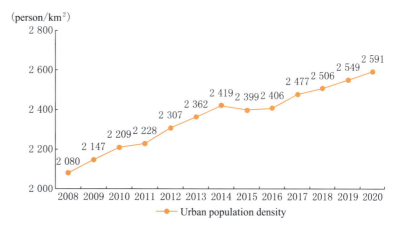

Fig. 4
China's urban
population
density
Source: Deloitte
(Including forecast).

Urbanization has brought about expansion of cities and related facilities, and I think it has brought opportunities and challenges at the same time. In order to solve the severe challenges brought by urbanization, China has launched large-scale smart city pilot projects since 2012. China has continuously expanded the scope, and upgraded this project into national strategy. In 2018, our government clearly put forward the goal of building 100 new smart cities on different levels. See the related strategies and policies in Table 1 and Table 2.

Table 1
Top-level strategies in China

2012	2013	2014	2015	2018
Comprehensively use modern science and technology, integrate information resources, coordinate business application systems, and strengthen urban planning, construction and management. —*Ministry of Housing and Urban-Rural Development of China*	The development of intensive, intelligent, green and low-carbon new urbanization will stimulate domestic demand and drive industrial transformation and upgrading. —Ministry of Housing and Urban-Rural Development of China	Use new-generation information technologies such as the Internet of Things, cloud computing, big data, and spatial geographic information integration. —National Development and Reform Commission	Promote the in-depth integration and iterative evolution of a new generation of information technology and urban modernization, and realize a new ecology of coordinated development between the country and the city. —Cyberspace Administration of China	Services for the people, transparent and efficient online government, integrated and innovative information economy, precise and precise urban governance, and safe and reliable operation system. —State Council

2. About "new infrastructure"

The implementation of smart city is a continuing challenge and a subject of high political concern. From the beginning of 2018, our government has been implementing policies on building new infrastructure. The so-called "new infrastructure" refers to the construction of a new type of infrastructure. Unlike the traditional infrastructure including roads, bridges and houses, "new infrastructure" mainly focuses on the infrastructure construction of technologies. According to the official definition, "new infrastructure" covers seven major fields: 5G networks, the industrial

提升社区和城市品质

Table 2
Policy support in China

Release Time	Policy	Release Time	Policy
2012.11	Interim management measures for National Smart City pilot project	2013.08	Opinions on promoting information consumption and expanding domestic demand
2012.11	National Smart City (District, Town) Pilot Index System	2014.03	National New Urbanization Plan (2014—2020)
2014.08	Guiding opinions on promoting the healthy development of smart cities	2017.01	Action Plan for Promoting Smart Transportation Development (2017—2020)
2015.01	Guiding opinions on promoting the development of smart tourism	2017.07	Development plan of new generation artificial intelligence
2016.11	Notice on organizing the evaluation of new smart cities and pragmatically promoting the healthy and rapid development of new smart cities	2017.09	Technical Outline for the Construction of Spatio-temporal Big Data and Cloud Platform for Smart City (2017 Edition)
2016.12	New Smart City Evaluation Index (2016)	2017.09	Action plan for smart transportation to make travel more portable (2017—2020)

internet, inter-city transportation and inner-city rail systems, data centers, artificial intelligence, ultra-high voltage, and new energy vehicle charging stations, involving communication, transportation, people' life, industries in the future. According to our research, we believe that "new infrastructure" is one of the most important areas to develop in the next two years.

3. Role of "new infrastructure": accelerating the process of smart city

First, "new infrastructure" promotes the intellectualization of social governance and accelerates the construction of a smart society. We believe that the modernization of urban governance system and governance capacity needs the construction of "new infrastructure" especially when China's prevention and control of the COVID-19 pandemic enters the new normal state. This also brings a good opportunity for smart city projects to further develop and integrate efficient and smart urban management.

Secondly, "new infrastructure" accelerates intelligent production and promotes the development of digital economy. "New infrastructure" makes production decisions more intelligent. Any enterprise can use advanced cloud computing, AI, big data and other types of new infrastructure at low cost. They can focus on their own business and market development without the limit of IT resources.

Thirdly, "new infrastructure" facilitates citizens' lives. In the beginning of 2020, "new infrastructure" helped us fight against the pandemic and keep a high-quality economy development. During the period, "5G + Education" became popular. "New infrastructure" also enabled the allocation of medical resources to break space constraints. Besides, the resumption of work, production and other kinds of activities, all to a certain extent depends on new infrastructure, especially E-commerce.

4. Classification of AI smart city landing scenarios

Together, the AI smart city landing scenarios form a "one core, three systems" industrial development framework. This framework has Artificial Intelligence, including AI Algorithm, AI Product, AI Service and AI System as its core, and "AI+ Manage", "AI+ Ecology" and "AI+ Life" as its constitution forms/three systems. The "smart" industrial planning is led by the government and guided by the intelligent industrial chain model, so as to build an artificial intelligence industry model for the development of cities, vigorously develop artificial intelligence technology industries, and improve cities' construction with intelligent management, intelligent ecology and intelligent life.

5. Application areas: driven by country and market demand

The Smart City Structure Model is divided into three parts, namely infrastructure, smart center and application services.

Fig. 5
Smart city structure model

提升社区和城市品质

6. Smart buildings: case study of Shanghai "Lingang" Virtual City

SenseTime is participating in the construction of "Lingang" Virtual City in Shanghai. Around RMB 5.6 billion has been invested into the important program, which was officially launched in 2019. In 2017, Shanghai Lingang started up the construction of "Smart Lingang BIM+GIS Urban Big Data Platform", and built a refined "virtual Lingang" through BIM + GIS. The platform is the first city-level data platform for the integration of urban geographic building facilities, covering 315 square kilometers of urban space of Lingang, and copying the architectural geographical construction of the whole city as it is. The platform can perceive the urban population heat map, traffic flow, parking garage status, video surveillance and other urban operation dynamics in real time. It can also use drones to carry out automatic image recognition and analysis, intelligently find abnormal urban problems, and deduce future development prediction.

Fig. 6
Shanghai
"Lingang" Virtual
City

7. Changes of SenseTime's products map

SenseTime is a leading global company focused on developing AI technologies that can advance the world's economies, society and humanity for a better tomorrow. We have made a number of technological breakthroughs. With our roots in the academic world, we keep investing in fundamental research to further our understanding and advance the state-of-the-art AI technologies. At SenseTime, we have a global team of talented individuals dedicated to R&D. Since 2015, our products map has been evolving, but we are always dedicated to improving governance through constructing smart city, empowering industries including retail, finance, tourism, manufacturing and autonomous driving, and benefiting people through developing smart hardware, Internet finance and so on. We have always been insisting on originality and trying our best to let AI lead human progress. We hope that AI technologies can promote the sustainable development of society and update the world.

Mobile Connectivity and Smart Transportation

Xu Shoulong

Operation Director of Mobile Connectivity in SAIC Volkswagen

In SAIC Volkswagen, my job is about how the vehicles provide entertainment through communications, about V2X, and about supporting autonomous driving of vehicles in China. Meanwhile, I'm a PhD student right now, doing some research in smart transportation. I want to share my thoughts with you about the interrelationship between mobile connectivity and the smart transportation.

1. Mobile connectivity empowers smart transportation

First, I want to elaborate on what I think about the relationship between the car, the Internet, the road, the cloud, and the smart brain (Fig. 1). In the industry, we have long been focused on the car

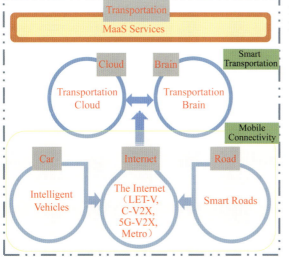

Human-Car-Road under Mobile Connectivity for Better Transportation

- Car: intelligent vehicles in the era of smart transportation
- Road: infrastructure for smar transportation
- Internet: telecommunications featuring 5G Internet of Cars and Internet of Things
- Cloud: Tiered and smart Cloud for transportation with computational services
- Brain: Smart Brain for decision-making, monitoring and operation based on big data
- Transportation: Fast and timely MasS Services and new operations of smart transportation

Fig. 1
The relationship between mobile connectivity and smart transportation

itself and wondering if we can connect the car with the driver. But now let's talk about whether we can have vehicles relying solely on themselves to do some thinking, to have some senses and move forward on the road by means of artificial intelligence. What we want to do is to move vehicles out of labs and use telematics to combine more of the intelligence with infrastructure, other cars, V2X and other objects on the road or in the environment to make the vehicles more intelligent in transportation instead of confining their development only to the lab level. In doing so, we expect the roads to facilitate the mobility of vehicles as a means of service by using the smart brain or the cloud.

2. Tiered development of car, internet and road

Second, I'd like to share some of my thoughts about the structure of the current vehicle industry. As we now see, technological advancement has improved our efficiency in using telematics and realizing connectivity. However, I don't think that is enough because without changing the fundamental way in developing transportation, we cannot make much success out of it.

As previous speakers mentioned, there is a limitation. So far, it's not easy to achieve complete automation of driving. There is an idea in the industry which is about hybridity, involving the car, the driver and other factors. So how can we deal with such a hybridity? This question is what we mainly think about at this moment. Therefore, I want to talk about the relationship between the connectivity and smart transportation. In Fig. 2, you can see there are three different standards in the bottom respectively for the car, the Internet and the road. Referring to the researches done by other scholars,

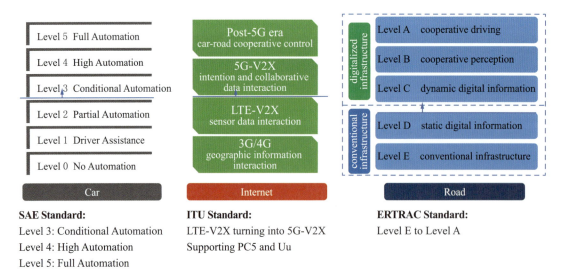

Fig. 2
Tiered development of car, internet and road

we have found out that there is already progress in China, Japan, Europe and the US. In different areas, we have different standards. From Fig. 2, you can see there are 5 levels according to SAE. Some commercials, different OEMs or different car-makers claim that they have reached level 4 or level 5. Tesla might be one of them. But actually, in the industry, what we always talk about is level 2, level 2 plus or level 2.5.

If we reach level 3, that means in some scenarios the car can drive itself. But when the driving situation is beyond the car's ability to control, then it will handle back the control power to human. But how can the car identify when to handle back that? It is actually still under discussions because we can set rules for AI to guide itself, but when it comes to human, things will be more complicated: What happens if the driver is not ready, gets distracted, or fundamentally incapable of handling such a complex situation? The answer to this question remains to be discussed.

I hold the idea that we are still trying to reach level 3. Some of the emerging OEMs are talking about jumping over level 3 to level 4. But I think companies still need to think about how to reach level 3 in a more reasonable manner. So that is the current situation with regard to the car.

In terms of communications, there are a lot of discussions about 5G and its advantages. I don't want to spend too much time on this topic here, because the industry itself and the countries are already spending so much time and effort in this field, but how can we really take advantage of 5G? This is both an industrial and academic issue. I have research experience with China Mobile and the other well-known companies. What they're doing now is trying to make the remote control, which means they will have an operator sitting behind a screen in a remote place, trying to operate the vehicles, instead of relying totally on 5G to do the job in those specific scenarios.

As for the roads, there are some standards set by European Road Transport Research Advisory Council (ERTRAC). They categorize roads to be A, B, C, D and E five levels. Honestly, I think we still lag behind in the development of roads and infrastructure. To solve this problem requires a lot of money, especially government investment. What the government should do to adopt a comprehensive strategy to ensure the benefit to the driver and other people is still not clear at the moment.

We've talked about three different elements and three different standards. What if we put them together?

3. Cooperative development of car, internet and road

Third, I'd like to talk about how the three areas connect with each other as well as the standards of the cars, Internet and roads. As shown in Fig. 3, we can see we are now in the middle stage from

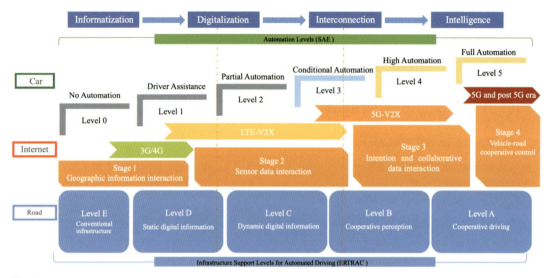

Fig. 3
Cooperation development of car, internet and road

informatization to intelligence, in the level 2 or 2.5 of car automation, stage 2 of Internet and level C of road. There is still a lot of work to do.

4. Smart car and smart road

Fourth, it's about the smart car and smart road. Now, the smart car is half autonomous, but the smart road still lacks investment and development. Besides, Internet is everywhere with a high

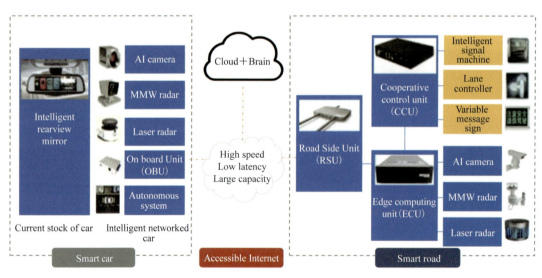

Fig. 4
Smart car, smart road, accessible internet and cloud plus brain

speed, low latency and a large capacity. We can see the details in Fig. 4. But still, we need better infrastructure to support our road and achieve smart road. And we should make the whole things as a good system.

5. Existing problems

At last, Fig. 5 shows existing problems based on my previous presentation. Different car-makers have done a lot in collecting data, but what we are actually building up right now are isolated islands. We need to work together. The first problem is that the current standards don't fully cover the vehicle, road and management. Despite the progress that has been made in various fields, we still lack collaborative application, which is a big challenge. So, the second problem is about how to create the application scenarios and how to merge different factors together. The last problem is the business models. Of course, the government can invest money in this area, but it is not the best solution. Only profitable business and operation models can actually attract companies to invest, to bring in the money, and to create an eco-system. Based on my own research and experiment, I found that lots of companies were willing to invest in autonomous vehicles and smart cities and what they are really interested in is how to earn money from this business. But the business model today is still not clear and profitable enough.

Fig. 5
Existing problems

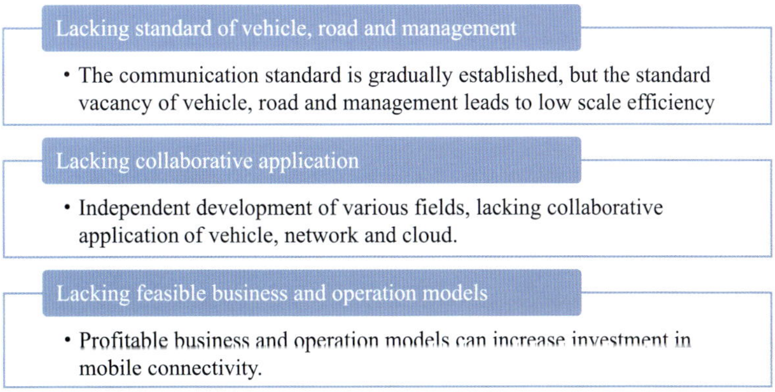

Lacking standard of vehicle, road and management
- The communication standard is gradually established, but the standard vacancy of vehicle, road and management leads to low scale efficiency

Lacking collaborative application
- Independent development of various fields, lacking collaborative application of vehicle, network and cloud.

Lacking feasible business and operation models
- Profitable business and operation models can increase investment in mobile connectivity.

How can we solve those challenges and move forward? We need to work together with our talents from different areas. I look forward to living in the smart city with mobile connectivity and smart transportation.

New Urban and Industrial Planning Under the Influence of Smart City and Intelligent Transportation

Hu Chuyan

CTO of Urban Space

1. Development stages of smart city

The global smart city market is vast. Public safety requirements, smart government affairs and transportation will become the main drivers of market growth. At present, most countries in the world are actively involved in the construction and development of smart cities. China, among all these countries, is the most popular one for smart city construction, with the number of pilot projects accounting for 48% (See Fig. 1). According to the latest research report released by Markets and Markets, a market research organization, the global smart city market was worth US$308 billion in 2018, and this figure is expected to grow to US$717.2 billion by 2023, with a compound annual growth rate of 18.4% .

Fig 1
The proportion of global smart cities under construction by region

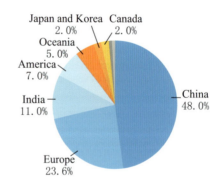

China's smart city construction has gone through three stages of development: from the decentralized construction phase of the introduction of smart city concepts, to the standardized development phase of smart city pilot exploration, and then to 2016 formally enter a new smart city with people-oriented, effectiveness-oriented, coordinated planning and collaborative innovation development stage. Today, Chinese smart city construction has entered the third stage, committed to

提升社区和城市品质

building an integrated operation pattern.

2. Smart city vs. land space plan

Under the New Era, Chinese urban planning is going through both institutional and content reform. Land space planning came into being. Since 2010, a spatial planning system has gradually come into being, as we have always heard one master plan replaced multiple plans. As time goes by, we have developed three goals—production, living and ecology, and the spatial planning system has been improved. Great changes have taken place in 2017. Ministry of Natural Resources initiated a new reform on institution. From then on, we have a new planning system. In this system, space planning is the base of the concept, led by the national development plan. However, we need to be aware that space planning should take more factors into consideration, including not only the current needs but also the connection between people and smart city in the future.

We know that one master plan has replaced multiple plans and land space planning has been developed. For this kind of change, big data platforms value decisions in land space planning, which has laid a solid foundation for the construction of smart city. We realize that the combination of land space planning and urban operation big data platform is an important guarantee for building smart cities. With the mature analysis model, we can provide people with customized platform services. By means of big data platform, we develop our land use planning and urban master plan.

3. Prospect of intelligent connected cars

Intelligent transportation is an important application of smart city. There are four levels of intelligent application. Intelligent car is still in stage L1-L2; the L3 intelligent networked car is still in the research and development period. But we are glad to see that intelligent cars have entered the market in cities including Shanghai and Beijing. An industry research has showed that intelligent connected cars are still in the research and development period, and key technologies will continue to improve in the future.

Intelligent cars are not just a means of transportation tool. In Jiaxing, an industrial city not far from Shanghai, we have built platforms to see what the intelligent cars can do. During the whole process, we found that for a smart city, the car is a connection point for other facilities other than a mere means of transportation. The car will take on all the affairs during the trip, most of which are not solely part of the trip scene. We should think more to bring out the market outcomes and make the

China's new car market size and growth of intelligent and connected vehicles, 10 000 units

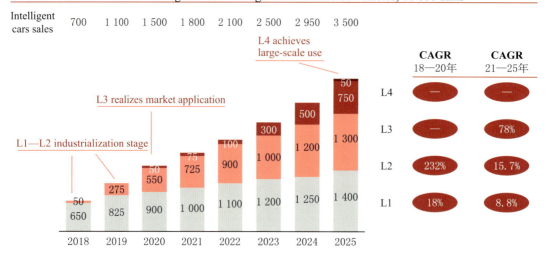

Fig. 2
China's new car market size and growth of intelligent and connected cars

project a big success. Besides, the driving data of vehicles can be fed back to urban road management. In that case, we should do a lot of road designs, which are fit for the new kind of car. On the planning side, we should put more efforts into infrastructure development.

4. Smart city and intelligent transportation

Vehicle-road collaboration (V2X) construction has become the starting point for the intelligent road traffic in cities. When it comes to the detailed planning work, we should adapt it for real conditions. The planning needs to consider vehicle-road collaborative applications, including warnings of dangers, traffic signal broadcast and coordinated control, etc. What's more, in order to make the new smart city infrastructure suitable for autonomous vehicles, we need to improve the lane markings, roadside sensors, smart signage, and 5G construction.

We believe that new urban construction can promote the coordinated development of intelligent cars and smart cities. We need to explore the trend of urban smart infrastructure construction. We should work hard to explore the application scenarios of smart cars and smart transportation. We also need to think about the construction model of multiple subjects and the future of technological innovation. I hope we can give it a try and maybe we will have more resources to work together on this study.

Promote the Construction of "Future Space" and Build Innovative Ecological Chain of Intelligent Vehicle-Road-Network

Zhang Xi

Professor of Shanghai Jiao Tong University

I would like to talk about how we promoted the construction of "Future Space" in Fengxian District, Shanghai, and how we built an innovative ecological chain of intelligent vehicle-road-network.

1. Smart city— "future space"

In Fengxian District, we aim to build a "Future Space" with "Integration of Living-Life-Production-Ecology". Here, we have policies such as being Open and Creative, Smart Ecology, Integration of Industry and City, and building a space Suitable for Business and Living.

We have a "4+2+1" Fusion Application (Fig. 1).

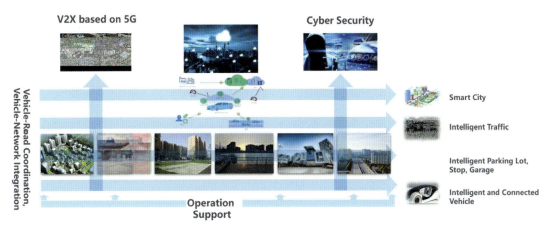

Fig. 1
Fusion application of "4+2+1"

We have realized cyber security in intelligent vehicles, so we cooperated with scientists from Shanghai Jiao Tong University (SJTU), focusing on cyber security.

2. Significance of "future space"

We created new economic forms (Fig. 4) in Fengxian District and extended to the whole Shanghai.

- Driving, Business, and Entertainment in the car
- Intelligent Vehicle and Core Parts
- Software, Service, and V2X: We have realized algorithms in the vehicle software.
- Roadside System and 5G Station: We have developed a roadside system. The system is capable of recognizing pedestrians, electric bicycles and driving cars, sending messages to the car. We have already established the infrastructure in Fengxian District, using our own ecologies.
- On-Board T-Box: We also call it OBU in the car. It can transform the signals in the cars into the roadside.
- Big Data: In the Cloud, we can pick big data from the cars. Finally, we can provide useful services for the government, car makers, and companies like Huawei.

The first thing is not only about the infrastructure. It's not for the hardware, but the software or the signals. We have built the common standards for thevehicles and then all the companies involved can share the signals and obey the same standards.

3. Practice of SJTU

We referred to the model of "Stanford University-Silicon Valley" to build an industrial cluster

Fig. 2
The whole travel chain in the area surrounding Shanghai Jiao Tong University

near our campus. SJTU is in Minhang District, and Fengxian District is just across Huangpu River. The area surrounding SJTU resembles the Stanford University-Silicon Valley area to some extent. We brought our ideas into reality in the area near our campus, and we engaged many scientists in the process. The two areas are similar in some ways.

We have built a demonstration zone of a whole travel chain near our campus. In this zone, there are highways, BRT, underground garages, and an industrial park.

There are six typical scenarios that interwork in this zone: Community, Industry Park, Campus, Scenic Spot, Commercial Area, and Urban Area. They can be connected by autonomous driving. Together, they form the base in the area surrounding SJTU.

Fig. 3
Interworking of six typical scenes

I would like to introduce some interesting technologies. In China, the pedestrians and electric bicycles on the road seem very complicated. Therefore, autonomous driving needs to pay attention to the pedestrians. There are no relevant laws to obey, which makes the situation more complicated. In 2018, we focused on the human factors for the first time. We have recognized the process of the pedestrians, separated those pedestrians into over 20 points, and developed algorithms to judge whether they are going to cross the road or not.

Besides, we made use of social sciences. Psychology sometimes decides the pedestrians' behavior: to go ahead or backward. We invested much in the decision-making controller in the autonomous driving cars.

We have two scenarios. First, when a child crosses the road, sometimes he/she suddenly stops, having no idea when the vehicles will come. When such condition occurs, vehicles have to steer away from the child. Second, if the child is tracking a football, he/she would be focusing on the football without noticing the coming car. You have to judge whether to go straight or stop on the road.

We have also built the Metropolitan Intelligent Transportation National System. It was established thanks to the collaboration between SJTU and Argonne National Lab in the US under the joint sponsorship of China's SAT Ministry and the US Department of Energy (DOE). We have established the biggest model into this traffic world.

We realized that the autonomous driving needs to integrate into the environment. Cars bring some coupling effects to the traffic, and the traffic influences the decision-making of cars. We need to build the supporting environment, not only for the autonomous driving, but for the smart city. We have established buildings, highways, or exits or where to set these system exits. These can be the benchmark or references to this establishment.

Finally, we have put entire Beijing scenarios into the system, including tens of thousands of roads, intersections, and the night timing. They will be the types of the electric cars or oil cars and the population. All these are factors that we consider in this system. As a result, that will be very close to the real conditions.

Towards Collaborative Development of Intelligent Vehicle in Smart City

Yu Junli

Research Assistant Professor, China Institute for Urban Governance

Today, we have learned some knowledge about AI technology and I am about to discuss another one.

1. Solow Endogenous Growth Model

First of all, please allow me to introduce the economic model. It's Solow Endogenous Growth Model. On the left hand of the equation is output, namely GDP and productivity. On the right hand is Alpha which refers to productivity, and function which includes capital, labor, land and others. This is a basic economic growth model.

Fig. 1
Solow
Endogenous
Growth Model

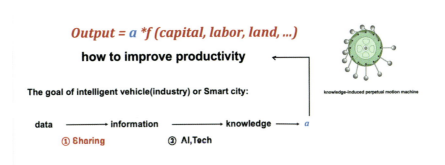

In arrangement of vehicle in a smart city, we have many data which share and form the information. We use AI technology to facilitate the information flows. Knowledge is a new productivity. If you don't change the factor "function" yet add "knowledge" to the last channel, you can introduce promotion machine which will improve the quality of welfare in the city. So, we can say knowledge is new productivity and a factor to drive city economical welfare development.

2. Subjects in intelligent vehicle and smart city

There are three types of subjects in intelligent vehicle and smart city: enterprises, consumers (users, drivers, and others), and government. However, there is an imbalance between supply and demand. For example, if enterprise A supplies the data to enterprise B, then they have a sharing platform. With the data, enterprise B can improve vehicle quality. However, enterprises are unwilling to cultivate their potential competitors, so the incentive for sharing is absent.

Another subject is consumer. They are allowed to get this data of information, but are unwilling to pay for information. They have no capability to build the data.

The third subject is government. It has funds, capability and other elements, but it has multiple identities maybe as a monitor, a builder, and many others. As a result, the three subjects all have insufficient incentive for construction of data sharing platforms.

What should we do to address this dilemma? First, we must distinguish the three parties and make it clear who build this platform, who share or learn intelligent vehicle usage data, and who supervise or monitor the platform. Second, we should clearly define property rights about who own the property rights. Is it user, the industry or government?

3. Case reference

We have an example from European Union. The EU launched the General Data Protection Regulation (GDPR) in 2018. It claimed that intelligent vehicle users, the subject, had rights of information self-determination. And vehicle manufacturers or firm and software developers are responsible for the control, while government agencies for supervision. As you can see here, government agencies, stakeholders and the European Commission set up a working group to discuss data protection issues.

Now I change it to Chinese context and I want to focus on payment industry. Everyone has a bank card. Here we have a bank card union called UnionPay, and China Banking and Insurance Regulatory Commission, a government agency, which can be the monitor. In this model of framework, users will share the data to the UnionPay, which will provide the learning of information like who was the card holders, the quality and others. The government supervises and monitors.

FORUM

分论坛

Liveable Cities
宜居城市

主持人 · HOST

陈杰 · Chen Jie

上海交通大学住房与城乡建设研究中心主任，
国际与公共事务学院/中国城市治理研究院教授

Director of Center for Housing and Urban-Rural Development in SJTU,
Professor of China Institute for Urban Governance and School of
International and Public Affairs, SJTU

宜居：生活的目标与营商的要件

倪鹏飞

中国社会科学院城市与竞争力研究中心主任，中国城市经济学会副会长

1. 宜居是人类矢志不渝的理想追求

人类自诞生以来，生存和发展都离不开居住，内心深处都希望获得更好的居住条件。因此，人类未来会追求更美好的居住条件。宜居是一个永恒的命题，是人类矢志不渝的追求。

从古代诗人的诗句中可以看出，人们追求的宜居不仅是环境、物质层面的，还有精神层面的。最美好的宜居就是诗意栖息，即经济上丰衣足食，环境风景如画，社会和谐融洽，心灵自由安详。古代人尤其注重心灵层面的宜居。西方哲人荷尔德林（Friedrich Hölderlin）说："人，诗意地栖居在大地之上。"在中国古代，白居易说过："身心安处即吾土。"苏轼说："此心安处是吾乡。"这些诗句都体现出人们对宜居理想的追求。宜居是人类永恒的终极追求，是永远重要的话题。

2. 人类及住区发展框架由四要素组成

近期城市发展经济学的理论研究表明，城市发展是由四个要素不断演化并相互推进的机

图 1
人类的生存与延续的
动力演化机制

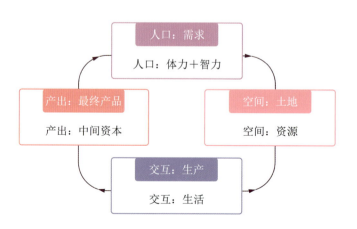

制。发展经济学在过去往往忽视了空间以及空间上的公共主题，如今的研究结合空间这一要素，是城市发展经济学的一大创新。人类发展实际上是人类内在需求和能力供给在一定的空间内相互活动，创造出最终消费的产品和包括技术、制度在内的中间产品，是一个扩大、深化循环的演化过程。基于这一演化机制，根据流动、固定、分散、聚集四大特点，人类住区先后经历了渔猎采集的分散流动、农业时代的分散固定、工业时代的聚集固定三个生息阶段，未来将进入智能时代的聚集流动的生息阶段。通过这样的时间梳理，我们能更加深入地分析城市宜居问题。

3. 宜居是城市生活环境的重要目标

如今中国已完成城市化上半程，开启城市化下半程。从人口、空间、交互、产出这四个要素分析，下半程相较于上半程发生了重大变化。就人口，尤其是人口需求而言，城市化上半程，是人进入城市谋生，而城市化下半程，是人居住在城市里生活。

两千多年前，亚里士多德曾有两个关于城市的论断，非常恰当地描述了城市化的上半程和下半程。他说，在第一个阶段，人来到城市是为了谋生，而在第二个阶段，人是到城市里居住，不仅仅是为了就业、赚钱，而是为了享受更好的生活，享受城市里的公共服务和基础设施。所以，在城市化下半程，或是"十四五"期间和未来相当长的一段时间内，美好生活是居民最重要的需求，宜居的环境则是实现美好生活和高质量生活的重要目标。

过去，我在研究城市竞争力时发现，国外，尤其是发达国家，特别重视生活环境，对经济的竞争力则不是很重视。随着研究的深入和中国的发展，我发现，我们进入城市化下半程后，宜居具有双重作用，一是满足生活本身需要，二是实现高质量生活。从供给角度而言，新产出力量实际上就是供给。此外，推动经济增长和城市发展的要素也发生了重大变化。

4. 宜居是城市营商环境的基本要件

中国城市发展与竞争的逻辑已经发生变化。在城市化上半程或早期，城市的发展是劳动力、土地和外来资本之间的吻合，特别是在制度创新的基础上实现吻合，从而促进了中国城市的崛起。中国在过去30多年的城市崛起阶段先后经历了以劳动力转移为主导的小城镇发展阶段、以外资和跨国公司为主导的外向型经济发展阶段，以及土地城镇化或是以土地经营为主导的城市化阶段。这是城市化上半程。但进入下半程，土地、资本、劳动力等影响城市经济发展的决定因素逐渐发生变化：土地由于房地产价格不高受到影响，部分外企倒闭撤离等导致外来投资有所下降，以及劳动力红利消失。

此外，在城市化下半程，推动城市发展或者经济增长的一级动力从劳动力转向人才，带来了一系列发展和竞争的逻辑变化。过去，政府倾向于采用优惠的政策，包括土地政策和其他的财政政策，招商引资，把企业吸引到城市，发展产业，创造税收，然后投资基础设施建设，改善生活环境。现在，人才和科技创新是决定城市进一步发展的关键。首先要吸引高端人才，才能吸引高端要素，包括科技、创新等要素，然后才能吸引或培育高端产业，创造更多税收。这形成了一个循环，循环以改善生活环境为起始，然后吸引高端人才，创造高端产业，最终创造更多的收入并促进经济增长。因此，首先要改善生活环境，使生活环境更加宜居，这样才能吸引高端人才和高端要素，才能吸引和培育高端产业，从而完成新一轮的创新循环。

图 2
中国城市发展与竞争
逻辑变化

因此，宜居是城市营商环境的基本要件，是城市经济发展的根本性基础。宜居既是生活的目标，也是生产或营商的要件，所以宜居在城镇化第二个阶段、"十四五"规划期间以及未来变得更加重要。

5. 中国城市的生活环境亟待宜居性提升

我所在的中国社会科学院财经战略研究院最新发布了一份有关城市生活的《中国城市竞争力报告 No.18：劲草迎疾风：中国的城市与楼市》，主要包括物质、经济、基础设施、公共服务等方面。报告采用文化、医疗、健康、气候、环境、消费、居住、体育、休闲、文化设施等方面作为指标，评估全国 291 个城市的数据。结果发现，中国城市生活环境整体水平还有待提升。沪粤港澳台等东南沿海地区城市生活环境较好，而全国大部分地区表现不佳，区域上呈现"南强北弱，东部领先"的态势。从城市层级而言，一、二线城市在行政层面存在优势，公共服务、基础设施和收入水平都较高，宜居环境较好，但是面临房价高企、环境污染威胁；三、四线城市居住成本较低，气候舒适度较好，但公共服务和收入就业水平亟待提升。

总体而言，中国城市的宜居环境还不是尽善尽美，各层级城市都有弱项。三、四线城市或是层级较低的城市，由于公共服务和公共基础设施较不完善，生活环境较差，但这有助于推动城市改进宜居环境。

6. 建设宜居城市是城市化下半程的政策重点

宜居是生活和生产的关键，城市化下半程应该把建设宜居城市作为推进城市化的重点。以人为本的宜居城市是最大化保证全体居民个体创造、分享幸福和发展成果的出发地和落脚地，确保居民能分享幸福和发展成果，发挥个性和创造力。

具体而言，可以在以下方面进行改进：改善城市的自然环境，完善基础设施，提高政府服务水平，规划、提供和管理私人服务，确保大多数居民能便捷、舒适地享用这些设施与服务，从而达到居民身心健康、精神愉悦、生活幸福、素质文明提升的目的。这将是后续的政策重点。除了提供高质量的基础设施和公共服务外，建设宜居城市还需要做很多工作。总体方针是确保全体居民发挥个性和创造力，分享幸福和发展成果。

城市化进程中的公平与效率：土地增值归属

朱介鸣

同济大学规划设计院总规划师、建筑与城市规划学院教授

中国人多地少，土地相当有价值，土地增值成为一个大问题。城市规划以土地规划为主，所以在城市化进程中，土地增值尤为重要。

我将围绕土地增值讲四个方面的内容。首先，土地增值的归属实际上是一个意识形态问题。第二，土地租金造成"城乡差别"逆转和"乡乡差别"。"城乡差别"逆转主要发生在一线城市，而"乡乡差别"是最近新出现的现象。第三，我将探讨城市化进程中的土地寻租现象。最后是关于建设用地指标分配的公平和效率问题。

1. 土地增值归属：意识形态争论

（1）意识形态的问题。

19世纪，美国有一位社会改革家叫亨利·乔治（Henry George），他提出土地增值100%归公。他认为，土地增值是由于政府的投入和城市规模的扩大而带来的，而土地业主并没有做出什么努力，可以说是"不劳而获"。有人提出异议：虽然可以通过改善地段、加强水利建设等措施改善农地，从而使土地更加肥沃、产出更高，但是农地的增值非常有限。不过对于城市用地而言，其价格比农地高很多，且往往与区位有关，区位越好，价值越高，而区位的好坏又与政府对基础设施等方面的投入有关。因此，亨利主张土地增值100%归公。

此外，经济学家斯蒂格利茨（Joseph E. Stiglitz）也用经济学模型证明，城市规模和人口规模的扩大、政府对基础设施和社会设施的投入能引起土地增值。

20世纪50年代，距离二战结束后不久，英国保守党要求土地增值税为0%，以保护业主的利益，而工党要求土地增值税为100%，认为土地增值应该由社会共享。在此之后，土地增值税不是0%，也不是100%，而是在40%—50%之间，工党倾向于高一点，保守党倾向于低一点。这是出于政治方面的考量。

土地增值100%归公并不合适，不能吸引风险投资，所以亨利的想法没有得到实施。90

年代中期，我的一个朋友在上海浦东联洋社区买了房子，他很担心自己买错了，因为那时候浦东地区才刚开始开发，区位并不好，对他来说是风险投资。事实证明他的选择是正确的，现在联洋社区的房价极高。如果当初无人敢投资，开发商就没法对浦东地区进行开发建设。股票市场也是一个很好的例子。如果股票市场投资增值 100% 归公，那就没有人敢投资股票，毕竟股票就是风险，是向市场集资给生产单位筹集经费。因此，土地增值 100% 归公和 0% 归公都是不合理的，需要取一个中间值。

（2）新加坡的土地增值。

从图 1 中可以看出，1975 年至今，新加坡的住房屋价格指数可以分成两个阶段：1975—1996 年、1996 年至今。从 1975 年到 1996 年，住房价格总体一路飙升，基本上无风险。但是从 1996 年开始，住房价格波动较为频繁。过去的亚洲金融危机、互联网泡沫和全球金融危机，以及现在的反全球化现象，都对住房价格产生了极大的影响。

图 1
新加坡商品住房价格
指数（1975—2020）

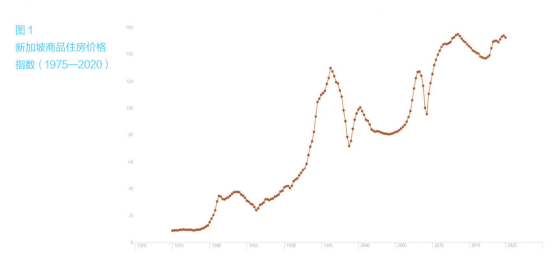

1975 年，新加坡的住房价格指数为 8.9，1996 年升至 129.7，21 年间增长了 13.6 倍。上海好像没有住房价格指数，但住房价格也同样猛涨。2020 年，新加坡的住房价格指数为 152.1，自 1996 年后的 24 年仅增长了 17.3%，与前一阶段差距很大。1975 年至 2020 年，新加坡的住房价格指数平均年增长率为 6.5%，第一阶段的平均年增长率为 13.6%，而第二阶段仅为 0.7%。前一阶段的风险较小，可见土地增值在城市化快速发展期相当显著，所以土地增值是非常值得研究的课题。

2. 土地租金造成"城乡差别"逆转和"乡乡差别"

（1）"城乡差别"逆转。

土地租金造成"城乡差别"逆转，这不是坏事。如今在北京、上海等一线城市，农民的收入比城市居民高，因为他们拥有国家免费分配的宅基地，可以出租集体建设用地获得收入。城市居民和农民享有均等的就业机会，但农民有宅基地和额外的租金收入，而城市居民没有，从而造成了"城乡差别"逆转。

例如，上海七宝镇联明村的"联明雅苑"是村里在集体用地上开发的公租房，按市场价收租金。据媒体报道，村里每户家庭每年能拿到2—3万元的分红。这就是村民的额外收入。

（2）"乡乡差别"。

"乡乡差别"可能更严重。我的团队在广东做了一项调查，发现在一个城市化程度很高的村子，土地租金收入占家庭总收入的25%，工作收入占75%。村里还有很多农民工，他们不仅在城市里打工，也在郊区打工，但是本地农民由于有村里的土地租金和自己的住房租金，收入是农民工收入的150%。另一个村子里，农民土地租金收入占比更多，达50%，因为这个村区位更好，城市化程度更高，本地农民收入是农民工收入的220%。土地对农民而言是一种资产，在区位好的农村，土地的价值很大，而区位不好的农村，比如内地的农村，土地并不值钱，因为没有租赁需求。这就是土地租金造成的"乡乡差别"。

昆山很多乡镇企业已经破产、转型或关闭，农村的少量集体经营收入几乎全部来自土地租赁收入。村土地物业租赁平均年收入为162万元，最低的村土地收入为零，如周庄等区位不好的村子。靠近城区的村则收入较高，最高的村土地收入达1 960万元。村土地租赁收入差距之大可见一斑。

"食租"阶层由此产生。据新加坡《联合早报》报道，单靠收租金，深圳渔民村每户居民平均年收入在60万元以上。我们在大学工作也没有60万元年薪。可见他们的租金收入相当高。

3. 城市化进程中的土地寻租

"食租"现象不止农村，城市也十分显著。城市化进程中的土地寻租是我的研究对象之一。土地寻租并不是真正的经济发展，不利于经济发展效率的提高，属于"不劳而获"的收入。

（1）城市政府土地财政。

众所周知，政府在拼命征地，通过出让土地获得租金，然后用获取的资金投资基础设施。但有些新区的开发效率很低，出现了"鬼城"的现象。经统计，在全国范围内规划的城市新区可容纳34亿人口。政府开发了这么多土地，但人们并没有这么多租赁需求。那政府为什么要追求土地财政呢？

有这样一个案例，在内地的一个三线省会城市，当地政府计划建造中央商务区（CBD）发展第三产业，但实际上并没有这样的需求，也不会有租户。后来政府授权一个土地开发商开发该地区所有的商品房，作为交换，开发商需要为政府建造几栋高层办公楼。但是，建造完两栋高层办公楼之后，楼房没有市场，即使价格从每平方米 18 000 元降至 12 000 元，依旧没有买方，因为市民没有金融投资的需求。实际上，政府是借土地财政达成其政治目的，向人们表明，这个城市也有中央商务区，城市发展程度不比上海差。

（2）村集体的土地寻租。

村集体的土地寻租就是租地发展工业。这一现象在上海郊区十分显著，广东、苏南也有此现象。这会造成农村空间环境细碎化，造成农地和建设用地高度混杂，从而导致生态环境的恶化。村集体不惜以牺牲生态环境为代价获得租金的收入。村子和城市不一样，城市是一个整体，而村是行政基本单位。一个镇大概有十个行政村，每个行政村都在出租土地，于是工业用地随处可见。

（3）城市国有单位的土地寻租。

上海虹口区有些工业用地空置多年，没有人开发。这是因为国有企业不愿意把土地交还给政府。国有企业倒闭后，不需要的工业用地照理应该归还给政府。但他们既没有归还土地，也没有继续开发，造成工业用地的空置。后来政府和用地单位达成协议，计划将空置的工业用地变为商业用地，只是需要用地单位交出 50% 的土地出让金，政府和用地单位共享租金收入。这是合情合理的，因为土地本来就是国家所有，而非单位所有。由于政府只拿到一半土地出让金来建造地铁等基础设施，于是出现了老城区超高密度改造的现象，上海的城区密度之高就是出于此原因。

图 2 是 1989—2009 年昆山的城市化发展情况，大量农地被"肢解"，虽然收益很好，但引发了生态环境问题。

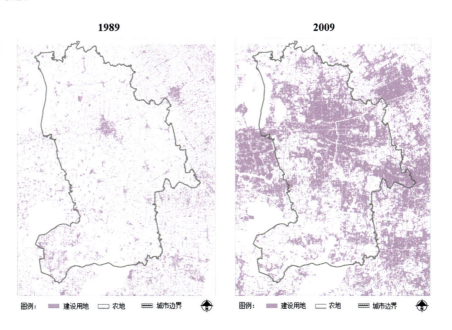

图 2
1989—2009 年昆山的城市化发展情况

另一个例子是，在上海老城区新天地太平桥区域，开发商起初计划保护老城区，邀请同济大学的罗小未教授对当地进行研究调查。罗教授在新天地社区做了深入的研究，发现这里有着悠久的人文历史。但后来开发商发现，改造成本和拆迁成本巨大，需要给当地居民和单位一笔高额赔偿金，比欧洲保护古建筑所花的成本还要高，所以成本成了大问题。最后开发商还是建造了高层住房，现在新天地地区房价极高。这就是国内特殊的产权状况。

我觉得老房子很有味道，城市里如果都是高层建筑，就会显得这个城市平庸无味，具有历史感的老房子可以增添城市的人文气息。拆掉老房子、建造高层住房，居民和开发商很满意，但学者不满意，他们惋惜具有历史感的老房子消失了。总而言之，这些现象是受土地寻租的驱动。

4. 建设用地指标分配的公平和效率

国土空间规划中的建设用地指标已经在国内沿用了二十多年。指标的分配自上而下，由中央分配，城市要发展，就需要建设用地指标。指标的分配通常涉及竞争，因为每个地方都想要建设用地指标，有指标才能开发土地，让土地变得值钱。这实际上是城市化发展的红利，即城市化发展使得土地变得值钱。

建设用地指标的分配存在不公平的现象。大城市获得的指标比小城市多，靠近城区的村子获得的指标比离城区远的村子多。但我认为，既然土地是国有的，建设用地指标就应该公平分配，按人均分配，而不应该差别对待。

"建设用地指标交易市场"指的是，对指标有需求的城市可以与其他城市进行交易。例如，甘肃可能因为城市化发展速度慢而不需要很多建设用地指标，于是可以将这些指标卖给上海，这样甘肃获得了财政收入，而上海得到了指标。这有助于提高城市化发展的效率，让城市不会过度依赖于获取土地财政或是建造"鬼城"。

目前西方出现了反城市化的现象。为了追求效率，反而牺牲了公平，但公平极为重要。我们团队在松江区做了一项研究。图3中，深色的是建设用地，白色的是农地。这样的规划十分混乱，规划局需要重新规划。右图我们称为"紧凑城市"，城市与乡村泾渭分明，这样的规划比较合理。

城市规划中存在很多问题。首先，北面靠近城区的村子建设用地开发多，南面的村子由于区位不好，建设用地较少，导致村与村之间收入差距很大。从建设用地的公顷数来看，最低的只有62，而最高的有209。当时松江区集体建设用地有2 560公顷，后来政府对指标减量化，将建设用地指标分配给其他地方，松江区集体建设用地减到了960公顷。结果，建设用地指标原本就少的地方又减少了许多指标，北面的村仍有许多建设用地，南面的村几乎没有建设用地。生态环境属于公共物品，为什么唯独让南面的村做出牺牲？市场本就不均衡，城

图3
规划不均衡的松江区以及"紧凑城市"的面貌

市规划跟着市场的逻辑走，因此也非常不均衡。从建设用地的数量上来看，最多的村有283，而最少的只有3。这导致村与村之间的贫富差距加剧。其实规划的措施是合理的，但制度设计存在问题。我认为，在实施的过程中应该更加注重公平。

　　集体建设用地指标的均衡分配和交易有利于城市空间重构。实际上，在实施的过程中会遇到很多冲突，很多地区不愿意被拆迁。大家都希望拥有宜居的生活和生态环境，但追求宜居环境的过程应该是公平的，要让所有人都能够从中受益，这才是有效的方案。

城市空间形态与城市宜居性：集聚不经济的视角

孙斌栋

华东师范大学中国行政区划研究中心主任

我将从集聚不经济的角度介绍城市空间形态与城市宜居性的相关研究，这些研究是我和我指导的学生团队历时几年一起完成的。

1. 研究问题

（1）集聚经济与集聚不经济。

集聚经济的概念并不陌生，它最早来自冯·杜能（Johann Heinrich von Thünen）的孤立国单中心城市模型。后来马歇尔（Alfred Marshall）提出集聚经济外部性的三个好处：劳动力市场共享，靠近供货商和顾客，人力资本积累引发的知识外溢。以克鲁格曼（Paul Krugman）和藤田昌久（Masahisa Fujita）为代表的新经济地理学派将集聚经济的研究推向高峰，该学派认为集聚经济有助于规模报酬递增。现在学界公认集聚经济可以带来三个好处，即共享、匹配和学习。这些都是理论研究，相关实证研究一般将城市的规模或密度作为变量来检验集聚的经济效益。目前在政策方面讨论比较多的是大城市和小城市孰优孰劣。一般支持大城市的学者都认可集聚经济，但任何事物都是辩证的，过于集聚会带来不经济，包括交通拥挤、地价高企、空气污染以及社会冲突等问题。

在实践中出现了集聚不经济现象，比如北美集聚到了一定程度之后发生了郊区化和多中心化。集聚不经济导致了单中心往外扩散，在郊区形成了多中心的结构。今天讲的都市圈实际上就是多中心城市结构的缩影。北美、日本的都市圈是功能性的城市。学术界和政治界都在讨论都市圈，其概念已经泛滥，甚至已经被错误地理解。现在的都市圈已经远远超出最初学术地理界的通勤圈概念，很难定义。西欧的多城市中心区域以及城市群都是多中心结构。中国的生产力布局也应该有多中心结构，不应该只集中在东南沿海地区。但是相对集聚经济来讲，对集聚不经济的研究非常少，尤其是对集聚不经济的非经济效益的关注更加少。

（2）西方发达国家积极倡导紧凑的城市空间形态。

以北美为代表的西方发达国家积极倡导紧凑的城市空间形态，即集聚的城市形态。世卫组织（WHO）有一份文件曾提出优先考虑紧凑，认为紧凑有利于健康。该文件指导的是所有国家，但其科学规律和经验却来自北美国家，因此十分片面。北美的新城市主义派和低碳主义派给中国开药方的时候也特别强调紧凑。我们的怀疑是：中国已经非常紧凑了，难道还要更加紧凑吗？因此他们的观点存在一定问题，或者有非常危险的倾向。这是我们研究的重要动力。

世卫组织讨论文件（2018年4月9日）

健康体育活动
加强身体活动，造就健康世界：
2018—2030年促进身体活动全球行动计划草案
draft global action plan on physical activity 2018—2030

行动2.1　加强各级相关政府城市规划政策和交通规划政策的整合，强调紧凑型混合土地利用原则，使邻里街区更为紧密，从而在城市、郊区和农村社区便利和促进步行、骑自行车、涉及使用轮子的其他出行方式（包括轮椅、滑板和轮滑）和使用公共交通。

关于紧凑有不同的说法，但最主要的变量是人口密度。高密度比低密度更加紧凑。西方认为紧凑可以提高城市宜居性的逻辑是：人和人之间、人和事物之间的距离比较近，所以人们可以非机动化出行，从而减少交通拥堵，空气质量也得到改善。此外由于人们步行，健康得以改善，而且步行会导致互相来往、见面机会较多，可以促进社会资本提高，从而增加幸福感。

图2
紧凑提高城市宜居性
的作用机制

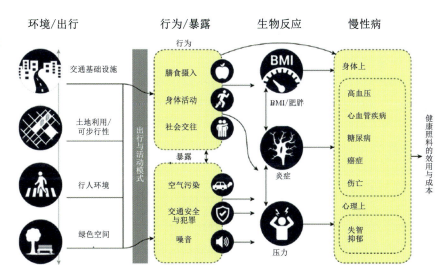

图 3
中西社区对比

中国社区　　西方社区

（3）紧凑的空间形态能提升中国城市宜居性吗？

与北美不同的是，中国的东部人口密度非常大。中国的住宅是高楼大厦，而西方的住宅是低密度的田园别墅。城市密度不同，居住形态不同，对紧凑的要求当然也不同。

上海和东京两座城市面积一样，东京人口比上海多。但是在人口分布形态方面，东京更加均衡，上海更加集聚，尤其是市中心。用更细的尺度来看，上海的紧凑度已经远远高于东京。但由于人口分布不均匀，上海的人口承载能力却不及东京。

2. 研究假说：紧凑的空间形态对中国城市宜居性的影响

我们的研究假说是城市空间形态会影响城市宜居性，研究将人口密度作为紧凑最主要的变量。西方认为紧凑会让城市更宜居，促进非机动化出行，改善空气质量以及提高社会资本，包括有助于减肥和健康，增加居民的幸福感。但我们认为，中国的紧凑程度已经很高，更加紧凑可能会带来事与愿违的效果，即不经济。

为什么过度紧凑不利于城市宜居性？交通拥堵就是一个例子。在过于紧凑的情况下，不一定所有人都会放弃驾驶小汽车。即使有些人放弃了，还是会有更多车辆集聚在紧凑的空间里，反而加剧了交通拥堵和空气污染。城市居民现在都居住在高楼中，城市是生人社会，人与人之间交流少，反倒不利于提高社会资本，不如原本低人口密度的社会。此外，人口密度

图 4
紧凑的空间形态对城
市宜居性的影响

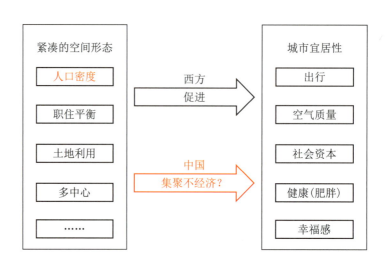

高的地区周围活动场所少，场所可达性差，则运动机会少，必然会导致肥胖。高密度也意味着高强度工作和快节奏生活，会加重心理压力。从心理学的角度看，心理压力大会导致吃饭速度更快，睡眠时间变短，损害人们的健康。

3. 实证结果

由于一直坚持实证态度，我们更多的研究工作是在实证方面。如果没有证据支撑，理论再多也毫无意义。我将介绍四个方面的实证。

（1）紧凑与出行。

本段提到的研究基本都来自我们已发表的论文。第一个研究的数据来自中山大学社会科学调查中心完成的 2014 年"中国劳动力动态调查"（CLDS），研究发现城市人口规模和城市人口密度（包括社区人口密度）的提高，都会导致通勤时间延长。这个结论是通过控制其他必要变量，利用三个不同尺度的多层模型分析得出的，较为可靠。第二个研究的数据基于复旦大学长三角地区社会变迁调查（FYRST），使用上海的个体居民数据和多层模型进行研究，结果表明街道人口密度的提高会带来通勤时间的显著延长。

（2）紧凑与空气质量。

一般来说城市越紧凑，开车的人应该越少，空气质量应该得到改善。但实际上这只是问题的一方面，另一方面也正是因为紧凑，原本分散的车辆会集中在小的空间里，所以紧凑的地方反而污染更严重。总体而言，污染可能没有显著增加，但在车辆集中的地点，污染是增加的。此问题在中国尤为突出。尽管在目前一些地区即使人口、建筑密度高，人们不开车或不购车的可能性还是很低，但在不久的将来，很多人富裕之后为了出行方便或者炫富都会买车。我们的研究采用上海的数据，发现街道尺度的人口密度与 PM2.5 浓度呈正相关关系。

（3）紧凑与社会资本。

这项研究同样采用 2014 年"中国劳动力动态调查"（CLDS）的 3 856 个城市居民的数据，不仅检验了紧凑对社会资本的直接作用，也用结构方程进一步探讨了其作用机制。我在前述的研究中没有提到机制探讨，因为机制探讨难以做到，它取决于数据的可得性。此项研究获得的数据较好，能使我们检验其作用机制。在社会资本这一重要定义中，我们将社区内的熟人数量、居民之间的信任、互助和团体参与情况这四个方面作为社会资本的因变量。研究发现人口密度高的情况与至少三个社会资本的因变量是不相关的，包括熟人、信任和互助。结构方程的检验显示，社区人口密度高会降低居民的安全感，从而降低交流频率，进而降低社会资本。

（4）紧凑与健康。

这个方面是我近几年的研究重点，主要是肥胖问题，共有三个研究。

第一项研究开展于 2016 年，数据来自中国家庭追踪调查（CFPS）2010—2012 中 15 356 个观测值，研究方法为结构方程。研究发现社区人口密度提高会增加居民肥胖率。图 6 显示，人口密度确实会降低小汽车出行概率，从而降低肥胖率，因此左上方这条路径是负值。但从净效应看，人口密度仍然和肥胖率呈正相关。此外还有一些潜在机制：

第一，中国已经十分紧凑，更高的紧凑度不会在中国实现与欧美一样的效果，即增加非机动化出行。

第二，人口密度高时，无论采用什么出行方式，包括步行和骑自行车，出行距离短都会导致运动消耗减少。

第三，高密度地区还会导致室外活动空间和体育活动减少。我们的研究证明高密度社区居民的静态活动时间长，比如在家中打牌、看电视、学习和看书，而体育活动较少。

第四，人口密度高会导致城市生活节奏加快。我们的模型发现，吃饭快、睡眠少的人更容易肥胖。人口密度高的地区往往餐饮设施密集，比如小吃店和冰淇淋随处可见，人们外出就餐频率较高，进而增加了肥胖率。

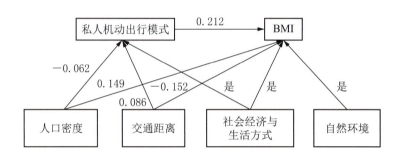

图 5
社区人口密度对
BMI 的影响机制

第二项紧凑与健康的研究采用了 2012 年中国劳动力动态调查的数据。研究发现城市人口密度与表示肥胖的指数 BMI 呈 U 型相关。即人口密度很低时，提高密度可以降低 BMI，但是密度超过了最佳点之后，BMI 是随着密度增加而提高的。

随着我们研究不断深入，采用的数据也越来越可靠。第三项研究采用的数据来自 2004 年、2006 年、2009 年和 2011 年美国北卡罗来纳大学教堂山分校（University of North Carolina at Chapel Hill）和中国疾病预防控制中心营养与食品安全所协作开展的中国家庭营养与健康调查（CHNS），使用了固定效应模型。为检验空间形态与肥胖的关系，我们将反映腹部脂肪累积的腰臀比指标作为衡量肥胖的标准，因为身体质量指数（BMI）适合用于衡量欧美人的肥胖情况，而腰臀比更能反映东亚人的肥胖情况。中年男性尤其是知识分子有久坐的习惯，导致腹部脂肪积累迅速。经常开私家车的中年人腹部脂肪积累也较多，是体重增加的主要原因。研究结果显示，社区人口密度与腰臀比呈 U 型。人口密度低时，提高密度会降低腰臀比，但是超过最佳密度值，人口密度再提高，腰臀比就会上升。值得注意的是，中国一些城市的社区人口密度已经开始超过了最佳值，居民肥胖率开始增加。我们的研究机制已

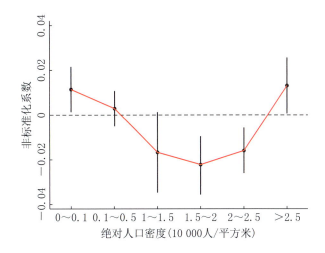

图 6
社区人口密度与腰臀
比呈 U 型

经得到检验，说明高人口密度会提高腰臀比的原因在于高人口密度会减少居民的体育活动时间。

4. 总结与启示

（1）结论。

这一系列关于城市宜居性的研究揭示高人口密度会降低幸福感，而且我们的研究首次揭示：紧凑的城市空间形态与城市宜居性的倒 U 型规律。也就是说，随着紧凑程度的提升，城市可能会从低人口密度的不宜居状态变成适度紧凑的宜居状态，而如果紧凑程度过高，城市又会变得不宜居。这可以为宜居城市建设提供一定的学术依据。集聚经济和集聚不经济同样重要，但经济学家更关注集聚经济，对集聚不经济的研究和文献相对少很多。所以我想在此呼吁学界加强对集聚不经济的探讨。

（2）政策建议。

北美城市人口密度较低，即处于倒 U 型的左边，因此提高紧凑度能提高北美城市宜居性。但是中国的城市过于紧凑，处于倒 U 型的右边，已经处于不宜居的状态。因此，中国的城市

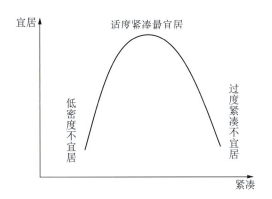

图 7
紧凑的城市空间形态
与宜居呈倒 U 型

规划建设要有自己的建设标准，尤其是不能让开发商主导。因为开发商不会考虑健康问题，只追求收益，只想提高人口密度。但作为学者，我认为高人口密度不利于健康。中国城市需要的是适当的紧凑，中国的城市建设不能被世卫组织的健康导则误导，而是要基于国情，提出中国自己的宜居标准或建设模式。

气候变化风险与韧性城市：自然 vs. 个体

张晓玲

香港城市大学公共政策系教授，中国区域可持续发展专业委员会副主任

1. 可持续发展历史进程中的"变"与"不变"

人类的发展和变迁经历了持续的变动，比如来自社会、经济、环境、文化等的挑战，逆全球化、技术、政府和市场各种力量的对冲，以及文化等领域的影响。在各种力量交错与对冲的环境中，需要持续地考量整个可持续发展历史进程中的"变"与"不变"。

首先，从人口数量看，第一次农业革命到第一、第二次工业革命，到当前的第三、第四次工业革命，以及即将到来的基于人工智能的技术革命，人口数量从最开始的较低水平发展到现在的人口大爆炸。不讨未来人口也许会持续衰减。其次，从技术水平层面来看，人类从原来依赖植物和动物驯养，到发明蒸汽机、电力、机器及现代交通，再到当下的因特网和基因技术，人类对于资源、能源的需求强度呈现从低到高的趋势。然而，大自然的供给能力从最开始的较高水平变成了现在的相对不足，劳动力分工因此从原始的部落分工变成了现在的

表1
可持续发展历史进程中的变化

	第一次农业革命	第一、第二次工业革命	第三、第四次工业革命
历史时期	公元前 2000—1000 年	17 世纪—20 世纪 40 年代	20 世纪 80 年代至今
人口数量	小	快速增长	人口大爆炸
技术水平	植物和动物的驯养	蒸汽机、电力、机器、现代交通	因特网、基因技术等
资源和能源需求强度	低	快速增强	高
资源和能源供给能力	高	降低	不足
劳动地理分工与全球不均衡发展	生产专业化的初始阶段以及部落内部的劳动分工	殖民主义兴起以及第一次世界劳动分工	整合的全球生产网络，北半球 vs. 南半球

图 1
经济增长与可持续
发展

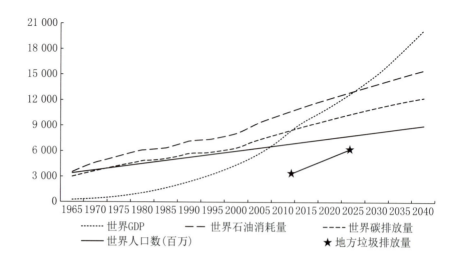

全球化生产。下一步，即将到来的是初见端倪的"逆全球化"阶段。这些历史进程让人们开始逐渐着眼于当下逐渐增加的全球人口、经济碳排放、化石燃料和垃圾等问题。

那么，增长的边界在哪里，城市的边界在哪里，人类社会是否可以抵御这样一次又一次自身行为挑战大自然系统性边界带来的问题与风险？比尔·夏普（Bill Sharpe）在 2013 年提出了"三条路径"的理念，理想状态应该是第三条道路，命名为"绿色道路的胜利"。

图 2
三条路径图

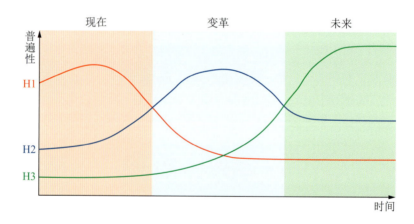

2. 气候变化风险下的韧性城市

科学家、经济学家、管理学家希望用线性思维去考量，做线性的假设，但是事实上社会经济以及城市发展是一个系统思维。普林斯顿大学经济学家丹尼尔·卡尼曼（Daniel Kahneman）曾提出快乐水车理论，指的是个体通过购买、不断消费得到满足，会使得经济内部循环增强，代价就是对环境和资源能源的消耗，不过技术进步能够在一定程度上降低这样的消耗。

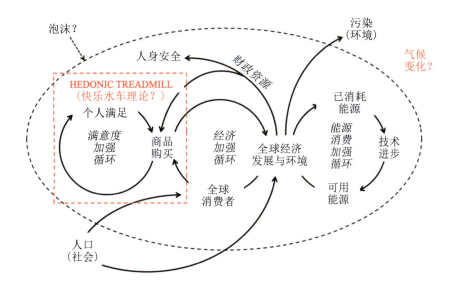

图 3
系统思维：一个简化
的模型

不可否认，经济发展造成的环境污染、气候变化给人类带来了很大的挑战，包括气候变化风险、经济衰退以及社会人口老龄化的问题，这体现了自身和社会的平衡，以及短期和长期之间平衡的两难问题。

在这样的语境和背景下，我提出了"气候变化风险下的韧性城市"的课题。2013 年，洛克菲勒基金会评选出全球 100 个韧性城市的列表，大多是沿海或者接近河流河谷的、在地理空间上比较边缘的城市。

这些韧性城市究竟具备哪些特殊品质，使其能够承受、响应和适应来自外部的冲击和压力？需要考察的包括：反思型城市、资源型城市、稳固型城市、冗余型城市、弹性的城市、包容性城市以及全球化的融合型城市。

关于可持续城市理念，第一阶段是"静态的环保"，最早在《寂静的春天》①中提出；第二阶段是"可持续性"，正如刚刚提到的线性系统内实现循环增长的可持续城市；然后到最前沿的第三阶段的韧性和复原力城市。韧性意味着从不确定的未来规划中长远地"计划不确定"。韧性空间的战略内涵需要考虑如何实现从短期行动到长期战略，从部门或个人到竞争协作的方法的转变。也就是说，与前面两种易受攻击的系统相比，韧性城市考量的是城市在遭受洪涝或者雾霾等冲击后，如何能使其加速修复或使之可逆转。

我的团队正在细化研究这一问题，从系统的角度来进行关联性的思考，包括一些著名的物质能源流动分析的模型。我们发现复杂性的动态现象具有一个共同特征：在互不相关的时空尺度水平上，发生不确定性关联事件的可预测性较低，并且往往来自不同的学科背景，比如还未消退的新冠肺炎疫情、气候变化风险等。复杂性的动态现象体现在当地的反映是：自

———————————

① 《寂静的春天》（*Silent Spring*）是美国科普作家蕾切尔·卡逊（Rachel Carson）创作的科普读物，首次出版于1962 年。

图 4
系统思维：基于关联
性的复杂模型

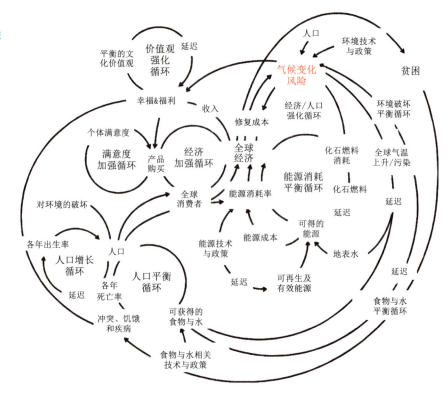

图 5
动态现象流动分析
模型

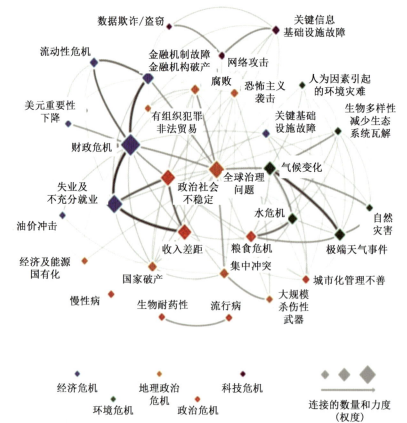

然和社会试图在一个混乱的世界中自我组织，并且趋向于达到一种平衡状态，因此，城市、社会自然生态系统和个体之间的关系也变得越来越复杂。如果想真实地理解城市，不仅仅要将其视为放置在空间中，也应该把它们作为网络和流量系统来考察。

从个体层面来说，新冠肺炎疫情刚好符合这次的讨论主题。在这一背景下，个体的韧性重点体现于持久，为了度过危机，需要内在的力量和强健的体魄。从城市层面来说，同样需要持久性，城市需要在不同的变化和发展方式中不断调整、适应，以应对风险或危机。所以，首先需要建设"风险之城"，这是基于短期规划甚至恐慌反应而做出的决定。此外还应该建设"希望之城"，这是基于长期规划，与合作伙伴达成共识做出的决定，能够化风险为机遇。

3. 基于自然的解决方案

城市是缓解和适应气候变化的关键，但是城市其实面临着人与自然的双重威胁，于是本世纪初世界自然保护联盟（IUCN）提出了基于自然的解决方案（NBS）这一概念。基于自然的解决方案是保护、可持续管理和恢复自然和改良生态系统的行动，有效和适应性地应对社会挑战，同时提供人类福祉和生物多样性利益。[①] 这一解决方案描述了人类需要利用自然过程而非技术过程来达成针对社会各种挑战的创新努力，包括适应气候变化、保护生物多样性、生态系统管理和维系可持续生计，也即"以子之矛，攻子之盾"。

要采用基于自然的方案重塑人与自然在城市韧性发展中的作用，应当思考以下关键问题：第一，如何最大化 NBS 行动的有效性，比如城市绿地是谁的绿地，怎样使用？第二，如何从自然系统中学习并转化为城市实践？第三，NBS 在何时何地比传统的解决方案更有效，例如基于自然的沿海湿地工程？第四，如何将 NBS 嵌入地方一级的城市空间规划和决策中，比如构造更多生活实验室，构建更多城市绿色基础设施？第五，如何设计将 NBS 转变为可融资的机会，如何扩大规模并发挥私人资本的杠杆效用？

如果要构建一个理论，那么就应该结合对韧性城市价值的理解提出解决方案。基于此，从认识论、方法论和价值论的角度重新界定"人"与"自然"，并提出自然、本土、新

图6
NBS 系统的核心
构成

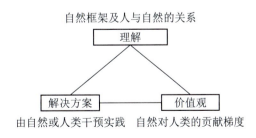

自然框架及人与自然的关系

理解

解决方案 —— 价值观

由自然或人类干预实践　自然对人类的贡献梯度

---

① Cohen-Shacham, E., Walters, G., Janzen, C. and Maginnis, S. (eds.), 2016, *Nature-based Solutions to address global societal challenges*, Gland, Switzerland: IUCN, pp. xiii + 97.

颖、绿色、文化这五个范式，以及每种范式的一个优缺点。每种范式各有利弊，关键在于找到适应当地生态系统发展的 NBS 解决方案，不断地在城市发展与韧性的关联中找到一个连续体。

五种不同的范式各具有两种门槛，这种门槛取决于对城市系统 NBS 的区分。NBS 范式有以下优点：第一，范式的区分有助于加强 NBS。第二，可以减少 NBS 实现的随机性，强化解决方案和结果，避免随意使用和对环境的无意识破坏。第三，提供了一个平台和一个连续体，范式的连续性有助于应对人与自然系统耦合日益糟糕的局面。第四，为政策制定者和从业者

表 2
重新定义"自然"和"人"在可持续发展中的作用的五个范式

| 范式 | 认知论 | | 方法论 | 价值论 |
	自然	人	自然与人的角色	NCP
自然范式	最佳情况，尽可能原始和原封不动	良好生态的潜在危险	让大自然回到最佳状态；尽量减少人们的干预，避免任何影响；在有人干预的地区撤退（什么也不做）	地球母亲的内在价值
本土范式	可预测的情况，尽可能具有历史意义	复原历史的潜在推动者	恢复历史状态；刺激自然继承恢复自然扰动；减少人的干扰	进化与生态过程
新颖范式	不可预测的情况，尽可能健康	生境创造的潜在促进者	探索设计的实验采用适应性管理	生境的创建和维护，工具功能
绿色范式	精心处理的情况，尽可能减少负面影响	潜在的负面影响的缓解者	减少，再利用，回收；尽可能减轻负面环境影响；尽可能绿色	调节功能，身体、心理、社会和情感健康、生活方式
文化范式	尽可能多地照顾文化产品	大自然的管理者	鼓励参与生态系统的恢复或建设；教育人们爱护自然	自然与人之间的互动

表 3
五种范式的聚焦点及优劣势

范式	焦点	优势	劣势
自然范式	自然的是最好的	需要的投资最小	大自然不可预知的"惊喜"
本土范式	历史生态系统是最好的	当地物种更好地适应	历史条件和自然继承可能需要很多时间
新颖范式	功能实验是最好的	量化的目标和效益	实验结果没有客观标准
绿色范式	"绿色的"比"非绿色的"好	相对容易和快速的实施	绿色化不一定是生态化
文化范式	培养对自然的关爱是最好的	强化人与自然的关系	耗时，对自然的潜在损害

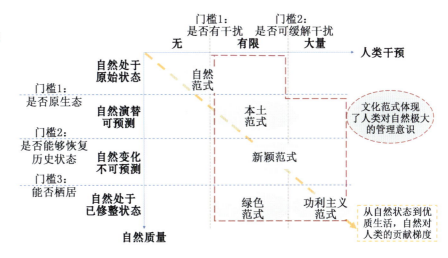

图 7
具有相互关联的思想
和方法的连续体

提供了一个连续共同体，可以在不同环境中绘制当前 NBS 实践的状态，并考虑行为改变的可能性。

4. 基于个体韧性的解决方案

基于个体韧性的解决方案这个理论是我和上海交大城市治理研究院的潘浩之老师一起合作的研究。从城市的韧性框架可以看到，城市的风险暴露和脆弱性可能会损害城市发展，因此需要考虑如何使城市适应风险并逐渐恢复发展弹性。比如在发生疫情、城市洪涝和台风等黑天鹅事件后，需要考虑如何使城市恢复到原有发展状态。

我认为构建韧性的关键并不在于城市规划本身，而在于个体。

第一，这一研究板块体察个体和地区的时空动态韧性指数也就是复原力指数，即找到每个个体的机会、可能性和脆弱性，从而考察其相关的、在个体空间里某一个时空坐标系统下的可及性。拿职住分离现象举例，我现在住在香港，每天大概花多长时间赶到工作岗位，回家休憩又需要多久，在此过程中所花费的时间就是我们定义的可及性指数。简而言之，可以理解为工作、教育和生态系统服务的可及性。

第二，研究时空区域资本所有权指数，即通过汇总个体到城市以及区域层面的总资

图 8
城市韧性框架

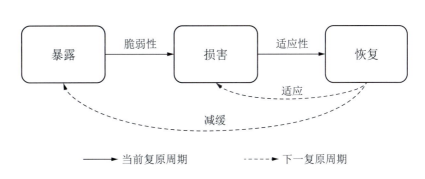

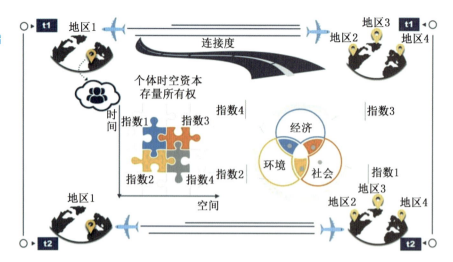

图 9
个体时空动态韧性指
数（IRI）构建

本，对其进行量化，从而构建一个多维的个体时空动态韧性指数（individual resilience index，IRI），这样就可以将传统的、静态的可持续性发展指标视为一种适用于个体和城市的固定、可移动的资本，将个体"可达性"作为"空间资本"的"空间"所有权来同步衡量。

第三，通过"脆弱性"和"机遇"两个指标衡量个体作为"时间资本"存量所有权的"非衰减性财富"。这一潜在跟踪结果可以帮助讨论微观个体、中观城市以及更广泛的区域层面的韧性治理框架。

时空动态韧性指数的建立实际上取决于治理和管理理论的木桶原理。一个城市的发展是否具有持续的核心竞争力，重点不在于它的长板，而在于短板。也就是说，需要尽快构建个体时空动态韧性指标，计算和追踪个体再汇总到整体城市的基于脆弱性和机会贫困方面的发展水平。

图 10
IRI 指数跟踪结果

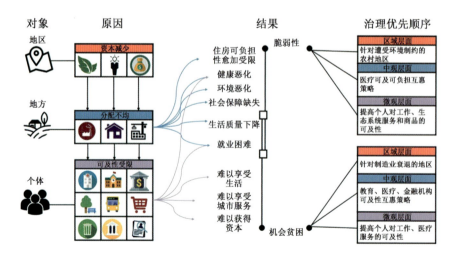

5. 个体的"可及性限制"造成"机会贫困"

我们设计了一种方法来描述 IRI 如何影响地方的脆弱性和机会贫困。例如，假设一个城市的生态基础设施贫困可能是由经济资本不足引起的，并因公共资本在固定资本投资中的不平等分配而加剧。对个体而言，生态系统服务的"可及性限制"，是由当地的自然资本不足和分配不均等，从地区到地方的涓涓细流而形成的一种累积性效应，并且会因为分配不均而产生某种后果。例如在我们耳熟能详的教育方面，为什么学区房往往集聚在某些区域？为什么公共绿地往往跟遍布高楼大厦的中央商务区（CBD）相连？为什么贫困人群却不能随时随地享受这些公共利益？这些问题可以帮助我们思考一个城市的可及性限制或机会贫困的来源。类似的累积性设计，可以帮助我们进一步思考城市的韧性体现在"短"还是"长"。再举个例子，当疫情来临，城市的医疗基础设施和生态系统服务的"可及性受限"，可能会导致个体健康状况恶化。如果当地的资本分配更加不均等，可能会加剧脆弱性的发生，造成脆弱性和机会贫困的双重损失，进而加剧整个城市社会的不稳定性和不确定性。

基于以上理论，我们通过两个基于个体的动态时空韧性的框架（ISRF）界定了基于个体的时空动态韧性的贝叶斯量化评估模型。通过对全国的交通、教育、医疗、城市服务和生态系统服务进行可及性测算，采用了一定的校准技术，通过贝叶斯网络的初步分析，得到个体

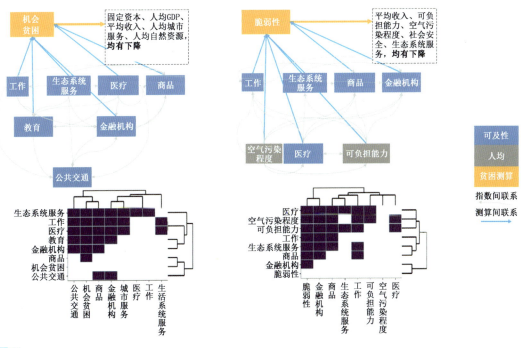

图 11
两个基于个体的动态时空韧性框架

图 12
可及性校准

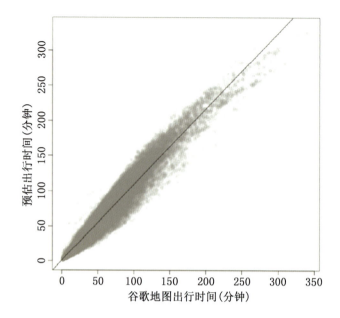

图 13
贝叶斯网络模型与初
步结果

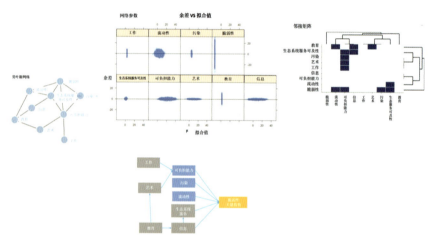

图 14
个体动态时空韧性热
力图（机会 vs. 脆弱
性关系图）

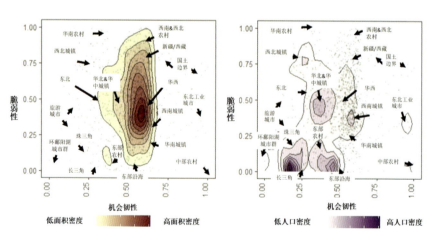

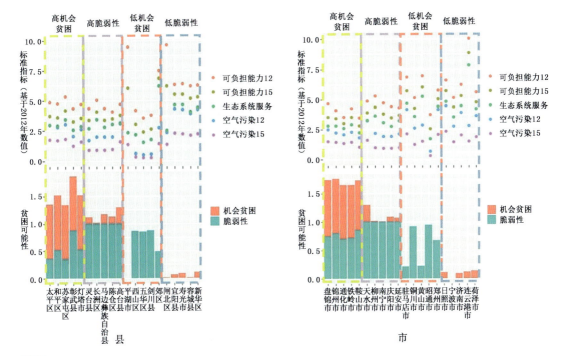

图 15
城市层面：动态时空韧性分布内部关联性

的动态时空韧性热力图。从图中可以看到，"机会"和"脆弱性"之间存在非常明晰的关联，也可以让我们从城市层面动态地理解韧性的内部关联和系统性。

图 15 显示了中国最高机会、贫困度以及最高脆弱性城市和县域的位置，使用的关键指标包括可负担能力、生态系统服务可及性和空气污染程度。

6. 四个城市"机会"和"脆弱性"的研究结论

第一，2012 年，在城市一级，低机会贫困城市和低脆弱性城市总体上具有更好的可承受外在风险压力和获得生态系统服务的能力。

第二，在低脆弱性和低机会贫困的高排名城市中有相反趋势，即低机会贫困城市有时伴随着高脆弱性，而低脆弱性城市往往与低机会贫困重叠，对此可能的解释是低脆弱性城市通常拥有良好的基础设施和便利措施，因此不太可能因为经济衰退而遭受极端机会贫困。正如俗语有云，"东边不亮西边亮"。

第三，中国县域单位的机会脆弱性关系往往非常复杂。一般而言，高机会贫困县域的脆弱性比城市低，因为这些县的平均负担能力相对更好，例如中国东北的彰武县。但我们的结论还需要进一步细化来得出更多发现。

第四，城市的脆弱性和机会的关系处于不断的动态变化中，机会贫困往往与经济衰退高度相关。例如 2012—2015 年间，机会贫困主要发生在国有企业和传统制造业衰退的地区，即部分东北和沿海传统制造业城市。

7. 韧性城市应对框架

面对这些结论，我们应该如何更好地应对？

韧性城市系统包括科学、经济、社会以及治理几个层面，而适应和改变处于最顶端的层面。如果将自然和个体融入一个框架里，可以通过如图 16 所示的方式更好地应对。框架的初始点是不确定性导向的规划，关键在于韧性城市转变，最重要的是进行预防，在治理层面包括公平、一体化和经济应对，在规划层面注意适应性、规划和可持续发展。

图 16
自然 vs. 个体的韧性
城市应对框架

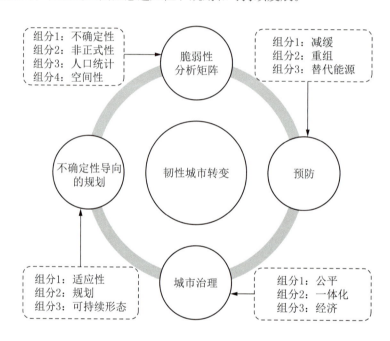

8. 结语

第一，对中国城市而言，我们的研究考察的不只是城市本身的问题，还有城市和市民，正如 2010 年上海世博会主题所言，"城市，让生活更美好"。通过寻找个体和自然韧性的"木桶短板"：比如通过对个体时空韧性指数的贝叶斯评估，以及对整个中国城市地区的脆弱性和机会贫困的映射，我们的研究发现在城市甚至区域一级，最易发生脆弱性和机会贫困的地区往往集中在中国西部农村和山区、老牌工业城市以及这些城市群所依托下的易衰退的地区和周边环境。

第二，我认为城市科学家和城市治理学者应当共同努力，去寻找城市治理或代理中的冗余、模块化、多样化的弹性（组件）或连接：比如通过界定"直接导致机会贫困 / 脆弱性"的指标和领域，分析多种指标的共同受益方；通过连接医疗保健机构、教育机构、保险机构和金融机构来共同抵御风险，即所谓的联防联控；在个体医疗保健可负担性和教育可及性不足的情况下，共生共治此类风险。

第三，韧性城市发展阶段需要重新定义，可以划分为城市系统、社区系统和个体系统。疫情给我最大的感受是个体系统的防疫问题。我们需要内化和内生再定义后的系统，使"自然资本""社会资本"，甚至"个体资本"要素，通过依赖自然本身的韧性，变成一种物理的内置系统来达成集体行动。比如，建设气候变化风险下的韧性城市，根本上是集成"自然 + 个体"的智慧城市解决方案，是一个集体行动的达成，其中也包括对技术极大化达成。对于个体层面，我认为关键在于提升个体"机会可及性"和降低个体"脆弱性"。"大国大城"还是"小国寡民"，取决于个体的选择：是否到大城市寻找工作、教育和其他方面的机会。

第四是韧性成本，韧性和可适应性非常抽象，韧性城市由此变成非常昂贵的公共品。在韧性城市昂贵且稀缺的情况下，要在人类精心设计选择和自然自我组织之间找到永续的权衡，其目标是：让城市使得人与自然和谐共生。

东亚地区空间规划与可持续发展

沈振江

日本国立金泽大学环境设计学院教授，日本工程院院士

1.《空间规划与可持续发展》书籍介绍

空间规划与可持续发展国际学会（SPSD）曾出版了一本书——《空间规划与可持续发展》，内容与这次论坛的主题相接近，也是我要介绍的"东亚地区空间规划与可持续发展"。

从空间规划的角度来讲，关于可持续城市形态有四种流派：美国的城市控制（urban containment）流派，主要涉及土地利用，由国家来限制规划和建设；英国提出的紧凑城市（compact city）流派；美国提出的生态城市（eco-city）流派；以及欧洲的新传统城（neo-traditional development）流派。可持续发展形态有一些重要评价指标，分别是紧凑度、交通可持续度、密度、土地利用的混合度、多样性、节能性、环保性。

城市形态是城市中多个利益相关方相互作用的结果，其中公共部门和私人部门起重要作用。私人部门对于土地利用有两方面的影响，一方面追求低成本导致城市扩张，另一方面通过集聚追求更高利润，使得企业运营更高效。公共部门相比起私人投资者有不同的考虑，这是因为其最主要的作用是提供公共服务，期待节约财政达到建设高效。

在空间规划过程中，公共政策对于控制可持续发展形态非常重要。我今天介绍的这本书主要研究如何利用公共政策控制城市发展的形态，其中包含东亚地区如日本、韩国、中国以及中国台湾省的空间规划和可持续发展研究的实际案例。

2. 可持续发展与空间规划案例研究

从东亚城市的可持续发展进程来看，相对发达的国家，如日本和韩国，已经度过了城市增长期，现在处于城市衰退时期，面临着人口减少、中心区衰退、城市机能再生的问题。对于还处于城市增长期的国家来说，如中国、泰国、越南等，处理好投资的问题很重要，特别是企业投资，并且需要处理好城市内就业、居住和交通问题。此外，在城市开发的过程中，

为达到可持续发展目标，在兼顾经济增长目标的基础上，也需要考虑人类社会的公平发展需求和生态需求之间的平衡。对于已经比较发达的国家，它们主要面临的是人口减少、中心区衰退的问题，因此要通过城市再生，来提高城市的中心性。

这本书分成两个部分来讲空间规划与可持续发展，每个部分都有发达国家和发展中国家与地区的一些经验。第一个部分是城市化与可持续发展社会。在城市化过程中，可持续发展是很重要的目标，过程中会面临开发的问题，还有开发之后的城市扩张与城市人口增长等问题。另外社会、生态、农业之间的相互关系也很重要。第二个部分是关于生态系统可持续发展，讲述可持续发展也许会给经济发展带来限制。因此要实现社会的稳定发展，也需要考虑到生态以及农业的因素。

从开发压力的角度来看，如何处理土地利用的规划与实施非常重要，在投资层面则需要考虑住宅的开发以及交通因素。在城市发展的压力之下，也要考虑对周边土地的利用产生的矛盾，加强绿色城市设计的规划。此外还要尽量减少对农地、生态的占用和对生态系统的破坏，在这个过程中的公共政策能起很大作用。对于欧洲、北美和亚洲的发达国家，公共政策规划非常重要。

对于目前处于衰退期的国家，像日本、韩国，就需要增加中心性，促进中心区人口回流，解决老龄化社会问题，并在中心区进行城市更新。中国和日本对于城市更新的定义略有不同，城市更新在中国更注重住宅问题，日本多用城市再生一词。城市更新在日本更注重中心区的城市功能本身，吸引代表新的经济活动的企业进入中心区，而这也需要在公共政策上多付出一些努力。

韩国科学技术院（KAIST）针对可持续发展形态提了一个建议[①]：东亚地区要合起来考虑发展问题，因此共享空间数据库是很重要的。欧洲做了一个非常好的示范，东亚地区还有待加强。

韩国交通研究院（KOTI）也做了一个案例分析[②]，发现韩国近年有 39 个地方城市面临着城市衰退的局面。特别是郊区再开发的过程中，私营企业由于追求利润会选择比较便宜的郊区土地，城市形态扩张之后，中心区的功能受到很大影响，从而导致城市衰退。所以在韩国，如何使得中心区再生目前是个很大的问题。

此外，日本国土交通省（MLIT）的研究还说明日本正面临着边缘乡村消亡的问题[③]，需要政策来提供农业补助，解决农业地区老龄化问题，促进城市区人口到农村从事农业。在日本、

① Ye, Kyung-rock, 2013, "The Possibility of Sharing Spatial Data and Research Cooperation Within East Asia Countries", 10.1007/978-94-007-5922-0_2.

② Lee, Bum-hyun, 2013, "A Study on Classification of Downtown Areas Based on Small and Medium Cities in Korea", 10.1007/978-94-007-5922-0_3.

③ Yamashita, Ryohei & Ichinose, Tomohiro, 2013, "Significance and Limitations of the Support Policy for Marginal Hamlets in the Strategy of Self-sustaining Regional Sphere Development", 10.1007/978-94-007-5922-0_4.

韩国这种相对来说比较发达的国家，目前主要存在两个问题：地方城市的衰退和大城市圈过于集中。

此外，从首都圈开始，从东京到日本的直辖市、中等城市，再到农村，老龄化问题都很严重。[①]因此，国家需要研究区域性的规划圈该怎么考虑，以及从广域到微观的生活圈的空间规划该如何协调。

城市的功能更新也非常重要。智慧城市建设大家应该都很熟悉，日本也有很多智慧城市建设的样板城市[②]，它们利用政府的补助，通过环境共生、智慧能源等各种各样的项目入手，更新城市的功能。

综上所述，发达国家遇到的问题是城市中心区衰退、大城市的城市更新问题，以及边远农村的消亡问题。并且在发达国家，目前努力通过公共政策来调整城市形态促进可持续发展的经济社会的形成。

3. 发展中国家职住问题亟待解决

第一个案例是中科院地理所做的北京住宅需要、职住结构分析研究[③]。主要是通过推进公

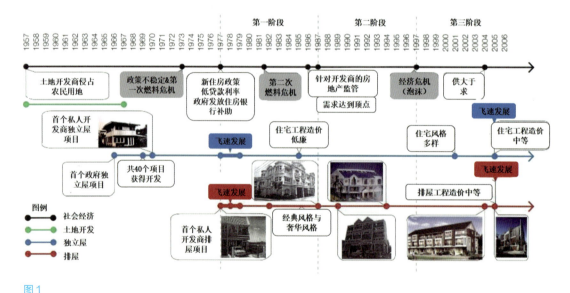

图 1
泰国排屋发展

---

① Nishino, Tatsuya, 2013, "Continuity of Relations Between Local Living Environments and the Elderly Moved to a Group Living", 10.1007/978-94-007-5922-0_5.

② Balaban, Osman, 2013, "The Use of Indicators to Assess Urban Regeneration Performance for Climate-Friendly Urban Development: The Case of Yokohama Minato Mirai 21", 10.1007/978-94-007-5922-0_6.

③ Gao, Xiaolu, 2013, "Modeling Housing Demand Structure: An Example of Beijing", 10.1007/978-94-007-5922-0_10.

共租赁住宅的做法分析住宅需要结构，再研究如何进行福利住宅和租赁住宅的开发。这是北京目前面临的一个大问题。

第二个例子是泰国，我认为泰国曼谷的开发过程和中国北京有相似之处。私营企业追求利润，于是在一些它们认为有利可图的地方开发住宅。经过几十年的开发，住宅和工作的地点相隔很远，这是很不合理的。所以在泰国，特别是曼谷大都市圈，交通问题非常严重[①]。同样的问题也存在于北京和中国其他的一些省会城市。

4. 发达地区交通问题解决思路多样

在发达国家和相对较发达的地区，一方面人口减少导致交通压力目前比发展中国家小，这在一定程度上减轻了职住交通的问题。另一方面，它们也从别的角度来处理土地和交通问题。例如，中国台湾地区促进了全岛自行车环路建设[②]，在处理好职住问题之后，在交通规划

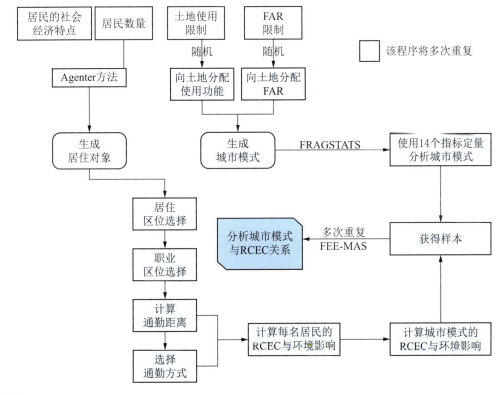

图2
北京城市模式、交通耗能与环境影响模拟研究

---

① Klinmalai, Siwaporn & Kanki, Kiyoko, 2013, "Characteristic of Sustainable Location for Townhouse Development in Bangkok and Greater Metropolitan Area, Thailand", 10.1007/978-94-007-5922-0_9.

② Pai, Brian & Hu, Tai-Shan, 2013, "The Role of the Knowledge Community and Transmission of Knowledge: A Case of Bicycle SMEs in Taiwan", 10.1007/978-94-007-5922-0_11.

方面有一定的余力来考虑娱乐性和健康性。

还有一个重要方面是要尽量减少交通量和交通距离，这对可持续发展，特别是低碳排放非常有益。图 2 是清华大学做的一项模拟性的政策研究 [1]，主要研究的是北京如何通过改善交通和职住关系减少碳排放。

除了上面提到中国台湾建设休闲娱乐性全岛自行车交通网络，日本也正在进行环境友好的智慧交通相关的研究 [2]，其中也有考虑如何通过倡导步行减少交通压力的做法。日本希望通过个人步行道具来提高步行便利性。

步行可达性研究目前是发达国家的热门课题。在中国，城市建设较好的地方，比如厦门，也很重视步行可达性研究。[3]

5. 城市化需要寻求社会、经济与生态、农业的平衡

随着社会经济的发展，人们逐渐形成可持续发展的社会。城市化有城市增长的过程，也有城市衰退的过程。在这个过程中，发达国家和发展中国家遇到的问题有所不同，比如亚洲地区有面临城市增长的开发压力的国家，同时也面临着中心衰退问题的国家，不同的国家在做不同的努力。

另一个可持续发展的重要问题是社会经济发展与生态、农业的平衡问题。不同地区在做不同层次的努力。比如为减少碳排放，日本建筑研究所（Building Research Institute）通过在建筑本身增加绿化，改善城市微观的温热环境以及个人居住的生态环境。[4]

日本建筑研究所还做了一些别的努力，如"海绵城市"。[5] 这个项目考虑的是如何吸收雨水，尽量不把雨水排放到河道，从而减少城市灾害的发生。该研究对降低城市脆弱性、提高城市恢复力颇有助益。

在中国，北师大开发了城市生态分析管理系统。[6] 日本之前有过类似工作。日本是个狭长

---

[1] Long, Ying & Qizhi, Mao & Shen, Zhenjiang, 2013, "Urban Form, Transportation Energy Consumption, and Environment Impact Integrated Simulation: A Multi-agent Model", 10.1007/978-94-007-5922-0_13.

[2] Ando, Ryosuke & Li, Ang & Nishihori, Yasuhide & Kachi, Noriyasu, 2013, "Acceptability of Personal Mobility Vehicles to Public in Japan: Results of Social Trial in Toyota City", 10.1007/978-94-007-5922-0_12.

[3] Wang, Hui, 2013, "Mapping Walking Accessibility, Bus Availability, and Car Dependence: A Case Study of Xiamen, China", 10.1007/978-94-007-5922-0_14.

[4] Kato, Masashi, et al., 2013, "Effects of green curtains to improve the living environment", https://doi.org/10.1007/978-94-007-5922-0_15.

[5] Kikuchi, Sachiko & Koshimizu, Hajime, 2013, "A Comparison of Green Roof Systems with Conventional Roof for the Storm Water Runoff", 10.1007/978-94-007-5922-0_16.

[6] Xu, Lin-yu & Yang, Zhi-feng, 2013, "Evaluation and Regulation of Ecological Security When Implementing Urban Planning: Review and Suggestions for Spatial Planning and Sustainable Development in China", 10.1007/978-94-007-5922-0_17.

的山型国家，水源地位于山顶，需要保护，中游发展旅游，到进海口的地方大多数和城市用水结合在一起，城市地区防御城市洪灾也十分重要。可见，除了森林之外，水生态也是日本的一个重要问题。

在生态层面，中国台湾台中地区一些城市正在提倡的生态网络合作，主要从区域角度考虑形成绿色网络。[1]日本的绿地机构做的研究与此类似，主要从区域、城市和社区级别研究生态网络的建设。

社会、城市发展与农业之间存在着尖锐的矛盾，比如农业发展正面临土地开发的压力，以及来自城市发展改变耕地功能的压力，但也有一些成功案例。

图3是北京市周围的农作物情况。由于种植小麦经济效益不大，北京周围一些农村转而种植一些可作为产油原料的、经济效益更高的农作物。[2]

图3
北京周边农作物及用地情况

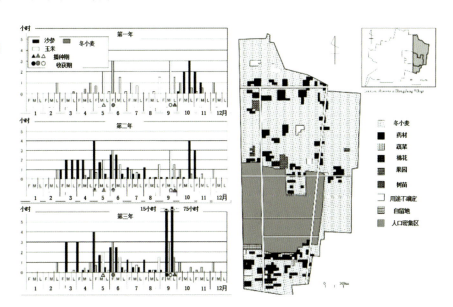

此外，北京农业大学也做了一个关于北京的研究，提倡在城市发展景观农业。[3]当时北京的污染比较严重，我认为在北京进行都市景观农业的规划以减少碳排放是个非常好的建议。

发达国家的农业管理还包括森林管理。森林是私有地，一些地区由于老龄化问题，如今的管理十分混乱，甚至荒废了管理，无法落实森林的所有者和所有范围，形成一个很大的管理问题。

---

[1] Liu, Li-wei & Ko, Pei-yin, 2013, "Imagination and Practice of Collaborative Landscape, Ecological, and Cultural Planning in Taiwan: The Case of Taichung County and Changhua County", 10.1007/978-94-007-5922-0_7.

[2] Wang, Dai & Si, Yuefang & Zhang, Wen-zhong & Sun, Wei, 2013, "An Investigation of Changes in the Urban Shadow of Beijing Metropolis Under Agricultural Structural Adjustment in China", 10.1007/978-94-007-5922-0_18.

[3] Zhang, Feng-rong & Zhao, Hua-fu，2013, "The Spatial Planning of Agricultural Production in Beijing Toward Producing Comfortable and Beautiful Living Environment", 10.1007/978-94-007-5922-0_19.

图 4
陕西新农村建设研究

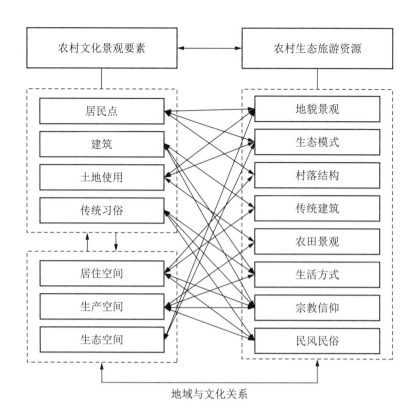

图 5
韩国多光谱卫星影像
土地覆盖分析

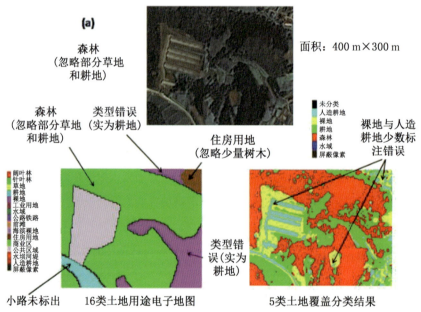

清华大学进行了关于如何在陕西地区发展新农村建设的研究，目的是为了建设符合当地生态的住宅。[1]

---

[1] Dang, Anrong & Zhang, Yan & Chen, Yang, 2013, "Sustainable-Oriented Study on Conservation Planning of Cave-Dwelling Village Culture Landscape", 10.1007/978-94-007-5922-0_8.

图 5 是韩国的森林管理案例[1]，希望通过遥感数据观察吸收碳排放的效果。但在研究过程中同样发现森林管理存在很大问题，需要明确谁拥有这片土地，并研究政府应该如何促进所有者进行森林管理。

6. 城市发展需要降低城市脆弱性、提高城市恢复力

无论是发达国家还是开发压力大的发展中国家和地区，都面临城市脆弱性和城市灾害的问题，比如洪涝、地震等，都需要进行城市基础设施建设，以此降低城市内部脆弱性。社会合作也同样重要，相对而言发达国家在这方面做得更多。

图 6 是日本国土交通省国土技术政策综合研究所（National Institute for Land and Infrastructure Management，MLIT）在国土空间规划层面做的研究[2]，也是关于城市脆弱性的案例。日本纬度偏北，豪雪地区多见，加上日本的老龄化问题，雪灾也是关乎城市脆弱性的一

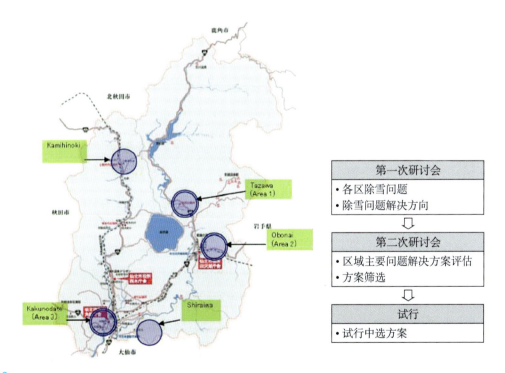

图 6
日本豪雪地区问题研究

---

[1]　Kim, Jung-Rack & Lin, Shih-Yuan & Chang, Eunmi & Lee, In-Hee & Yun, He-Won, 2013, "Land Cover Analysis with High-Resolution Multispectral Satellite Imagery and Its Application for the CO_2 Flux Estimation", 10.1007/978-94-007-5922-0_21.

[2]　Yuhara, Asako & Ye, Kyung-rock, 2013, "Sustainable Communities in Hilly, Mountainous and Heavy Snowfall Areas", 10.1007/978-94-007-5922-0_24.

大问题。日本很多农村的老龄人由于无法除雪，冬季死亡率升高。

还有一些案例主要是从历史的角度来研究如何保护城市生态，特别是水环境，图7是重庆关于水环境脆弱性所做的研究。[①]

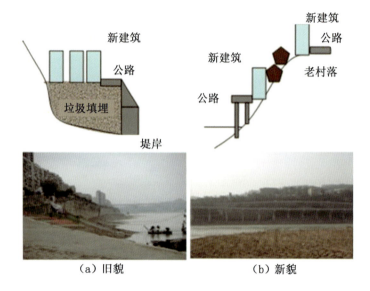

（a）旧貌　　　　　　　　（b）新貌

7. 总结

通过韩国、日本、中国和中国台湾地区等东亚国家地区的案例，主要观察如何通过公共政策的努力来达成可持续发展的城市形态。因此我们考虑的角度包括如何在经济开发压力下形成可持续发展的社会，如何寻求生态和农业的平衡，还讨论了发达国家和正在开发的地区的不同层次的问题。

东亚地区的空间规划，其实正同时面临城市增长和城市衰退的问题。由于不同区域的发展历程各不相同，因此也有了不同的政策和做法。发展中国家的土地分配利用模式要更注重经济需要的空间分配，发达国家要更注重中心区衰退和解决人口减少的问题。此外，随着技术的发展，也要更注重联合相关技术发展的企业资本进行城市中心区的更新，加强中心性的问题。

① Huang, Guang-wei & Shen, Zhenjiang, 2013, "A Vulnerability Study from Water Perspective on the Largest City of China", 10.1007/978-94-007-5922-0_25.

后疫情时代的城市与房地产反思

程天富

新加坡国立大学城市与地产研究院院长

1. 城市规划和愿景的未来变化

在提及"宜居城市"这一概念时，每个城市都有自己的憧憬和想法，都在朝着打造更美好的生活这一目标而努力。针对如何去打造以人为本的美好社会，新加坡建屋发展局（Housing and Development Board，HDB）近期推出了未来 10 至 15 年的组屋发展蓝图，以智能生活、优质生活、和谐生活为主题构建未来市镇。新冠肺炎疫情爆发将会对建屋发展局的原有策略产生一些影响。在疫情发生之前，很多宜居城市方面的城市规划主要围绕较为正面的愿景描述，如"美好生活""宜居城市"或者"环境绿化"等。但此次疫情过后，城市规划的策略上必须进行一些改变和修正。城市规划者在疫情之后采取了更为主动的策略，他们不单单关注构建宜居城市，也更关注打造具有韧性与灵活性的城市。一个具有韧性与灵活性的城市，可以根据形势及时作出调整，更好地适应环境的变化。环境变化、气候变迁，人口结构的变化等都是极为紧迫的城市问题，城市规划者必须加以应对，寻找解决方法。

在这种背景下，未来的宜居城市规划可能需要有所改变，从打造正面愿景转向更为主动地去适应环境问题。也就是说，未来的宜居城市规划会针对气候变化、人口结构变化进行调整，尤其是会融入疫情过后的社会和城市发展，以及空间应用方面的一些思考。可以说，此次疫情打乱了城市规划的整体布局，因为它不单单对经济产生冲击，影响了人们的生活步调，也将改变未来经济发展的走向。

此前，探讨城市规划时通常会从城市经济学的角度出发。城市经济学是一门研究个人对空间选择的学科，主要关注空间选择的效益最大化，即如何在不影响环境绿化的前提下，最大化地利用有限的土地资源，从而为经济发展、工作、休闲以及个人住宅提供空间。在城市经济学的视角下，集聚效应显得尤为重要。集聚经济旨在让多家企业集中在市中心，享有特定区域的优势和好处，也能惠及其他聚集在一起的企业。企业的集聚可提高生产力，就可能进一步减低投入成本。与之类似，城市人口大多是比较群聚的社群。人们在工作时以及社交时，都希望能面对面地进行互动。这影响了城市规划的大方向，例如大家的工作地点通常聚集在市中心，居住地则位于离市中心较远的地区。在这种情况下，人们早上都会通勤到市中心去工作。虽然这种规划可以实现经济效益的最大化，但它也会带来一些负面的城市问题，比如交通堵塞、环境污染等。由于人们需要在同一个时间段通勤到市中心的工作地点，城市的公共交通等基础设施难免要承受大量负荷。但到了周末或者下班之后，这些基础设施却大多未能得到有效利用，整个市中心变得空旷寂静。

这些都是我们以往进行城市规划时需要关注的因素，换句话说，我们需要考虑如何才能让城市体系更有效地运转。在基础设施方面，我们通常也会考虑到怎样解决上述问题。这次疫情爆发后，人们可能需要重新考量集聚经济的效应，以及集聚经济以后能否带动社区发展。为了追求集聚效应，城市空间一般仅限于单一用途，而单一用途的空间所产生的集聚效应难以适配不同的时间与空间。此次新冠肺炎疫情对于城市发展和房地产空间布局产生了相当大的影响，未来五十年乃至百年的城市规划都需对集聚经济重新进行反思。

2. 新冠肺炎疫情对城市的影响

相比城市的集聚效应，如图 1 所示，人口密度越大的地区，疫情传播的风险也就越高。因此，如今的城市经济学与公共卫生的防疫需求其实存在冲突。我们需要思考如何才能解决问题，让城市人口在不受传染的情况下继续交流，并继续发挥集聚效应，更好地利用城市空间。

图 1
各国人口密度与新冠肺炎确诊病例之间的关系
资料来源：世界发展指标，世界银行。

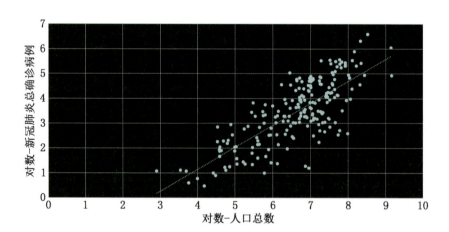

我在此分享三篇有关疫情影响的研究。第一篇研究是来自上海科技大学的 "Human Mobility Restrictions and the Spread of the Novel Coronavirus（2019-nCoV）in China"，主要关注城市空间与隔离措施，以前的城市设计往往忽视了这一视角。在第一篇研究中，我的一位前博士生及其团队对武汉的封城策略进行了研究。

图 2 显示，武汉封城之后，城际人口流动和城内人口流动大幅减少。可以说，武汉的封城策略非常的有效，明显减缓了疫情的传播速度。此次疫情期间，我们发现社区隔离、社交隔离非常重要，若没有这些隔离措施，此次疫情的传播速度恐怕会更快，带来更加严重的后果。

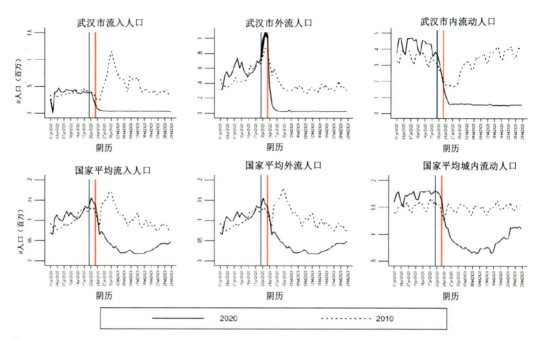

图 2
中国城际人口流动与城内人口流动情况

第二篇研究是收录于社会科学研究网络（SSRN）的"Containing the Virus or Reviving the Economy？Evidence from Individual Expectations during the Covid19 Epidemic"，主要针对管控疫情与重启经济的取舍。该研究发现，疫情会对人们的心态和对经济的预期产生非常负面的影响。也就是说，疫情爆发后，人们对于经济前景的看法会变得非常悲观。目前很多国家的政府正在解封经济和控制疫情之间作抉择。在二者间达成平衡非常重要，因为疫情无法得到控制的话，经济必然会受到影响，经济复苏后，人们的生活、工作和就业等方面才会得到改善。

第三篇研究是来自新加坡国立大学城市与地产研究院（IREUS）的"Application of Artificial Intelligence（AI）to Forecast the Spread of Coronavirus Disease 2019（Covid-19）"，主要探讨了疫情发展的预测。为什么此次疫情的传播速度如此之快？社区传播的问题又该如何去解决？其实我们以前已经历过类似的疫情，尤其是 2003 年 SARS 疫情时，我们当时也面临类似的问题。但 SARS 疫情时，病毒的感染者在病情发展至后期后才具有较强的传染性，比较利于我们去预测疫情的传播速度。但此次新冠肺炎疫情中出现了很多无症状感染者，他们也会引起疫情的传播。这就使得问题更为复杂，控制社区感染，减缓疫情的传播速度就显得极为重要。

第三篇研究主要关注如何去预测无症状感染者的传播风险。研究中进行了一些简单的预测，如图 3 所示，如果没有自我隔离措施，疫情的传播速度将会更快。而推行自我隔离措施后，病毒的传播和感染病例的集中性会得到一定程度的控制。

图 3
自我隔离对疫情传播
的影响

早期感染率和分布　　　　没有自我隔离　　　　有自我隔离

总而言之，上述三点都是疫情时代城市规划必须关注的重要因素。一定程度上，这次疫情使已制定好的城市规划和经济政策面临危机，打乱了此前的策略。此次疫情过后，如何有效利用隔离政策，如何在经济复苏和控制疫情之间取得平衡都需要进一步的思考。在这里我也介绍一些新加坡的应对措施。为控制疫情，新加坡推出了多个阶段的防疫限制措施，先是自 4 月份起实施阻断封锁措施，要求人们居家隔离，在家中工作和上课。新加坡于 6 月 2 日起开始启动第一阶段解封，并积极采取各类措施，包括分组及远程办公，业务持续规划，合力追踪系统等，防止第二波疫情的爆发。到现在为止，新加坡的疫情在一定程度上已经得到控制，近期的新增病例多以输入型病例为主。

3. 新冠肺炎疫情对房地产和空间应用的影响

许多公司和机构纷纷推行远程办公，在疫情期间，已有超过 80% 的劳动人口通过远程方式进行办公。这种趋势将对我们的空间需求产生影响，在疫苗研发取得突破、疫情得到控制之后，鉴于已有如此之多的劳动人口接触过远程办公，我们的办公模式可能也无法恢复到疫情前的状态。目前，Twitter、微软（Microsoft）、谷歌（Google）等很多大公司已出台政策，鼓励员工继续居家办公。他们的大部分目前仍在居家办公员工，已经适应了这种模式。

因此，此次疫情将给办公楼市场和空间规划带来以下三点主要影响。第一，"去中心化"现象将会愈发普遍。第二，中央商务区的重新发展和综合性发展将进一步提速。目前中央商业区是一个以商业用途为主的比较单一的综合中心，当大部分员工都已远程办公时，空闲出来的办公空间该如何去利用，旧的办公楼又该如何重新开发，这些都是非常重要、值得我们去思考的问题。第三，空间的灵活应用将得到更多关注。

具体而言，"去中心化"是指，当更多公司实行"业务稳定与延续性计划"时，尤其在疫情期间实行分组工作制，劳动力密度和集中度减小，中央商业区的集聚效应减弱的情况。目前很多公司已将员工分成不同小组，让他们在不同时段回到办公室工作，以降低疫情传播风险。很多公司已经开始采取"去中心化"措施，把部分设施搬迁到中央商务区（CBD）以外。因为目前来说，不单单工作场所存在疫情传播风险，员工在乘坐公共交通通勤上班时也面临一定的风险，解决上述疫情传播风险已非常重要。很多公司已开始把一些后勤营运部门搬迁到中央商务区以外，目前来说，新加坡中心商业区以外的一些办公楼，比方说纬壹科技城（One North）、巴西班让商业城（Pasir Panjang）等都已吸引许多科技公司落户。这些公司已无需追求临近市中心其他企业的集聚效应，他们的许多员工已采取远程方式办公，无需聚集在市中心，而是可以通过网络的方式联系交流。

至于第二点中央商务区空间使用的再规划与重新发展，目前来说我们的中央商务区非常单一，主要以办公楼和商业活动场所为主。疫情之后，我们需要对这种单一的商业用途进行重新考量，因为大部分人以后可能都不愿、也无需再回到中心商业区工作，办公楼空间面临如何处置的问题。那么接下来中央商务区的规划可能更多的会以综合性用途为主，并减少通勤和交通方面的问题。换言之，未来的中央商务区可能朝综合性方向发展，在小范围的土地内融合办公楼、住宅、购物休闲场所。中央商务区的员工无需再进行通勤，交通拥挤问题也将有所缓解，城市空间也得到更好的利用。

新加坡市区重建局（URA）目前也在推行中央商务区奖励计划（CBD Incentive Scheme），鼓励业主对旧的商业区进行重新规划与发展，将这些中心打造成更具活力、具备更多用途的城市空间。

此外，办公楼的空间设计也需重新进行调整。目前来说，办公楼的设计通常都较为长期性，办公空间的租赁期限较长。此次疫情之后，很多人开始转而考虑租期更短、更具灵活性的办公空间。而且在疫情爆发之前，很多共享经济企业已开始提供更加灵活的共享办公空间。在疫情结束后，我们会发现，此类共享办公空间可能更加适合未来的办公需求。

最后，此次疫情揭示，云端科技、数据中心对于企业至关重要。如果企业在此前在这方面有着较好的基础，疫情对它们造成的冲击其实相对较小。反观在这方面缺乏积累，较为传统的企业，疫情对它们造成的影响则相对更为严重。

韧性基础设施、新旧基建融合与可持续性投融资

叶　臻

伦敦大学学院巴特雷建设与项目管理学院基础设施投融资课程主任，厦门大学金融学讲座教授

林楷蓓

剑桥大学土地经济系房地产金融专业研究生

梅一钦

伦敦大学学院巴特雷建设与项目管理学院基础设施投融资专业研究生

本次报告从城市化和发展包容性的角度出发，对正负外部性、新旧基建融合和金融创新几个角度探讨如何构建更具可持续性的韧性基础设施。我们认为构建韧性需要在生态和人文两个领域设计更具包容性的设施。其中城市数据化是新旧基建市政融合的主要载体。在中国，基础设施作为一种资产类型对其可以进行适度的金融创新，通过引入不同类型所有制进入基础设施投融资领域，通过绩效管理提升资产效率。基础设施的韧性固然重要，我们更需要更为精细地管理基础设施，使基础设施更具包容性和长期的发展潜力。

1. 韧性基础设施的正负外部性和包容性

长城是人类古代工程的杰出代表，它屹立数千年不倒，用途也从最初的国防基础设施转变为如今的旅游设施。其实，人类社会建造的许多历史遗迹，如金字塔，最初目的都是为了永久存在。人类不惜代价去建造它们，但伴随这些巨大结构的城市却已不复存在。毫无疑问，这些历时千年的建造物仍然具有我们今天所讨论的建筑韧性，但其建造成本的合理性和功能性值得去探讨和反思。

基础设施的韧性可从狭义与广义两方面来审视。狭义上的韧性，是指城市中提供系统性互联互通的重要基础设施的延续性，及其面对重大灾害的耐受能力。广义上的韧性，则是指基础设施具有发展的可持续性、生态和人文的包容性及可适应性。从金融学的角度看，韧性基础设施对可持续性投融资的作用体现在两方面，一是韧性基础设施可以延缓股权资金成本上升，二是可缓解因重大事件造成预期现金流不足以覆盖债务而产生破产风险。韧性基础设施作为一种资产类型在当今世界金融创新和城市治理中扮演着重要角色。

许多城市的部分基础设施并不具备广义上的韧性。如部分地铁与快速公交系统（BRT）的电梯只有上行却没有下行，这种情况会给老年人和残障人士带来诸多不便，是典型的缺乏人文包容性的案例。再如侧道入口的多条车道限高杆设置不合理，车主可能因看不见或不知道自己车的高度，而在转弯驶入支路时进入不限高车道从而造成主干道堵塞。在城市高速发展的进程中，不乏这类缺乏考虑、设计缺乏韧性的基建。我们既要改造，也要避免低效率的重复建设。合理规划的韧性基建可提高城市可持续发展能力，以适应不断演化、进步的城市体系，这样未来城市才能变得更为宜居，才能通过正外部性吸引更多的人和资本。

在人文韧性方面，英国的经验值得我们借鉴。2005 年，英国通过对《反残疾歧视法》（Disability Discrimination Act，DDA）的修正案，这一措施使得许多使用上百年的基础设施得到了改造。例如，全世界历史最为悠久、运营时间近 160 年的伦敦地铁改造了大多数设施，还为残障人士提供了支持上行和下行的电梯。

现代化进程中基础设施的负外部性要求我们系统应对"城市病"。中金公司的一份研究报告认为，"城市病"是指人口向城市集中，但城市基础设施相对欠缺而引起的一系列社会问题。这些问题具体体现在交通拥堵、城市内涝、空气污染、水体污染、固废危废堆积等方面。例如，水体污染方面，住建部在 2016 年 2 月排查了全国 295 个地市，排查出城市黑臭水体 1 811 个，平均每座城市 6.13 个。交通拥堵方面，高德地图 2018 年发布的报告显示，在其监测的 361 个城市中，15% 的城市通勤高峰面临拥堵，59% 的城市通勤高峰处于缓行状态，仅有 26% 的城市通勤高峰不受拥堵问题困扰。[①]

正外部性和负外部性的存在，使得我们必须考虑之前提到的韧性基础设施的可持续性、生态和人文包容性及可适应性。需要设计更为包容的韧性基础设施，还必须考虑到基础设施对于儿童、老年人、残障人士等群体的包容度。

2. 城市数字化与新旧基建的市政融合

建造具有韧性的基础设施不可避免地涉及新旧基建的融合问题。我们认为新基建的定义不应只局限于支持科技发展的基础设施从而蜕变为一种新的产业政策。新基建是城市更新的核心，可以增加城市韧性，解决上述的"城市病"问题，是提高城市发展效率以及引领未来城市可持续发展的主要推动力。其中的关键在于如何更好地构建数字化城市，以数据为核心连接新旧基建，使新旧基建更好地无边界融合到城市的管理和运营体系中。

（1）城市数字化。

2019 年末，中国的城镇化人口超过 60%；摩根士丹利在其《中国城市化 2.0》的报告中

---

① 数据来源：中国环境监测；凤凰财经；能源世界；中金公司研究部。

预测，2030 年，中国城市化人口将升至 75%。随着城市化率的不断提高，大城市运行负荷加重，中国城市化已经步入中后期的特殊阶段。[①] 缺乏韧性的钢筋水泥建筑已无法满足当代城市人口多样且复杂的生存、居住需求。在此背景下，由新基建所驱动的城市更新显得尤为重要。新基建可促进城市的智慧升级、智能化发展，通过建设数字城市，精细化城市管理，从而提升城市韧性。

新基建是数字经济的必要生产要素，数据的生产、传输、储存与使用是过程，最后的产出则是基于城市数据的新型治理模式。数据产出帮助增强城市韧性，达成产业优化及其他方面的可持续发展目标。城市每天产出且消耗大量数字信息，只有利用新基建配套设施，建立全面、有效、标准的数据治理系统，才能充分释放新基建的数据价值。

在工业上，我们能看到明显的生产流程数字化的趋势，比如工业物联网的巨大价值。其中，数字孪生（data twin）在工业生产中的运用能极大程度上优化资产性能、提高生产效率。数字孪生是一种用数字结构解读物理状态的工具，原理是通过集成反馈物理数据，用人工智能、机器学习进行数字化分析，在信息平台内建立模型、产生数字副本。在城市管理上，数字孪生可以通过捕捉时间和空间影像，建立城市副本，以此优化城市可持续发展。目前新加坡等一些城市已经在开发数字孪生城市系统，用于城市智慧化管理。未来更多的城市都将会利用这些技术。当然，这些数据运营，特别是规模巨大的城市数据的运营、管理，都必须以完备的新基建系统为支撑。另一方面，我们必须意识到新旧基建融合过程中的数据生产和使用所消耗的能源必须是具备可持续性的可再生能源，从而减少长期的气候变更风险。

（2）新旧基建的市政融合与金融创新。

在内循环背景下，未来新型基础设施领域的投资重心或许会向市政建设方向转移。新基建中包括很多以高科技创新应用为主的领域，如为人工智能、新能源汽车、5G、机器人等战略新兴产业提供设施。此类基建领域面临着如何与旧基建中的城市建设、公共事业和社会保障融合的问题。比如，在城市建设设计中，未来机器人和人机交互将发挥何种作用，自动化驾驶与先进轨道交通间又该如何避免重复建设，庞大的数据如何实施保护，新基建中的人工智能和大数据如何进一步提高传统基础设施的运营效率，如何利用大数据预测基础设施的风险等问题。

我们近期的实证研究表明，从金融学的角度来看，以贝塔（β）系数衡量市场风险，中国新基建市场的风险倍数略高于旧基建，新旧基建的市政融合问题变得尤为重要。新基建的市场风险倍数之所以高，主要有以下三点原因：第一，新基建的预期现金流存在较大的不确定性；第二，新基建还未能完整地融合到旧基建的改造中；第三，新基建的资产定价和市场竞争结构有所不同。

---

① 参见仇保兴：《复杂科学与城市转型》，2012 年。

2019 年，另类资产领域数据和情报提供商普瑞奇（Preqin）对全球基础设施投资的调查显示，超过半数的投资者最为关注资产定价和市场竞争结构。过高的资产定价导致未来收益下降，使得后进资本参与后无法有效退出。市场缺乏竞争机制则将导致垄断和缺乏创新。从资产定价和市场竞争结构两方面看，新旧基建的融合需要更多考虑市场结构和创新的关系。其中，所有权和基础设施绩效是理清两者关系的核心，金融创新则是解决上述问题的重要工具。

从所有权的角度看，一定程度的金融创新可以解决因所有权不清晰而导致的所有者缺位和资产利用效率低的问题。基建的项目所有权可分为土地所有权以及资产所有权。从运营层面来看，现金流收入的所有权与资产运营息息相关，良性运营的资产可以给股东带来一定收益。通过引入不同类型所有制进入基础设施投融资和绩效管理来提升资产效率。英国高速公路管理局（Highways Agency）成功管理 M25 伦敦环城高速公路的经验值得我们借鉴。其通过与私营机构合作，利用公路维护公司和绩效合同，实现了在更短的时间内维护路面设施及其韧性。

从投资的层面来看，通过包括资产证券化、基建 REITs 在内的金融创新产品的优化，可以让更多投资者享有优质资产运营带来的现金流收益，同时也能实现资本反哺，提升资产的利用率和管理效率。

因为基建项目具有投资周期长、资金规模大、退出机制尚未完全清晰等特殊性，许多社会资本对于大型基建的投资望而却步。尤其在中国，退出渠道非常有限，市场机制不够完善，成熟机构投资者少。但自 2020 年 4 月以来，国家发改委明确指出新基建的发展方向，推进基建 REITs 平台的完善，越来越多的民间资本在积极寻求机会加入新基建投资的赛道。基建 REITs 的建设给现有股权投资人提供了更多的退出机制选择，也给项目增加了融资渠道。新旧基建的资本化发展有利于促进底层项目的建设与运营，形成良性循环。

目前我们可以看到明显的投资趋势包括，以政府主导投资、政府带动民间投资以及纯民间投资。民间资本也以 PPP 等方式不断参与大型项目的主体建设及运营。在企业端，也有更多公司专注于基建智能化升级的核心技术。

（3）基础设施作为资产类型的特征。

从全球视角来看，基础设施作为比较稳定的资产类型，正受到全球投资人的密切关注。如图 1 所示，通过对过去十年标普全球（S&P Global）数据的资产定价模型（CAPM）回归，我们推导出基础设施的股权资金回报率在 9% 左右。虽然全球基础设施的年化回报率（3%）远低于标普 500（S&P 500）的年化回报率（11%），但其年化回报波动率（15%）也低于标普 500（17%）。再加上基础设施投资具有稳定的分红比率（稳定的运营现金流收入）和真实资产效应，投资机构正愈发偏好这一资产类型。

图 2 测量了全球证券、债券、房地产信托以及基础设施投资自 1989 年以来的累计回报率，数据证实了基础设施介于债和股间的中间资产特性。图 3 用 5 年期滚动标准差测量了上述几种资产投资的波动率，尤其是在 2008 年金融危机中，基建的风险波动上升比率明显低于

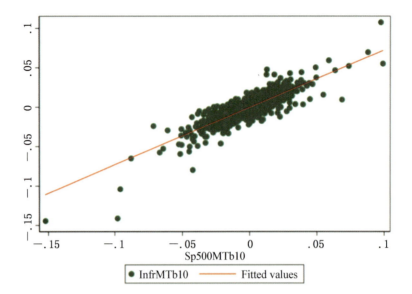

图 1
全球基础设施的资产定
价模型（CAPM）回归

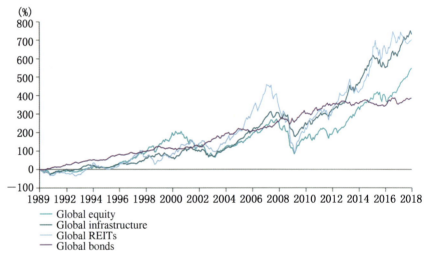

图 2
1990—2017 年全球
资产累计回报率（转
换为统一当地货币）
资料来源：
Vanguard Research
2018，The role of
infrastructure in a
portfolio.

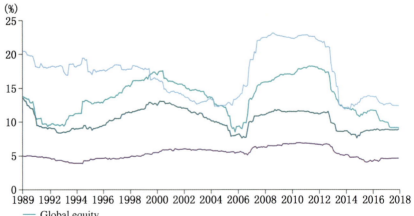

图 3
波动指标年标准差—
5 年窗口滚动相关

REITs 和股市。在市场波动大的时候基建投资更加稳定。在波动性大的情况下，基建作为弱周期产品，能减缓下行风险，在资产组合中尤显重要。

3. 韧性基础设施的长短端风险

从全球债务角度来看，韧性基础设施可以延缓重大事件造成的预期现金流不足以覆盖债务的破产风险。根据全球工程咨询机构 Arup（奥雅纳）的研究，2020 年新冠肺炎疫情之前，全球大多数收费公路的偿债覆盖率（DSCR）在两倍以上。而疫情之下，全球收费公路日交通流量大幅下降。从首次禁止聚集活动开始，除澳大利亚减少 40% 外，意大利、法国、西班牙等发达国家的日交通流量均减少 80% 左右，收费公路的 DSCR 也减少至略多于一倍，临近破产边缘。由此可见，重大事件造成的预期现金流不足，短期内直接加大全球收费公路的破产风险。

表 1
全球收费公路的偿债覆盖率

资　产	债务契约	违约阈值	分布锁定阈值	2019 年 12 月 31 日
公司债券	ICR	1.25x	N/A	4.44x
TQ	ICR	1.20x	1.40x	2.31x
95 号快车道	DSCR	N/A	1.45x	2.92x
495 号快车道	DSCR	1.15x	1.45x	3.40x
Cardinal Hold Co	DSCR	N/A	1.30x	1.76x
A25	DSCR	1.05	1.175x	1.81x
ED	ICR	1.15x	1.40x	4.99x
Hills M2	ICR	1.15x	1.30x	10.19x
LCT	ICR	1.15x	1.30x	2.73x
CCT	ICR	1.15x	1.30x	5.87x
M5	DSCR	1.10x	1.30x	2.09x
M7	DSCR	1.10x	1.30x	4.83x
M4	DSCR	1.10x	1.30x	1.93x

因此，在设计规划韧性基础设施时，从金融学的角度来看，必须考虑到百年不遇的大事件对偿债覆盖率的冲击，把小概率的事件冲击纳入未来现金流的分布参数中，从而更好地控制未来投资的债务风险。不能不惜代价地建设特大项目，而需要更为精细的资产管理，并积极提高基础设施利用效率。

英国、新加坡等许多国家按照具体路段使用情况和拥堵程度对公路进行定价。伦敦对拥堵区实行收费，对不同路段和车辆进行差异性处理，将费率与排放量、清洁能源挂钩。这些实践有助于运营现金流平滑化，有利于提高基础设施利用率。

从资本市场的角度看，全球资本市场目前主要通过环境、社会与企业治理（ESG）三方面的规则来影响基础设施投融资的可持续性。首先，有限合伙人（LP）及资金提供方对于ESG的关注度在不断增加，从可再生能源到有社会责任的初创公司，ESG正在成为风险管理的主要核心和创造潜在价值的驱动力。其次，更大的压力来自投资者和发行人对ESG的披露要求。信息透明度以及对ESG标准和框架的可靠性通过LP投资协议传导至资本市场各方。正如同气候变更协议影响了产业政策，ESG正在通过金融行业的规制和框架协议影响资本游戏的规则，各种评级机构日渐重视ESG，并将其纳入综合信用评估体系。

从长期视角来看，气候变更和碳中和目标将作用于长期资金成本，使得投资回报率下降，这一情况对可持续投融资的作用尤为重大。可以预见，随着中国经济的发展，未来的基础设施投融资所需要考虑的风险因素会更多，设计上的要求更高，受到的规制也会更多。以往以国家为主体的基础设施投融资模式为中国经济和社会发展做出了巨大的贡献，随着中国经济进入资本和创新双驱动的时代，适度的金融化基础设施能更好地提升资本效益和资产运营效率，形成良性循环。同时，我们需要在生态和人文两个领域建设包容性更强的韧性基础设施，通过金融创新使得基础设施具有长期投资的可持续性，以应对具有更多不确定性的未来。

4. 总结及政策建议

对于可持续性投资而言，韧性基础设施可以延缓长端股权资金的成本上升，并能够防范因重大事件造成的预期现金流不足以覆盖债务的破产风险。结合目前国家提倡的新基建，我们必须梳理好新旧基建的融合问题，理清基础设施的市场结构和创新之间、所有权和绩效提升之间的关系。新基建带来的技术创新有助于提升旧基建的效率并更好地预测风险。气候变化和ESG则可以通过影响资金成本和游戏规则，从而影响基础设施投资的长期和短期收益。设计韧性基础设施时必须考虑百年不遇的大事件，把小概率事件的冲击纳入未来现金流的分布参数中，从而更好地预测未来的债务风险。

我们需要设计更具包容性和可适性的韧性基础设施，以便在外循环的流通中更好地嵌入国际社会和当地发展，从而减少未来全球资本市场融资成本上升的风险。不惜代价地建设基础设施并不能带来更高的边际收益，反而会加剧系统性金融风险。在基础设施达到一定规模后，适度的金融化可以进一步提升基础设施的韧性和利用效率。对于可持续的投融资而言，引入不同类型所有制进入基础设施投融资领域，并通过绩效管理提升基础设施资产的利用效率至关重要。最后，基础设施的韧性固然重要，我们更需要更为精细地管理基础设施，使基础设施更具包容性和长期发展潜力。

Livability: The Purpose of Life and an Essential for Business Development

Ni Pengfei

Director, City and Competition Research Center, Chinese Academy of Social Sciences; Vice President, China Society of Urban Economy

1. We have been pursuing a livable life

Since the beginning of human history, seeking better living conditions has been an indispensable part of our survival and development. Therefore, throughout our life, we have been pursuing a livable life, and we will keep pursuing better living conditions in the future.

As can be seen from ancient poems, a livable life not only means a better living environment, but also means inner freedom and peace. Poetic dwelling is everyone's dream, meaning adequate food and clothing, beautiful environment, harmonious society, and inner freedom and peace. In ancient times, people valued inner freedom and peace the most. A western philosopher Friedrich Holderlin once put it, "Poetically man dwells." In ancient China, Bai Juyi and Su Shi believed that "Home is where the heart is" and wrote poems that highlighted people's pursuit of a livable life. A livable life is the ultimate pursuit of humankind.

2. The human and housing development framework is made up of four elements

Recent studies on urban development economics show that urban development depends on four interacting elements that keep evolving. Traditional urban development economics ignores the role of space, while today's urban development economics takes space as one of the four elements promoting urban development. In fact, human development is an evolutionary process. During this process, human demands and supplies interact with each other in a particular space, creating final products and intermediate products including technologies and systems. Based on the evolutionary process of human development and the features of human settlement, we can divide it into four periods: in the hunting and gathering period, humans lived in different places and moved from one place to another;

later in the agricultural era, they still lived in different places but preferred staying in one place for quite some time; in the industrial age, large groups of people migrated to cities, working and living there; and in the future featuring artificial intelligence, humans will not stay in one place for a long period of time. After figuring out different periods of human and housing development, we can better analyze urban livability.

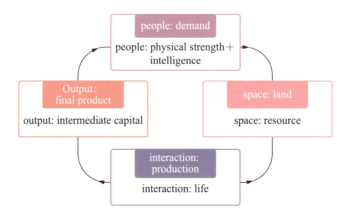

Fig. 1
Human survival and development framework

3. Livability is an important goal that we should achieve in the process of improving urban living environment

So far, China has finished the first half of its urbanization and is moving towards the second half. In terms of people, space, interaction and output, great changes have taken place in the second half. First of all, people have changed their needs from making a living to enjoying life in cities.

Over 2000 years ago, Aristotle's two statements about cities explained well the first and second half of urbanization. He said that at first, men came to cities in order to earn a living, but then in the second half of urbanization, they decided to stay in cities because of the better living environment there. That is to say, they came to cities not only for jobs and money, but also for better access to public services and infrastructure. Therefore, in the second half, during the 14th Five-Year Plan period and even in the long term, a better life will remain the most important need of residents, and a livable environment will continue to be critical for a better life.

From my studies on city competitiveness, I find that foreign countries, especially developed countries, value living environments more than economic competitiveness. As China enters the second half of urbanization, I find that livability can both help residents meet their basic needs and improve their quality of life. In fact, supply is the driver of output. Moreover, the drivers of economic growth and urban development have changed significantly.

4. Livability is an essential for a city's business development

The model of urban development and competition in China have changed. In the first half or early stage of urbanization, a city's development was influenced by the balance between labor, land and foreign capital, especially on the basis of institutional innovation. China's urban development was thanks to such balance. Over the past 30 years, China has experienced three stages of urban development. In the first stage, urban development depended on labor transfer; in the second stage, the driver of urban development shifted to the export-oriented economy driven by foreign capital and multinational corporations; and in the third stage, urbanization featuring the conversion of land use from non-urban to urban uses or urbanization focusing on land management promoted urban development. This is the model of urban development in the first half of urbanization. However, in the second half, land, capital, labor and other factors affecting urban economic development are all changing: land development is weakened by low real estate prices; foreign capital is cut due to some foreign enterprises' closure and withdrawal; and labor dividends are disappearing.

Additionally, the main driving force of urban development or economic growth has shifted from labor force to talents, bringing about a series of changes in the model of urban development. In the past, governments tended to adopt preferential policies, including land policies and fiscal policies, to attract investment and encourage companies to develop in cities, so that they can develop industries, generate tax revenues, and invest in infrastructure to improve the living environment. Nowadays, talents and technological innovation are keys to promoting a city's development. To promote a city's development, the first step is to attract high-end talents. They will help develop high-end industries involving science and technology and innovation, thus creating more tax revenues. This forms a cycle that begins with the improvement of the living environment in a city; then, the city works on attracting high-end talents to boost high-end industries; and finally, the city enjoys more revenues and a growing economy. Therefore, we need to first improve our city's living environment and make

Fig. 2
Changes in
China's model
of urban
development and
competition

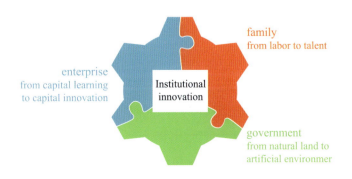

this city more livable, so that the city will be an attraction to high-end talents. As a result, high-end industries will be boosted and a new round of innovation will start.

Therefore, livability is essential for a city's business and economic development. Livability is not only a goal of life but also an essential for production or business. Therefore, in the second stage of urbanization, during the 14th Five-Year Plan period and in the future, livability will play an increasingly important role.

5. China's cities need to be more livable

Not long ago, the National Academy of Economic Strategy at the Chinese Academy of Social Sciences released a report on urban life and it was entitled "Annual Report on China's Urban Competitiveness (No.18): China's Cities and Property Market". This report analyzes data from China's 291 cities in terms of culture, medical care, health, climate, environment, consumption, housing, sports, recreation and cultural facilities. According to this report, the living environment of China's cities needs improvement. It finds that the living environment of coastal provinces and cities in southeastern China, such as Shanghai, Guangdong, Hong Kong, Macao and Taiwan, is relatively good, while that of other areas is poor. It shows that southern areas have a better living environment than northern areas do, and eastern areas take the lead. First- and second-tier cities have high-level urban administration and management, better public services and infrastructure, more livable environment and higher income, but they are faced with high house prices and severe environmental pollution. The third- and fourth-tier cities have lower living costs and the climate there is relatively more comfortable, but they have inadequate public services and lower income.

Overall, China's cities need to be more livable. The inadequate provision of public services and infrastructure in third- and fourth- or even lower-tier cities will drive them to strive to turn themselves into livable spaces.

6. Building livable cities is the focus in the second half of urbanization

Livability is key to urban life and productivity. Therefore, in the second half of urbanization, the focus is to make cities more livable. A people-oriented livable city allows all the residents to participate in city construction, takes advantage of their creativity and ensures that they will enjoy the benefits of urban development.

More specifically, a city needs to work in the following aspects: improving the natural environment, infrastructure and government services; planning, providing and managing private services; ensuring that most residents have easy access to the infrastructure and services, thereby benefiting their physical and mental health and improving their wellbeing. These are what a city needs to focus on in follow-up work. In addition to providing high-quality infrastructure and public services, much more needs to be done to build livable cities. The general guideline is to focus on the demands of all the residents, allow them to participate in building livable cities and ensure they will share the benefits of urban development.

Equity and Efficiency in Urbanization: Land Appreciation

Zhu Jieming

Chief Planner of Shanghai Tongji Urban Planning and Design Institute,

Professor of College of Architecture and Urban Planning, Tongji University

China has a large population but limited land resources. This makes land a valuable asset. Land needs to increase value. Since land-use planning is the main part of urban planning, land appreciation is of vital importance in urbanization.

I'm going to cover four areas on land appreciation. First, I'll talk about who should enjoy the gains of land appreciation. Second, I believe land rent has reversed the urban-rural divide in China's first-tier cities, and has recently widened the gap between rural villages. Third, I'll focus on rent seeking in urbanization, and finally I'll share my thoughts on the equity and efficiency in land development quota allocation.

1. Who should gain from land appreciation

(1) An ideological issue.

In the 19th century, an American social reformer Henry George proposed that gains derived from land appreciation should go back to the government, because the increase in value was brought by urban expansion and government investment, whereas landowners contributed nothing and thus were in a position to receive such gains. This proposal was met with some skepticism. Some argued that while the measures to improve water conservancy facilities could indeed make farmland more fertile and productive, the resulting increase was still quite limited. Compared with farmland, urban land is much more valuable, and the better the location, the higher the value. Government investment in infrastructure in turn raises the value of a piece of land. Therefore, Henry George argued that benefits from land appreciation should go to the public coffer.

Later on, Joseph E. Stiglitz, an American economist, also came up with an economic model that proved that urban growth, population increase, and government spending on infrastructure and public utilities could raise land value.

In the 1950s, shortly after the end of World War II, the Conservative Party in Britain championed a zero percent tax on land appreciation in order to protect the interests of landowners, while the Labour Party pushed for a 100 percent tax, arguing that appreciation in land value should be shared by all. Since then, the tax rate in Britain has stayed between 40 and 50 percent, with the Labour Party asking for a higher rate and the Conservative Party a lower one, due to their different political propositions.

It is not right for all the gains of increased value to go to the public because doing so dampens venture investment. As a result, Henry George's idea was never taken up. In the mid-1990s, a friend of mine made a housing investment in Lianyang Community in Pudong District. Given that the area was just beginning to develop at the time, and that the location was not good, my friend was very concerned that the investment might be too risky. Now his concerns appear to be unnecessary. The housing prices there are now extremely high. If no one had invested in the area, the developers would not have been able to develop Pudong in the first place. The same is true of the stock market. If a 100 percent tax were imposed on stock appreciation, no one would dare to buy stocks. It is risky, after all, to put our hard-earned money in a public traded company. Therefore, it is not right for tax on land appreciation to be either at 100% or zero percent. We should aim for a reasonable rate.

(2) Land appreciation in Singapore.

Fig. 1 shows that housing index in Singapore can be divided into two stages: from 1975 to 1996, and from 1996 to the present. Housing prices were on a rising streak in the first period and the housing market was largely risk-free. Starting from 1996, housing prices have fluctuated more frequently, affected by the Asian financial crisis, the dot-com bubble, global financial crisis, and the current anti-globalization movement.

Fig. 1
Residential
housing
price index
in Singapore
(1975—2020)

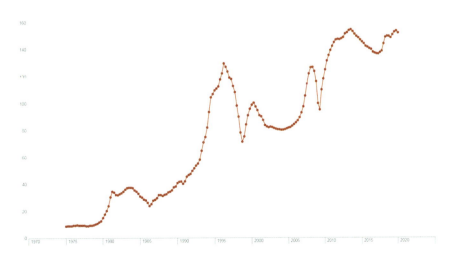

Singapore's housing price index was 8.9 in 1975, but rose to 129.7 in 1996. This is 13.6 times increase in a duration of 21 years. We don't have a housing index in Shanghai, although housing prices there have also soared. Singapore's housing index was 52.1 in 2020, up 17.3 percent from 1996, a far more minimal increase compared with the previous stage. From 1975 to 2020, the average annual growth rate of housing prices was 6.5%, with 13.6% in the first stage and 0.7% in the second. This shows that land value can rise sharply during rapid urban growth, making land appreciation a worthy area of further research.

2. Land rent has reversed urban-rural divide and widened the gap between rural areas

(1) Reversal of urban-rural divide.

Land rent has reversed the urban-rural divide. That's not bad. In Beijing, Shanghai and other first-tier cities, farmers earn more than urban residents, because they own homesteads allocated by the state and can receive rents from collectively owned land. Farmers and urban residents all make money from their regular jobs, but the farmers have additional source of rental income. This is why the urban-rural difference is being continuously narrowed.

For example, the Lianmingyayuan complex in Lianming Village, Qibao Town, is a public rental house built on collectively owned land. The rent is charged at the market price. According to media reports, every household in the village receives an average dividend of 20 000—30 000 yuan a year as their extra income.

(2) Gap between rural areas.

The widening gap between rural areas is arguably a more serious problem. We once did a research in Guangdong, and found that in a highly urbanized village, a family can get 25 percent of its income from land rent, and 75 percent from their regular jobs. Compared with some migrant workers who also live in the village, local farmers can earn 1.5 times more than the income of these migrant workers, thanks to their extra rental income. In another village, which is better located and more urbanized, farmers' rental income can account for as much as 50 percent of the total, making their total earnings 2.2 times more than that of the migrant workers. Land is an asset for farmers, particularly so in well located villages, but in poorly located villages, for instance, in China's inland cities, land is not considered as a premium asset because there is low rental demand. That is why land rent has caused the difference between rural areas.

In Kunshan, since many town/village-owned enterprises have either gone bankrupt, transformed or closed, whatever collective operating income that remains comes almost entirely from land rent.

Generally speaking, a village receives 1.62 million yuan a year on average as its rental income. Poorly located villages, such as Zhouzhuang, get virtually no rental income, while the villages that are located close to urban areas can get as much as 19.6 million yuan. This example just gives us a glimpse of the gap in the rent charged in different villages.

This is the reason why a new social class — the rentier class — comes into being. According to Singapore-based Lianhe Zaobao, a household in Fishermen Village in Shenzhen can earn an average 600 000 yuan from their rental income alone. It is a really stupendous figure. To put the figure in context, we can't earn 600 000 a year teaching at a university.

3. Rent seeking in urbanization

The rentier class exists not only in rural areas but also in urban areas. Rent seeking that emerges in the process of urbanization is one of my research objects. Rent seeking does not represent economic growth. It does not help with the efficiency of economic growth. It is actually a kind of "unearned" income.

(1) Land financing by governments.

Governments in the cities are known for their propensity to appropriate land. They sell land for rent, with which they invest in infrastructure. But the areas sold are actually not well developed later on, and look as empty as ghost cities. It is estimated that the total of planned new urban areas nationwide can accommodate as many as 3.4 billion people. The amount of newly developed land is not matched with the actual rental demand. Then we have to ask ourselves: why are the governments still obsessed with land financing?

Here is a simple example: in a third-tier provincial city in the mainland, the local government planned to build a central business district to develop the tertiary industry, though they knew there might be no such demand. The government gave a land developer authorization to develop commercial real estate in the area, and asked the developer to build a couple of high-rise office buildings for the government in return. However, after two office buildings were constructed, there was no investment demand. Even after the developer cut the housing prices from 18 000 yuan per square meter to 12 000, there were still no buyers. The government was simply using land financing as a tool for political purposes. They wanted to show to the public that they also had a central business district that was no less developed than Shanghai.

(2) Rent seeking in rural areas.

In rural areas, rent seeking comes in the form of renting out the land for industrial purposes. It is particularly common in the suburbs of Shanghai, and also seen in Guangdong and southern Jiangsu. Doing so has made rural space more fragmented, with the farmland and construction land existing side by side, thus damaging the ecological environment. The rental income is obtained at the cost of the environment. A village is different from a city: a city is governed as a whole unit, but each village has its own administrative body. There are about ten administrative villages in a town. When each administrative village is renting out land, it is no wonder that industrial land is seen everywhere.

(3) Rent seeking by state-run enterprises.

In Hongkou District in Shanghai, some industrial land has remained vacant for years without being developed. That's because the state-run enterprises who owned the land were reluctant to hand it over to the government. They are obligated by law to return the industrial land to the government if their business fails. But the truth is that they did not return nor develop the land, just leaving it vacant for years. The government finally reached an agreement with these enterprises to develop the vacant land for commercial purposes, on condition that these enterprises had to hand over 50% of the land transfer fees to share the rental income with the government. This is a sensible proposal because the land is owned by the state, not by these enterprises. Since the government can only use half of the land transfer fees to build infrastructure, such as the metros line, the old town is often redeveloped in an intensive manner. That's why Shanghai's urban density remains so high.

Fig. 2 shows the urbanization of Kunshan: a large amount of farmland was divided and damaged, which might trigger ecological and environmental problems despite good economic returns.

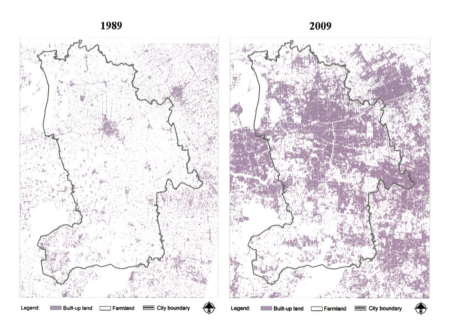

Fig. 2
Urbanization in
Kunshan from
1989 to 2009

Here is another example, which took place in Taipingqiao Area of Xintiandi in Shanghai. The developer originally planned to preserve the area's old town. They even invited Luo Xiaowei, a professor from Tongji University, to conduct research there. After an in-depth study, Professor Luo provided actual evidence of the area's heritage. However, the developer found out that it would cost a lot to renovate the old buildings and relocate the local residents. The amount of compensation involved is even higher than that required for preserving old buildings in Europe. As a result, the developer eventually chose to build high-rise apartments there, which contributed to the high housing prices of the area. Such are unique circumstances China finds itself in.

The old houses give a city a distinctive cultural flavor. If the city is full of tall buildings, it will look dull and unattractive. The demolition of old houses and construction of high-rises may work in the interest of local residents and developers, but not for people like me. It is such a pity for a city to lose its historic buildings. In conclusion, all the phenomena I've mentioned are driven by rent seeking.

4. Equity and efficiency in land development quota allocation

Land development quotas from territorial spatial planning have been used for more than 20 years in China. Quotas are allocated by the central government for a city's development. Cities often compete with each other for the quotas, in order to have the right to develop the land and make it valuable. It is actually a bonus of urbanization.

However, inequalities exist in the allocation of land development quotas. Big cities often get more quotas than small cities, and villages close to urban areas get more quotas than those far from urban areas. I think since land is state-owned, the quotas should be allocated per capita without discrimination.

The land development quota trading market means that cities can trade with other cities for quotas. For example, Gansu may not need many quotas due to its slow urbanization, so it can sell some quotas to Shanghai. In this way, Gansu will get fiscal revenue, and Shanghai will get the quotas it needs. It will make urbanization more efficient, so that cities won't rely too heavily on land financing or focus on constructing ghost cities.

Anti-urbanism now appears in the West. Efficiency is pursued at the cost of equity, which is actually important. Our team once carried out a study in Songjiang District in Shanghai. In Fig. 3, the dark areas are construction land, while the white areas are farmland. Such planning is chaotic. We need to go back to the drawing board. The picture on the right shows what we call a "compact city",

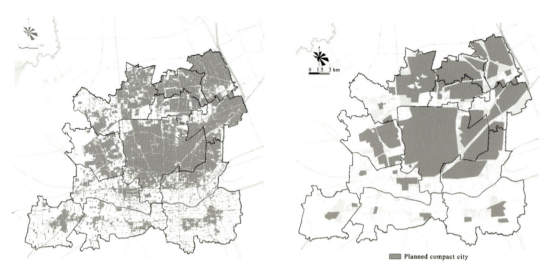

Planned compact city

Fig. 3
Unbalanced planning of Songjiang District and "Compact City"

in which urban and rural areas are distinct from each other. It looks much more orderly.

Many problems can emerge in urban planning. First of all, the villages that are located near urban areas in the north were given higher quotas, while those in the south received fewer quotas due to their poor location. This resulted in the widening income gap between villages. Similarly, the area of construction land given to each village ranges from a low of 62 to a high of 209 hectares. Songjiang District used to have 2 560 hectares of construction land. When the government cut the overall quotas and directed land development quotas to other places, the area of construction land in Songjiang was reduced to 960 hectares. But the reduction was disproportionately felt in different places. Those with few quotas received ever fewer quotas. There was still sizeable construction land in the northern villages, while the southern villages were left with virtually no construction land. Why were those southern villages treated unfairly? The property market is not driven by balanced demand. When urban planning is made in line with the market, such imbalance appears even more pronounced. After the reduction, some villages still get 283 hectares of construction land, compared with some that only get 3. This reform further widens the gap between villages. The intentions of reform are good, but the design is problematic. In my opinion, more attention should be paid to the equity of allocation.

A balanced allocation scheme and trading of land development quotas will promote urban restructuring. But the implementation of the scheme may be prone to conflicts because people are generally reluctant to be relocated. We all want to have a livable environment, but the means with which we achieve this goal should be equitable and benefits everyone.

Urban Forms and Urban Livability: From the Perspective of Diseconomies of Agglomeration

Sun Bindong

Director, China Administrative Planning Research Center, East China Normal University

I will introduce our studies on urban forms and urban livability from the perspective of diseconomies of agglomeration. A team of my students and I have spent several years on these studies.

1. Research questions

(1) Economies and diseconomies of agglomeration.

The concept of economies of agglomeration is not new. It originated from Johann Heinrich von Thünen's model of the single central city in the Isolated State. Later, Alfred Marshall proposed three external benefits of economies of agglomeration: labor pooling, proximity to suppliers and customers, and knowledge spillover brought by human capital accumulation. The school of new economic geography, with Paul Krugman and Masahisa Fujita as its two leading figures, believes that economies of agglomeration are conducive to increasing returns of scale. Scholars have agreed that economies of agglomeration can bring three benefits, namely, sharing, matching and learning. In addition to theoretical studies, relevant empirical studies have looked into the size or density of cities and used them as variables to measure the economic benefits of agglomeration. There has been much discussion about whether big cities are better than small ones. Generally, scholars who favor large cities acknowledge economies of agglomeration. Still, as a coin has two sides, excessive agglomeration will cause diseconomies, such as traffic congestion, high land prices, air pollution, and social conflicts.

Diseconomies have occurred in practice, for example, North America experienced suburbanization and multi-centralization after agglomeration reached a certain level. The diseconomies of agglomeration make single city centers disperse outwards and form multi-center structures in the suburbs. The metropolitan area we refer to today is actually the epitome of the polycentric urban structure. Metropolitan areas in North America and Japan are functional cities. Both the academic and the political communities have been discussing the issue of metropolitan areas. The concept of a metropolitan area has been expanded or even misunderstood. Now, a metropolitan area has been extended far beyond the original concept of commuting zones in geographical studies. It is difficult to agree on a common definition. Polycentric urban regions and city clusters in western Europe all have polycentric structures. Even China's productivity layout should have a polycentric structure, instead of concentrating only on the southeast coastal areas. There are far fewer studies on diseconomies than on economies of agglomeration. In particular, much less attention has been paid to the non-economic effects of diseconomies of agglomeration.

(2) Developed countries in the west actively advocate the compact urban form.

Developed countries in the West, especially those in North America, have been active in advocating the compact urban form, namely urban agglomeration. A World Health Organization (WHO) document mentioned prioritizing compactness to promote health. The document intends to provide guidance to all countries, but the patterns and experience supporting it came from only North American countries. Therefore, it is very one-sided. New Urbanism and Low Carbonism in North America also emphasize compactness in their suggestions for China's urbanization. But should China have more agglomeration since it has been very compact? I have doubts about this. Their views have flaws and may lead us to dire consequences. So, to refute their arguments is an important motivation for our research.

There are different definitions for compactness, but its main variable is population density. Cities with high population density are more compact than those with low density. The West believes

Fig. 1
WHO health
guidelines

WHO Discussion Paper（9 April 2018）
Physical activity for health More active people for a healthier world: draft global action plan on physical activity 2018—2030
Action 2.1   Strengthen the integration of urban and transport planning policies to prioritize the principles of compact, mixed land use, at all levels of government as appropriate, to deliver highly connected neighbourhoods to enable and promote walking, cycling, other forms of mobility involving the use of wheels (including wheelchairs, scooters and skates) and the use of public transport, in urban, peri-urban and rural communities.

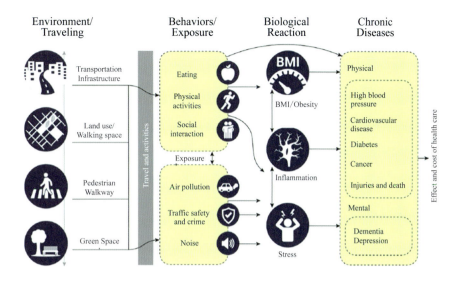

that compactness can improve urban livability because the distances between people and things are shorter, so people can travel in a non-motorized way, thus reducing traffic congestion and improving air quality. In addition, walking can improve health and lead to more interaction and meetings, which increase social capital and happiness.

(3) Can the compact urban form promote urban livability in China?

Unlike the United States, China, especially its eastern part is densely populated. City dwellers in China cram in high-rise buildings, while their western counterparts live in sparsely distributed idyllic villas. Cities have different levels of population density and residences, so they certainly require different levels of compactness.

Shanghai and Tokyo have similar land areas, but Tokyo has a population larger than Shanghai's. Population distribution of Tokyo is more balanced, while Shanghai's is more concentrated, especially in the city center. On a finer scale, Shanghai has already been far more crowded than Tokyo. However, due to its uneven population distribution, Shanghai accommodates a smaller population than Tokyo.

Chinese residence

Western residence

2. Hypothesis: the impact of compactness on urban livability in China

Our research hypothesis is that urban forms will affect urban livability, and population density is taken as the major variable of compactness. The West believes that compactness will make cities more livable, promote non-motorized travel, improve air quality, and increase social capital. For example, some scholars believe that compactness helps people lose weight, is good for their health, and brings them happiness. But we believe that China has already been very compact and that more agglomeration can backfire, causing diseconomies.

Fig. 4
Influence of
compact urban
form on urban
livability

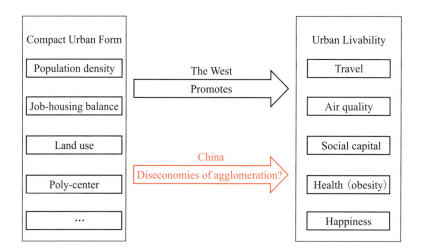

Over-compactness is detrimental to urban livability because of the following reasons. Traffic congestion is an example. When cities become excessively compact, it is possible that some people will keep driving cars. Even if some give up, more cars will converge in crowded places, exacerbating traffic congestion and air pollution. Urban residents now live in high-rise buildings. Cities are stranger societies where people have little communication, which is less conducive to social capital than the non-urban societies with lower population density. In addition, densely-populated areas provide fewer places for physical activities and these places are less accessible. Therefore, fewer opportunities for exercising will inevitably lead to obesity. Higher population density also means higher work intensity, faster pace of life and more stress. From a psychological point of view, stress can cause faster eating, less sleep, and damage to health.

3. Results of empirical research

Since we always pursue empirical studies, more of our research work on urbanization is also empirical, given that theories are pointless if there is no evidence to support them. I will present four aspects of empirical evidence we have found.

(1) Compactness and travel.

The studies mentioned in this paragraph are from our published papers. Using data from the 2014 Chinese Labor-force Dynamics Survey (CLDS) completed by the Center for Social Science Research at Sun Yat-sen University, the first study found that increases in both urban population size and density (including population density in neighborhoods) will lead to longer commuting time. This conclusion is relatively reliable because it is drawn by controlling other necessary variables and using three multi-layer models of different scales. The second study used data of Shanghai residents in the Fudan University's Survey on Social Change in the Yangtze River Delta Region (FYRST), and was built on a multi-level model. The results show that the rise in street population density leads to a significant increase in commuting time.

(2) Compactness and air quality.

In theory, a more compact city means fewer cars and better air quality. But that is only one side of the picture. It is precisely because of compactness that sparsely located vehicles tend to concentrate in compact spaces, causing more pollution. The total amount of pollutants may not increase. But in places with high vehicle concentrations, air pollution is getting worse. Such problem is particularly acute in China. At present despite the high population and building density in some areas, the possibility of people not driving or not buying a car is very low. But in the near future many people will buy cars to travel or flaunt their wealth after becoming rich. Using data from Shanghai, our study found a positive correlation between population density at street level and the PM 2.5 concentration.

(3) Compactness and social capital.

Using data from 3 856 urban residents in the 2014 China Labor-force Dynamics Survey (CLDS), this study not only examined the direct effect of compactness on social capital, but also further analyzed the mechanism of the effect with structural equation modeling. The mechanism exploration was not in any of the aforementioned studies, because it is difficult to do and dependent on the availability of data. The data collected for this study was good enough for us to examine the effect mechanism. When defining the key concept of social capital, we used the number of acquaintances in a community, the trust between residents, mutual help and group participation as dependent variables. The research found that high population density is not related to at least three dependent variables, including acquaintance number, trust, and mutual help. Results of the structural equation modeling analysis reveal that high population density reduces residents' sense of security and the frequency of communication, hence leading to the decline of social capital.

(4) Compact and Health.

Three studies have been conducted in this aspect. My research over the past few years has focused on compact and health, especially the obesity problem.

Carried out in 2016, the first study used data from 15 356 observation values in the China Family Panel Studies (CFPS) from 2010 to 2012, and the structural equation as the research method. It found that higher population density in neighborhoods increases obesity rates. Fig. 6 shows that population density does reduce the possibility of car travel and therefore brings down the obesity rate. So, the path on the upper left has a negative value. However, in terms of the net effect, population density is still positively correlated with the obesity rate. There are also some other potential mechanisms:

First, China has already been very compact, so more agglomeration will not induce the same effect, namely increasing non-motorized travel in China as it has in the US and Europe.

Second, shorter travel distances in densely populated cities will lead to less exercise no matter what kind of travel mode is used, including walking and cycling.

Third, high population density also causes less outdoor space and fewer physical activities. Our research demonstrates that residents of highly-populated neighborhoods spend less time in physical activities and more time in static activities, such as playing cards at home, watching television, studying and reading.

Fourth, high population density leads to a faster pace of life in cities. We found that people who eat quickly and sleep less are more likely to become obese. Highly-populated areas tend to have a concentration of catering facilities, such as snack bars and ice cream shops, so people dine out more

Fig. 5
The influence mechanism of community population density on BMI

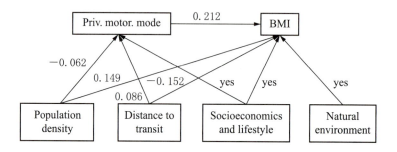

often and obesity rates increase.

The second study of compactness and health used data from the 2012 CLDS. A U-shaped relationship was found between urban population density and the BMI index which indicates obesity. When population density is very low, increasing density can reduce the BMI index. But after the density exceeds its optimal value, BMI rises in lockstep with it.

As we went further, the data we used became more reliable. In the third study, we used data from the China Health and Nutrition Survey (CHNS) conducted in 2004, 2006, 2009 and 2011 by the University of North Carolina at Chapel Hill and the National Institute for Nutrition and Health of the Chinese Center for Disease Control and Prevention. We adopted a fixed-effect model. To examine the relationship between urban forms and obesity, we used the waist-to-hip ratio, an indicator of abdominal fat accumulation, to measure obesity, because it shows s more accurate results for East Asians than the body mass index (BMI) which is suitable for measuring obesity of Europeans and Americans. Middle-aged men, especially intellectuals, have sedentary habits, resulting in rapid accumulation of abdominal fat. Middle-aged people who drive frequently also have more abdominal fat, which is the main reason for weight gain. The results show that population density and the waist-hip ratios in neighborhoods have a U-shaped relationship. When population density is low, increasing the density decreases the waist-to-hip ratio. But after the density surpasses the optimal point, the ratio rises in lockstep with it. It is worth noting that in some Chinese cities, population density in neighborhoods has begun to exceed their optimal levels, and obesity rates have started to increase. The mechanism in our study has been tested true, showing that higher population density elevates the waist-to-hip ratio by cutting the time people spend on physical activities.

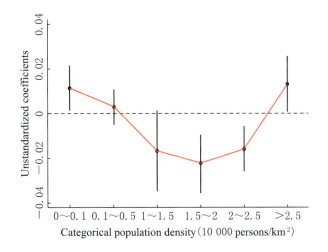

Fig. 6
The U-shaped relationship between population density of neighborhoods and the waist-to-hip ratio

4. Summary

(1) Conclusion.

In general, these studies on urban livability reveal that high population density lowers happiness. In addition, an inverted U-shaped pattern between the compact urban form and urban livability was found for the first time. In other words, with the increase of compactness, urban livability rises from a low level to a moderate one. But if a city is excessively compact, it becomes unlivable. This can provide some scientific basis for enhancing urban livability. Economies and diseconomies of agglomeration are equally important, but economists focus more on the former one, whereas very few studies and literature are about the latter. So, I look forward to more scholarly discussion about the diseconomies of agglomeration.

Fig. 7
An inverted U-shaped relationship between the compact urban form and livability

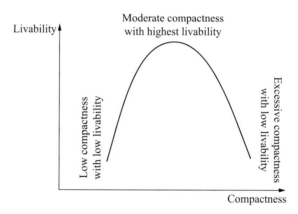

(2) Suggestion for policy making.

North American cities have relatively low population density. They are on the left side of the inverted U shape, so more compactness brings higher livability. But Chinese cities are too compact, so they are on the right side of the inverted U shape, which means they have become unlivable. Therefore, China should formulate its own standard for urban planning and development, and prevent the dominance of real estate developers. These profit-driven developers do not care about residents' health, so they want to increase population density. But as a scholar, I think high population density is not good for health. What cities in China need is moderate compactness, so the country's urban development should not be misled by WHO's health guidelines and should be guided by its own standards for urban livability or development models formulated on the basis of China's situation.

Resilient Cities Against Climate Change: Nature vs. Individual

Zhang Xiaoling

Professor of Department of Public Policy, City University of Hong Kong,

Deputy Director of China's Regional Sustainable Development Commission

1. The "changed" and "unchanged" in the process of sustainable development

In the development process, human beings have experienced continuous changes in social, economic, environmental and cultural aspects, for example, the emergence of deglobalization technology and the conflicts between governments and markets. Amid such a complicated situation, it is necessary for us to consider what has changed and what remained as it was in the development process.

Table 1

Changes in the process of sustainable development

	The first agricultural revolution	The first and second industrial revolutions	The third and fourth industrial revolutions
Historical Eras	2000—1000 B.C.	17th century — the 1940s	The 1980s — present
Population	Small size	Rapid growth	Population explosion
Technological development	Plants and animals	Steam engines, electricity, machinery, transportation	Internet, gene technology, etc.
Resource and energy demand	Low	Increase rapidly	High
Resource and energy supply	abundant	Depleting	Inadequate
The spatial division of labor in the process of global development	Division of labor within tribes: the initial stage of production specialization	The rise of colonialism led to the first international division of labor	Integrated global production network, in both the northern andsouthern hemispheres

From the first agricultural revolution to the first and second industrial revolutions, even to the coming technological revolution based on artificial intelligence (AI), the global population has grown from one with a small size to the current population explosion. But the population may decline and stay on a declining trend in the future. In terms of technological development, humans are increasingly dependent on resources and energy. For example, in the past, humans lived on the domestication of plants and animals. Then, they invented steam engines, electricity, machinery and modern transportation. Now, humans rely more on the Internet and gene technology. However, the resource and energy supply of nature has changed from being abundant to relatively inadequate now, and the division of labor has therefore expanded from the primitive tribes to the whole world. Now, the era of "deglobalization" is on the way. These changes have led people to look at the issues concerning increasing global population, economic carbon emissions, fossil fuels and waste.

So, where are the growth boundaries? Where are the city boundaries? Can the earth survive the problems and challenges caused by human's threatening nature's limits? According to the Three

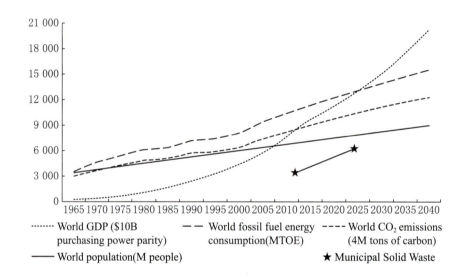

Fig. 1
Concerns on global issues

------- World GDP ($10B purchasing power parity)   — — World fossil fuel energy consumption(MTOE)   ---- World CO$_2$ emissions (4M tons of carbon)

——— World population(M people)   ★ Municipal Solid Waste

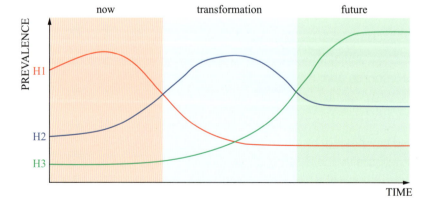

Fig. 2
Three horizons chart

Horizons Framework developed by Bill Sharpe in 2013, the third horizon is the ideal one, namely, "Victory in the Green Path".

2. Resilient cities against climate change

Scientists, economists, and managers can definitely use linear thinking and make linear assumptions, but social, economic and urban development requires systems thinking. Daniel Kahneman, a professor of economics at Princeton University, proposed hedonic treadmill theory. The theory explains that when a person seeks satisfaction from buying goods, he fuels the economy at the expense of the environment and resources, although technological progress might reduce such damage and consumption to a certain extent.

Fig. 3
Systems thinking
for economic
and urban
development

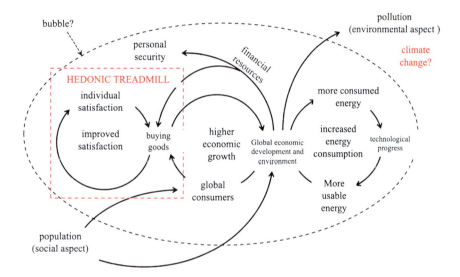

It is undeniable that environmental pollution and climate change caused by economic development have brought great challenges for us, such as economic recessions and an aging population, which reflects the dilemma of striking a balance between individual and social development, and immediate and long term needs.

In this context, I proposed the topic "Resilient Cities Against Climate Change". In 2013, Rockefeller Foundation announced its list of the 100 most resilient cities in the world. It turned out that most of these cities were along seas, rivers or valleys.

What enabled these cities to survive, adapt and thrive in the face of acute shocks and chronic stresses? Cities can be divided into different types as follows: reflective, resource-based, robust, redundant, flexible, inclusive and integrated cities.

The concept of sustainable cities experienced three stages. The earliest is "environmental protection" as proposed in *Silent Spring*, the second is "sustainable development" as mentioned above in the linear system, and the third stage is the cutting-edge concept of resilient cities. Resilience means planning the future despite uncertainties. Building resilient cities require considering how to shift from short-term actions to long-term strategies, from efforts by separate sectors or individuals to collaborative approaches. That is, compared to the previous two vulnerable systems, resilient cities look at how to help cities speed up recovery or help them recover to the original status after being struck by disasters, such as floods and smog.

My team is trying to deal with this topic from the perspective of systems thinking, which entails the use of some well-known models of material and energy flow analysis. We find a common feature in complex dynamic phenomena. We find that in unrelated spatial and temporal scales, uncertain related events are less predictable and always occur in different fields, such as COVID-19 and climate change. The complex dynamic phenomena can be considered as: nature and society try to organize themselves and reach an equilibrium in a chaotic world. As a result, the relationships between individuals, cities, and social and natural systems are becoming more and more complex. To thoroughly study cities, it is necessary to focus on spatial scale, and consider cities as networks and traffic systems.

As for the individual level, COVID-19 is a good example. Surviving the COVID-19 requires individual resilience, namely, physical strength and a strong body. At the city level, resilience is also needed. Cities need to adapt themselves to the changes in development, so as to cope with risks or crises. To this end, the primary solution is building "a city against risks", which is based on short-term planning or even decision-making in panic. The better solution is building a "city of hope" based on long-term planning made by consensus decision-making with partners, hence turning risks into opportunities.

3. Nature-based solutions (NBS)

Cities, the key to mitigating climate change, are facing threats from both humans and nature. NBS was proposed by the International Union for Conservation of Nature at the beginning of this century:

"Nature-based Solutions are actions to protect, sustainably manage, and restore natural and modified ecosystems that address societal challenges effectively and adaptively, simultaneously providing human well-being and biodiversity benefits."[1]

① Cohen-Shacham, E., Walters, G., Janzen, C. and Maginnis, S. (eds.), 2016, *Nature-based Solutions to address global societal challenges*, Gland, Switzerland: IUCN, pp. xiii + 97.

Fig. 4
Systems thinking
for models based
on correlation

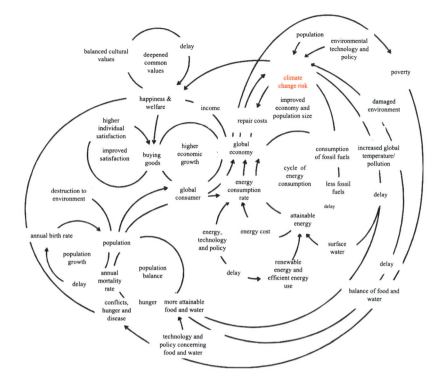

Fig. 5
Models of
material and
onorgy flow
analysis

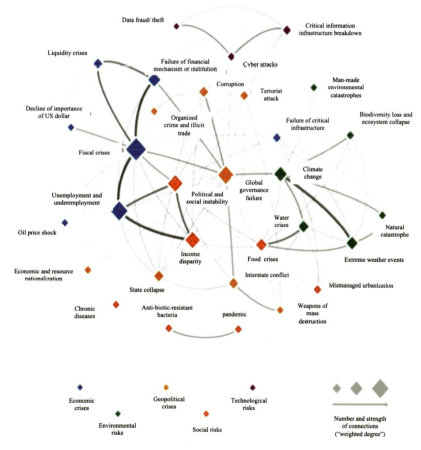

Fig. 6
The core of NBS
theory

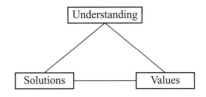

Note: Understanding means to know NBS theory and the relationship between human and nature; solutions shall be realized by mankind and nature's practices; values represent the contribution of nature to human beings.

Table 2
The role and relationship between nature and human in the five patterns

Pattern	Understanding		Solutions	Values
	Nature	Individual	The role of nature and individual	NCP
Natural	Best and original	Potential risks for environment	Keep nature in the best situation by reducing the impacts from humans; Retreat from places where humans stay, that is, do nothing	The value of the earth
Native	Predictable and historical	Promote recovering history	Keep nature in the primitive status; Help nature recover; Reduce human interventions	Evolutionary and ecological process
Novel	Unpredictable, and try to be as healthy as possible	Potentially promote creating a new ecological environment	Explore adaptive management in experiment	Create and maintain the ecological environment; The function as a tool
Green	Taken good care of, and try to reduce negative impacts	Alleviate potential negative impacts	Reduce consumption; Recycle; Reduce negative impacts on the environment; Adopt green practices	Adjustment for physical and mental status; Lifestyle
Cultural	More efforts on cultural goods	Governor of nature	Encourage individuals to help restore ecological system; Educate individuals to protect the nature	Interactions between nature and individuals

Table 3
The key value of five patterns and their pros and cons

Pattern	Key value	Advantage	Disadvantage
Natural	Being natural	Least investment required	Unpredictable occurrence in the nature
Native	Historical ecological system	Easy to adapt for local creatures	It takes a lot of time to complete natural succession of historical conditions
Novel	Functional experiment	Quantitative objective and result	No standard for experimental results
Green	"Green" is better than "Ungreen"	Relatively easy to implement and the process is fast	Being "green" does not necessarily mean being "ecological"
Cultural	Cultivating individuals to protect the nature	Strengthen the relationship between human and nature	Time-consuming; Potential risks for the nature

NBS describes innovative efforts needed for addressing challenges in society, including climate change, biodiversity conservation, ecosystem management and construction of sustainable livelihoods, all of which should be realized in a natural way rather than a technological way.

In order to reshape the role of humans and nature in the development of resilient cities, the following issues should be considered: First, how to maximize the effectiveness of NBS? For example, who should take charge of urban green spaces, and how can we use the spaces? Second, how can we draw experience from the natural system and translate it into urban practice? Third, under which circumstance is NBS more effective than traditional solutions? For example, nature-based

Fig. 7
The relationship between the five patterns

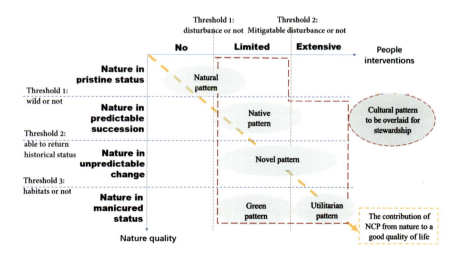

coastal wetland projects? Fourth, how can we integrate NBS in urban spatial planning and decision-making at the local level, such as building more living laboratories and green infrastructure in cities? Fifth, how can we turn NBS into financing opportunities, scale up the use and leverage private capital?

The development of the NBS theory should be combined with an understanding of the value of resilient cities. On this basis, the concepts of "human" and "nature" are redefined: five patterns were proposed, including natural, native, novel, green and cultural patterns, as well as advantages and disadvantages of each pattern. Since each pattern has its pros and cons, it is important to find the appropriate NBS according to the development of local ecosystems, so as to find a balance between urban development and city resilience.

Here are the advantages of NBS: First, the patterns are classified into five categories, which enables different cities to find their NBS according to their features; Second, it unifies the solution and results, which avoids random use and unconscious destruction to the environment; Third, the patterns provide a platform a continuum for human and nature to adapt to each other; Fourth, these patterns provide a continuum for policymakers and practitioners to map appropriate NBS practices in different situations and consider the possibilities for behavioral changes.

4. Individual resilience based solutions (IRBS)

The theory of individual resilience-based solutions was jointly proposed by Haozhi Pan from Shanghai Jiao Tong University China Institute of Urban Governance and me. As can be seen in the city resilience framework, the city's exposure to the outside world and vulnerability might impede its development. Therefore, we need to consider how to help cities adapt to risks and become resilient in the face of Black Swan events, such as epidemics, floods, and typhoons.

I believe the key to helping cities build resilience lies not in urban planning but in individual resilience.

Fig. 8
City resilience
framework

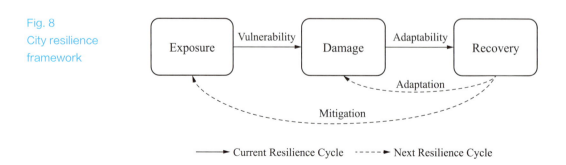

提升社区和城市品质

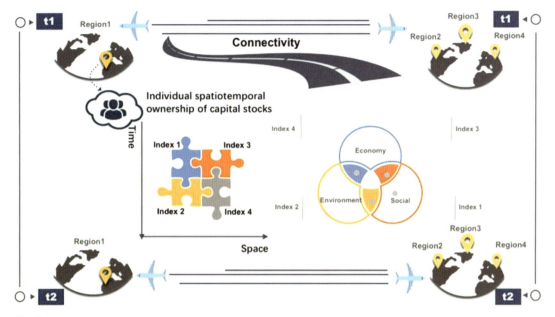

Fig. 9
Construction of individual resilience index (IRI)

First, the theory looks at individual and spatial-temporal dynamic resilience index. It means that we ought to find an individual's opportunity, possibility and vulnerability, so as to examine his or her accessibility within a spatial-temporal coordinate system within the individual space. Let me take homework separation as an example. Now I live in Hong Kong, and the commute time of traveling

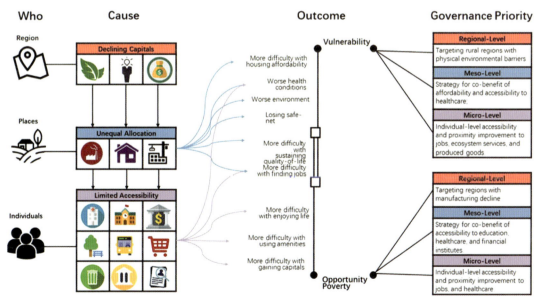

Fig. 10
Study results using IRI

to work and returning home every day represents the accessibility I mentioned above. In short, accessibility can be understood as the access to work, education, and ecosystem services.

Second, the theory looks at individual spatiotemporal ownership of capital, that is, the total costs that it takes an individual to travel to a city or a region in a city. It means that we need to quantify the factors and construct a multi-dimensional individual resilience index (IRI). Then we can interpret traditional static indicators as fixed and mobilized capital that can be applied to individuals and cities, hence measuring capital by using individual accessibility as the spatial ownership.

Third, the theory uses "vulnerability" and "opportunity" as factors to measure the "non-decaying wealth" of individuals as time capital stock ownership. The results of this study can help discuss the resilience governance framework at the individual level, city level, and regional level.

Constructing individual spatial-temporal resilience index actually depends on Liebig's law of the minimum in the field of management and control. It means that the sustainable competitiveness of a city depends on its weakness, rather than its strength. In other words, it is necessary to construct individual spatial-temporal resilience index to calculate and track the weakness of individuals and cities arise from vulnerability and opportunity poverty that impedes their development.

5. Limits of individual accessibility leads to opportunity poverty

We designed a model to describe how IRI affects local vulnerability and opportunity poverty. For example, if we suppose that the shortage of ecological infrastructure in a city is caused by its insufficient economic capital, and this shortage is exacerbated by unequal distribution of public capital in fixed capital investment. For individuals, the accessibility limits of ecosystem services, accumulated in regions and spread to local areas, are caused by the local natural capital shortage and unequal distribution. The limits tend to lead to unfavorable consequences, which gets us pondering over the following questions: why do school district houses cluster in some areas? Why are central business districts (CBD) always surrounded by public green spaces? Why can't the poor have access to these common benefits as they want? These questions remind us of a city's accessibility limits or sources of opportunity poverty. These questions encourage us to think further about what the city resilience is. Another example is that in the event of an epidemic, the accessibility limits of healthcare infrastructure and ecosystem services in a city may lead to deterioration in individuals' health. Unequal local capital distribution may increase vulnerability, lead to losses because of vulnerability and poverty caused by lack of opportunity, hence further aggravate the instability and uncertainty of urban areas.

Therefore, we have constructed a Bayesian evaluation model on the basis of individual-based

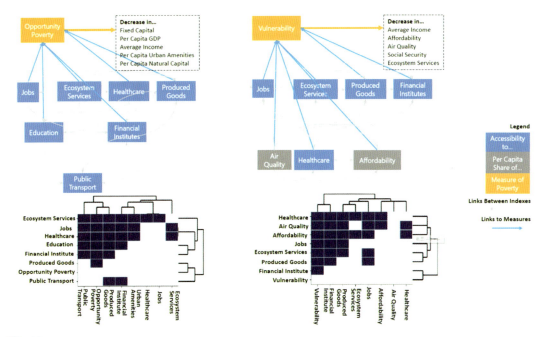

Fig. 11
ISRF base on individuals

spatial-temporal resilience frameworks (ISRF). We analyzed with Bayesian network and adopted calibration procedures to measure the accessibility of transportation, education, health care, urban services and ecosystem services across the country. Finally, we achieved the thermodynamic diagram of individual spatial-temporal resilience. As depicted in this diagram, we can see a very clear correlation between "opportunity" and "vulnerability", and it also provides us with a dynamic

Fig. 12
Calibration procedure

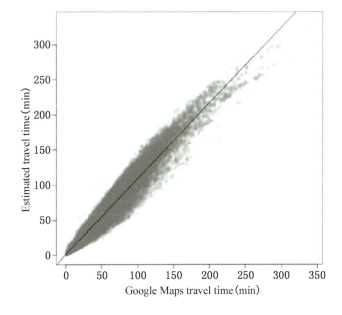

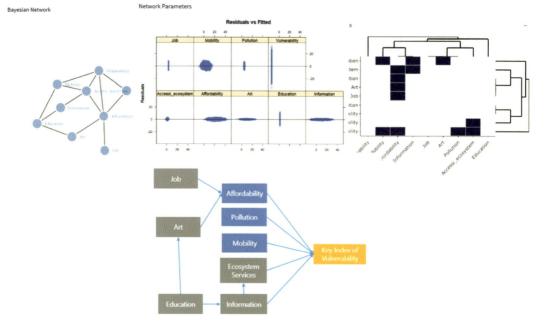

Fig. 13
Bayesian network model and study results

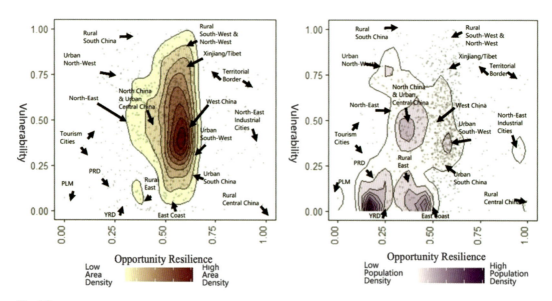

Fig. 14
Thermodynamic diagram of individual spatial-temporal resilience

understanding of the interconnectedness and systematicness of resilience at the city level.

As is depicted in Fig. 15, we can find the regions in China with the highest density of opportunity, poverty and vulnerability, measured by key factors such as affordability, ecosystem services, and air pollution.

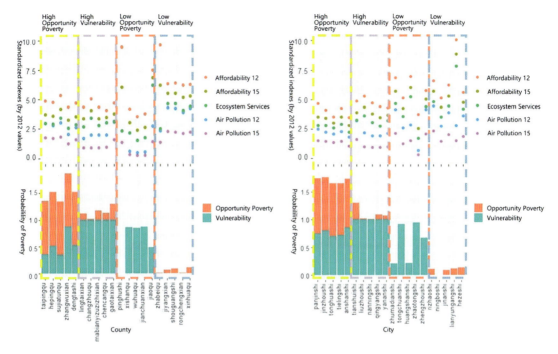

Fig. 15
Interconnectedness and systematicness of resilience at the city level

6. Conclusions about urban "opportunity" and "vulnerability"

First, cities with low opportunity poverty and low vulnerability do better in resisting risks and pressure, and have better access to ecosystem services in 2012.

Second, cities with low opportunity poverty tend to have high vulnerability, and cities with low vulnerability tend to have low opportunity poverty. The reason might be that most cities with low vulnerability have better infrastructure and facilities, which shelter them from extreme poverty in the face of recession.

Third, the relationship of opportunity and vulnerability in China's counties is very complicated. Generally speaking, because of better affordability, counties with high opportunity poverty tend to have lower vulnerability than cities, such as Zhangwu County in Northeast China. But we need further study to refine our study results.

Fourth, the relationship between vulnerability and opportunity in cities constantly changes, and opportunity poverty is often highly correlated with an economic recession. For example, from 2012 to 2015, opportunity poverty mainly occurred in the areas where state-owned enterprises and traditional manufacturing industries declined, namely part of the cities in northeast China and coastal areas dedicated to conventional manufacturing.

7. City resilience framework

Based on these conclusions, how can we better respond to the risks and pressure?

Building resilient cities requires efforts in science, economy, society, and law and governance, with adaptation and mitigation at the core. If we integrate nature and individuals into this framework, we can respond in the ways as Fig. 17 shows. In this framework, the starting point is planning with uncertainty, the key is resilient city transformation, and the most important part is risk prevention. Regarding city governance, equality, integration and sustainable economic development are required.

8. Conclusion

First, our study looks at not only the cities but also the citizens in China. As the theme of the 2010 Shanghai World Expo puts it, "Better City, Better Life". To this end, we can look for "the minimum part" of individual and natural resilience. For instance, by virtue of Bayesian assessment of individual-based spatial-temporal resilience frameworks and the mapping on vulnerability and poverty of China's urban areas, we found that China's west rural areas, mountainous areas, traditional industrial cities, and places surrounding these city clusters facing recession are most prone to vulnerability and poverty opportunity.

Fig. 16
Natural and
individual city
resilience
Framework

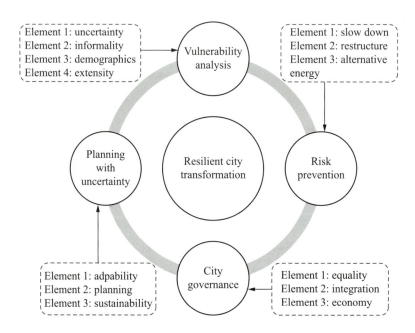

Second, I believe that scientists and scholars dedicated to urban governance should work together to find redundant, modularized, and diversified components or parts in urban governance. For example, they can define indicators directly contributing to and areas most prone to opportunity poverty and vulnerability, analyze the common beneficiaries of multiple indicators mentioned above, and persuade health care, education, insurance and financial institutions to jointly resist risks, namely so-called joint prevention and control. In this way, these kinds of risks could be dealt with despite inadequate individual health care affordability and education accessibility.

Third, we need to redefine the stages of resilient city development, which can be divided into three phases: city, community and individual. The deepest feeling that this pandemic left on me is the inadequate individual-based prevention. We need to internalize the redefined system to combine natural capital, social capital and individual capital, and rely on individual resilience to construct a built-in system for collective action. For example, building resilient cities under the risk of climate change is a smart city solution that integrates nature and individuals. It requires collective actions, such as the realization of technology maximization. In terms of the individual level, I think the key is to improve opportunity accessibility and reduce vulnerability. The population size in cities depends on the individual's choice: whether to seek work, receive education and look for other opportunities in big cities.

Fourth, resilience and adaptability are so abstract that resilient cities become extremely expensive public goods. In a world where resilient cities are expensive and scarce, the ultimate goal must be to find a sustainable trade-off between carefully designed human choices and nature's self-organization: building cities that allow people to live in harmony with nature.

Spatial Planning and Sustainable Development in East Asia

Shen Zhenjiang

Professor of Division of Environmental Design, Kanazawa University, Japan

1. Introduction to the Book *Spatial Planning and Sustainable Development*

Spatial Planning and Sustainable Development is a book published by the International Community of Spatial Planning and Sustainable Development (SPSD). It is closely related to the theme of this forum and discusses spatial planning and sustainable development in East Asia, which is also the topic I am going to address today.

I could identify four schools of thought regarding the sustainable urban form in spatial planning. They include (1) the urban containment policy in the U.S., where the government draws up plans for land use and restricts urban sprawl; (2) the compact city concept brought up by the British; (3) the eco-city model proposed by a group of Americans; and (4) the neo-traditional development originated in Europe. Urban sustainable development can be assessed by a number of criteria, including compactness, transportation sustainability, density, mixed land use, diversity, energy conservation, and environmental protection.

Urban form is the result of interaction among multiple stakeholders. In this process the public and private sectors play an important role. The private sector affects land use because on the one hand, private businesses tend to set up their business in the cheapest area, which leads to urban expansion; on the other hand, they want to increase their scale in order to maximize their profits and operation efficiency. In contrast, the public sector has different motives. As the main provider of public services, the public sector aims to achieve efficient urban construction without increasing financial costs.

Public policy can play a vital role in shaping the urban sustainable development. The book I am going to introduce today focuses on using public policy to steer urban development. It provides useful examples and practices of spatial planning and sustainable development that have taken place in East

提升社区和城市品质

Asia including Japan, South Korea, China's mainland, and Taiwan of China.

2. Case studies on sustainable development and spatial planning

In terms of degree of urban sustainable development in East Asia, developed countries, such as Japan and South Korea, have gone through the phase of urban growth and are now facing urban decline. They have to cope with decreasing population, decaying city centers, and have to find ways for urban regeneration. In comparison, countries in the midst of urban growth, such as China, Thailand and Vietnam, often have to concern themselves with providing a favorable environment for investments, especially business investments, and addressing problems in employment, housing and transportation in cities. In addition, in order to attain sustainable development goals, cities often have to balance economic growth, social equality and environmental protection. For the developed countries, whose major problems are population decline and urban decay, the major task is to revive the cities so they can better serve their urban functions.

The book comes in two parts, each part collating experiences of developed and developing countries and areas in spatial planning and sustainable development. The first part is on urbanization and sustainable society. Sustainable development is one of the vital goals of urbanization. In this process, we not only have to deal with problems that emerge in the process of urbanization, but also have to cope with urban expansion and urban population growth that follows the development. It is also important to balance the development of society, ecology and agriculture. The second part of the book is about the sustainable development of the ecosystem. Although sustainable development might hinder economic growth, governments need to take into account ecological and agricultural factors for the sake of steady social development.

In terms of land development pressure, cities need to work out and implement sound plans regarding the land use. They have to foster real estate development and consider traffic problems from an investment point of view. Despite the pressure of urban development, they have to consider how to avoid conflicts arising from improper use of land, design a greener city and minimize the appropriation of farmland and destruction of the ecosystem. Public policies can play a leading role in this process, particularly so for developed countries in Europe, North America and Asia.

It is important for countries facing urban declines, such as Japan and South Korea, to strengthen centrality of cities by encouraging influx of population into downtown areas, solving problems in an aging society, and facilitating urban renewal in city centers. China and Japan define urban renewal differently. The Chinese focus on housing while the Japanese, describing it as urban regeneration, emphasize more on the revival of urban functions of city centers and attracting businesses of emerging industries to downtown areas. Public policies also play a role on this front.

The Korea Advanced Institute of Science and Technology (KAIST) once proposed that in order to promote urban sustainable development[①], East Asian countries need to build a shared spatial database for holistic planning. Europe has set a good example in this regard, and we have some catching up to do.

The Korea Transport Institute (KOTI) also made a case study and found that up to 39 South Korean cities have been threatened by urban decline in recent years.[②] In particular, as the suburban land is being redeveloped, private enterprises tend to choose cheaper land in the suburbs to maximize their profits, which leads to urban sprawl and the declining function of its central area, and eventually to urban decline. South Korea is thus in urgent need to figure out a way to regenerate its downtown areas.

A study by the Ministry of Land, Infrastructure, Transport and Tourism of Japan (MLIT) also shows that the Japan's remote rural areas are dying,[③] and calls on the policy maker to give more agricultural subsidies, address the aging problem in agricultural regions, and to encourage more people to work in rural areas. For developed countries such as Japan and South Korea, they mainly grapple with two major problems: urban decline and the over-concentration of metropolitan areas.

In addition, aging is so grave in Japan that it not only exists in and around Tokyo but is seen in Japan's municipalities, mid-sized cities, and the rural areas.[④] Therefore, Japan needs to consider how to remake its regional planning and how to coordinate the spatial planning of people's life circles, not only on the macro level, but also on a micro level.

Renewing urban functions is also an area that cannot be neglected. Everyone now talks about smart city. Japan has also set up smart city pilots across the country.[⑤] These cities invest government subsidies in various projects, such as environmental symbiosis and smart energy, to update their urban functions.

① Ye, Kyung-rock, 2013, "The Possibility of Sharing Spatial Data and Research Cooperation Within East Asia Countries", 10.1007/978-94-007-5922-0_2.

② Lee, Bum-hyun, 2013, "A Study on Classification of Downtown Areas Based on Small and Medium Cities in Korea", 10.1007/978-94-007-5922-0_3.

③ Yamashita, Ryohei & Ichinose, Tomohiro, 2013, "Significance and Limitations of the Support Policy for Marginal Hamlets in the Strategy of Self-sustaining Regional Sphere Development", 10.1007/978-94-007-5922-0_4.

④ Nishino, Tatsuya, 2013, "Continuity of Relations Between Local Living Environments and the Elderly Moved to a Group Living", 10.1007/978-94-007-5922-0_5.

⑤ Balaban, Osman, 2013, "The Use of Indicators to Assess Urban Regeneration Performance for Climate-Friendly Urban Development: The Case of Yokohama Minato Mirai 21", 10.1007/978-94-007-5922-0_6.

To sum up, developed countries are mainly confronted with the urban decline, the need for urban renewal, and the disappearance of remote rural areas. They mainly use public policies to adjust their urban forms and to promote a sustainable economy.

3. Work Commute in Developing Countries

The first case is a study on the housing demand and business and residential area distribution in Beijing.[1] It is conducted by the Institute of Geographic Sciences and Natural Resources Research, Chinese Academy of Sciences. The study analyzes the housing demand in the city with a view to promote the development of public housing and rental housing, and ultimately alleviate the housing problem in Beijing.

The second case is about Thailand. I believe Bangkok shares a lot of similarity with Beijing in terms of its urbanization process. To maximize their profits, private companies in Thailand develop residential areas in places that they believe are profitable. Consequently, after decades of development, people often live unreasonably far away from their workplaces. This leads to severe traffic congestions in Thailand, especially within the Bangkok Metropolitan Region.[2] Similarly, similar problems also exist in Beijing and many other capital cities in China.

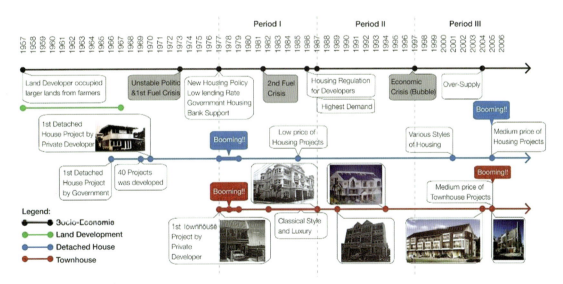

Fig. 1
Townhouse development in Thailand

①　Gao, Xiaolu, 2013, "T Modeling Housing Demand Structure: An Example of Beijing", 10.1007/978-94-007-5922-0_10.

②　Klinmalai, Siwaporn & Kanki, Kiyoko, 2013, "Characteristic of Sustainable Location for Townhouse Development in Bangkok and Greater Metropolitan Area, Thailand", 10.1007/978-94-007-5922-0_9.

4. Innovative solutions to traffic problems in developed areas

Developed countries and regions have fewer people, so they have less of a traffic problem and commute problem. But they also use innovative approaches in land and traffic issues. For example, Taiwan of China has built a round-the-island cycling route,[①] which is an effective solution and comes with recreational and health benefits.

Another important solution is to reduce car use and minimize commuting distance, which is conducive to sustainable development and helps carbon emission reduction in particular. Fig. 2 shows a simulation policy study conducted by Tsinghua University.[②] The study tries to figure out how

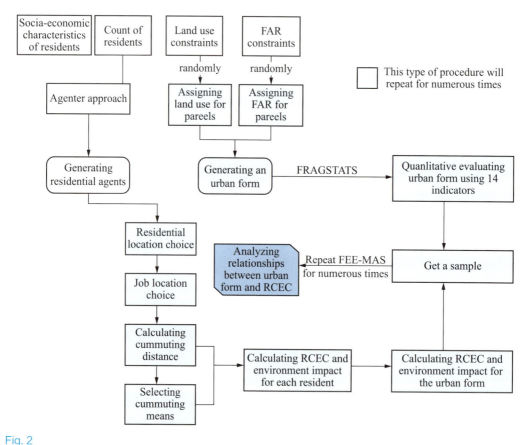

Fig. 2

Simulation study of Beijing's urban pattern, traffic energy consumption and their environmental impacts

---

① Pai, Brian & Hu, Tai-Shan, 2013, "The Role of the Knowledge Community and Transmission of Knowledge: A Case of Bicycle SMEs in Taiwan", 10.1007/978-94-007-5922-0_11.

② Long, Ying & Qizhi, Mao & Shen, Zhenjiang, 2013, "Urban Form, Transportation Energy Consumption, and Environment Impact Integrated Simulation: A Multi-agent Model", 10.1007/978-94-007-5922-0_13.

Beijing can reduce carbon emissions through improved traffic conditions and shorter commute to work.

Similar to what has been done in Taiwan of China, Japan is also researching on environmentally friendly smart transportation and attempts to find out how to promote walking as a way to relieve traffic congestions.[1] Japan hopes to make walking more convenient through personal mobility vehicles (PMVs).

Research walking accessibility is now a popular research topic in developed countries. The topic has also attracted the attention of cities with well-developed urban infrastructure in China, such as Xiamen.[2]

5. Urbanization requires a balance between socio-economic development and the protection of environment and agriculture

With the development of economy, humankind gradually forms a sustainable society. Urbanization is a process that involves both urban growth and urban decline. Developed and developing countries come across different problems in this process. In Asia, some countries are facing the development pressure of urban growth while other countries are dealing with urban decline.

Another problem related to sustainable development is to address the balance between socio economic development and the conservation of ecology and agriculture. Countries are making various efforts on this front. For example, in Japan, the Building Research Institute (BRI) has tried to reduce carbon emissions by promoting green buildigs, which can improve the city's micro thermal environment and create a better residential environment for the citizens. [3]

The BRI has also been trying to build "sponge cities", [4]which can collect rainwater to prevent it from going into rivers, thus reducing the risk of flooding and other urban disasters. The project will help reduce vulnerability of cities and enhance urban resilience.

In China, Beijing Normal University has developed an urban ecological analysis and

---

[1] Ando, Ryosuke & Li, Ang & Nishihori, Yasuhide & Kachi, Noriyasu, 2013, "Acceptability of Personal Mobility Vehicles to Public in Japan: Results of Social Trial in Toyota City", 10.1007/978-94-007-5922-0_12.

[2] Wang, Hui, 2013, "Mapping Walking Accessibility, Bus Availability, and Car Dependence: A Case Study of Xiamen, China", 10.1007/978-94-007-5922-0_14.

[3] Kato, Masashi, et al., 2013, "Effects of green curtains to improve the living environment", https://doi.org/10.1007/978-94-007-5922-0_15.

[4] Kikuchi, Sachiko & Koshimizu, Hajime, 2013, "A Comparison of Green Roof Systems with Conventional Roof for the Storm Water Runoff", 10.1007/978-94-007-5922-0_16.

management system, [①]something Japan has been trying to do before. Japan is a narrow-shaped and mountainous country. Its water sources are usually located on the top of mountains, which requires protection. Regions along the midstream of rivers are often developed into tourist destinations. In mostestuarine cities, the sea water is often mixed together with water to be used in cities. Flooding can be disastrous in urban areas. Along with forest conservation, water protection has become an important part of Japan's ecological conservation.

The ecological network cooperation advocated by cities in central Taiwan of China aims to form a green network on a regional level. [②]The Urban Greenspaces Institute in Japan has carried out similar studies with a focus on the construction of ecological networks on community, city and region levels.

There are sharp conflicts of interest between society development, urban development and agriculture development. Some farmland may be encroached by property development, some may be converted into other uses. However, there are also some successful stories.

Fig. 3 shows the crops planted in the surrounding areas of Beijing. The main crops that used to be planted there were wheat, but now they are replaced by cash crops, such as oil plants. [③]

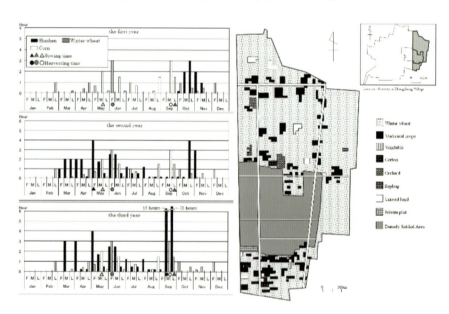

Fig. 3
Crops and land
use in rural
Beijing

① Xu, Lin-yu & Yang, Zhi-feng, 2013, "Evaluation and Regulation of Ecological Security When Implementing Urban Planning: Review and Suggestions for Spatial Planning and Sustainable Development in China", 10.1007/978-94-007-5922-0_17.

② Liu, Li-wei & Ko, Pei-yin, 2013, "Imagination and Practice of Collaborative Landscape, Ecological, and Cultural Planning in Taiwan: The Case of Taichung County and Changhua County", 10.1007/978-94-007-5922-0_7.

③ Wang, Dai & Si, Yuefang & Zhang, Wen-zhong & Sun, Wei, 2013, "An Investigation of Changes in the Urban Shadow of Beijing Metropolis Under Agricultural Structural Adjustment in China", 10.1007/978-94-007-5922-0_18.

China Agricultural University has also carried out a study in Beijing to promote urban landscape agriculture development. [①]Beijing was suffering from severe pollutions at the time, so I find it a very good idea to develop landscape agriculture in Beijing to reduce carbon emissions.

Agricultural management in developed countries also entails forest management. Forests are often privately owned. In some areas, due to the aging population, forests are not managed in an effective way, and neglection is common. One huge challenge is to establish the ownership and boundaries of these private forests.

Tsinghua University conducted a research on new rural construction in Shaanxi Province, with an aim of building houses that fit the local environment. [②]

Fig. 4
A Study on new rural construction in Shaanxi Province

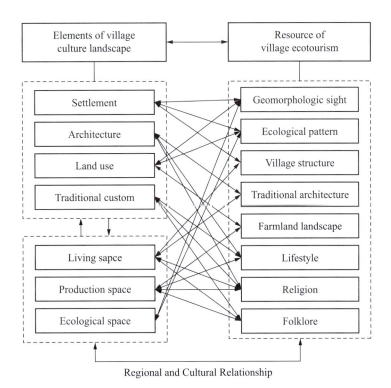

Regional and Cultural Relationship

Fig. 5 shows a case in South Korea that tracks the effect of carbon absorption through remote sensing data. [③] While doing the research, the researchers also identified a lot of loopholes in forest

① Zhang, Feng-rong & Zhao, Hua-fu, 2013, "The Spatial Planning of Agricultural Production in Beijing Toward Producing Comfortable and Beautiful Living Environment", 10.1007/978-94-007-5922-0_19.

② Dang, Anrong & Zhang, Yan & Chen, Yang, 2013, "Sustainable-Oriented Study on Conservation Planning of Cave-Dwelling Village Culture Landscape", 10.1007/978-94-007-5922-0_8.

③ Kim, Jung-Rack & Lin, Shih-Yuan & Chang, Eunmi & Lee, In-Hee & Yun, He-Won, 2013, "Land Cover Analysis with High-Resolution Multispectral Satellite Imagery and Its Application for the CO_2 Flux Estimation", 10.1007/978-94-007-5922-0_21.

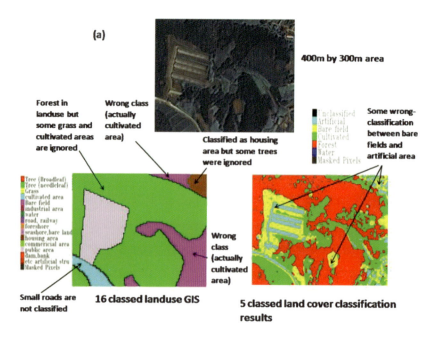

Fig. 5
A land cover
analysis by
multispectral
satellite images in
South Korea

management. The ownership of forests should be clarified and governments need to figure out ways to encourage forest owners to engage in management of their own lands.

6. Urban development requires people to reduce urban vulnerability and improve urban resilience

Whether we discuss developed courtiers, or developing countries and areas with high development pressure, they all face urban vulnerability and urban disasters, such as floods and earthquakes. Thus, they need to strengthen urban infrastructure to reduce the vulnerability of cities. Social cooperation is also important. Relatively speaking, developed regions have set a good example in this respect.

Fig. 6 shows a study conducted by the National Institute for Land and Infrastructure Management (MLIT) under Ministry of Land, Infrastructure, Transport and Tourism of Japan. It was a study related with territorial spatial planning and urban vulnerability. [1] As a high latitude country, Japan is prone to heavy snowfalls. Snowstorms can become a severe threat to old people. Many old folks living in rural areas have difficulties in clearing snow in winter and death rates are particularly high in winter.

---

[1] Yuhara, Asako & Ye, Kyung-rock, 2013, "Sustainable Communities in Hilly, Mountainous and Heavy Snowfall Areas", 10.1007/978-94-007-5922-0_24.

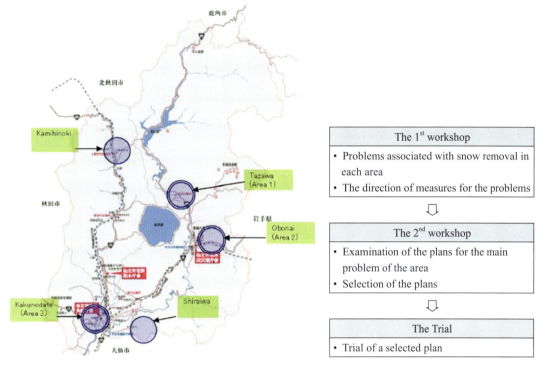

The 1st workshop
• Problems associated with snow removal in each area
• The direction of measures for the problems

⇩

The 2nd workshop
• Examination of the plans for the main problem of the area
• Selection of the plans

⇩

The Trial
• Trial of a selected plan

Fig. 6
A study on heavy snowfall areas in Japan

Other studies use a historical perspective to learn how to protect urban ecology, especially the waters. Fig. 7 shows a research on water vulnerability in Chongqing, China. [1]

Fig. 7
A study on water
vulnerability in
Chongqing

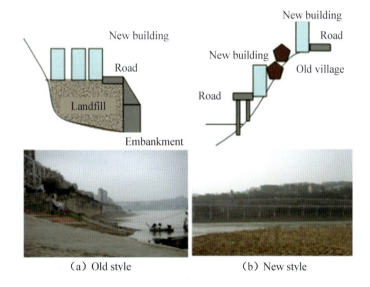

(a) Old style   (b) New style

---

[1] Huang, Guang-wei & Shen, Zhenjiang, 2013, "A Vulnerability Study from Water Perspective on the Largest City of China", 10.1007/978-94-007-5922-0_25.

6. Conclusion

So far, we have analyzed cases in East Asia, including South Korea, Japan, China's mainland, and Taiwan of China, to see how they achieve sustainable urban development through public policies. The approaches used include forming a sustainable society under the urgent need of economic growth and balancing socio-economic development and the conservation of the environment and agriculture. We also discussed different types of urban problems in developed and developing countries.

In fact, spatial planning in East Asia is challenged by both urban growth and urban decline. Countries and regions at different stages of development have adopted various policies and practices. Developing countries often prioritize economic needs in land use while developed countries have to tackle urban decline and the shrinking population. In addition, with the advancement of technologies, we should also engage technology companies to enhance urban functions and contribute to the renewal of urban centers.

Reflection upon Urban Planning and Real Estate in the Post-COVID-19 Pandemic Era

Tienfoo Sing

Director, Institute of Real Estate and Urban Studies, National University of Singapore

1. Future changes in urban planning and vision

When it comes to the concept of a "livable city", every city has its own vision and ideas, and is striving towards the goal of creating a better life. Regarding how to build a people-centered better life, the Housing and Development Board (HDB) in Singapore recently has unveiled a blueprint of housing development for the next 10 to 15 years, which aims to build a future city featuring smart, quality and harmonious life. The COVID-19 pandemic will definitely have impacted on HDB's existing strategies. Before the outbreak, a lot of urban planning for livable cities centered on more positive visions, such as "better life", "livable cities" or "environmental greening". But in the wake of the COVID-19 pandemic, changes and revisions in these urban planning strategies will become necessary. Urban planners have taken a more proactive approach after the pandemic broke out, focusing not just on building livable cities, but also on building resilient and flexible cities. A city with resilience and flexibility can make timely adjustments according to the situation, thus better adapting to changes in the environment. Environmental change, climate change and demographic change are all pressing problems that require urban planners to address.

In this context, urban planning for livable cities in the future needs to transform from creating a positive vision to more proactively adapting to environmental issues. In other words, planning on livable cities in the future will be adjusted in accordance with climate change, demographic change, social and urban development after the pandemic in particular, as well as new thinking on urban space utilization. It is fair to say that the pandemic has disrupted the overall layout of urban planning, because it not only has brought a huge impact on the economy and people's pace of life, but will also change the direction of economic development in the future.

Previously, urban planning was usually based on urban economics. Urban economics is a discipline that researches into individual's choice of space. It mainly focuses on maximizing the benefits of space choice, that is, how to maximize the use of limited land resources without affecting the greening of the environment, so as to provide space for economic development, work and leisure places, as well as personal housing. From the perspective of urban economics, the agglomeration effect is particularly important. Agglomeration economics aims to bring together a number of businesses in a downtown area to help them benefit from the advantage of a particular area, as well as to facilitate other businesses that are clustered together. The agglomeration of companies can increase productivity, which may further reduce the cost of input. Similarly, people living in cities tend to be more social. People want to have face-to-face interactions with others, both at work and at social events. This affects the general direction of urban planning. For example, people usually work in the city center, but live in areas far away from it. In this case, they have to commute to the downtown area for work in the morning. Although this type of planning can maximize economic benefits, it will also bring about urban problems, such as traffic congestion and environmental pollution. As people commute to work in the city center at the same time, the city's infrastructure, such as public transportation, is inevitably under heavy load. But by the end of the week or after work, much of this infrastructure is left unused, leaving the city center empty and quiet.

These were the factors that we took into account when doing urban planning in the past. In other words, we need to think about how to make urban systems work more efficiently. And we usually think about how to solve these problems when building infrastructure. In the post-pandemic era, people may need to rethink the effects of agglomeration economics and whether it can boost community development in the future. In order to pursue agglomeration effects, urban space is generally limited to one single purpose, and the agglomeration effects produced by such space can hardly change with time and circumstances. The COVID-19 pandemic has exerted significant influence on urban development and the spatial layout of real estate. In the next 50 years or even 100 years, urban planning needs to reflect upon agglomeration economies.

2. Impact of the COVID-19 outbreak on cities

In contrast to the clustering effect of cities, as shown in Fig. 1, the more densely populated an area is, the higher transmission risks it faces. As a result, today's urban economics is actually in conflict with the public health requirements to control the pandemic. We need to think about how we can solve the problem so that urban populations can continue to communicate without being infected, and how we can continue to unleash agglomeration effects and make better use of urban space.

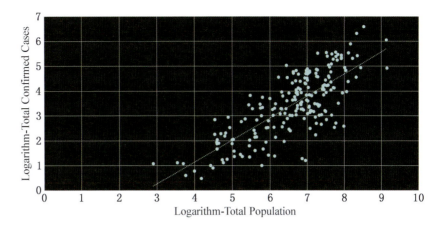

Fig. 1
Relationship
between
population density
and COVID-19
confirmed cases
in each country
Source: World
Development
Indicators, The World
Bank http://www.
worldometers.info/
coronavirus/#
countries(19July2020)

Next, I would like to share three-studies on the impact of the COVID-19 pandemic. The first one, "Human Mobility Restriction and the Spread of the Novel Coronavirus (2019-NCoV) in China", is conducted by a team from Shanghai Tech University and focuses on urban space and quarantine measures, a perspective often neglected by urban planners in the past. In this study, a former PhD student of mine and others in the team studied Wuhan's city-wide lockdown strategy.

Fig. 2 shows that after Wuhan's lockdown, both the inter-city population flow and intra-city population flow decreased significantly. We can conclude that Wuhan's lockdown strategy is very effective, which has significantly slowed down the spread of the pandemic. During this outbreak, we have found that community quarantine and social distancing are very important. Without these

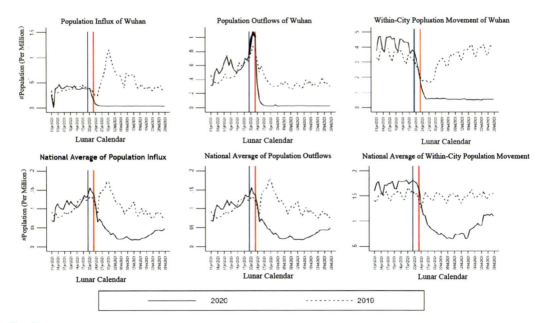

Fig. 2
Inter- and intra-city population mobility in China

restriction measures, the spread of the pandemic would have been faster, resulting in much more serious consequences.

The second study is "Containing the Virus or Reviving the Economy? Evidence from Individual Expectations during the COVID-19 Epidemic". Its findings have been published on Social Science Research Network (SSRN). This study focuses on the trade-off between managing the pandemic and reopening the economy. The study finds that the outbreak can have a very negative impact on our mindsets and expectations of the economy. In other words, after the pandemic broke out, people are very pessimistic about the economic outlook. At a time when many governments are choosing between reopening their economies and containing the pandemic, it is vital to strike a balance between the two tasks. Because if the pandemic cannot be controlled, the economy will inevitably be affected. Only when the economy starts to rebound, will our daily life, work, employment and so on be improved therewith.

The third study, "Application of Artificial Intelligence (AI) to Forecast the Spread of Coronavirus Disease 2019 (COVID-19)" is conducted by the Institute of Urban and Real Estate Studies of the National University of Singapore. It mainly discusses the predictions of the development of the pandemic. Why does this pandemic spread so quickly? How-can we prevent community transmission? In fact, we have been through similar pandemics before, for example, SARS in 2003. At that time, we were faced with similar problems. However, in the SARS pandemic, people infected with the virus only had strong transmissibility when they had severe symptoms, which was easier for us to predict the spread speed of the disease. But this time, there are many asymptomatic cases that can also spread the disease. This makes things more complicated. Therefore, it is vital to control community transmission and slow down the spread of the coronavirus.

Fig. 3
Impact of self-quarantine on the spread of the pandemic

Distribution of Infections at Early Stage   Without Self-Quarantine   With Self-Quarantine

提升社区和城市品质

The third essay focuses on how to predict the transmission risks of asymptomatic cases. The study makes some basic predictions, as shown in Fig. 3, and it finds that the pandemic would have spread faster without self-quarantine measures. With self-quarantine measures, the spread of the virus and the concentration of infected cases will be controlled to a certain extent.

All in all, the above findings are important factors that must be taken into consideration for urban planning in the pandemic era. To some extent, the outbreak has put established urban planning and economic policies at risk, interrupting our previous strategies. In the aftermath of the outbreak, further reflection is needed on how to use quarantine measures effectively and how to strike a balance between economic recovery and pandemic response. I would also like to share with you some of Singapore's response measures. To control the outbreak, Singapore has rolled out restriction measures in several stages, starting with a lockdown in April that required people to stay, work and attend classes at home. On June 2, 2020, Singapore started the first phase of the reopening and implemented various measures, including working in shifts and remote working, business continuity planning, and joint force tracking system, to prevent a potential second wave of the outbreak. So far, the outbreak in Singapore has been basically controlled, with most of the recent new cases being imported cases.

3. Impact of the COVID-19 Outbreak on Real Estate and Space Utilization

Many companies and organizations have introduced remote working, with more than 80 percent of the workforce working remotely in the midst of the pandemic. This trend will have great influence on our space demands. Given that a large part of the workforce has experienced remote working, the way we work may change forever after the pandemic is largely controlled thanks to breakthroughs in vaccine development. Many big corporations, including Twitter, Microsoft and Google, have come up with policies encouraging employees to continue to work from home. Most of their employees, who are still working from home, have adapted to the model.

Therefore, the COVID-19 pandemic will mainly bring the following three impacts on the commercial property market and space planning. First, "decentralization" will become more common. Second, the redevelopment and comprehensive development of the central business districts (CBDs) will gain more momentum. At present, a central business district is a comprehensive center for merely commercial purposes. When most people work from home, how to use the spare office space and how to redevelop the old office buildings are issues of great importance, deserving our thinking and studying. Third, more attention will be paid to the more flexible utilization of urban space.

Specifically, "decentralization" refers to the reduced concentration of the workforce and the decline of the agglomeration effects of a CBD, as more companies implement "business stability and continuity plans", especially during the outbreak when they implement work in shifts strategies. Many companies have divided staff into smaller teams and sent them back to the office at different times to reduce the transmission risks. Meanwhile, many companies have started to "decentralize", moving some of their facilities out of a CBD. At present, not only is the workplace at risk of spreading the diseases, employees who commute to work by public transportation are also at risk. It is very important to address these problems. Many companies have begun to move logistic and operation departments out of the CBD. For example, some office buildings outside Singapore's CBD, such as One North and Pasir Panjang, have attracted many technology companies. These companies no longer have to pursue aggregation effects from other businesses close to the city center. Many of their employees have been working remotely and can communicate via the Internet without the need to congregate in the city center.

As for the re-planning and re-development of the space utilization of CBDs, there is a problem that they have not been used for diversified purposes at present but mainly for office buildings and commercial activities. After the outbreak, we need to tackle this problem, because most people may not want to or need to go back to work in CBDs. We need to find out a solution to the spare office space. In the future, the planning of CBDs will more likely focus on mixed-use and mitigating problems related to commuting and transportation. In other words, CBDs in the future will develop towards a comprehensive direction, integrating office buildings, residences, shopping and leisure areas in a small area. People working in CBDs will no longer have to commute, congestion will be reduced and urban space will be better utilized.

Singapore's Urban Redevelopment Authority is also working on a CBD Incentive Scheme to encourage property owners to redesign and develop old commercial districts into more vibrant and versatile urban spaces.

In addition, the space design of office buildings also needs to be adjusted. At present, office buildings are usually designed to be used for a long period of time, and leases of office space also last for a long term. In the wake of the outbreak, many people will turn to more flexible office spaces with a shorter-term lease. And even before the outbreak, many sharing-economy companies had begun to offer more flexible shared workspace. When the pandemic is over, we will find that such shared workspace may better fit office needs in the future.

Finally, this pandemic has revealed that cloud technology and data centers are vital to businesses. If companies already have a good foundation in this area, the impact of the pandemic on them is relatively smaller. On the contrary, if companies suffer from the lack of investment in this area, the impact of the pandemic on these traditional entities is more serious.

Resilient Infrastructure, Integration of New and Existing Infrastructure, and Sustainable Investment and Finance

Ye Zhen

Director, Infrastructure Investment and Finance, Batley School of Construction and Project Management, University College London (UCL); Visiting Professor of Economics and Finance, Xiamen University

Lin Kaibei

Graduate student majoring in Real Estate Finance, Department of Land Economy, University of Cambridge

Mei Yiqin

Graduate student majoring in Infrastructure Investment and Finance, Batley School of Construction and Project Management, UCL

In the context of rapid urbanization and inclusive development, this article discusses how more sustainable and resilient infrastructure can be built from the perspectives of positive and negative externalities, integration of existing and new infrastructure, and financial innovation. We believe that a resilient city requires more inclusive infrastructure featuring ecological and social inclusiveness. In this regard, data-driven cities should become a main platform for the integration of existing and new infrastructure. Infrastructure in China, as an asset type, can be integrated with financial innovation. By introducing various types of ownership into infrastructure investment and financing, we can improve asset utilization through performance management. Infrastructure resilience is important, but we still need to manage infrastructure in a more sophisticated way to make it more inclusive and sustainable.

1. Positive and negative externalities and inclusiveness of resilient infrastructure

The Great Wall of China, one of the largest man-made existing structures, has stood the test of time for thousands of years. Originally built for defense, it is now a tourist attraction. Actually, many construction projects from ancient times, including the pyramids, were built with an intention of extreme longevity. Our ancestors built them at all costs, but the cities that accommodated these gigantic structures no longer exist. There is no doubt that these millennial-old structures still have the resilience we are talking about. But is it reasonable to build them regardless of costs, or are they well-functioning? We still need to think about these questions.

We believe that infrastructure resilience can be defined from both narrow and broad views. Infrastructure resilience, in a narrow sense, refers to the continuity of critical infrastructure in a city that provides systematic connectivity and its ability to withstand major disasters. In a broad sense, resilience refers to the sustainability, adaptability, and ecological and social human inclusiveness of infrastructure. From the perspective of finance, building resilient infrastructure benefits sustainable investment and finance in the following two aspects. For one thing, it can defer the rising costs of equity capital. For another, in case of a major event that leads to a shortfall in expected cash flows, resilient infrastructure can reduce the risk of bankruptcy for businesses. We can see that resilient infrastructure, as an asset type, plays a critical role in financial innovation and urban governance.

Many urban infrastructure facilities are not resilient in broad terms. For example, elevators in many subway stations and bus rapid transit (BRT) systems only go up but not down, which brings inconvenience to the elderly and the disabled. This is a typical case of inadequate inclusiveness for disadvantaged groups. Clearance bars in the picture at the side entrance are another example. They are inconvenient because drivers who might not see the bars or not know the height of their cars may be blocked by the bars when they turn into the side road, thus causing congestion on the trunk road. In the process of rapid urbanization, we have seen many such "inconsiderate" infrastructures. We should not only renovate them, but avoid inefficient and repetitive construction. Properly planned resilient infrastructure can make cities more sustainable and adaptive to ever-changing urban systems, which will increase positive externalities so that cities of the future will be more livable and attract more people and capital.

As to social inclusiveness, the United Kingdom has much to offer. In 2005, the country passed an amendment to the Disability Discrimination Act (DDA), which enacted improvements to much of the country's century-old infrastructure. For example, the London Underground, the world's oldest underground passenger railway in operation for nearly 160 years, has most of its facilities transformed, providing up and down elevators for the disabled.

Meanwhile, negative externalities of infrastructure in the process of modernization require us to deal with urban diseases systematically. According to a report from China International Capital

Corporation (CICC), an investment bank, urban diseases refer to a series of social problems caused by the imbalance between the growing urban population and inadequate infrastructure. These problems include traffic congestion, urban water-logging, air pollution, water pollution and accumulation of hazardous and solid waste. Take water pollution for example. In February 2016, China's Ministry of Housing and Urban-Rural Development surveyed 295 cities and found a total of 1 811 black and malodorous water bodies, an average of 6.13 in each city. In terms of traffic congestion, a 2018 report from Amap, a Chinese navigation service provider, showed that during rush hours, 15% of the 361 cities it had monitored were plagued by congestion, 59% were in slow traffic, while only 26% witnessed smooth traffic flows.[1]

Given the positive and negative externalities, we must take into consideration the sustainability, inclusiveness and adaptability of resilient infrastructure. More inclusive infrastructure, friendly to vulnerable groups like children, the elderly and the disabled, needs to be put in place.

2. Urban digitization and integration of existing and new municipal infrastructure

An inevitable problem in building resilient infrastructure lies in the integration of new infrastructure (NI) into the existing system. We believe that NI should not be confined to supporting technological development, thus evolving into a new industrial policy. Instead, NI is at the heart of urban renewal. It can improve urban resilience and prevent urban diseases from going from bad to worse. It is a critical driver for improving urban efficiency and future sustainable development. The key lies in how to better build a digital city and connect existing and new infrastructure with data at the core, so that NI can be better integrated into a city's management and operation system.

(1) Urban digitization.

By the end of 2019, the share of the urban population in China's total population has exceeded 60%. According to the prediction of Morgan Stanley in its "China's Urbanization 2.0" report, 75% of the country's population will live in urban areas by 2030. The continuing urbanization has also put great pressure on big cities, as the country's urbanization has entered a special stage[2]. Concrete buildings without resilience have failed to meet the diverse and complex living and housing needs of today's urban residents. In this context, urban renewal driven by NI is of great importance, because NI will facilitate smart upgrading, data flows, and sophisticated management of cities, thus making them more resilient and sustainable.

---

[1] Sources: China National Environmental Monitoring; IFeng Finance; Energy World; Research Department of CICC.

[2] Qiu, Baoxing, 2012, "Complexity Science and Urban Transformation".

As a key factor of production to the digital economy, NI involves generation, transmission, storage and use of data, and creates a new data-based governance model. This can help achieve sustainable development goals, like boosting urban resilience, and optimizing the industrial structure, etc. Cities produce and consume a large amount of digital information every day. To fully tap into the potential value of these data, we need to leverage NI supporting facilities to establish a comprehensive, effective, and standardized data governance system.

In the industrial sector, we've already witnessed an inspiring trend towards the digitalization of industrial production. For example, the emerging use of the Industrial Internet of Things (IoT) has delivered concrete value at scale. One example is the application of digital twins in industrial production, which can greatly optimize asset performance and improve production efficiency. A digital twin is a digital representation of a physical asset. It takes real-world data about a physical item as inputs, analyzes these data with the help of artificial intelligence and machine learning, and creates a virtual simulation model and a digitalized copy of the asset. Digital twins also benefit urban management. By modeling the city in the real world, its digital city twin will help city planners visualize various options for urban planning and choose the best solution for the city's sustainable development. Cities like Singapore are developing such digital twin systems for smart urban management. And we believe that more cities will embrace these technologies in the future. Of course, data operations and management, especially those in big cities, require the support of well-established NI systems. At the same time, we should ensure that when we integrate existing infrastructure with NI, energy consumed for data generation and usage must be renewable and sustainable, thus reducing the long-term risk of climate change.

(2) Integration of existing and new municipal infrastructure and financial innovation.

As China has put more emphasis on domestic demand and technological innovation, NI investors may shift their future focus to municipal engineering. NI encompasses a range of strategic emerging sectors where high-tech innovation and application play an essential role, such as artificial intelligence, new energy vehicles, 5G, robotics, etc. Such new sectors are faced with the problem of how to integrate with urban construction projects, public utilities, and the social security system. For example, we need to think about the following questions: what role robots and human-machine interaction will play in urban planning in the future; how to avoid redundant construction of equipment and facilities for autonomous vehicles and advanced rail transits; how to protect huge amounts of data; how to apply AI and big data to improve the operational efficiency of old infrastructure; and how to use big data to predict infrastructure risks.

In finance, the beta coefficient (β) is a measurement of market risks. According to our research, in China's infrastructure market, NI has a higher β compared with old infrastructure. So, we should pay more attention to the integration between existing and new infrastructure. Three reasons can explain why NI has a higher β. First, expected cash flows of NI face considerable uncertainty. Second, NI has not been fully integrated into the renovation of old infrastructure. Third, asset valuations and the market competition structure of NI are different.

According to a 2019 survey of global infrastructure investment from Preqin, a data and insights provider to the alternative assets' community, more than half of investors are most concerned about asset valuations and the market competition structure. The reason is that overpricing assets will result in fewer future returns, making it hard for latecomers to withdraw from their investments. Also, a lack of competition in the market will lead to monopoly and innovation stagnation. In terms of asset valuations and the market competition structure, we need to take more into consideration the relationship between market structure and innovation during the process of integrating NI into the existing system. The keys to figuring out the relationship between the two are ownership and infrastructure performance, while financial innovation serves as an important tool to solve the problems mentioned above.

In terms of ownership, moderate financial innovation can solve the problem of owner absence and low efficiency of asset utilization caused by unclear ownership. Ownership of infrastructure projects can be divided into the ownership of land and that of the asset. In terms of asset operation, the ownership of cash flows is closely related to the operation of assets. Assets with good operations can bring returns to shareholders. Therefore, we can improve asset efficiency by introducing different types of ownership into infrastructure investment, financing and performance management. In this regard, we can learn from the Highways England's (formerly the Highways Agency) management of the M25 motorway. The Highways England is a government company charged with operating, maintaining and improving England's motorways and major A roads, including M25 motorway, a major road encircling almost all of Greater London. The Highway England has worked with private road maintenance companies, and signed performance contracts with them, which enables the agency to maintain resilient road infrastructure much faster.

In terms of investment, optimizing financial innovative products, including asset securitization and infrastructure real estate investment trusts (REITs), will enable more investors to enjoy the cash flow income brought by the operation of high-quality assets. In return, it can also improve the asset utilization ratio and management efficiency.

However, many private investors are reluctant to invest in major infrastructure projects because of their longer investment cycle, larger investment scale, and ambiguous exit mechanism.

This is particularly true in China, where investors are faced with limited exit channels, imperfect markets, and inadequate mature institutional investors. But the good thing is, since China's National Development and Reform Commission put forward a blueprint for NI and improving the infrastructure REITs platform in April 2020, more and more private investors have been seeking opportunities to invest in NI. Infrastructure REITs provide more options for existing equity investors to exit and open more financing channels for infrastructure projects. Infrastructure capitalization is conducive to promoting the construction and operation of underlying projects, thus creating a virtuous cycle for the development of infrastructure.

Currently, we have witnessed diversified investment activities in the infrastructure sector, including government investment, government-led private investment, and purely private investment. Private investors also have engaged more in the construction and operation of large-scale projects through public-private partnerships (PPP). And more and more companies are focusing on the core technologies for making infrastructure more intelligent.

(3) Characteristics of infrastructure as an asset type.

Infrastructure, generally marketed as a stable asset type, is gaining more and more attention from global investors. As is shown in Fig. 1, according to a capital asset pricing model (CAPM) regression of S&P Global data over the past 10 years, we have deduced that the return on equity for infrastructure investment is around 9%. While global infrastructure's annualized rate of return (3%) is much lower than that of the S&P 500 (11%), its annualized return volatility (15%) is also lower than that of the S&P 500 (17%). In addition, since infrastructure investment is a form of "real assets" and has a stable dividend payout ratio (or stable operating cash flows), investor enthusiasm for

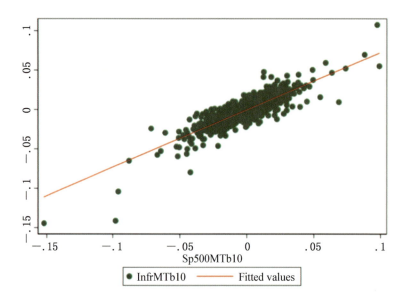

Fig. 1
Capital Asset
Pricing Model
(CAPM)
regression
for global
infrastructure

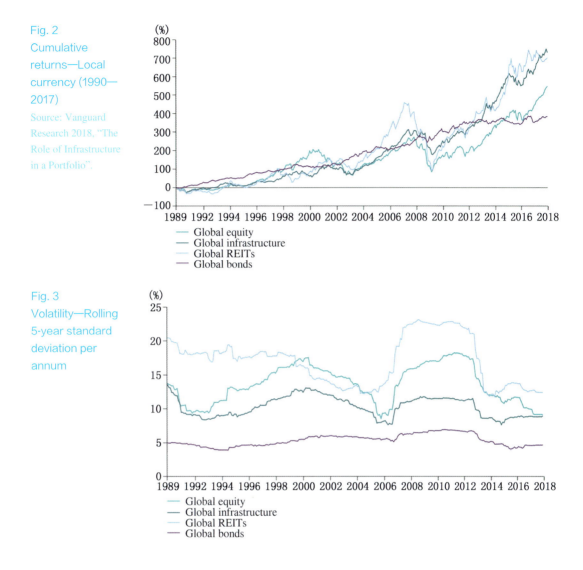

Fig. 2
Cumulative
returns—Local
currency (1990—
2017)
Source: Vanguard
Research 2018, "The
Role of Infrastructure
in a Portfolio".

Fig. 2 chart:

(%)
800
700
600
500
400
300
200
100
0
−100
1989 1992 1994 1996 1998 2000 2002 2004 2006 2008 2010 2012 2014 2016 2018

— Global equity
— Global infrastructure
— Global REITs
— Global bonds

Fig. 3
Volatility—Rolling
5-year standard
deviation per
annum

Fig. 3 chart:

(%)
25

20

15

10

5

0
1989 1992 1994 1996 1998 2000 2002 2004 2006 2008 2010 2012 2014 2016 2018

— Global equity
— Global infrastructure
— Global REITs
— Global bonds

infrastructure is rising.

Fig. 2 shows the cumulative returns of global equities, bonds, REITs and infrastructure investments since 1989. The data confirm that infrastructure is more like an intermediate asset compared with equity (a longer-term investment) and debt (a shorter-term investment). Fig. 3 shows the rolling 5-year annualized standard deviation of the above-mentioned asset investments. It is worth noting that in the 2008 financial crisis, the rising ratio of infrastructure volatility was much lower than that of REITS and of the stock market. Therefore, infrastructure investment is more resilient in the midst of high market volatility. And under such circumstances, infrastructure plays a significant role in asset portfolios because as a non-cyclical asset, it can reduce downside risks.

3. Long-and short-end risks of resilient infrastructure

From a global debt perspective, resilient infrastructure can defer the risk of bankruptcy for businesses if their expected cash flows are insufficient to cover the debt due to a major event. According to a research by Arup, a multinational engineering consulting firm, the debt service coverage ratio (DSCR) of most of the world's toll roads in 2020 was more than 2 before the COVID-19 pandemic. However, in the wake of the pandemic, the daily traffic of global toll roads decreased significantly. Since the initial ban on gathering in March 2020, developed countries like Italy, France, and Spain have seen daily traffic decreased by about 80%, with Australia being the exception seeing a 40% decrease. The DSCR of global toll roads has also reduced to slightly above 1, on the edge of bankruptcy. Thus, we can see that insufficient expected cash flows caused by a major event can directly increase the bankruptcy risk of global toll roads in the short term.

Therefore, from the perspective of finance, when designing and planning resilient infrastructure, we need to take into consideration the impact of once-in-a-century events on the DSCR, and include small-probability events impact into distributed parameters of future cash flows, so as to better control

Table 1

DSCR of toll roads around the world

Asset	Debt covenant[2]	Default threshold	Distribution lock-up threshold	31 December 2019
Corporate debt	ICR	1.25 x	N/A	4.44 x
TQ	ICR	1.20 x	1.40 x	2.31 x
95 Express Lanes	DSCR	N/A	1.45 x	2.92 x
495 Express Lanes	DSCR	1.15 x	1.45 x	3.40 x
Cardinal Hold Co	DSCR	N/A	1.30 x	1.76 x
A25	DSCR	1.05	1.175 x	1.81 x
ED	ICR	1.15 x	1.40 x	4.99 x
Hills M2	ICR	1.15 x	1.30 x	10.19 x
LCT	ICR	1.15 x	1.30 x	2.73 x
CCT	ICR	1.15 x	1.30 x	5.87 x
M5	DSCR	1.10 x	1.30 x	2.09 x
M7	DSCR	1.10 x	1.30 x	4.83 x
M4	DSCR	1.10 x	1.30 x	1.93 x

debt risks of future investment. Instead of building mega infrastructure projects at all costs, we should manage assets more sophisticatedly, and improve the utilization efficiency of infrastructure.

Many countries, such as the UK and Singapore, have implemented road pricing schemes according to the use of roads and traffic congestion. London has introduced differentiated congestion charges to different zones and vehicles. Vehicles failing to meet emission standards may face additional charges, while those using clean energy may enjoy discounts or exemptions. These practices help smooth operating cash flows and improve infrastructure utilization.

From the perspective of capital markets, environmental, social and governance (ESG) factors are becoming a major standard for global capital markets to influence the sustainability of infrastructure investment and finance. ESG is gaining increasing attention from limited partnerships (LPs) and funding providers. From renewable energy to socially responsible startups, ESG is becoming a key to risk management and a driver of potential value creation. Also, investors and issuers have higher requirements for ESG disclosure. Information transparency and the reliability of ESG standards and frameworks are transmitted to all parties in capital markets through LP Agreements. As climate change agreements have influenced industrial policies, ESG is changing the rules of capital markets through regulations and framework agreements in the financial sector. Various rating agencies are increasingly paying attention to ESG and including it into their comprehensive credit evaluation system.

In the long run, climate change and carbon neutrality goals will affect long-term capital costs, and reduce the return on investment, which is particularly important for sustainable investment and finance. It can be predicted that as China's economy continues to thrive, infrastructure investment and financing in the future should consider more risk factors, face higher design requirements and stricter regulations. The previous infrastructure investment and financing model, which was dominated by the public sectors, has made a great contribution to China's socio-economic development. But as China's economy is now driven by capital and innovation, giving better play to the private sectors in infrastructure investment and financing can improve capital efficiency and asset operation, hence creating a virtuous cycle. At the same time, we need to build resilient infrastructure that has stronger ecological and social inclusiveness, and make infrastructure sustainable for long-term investments through financial innovation to cope with a more uncertain future.

4. Summary and policy recommendations

As to sustainable investment, resilient infrastructure can defer the rising costs of long-end equity funding, and protect against the risk of bankruptcy when expected cash flows are insufficient to cover the debt due to a major event. In light of the NI plan advocated by China's central government, more efforts are needed to facilitate the integration of existing and new infrastructure, and to figure out the relationship between the market structure and innovation, and the relationship between ownership and performance improvement in the infrastructure market. Technological innovation brought by NI is helpful to improve the efficiency of existing infrastructure and to predict risks. Climate change and ESG can affect the long-term and short-term returns of infrastructure investments by affecting capital costs and market rules. When designing resilient infrastructure, we must take into consideration the impact of once-in-a-century events, and include small-probability events' impact into distributed parameters of future cash flows, so as to better predict debt risks of future investment.

We need to design resilient infrastructure that is more inclusive and adaptable to better engage with the international community and benefit local development, thus reducing the risk of future increases in financing costs of global capital markets. It is clear that building infrastructure at any cost will not deliver higher marginal returns. Instead, it will exacerbate systematic financial risks. After infrastructure investments have reached a certain scale, moderate financialization will further improve infrastructure resilience and utilization efficiency. As to sustainable investment and finance, it is crucial to introduce different types of ownership into infrastructure investment and finance, and improve the utilization efficiency of infrastructure assets through performance management. Last but not least, while infrastructure resilience is important, we still need to manage infrastructure more sophisticatedly to make it more inclusive and sustainable.

FORUM

分论坛

Future Communities
未来社区

主持人·HOST
彭勃·Peng Bo
上海交通大学国际与公共事务学院教授
Professor of School of International and Public Affairs in SJTU
田毅鹏·Tian Yipeng
吉林大学哲学社会学院教授
Professor of School of Philosophy and Social Sciences in Jilin University

未来社区：新样态、新治理

文 军

华东师范大学社会发展学院教授

1. 未来社区的含义与特征

自 20 世纪 80 年代以来，学术界和社会学界就开始探索"未来社区"这一议题。"社区"一词由来已久，随着时间的推移其概念也在获得不断的反思与重构，甚至可以说它本身已逐渐衍生为一种"理想类型"，一个达至社会理想的关键因素。所以从广义维度看，"未来社区"并非一个全新的概念：第一，对于未来的设想与追求贯穿于人类历史发展的每一个时期、每一个阶段，而作为一种社会理想图景的建构，"未来社区"理念也始终以各种形式不断得到呈现。第二，鉴于地域文化、发展阶段、价值理念、自身资源等方面存在的差异性，同一时期内不同地方的社区形态也不尽相同。

既有的"未来社区"发展脉络大致可总结为"技术论"与"生态论"下的二重论断，这两种思想同时也分别对应着联合国先后掀起的两波发展热潮。

图 1
千年发展目标
（MDGs）

图 2
可持续发展目标（SDGs）

"技术论"是在联合国千年发展目标（MDGs）的指引下，在全世界范围内掀起的"以经济促发展"、"以科技谋创新"，借助生产力的高速增长带动人类共同富裕的第一波浪潮。当然，正是由于这一时期物质资料与现代技术的不断累积，为后续以 5G、物联网、人工智能等为代表的"新技术"奠定了坚实的基础。同时也迎来了诸如"智能社区""智慧社区"等"未来社区"形态的建设构思。

"生态论"对应在联合国可持续发展目标（SDGs）的指引下，社区建设开始转换视角，强调在制定未来框架的同时兼具人本性、生态性及可持续性。生态视角逐渐成为引领"未来社区"建设浪潮的新航标：第一，"生态论"编织了人类生活的丰富性，不仅倡导将可持续发展置于"未来社区"的中心，还致力于促进具有包容性的社会发展观的形成；第二，"生态论"着重开发社区的生态背景和人文价值理念，主张关注个人、家庭、组织与社区环境间关系的和谐发展，将人"置于"自然中，而不是凌驾于自然之上。

从"技术论"向"生态论"转变的原因主要有以下两点。第一，虽然"技术论"指引下的社区建设取得了巨大成就，但却在一味强调增长、技术与进步的同时使"发展与环境""发展与人"相分离，造成了资源短缺、环境污染与生态破坏等三大频发的全球性危机；第二，自然风险逐渐过渡为"社会风险""制度风险"与"技术风险"，而单纯依靠技术发展模式无法有效应对。新冠肺炎疫情的大流行就是这种"复合风险"的真实写照。

从中国的实践来看，社区建设的目标定位在建设"社会生活共同体"，其要义在于使社区建设的功能、价值和意义回归居民的日常生活。因此，从居民日常生活出发建构社会共同体，其指向一方面包括作为社会组织形态的社会共同体，比如中国社区建设的第一阶段，在 20 世纪 80 年代和 90 年代强调基础设施和环境的改善，聚焦在物质层面的建设，我们可以称之为社区建设的 1.0 版本。第二阶段，也是目前中国大部分社区正在强调实施的运用各种技术性手段并配之以各种管理制度的社区建设，其中"网格化管理"就是一个典型，其核心特征就是突出"制度—技术层面"的建设，我们可以称之为社区建设的 2.0 版本。第三阶段的社区建设，我认为最为重要的是作为精神文化形态的社会共同体，也就是中国社区建设未来要聚焦的社会文化和心理情感层面，我们可以称之为社区建设的 3.0 版本。"未来社区"的建设应该将更多的精力放在"以人为中心"的社会文化层面建设中来，以保持其可持续发展的态势。

因此，就核心理念而言，"未来社区"将从关注技术、制度等客体要素转向关注社区发展的核心主体——"人"。假设没有对"人"的重视，那么现代化信息、知识，甚至是组织、社区都可能倾向于忽视他人、排斥弱者，使社区成为彼此封闭的"利益体"。所以在谈技术赋能社区时，需要注意到技术在任何时期都只是工具，而"人"才是必要基础。"未来社区"亟须迎来价值与功能的双重转型，逐步转变成更具人文关怀、智慧性、可持续性的生态社区。

2. 未来社区的主要样态

一是网络虚拟化。数字化、网络化、虚拟化技术的扩展构成了"未来社区"的发展基础。其具有改变传统交互方式并提高经济、社会和环境效率的能力。另外，在应急管理中，我们看到从风险预警、评估到风险防控，人工智能在其中扮演着不可或缺的角色。

二是绿色可持续。绿色、协调、可持续构成了"未来社区"的发展意涵。"未来社区"需要考虑到经济、社会和环境等领域的可持续性，不断开拓生活富裕、生态良好的文明发展之路，在满足自身发展需求的同时，留下蓝天碧海、绿水青山。

三是组织多样性。组织多样性构成了"未来社区"的发展形态。正是由于多样性的存在，在面对社会危机时才不会引致整个社区系统的崩溃。相较于以往的"纵向传导"，"未来社区"将导向于一种"横向互动"模式，多元主体之间的经验分享与风险共担将使得社区治理更富成效。

四是生活幸福感。居民的获得感、富足感与幸福感将构成"未来社区"的发展目标。除了针对不同人群建立起相应的社会支持系统以满足居民需求之外，还要注重对其"精神层面"的关注，强化社区情感共同体建设，增进民众的归属感、认同感。

五是发展不确定性。社会发展的不确定性、不稳定性和不可预测性构成了"未来社区"的发展动力。在现代化语境下，社会发展越来越具有风险和不确定性。风险社会并不是一个历史分期意义上的概念，而是对人类所处时代特征的一种形象的概括和描述，同时具有一定的现实性和实践性。我们需要转换视角，适应不确定的未来发展，同时激发出更多潜力与创造力。

总的来看，"未来社区"的具体表现形态至少可以从两个维度展开思考：一是将"未来社区"视为"发展议题"，二是将"未来社区"视为"发展背景"。第一种视角倾向于关注"未来社区"的自身特性。社区何以可能，又以何为社区成员提供先进的生活理念与生活方式以及智能化、信息化、绿色化的配套基础设施，如何激励社区成员参与社区事务甚至更大范围的社会事务。第二种视角倾向于将"未来社区"视为一种发展背景。强调社区是各种要素共同型塑的产物。其中一些影响是直接的，例如社区成员、社区组织等，而另外一些则是间接的，例如地方文化、宏观政策等。每一部分单独拆开来看并无特殊之处，但当它们互相嵌入共同成为一个社区的时候，就会深刻地影响到未来的发展轨迹与发展样态，因此要重点关注不同要素之间的组合方式和融合方式。

3. 未来社区的治理逻辑与策略

全球化进程的加速不仅放大了传统自然风险，还进一步引发了诸如制度、科技等现代化风险，如今各种风险又开始呈现出一种"联动效应"。本次新冠肺炎疫情的发展已然呈现出"发生不确定性""影响不确定性"以及"响应不确定性"的特点。对此，在"未来社区"中应该如何应对一系列风险事件？"未来社区"的概念意涵与发展样态又能提供哪些切实的解决方案呢？概括来说，主要包括以下几方面要点：

第一，从"依赖技术"到"指引技术"。虽然技术发展是必然趋势，但是近年来愈发凸显的社会风险也使我们认识到所有现代化事物所具有的"双面性"。对此我们迫切需要实现从"依赖技术"到"指引技术"的转换，不将未来的社区治理完全交给技术，而是注重制度能力、价值理念建设，实现"数治"和"人治"的有机统一。

第二，从"线性增长"到"复合发展"。一味追求物质财富的积累是片面的增长观，"未来社区"治理需要从"线性增长"迈向"复合发展"，将重心转移到人际关系、社会关怀、民族团结、生态发展等包容性逻辑中。就"美好生活"终极目标来看，"复合发展"将比传统"线性增长"方法更有意义，也更容易应对这个时代所遭遇的复杂问题。

第三，从"基于生态系统适应"到"基于社区适应"。源于环境科学的"基于生态系统适应"旨在有效应对愈发严重的气候危机。在此基础上提出的"基于社区的适应"模式更是为应对社会风险的复杂性与多变性提供的一种切实有效的解决策略。其主张建立由"社区主导"的风险防范计划，凭借社区的"内生力量"进行自我组织与自我治理，从横向协作的组织关系维度出发，既自我规划、自我服务以满足本地需求，又自我支持、自我援助以释放社区能量。由此，整个社区层面的活力、创新力、协作能力、响应能力都会得到提升。

第四，从"分散治理"到"整体治理"。原本为减少技术风险而产生的"替代技术"在现阶段却被发现会造成更为严重的社会问题；原本用于治理工业污染而产生的"反污染系统"也引发了规模更加庞大的系统性危害。传统治理模式对待每一个问题的方式都是孤立的，解决策略也是"头痛医头，脚痛医脚"式的，长此以往便形成一种典型的"分散治理"思维。相比之下，"未来社区"将采取"整体治理"逻辑，充分认识到社会问题的系统性、复杂性。在各种社会问题之间建立起从知识到行动、从理论到实践的综合应对体系。

第五，从"地方治理"到"全球治理"。"未来社区"治理将与全球化息息相关。若要有效应对全球性灾害，全球风险意识和集体行动是绝对必要的。社区问题之所以积习难除，难以解决，本质上是因为每一项风险既在地方社区中出现，同时也是全球社区的共同产物。然而就全球治理现状而言，无论是难民危机、全球气候危机还是瘟疫、大流行性疾病，全球协作模式都严重匮乏。"放眼全球，立足本地"的口号对于"未来社区"治理来说已经远远不够了，面对未来我们既要"全局思考、全局行动"，又要"局部思考、局部行动"，树立起一种全球治理观。

4. 关于"未来社区"的几点反思

第一点是"未来社区"如何规避千篇一律的建设。"未来社区"的发展目标、发展理念、发展前景、发展思路、发展策略已有了相对清晰的规划，甚至在建筑外观、建筑形式层面都给予了一定的要求。但高度规范化的指标体系亦带来一丝担忧：随着"未来社区"项目的高位推进与基层落实，是否会带来一系列制式统一，从风格、样貌到基本功能都相对趋同，失去多样性和差异性的"未来社区"？

第二点是"未来社区"究竟表征一种清晰的发展图景，还是社区的理想类型，"未来社区"与"智慧社区"的区别在哪里？"未来社区"的概念框架虽然开始被倡导、关注，但是总能隐约看到"智慧社区"的影子。如果说"智慧社区"只实现了部分功能，那么"未来社区"的完整性又会如何体现？特别是在"智慧社区"体系建设不断健全的过程中，"未来社区"如何与"智慧社区"相区别？从这个角度看，"未来社区"是否仍然是一种"理想类型"？是否仍然是"政治命名"的产物？

第三点是为有效应对"未来社区"所面临的社会风险，国家体制、社会机制与现代技术如何进一步契合与协同？技术发展是始终先于国家体制与社会机制建设的，例如疫情期间广泛使用的大数据监控技术，其实早已应用于企业数据分析和网络平台的服务过程中了。此外，传统应急管理制度缺乏与技术平台的磨合，体制内技术人才缺失，数字防控体系尚未健全，社会层面对新兴治理技术不适应等问题频频出现。这些难题都在引导我们去思考未来的风险治理应如何促进三者间的有效协同，又该如何弥合"技术"与"制度"之间的鸿沟。这是我们要进一步去思考的三个问题。

未来社区：现在时将来时的互观

郎友兴

浙江大学公共管理学院教授

未来社区的概念当然不是什么新的概念，在美国、新加坡等国都有了不少实践。在中国几十年的社区建设过程中，也渐渐形成或出现了一些理念、做法，例如，智慧社区、社区O2O、低碳社区、社区微更新、缤纷社区、15分钟社区生活圈。在中国，未来社区概念的创新之处或许就是这些既有概念、做法整合在了一起，获得了一个整体性和系统性的统筹视野。不过，从官方的行动来看，浙江省领先于全国。在2019年3月，浙江省政府发布《浙江省未来社区建设试点工作方案》，首次提出未来社区的概念。

1 以未来社区反思现有社区建设状况

对照未来社区对老旧小区综合进行改造与提升。《浙江省未来社区建设试点工作方案》里提出了构建未来邻里、教育、健康、创业、建筑、交通、低碳、服务和治理九大场景。就目前来说，比如杭州，重点还是要解决社区的基础设施问题，或者说，通过未来社区的建设，带动并推进周边社区基础设施建设，提供良好的社区服务，甚至推动产业转型上的联动发展，进而推动整个区域发展。

关键依然是社区治理体系问题。目前不少社区，在治理主体关系上、居民的参与方面、归属与认同感方面普遍存在程序不一的问题。一是物业、业委会、居民之间存在多种矛盾；二是社区服务精细化程度不足；三是人文关怀缺失，人文氛围、传统文化等文化软实力较弱；四是居民的参与性不足；五是居民归属感、认同感弱。

这些问题的存在也可能影响到未来社区的建设，比如如何将未来社区的绿色、开放、共享等先进理念植入现有社区之中，从而引导居民群众、小区相关联单位共同参与老旧小区改造，实现决策共谋、发展共建、建设共管、效果共评、成果共享，助力居民创建有归属感、舒适感和未来感的社区环境；以及如何以未来社区的人本化理念来推动社区人文环境的建设等。

2. 从现实看未来社区建设可能存在的问题

第一，概念及其涵盖面的界定。因为未来社区的概念外延太广，几乎涵盖了城市生活的方方面面。也没有比较官方的对于"未来社区"的定义，浙江官方的说法就是"三化九场景"（图1）。现在农村也搞未来社区，例如浙江衢州。

第二，未来社区可能会出现千人一面的现象，类同性现象严重。不少地方推进了规划效果图，似乎有千人一面之感。

第三，未来社区如何融入城市之中，成为城市有机整体的一部分。是否出现这样的情形：未来社区能够自成体系，却无法与周遭发生呼应，更无法融入生活圈。未来社区不应该成为一件衣服中的一块补丁，尽管这块补丁是很新很时尚的。

图1
浙江省"未来社区"的
"三化九场景"

未来社区治理的结构性因素

景跃进

清华大学政治学系教授

我们在谈到中国未来社区的时候，基本上沿袭了现有的框架和思路设想，尽管技术有所突破，但是在治理的机制和体制方面保持了延续性。今天我就从两个方面来探讨这个问题，即两个会制约我们对未来社区想象空间的结构性因素。这两个因素可以被概括为横向坐标和纵向坐标。

1. 横向坐标

第一个，横向坐标。今天看来，中国政治生活中最重要的横向坐标是党政关系。在计划经济时期，党政不分是高度集权体制的一个基本特征。党政关系破局以后，政府与企业的关系、中央和地方的关系、政府与市场的关系，以及国家和社会的关系，有了分化的空间。党的十八大以前人们经常谈论的是政治体制改革、经济体制改革、村民自治等等，这在党政分开的语境之下容易得到充分的理解。十八大以后发生了一个重大的变化，在党政关系的处置方面明显不同于当初强调的党政分开。当党政关系重新回归它的原点，先前在党政分开条件之下所考虑的国家和社会的关系、政府和市场关系、央地关系等是否需要重新考量？在对未来社区的想象中，是否需要将党政关系变化这一新变量纳入其中？这个问题还没有引起足够的重视，或者说很多人尚未意识到这一变量的潜在意义。

我对农村基层治理这一块比较了解，当时在推进村民自治的时候，有两个具有普遍性的重要问题，到现在依然存在。其中一个问题是，如果村民搞海选，党支部不再推荐村委会候选人，候选人对全体村民开放。在这种情况下，村党组织的领导作用如何发挥，与村委会的关系如何处置，构成了一个制度性、结构性的问题。一些地方出现的村两委矛盾便是一个经验表征。现在重新强调农村党组织的领导地位，并采取各种组织举措加以保障，那么我们就需要反向提问，在保障和实现党的领导的前提下，村民自治如何落实？核心问题是村民选举如何不流于形式？

由此可见，宏观层面党政关系的变化直接制约了基层治理的探索空间。尽管在法理上，社区不是政府，社区治理不能等同于政府治理，但在党政体制下，高层与基层的党政关系是同构的。由此不难理解为何在实践层面社区治理常常难以避免行政化色彩。所以，考虑中国未来社区发展必须将党政关系这一结构性变量纳入进来，这个变量会长期作用于城乡社区治理体系和治理结构。

2. 纵向坐标

第二个是纵向坐标。随着城市化进程加快、信息技术飞速进步，国家和社会的关系有一个重要的变化，那就是从原来的汲取农村资源到现在的国家反哺，在资源反哺的过程中国家权力再次下乡。如果说横向维度的党政关系经历了"党政不分—党政分开—党政融合"三个环节的变化，那么在纵向维度，国家权力向乡村社会的渗透，呈现出"国家与社会一体（人民公社体制）—国家权力从乡村社会撤退—国家权力再次进入乡村"的螺旋式循环。在这个过程中，乡村治理的单元问题成为一个重要的分析变量。

比如在搞村民自治的时候，最初的村委会是在自然村（屯）层面出现的，以解决公社制度解体之后出现的失序问题，维持社会治安，但对于国家来讲，它需要解决的是宏观性的结构问题，人民公社转化为乡镇以后，生产大队这一级需要做相应的转变，所以国家制定的村民自治法律将村民自治的单元提升到行政村一级。在加速城镇化和新农村建设的过程中，出现了大量的并村现象。农村基层治理单元的规模扩大，从一个不同的角度推动了村委会的行政化。在城市社区领域，类似的现象以不同的机制呈现：信息技术的大量运用极大地提升了政府的治理能力和自信心，政府对基层社区的渗透能力与之前相比，完全不可同日而语。一个越来越明显的趋势是，在大数据和云计算的助力下，原先的各级政府以及政府与社区的关系正在得到全新的重构，一个将不同层级的政府和社区整合起来的治理综合体正在浮现：在这个治理综合体中，原先被认为是实行社区自治的基层治理单元，现在被转化为其中的一个节点；也就是说，基层治理单元独立性被弱化，在很大程度上被消解了。

3. 未来社区治理要考虑的问题

在这样的背景之下，我们提出几个问题：第一个问题是如何理解村民自治和社区自治，是否要对自治进行重新界定。第二个问题，在高度行政化的过程当中，基层治理单元自主性和独立性被弱化。在这种情况下，如何发挥社会的作用？这是目前体制遇到的两个基本问题，在关于未来社区的想象中也不能回避，必须正面对待。从宏观角度上来讲，"政府—市场—社会"的三元框架在全世界各国都是一样的，现在十九届五中全会提到了"有效市场和有为政府的结合"。而"社会"这一块如何在中国去展现，它应该展现的是什么样的面貌，如何将"社会"更好地融入未来国家治理框架之中，需要我们进一步的思考。

构建"共治"+"智治"的社区治理下城模式

杨晓萍

浙江省杭州市下城区民政局局长

下城位于杭州的核心地区，也是杭州的老城区，面积是 31 平方公里，下辖 8 个街道，75 个社区，常住人口有 528 000 人，是一个典型的以老旧小区为主体的城区，社区治理工作一直走在全市前列。近年来，我们一直在思考社区治理该如何适应新的发展，比如顺应数字化浪潮，借助信息化、智慧化的手段助推社区治理再上新台阶，帮助解决社区治理中亟待解决的几个传统问题，如何凝聚人、吸引人、引领人，扩大社区参与面，真正让社区自治回归居民自治等，积极寻求解决的方法。

1. 夯实"共治"+"智治"下城治理模式的群众基础

一是夯实治理模式的群众基础。我们一直希望能够在城市社区也培育熟人社会、能人治理的居民自治的土壤。现在，社区工作者是社区治理过程中的中坚力量，但是随着社区工作者逐步向专业化、职业化发展，他们也是一支由财政供养的、除了行政事业编制之外的特殊编制人员。在居民群众的眼中，社区工作者与街道干部、机关干部并没有太多实质性的区别。为此，我们提出了居委会成员中"本土化率"的概念。在上一届的居委会换届选举过程中，我们推选产生了 295 名居民领袖来担任我们居委会的成员，其中有 19 人担任居委会主任，居委会本土化率实现 71.78%。我们希望在社区治理过程中，利用这些老杭州、老街坊、老邻里的这种关系，凭借本土化语言和愿意为街坊邻里服务的热忱，有效推动邻里矛盾调解、小区停车难等社区难点问题的解决。比如我们曾引入"开放空间"议事法，通过上门沟通、多轮商议、民主表决等途径，有效地统一住户思想，解决了困扰居民多年的餐饮油污堵塞污水管问题。

二是完善自治路径、全周期居民参与的保障机制。首先从财政资金上来说，是按照常住人口每人每年 10 元的标准，配备社区自治的项目金，全区的预算基本上是在 528 万元到 600 万元之间。在一些具体事务上，我们是通过事前的判断（征集民意）、事中的参与、事后的评估修复这三个机制来保障居民在社区工作中能够做到全流程、全周期的参与和管理。

三是设计可见可闻、贴近民需的居民自治内容。我们在每年自治金项目的设计过程中，优先考虑与居民民生相关的实事项目。如社区图书馆的修建、公园的维修或是停车库的整治等。这些项目的启动，能够吸引更多的居民，凝聚更多的力量，使居民对社区治理成果有更深的幸福感和获得感。

2. 健全"共治"＋"智治"下城治理模式的工作保障

一是优化制度设计，助力社区发展。首先，我们对现有社区的制度进行了优化，厘清了工作职责。目前下城区的社区主要有社区党组织、社区居委会、公共服务工作站和居务监督委员会这几个组织。对于居委会，我们希望能够通过本土化率的提高，真正回归到居民自治，发挥它的自治功能；而公共服务工作站更多的是承接政府公共服务，并向社区基层延伸；居务监督委员会则主要负责工程监督。通过厘清组织职责边界，实现科学平衡发展。其次，我们构建了一个比较好的评估体系。目前，我们主要从邻里友善度、居民参与度、居民满意度、社区服务力、社区组织力等几个维度来引领社区的发展，减轻社区考核的负担。同时，按照浙江政务服务"最多跑一次"的工作要求，来严格推行社区事项准入制。最后，我们积极培育了"公羊会""武林大妈""红色义工站"等一系列的社会组织品牌，扶持社区优质公益项目。目前，全区的社会组织已经达到 2 600 余家，在社区的老年人、妇女、儿童、残疾人、失业人员、困难家庭扶助，青少年社区矫正，以及社区禁毒等方面发挥着更具专业化的力量。

图 1
现代城市社区智治在线系统

二是研发智治在线，助力智慧治理。我们主要目标是在社区打造一个以精密智控、精准服务、全周期管理为目标的社区自治在线平台。这个平台与城市大脑、浙江基层治理等四个平台之间能够进行快速流转，从而实现部门数据之间的打通，为社区治理构建一个实时动态的基础信息和基础数据库。同时，这个平台还对民政、社保、残疾人保障等民生服务保障类政策进行汇集，形成政策数据库。此外，还可以对个人身份信息进行比对分析，从而实现提前、主动和及时的预警，有效减轻社工的负担，帮助社工更具针对性地进行走访，从原来靠经验判断到如今依托数据分析技术，化被动应付为主动服务。

三是融合线上线下，助力减负增效。无论是自治还是共治，最重要的还是居民参与，要有线上线下的融合。为此，我们也搭建了多个专业化的平台，如社区居民能够使用的"亲邻 e 站"手机客户端和社区工作人员使用的社区工作小程序，也有"社区自治在线"等综合性的平台。"亲邻 e 站"小程序是居民说事议事评事的平台，通过计算机自动算法对平台上居民的反馈进行数据处理，从而形成搜索热词，让社区居民随时了解评论事务的进展情况，提高社区的工作和沟通效率。

此外，针对我们老龄化程度较高的人口特点（全区老龄化比例已经接近 28%，有三个街道老龄化比例已经超过 31%），我们把养老服务作为平台打造的重点方向，养老服务机构实现线上派单，改变过去招投标制定商家的做法。为解决老人对智慧化设备适应能力不强的问题，我们推出"养老顾问"制度，请具有专业养老知识和社会工作经验方法的专业人员上门为老人科学定制一对一的养老服务，形成线上需求。老人遇到困难只需拨打统一电话。平台实现所有服务"一号呼应"、服务供给"一图全览"以及服务流程"一网闭环"。

3. 优化"共治"+"智治"下城治理模式的实现路径

一是延伸基本公共服务。梳理区、街道、社区三级行政审批和公共服务职能，规范街道、社区两级便民服务中心建设；采取 24 小时在线贴心政务服务，审批服务事项"全时办"；成立全省首家物管站，推进老旧小区综合改造，首创"小区管家"服务模式等。

二是建强专业服务队伍。目前全区社区工作者中取得助理社会工作师及以上资格的有 603 人，占比 63.08%。下城区致力于建立社会组织和社会工作人才信息资源库，重点培养职业化、专业化的社会组织运营、管理和督导人才；推进社工转型，由"项目社工"成立的社工机构承接的街道、社区公共服务项目总金额累计达 1 180 万元。

三是营造社区公共精神。我们推广下城"最美现象"，形选树如孔胜东、黄飞华、鲍倩等"居民模范"，培育塑造各具特征的社区精神。开展邻居节活动，倡导文明礼让、邻里和睦、守望相助的社会新风尚。组织"重家庭、立家训、传家风"活动，大力建设"好家风"。积极建设广场文化、楼院文化、家庭文化、节庆文化，丰富居民文化生活，进一步提升居民群众的社区荣誉感。

从治理难到治理易：未来社区治理之道

陈伟东

华中师范大学政治与国际关系学院教授

1. 基层社区治理的难点

我想讨论的这个问题是，现在基层社区治理难在哪里，以及我们怎么样走向未来的社区治理。首先，我是从组织的资源能力这个角度来谈的，即组织自主的、高效的配置资源，以完成各种功能性活动的能力。

我从 2000 年开始做社区调查研究，感受到现在的社区治理难在两个方面："天然难"和"人为难"。"天然难"是指社区要面对所有的问题，所谓"上管天、下管地、中间管空气"。尽管很多人平时不一定去社区，但是他们往往在遇到问题的时候，就会找社区。但是，在我看来，社区更难的是制度性失能。有一句俗话叫做"英雄无用武之地，巧妇难为无米之炊"。"人为难"主要体现在两个方面，一个是"巧妇难为无米之炊"，缺乏资源；另一个是"巧妇有米也难炊"，有资源却没有自主权，存在专业能力不足、时间精力不够、行为失范等问题。现在基层社区治理过程中始终没有解决的一个难题，就是通常我们所讲的"看得见的管不着，管得着的看不见"。

2. 基层社区治理的解释变量

我主要从组织的资源能力，提出六个解释变量。

"巧妇难为无米之炊"主要体现在两个解释变量上：一是组织数量越多，资源越多，治理越易；反之，组织数量越少，资源越少，治理越难。尽管现在社区中有很多单位，但是大多数并不参与社区治理，资源利用率很低。二是组织种类越多，资源越丰富，治理越易；反之，组织种类越单一，资源越贫乏，治理越难。而"巧妇有米难炊"主要是因为下面四个变量：三是组织自主性越强，资源能力越强，治理越易；反之，组织依赖性越强，资源能力越低，治理越难。现在社区自主性相对较低，作为特别法人，社区却没有相应的财政自主权，"居财街管、村财乡管"，目前全国各地还没有关于社区财政自主权的文件。四是组织越专门化，资源能力越强，治理越易；反之，组织任务越繁杂，资源能力越弱，治理越难。五是组织越专业化，资源能力越强，治理越易；反之，组织专业性越低，资源能力越弱，治理越难。六是组织越规范化，资源分配越公平，治理越易；反之，资源分配越不公，治理越难。

3. 未来社区治理之道

我们要迈向未来的社区治理，一是要社区开放化，实现政府开放、社区开放，多元组织参与，从而实现资源下沉、治理有效；二是社区治理自主化，形成能动的基层；三是社区治理法制化，促进资源分配制度化；四是社区治理精细化，推动社区治理精细分工，组织任务专门化；五是社区治理专业化。

最后，我们讲"共享"是 21 世纪新的生产方式和生活方式，那么共享权力和资源，也是未来社区一种新的治理方式。

复杂韧性系统分析：阿苏国立公园与当地社区合作来维持草地生态系统

上野真也

日本熊本大学名誉教授

1. 目标、背景和方法

本研究旨在通过对社会生态系统韧性的研究，加强对自然资源和社区的区域管理。

研究背景是乡村地区存在许多困难，但从城市治理的角度来看，城市发展依赖于农村环境的健康维护，特别是农村地区的水资源和补给区。近年来，由于草地资源经济价值丧失，草原面临着巨大困难。草原对于维护良好的生态环境非常重要。因此，如何保护草原在日本和我所在的地区都是非常重要的问题。

本研究的研究方法包括农村社区自然资源管理能力的实地研究、社会资本问卷调查、复杂韧性系统的韧性思维和系统动态思想的运用。

熊本的气候条件与上海类似。阿苏区位于九州岛的中心。作为一个水资源区，它涵养了九州岛一半的人口。

2. 生态演替：适应性循环

生态演替是一种适应性循环。刚开始是裸露的土地，然后长出了苔藓，再然后有了一年生植物，形成一片草原。然后再长出多年生草。有了草之后，小树和不耐阴树木就会慢慢长出来，形成森林。最后，在最终状态中，出现了耐阴树种。在日本，这种从光秃秃的土地到森林的演替非常容易形成。但为了保护这里的草原，我们就需要阻止不耐阴树木的生长。这意味着我们每年都要在山上或草地上放火烧掉这些树木。这就是为什么我们一万年来能一直保留最大草原景观的原因。但是这么做成本很高，需要很多劳力。

20世纪60年代以来日本最大的变化是不再利用草地资源了。在能源革命之前，我们用木柴或木炭做饭取暖，还使用堆肥和绿肥，但现在我们普遍用的是化肥。绿肥是一种环保型肥料。如图2所示，使用草地的需求下降得非常快。所以我们才要人为地增加对草地资源的

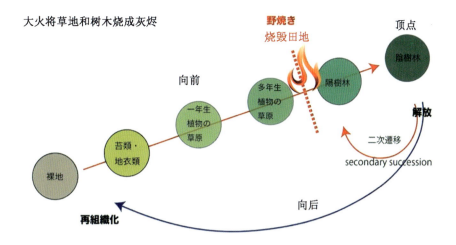

图 1
生态演替

大火将草地和树木烧成灰烬

野烧き
烧毁田地

顶点

陰樹林

向前

陽樹林

解放

二次遷移
secondary succession

裸地

苔類・地衣類

一年生植物の草原

多年生植物の草原

再組織化

向后

利用。

　　图 3 中的阿苏地区处在一个非常美丽的季节。你可以看到美丽的草原，远处还有许多牛。如图 4 所示，我们一般在 2 月、3 月间放火烧山。当地社区居民齐心协力，在该地区所有山脉间放火。在 5 月或 6 月之后新草长出来时，农民就会在草区放牛。这就形成了一个非常健康的草地利用系统。

3. 社区功能和社会网络

　　这一系统得到了社区网络的支持。社区居民建立了必要的人际网络。居民们组建了许多重要的组织，如社区和各种协会。他们在社区拥有自主权。社区居民共同承担着保持自然资源、增加生产和促进旅游业发展等多种职责。即使是在洪水或地震等危机时刻，他们也会齐心协力，为社区大家庭提供帮助。

　　社区内部的网络也非常重要，特别是需要覆盖范围广泛的环境管理领域。在社区间网络

图 2
社区森林和草地利用
变化

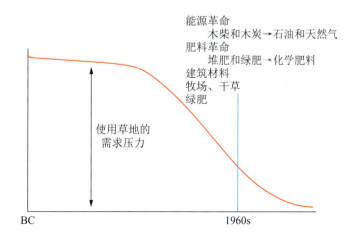

能源革命
木柴和木炭→石油和天然气
肥料革命
堆肥和绿肥→化学肥料
建筑材料
牧场、干草
绿肥

使用草地的需求压力

BC

1960s

图 3
阿苏国立公园

图 4
阿苏国立公园内放火
烧山

之上是地方政府，他们会负责这一问题。在阿苏地区，有 7 个行政区、市、町和村政府。它们作为内部政府网络协同工作。层层递进的管理网络对于保持自然资源的良好管理非常重要。

图 5 是一项社会调查的结果，显示了每个问题的偏差值。我做的全日本调查显示平均值是 50。虽然阿苏地区许多社区人口数量减少很快，老龄化趋势也很严重，但却在许多项目中得分都很高（见图 6）。目前，管理工作基本覆盖了 60 岁以上的人群。代际趋势（见图 7）表明，与老年人相比，年轻一代所占的比例较小。生活方式的改变对当地活动有很大的影响。

图 5
每个问题的偏差值

问候和会话的程度
关联的程度
邻居的数量
与朋友见面的频率
谈论政治的频率
参与居民协会的活动
参与志愿者活动
参与犯罪预防和灾害预防活动
参与农场道路和水路管理活动
你有可以咨询的人吗？
你有会照顾你的人吗？
对当地人的信任
解决当地问题的能力
归还丢失钱包的概率
为社区活动提供劳动
社会责任

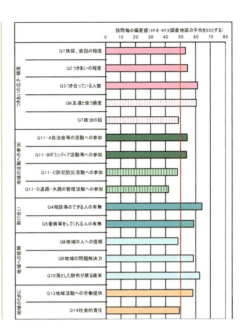

图 6
阿苏地区人口构成

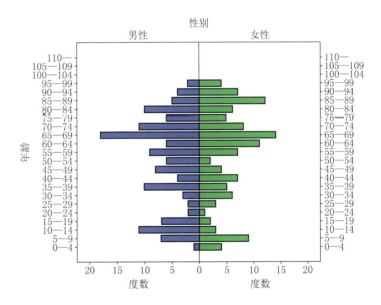

图 7
代际趋势

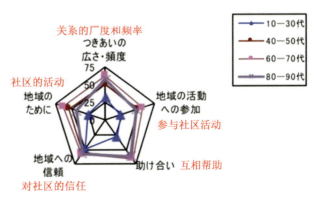

4. 草地向森林过渡的模拟

图 8 为草地向森林过渡的模拟。1982 年，我们这里的草地范围还很大，但现在部分森林面积在扩大。预计到 2050 年，森林面积会进一步增加。众所周知森林对环境有益。但在阿苏，草地才是最有利的景观，而非森林。我们需要想办法在未来保护这些草地。

图 8
草地向森林过渡的
模拟

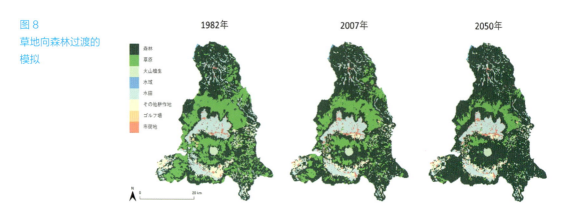

图 9 显示了生态系统的过渡。通常，生态系统一开始会迅猛发展，然后在某一时刻达到养护期。在这个养护时期内，我们通常会通过政府补贴和其他一些措施来维持这一阶段。但最终，这个养护期会到达极限。然后就会突然发生破坏性或创造性的变化。所有的自然资源都被重新释放到了市场上。然后重新调整的周期就又开始了。这是创新的开端。

图 9
社会生态系统基本
变化

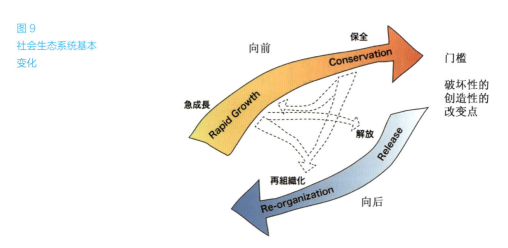

这一趋势是生态系统中一个非常常见的模型。如果置之不理，天然的草地状态就会变成森林系统。如图 10 所示，如果一直停留在状态 1，非常好。但如果环境发生变化，就很难一直维持在状态 1。突然间，系统会进入状态 2。一旦你转移到一个新的状态，就再也回不去了。

图10
将系统模拟为球的盆
体模型

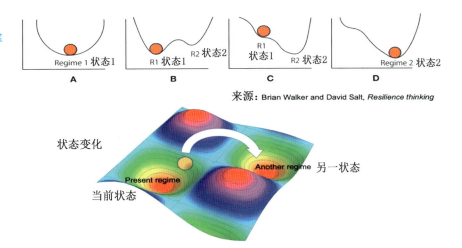

来源：Brian Walker and David Salt, *Resilience thinking*

状态变化

另一状态

当前状态

图 11 显示的是阿苏地区某个村庄的情况。虽然我们仍然每年春天放火，但一些牧场和草原已经停止运转了。这幅图中描绘了一个悲观的未来，但我认为每个牧场或草地就像一个个模块，是孤立的。如果我们和社区居民一起努力，也许就能够改变现状。

图 11
南阿苏村的状态
是否发生了变化
（1999—2019）

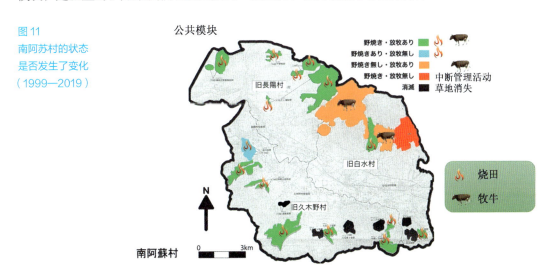

5. 未来情景

首先，我们需要通过社区活动来维护草原。其次，目前我们正在做社区活动，还与城市志愿者展开合作和捐赠，但我们需要更多的改进。

6. 基于社会生态韧性思维的干预措施

首先，我们要增加对社会生态系统的了解。这是一个复杂的适应系统，而非简单的线性链条。其次，我们需要加强社区自治，在未来更多地依靠社区活动。

7. 授权社区维持当前状态

如图 12 所示，目前有两种循环模式：一种循环可以加强地方治理，而另一种循环可以减少社区治理。这两种不同模式结合在一起便创造了一个平衡的循环。如果我们能加强信任循环，也许就能改变移动或过渡的方式。但如果我们失败了，递减循环就会变得更强。因此，我们提出了社会资本循环，用以加强信任循环。

图 12
两个循环的平衡

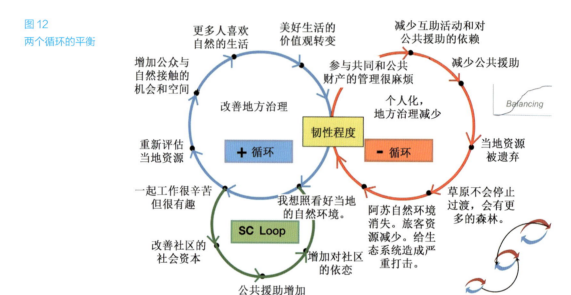

15 分钟社区：社区公共空间再造

拉斯穆斯·唐-格鲁内

丹麦哥本哈根城市规划设计事务所主任

今天我想谈一谈 15 分钟城市，或叫 15 分钟社区，以及为什么它在我们谈论城市社区时相当重要。

1. 盖尔方法：建设以人为本的城市

我来自盖尔，盖尔是基于扬·盖尔教授的研究而成立的一个事务所。我们以"建设以人为本的城市"为使命，结合学术角度并联系人类行为来分析社会的实际环境。比如人类行为会基于实际环境发生什么样的变化？其中一些有关我们研究的著作也可以在中国买到，也有中文版。

我们所理解的城市发展方式不同于传统的规划流程。传统的规划流程是先搭建建筑，完善交通和基础设施建设，再研究如何为社区生活提供支持。

我们与之相反。我们首先会想："我们想要为什么样的生活和社区提供支持？"再去看为此我们需要什么基础和条件，最后就能理解我们需要什么样的建筑，以及进一步的发展方向应该是如何的。所以，生活应该是被放在第一位的。也就是，我们想要什么样的城市生活？

我们从个人的角度进行了很多研究，什么是对个人有利的？但我们又同时从集体的角度出发来思考，这能为整个城市和社区带来什么好处？同时，我们还将其与联合国可持续发展目标联系了起来。

比如在哥本哈根，我们所做的就是努力实现哥本哈根的城市愿景，即建设"人性化大都市"。我们所设想的哥本哈根发展愿景以市民为重心，在过去 15 到 20 年里，哥本哈根在这一方面已经取得了长足的发展。在哥本哈根内城，我们规划建设了许多类似这样的地方。在这里，城市正在慢慢改变，在重点关注行人和骑行者的同时也为社区提供了许多支持。当然，海港沿岸的环境非常好，干净的海水也很适合游泳。这些都吸引着很多人来到这里，驻足游玩，成为这座城市一道靓丽的风景线。

图 1
哥本哈根海港

2. 盖尔案例：15 分钟本地社区

在世界各地，包括中国，我们进行了很多有关"舒适生活圈"或"社区生活圈"这一概念的研究和实践，在有些地方这也被称为"15 分钟本地社区"。这背后的理念是，要更多关注社区在 15 分钟可达范围内能提供什么样的服务设施，从而发展一种可持续的社区生活方式。也就是说，你可以利用好整座城市。

而上海就是一个很好的例子。我们需要利用好上海这座城市的全部资源，明确若要实现上述的社区生活方式，我们在本地社区需要做些什么。在中国，我们目前正与能源基金会和我们的合作伙伴宇恒可持续交通研究中心进行合作。例如，我们重点开展了"五步提升城市品质"的工作，这也是一种思考未来城市的方式。接下来我想再举几个例子。我们之前的一项重要工作是与上海市城市规划设计研究院合作编写《上海市街道设计导则》。这份街道设计原则着眼于城市和标识方式，并要确保城市和街道也被视为公共空间。这些地方也是生活的一部分，也就是说我们走在街道上也是为了感受生活，而不仅仅是为了交通或出行。

我们也有很多工作是围绕人们熟知的"慢行"这个概念，也就是强调慢节奏的出行方式，

图 2
四项基本策略

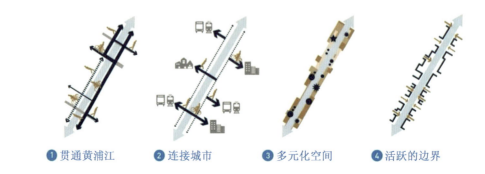

❶ 贯通黄浦江　　❷ 连接城市　　❸ 多元化空间　　❹ 活跃的边界

而不必一直处于快节奏。比如在上海，盖尔已经与不同政府部门展开了合作，共同研究黄浦江沿岸公共空间的设计规划，并参与了其中的四项工作（图2）。我们已经开发了许多类似这样的地方，并为许多这样的活动提供了支持。经过数年的发展，如今上海黄浦江沿岸45公里的公共空间已实现了贯通。这些地方能够更好地支持本地社区发展，不仅方便休闲娱乐，也为市民提供了社交活动的场所。

对我们来说十分重要的一点是，我们要先决定需要打造什么样的社区实际环境，才能为本地社区提供支持，因为15分钟社区的发展非常依赖于周围的实际环境。我们非常荣幸地看到，习近平主席在2019年走访了黄浦江，并谈到公共空间是当今城市发展中非常重要的一部分。我们在设计南京路时也遇到了同样的情况，南京路的末段南京东路之前仍是允许汽车通行的，但经过评估，我们发现在南京路，行人的人流量更大，所以其实走南京东路的基本都是行人。另外，过去和平饭店前有很多车道，但这里其实也是人们本地化社区生活的一部分，他们需要在这里生活和工作。

因此2015年，我们提出了针对这条路的改造设想，并开始逐步实施，这就是这条路今天的样子。这些地方不仅有企业，还有来来往往的本地人，因此对本地社区的建设十分重要。

3. 新冠肺炎疫情对 15 分钟社区的影响

最后，当我们在讨论15分钟社区时，也应该要从过去半年的新冠肺炎疫情中汲取教训。在盖尔，我们针对欧洲和美国的情况进行了调查和分析，也研究了一些亚洲的情况。如

图3
本地活动场所人流量
有所增加

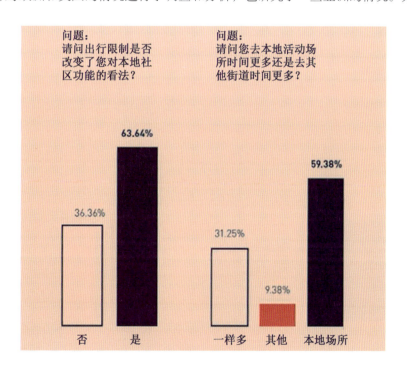

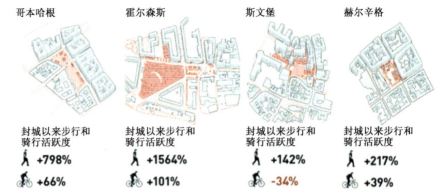

图 4
在丹麦的四个城市
中，步行和骑行活跃
度都在增长

哥本哈根　　　　霍尔森斯　　　　斯文堡　　　　赫尔辛格

封城以来步行和　封城以来步行和　封城以来步行和　封城以来步行和
骑行活跃度　　　骑行活跃度　　　骑行活跃度　　　骑行活跃度
🚶 +798%　　　🚶 +1564%　　　🚶 +142%　　　🚶 +217%
🚲 +66%　　　　🚲 +101%　　　　🚲 -34%　　　　🚲 +39%

果您感兴趣，可以在 covid19.gehlpeople.com 上下载完整报告。本研究的重点是分析新冠肺炎疫情期间公共场所人流量的变化情况。疫情期间确实有很多人选择居家不出，或需要居家办公，但有一个现象是，尽管中心购物街和许多办公园区的人流量明显下降，15 分钟社区内的公共场所人流量仍有所上升（图 3）。

我们可以看到，丹麦这四个城市的出行活跃度都在增长（图 4），尤其是步行和骑行，即所说的"慢行"。这些市民都是在本地社区就近出行，而不是到很远的地方。因此我们需要在本地社区为他们提供支持，打造建设公共空间，确保他们能享受良好的社区生活。

我们尤其会谈到 5—15 分钟步行（图 5），也就是 5 到 15 分钟步行的可达范围内有什么？这是全球都愈发关注的一个问题。我的祖国丹麦虽然已经做得很好了，但是我们仍在探索 5—15 分钟的可达范围内能进一步提供什么支持，这也是我们现在正在中国做的一些工作。

我们看到步行和骑行正成为越来越常见的出行方式，这也表明人们需要能够就近享受到本地社区的设施与服务。比如，北京的自行车高速公路上就有大量骑行者，在上海也是同样的情况。我认为这在今后会成为人们更加关注的问题。

图 5
5—15 分钟步行

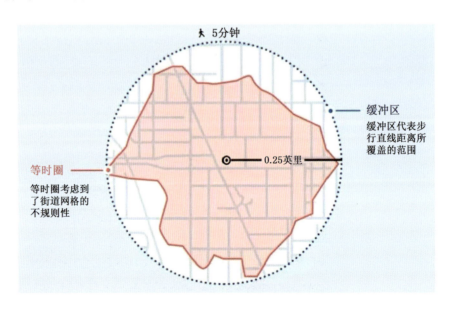

"公共空间、公共服务与公共秩序"三位一体建构：多功能社区服务综合体建设与社区发展

唐亚林

复旦大学国际关系与公共事务学院教授

1. 社区治理的转向：从社区自治走向治理与发展兼具的社区发展

20 年前，我们比较强调社区自治，到今天，我们更多的是把"社区""治理"和"发展"联系在一起，不是一个简单的靠推进如社区民主选举这种单兵突进的做法。是什么原因导致社区的"治理"和"发展"成为我们工作的重心呢？有五个方面的原因。

第一个是时代变迁。基于多年来对以民主选举与社区管理为核心的社区治理绩效的反思，我们发现单兵突进的以社区民主选举为导向的社区自治成效不彰，社区治理出现了从突出政治性到强调服务性再到如今强调以政治性引领服务性的转变，并走向了以生活需要为主的生活共同体的建构这一新趋势。第二个是需求导向。社区治理基于民众需要的多样化与多层次内容的变化，走向了以交往需要为主的关系共同体的建构。第三个是特色创新。基于社区自治形态的特色化认识的深化，如通过载体、项目、机制等的创新，社区治理走向了以个性化需要为主的体验共同体的建构。第四个是管理精细。基于城市基层精细化管理的思考，在社区环境、社区治安、社区卫生、社区文化等领域，推进以垃圾分类、15 分钟公共文化服务圈建设、老旧小区及其适老化改造为核心的精细化治理与服务等进程，社区治理走向了以精准需要为主的生态共同体的建构。最后一个是政治统治。这也是最为核心的，基于强化政权根基建设的有效性思考，社区治理走向了以联动需要为主的协作共同体的建构。

综合而言，社区治理的发展趋势，出现了从过往由政府负责指导的、以选举为核心的、以稳定安全秩序为价值诉求的、以功能性服务为重点的社区自治，走向了社区组织负责、政府出资、专业社会组织指导、群众广泛参与协商、科技手段赋能的，解决民众实际生活问题和建构安全秩序的共同参与平台的搭建与运作机制体系的建构，也就是从社区自治走向治理与发展兼具的社区发展。

2. 需求导向与功能满足的对接：多功能社区服务综合体建设的兴起与社区公共空间的再造

近年来，各地在推进社区服务与社区治理等方面，出现了将面向基本同类居民群体、涵盖各种服务功能却分散在诸如党群服务中心、社区服务中心、社区文化服务中心、社区卫生服务中心等各类服务设施空间进行重新整合的趋势，重点按照共享集约、便捷可及、成本可控、服务高效等原则，推进一定区域范围内公共服务设施空间布局的科学化、标准化与效用化建设，其表现形式就是多功能社区服务综合体建设与社区公共空间再造的兴起。

是什么原因推动了社区多功能服务综合体的建设进程呢？首先是实践发展需要。在上海的各区，相继出现了诸如浦东新区"家门口服务体系"、杨浦区"睦邻中心"和徐汇区"邻里汇"的建设的实践，其主要做法也在于将面向社区居民的各类服务功能进行整合，这是实践推动的创新活动，也可以说是社区治理已经发展到新阶段的必然需求。在全国各地，也出现了这一新趋势，比如成都比较早地推进了社区多功能综合体建设进程。更早的话，我们可以追溯到"十二五"规划关于乡村文化建设中乡镇文化综合服务站建设的安排，但是那个时候更加强调的是用有限的资源来推动乡村文化的发展。

从文件规定来看，2020 年 6 月中共上海市委办公厅、上海市人民政府办公厅印发了《关于进一步提升社区治理规范化精细化水平的若干意见》，其中提出推广社区服务综合体建设，并推动各区根据"共享集约、便捷可及"原则，因地制宜、合力布局，加快推进社区综合服务设施标准化建设，实现社区全覆盖。将社区服务综合体的建设提上日程，一是为了回应民政部的新要求，二是为了解决社区发展实践中存在的问题，如服务设施分散、利用效率不高、部门协作机制缺失、党员群众覆盖不足等。

第二是满足需求导向。上海在推进基层治理创新过程中，特别强调要以需求导向、问题导向和结果导向三大导向为基层工作开展和社区治理创新的出发点。将需求导向与功能满足有机对接，将老百姓的需求作为推动治理创新的"指挥棒"，可以有效改进工作盲目开展的不足，提升民众的满意度和获得感。

第三是创新基层治理服务方式。在实际工作中，像浦东"家门口"服务体系在建设过程中，首先是让广大的基层社区工作者改变工作作风，直面广大社区群众，变管理者为服务者，并把居委会和党支部书记的工作场所进行功能化改造，变成直接面向群众的、集多功能于一体的综合性多功能服务空间。其次，浦东新区提出了社区服务涵盖党群服务、政务服务、生活服务、法律服务、健康服务、文化服务、社区管理服务七大类基本服务内容，要通过社区治理的政治功能、服务功能、组织功能、治理功能的整合和带动，实现对这些基本服务的有效供给和精准递送。

3. 寓公共服务与公共秩序于公共空间：多功能社区服务综合体的关系构造及复合形态

从理论关怀上来看，在多功能社区服务综合体的关系构造和复合形态的背后，是国家治理重心下移与基层社会秩序的重构。

一般而言，基层社会秩序主要包括环境秩序、交通秩序、安全秩序、服务秩序、空间秩序五大类。在城市治理重心下移的背景下，需要运用权力在一定区域空间内对人力、资源、服务、平台、技术等进行统合，以达到系统性地解决高效服务群众"最后一公里"问题之目的。在此过程中，多功能社区服务综合体的建设，既融合了面对社区同类群众的多样化服务，又可通过服务建构关系，即通过服务和人群的联结，形成新型交往关系、新型服务关系、新型协商关系与新型邻里关系。

与此同时，因服务与技术的嵌套、服务与平台的嵌套、服务与组织的嵌套等新型服务方式的创新，还出现了多功能社区服务综合体的复合形态，即将扁平化技术性虚体体系（微信群、App 应用、社区通、一网通）嵌套在科层制物理性实体体系（办公场所、服务场所、活动场所、健身场所）之上，建构了权力结构体系与治理空间体系的嵌套、管理网络体系与服务网络体系的嵌套、服务平台体系和资源网络体系的嵌套等复合形态，从而形成了突破时空限制的融多功能于一体的社区服务复合型空间。

4. 回到生活与交往共同体：社区发展与基层治理的融合模式

我们要看到社区治理、基层治理、社会治理与城市治理、地区治理、国家治理之间的有机统一关系，进而在促进社区发展与基层治理的过程中，推进生活与交往共同体的建构，这是社区发展与基层治理融合发展的最终归宿。

这种体现社区发展与基层治理相融合的生活与交往共同体的内在意涵是多方面的：一是构建基于阵地意识的生活与交往共同体。基层治理是带有阵地意识的，不仅是服务阵地、交往阵地、生活阵地，而且还是治理阵地、政治阵地，是构建人心政治的基础性阵地。二是构建基于社区发展的生活与交往共同体。社区发展有很多指标性的评价维度，比如服务性、参与性、交往性、礼治性、规则性的指标，这些指标维度是与广大社区民众日常生活需求密不可分的，直接反映生活多样性、便利度以及交往紧密性、情感性的程度，也反应社区居民的生活满意度、幸福度和安全度。三是构建基于社区发展与基层治理的融合模式。如今由党建引领的基层治理模式，将国家层面的执政党、政府与社会三分宏观权力架构转化为以基层党组织为统领的权力、空间、资源、治理、自治一体化模式，其背后反映的是中国共产党无论是在城市还是乡村，都要建构一种包括大生活、大福利、大党建、大治理的人心政治形态，其内涵主要包括党建引领、需求导向、重心下移、资源整合、服务优化、平台再造、技术赋能，功能复合、参与协商、以文化人等要素，并由此构建融服务、治理与发展于一体的复合型社区治理新形态。

超大型城市治理中的"小细胞"：以桃源街道三区融合视角下精品特色社区创建为切入点

黄　健

广东省深圳市南山区桃源街道办事处党工委书记

习近平总书记在深圳经济特区成立四十周年庆祝大会上指出，要树立全周期管理意识，加快推动城市治理体系和治理能力现代化，努力走出一条符合超大型城市特点和规律的治理新路子。桃源作为深圳的一个街道，在最近几年做出了一些探索和实践。桃源街道在广东省深圳市南山区的北部。南山区的经济总量目前在全国的所有区中排名第三，人口较多，整个区域的管理人口已经超过 400 万。桃源街道总面积为 35 平方公里，差不多相当于其他城市一个区的面积，人口约 30 万。在人口众多、经济体量大、各种要素密集，而且人流、物流、资金流、信息流快速交换的超大型城市中，城市治理所面临的挑战和困难是非常多的。

1. "三区叠加"全周期治理理念

什么是基层？我们现在所说的基层，或者是我们所说的社区，应该是传统治理格局上条块分割的一个概念。我们更多的是从物理的、地理的空间上来界定它，而没有从人的聚合的意义上来界定这样一个治理空间。实际工作中，很多的工作往往是跨社区的，甚至跨街道的。那么很多工作光靠条块分割的传统治理格局是做不到的，会有空白点存在。所以我们想让社区变得开放，同时要在社区里面做到资源能够真正整合，让资源能够进入社区、留在社区，同时在社区治理和社区服务中发挥它的作用，这就需要我们从结构的功能、系统的要素和运行的机制过程等多方面进行整合。我们根据桃源街道的特点，提出了一个"三区叠加"的全周期治理理念。

为什么叫三区？三区是公共社区、大学校区和产业园区的三区融合，这也跟桃源街道本身的特点有关。我们辖区有 12 个社区、21 个产业园区、7 所高校和 3 个科研院所，同时也有大量的城中村，因此辖区内各层次人群较多。为了更好地开展社区治理的相关工作，我们也借鉴了美国以及上海市杨浦区在前期采取的一些关于三区联动的举措。

2. 围绕"三区叠加"理念采取的举措

2017 年，我们开始提出把三区的各类资源进行充分的整合，开展融资源、融人文、融需求、融信息、融发展等各个方面的活动，使社区的各种小细胞能够充分地发挥它的作用，激发社区治理的大活力。实事求是地讲，我们经过几年的摸索，效果还是比较明显的。

在具体的做法上，我们总结了"一个核心""一套机制"和"一批阵地"的三个"一"做法。

"一个核心"就是核心引领，通过区域化党建引领三区资源。社区、校区、园区三区实际上有天然的分割，比如社区和校区层级的不对等，社区和园区运作方式不同，导致社区治理障碍重重。2019 年，桃源街道制定了深圳市街道层面第一个党建规划《桃源街道党的建设三年行动规划（2020—2022 年）》，提出要在 2020—2022 年着力形成区域统筹、条块协同、上下联动、共建共享的基层党建工作格局，我们希望的是形成一个以社区党委为核心的、协同自治的微循环生态系统。

"一套机制"就是我们在核心引领的基础上，建立了一整套完整的对话机制，比如我们推出了三区融合的联席会议制度等，通过一段时间的对话协商，来共同推动三区的资源整合，同时也解决三区发展中面临的各种各样的问题。因此，我们基本上形成了活动联办、资源共享、问题共商，助力三区产学研用落地的九大任务，出台了构建共建、共治、共享的工作方案，举办了三区融合的合作签约仪式。

除此之外，我们还建立了"一批阵地"来为融合发展服务。首先，在社区服务的层面，我们打造了街道的社会组织、创新的服务中心。一方面要让社会的力量参与进来，发挥多元主体的优势，引进专业的社会组织，为桃源民众提供优质的服务；另一方面，我们也积极培育辖区内的校区社会组织、园区的青年组织、社区内老年社团等，来为社区提供全方位的服务。在深度融合方面，我们成立了三区融合的促进中心和三区融合的产学研深度融合中心，来推动科研项目能够在园区落地。

3. "三区融合"工作推进中的难题

然而，在三区融合的过程中，我们基层街道仍然有着不少的困惑，比如说三区联动的基础和用户是不够的，街道和高校之间依然存在行政级别不对等、"小马拉大车"的状况，也就是说，三区融合的程度还是不够深入。另外，我们的区域化党建虽然有平台，但是能够发挥的作用还是有限的。最后，在社会治理层面，我们的系统性也还是不够的。我们也非常欢迎今天在座的各位专家学者有空能够来到桃源街道进行实地调研，帮助基层把脉问诊，解决一些问题。

城市社区共同生产何以可能：对社区生活垃圾治理的观察

孙柏瑛

中国人民大学公共管理学院教授

1. 研究背景

我的研究背景主要有四个方面。一是"韧性"社区治理从何而来？社区治理的过程中，要让社区公共事务治理富有动力、活力和能力是城市基层治理追求的目标，社会参与是共建共治共享的基本实现机制。二是从上海到北京等（超）特大城市启动了颇有声势的社区生活垃圾分类治理，党建引领、党政主导主责的自上而下驱动成为最主要的治理模式选择。三是在调研中发现，政府规模化、组织化启动社区生活垃圾分类治理之前十余年，北京一些社区存在自主性垃圾分类尝试。为何发生？驱动力来自哪里？如何实现了共同治理？四是尝试讨论自主治理的结构与功能，来探究项目运作成本—收益及其可持续能力，以及社区垃圾分类治理对自主治理方式的融合。在此基础上，我引入了社区共同生产的观念，其主要特征是组织与个人的统一、过程式参与、参与主体互动、社会资本形态以及社会创新，主要负责的事务有社区规划与更新（旧区改造）、社区日常事务、居民利益维系（加装电梯），这对城市化未来转型、建设美好社区起着重大作用。

2. 社区生活垃圾处理的三大模式机制

在我们调研走访的过程当中，发现社区生活垃圾的处理模式主要可以分为三大模式机制：党政主导型发动模式机制、物业公司启动模式机制和开发商 & 基金会启动模式机制。

党政主导型发动模式机制：社区生活垃圾分类处理作为党和政府城市治理一项重大政策推进，自上而下逐级下行执行，街道工委、办事处成为属地主责整合中心。政府一方面提供分类设施布点标准和分类标准；另一方面提供垃圾分类设施以及与后续运输、处理（焚烧）流程衔接。属地政府动员社区各主体在现有权力结构下的运行，监督物业公司承担垃圾分类事物的法定责任，协同联动。部门下达以街道为单位的垃圾分类（流量、构成）考核指标，

表 1

三个典型类型案例的情况

分析维度	党政主导发动（2019 年）	物业公司启动（2003 年）	开发商 & 基金会启动（2005）
社区属性	所有类型	商住小区	商住别墅小区
驱动主体	主责部门、街道	物业公司	开发商及所属基金会
产生动因	政策目标及社会动员	降低物业管理成本、服务质量、"零废弃"	环境友好社区生活形态
介入主体	物业公司、居业委、居民	专家团队、社会组织、居业委、居民	基金会、专家团队、居业委、居民
生产过程	宣传、分类环节	宣传、分类、设施投放、专门分拣、资源化处理	资金投放、居民合意、宣传、分类
联结方式	垂直任务下达、社会动员调动力量	组织间横向联结、与政府部门多项目合作	基金会撬动、多企业介入、与街道合作

每天、每周进行评估和排名。社区党委与居委会动员社会力量，如志愿者等。

物业公司启动模式机制：依据大城市社区垃圾管理的地方性法规规定，物业公司成为社区生活垃圾管理的责任人，具有成本—收益价值的市场逻辑的本源驱动与提高社区物业服务质量的诉求，打造社区物业服务品牌，实行项目制＋酬金管理。通过自主性的横向合作意愿，解决分类问题导向的多层次、多类型协作。他们工作的亮点在于引进了专家团队与专业技术化的处理手段，实现垃圾分类与处理的精细化流程管理及不同参与者的介入。

开发商 & 基金会启动模式机制：在高品质、居民规模小的社区中形成，具有社区共同体共同意愿的起点与基础。开发商及其基金会的驱动，价值上将其作为推动社区新生活方式的重要组成部分。主要采用商业模式来推动社区生活垃圾分类和消解，建立与垃圾企业联营和循环产品开发的合作机制，从而进行专业化处理。同时，将垃圾回收产生的有机肥料回馈给社区居民，增强参与动力。这种模式也得到了地方街道办事处的支持。这类计划已被列为政府试点项目，并获得政府补贴。

3. 简要的总结思考

为此，我想做一个简要的总结。第一，未来社区发展最为需要的是撬动社会参与力量和助推社区治理的主动参与。第二，社区事务治理存在着多元的、可以选择与替代的治理机制，包括行政、商业（公司化）、社会自组织、公益性模式，在社区治理过程中，面向市区公共事务物品及其类型，选择具有有效性以及可持续能力的治理政策工具。第三，政党和政府是社区开放式治理，助推社区合作治理的决定性变量，要发挥现有社区基准的治理结构的重要作用，提升对基层治理领导的多维能力。

未来社区研究的几个问题

田毅鹏

吉林大学哲学社会学院教授

1."未来社区"问题缘起

2019年3月,我在浙江调研,正逢浙江的"两会"召开,时任浙江省省长袁家军在"两会"上的报告中提到了"未来社区"的概念。随后,浙江省政府印发了《浙江省未来社区建设试点的工作方案》,对"未来社区"的概念提出了"139"的概括,"1"就是满足人民对美好生活的向往;"3"就是聚焦人本化、生态化、数字化;"9"是社会管理、社会治理方面的九个要素,如邻里关系、教育、健康、创业、建筑、交通等。我在实际调研的过程当中,也感受到了地方政府围绕着"未来社区"进行了 整套非常精致的设计,并且展开了一些实践。后来我围绕这个主题发表了两篇文章,一篇是《"未来社区"建设的几个理论问题》,发表在《社会科学研究》2020年第1期;还有一篇是《乡村"未来社区"建设的多重视域及其评价》,发表于《南京社会科学》2020年的第7期。

2."未来社区"建设过程中的"未来性"如何展开?

社区的概念是一个带有怀旧性的概念。社区消逝论者认为,传统社会的一些社会性会随着工业化、城市化、流动化而大量地流失,为了能够在现代社会剧烈变迁的背景之下,使这些社会性得以留存,需要构建"社区"的概念,这是"社区"概念产生之时最核心、最本质的一个问题。还有一派,比如说美国的芝加哥学派,他们在北美城市当中就发现,在工业社会中依然还有社区的存在,可以看出,社区研究很少从"未来性"的角度来谈。那么在"未来社区"这个话题的展开过程当中,要讨论"未来性"就必须处理好一系列的关系。

第一,社区的"未来性"与技术性的关系。社区"未来性"的展开,有一个非常重要的背景,那就是20世纪晚期产生的网络社会。网络技术深度地嵌入城市的发展过程当中,所以,"未来性"与技术性之间的关系是非常密切的。一方面,没有一定的技术变迁,社区的

"未来性"是无法显现的。事实上，现在已有的一些关于"未来社区"的版本，比如说低碳社区、生态社区等，都是与技术相关联的。另一方面，在学术界看来，"技术性"在很大程度上是对社区社会性的扼杀，随着技术的变动，社会关系将会发生一些重要的变动。所以说，未来社区的"未来性"与技术性的关系是一个非常值得强调和重视的关系：一方面，如何使技术性为"未来性"拓展它的路向、道路与途径；但另一方面又不因为技术性而过度地对社会的传统进行扼杀。

第二，社区的"未来性"与社会性的关系。社区社会性的含量是一个社区非常重要的衡量标准。一个好的社区和一个差的社区的区别，有硬件元素的原因，但更重要的是软件元素。一个社区，如果没有社会关系、没有社会互动、没有共同的集体行动，那么很难想象这个社区是一个好的社区，无论建筑多么豪华，硬件条件多么到位，但那只是水泥森林而已。所以，一个社区社会性的存留和激活，对于延续社区来说是非常重要的。但是在"未来性"的发展过程当中，随着城市化、工业化、技术的进步，人类的社会性会大幅度流失。这是由于在市场经济条件下，依托于市场的服务，替代了人与人关系的真实的互动，人们很多需求可以通过市场解决，那么社会性大面积的流失恐怕是一个不争的事实。所以"未来社区"在展示它的"未来性"的过程当中，要考虑如何最大限度地处理好它的"未来性"与社会性的关系。

第三，社区的"未来性"与传统性的关系。到目前为止，很多社区都形成了自己的特色，比如说工业社区、商业社区、城乡接合部或者是大学城等，它都有自己的一些传统。在"未来社区"的构建过程当中，也需要最大限度地保持它的传统。

第四，社区的"未来性"与生态性的关系。这一方面，也受到了国内外学界的重视。

总而言之，目前我们在规划"未来社区"的时候，我认为应该首先从它的一些基本的元素入手，处理好"未来性"与技术性、社会性、传统性、生态性以及其他一些元素的关系。只有把这些关系处理好，我们才能让城市更新、社区更新与传统、社会、生态、技术形成一个良好的互动。

营造公园社区的美好生活场景：成都市双流区黄水镇社区发展治理实践与思考

袁　莆

四川成都市双流区黄水镇党委书记

黄水镇是双流国际机场的新城区，近年来，我们坚守建设让生活更美好的城市的初心，以场景营造为抓手，弘扬社区发展的胜利新路径，加快构建"人城境业"高度和谐统一的大美公园社区。以下是我对公园社区发展治理生动实践的思考。

图1

四川成都市双流区黄水镇

1. 公园社区发展治理的生动实践

2018年2月，习近平总书记在成都首次提出"公园城市"理念。2020年1月，习近平总书记在中央财经委员会第六次会议上明确要求，"支持成都建设践行新发展理念的公园城市示范区"。这是党中央赋予成都发展的新战略定位。公园社区治理是一个全新的课题，对于基层来说，需要深入思考三大问题：

（1）为什么要建设公园社区？

公园城市实践习近平生态文明思想的城市表达，诠释了新时代人与自然和谐共生的价值取向。公园社区是公园城市的微观表达，包含着城市以人民为中心的价值追求。公园社区应当是形态优美、开放时尚的社区，业态融合、活力迸发的社区，生态怡人、绿色发展的社区，文态浸润、传承创新的社区，心态包容、向善向美的社区。

（2）是否有条件建设公园社区？

黄水镇具备建设公园社区的基础优势。黄水镇牧马山森林覆盖面积达 60% 以上，规划天府绿道超 300 公里，具有亚洲最大的湿地公园和国内最大的航空大地景观，人均公园绿地面积达 12 平方米。

黄水镇是古蜀农耕文化的重要发祥地，也是儒家文化、古蜀农耕文化、三国文化的重要承载地和古丝绸之路的重要交汇地。幅员面积达 68.92 平方公里，常住人口为 7 万人，2/3 以上的面积已经纳入城市规划区，是成都芯谷空港商圈的重要承载地。成绵乐高铁穿境而过，成都地铁 3 号线、10 号线、17 号线在此汇集。

（3）如何高水平建设公园社区？

公园城市示范区建设正有力驱动着黄水镇转型、蝶变。这里我给大家分享三种公园社区场景营造的故事。

第一个故事是营造生态场景，把噪音区变成"网红景区"。黄水镇云华社区，部分居民房屋长期位于飞机航线下。曾有群众投诉反映，生活在噪音区，公鸡逐渐变得不会打鸣，母鸡也不生蛋。为此，黄水镇于 2015 年实施了云华新村土地整理项目，122 户居民搬进了新区。新的难题就摆在了面前。如何实现生态价值多元化转变，让搬迁户的居民共同受益？

2017 年，黄水镇与四川航空公司合作，按照"自然生态本底 + 熊猫大地景观 + 健康绿道风光"的思路，打造了万亩空港花园，把昔日的噪音区变为游人如织的"网红景区"。当地的群众都成了房东、股东和老板，人均年收入都超过 8 万元，实现了业兴、家富、人和、村美。

第二个故事是营造产业场景，空壳社区变农商文旅体融合示范区。白塔社区过去基础配套差，产业落后。近年来社区依托毗邻牧马山历史文化保护区的优势，大力发展观光农业、精品民宿等特色产业，实现了农商文旅体融合发展。

如何让社区居民共享产业发展"红利"？黄水镇采取"龙头企业 + 股份合作社 + 农户"模式，出资 300 万元与本土企业合作打造"板坡·良舍"精品民宿项目，并依托新村建立了土地股份合作社，群众收入得以节节攀升。

当地居民算了一笔账，今年全家预计收入 35 万元，比三年前翻了一番。从"板坡·良舍"民宿项目中，可获得 3 万元分红，儿媳在该民宿打工，每月工资 4 000 元；五亩承包地入股土地合作社，可收入 1.5 万元租金、2 万元分红；此外还出租一套 150 平方米的新村房屋，年租金 6 万元。白塔社区像王洪彬这样的家庭还有很多，社区集体经济年收入超过千万，人均增收近 4 000 元。

第三个故事是营造服务场景，集中安置小区变新型城市社区。2014 年，9 600 多人搬入楠柳社区集中安置小区，黄水镇按照"15 分钟生活服务圈"标准，在一平方公里范围内配置了学校、医院、日间照料中心等公服设施，社区硬件上了新台阶。

而棘手的难题随之而来，如何实现居民生产生活方式同步转变？刚搬入新居时，小区内常出现乱丢垃圾、圈地种菜、物业费收缴难等现象。为此，黄水镇引进专业社会组织合作打造睦邻生活服务馆，开展 4:30 儿童课堂、社会公益、文艺培训等服务，引导群众从"村民"向"市民"转变。

针对部分群众的种菜愿望，我们创新打造了"共享菜地"，对一处 7.5 亩的闲置土地进行整理，划分出 80 块"微菜地"。按照志愿服务时长优先、文明家庭优先、物业费足额缴纳优先等条件，对报名群众进行筛选，并建立栽培管理和积分进退机制。"共享菜地"实施以来，物业费缴纳比例由原先不足 65% 上升到 95%，小区里不文明现象也明显减少。

这三个案例是成都市双流区社会发展治理的一个缩影，也是黄水镇满足市民美好生活向往，探索公园社区建设的真实情况。

2. 区发展治理面临的难题和思考

城市让生活更美好，建设践行新发展理念的公园城市示范区，社区是前哨。在公园社区的实践中存在着三方面的难题。一是社区支持定位与实际运行错位，导致"小马拉不了大车"，社区职能转换不到位，有的社区承担行政事务过多，弱化了自治与服务的功能。二是社区高品质公共服务缺位，导致"面子重于里子"，社区的管辖面积较大，服务人口过多，高品质公共服务欠账多，城市综合管理功能不完善。三是公园社区治理创新思路不开阔，导致"老办法解决不了新问题"。缺乏对城市治理规律的深入研究，公园社区发展治理缺乏系统规划，共建力度不足、共治方法较少、共享效果欠佳。

关于破解公园社区发展治理中的矛盾问题，我有三点思考。第一，社区更迭，乡愁与城愁要同调。城镇化进程中的生态失衡，让我们失去了往日的青山绿水。如果不重视绿色发展，就会导致城市生态病。因此必须坚持绿色发展理念，让居民看得见山、望得见水，记得住乡愁和城愁。第二，社区赋能，发展与治理要同振。社区既要治理，更要发展增强"造血"功能。必须坚持职住平衡、产城相融，创设更多的产业空间、就业空间，不断提升市民的获得感、幸福感、安全感。第三，社区融合，文化与生活要同美。打造社区共同体，聚合社区能量，需要唤醒文化基因。我们必须坚持以文化人，提供更多的公共文化服务，提升居民文化素养，实现社区与居民同步成长。

3. 构建公园社区未来美好生活场景

面向未来，黄水镇将坚持以人民为中心的发展思想，主动回应市民美好生活需求，以创新场景营造互助社区发展治理优势，高质量打造美丽宜居公园社区。

（1）强化顶层设计，建设可持续发展的理想社区。加强规划引领，坚持"先策划、再规划、后设计"的理念，按照成都市城乡社区发展治理总体规划"三步走"的目标，结合实际，制定公园社区治理"路线图"和"施工图"。坚持分类治理、精细治理和创新治理，建设全民友好、舒畅宜居的城镇社区，集约高效、活力共享的产业社区，以及青山绿水、美田弥望的农村社区。

（2）坚持精准对接，绘制社区场景地图。坚持以智慧社区建设为载体，摸清社区家庭，打造基础数据库。精心绘制社区场景地图，推动社区产品与美好生活需求精准匹配。加快建立多元服务共建模式，拓展完善市民参与层次。构建以基层党组织为引领的公共服务圈、群众自治圈和社会共治圈。

（3）坚持多元叠加，营造高品质社会生活场景。高质量打造公园社区的服务、文化、生态等七大场景，构建完备系统的宜居生活服务体系，积极培育社区服务新业态、新模式，结合本土文化再现形式和表达方式，打造市民文化家园。坚持"人城产"逻辑，以空港花田、空港中央公园等重大生态项目为载体，以场景营造＋产业植入＋专业应用为导向，打造生态价值转化示范亮点。按照景观化、景区化、可进入、可参与的标准，推进 TOD 综合开发，建设更多社区开放空间。依托熊猫国际家园等重大文明项目，推进"人文地产景"融合发展，完善社区发展治理和社区服务。以点带面，推动 5G 智慧治理，提升社区治理效能。

我坚信，未来的公园社区建筑是可阅读的，街区是适合漫步的，公园是适宜休憩的，市民是尊法诚信的，城市始终是有温度的。

生态社区活力体，宜居宜业新地标

沈　炜

上海市浦东新区三林镇世博前滩社区书记

1. 社区区域现状

首先，我跟大家简要介绍一下三林镇世博前滩社区的基本概况。三林镇前滩社区位于黄浦江南延伸段，东至济阳路，南至中环，西至黄浦江，北至川洋河，总面积是 2.83 平方公里，是以世博会为核心的黄浦江南部滨江区域的重要组成部分。前滩社区是以总部商务、文化传媒和体育休闲作为三大核心功能，在此基础上配备完善的商业、居住、酒店、教育、医疗等配套设施，力争打造宜居宜业的 24 小时活力城区。

整个前滩规划的总建筑面积是 350 万平方米，其中商业是 66 万平方米，办公室 147 万平方米，住宅是 90 万平方米，城市配套包括文化、教育、医疗等公共设施 40 万平方米，规划居住人口 2.35 万，就业岗位 10 万家。目前前滩区域规划建设的 100 个地块完工项目已超过半数。前滩社区规划有 6 个居民区，26 个小区约 9 000 户居民，目前已经入户的小区 9 个，交房 3 600 套左右，常住人口大概在 5 000 人。

随着建设步伐的不断加快，前滩的人气也是越来越旺。我们在与前滩产生交集的各个群体的交流过程中发现，大家对前滩的发展存在各种个性化和共性化的诉求，包括企业服务、生活配套、个人价值体现等方面。因此，我们提出了"国际范儿，中国味儿"的规划理念。

2. 规划理念

所谓的"国际范儿"，就是要对标国际标准的城市 3.0 建设，包括办公、商业、教育、医疗、社区、文体等各个方面。得益于我们前滩区域整体开发的模式，以及陆家嘴集团比较强大的开发和引资能力，前滩社区在成长的起步阶段就具备了较高的起点。在教育方面，我们有公办的九年一贯制学校：华师大二附中、前滩学校、冰厂田幼儿园、中福会幼儿园；民办九年一贯制学校：惠立学校、嘉宝幼儿园、霍林顿外籍人员子女学校，以及在建的上海纽约大学前滩校区。医疗方面有新加坡来福士医院，体育设施方面有东方体育中心，文化方面有信德文化中心，商业方面有太古里、晶耀前滩、四方城等。

而"中国味儿"是我们在对标国际标准之外，还应当大力地传承和发扬中国精神的内核打造。无论我们怎么开展工作，其实都离不开党建、群团、涉外、公益等与社区治理息息相关的元素，这些都是我们需要思考和探索的内容。我们认为，社区发展最重要的元素就是人，有赖于前滩社区建设和发展并举的现状，我们提出了"社区开拓者"和"社区规划者"的发展概念。

"开拓者"针对居民和社区的共同成长。无论是工作群体、居住人群还是旅游人群，都在参与前滩的初创期、成长期，给予他们"开拓者"的角色定位，更加凸显区域发展的自主性和灵活性，强化"大家的事情大家说了算"的行为模式，逐渐培养出强大社区自治共治能力。"规划者"针对自治共治的需求及能力。要发挥"小"政府的大作为，充分发挥区域人员知识水平高、能力强、自治意愿强、品质要求高等特点，调动他们参与决策区域发展，真正打造"我想要"的社区，形成拥有居民血液的社区发展蓝图。

3. 发展方向

目前，我们的工作重心是围绕两个生态圈和一个生态链的建设。具体包括：建立"供求互动"的社区生态圈，也就是前滩大联盟；构建"以人为本"的公益生态圈，也就是社区公益积分体系；打造全民参与的生态链，也就是前滩生活节。通过进一步打响前滩生活节这个品牌社区生态链，串联两个生态圈，组成社区全域生态圈，使之成为"和谐共存"的都市生态圈，即前滩大联盟的运作，社区公益积分的推广，前滩生活节品牌的打造三大块工作。

我们希望通过"自循环"生态系统，引导各类人群进入生态循环体系，通过需求导向、积分兑换、项目载体、共享空间等机制体制的搭建，形成"需求、资源、项目"自发的、闭环的循环生态。经过一至两年的运作，形成成熟的机制、队伍、项目等。

4. 工作框架

目前，我们工作的基本框架是"四个一"引擎拉动。

第一个"一"是一个工作平台：前滩大联盟，它是发挥社区领导力，搭建跨界合作的平台。在这个平台上，社区、园区、商区、企业、政府都可以找准自身定位和作用。联盟可以很好地发挥党建引领作用，整合更多的社区资源，参与社区治理，提升前滩社区党建联建和社区共治的水平。社区党委可以借助联盟力量积极回应社区问题和需求，充分调动共享资源，联合相关职能部门与企事业单位，共同探索社区治理新思路。目前，我们的成员单位已经达到了 26 家，包括公安、消防、社区事务受理、市场监督管理、卫生监督、医院、银行、学校、商业机构等，也涉及安全、卫生、金融、教育等多个领域。

第二个"一"是一套工作机制：公益积分项目，它是通过需求导向的"公益积分"规则，倡导"温暖社区、人人参与"的原则，打造熟人社区。一方面，我们针对社区资源的供给，提供契合居民实际需求的服务，并将需求合理导入公益元素，逐步实现付出与回报的统一；另一方面针对工作群体，更多体现公益岗位的适配性，契合白领青年群体的社会价值体现的需求。

第三个"一"是一支自组织队伍：前滩"开拓者"。在参与社区治理的过程中，让企业领袖、社区达人、社区志愿者等人群主动成为社区的开拓者。推动高质量发展、高品质生活项目的落地，形成具有自我发展、自我完善功能的生态体系。

第四个"一"是一个品牌项目：前滩生活节。它是一个实现各方参与配合、全民共乐的大舞台。一年我们有"四季"：民俗季、文化季、运动季和阅读季。"四季"中，每一个项目都由前滩大联盟成员单位策划、主办，每一位居住、工作甚至到前滩游玩的个体，都能够从前滩生活节中找到属于自己的一份惊喜。

在三林镇党委政府的领导和支持下，我们前滩社区党委围绕着产城融合、于基于业，打造都市重镇新高地、现代城市品质区的目标，积极发挥党建引领作用，在深入加强驻区单位共建联建，深化基层社区治理创新等方面，做出了诸多探讨，取得了显著的成效。未来前滩社区也将继续深化加强党的领导，整合更多的资源，参与社区治理，将前滩社区建设得更加美好。

基层治理的实践与反思

蒲亚鹏

上海市徐汇区虹梅街道党工委书记

1. 社区治理的背景

1996 年，上海基本形成了"两级政府，三级管理，四级网络"的社区管理模式。2015 年，街道办事处剥离了经济职能，重心转到社区治理。2017 年，提出"要打造共建共治共享的社会治理格局"，"加强社区治理体系建设，推动社会治理重心向基层下移"。2019 年，习近平总书记提出了"人民城市人民建，人民城市为人民"的重要理念，对基层提出了新的要求。

虹梅街道位于徐汇区西南部，东起桂林路，西迄莲花路，南抵漕宝路，北以蒲汇塘为界，占地面积 5.98 平方公里；有 13 个居委会，22 个居民小区，户籍人口 2 万余人，常住人口 4 万余人，来沪人员 2 万余人。漕河泾高新技术开发区徐汇部分，企事业单位约 4 000 余家，员工 25 万余人。

2. 基层治理的主要实践

2015 年，上海"1+6"改革之后，对基层治理提出了更高的要求。因此，我们对基层治理的很多理念机制需要进一步明确，基层治理的范畴与工作内容，也需要进一步的思考。基层，尤其是社区工作的一些基本范式和工作方法，需要在很多领域进行细化和完善。同时，在基层治理参与的过程当中，各类主体之间的关系、权责如何体现值得探讨。最后，我们要明确我们社区工作者本身的职责和要求。

今天，我以"小区"这样一个社区治理最基本的单元入手，介绍一下如何去开展基层治理的工作。虹梅街道尝试提出了"五维工作法"，即用资源匹配度、群体结构、居民参与程度、治理结构和治理取向五个维度来评判基层治理的具体情况。

这五个维度可以把小区的特性分成 32 个类型。比如，资源匹配度主要衡量小区硬件设施是否足以支撑小区居民的基本生活需求，分为资源匹配型和相对资源紧缺型两个类型。从群体结构来讲，主要是根据小区的人群来判断，判断小区居民属于相对同质性人群，还是异质性人群。对于居民参与度，我们把它划分为高参与度、低参与度。针对治理取向，有些我们是以传统情感联络的方法来治理，有些建立比较强的规则体系。治理结构则主要是看能不能形成以基层党组织为核心的同心圆结构。通过这样的五个维度，就把基层的治理分成32个可能性，对每一个小区进行画像。

第二个是两张清单。一张清单反映的是在居民区工作当中，政府，尤其是居委会应当承担的管理职责和行政职责。另外一张清单，主要体现的是从各种渠道反映上来的小区的各类问题。总体上，我们用两张清单和一个评估方法，把辖区内所有小区都按照治理的视角，给予相对准确、全面的画像。有了画像之后，我们会根据小区的情况采取一定的干预措施。

图1
两"清单"一"方法"的意义

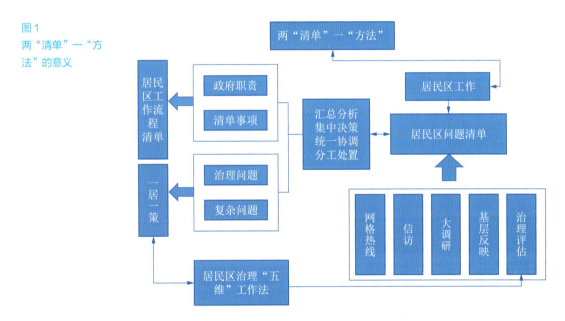

由图1可知，"两清单一方法"会对所有的事情都进行一个流程化的处理。比如说我们可以从网格热线、信访、大调研、基层反映等途径形成居民区的问题清单。问题清单通常分为两大类，一类属于政府职责和小区居委会辖内的管理事项；另外一类相对复杂，它的主体责任可能不是非常明确，可能需要由居民来承担。政府职责清单事项，主要是行政效率的问题，而其他问题主要就是治理的问题。

我们把清单进行分类之后，可以看到如图2所示，我们在小区内治理应该介入的核心领域，就是表中的非清单的长期事项。

基层治理的过程可以划分为两个领域，一个领域是从政府出发，调动各类行政资源、管理资源，解决好居民反映的各类问题。另一个领域是从居民自身出发，不断扩大居民参与度，提升治理效能，来解决居民区治理领域长期存在的一些问题。

当然，我们在基层治理的过程当中还有比较多的问题，比如公地悲剧和反公地悲剧，使

	清单事项	非清单事项	短期事项	长期事项	工作策略
政府职责	√		√		依流程运行
	√			√	
		√	√		解决问题，建立流程
		√		√	重点项目推进
居民区事务	√		√		依流程运行
	√			√	
		√	√		解决问题，建立规则
		√		√	居民区治理"五维"工作法

图2
居民区治理"五维"工作法

得公地配套设施没有得到良性的使用。在居民区当中还有一个非常核心的问题，就是小区随着时间的推移，收支会产生很大的问题。维持小区这样的资产良性运转，需要非常长期的、稳定的投入。现在的投入主要是小区维修基金、居民物业费、公益性收入和政府补贴这几部分。但从实际情况来讲，各小区之间的差异非常大，有些小区相对能维持辖区的收支平衡，硬件水平和服务水平能保持稳定，而大多数小区，尤其是老旧小区，如果没有政府的外力注入，光凭它自身的维修基金、物业费、公益性收入等，很难保证居民区的收支平衡，这样就会导致小区不断衰落。一旦小区衰落，就会形成恶性循环。这样的情况下，我们认为业主应该承担更主要的责任，但是实际上业主大会这样的主体，想发挥作用非常难，业委会在决策流程的操作上也出现过很多问题。

那么我们通过治理状态的画像，就能够提出有效的干预措施，并且在干预之后用治理评估方法进行再评估。目前，我们既有"邻里小汇"等小区公共空间的打造，也有"全岗通"等小区基本事务流程梳理，同时也在一些小区进行了居站分离的试点探索，更重要的是进一步完善"1+3"（党组织领导下，"三驾马车"议事）的议事规则，将基层治理规则标准化。

3. 基层治理的反思

未来，我们希望的方向是在基层治理过程当中形成可评估的治理，让治理过程显性化、治理内容结构化、基层工作专业化。从基层民主角度来说，要有具体的规则体系，鼓励居民参与实践，形成法治保障。最后，我们希望小区要有可持续的活力，包括家门口的基本公共服务、广泛的居民自治活动、充分的市场化活动等。

Future Community: New Features and New Governance

Wen Jun

Professor, School of Social Development, East China Normal University

1. Meaning and characteristics of the future community

Since the 1980s, the academia and the sociological community have been studying "future community". The word "community" has a long history. As time goes by, "community" as a concept has been constantly reinterpreted and reconstructed. It can even be said that it has gradually developed into an "ideal society" or as a key to an ideal society. Therefore, broadly speaking, "future community" is not a new concept. Why? First, people like to imagine the future and have aspirations to the future throughout the human history. As we envision the ideal society, the concept of "future community" has always manifested itself in various forms. Second, due to differences in the local culture, development stage, values and resources, even communities that exist in the same period can take on different forms.

The ways "future community" is developed can be roughly divided into two categories: one under the influence of "technological determinism" and the other under "ecocentrism". Each of them corresponds to a set of development goals set out by the United Nations.

Fig. 1
MDGs

Fig. 2
SDGs

Guided by the UN's Millennium Development Goals (MDGs), "technological determinism" is the first wave of efforts to achieve common prosperity across the world through "economic development", "science and technology innovation" and rapid productivity growth. Without doubt, the continuous accumulation of material goods and development of modern technologies at this stage have laid a solid foundation for the emerging "new technologies" represented by 5G, the Internet of things and artificial intelligence (AI). The idea of building "future community" such as "intelligent community" and "smart community" was also put forward at this time.

In comparison, guided by the UN's Sustainable Development Goals (SDGs), the "ecocentrism" has shifted the focus of community building. It stresses on the setup of a future framework and makes the development human-centered, ecological and sustainable. As time goes by, "ecocentrism" has become a bellwether of "future community". The reasons are as follows. First, it enriches human life. "Ecocentrism" puts sustainable development at the heart of "future community" and promotes inclusive social development concept. Second, it pays attention to sound ecological environment and human-centered values in the community, advocating the harmonious development of individuals, families, organizations and the community environment while putting people "as part of" nature, not above nature.

There are two main reasons for the shift from "technological determinism" to "ecocentrism". First, although great achievements have been made in community building under the guidance of "technological determinism", the blind pursuit of economic growth and technological progress has distorted the relationship between "development and environment" versus "development and human", resulting in the frequent global breakout of resource shortage, environmental pollution and ecological damage. Second, when natural risks evolve into "social risks", "institutional risks" and "technological risks", we cannot use technological means alone to effectively address these challenges. The COVID-19 pandemic is a vivid example of such "compound risks".

In view of China's practice, the goal of community building is to build a "social life community", which means community building needs to refocus its functions, values and significance on people's daily life. Therefore, using this as the starting point, we can design various social organizations and services in a better way. For instance, in the first stage of community development from the 1980s to the 1990s, communities in China focused on improving people's material life, such as the infrastructure and the environment. This is Community Building 1.0. In the second stage (from 1990s until now), most communities in China started to pursue development by making use of various technologies and management systems. The "Grid Management" was a typical example, which prioritized the use of technologies and management systems in community building. This is Community Building 2.0. In the third stage, the most important thing, I think, is to build social communities defined by their cultural characteristics, or to be more specific, by their psychosocial and sociocultural characteristics. This is Community Building 3.0. In the future, more attention should be paid to build "human-centered" social community, so as to ensure their sustainable development.

Hence, "future community" shifts its focus from objective factors such as technologies and management system to "people" as the central factor of community development. Without a concern for "people", modern information, knowledge, organizations and communities might ignore the interest of people and exclude the weak, making a community an enclosed "interest community". That is why whenever we talk about empowering communities with technologies, it is important to note that technologies are only tools, irrespective of its stage of development, and that "people" are the foundation on which community building relies. The "future community" urgently calls on us to reset its values and functions and make it an ecological community that is more human-centered, intelligent and sustainable.

2. Main features of the "future community"

First, "future community" is supported by the extensive usage of digital, online and virtual technologies. These technologies can transform traditional interactions and improve economic, social and environmental efficiency. In addition, as we have seen, AI has played an indispensable role in emergency management ranging from risk warning, risk assessment to risk prevention and control.

Second, "future community" is green and sustainable. It is underpinned by green, coordinated and sustainable development. Such community should take economic, social and environmental sustainability into consideration, constantly pursuing a model of sustainable development that leads to a higher living standard and healthier ecosystem. We need to preserve our blue sea, azure sky, lucid waters and lush mountains while meeting the development goals.

Third, "future community" encompasses various types of organizations. The diversity of these organizations is a necessary part of "future community". With such diversity, an entire community system could avoid collapse in the case of social crises. Compared with the previous model of "vertical management", "future community" adopts a "horizontal interaction" model, with multiple participants sharing experience and risks to make community governance more effective.

Fourth, "future community" pursues happy life. It regards people's sense of fulfillment, abundance and happiness as its development goals. In addition to establishing social support systems for different groups to meet the needs of their residents, "future community" also pays attention to the "mental well-being" of its residents, offering emotional care to enhance their sense of belonging and identity.

Fifth, although "future community" faces uncertainties in development, it is driving a desire to overcome the uncertainty, instability and unpredictability of social development. In a modern society, social development faces more and more risks and uncertainties. Risk society does not designate a developmental stage of society. It merely describes the characteristics of a certain period of time in which people live, albeit in a realistic and practical way. We need to shift our perspective, adapt to the uncertain future and unleash more potential and creativity.

In general, "future community" can be studied in at least two dimensions: one is to see "future community" as a "development issue"; the other is to regard "future community" as the "background for development". The former tends to focus on the nature of the "future community" itself. Why can we build a social life community? How to provide the community residents with advanced concepts about life and lifestyle, as well as intelligent, digital and green support infrastructure? How to encourage residents to participate in community affairs and a wider range of social affairs? The latter tends to see "future communities" as the background for development, stressing that community is shaped by various factors. Some of them, such as residents and organizations in the community, affect the community directly, while other factors, such as local culture and government policies, indirectly. Each factor is not special on its own, but together they will have a profound impact on the future development path and pattern of the community. As such, we should pay more attention to the ways these factors are combined and integrated.

3. Governance logic and strategy of future community

The accelerated globalization not only magnifies traditional natural risks, but also triggers modern risks in institution, science and technology and other fields. Even worse, various types of risks begin to show a "coupling effect". During the COVID-19 pandemic, we have witnessed uncertainties of things that may happen, uncertainties of their impact, and uncertainties of our response. In this sense, how should "future community" address these risks? What practical solutions can the elements of "future community" and its development pattern provide? Generally, these solutions include the following:

First, transform from "relying on technology" to "guiding technology". Although technology development is inevitable, the social risks that haven arisen in recent years have also shown that every modern thing has two sides. Therefore, there is an urgency to shift our reliance on technology to "taking the ownership of technology". Instead of leaving the future community governance entirely to technology, we should strengthen the build-up of institutional capacity and values and promote the integration of "ruled by data" and "ruled by man".

Second, transform from "linear growth" to "compound development". Pursuing the accumulation of material wealth is a biased view of growth. The governance of "future community" requires us to transform from "linear growth" to "compound development", which means we need to shift focus to the inclusive view that takes interpersonal relationship, social care, ethnic unity, ecological development into account. In terms of the ultimate goal of "better life", "compound development" holds more significance than the traditional approach of "linear growth", and will more easily handle the complex problems of our times.

Third, transform from "ecosystem-based adaptation" to "community-based adaptation". Ecosystem-based adaptation, which is derived from environmental science, aims to respond effectively to the worsening climate crisis, whereas "community-based adaptation" model, which is built on ecosystem-based adaptation, is a practical and effective strategy to deal with the complexity and variability of social risks. It advocates the take-up of a "community-leading" risk prevention program that relies on the "endogenous power" of the community to organize and govern itself. With horizontal collaboration, communities can conduct self-planning and self-service to meet local needs, as well as achieve self-support and self-assistance to unleash community energy. As a result, the entire community will be more dynamic, creative, collaborative and responsive.

Fourth, transform from "decentralized governance" to "integrated governance". "Alternative technologies", originally designed to reduce the technical risks, have caused more serious social problems at the present stage. The "anti-pollution system", originally targeted at industrial pollution, has also caused massive systemic harm. The traditional governance model treats each problem in an isolated manner, and the solutions proposed often work in haphazard manner, resulting in a typical "decentralized governance" mindset in the long run. In contrast, "future community" adopts a "holistic governance" mindset that fully recognizes the systematic and complex nature of social problems. It helps build a comprehensive response system composed of knowledge, action, theory and practice to address various social problems.

Fifth, transform from "local governance" to "global governance". The governance of "future community" is closely related to globalization. Global risk awareness and collective actions are absolutely needed in order to effectively respond to global disasters. The reason why community problems are so inveterate and intractable is that each risk is not only the product of local community and but also a product of global community. However, in terms of the current situation of global governance, the model of global cooperation is seriously deficient to tackle various challenges - be it the refugee crisis, the global climate crisis, or the plagues and pandemic diseases. The slogan of "think globally, act locally" is no longer enough for the governance of "future community". We need to "think globally, act locally" and "think locally, act locally". We need to establish a view of global governance.

4. Reflections on "future community"

First, how can "future community" avoid cookie-cutter construction? While we may have laid out the development goals, concepts, prospects, ideas and strategies of "future community", and may have even specified the appearance and forms of architectures located in such community, efforts to achieve standardization is also something of concern: with the associated fanfare and mass mobilization, will "future community" all look the same in terms of their standards, style, appearance and functions, and therefore lose its diversity and distinction?

Second, does the "future community" represent a clear vision of development, or an ideal type of community? What is the difference between "future community" and "smart community"? Although the conceptual framework of "future community" has been taken up and has gained wide attention, it is still somehow similar to "smart community". If "smart community" only fulfills parts of its functions, how will the integrity of "future community" be reflected? Especially in the process of building and improving the system of "smart community", how to distinguish "future community" from the "smart community"? From this perspective, is the "future community" still an "ideal society"? Is it still "the politics of naming"?

Third, in order to effectively deal with the social risks facing "future community", how can the state system, social mechanism and modern technologies be further integrated and coordinated? Technological development always precedes the construction of national institutions and social mechanisms. For example, the big data monitoring technology, which had widely used during the pandemic, has already been applied in the service process of enterprise data analysis and network platform services. In addition, new problems are emerging. For example, the traditional emergency management system isn't fully compatible with the technology platform; we still lack In-house technical personnel; the digital prevention and control system is not sound yet; and the society is yet ready to adapt to the emerging governance technology. How can risk management promote the effective collaboration of the three sides? How to bridge the divide between "technology" and "system"? These are the three questions that we need to think about further.

Future Community: Viewed in the Present and in the Future

Lang Youxing

Professor, School of Public Affairs, Zhejiang University

The concept of "future community" is nothing new, as the United States, Singapore and many other countries have made much efforts in practicing it. Over the past decades of community building in China, some ideas and practices have gradually taken shape, such as smart community, community O2O, low-carbon community, community micro-regeneration, colorful community and 15-minute community life circle. What makes China's approach innovative is that it has combined these existing ideas and practices to form a holistic and systematic perspective. At the government level, the Zhejiang Province is leading the way. In March 2019, Zhejiang Provincial Government issued "The Work Plan for the Pilot Project of Building Future Communities in Zhejiang Province", which for the first time put forward the concept of "future community" in China.

1. Reflections on current community building from the perspective of future community

We need to transform and upgrade old residential compounds in reference of communities of the future. "The Work Plan for the Pilot Project of Building Future Communities in Zhejiang Province" proposed building communities of the future in nine areas, namely neighborhood, education, health, entrepreneurship, construction, transportation, low-carbon environment, service and governance. At present, in Hangzhou, the focus of work is still to improve community infrastructures. In other words, by building communities of the future, the government can improve surrounding infrastructures, provide good community services, and even push the coordinated development of industrial restructuring, thus promoting the development of the whole region.

The key of work is still on the community governance system. Many communities are facing problems concerning the relationship between governing bodies, the participation of residents, and their sense of belonging and identity. First, contradictions still exist among property managers, owners' committees and residents. Second, many community services are not refined and detailed enough. Third, there is a lack of care for residents, and many communities still need to foster their soft power in terms of their cultural atmosphere and cultural traditions. Fourth, residents are not actively participating in community governance. Fifth, residents' sense of belonging and identity is weak.

Therefore, the question is how to apply the green, open and shared development that are found in communities of the future to today's communities so that residents and other relevant parties can participate jointly in the renovation of old communities. This will contribute to joint decision-making, co-management and co-assessment of communities and achieve shared benefits, thus building futuristic communities where residents can feel at ease and have a sense of belonging. Moreover, we should also think about ways to foster the humanistic atmosphere in communities through the human-centered philosophy of the future community.

2. Possible challenges in building future communities based on the present situation

The first challenge is to specify the definition and meaning of the concept. The concept of "future community" is so broad that it touches on almost every aspect of urban life, and there is no official

Fig. 1
"Three trends and nine areas of work" of "Future community" in Zhejiang Province

definition of this concept. The Zhejiang Government has defined it as "Three Trends and Nine Areas of Work" (Fig. 1). Some rural areas are also building communities of the future, such as the rural areas in Quzhou, a city in Zhejiang Province.

The second challenge is that communities of the future may look all the same, giving rise to the problem of homogeneity. Many cities in China have put forward their planning renderings which all look alike.

The third challenge is how to integrate communities of the future into the city and make it part of an organic whole. One possible scenario is that communities of the future might constitute an independent system, but cannot interact with the surrounding environment, let alone integrate into the life circle. Future communities should not be a patch on a piece of clothing, even if the patch itself is novel and fashionable.

Structural Factors of Future Community Governance

Jing Yuejin

Professor, Department of Political Science, Tsinghua University

When we talk about communities of the future in China, we basically follow the existing framework and ideas. Despite the technological breakthroughs, we have maintained continuity with governance mechanisms and systems. Today I'm going to examine this issue from the perspective of two structural factors that will constrain what we can imagine for future communities. These two factors can be summarized as the horizontal coordinate and the vertical coordinate.

1. The horizontal coordinate

The first one is the horizontal coordinate. Today, when it comes to politics in China, the most important horizontal coordinate is the Party-government relations. In the period of planned economy, the political system, without a division of labor between Party and government, was highly centralized. After the division of labor between Party and government, there is room for differentiation in the relations between the government and enterprises, between the central and local governments, between the government and the market, as well as the relations between the state and society. Before the 18th CPC National Congress, people often talked about the reform of the political system, the reform of the economic system, self-governance of villagers, and so on. This set of expressions can be fully understood in the context of the division of labor between Party and government. Since the 18th CPC National Congress, a major change has taken place. The handling of the Party-government relations is obviously different from the time when the division of labor was emphasized. When the Party-government relations return to where it was, do we need to reconsider the relations between the state and society, the government and the market, and the central and local governments, which were previously considered under the condition of the division of labor between Party and government? Do we need to include a new variable, the change in Party-government relations, in our vision of future communities? This issue has not received enough attention. Many people have not realized the potential significance of this variable.

I am familiar with primary-level governance in Chinese rural areas. At the time when villagers' self-governance was promoted, there were two major universal problems that still exist to this day. One of the problems is how to exert the leadership role of the village Party committee and how to deal with the relation between the village committee and the Party organization if the Party branch would no longer recommend candidates for the village committee, and all the villagers can be candidates. This has become an institutional and structural problem. An empirical representation of this problem can be found in conflicts between the village Party committee and the village committee in some places. Now the leading position of the Party organizations in rural areas is re-emphasized and various measures are taken to guarantee the position. Then we need to ask another question: how can we ensure the villagers' self-governance under the premise of guaranteeing and realizing the leadership of the Party organization? The core question is how to cast formalism off from the election in villages.

Thus, it can be seen that the change of the Party-government relations at the macro level has directly restricted the exploration of primary-level governance. Although legally, the community is not the government, and community governance cannot be equated with government governance, the Party-government relations at the high-level and the community-level share the same characteristics under the Party-government system. Therefore, it is not difficult to understand why community governance can't avoid administrative practices that are usually conducted by governments. As a result, the structural variable of Party-government relations must be taken into consideration in future community development in China. This variable will act on the governance system and structure of urban and rural communities for a long time.

2. The vertical coordinate

The second one is the vertical coordinate. With the acceleration of urbanization and the rapid progress of information technology, there has been an important change in the relations between the state and society. To be specific, the state once relied on the resources in rural areas to develop. Now it is helping rural areas to develop with poverty alleviation policies, during which the power again is decentralized. The Party-government relation in the horizontal dimension has gone through the changes from the one not being based on the division of labor between Party and government, to the one featuring the division of labor, and to the one focusing on Party-government integration. In the vertical dimension, the penetration of state power into rural areas presents the changes from the integration of state and society (the people's commune system) to the retreat of state power from rural areas, and to the re-entry of state power into rural areas. In this process, the unit of rural governance becomes an important variable.

For example, when villagers' self-governance was introduced, the village committee appeared at the natural village level to help solve the problem of disorder that arose after the dissolution of the people's commune system and maintain social security. But the state needed to solve macro-structural problems. After the dissolution of the people's commune and the emergence of the township, the production brigade also needed to be transformed accordingly. So, the state enacted the relevant villagers' self-governance law to change the unit of villagers' self-governance to the administrative village level. In the process of accelerating urbanization and new rural construction, a large number of villages have been merged. The expansion of the rural primary-level governance unit has promoted the administrative development of the village committee from a different perspective. In urban communities, a similar phenomenon is presented through a different mechanism. The extensive application of information technology has greatly enhanced the government's ability and self-confidence in governance. The government's ability to influence primary-level communities is completely unparalleled compared to what it was before. A growing trend is that, with the help of big data and cloud computing, the relations between different levels of governments and between governments and communities are being reconstructed in a new way, and a governance complex that integrates different levels of governments and communities is emerging. In this governance complex, the primary-level governance unit, which was originally adopted to implement community self-governance, has been transformed into one of the nodes; that is, the independence of the primary-level governance unit is weakened and largely dissolved.

3. Issues to be considered in future community governance

In this context, we will pursue further research on two questions. First, how can the villagers' self-governance and community self-governance be better understood; and should we redefine self-governance? Second, the autonomy and independence of primary-level governance units are weakened against the backdrop of growing administrative tendency, so how can society play its role? These can also be regarded as two fundamental problems of the present system, which cannot be avoided when it comes to the community of the future. From a macro point of view, countries across the world share a similar governance framework of "government, market, and society". And it is mentioned in the fifth plenary session of the 19th Central Committee of the Communist Party of China that "we should take into consideration both the efficient market and the effective government". We need to think further about what the role of "society" should be in China and how it can be better integrated into China's governance framework in the future.

Constructing a Xiacheng Model of "Joint Governance" and "Smart Governance"

Yang Xiaoping

Director, Civil Affairs Bureau, Xiacheng District, Hangzhou, Zhejiang

Xiacheng District is situated in the core and old-town area of Hangzhou. It covers an area of 31 square kilometers, comprising 8 streets and 75 communities, with 528 000 permanent residents. As a typical old residential district, we are leading the way in community governance in the city. We've been thinking about how to adapt community governance to new developments. For example, we want to use digitalization, information and intelligent technologies to help solve traditional and long-lasting problems of community governance. We are thinking of ways to bring more people on onboard and give them more voice in community management.

1. To consolidate public support of Xiacheng Model of "joint governance" and "smart governance"

First, we want to garner more public support. We want our communities to be governed and managed by people who are familiar to their operation and who are truly talented in community governance. At present, community workers mostly consist of people who expect to have a professional career in this line of work. They are the backbone of community governance and are paid by the government. The residents often regard community workers essentially the same as street cadres and officials. Therefore, we started to fill our residents' committees with more local residents. In our last election, we elected 295 residents, or 71.78% from our residents to serve as committee members, and put 19 of them as directors of the committee. We hope to tap into their familiarity with the neighborhood, their dialect strength and their enthusiasm to serve the neighborhood, and help us solve difficult community problems, such as neighborhood conflicts and residential parking difficulties. Let me give you a simple example of success we have achieved in this regard. The sewage pipes in our community used to be blocked by food grease for years. We introduced the "open space" discussion to gather residents' thoughts door-to-door, and had multiple rounds of discussion and democratic voting. Finally, we had this problem solved.

Second, improve the self-governance and guarantee mechanism for the full cycle of residents' participation. First of all, the community work is funded at a rate of 10 yuan per resident per year, which gives us a budget of 5.28 million to 6 million yuan. By soliciting public opinions in advance, by engaging them throughout the process and asking them to make evaluation of the work, we hope that residents can participate in and manage the whole process of community work.

Third, find content of work that is close to people's needs. In choosing which project to invest with the community money, we give priority to projects that are related to residents' livelihood, such as the construction of community libraries, park maintenance and parking garage renovation. The launch of these projects can draw on the initiative of the residents, and give them a deeper sense of happiness and fulfillment by taking part.

2. Improve the work support on Xiacheng Model of "joint governance" and "smart governance"

First, improve the system design to help communities develop. Westart by optimizing the existing system and clarified the job responsibilities of each subcommittee. At present, the work of Xiacheng sub district is mainly supported by the party organization, the residents' committee, the public service workstation and the residents' affairs supervision committee. By making the residents' committee local, we hope to empower them in community-level decision-making. The public service workstation is mainly charged to undertake the government's public services at the community level. The residents' affairs supervision committee plays more of a supervision role. By clarifying each of their responsibilities, we hope to develop in a balanced and scientific way. Secondly, we have built an effective evaluation system. At present, we use neighborhood friendliness, residents' participation, residents' satisfaction, community service ability, community organization ability as criteria to assess our work. At the same time, since Zhejiang government required all communities to provide one-stop services, we implemented strict access system for community affairs. Last but not least, we have set up our own social organizations such as Ram Union, Wulin Dama and Red Volunteer Station to support high-quality public welfare projects. At present, there are more than 2 600 social organizations in our community. They have played a tremendously helpful role in issues related with the elderly, women, children, the disabled, the unemployed and poor families and in community correction and drug control for teenagers.

Second, develop online platforms to help achieve smart governance. We hope to build a community online platform that can achieve precise and intelligent control, precise service and full-cycle management. This platform is expected to rapidly transfer data with the City Brain and four platforms of primary-level governance in Zhejiang, and build a real-time dynamic basic information base and database for community governance. At the same time, the platform can also collect data related to people's social wellbeing, civil administration, social security and protection of the disabled. In addition, it can analyze personal identity information to give early, active and timely warnings of problems, which then drastically reduce the work of social workers and help them make more targeted visits. As a result, rather than relying on intuition, the social workers can use data analysis technology, and become more proactive in service provision.

Fig. 1
The smart governance online system of Xiandaicheng Community

Third, integrate online and offline activities to help reduce burden and increase efficiency. Whether for self-governance or co-governance, it is important we involve residents both online and offline. That is why we start to build a number of professional platforms, such as the "Neighborhood e-Station" App for community residents, apps for community workers, as well as comprehensive platforms such as "Community Autonomy Online". "Neighborhood e-Station" is a platform for residents to put forward, discuss and evaluate community affairs. By using computer automatic algorithm, the platform analyzes residents' feedback and produces search hot words, so that the residents would know how the issues they care are handled, and raise the efficiency of community work and communication.

In addition, in view of Xiacheng's high proportion of old residents (close to 28% across the district, and more than 31% in three streets), the platform focuses on services for the old. Businesses that provide old age care are all now online accessible. To help old people adapt to smart equipment, we asked professionals experienced in elderly care and social work to provide customized one-on-one service at their home. The service is available as long as old people make a telephone call. It allows old people to track the status of the service provided and can link them with other services they might need.

3. Approaches taken in Xiacheng's Model of "joint governance" and "smart governance"

First, expand the range of basic public services. We have tried to organize the examination and approval services and the public service functions provided at the district, street and community levels in a coherent way. We have standardized the process in setting up convenience service centers at street and community levels. We now provide online government service and approval and service matters around the clock. We were the first to set up a property management station in Zhejiang. We have pushed for the transformation of old communities and became the first to offer "community housekeeper" services.

Second, strengthen professional service teams. At present, 603 community workers, which accounts for 63.08% of the total in the district, have obtained professional certification. Xiacheng District is committed to establishing an information resource database of social organizations. We want to train people so that they would be equipped with the knowledge and skills to run, manage and supervise social organizations. The district is also promoting the transformation of social workers. The street and community public service projects undertaken by our social workers are now worth 11.8 million yuan.

Third, foster the community spirit. We have set up role models including Kong Shengdong, Huang Feihua and Bao Jing to encourage more community residents to emulate their actions. We encourage our communities to be distinctive. Events such as the Neighbors' Day, have helped our residents appreciate the value of civility, harmony and mutual help. We have also used activities to try to instill into our community residents renewed appreciation of their family values and family traditions. We have gone all out to organize different cultural and recreational activities. We hope these efforts could enrich residents' cultural life and further enhance their sense of community.

Approaches to Easier Residential Community Governance in the Future

Chen Weidong

Professor, School of Politics and International Studies, Central China Normal University

1. Challenges in primary-level residential community governance

I would like to talk about the current challenges facing primary-level residential community governance and propose some approaches to easier residential community governance in the future. I will talk about them from the perspective of an organization's resource capability, which is the ability of an organization to independently and efficiently allocate resources to carry out various functional activities.

I have been studying residential community governance since 2000. From my research, I have found that residential community governance had been faced with two types of challenges: "intrinsic challenges" and "institutional challenges". "Intrinsic challenges" result from the fact that residential community administrators have to deal with all sorts of everyday problems for the residents. Whenever residents need help from their communities, they would always turn to the community administrators. However, in my view, "institutional challenges" are even more difficult to tackle. This type of challenges stem from the institutional failure in residential community governance. There is a saying that goes like this, "You can't make bricks without straw". "Institutional challenges" can be further divided into two sub-types. The first sub-type depicts a case in which communities lack the straw for making bricks, which is to say they do not have adequate resources. The second sub-type depicts a case in which the residential communities do have the straw, i.e., resources, but they lack the autonomy to make the bricks by themselves and may be faced with other problems. For example, the residential community administrators might lack professional competence, time, and energy to make the bricks, and they might violate certain regulations in the process of making bricks. Primary-level residential community governance has been beset by a long-standing conundrum, which we usually describe in the following way: The visible problems are hard to solve, but the solvable ones are hard to see.

2. Explanatory variables for primary-level residential community governance

We can use six variables based on the resource capacity of an organization to explain primary-level residential community governance.

The first two variables can illustrate why we cannot make bricks without straw. Firstly, the more organizations there are, the more resources there would be, making residential community governance easier. Although there are many units under a residential community administration, most of them do not participate in the governance of the community. Secondly, the more types of organizations there are, the more diverse the resources would be, making residential community governance easier. The following four variables explain why it is hard to make bricks even with enough straw. Thirdly, the greater autonomy an organization has, the stronger resource capacity it would have, making residential community governance easier. Residential communities in China have little autonomy. A special type of legal person as they are, they do not have the corresponding financial autonomy. Therefore, the finance of a residential community is managed by its governing subdistrict, and the finance of a village by its governing town. So far, local governments in China have not issued any document on the financial autonomy of residential communities. Fourthly, the more specialized an organization is, the stronger resource capacity it would have, making residential community governance easier. Fifthly, the more professional an organization is, the stronger its resource capacity would be, making residential community governance easier. Sixthly, the more standardized an organization is, the fairer the allocation of resources would be, making residential community governance easier.

3. Approaches to easier residential community governance in the future

I think residential community governance in the future should be:

1. more open: The government and the residential communities should engage diverse organizations in community governance, so as to decentralize resources and achieve greater effectiveness;

2. more autonomous, so as to allow primary-level administrators to act more actively;

3. more legalized and institutionalized, so as to facilitate the allocation of resources;

4. more specialized, so as to distribute tasks clearly;

5. more professional.

Finally, since "sharing" is a new production mode and lifestyle in the 21st century, powers and resources should also be shared for residential community governance in the future.

Analysis of Complex Resilience System: Sustaining Grasslands Ecosystems with Community in Aso National Park

Shinya Ueno

Professor Emeritus of Kumamoto University, Japan

1. Aim, background and approach

The aim of this research is to study on resilience of social ecology system to strengthen good regional management for the natural resources and community.

The background is that rural areas have many difficulties, but from the urban governance side, urban areas depend on the healthy maintenance of the rural environment, especially the water resources and the recharged areas. Recently, grassland has a very strong difficulty because the grass resources have lost their economic value. To keep the good shape, grassland area is very important from the environmental viewpoint. So how to keep the grassland is a very important issue in Japan and in my province.

The approach of this study includes field study on rural community's natural resources management ability, social capital survey with questionnaires, resilience thinking for complex resilience system and the use of system dynamics ideas.

Kumamoto has almost the same climate as Shanghai. Aso area is located at the center of the Kyushu Island. As a water resource area, it covers half of the population of Kyushu island.

2. Ecological succession: adaptive cycle

Ecological succession is an adaptive cycle. First, there might be bare land, and lichens come to the ground, then annual plants come up and form a grassland. Then perennial grass comes. After grass resumes, small trees and intolerant trees come and form the forest. Lastly, in the climax regime, shade tolerant trees come. In Japan, this kind of succession from the bare land to the forest is very easy. But to keep the grassland in our area, we need to stop the intolerant trees from resuming. That means

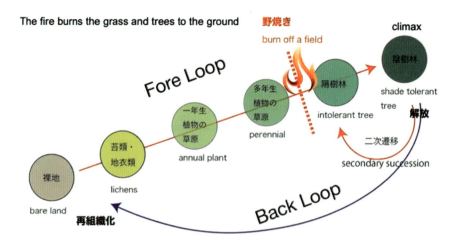

Fig. 1
Ecological
succession

The fire burns the grass and trees to the ground

野焼き
burn off a field

climax

Fore Loop

陰樹林

shade tolerant tree

解放

陽樹林

intolerant tree

多年生
植物の
草原

perennial

二次遷移

secondary succession

一年生
植物の
草原

annual plant

苔類・
地衣類

lichens

裸地

bare land

再組織化

Back Loop

we should put the fire on the mountain or grassland area every year to burn off the field. That's why we keep the biggest grassland scenery over the past 10 000 years. But it costs a lot and needs a lot of work forces.

The biggest change since the 1960s is that we don't use grass resources anymore. Before the energy revolution, we used firewood or charcoal for cooking or heating and used compost and green manure, but nowadays we use chemical fertilizer instead. Green manure is the kind of environmental disposal. As Fig. 2 shows, the pressure to use the grassland decreases very rapidly. That's why we have to cover this kind of pressure.

Fig. 3 shows a very beautiful season in the Aso area. You can see many cattle far away and very beautiful grassland. In Fig. 4, these fires on the grass of the mountains take place in early spring, in February or March. Community people work together and set the fire and burn all of the mountains in the area. After May or June, new grass comes and farmers brings the cattle to the grass area. This is very healthy grassland usage system.

Fig. 2
Changes in
the use of
community-
based forest and
grassland

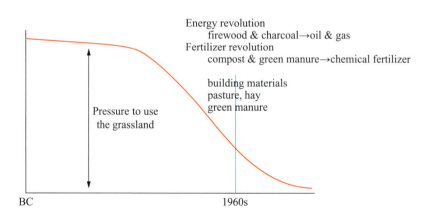

Energy revolution
　　firewood & charcoal→oil & gas
Fertilizer revolution
　　compost & green manure→chemical fertilizer

building materials
pasture, hay
green manure

Pressure to use
the grassland

BC

1960s

Fig. 3
Aso National Park

Fig. 4
Fires in Aso
National Park

3. Community functions and social networks

This system was supported by the community's network. In the community, they have the inter-personal networks they need. They form many essential associations such as the community and organizations. They have the autonomy in the community. And they share many functions to keep the natural resources, make more production and promote tourism. Even in a time of crisis such as a flood or earthquake disaster, they work together and help to provide for the community.

Intra-community networks are also very important, especially to cover the wide range area of environment management. Over the inter-community network are municipalities, a local government that takes charge of that issue. In the Aso region, there are 7 municipalities, cities and towns and village governments. They work together as intra-municipal network. This layers of network are very important to keep the management of natural resources in good condition.

The Fig. 5 is the result of a social survey showing the deviation value for each question. Number 50 is the average of the national survey that I did. In the Aso area, many points have a good score,

Fig. 5
Deviation value
for each question

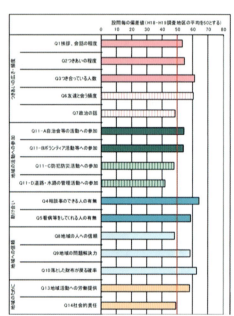

Fig. 6
Population
composition of
Aso Area

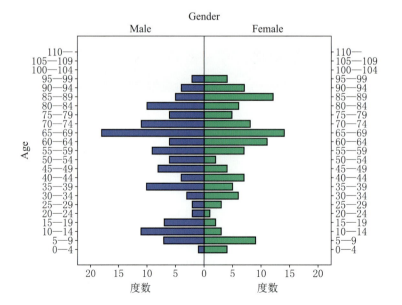

Fig. 7
Generational
Trends

even though their community's population decreases and ages very rapidly (See Fig. 6). Right now, the management work basically covers people over 60 years old. The generational trend (see Fig. 7) suggests that young generation shares a small proportion compared to the elderly. The lifestyle change has great effects on the activities in local area.

4. Transition simulation of grassland to forest

Fig. 8 shows the simulation of the grassland from grassland to forest transition. In 1982, we had many grassland areas, but nowadays a little bit forest area is expanding and in 2050 we will have more forests. Forest is good for the environment. But in this area, grassland is the most favorable landscape rather than forest. We need an idea to keep this grassland in the future.

Fig. 9 shows the concept of the ecosystems transition. Usually ecosystems start growing very rapidly, and at certain time they reach the conservation time. In this conservation regime, we usually try to keep the old regime with government subsidy, and other measures. But finally, this regime is reached to some threshold points. Suddenly, disruptive or creative changes will start. All of the natural resources are released to the market again. Then re-organization cycle will start. This is a beginning

Fig. 8
Transition
simulation of
grassland to
forest

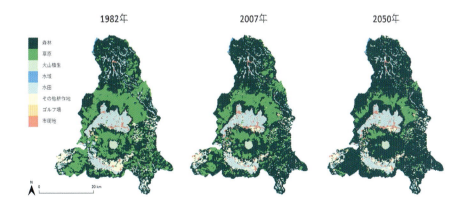

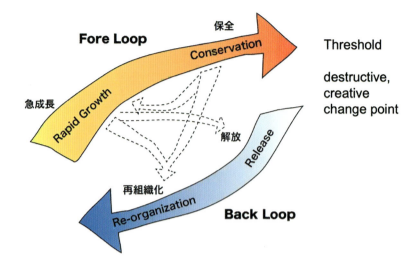

of innovation.

Tendency in an ecosystem is a common model. If we leave it, a natural grassland regime will change to a forest system. As Fig. 10 shows, if you stay in regime 1, it's okay. But if the circumstance or environment changes, it's very hard to stay in regime 1. Suddenly, your system will change to Regime 2. You cannot go back anymore once you move to another regime.

Fig. 11 shows the condition of a village in the Aso area. Still, we keep setting fire every spring, but some pastures or some grasslands have already stopped working. This picture shows the pessimistic future, but I think each pasture or grassland is isolated like a kind of module. If we work together with community people, maybe we can change the present condition to another condition.

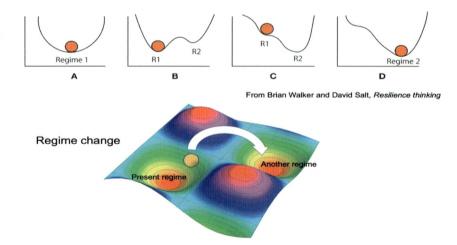

Fig. 10
The system as a
ball in the basin
model

From Brian Walker and David Salt, *Resilience thinking*

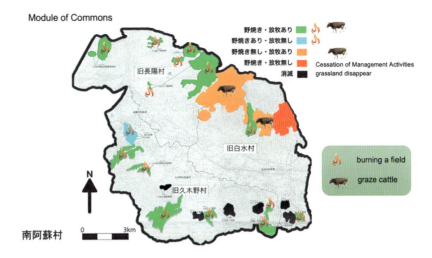

Fig. 11
Has the regime
of Minami-Aso
village changed
(1999—2019)

5. Future scenarios

Firstly, we need to maintain the grasslands through community activities. Secondly, we are doing community activities plus city volunteer collaboration and donations, but we need to improve more.

6. Intervention measures based on socio-ecological resilience thinking

Firstly, we have to understand social ecological system more. This is the complex adaptive system, not a linear chain. Secondly, we should strengthen community autonomy and rely on communities' activities in the future.

Fig. 12
The balance of
two loops

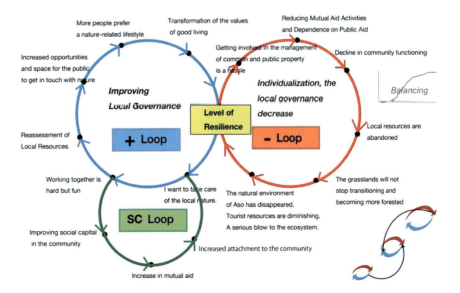

7. Empower community to keep present regime

There is a loop to strengthen local governance, and there might be another loop that tries to decrease community governance. These two different ones combined together create a balanced loop. If we can strengthen the trust loop, maybe we can change the movement or transition way. But if we fail, decreasing loop will become stronger. So social capital loop is put forward to strengthen the trust loop.

The 15-Minute Community: Reconstruction of Community Public Space

Rasmus Duong-Grunnet

Director of Gehl Institute of Urban Design, Copenhagen, Denmark

Today I will talk a little bit about 15-minute city or 15-minute community and why that is so important when we talk about communities in cities.

1. Gehl approach: making cities for people

First, I work at a group called Gehl that is based on the work by Professor Jan Gehl. With the mission of "Making Cities for People", we work with the academic discipline of looking at physical environment, linking it with human behavior. How can human behavior change, depending on physical environment? Some of the books concerning our research are also available in China and in Chinese.

The way that we understand development and cities is not to look at what's called traditional planning process where you build buildings, make traffic and infrastructure, and then try to figure out how we can support life community here.

We've turned it around. We start by saying, "what kind of life and community we want to support?" Then we look at the basis and conditions we need to do this. Then we can see the buildings and bigger developments we need in cities. So, we should always set life as the first thing. What life do we want in cities?

We work a lot with looking at individual situations. What is good for the individual person? But then we are also looking at what is good for the collective. How is this good for the whole city and community? We are linking it with the United Nations sustainable goals as well.

One case, for example, that we have done here in Copenhagen is to work on the vision for Copenhagen city. That is called "Metropolis for People". Basically, we have developed a vision for how Copenhagen should develop with a focus on people who live here, and Copenhagen has done a very nice development over the last 15 to 20 years. We have pushed for places like this in the inner city of Copenhagen. It's an area where the city has slowly changed, with a focus on pedestrian and bicycles, but also having space for community support. Of course, we have very nice environments along the Harbour now that is clean to swim in it. They also support those who come, stay and hang out and become part of something nice in your city.

Fig. 1
The Copenhagen
Harbour

2. Gehl case: 15-minute local communities

In China and throughout the world, we work a lot with this concept of "舒适生活圈" or a community life circle. In other places it's sometimes called the 15-minute local communities. The idea is to focus more on what is possible to reach in 15 minutes, because this allows you to develop a community and a sustainable way of living locally. That's to say you can use the full city.

Shanghai is a good example. We need to use all of Shanghai and see what I need locally to support this. The work we've been doing in China has been together with Energy Foundation and our collaborator CSTC. For example, we focused on the work about "Changing Cities in Five Steps". It's a way of developing a thinking about cities in the future. I'll just show a few examples. One of the most important things we've been part of is "Shanghai Street Design Guidelines", something we have worked on together with the Shanghai Urban Planning and Design Research Institute. The idea of the street design guidelines is to look at the city and the ways to sign and make sure that the city and the streets are also seen as public spaces. Life can take part here, so we can live in our streets, not just for traffic and mobility.

We also worked a lot with this concept that is known to lot of people now, which we call "慢

行 "in Chinese. That is to focus on slow mobility and how to move around without having to speed all the time. In Shanghai, for example, we've been able to work with various authorities, developing a way of looking at the Huangpu River public spaces. Gehl has been involved in 4 strategic work behind that (Fig. 2). We've been able to develop places like this and support more activities like this. This development has been implemented throughout the years. Now in Shanghai, we have 45 kilometers of connected public spaces along the Huangpu River. These types of places now are able to support local communities, not just for recreation, but also for activities, for coming together and for having a space where you can meet and socialize.

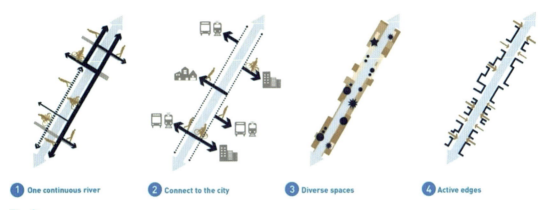

① **One continuous river**　② **Connect to the city**　③ **Diverse spaces**　④ **Active edges**

Fig. 2
Four basic strategies

For us, it's very important that we first decide what kind of physical environments we need to achieve before we can support this kind of local community. 15-minute community is very depending on the physical environment. We were very honored to see that last year President Xi went to visit the Huangpu River and talked about how public spaces are a very important part of urban development now. We see the same with Nanjing Road that we worked on, where we could see that East Nanjing Road, the last bit of Nanjing Road, was still for cars, but all the users were pedestrians. So how could we support the activity and life taking place there? In Nanjing Road, we made these measurements to show that pedestrians were much in favor. In front of the Peace Hotel, there were a lot of car lanes, but people need to have a local life here. They need to live and work here.

So back in 2015, we made a vision for how to develop this and slowly this is implemented. Today, it looks like this. These kinds of places where not only businesses but also locals can come and stay are important for local communities.

3. The impact of Covid-19 on 15-minute communities

My last point is that when we look at 15-minute communities, we should also learn from what has been going on the last half year for this COVID-19 situation we have been in.

From Gehl, we have been able to do surveys and analysis throughout Europe and in the U.S., with some information from Asia as well. The full report, if you're interested, can be downloaded at covid19.gehlpeople.com. The focus of this research has been what had happened in public spaces during COVID-19. Of course, a lot of people have stayed home and needed to work from home. But one thing is that local meeting places you have within 15 minutes in the community have gone up in their use (Fig. 3), even though the central shopping streets and many office parks have been with much less people.

Fig. 3
Local meeting places were more visited than before

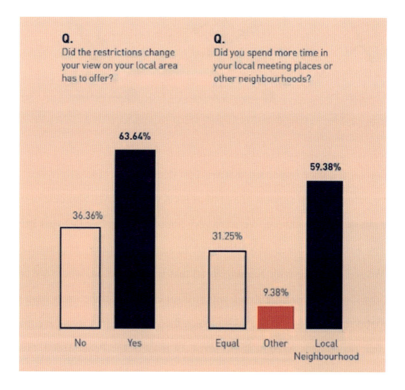

Therefore, we can see an increase level of activity across Denmark's four cities (Fig. 4). Pedestrian movement especially, and bicycle movement have gone up, which is " 慢行 ", namely slow mobility. Those people are not moving far away anymore. They're moving around locally. We need to be able to support them locally and make sure they can have spaces where they can have good community lives.

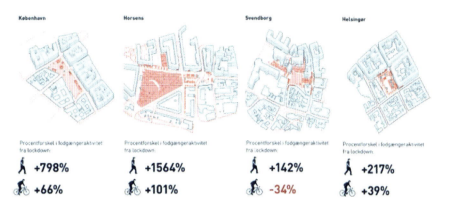

Fig. 4
Pedestrian and bicycle movement have gone up in use in Denmark's four cities

We typically talk about the 5—15 Minute Walk (Fig. 5). What is reachable within 5 to 15 minutes? This is where we are now seeing an increase in focus globally. In Denmark where I'm from, even though Denmark is quite good already, we are still pushing to see what we can be supported within 5 to 15 minutes. This is some of the work that we also involve in China now.

Fig. 5
The 5—15 minute walk

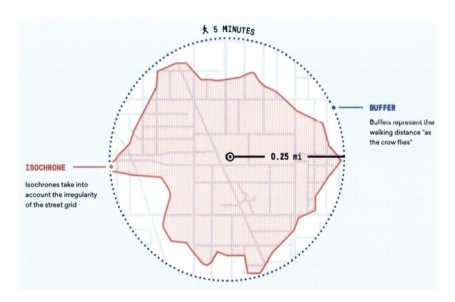

We see walking and biking going up as a way of moving. That also means people need to be able to reach local community functions closer by. In Beijing, for example, we see high numbers of users on Beijing's bicycle highway. In Shanghai we see the same things. I think from now on quickly, there is going to be a lot more focus on this.

The Co-development of "Public Space, Public Service and Public Order": Multi-functional Community Complex and Community Development

Tang Yalin

Professor, School of International Relations and Public Affairs, Fudan University

1. Transforming community governance: from community autonomy to a combination of governance and development

Twenty years ago, we emphasized more on community autonomy. But today, we tend to put "community", "governance" and "development" together. Community governance is no longer simply about selecting leaders to govern an area. What makes us shift the focus to community "governance" and community "development"? I believe five factors are at play.

First, change of the times. We have been thinking about the effects of using democratic elections and community management as the main way of community's governance, and we find that democratic elections are not effective on its own to promote community development. As a result, community governance has changed from being driven by politics to service and then to service guided by political principles, and has shown new trend of becoming a community of needs. Second, demand-driven orientations. Community governance has shown the trend of being a community of interaction because people now have diverse needs. Third, we now recognize it is important for a community to be distinctive. Through new innovative projects and mechanisms, we are trying to make a community of tailored experience. Fourth, the approaches used in management are getting more targeted and defined. In areas of the environment, safety, sanitary condition and cultural atmosphere, through the initiatives such as waste sorting, building a 15-minute public culture service circle and rebuilding old communities and making communities more friendly for senior citizens, we are trying to build a community of targeted needs. The fifth reason is the need of political guidance, which is actually the most important reason. We need to solidify the political foundations of community governance and build a community of collaboration.

To sum up, community governance used to be guided by the government. It relied on leaders elected by a community and focused only on safety and functional services. But now it is managed more by community organizations. With funding provided by the government, it brings in more actors and are empowered by technologies. It aims at building a platform and a system that can solve people everyday life problems. This shifts governance from community autonomy to governance that combines governance and development.

2. Connecting demand with functions: rise of a multi-functional community and reshaping public space

In recent years, to promote community governance and better cater to people's needs, different service centers, which were once separated and had their own focuses respectively, for example, Party member's center, Community Service Center, Community Cultural Activity Center, Community Health Service Center, etc., have gradually merged to form one comprehensive service center. This enables people to enjoy community services in a more convenient way, lower the cost and make full use of public spaces appropriately and efficiently without violating the urban design standards. As a result, multi-functional community complexes and broader public spaces are sprouting up.

What are the reasons that propel the rise of multi-functional community complexes? First, it is the direct result of rising up to the need of development. In Shanghai, we now see "Service at Your Doorstep" in Pudong New Area, "Neighborhood Center" in Yangpu District and "Community Care Center" in Xuhui District. These schemes are innovative in the sense that they try to offer different services in a centralized place in response of people's needs. Similar initiatives have also emerged in other regions of China. For example, Chengdu has already established a multi-functional community complex a while ago. The Township Cultural Service Station initiative put forward in the 12th Five-Year Plan was an even earlier attempt, though it was more about using limited resources to promote the development of rural culture.

Policy-wise, in June, 2020, the General Office of the CPC Shanghai Committee and General Office of Shanghai Municipal People's Government issued an official guideline entitled "Several Opinions on Further Improving Standardized Governance of Community". It promotes the buildup of a community complex and asks each subdistrict to roll out its own easily accessible community complex in an easily accessible, cost-efficient and standardized way. Putting community complex on the agenda is not only a new requirement by the Ministry of Civil Affairs, but also solves real problems in community development, for example, a community complex can raise the service efficiency, promote the coordination of different agencies and raise the initiatives of the people.

Second, a community complex can meet people's demands. In pushing for innovations of primary-level governance, Shanghai has made it clear that the community work at the grass-roots level should be more demand-driven, problem-driven and result-driven. Connecting demand with functions and making meeting people's needs the focus of innovation can effectively avoid service blind spots and raise people's satisfaction and sense of achievement.

Third, we have to innovate new forms of services provided in communities. For example, the "Service at Your Doorstep" project in Pudong asks every community worker to serve the people directly and change their roles from being a community manager to a service provider. The working places of residents' committee and Party secretary also turned into one-stop service centers directly serving the people. Pudong has divided community services into services concerning Party affairs, politics, daily life, law service, health service, cultural activities and community management. By consolidating the community's political function, service function, organizing and management functions, the community aims to provide these services in an effectively and timely way.

3. To provide public service and establish public order in public space: structures and service forms of multi-functional community complex

The decision to roll out multi-functional community complex is actually driven by the shift of power from national governance to lower level and the reconstruction of social order at the grassroots level.

In general, the social order at the grassroots level mainly concerns environment, traffic, security, service and public space. To adapt to the shift of governance focus, the community should work within its capacity to consolidate resources (including human resources), services, platforms and technologies so that it can provide residents with "doorstep" service. A multi-functional community complex not only brings different services under one roof, but also helps forge new relationships with people in the process of service provision, for example, relationship between service providers and residents, and relationship between residents in the same neighborhood. It also provides new ways for people to communicate and negotiate with each other.

A multi-functional community complex can also take up new forms because of new services supported by technologies, platforms and organizations. This is because virtual technologies (WeChat groups, APPs, etc.) are increasingly embedded in physical places (offices, services stations, entertainment centers, gyms, etc.). Based on this, the power structure can be embedded in governance space; the management systems can be embedded in service networks and service platforms can be embedded with resource networks. These changes help a community complex break the temporal and spatial constraints in service provision.

4. A community of living and interaction: combining community development and primary-level governance

We must recognize that the relationship between community governance, primary-level governance, social governance and urban governance, regional governance and national governance is an organic and coherent one. Based on this understanding, we should push for a community complex focusing on residents' daily life and communication with each other. This is the ultimate goal of co-development of community development and primary-level governance.

The rise of community complexes holds great implications. First, a community complex is intimately bound to a place. Primary-level governance cannot take place in a vacuum. It needs a place to provide services, for people to interact with each other and live a more enjoyable life, to govern and to get people united around a common cause. Second, a community complex seeks to achieve community development. A community can be measured in a lot of ways, for example, by the services it provides, by the degree of engagement of its residents in community activities, by the amount of people interaction and by how polite and rule abiding they are. These criteria are deeply connected with people's daily life and can reflect the richness, convenience and closeness of their life and their sense of satisfaction, happiness, and security. Third, a community complex should combine community development and primary-level governance. At the national level, power is distributed between the Party, the government and the society. At the primary-level, a community organization is guided by the Party in decision-making but also should be given more power, space, resource and governance autonomy to govern its affairs. The shift of power reflects the Party's efforts to serve people's needs and develop China into the greater welfare state. At the center of the vison, we need to strengthen Party building, adopt a demand-driven approach, shift governance focus, consolidate the resource and service functions, create new platforms, use new technologies, bring in more actors and hold more cultural activities. Only in this way, can we expect to build a new form of governance that combines services, government and development.

"Small Cells" in the Governance of Megacities: Taking the Three-District Integration by Taoyuan Subdistrict as an Example

Huang Jian

Secretary of the Party Working Committee of Taoyuan Subdistrict Office,
Nanshan District, Shenzhen City, Guangdong Province

At the 40th Anniversary marking the Establishment of the Shenzhen Special Economic Zone, President Xi Jinping pointed out that we must make efforts to build full-cycle management, accelerate the modernization of urban governance system and capacity, and strive to find a new governance path in line with the characteristics and development patterns of a megacity. As a subdistrict in Shenzhen, Taoyuan has made some explorations in this regard in recent years. Taoyuan is located in the north of Nanshan District, Shenzhen City, Guangdong Province. At present, the economic aggregate of Nanshan District ranks the third in China, and the total population of the district exceeds 4 000 000 people. Taoyuan covers 35 square kilometers, almost the size of a district of other cities. It has a population of about 300 000. Being part of a megacity with large population, large economic volume, various elements, and rapid exchange of people, logistics, capital and information, we face many challenges and difficulties in urban governance.

1. Full-cycle management philosophy

How is community-level governance defined? The traditional governance pattern, also known as the community-level governance, divides governance in geographical or spatial terms, rather than by population. But in reality, a lot of work is done across communities and districts. It is thus impossible for a single community to cover all the ground and gaps of governance. That is why we want to open our community, and at the same time, consolidate the resources we have and make them function. To this end, we need to consolidate our governance structures, all the systematical elements and operational mechanisms. In view of the local conditions of Taoyuan, we have come up with a full-cycle management philosophy named Three-District Integration.

Why do we call it Three-District Integration? Well, the name derives from the public community, university campus and industrial park that are located inside Taoyuan. Altogether, we have 12 communities, 21 industrial parks, 7 universities and 3 scientific research institutes, as well as a large number of urban villages under our jurisdiction. Therefore, people who choose to live in Taoyuan come from a diverse range of backgrounds. To govern this community, we started by looking at similar measures used in the Yangpu District of Shanghai and even governance experience from the United States as a reference in their early stages.

2. Measures taken on the basis of three-district integration

In 2017, we proposed to consolidate all types of resources in the three districts, including culture, demand and information, so that each small cell in the community could play its role and contribute to the vitality of community governance as a whole. I'm happy to report that after years of exploration, we've made some progress in urban governance.

we would describe our practices as driven by a core community-level Party leadership, a set of mechanisms and a cluster of service centers.

First of all, we need a community-level Party leadership to provide guidance on the integration work. The public community, university campus and industrial park belong to different administrative divisions. For example, the community and the university are governed differently and the way a public community is run is different from that of an industrial park. These factors add to our governance challenges. In 2019, we made a "Three-year Action Plan for Party Building in Taoyuan Subdistrict (2020—2022)", which is the first of its kind by subdistrict-level Party in Shenzhen. The plan put forward a Party building blueprint at community-level. We hope through the plan, we would achieve coordination of departments and regions not only horizontally but also vertically and form a micro-circulation system with the community level Party committee as the core and different actors assuming joint responsibility of governance.

A set of mechanism describes the dialogue mechanism we have with our partners. For example, we launched a joint meeting system for the integration of the three districts, through which we could jointly promote resources integration and discuss ways to solve various problems in the development of the three districts. We have already started to jointly organize events, share resources, hold joint discussions, and support the incubation of joint projects. We have also issued a work plan of cooperation for shared benefits and signed a joint agreement for the cooperation of the Three-District Integration.

We have also set up a cluster of supporting services to drive integrated development. At the community level, we set up a social organization and innovative service center, in order to bring in more actors from society and professional organizations to provide quality services. At the same time, we try to foster our own social organizations, for example, organizations set up by university students, by employees working at the industrial park and by senior citizens in the community, to cater to a diverse range of interest. To push for deeper integration, we set up a promotion center and an integration center so as to incubate research projects that can tap in to the synergy of the industry and academia.

3. Difficulties in promoting the three-district integration

We still face plenty of problems as we push forward the integration of the three districts. For instance, people may not be enthusiastic toward this initiative; as a community, we cannot govern over a university. To sum up, the degree of Three-District Integration is still not as deep as we wish, the role played by the regional party is limited and the structure of governance is still not systematic. That is why I'd like to invite all the experts and scholars present today to come to Taoyuan for fieldwork and I very much appreciate your advice to help us improve.

How to Achieve Co-production in Urban Communities: An Investigation of Community-based Household Waste Management Practices

Sun Baiying

Professor, School of Public Administration and Policy, Renmin University of China

1. Research background

My research focuses on four aspects. Firstly, how can a community achieve resilience in governance? I would argue that the goal of urban primary-level governance is to make it more dynamic and self-sufficient. Social participation is the key to achieve collaboration, participation and common interests. Secondly, mega-cities such as Shanghai and Beijing have launched massive community-based household waste sorting campaigns. These initiatives were driven by the Party and the government from top-down and implemented and supervised by the local community subdistrict offices. Thirdly, from our research, we found that before the start of these government-initiated waste sorting schemes, some communities in Beijing had carried out their waste-sorting activities on their own initiative 10 years earlier. We are wondering why these communities launched such activities? What were their motivations? How did they achieve co-governance? Fourthly, we want to focus on the structure and function of self-governance to see if it has the capacity to achieve cost-benefit and sustainability; we also want to discuss possibilities of integrating waste sorting and self-governance. Based on this, we would like to advocate the concept of community co-production, which is a process-oriented innovation-driven approach that seeks to involve both civil organizations, individuals and the social capital in the cause. All of them have a stake in community planning and reconstruction (old district renovation), managing daily community affairs, and servicing the residents' needs, for instance, whether to install elevators in the community. Their participation is the key in promoting change in urbanization and communities.

2. Three models of community-based household waste management

Based on our investigation, we have identified three models used in community-based household waste management practices. They include:

Party-government-led model: The Party and the government have made community waste sorting an important area of work in urban governance. They have also adopted a top-down approach with subdistrict committees and offices become the main bodies supervising waste sorting practices. The government on the one hand is the standard maker of waste sorting and dumpster distribution standards. On the other hand, it provides waste sorting facilities and oversees the coordination of subsequent transportation and disposal (incineration) processes. The local government would mobilize the whole community it governs and urges the property management companies under their

Table 1
Typical cases of the three models

Items	Party-government-led model (2019)	Property company-led model (2003)	Developer-foundation-led model (2005)
Type of community	All types	Developed community	Upscale small communities
Main bodies	Subdistrict committees and offices	Property companies	Developer and all foundations
Motives	Policy requirements and social mobilization	Low cost and high quality of community property service	Concept of the environment-friendly community
Participants	Property management companies, residents' committees, property owners' committees and residents	Experts, social organizations, residents' committees, property owners' committees and residents	Foundation, experts, residents' committees, property owners' committees and residents
Process	Promotion and sorting	Promotion, sorting, facilities equipment and technical waste disposal	Investment, residents' participation, promotion and sorting
Methods	Top-down implementation and social mobilization	Horizontal cooperation within property companies and cooperation with government's departments	Cooperation with joint ventures and subdistrict offices supported by foundations

jurisdiction to undertake their legal responsibility of waste sorting. The authority issues the waste sorting assessment index (including amount and composition of garbage) by community, evaluates their performance and ranks them on a daily and weekly basis. Community Party committees and the residents' committees also mobilize support from the society, by recruiting volunteers.

Property-company-led model: some regional rules and regulations have specified property management companies as the principal actor in community household waste management. Property companies are created to serve people's needs in a community. They are market driven in that they collect fees from community residents per household in exchange for the services provided. Through horizontal cooperation, the property companies can achieve multi-level and multi-type cooperation. One feature of this model is that property management companies have the freedom to bring in external experts and use their technical expertise to make sorting and processing as two distinctive activities in waste disposal.

Developer-foundation-led model: This model is typically used in upscale small communities. The developers and the foundations set up by these communities are the main actors and they tap into the collective will of the community residents to embrace a new way of life. They set up joint venture with professional companies to handle garbage disposal and processing of recycled products. The organic fertilizers generated by waste recycling are used back in the community as an incentive for further partnership. This model is even supported by the local subdistrict office. Such schemes have been listed as government pilot projects and receive government subsidies.

3. Brief summary

I'm now going to make a brief summary. First, what the future community needs most is to involve more actors in community governance. Second, we have a range of governance tools in community management, be they political-driven, commercial-driven, civic-drive, or welfare-driven models. Based on the situation we face, we need to select the tools that can work in the most effective and sustainable manner. Third, the Party and the government are the pushing force for a community to achieve open and cooperative community governance. We need to do more governance restructuring and enhance the multi-dimensional leadership in primary-level governance.

Relationships Worth of Attention in Researching Future Community

Tian Yipeng

Professor, School of Philosophy and Sociology, Jilin University

1. The origin of "future community"

In March 2019, I conducted a social science project in Zhejiang province. It happened to be the time the annual two sessions of the province were held. Yuan Jiajun, the then governor of Zhejiang Province, introduced in his report the concept of "community of the future". Shortly afterwards, the Zhejiang provincial government issued "The Work Plan for the Pilot Project of Building Future Communities in Zhejiang Province", which gave a detailed description of the concept. According to this work plan, community of the future is driven by the goal to meet people's needs for a better life. It focuses on people-oriented, ecological and digital development and deals with nine areas of work in social management and governance, such as neighborhood relations, education, health, entrepreneurship, architecture and transportation. I have observed first-hand in my investigation how the local government has developed a set of refined principles around "community of the future" and the efforts towards its achievement. I also wrote two articles on this topic. One, entitled "Theoretical Problems in the Construction of Future Community", is published in the first volume of *Social Science Research* in 2020. The other, entitled "Multiple Horizons and Evaluation of Rural 'Coming Community' Construction", is published in the seventh volume of Nanjing Journal of Social Sciences in 2020.

2. How does "futurity" unfold in the process of building a "future community"?

Community is a nostalgic concept. Those who believe that communities are destined for extinction claim that a traditional society will lose its social characteristics due to industrialization, urbanization, and the mobility of its population. That is why we need to build a "community" in order to keep its sociality against the drastic changes of a modern society. This is also the very reason why the concept was proposed. However, another school, represented by the Chicago School in the United States, claims that communities can well exist despite the arrival of an industrial society in some North American cities. It is thus clear that community studies rarely approach the topic from a "futuristic" angle. I believe in researching "community of the future", it is necessary we address a series of relations.

First, the relations between the "futuristic" and technological nature of a community. The "futurity" of a community came to our attention at an interesting time, which was during the advent of the internet society at the end of the last century. Internet technology is deeply embedded in the progression of urban development, so "futurity" shares a very close relationship with and technology. On the one hand, without technological advancements, there is no futurity to speak of. In fact, existing versions of "community of the future", such as low-carbon community and eco-community, are all connected to technology. The academia often perceives technology as a threat to the sociality of a community. They believe that as technology develops, social relations are bound to undergo important changes. The relations between the "futuristic" and technological nature of a community are thus a worthy topic of research: we need to consider how to use technology to enable "futurity", while not to strangle the traditions of a society with technological development.

Second, the relations between the "futurity" and sociality of a community. Sociality is a very important measure of a community. A good community differs from a bad one not only in infrastructure terms, but more importantly, by its intangible elements. If a community is devoid of any social relations, interaction and collective action, it hardly makes a good community. No matter how luxurious its buildings are and how much infrastructure is in place, it's a concrete jungle at best. Therefore, sociality is vital to a community's continuity. However, as our society becomes more futuristic, as urbanization, industrialization, and technology progress, it is inevitable we lose some of our sociality. This is because in a market-oriented economy, market-dependent services may replace the interactions of individuals. Since all needs are fulfilled by the market, then the loss of sociality is arguably unavoidable. It is therefore important to coordinate the relations between the "futurity" and sociality of "community of the future" as "futurity" unfolds.

Third, the relations between the "futurity" and traditions of a community. Many communities have developed their own distinctive characteristics, by being either an industrial community, a business community, a hybrid rural-urban community or a university town. In building a "future community", it is necessary we keep the traditions of a community to the best of our ability.

Fourth, the relations between the "futurity" and ecology of a community. This aspect has attracted a lot of attention from scholars in China and elsewhere.

On the whole, when we are planning "community of the future", I think we should start from its basic features and take good care of the relations among the futuristicity, technology, sociality, traditions and ecology. Only when these relations are well handled, can we achieve the urban and community renewal and expect to have good interactions of its tradition, society, ecology and technology.

Building a Park Community: Practices and Reflections on Development and Governance of Huangshui Town, Shuangliu District, Chengdu

Yuan Pu

CPC Committee Secretary of Huangshui Town, Shuangliu District, Chengdu, Sichuan Province

Huangshui is a newly consolidated town located near Shuangliu International Airport. In recent years, driven by the mission to build "better town, better life", we have been trying to make the town a beautiful park community as a way to achieve harmonious coexistence with nature. I'd like to share with you my reflections on the practices adopted in governing and developing a park community.

Fig. 1
Huangshui Town, Shuangliu District, Chengdu City, Sichuan Province

1. Practice of the development and governance of park community

In February 2018, during a visit to Chengdu, President Xi Jinping proposed to make the city a "Park City". In January 2020, at the Sixth Meeting of the Central Committee for Financial and Economic Affairs, President Xi Jinping once again made it clear that the central government support "Chengdu's decision to build a pilot park city as a way to put into practice the new concept of development". The CPC Central Committee has laid out new strategic positioning of Chengdu. However, governing a park community is something new for a community-level government. We must take into account three major issues.

(1) Why do we need to build a park community?

The practice of a park city is the embodiment of President's Xi Jinping's thoughts on ecological civilization and reflects the pursuit of harmonious coexistence between human and nature in the new era. A park community is a miniature version of a park city and demonstrates our aspirations for a people-centered city. We believe a park community is a beautiful and open community. It brings different business formats together and pursues eco-friendly and green development. It promotes traditions as well as innovation. It is an inclusive and friendly community.

(2) Does huangshui town have the conditions to build a park community?

Huangshui Town has natural advantages in building a park community. The Muma Mountain, which is located inside the Town, has a forest coverage rate of over 60%. The Tianfu Greenway, being planned by the town right now, runs over 300 km in length. Huangshui Town also has Asia's largest wetland park and Chinese largest aviation landscape. Its per capita green area now stands at 12 square kilometers.

Huangshui Town is rich in cultural history. It is the birthplace of ancient Shu farming culture and home to Confucianism, farm culture of ancient Shu and the Three Kingdoms culture. It's also part of the ancient Silk Road. The town covers an area of 68.92 square kilometers and has a permanent population of 70 000 people. More than 2/3 of its area has been designated as urban planning area. It is an essential part of Chengdu Konggang Business District. The Chengdu-Mianyang-Leshan high-speed railway passes through the town and Chengdu Metro Line 3, Line 10 and Line 17 converge here.

(3) How to build a high-level park community?

Building a pilot park city will undoubtedly drive Huangshui Town's revitalization and transformation. Let me share with you three stories on what we have done to make this vision a reality.

The first story is about making our community an ecological paradise. We have managed to turn a once noisy village into a popular scenic spot. Yunhua Community is located in close proximity to the airport. Residents there used to complain heavily about the noises, to the effect that the roosters they raised had stopped to crow and the hens had stopped to lay eggs. In response to their concern, Huangshui Town started a relocation scheme in Yunhua Village in 2015 and eventually moved 122 households into a new area. But how to transform the ecological value into economic gains in a way that benefits people who choose to stay and those who have moved out?

In 2017, Huangshui Town began to work with Sichuan Airlines to transform the place into a garden area that combines natural scenery, panda habitats and greenway. The once noisy village was turned into a popular scenic spot covering over 6.6 square kilometers. The local residents also participated in the transition as they engaged in the new business formats brought by the tourists. Their annual per capita income now exceeds RMB 80 000 and all began to live a more prosperous life.

The second story is about creating an industrial base here. We have transformed Baita community, a once poor community into a demonstration site of agriculture, commerce, culture and tourism. There were little industrial activities in Baita community in the past. In recent years, by taking advantage of its proximity to the Historical and Cultural Reserve of the Muma Mountains, the community has made efforts to develop sightseeing agriculture and high-quality homestays, so as to tap into its agriculture, business, culture and tourism potentials.

But how to make sure the residents can receive dividend brought by the development? We started to involve the local businesses, equity joint agency and residents into some initiatives. For instance, the Community government worked with local businesses and invested RMB 3 million into high-quality homestays called "Banpo · Homestay" that are run by local residents. A rural land stock cooperative agency was also set up. In this way, local residents can enjoy continuous stream of income.

According to a resident of Baita community, his family is expected to make a total of RMB 350 000 this year, double the amount they made three years ago. He could receive RMB 30 000 as dividend from the Homestay, his daughter-in-law takes home a monthly salary RMB 40 000 by working in the homestay, the family also gets RMB 15 000 as land rents by joining in the rural land stock cooperative agency, RMB 20 000 as dividend and RMB 60 000 by renting out their apartment in the new village. Examples of Wang abound in Baita community. The community's collective now makes RMB 10 million in revenue each year, so that each family can expect a per capita income of up to RMB 4 000.

The third story is about creating convenient services for our residents. We have tried to turn rural communities into new urban communities. In 2014, over 9 600 residents were resettled in Nanliu Community. Using the 15-minute community life circle as reference, we invested in its infrastructure, by building schools, hospitals, and day care centers so that residents could have easy access to these public facilities within 15 minutes.

But soon problems emerged. We found it hard to change their habits for their new way of living. Littering was common. Some started to plant vegetables in public land and it was also different to collect community management fees on time. We started to work with a professional property management company. We set up a "Community Life Service Hall" that offered services such as extracurricular classes, welfare services, and literature and art classes. We were hoping these measures could help people's transition to live an urban life,

In response to people's vegetable planting habits, we set aside an idle land of 5 000 square meters as "shared vegetable planting field". We divided it into 80 "micro-vegetable fields" and gave them to those who had either served as volunteers for the community, or selected as model families, or paid their property management fees on time. A training scheme and a point system was also put in place to make sure the selected families took their planting duty seriously. Since the implementation of planting scheme, 95% households had made their property management fee on time, up from 65%, and uncivilized behaviors have also declined.

The three stories are but only small episodes in our efforts to achieve good development and governance of Shuangliu District in Chengdu. They reflect how Huangshui Town has been working to live up to people's expectation for a better life in a park community.

2. Difficulties and reflections about the development and governance of a park community

Better city, better life. A community is doubtlessly at the frontline in building a park city. We have identified three problems in our practices of building a park community. Firstly, we must not set up unrealistic expectations. If a community office assumes to many administrative responsibilities, it may not perform each type of work in effective and fully autonomous way. Secondly, we must make sure the services are put in pace and are accessible to the people. In a city with large jurisdiction and population, a community may easily find itself ill-equipped for the challenges involved and thus cannot fulfil its service commitments to its people. Thirdly, we must be bold and innovative enough in governing a park community. We cannot expect to solve new problems using the old ways. Without in-depth knowledge of the pattern of urban governance, without systematic planning, without participation of multiple stakeholders, there is no way we can achieve good results.

I'd also like to offer three solutions for the problems that may emerge in the development and governance of a park community. First, we must also put green development at the heart of everything. Urbanization has led to ecological degradation and has deprived us of the green mountains and clear waters. Neglecting the importance of green development would make a city ecologically sick. Therefore, we must adhere to the principle of green development, so that people can enjoy the views of the mountains and the water forever. Second, we must empower our community and combine development with governance. When we govern a community, we also need to make it stronger so that it could develop in a sustainable way. We must make sure people don't have to make long commute to work and the industry development compatible with urban development. We must create more businesses and jobs so that people living here will feel fulfilled, happy and safe. Third, we must never forget about the role culture plays in this process. For community revitalization, we need to promote the local culture. We must continue to provide more public culture services, let the residents see the beauty of local culture, and achieve the simultaneous growth of communities and people.

3. Building a beautiful life for a park community

Looking forward, Huangshui Town will continue to put people in the center of its development strategy, actively respond to their aspirations for a better life, and build on its development and governance strength to make a beautiful and livable park community of high quality.

(1) Strengthen the top-down design and build an ideal community of sustainable development. Everything starts with a good design. Guided by the Chengdu Master Plan of Urban and Rural Community Governance and Development, we will first draw up a "road map" and a "construction plan" based on our specific conditions; We will take targeted, detailed and innovative governance measures to build urban communities that are friendly to all. We want to build an efficient and dynamic industrial community of scale, and a community with green mountains, clear waters and beautiful farmland.

(2) Drawing up a community blueprint. We want to build a smart community. We are now in the process of building a database of all households living in the town. We will make our service offerings more tailored and our infrastructures fully capable to meet people's aspirations for a better life. We will accelerate the establishment of a multi-service model and expand their access to the services offered. Under the guidance of community-level Party organization, we will build a public service circle, residents self-governance circle, and a social joint governance cycle.

(3) Improve life quality by combining multiple elements. We will build a comprehensive life

service system that combines service, culture and environment and other elements. We will also develop a new service model and build a culturally enriched community with local flavor. We will create more business ventures in Konggang Garden and Konggang Central Park to turn ecological value into economic benefits. In order to involve as many stakeholders as possible in the management and operation of new beautiful scenic spots, we will promote transit-oriented development (TOD) to expand community space. We will use major projects such as the International Panda Theme Park to promote the integrated development of culture, real estate, and landscaping. We will promote smart governance in 5G era and improve the effectiveness of community governance.

I'm convinced that with these efforts, we will one day have a park community that has beautiful buildings, tranquil streets, nice parks and satisfied and happy residents.

Building a Community into a First-class Area for Living and Working

Shen Wei

Secretary of Qiantan Community, Sanlin Town, Pudong New Area, Shanghai

1. About Qiantan Community

First of all, please allow me to give you a brief overview of Qiantan Community in Sanlin Town, Shanghai. Located along the southern extension of Huangpu River, Qiantan Community is bordered by Jiyang Road in the east, and Middle Ring Road in the south, with Huangpu River to its the west and Chuanyang River to its north. With a total area of 2.83 square kilometers and with the World Expo buildings at its center, it is an important part of the riverside area. Business, culture and media, and sports recreation are three core functions of Qiantan. The community is well equipped with commercial, residential, hotel, education, and medical facilities and provides residents with round-the-clock services.

Qiantan Community has a total of planned construction area of 3.5 million square meters, including 660 000 square meters for commercial use, 1.47 million square meters for offices, 900 000 square meters for residential use, and 400 000 square meters for culture, education, medical purposes. It is expected to accommodate a residential population of 23 500 people and provide 100 000 jobs. At present, more than half of the 100 land parcels in Qiantan has completed construction. Qiantan Community plans to house 6 residential areas, comprising 26 residential compounds with about 9 000 households. At present, 9 residential compounds have been put in use, 3 600 apartments have been delivered and 5 000 people have moved in.

With the accelerating pace of construction, Qiantan Community has drawn more people to settle down here. By communicating with various groups that live or work in Qiantan, we have been able to build better understanding of their expectations, either individually or collectively. These concerns are centered around the corporate services, living facilities, and personal value pursuits. In the light of this, we have put forward the concept of "making Qiantan international as well as distinctively Chinese".

2. Planning concept

By being "international", Qiantan aims to benchmark the international standard of Smart City 3.0 in its business, education, medical care, community building, cultural and sports activities. Thanks to its holistic development model and the strong R&D and financing capabilities of businesses in Lujiazui, we have been able to gain a head start in development. In terms of education, a number of public schools, such as The New Bund School of No.2 Secondary School of East China Normal University, Bingchangtian Kindergarten, and China Welfare Institute Kindergarten have set up their campuses here; we also have a number of private schools located here, including Huili School Shanghai, Julia Gabriel Centre, Wellington College International Shanghai and the Qiantan campus of NYU Shanghai, which is under construction at the moment. People here can go to Singapore Raffles Hospital for medical treatment, do sports at Oriental Sports Center, carry out cultural activities at Xinde Cultural Center, and shop at Taikoo Li, Crystal Plaza and Sifang City Plaza.

By "being Chinese", Qiantan aims to inherit and promote the Chinese traditions in addition to be guided by the international standards. Our work is closely guided by community governance, such as Party building, organizing work of civil organizations, foreign affairs and public welfare. These are the factors that we need to pay attention to. We believe that community development should be people-oriented. That is why we put forward "community pioneer" and "community planner" as two important concepts guiding our community efforts.

"Community pioneer" means that the residents and communities should grow and develop together. Whoever works here, lives here or travels here can participate in the growth of Qiantan Community. Giving them the role of "community pioneer" reflects the autonomy and flexibility of community development and will reinforce the idea that "everyone has a stake in the community", which will gradually foster the community's strong self-governance and joint governance ability. "Community planner" reflects the requirements and capabilities for self-governance and joint governance. Considering that people in Qiantan Community have a strong will for self-governance, strong capabilities of self-governance and a high demand for the quality of life, we need to involve them in decision making. In this way, we can truly build a community by all and for all.

3. Development direction

At present, we focus on developing two ecospheres and one ecological chain in Qianlin.

Specifically speaking, we aim to build Qiantan Group into a community ecosphere balancing supply and demand; we want to put in place a people-oriented ecosphere featuring a public welfare points system and launch Qiantan Life Festival that engages all residents. We want to make Qianlin Life Festival an influential link of the two ecospheres so that we can form an ecosystem for the whole community.

We hope to form a "self-sustainable" ecosystem that involves different groups. By building a shared space for the projects set up, run and financed by the residents themselves, we hope to form closed-loop circular ecology. In 1—2 years, we hope to incubate some mature mechanisms, teams, and projects.

4. Working framework

At the moment, our basic framework is driven by four engines.

The first engine is Qiantan Group. It is a platform for community work and cross-sector cooperation. The Group represents all the communities, parks, business districts, enterprises and governments located in Qianlin. It plays a guiding role, integrates community resources and improves Party building and community governance in Qiantan community. Through Qiantan Group, the community Party committees can address community problems and needs directly, mobilize shared resources, and jointly explore new ideas of community governance with relevant departments, enterprises and institutions. At present, 26 entities representing a wide array fields have registered as members. They include public security, firefighting agencies, community affairs organizers, market supervisors, public health supervisors, hospitals, banks, schools, and other commercial institutions.

The second engine is the public welfare points system. It is driven by demand and sets out to engage everyone in building a warm community. We provide community resources in response to the actual needs, and bring into play public welfare elements. Meanwhile, for those interested in community work, we provide jobs that meet the needs of the white-collar young people.

The third engine is a team of Qiantan Pioneers. We want to tap into the initiative of corporate leaders, community experts, community volunteers and other groups, so that they can be pioneers of community governance. They will help us promote high-quality projects and make our ecosystem more self-sustaining.

The fourth engine is the Qiantan Life Festival. We want all residents to have fun and enjoy themselves at the Festival. We have come up with four themed events for the festival that focus on folklore, culture, sports and reading respectively. Each event is planned and hosted by a member registered on Qiantan Group. Whoever lives, works or visits Qiantan can have fun at the Festival.

With the leadership and support of the Sanlin Town Party committee and governments, we have been working towards deeper integration of city and industry. We have made efforts to raise people's quality of life. We have actively played a role of the Party leading, strengthened connection of local parties and become more innovative in ways of primary-level community governance. We have made some explorations and obtained remarkable results. In the future, we will continue to strengthen the leadership of the Party, bring in more resources to promote community governance, and work towards a better future for the Qiantan community.

Reflections on Practices of Primary-level Governance

Pu Yapeng

Secretary of Party Committee of Hongmei Road Subdistrict, Xuhui District, Shanghai

1. Background of community governance

In 1996, Shanghai formally set up a community governance model headed by the municipal government and the district government and implemented and overseen by subdistrict and neighborhood governing offices. In 2015, all the subdistrict offices in Shanghai shifted their focus from economic management to community governance. In 2017, the Chinese government called for "a social governance system based on collaboration and broad participation with the goal to bring benefits to all" and proposed an initiative to "strengthen the system of community governance, and delegate the power of social governance down to primary level". In 2019, President Xi Jinping called upon China to build "cities built by the people and for the people", setting a higher standard for primary-level governance.

Hongmei Subdistrict, where I'm working, is located in the southwest of Xuhui District. It covers an overall area of 5.98 square kilometers, stretching from Guilin Road in the east to Lianhua Road in the west, and from Caobao Road in the south to Puhuitang in the north. There are 13 neighborhood committees and 22 residential compounds with more than 40 000 residents. 20 000 of these people have chosen Hongmei as their official household registration place. Our subdistrict is also home to Caohejing Hi-Tech Park, which houses more than 4 000 enterprises and institutions and employs over 250 000 people.

2. Practices in primary-level governance

Following a series of reforms for better community governance in 2015, we started to set a higher bar for primary-level governance. Therefore, we need to further define primary-level governance and its mechanisms, and reconsider how to do a proper work within the remit of community governance. Primary-level governance, especially community work, requires specific and refined models and processes. Meanwhile, we need to clarify the rights and responsibilities of each stakeholder that participates in primary-level governance. Lastly, it is necessary to clarify what community workers should do to fulfill their responsibilities.

Today, I'm going to take residential community, the most basic unit of primary-level governance, as an example to discuss ways of community governance. My subdistrict office has introduced five parameters, namely resources supply, demographic structure, participation level, governance structure and governance orientation, to evaluate the performance of community governance.

According to these five parameters, the residential neighborhoods can be divided into 32 types. For example, resources supply measures whether the facilities in a residential compound are able to meet the basic living needs of its inhabitants and label a community as resource-sufficient or resource-insufficient. Demographic structure evaluates the socio-economic status of the inhabitants in a community and determines whether they come from homogenous or varied backgrounds. The participation level measures residents' engagement in community activities as either high or low. In terms of governance orientation, some communities are better positioned to utilizing connections in community governance while others rely on robust rules and regulations. Governance structure assesses whether a community is able to function effectively and coherently under the leadership of the primary-level Party. With these five parameters, we can draw up an accurate profile for each community from a total of 32 possibilities.

Fig. 1
The system of five parameters and two lists

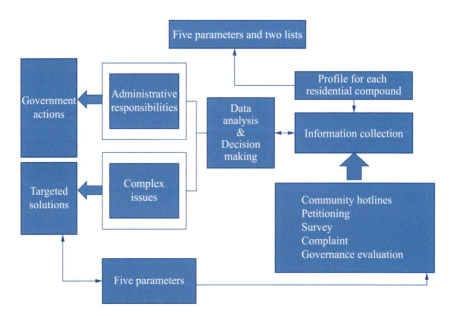

提升社区和城市品质

In addition to the five parameters, we have also established a two-list system. One list details what administrative responsibilities the local government, especially the residents' committees, should undertake in community governance. The other list records various problems that a community might face based on information collected from multiple channels. With these five parameters and the two lists, we are able to produce an accurate and comprehensive profile for each residential compound in our subdistrict, laying the way for better community governance. We can also take targeted measures to improve its governance based on a specific profile.

As you can see from the figure above, the system of five parameters and two lists defines what to do in each step in a clear way. For example, we can thus draw up a list when residents report problems in their residential areas either through community hotlines, or petitioning, or from our surveys, or by making direct complaints. All problems are then divided into two categories: one category include ones that can be solved by local government and residents' committees, and the other is more complex because it includes problems whose responsibilities are hard to define and may require the residents to step in. The first category concerns administrative efficiency, while the other entails governance issues.

Based on the two categories, what needs our intervention in community governance is the long-term issues that are not included in the list, as shown in Fig. 2.

In primary-level governance, governments and residents both have an important role to play. Governments are responsible for mobilizing available resources in administration and management

	In the list	Out of the list	Short term	Long term	Strategies
Government responsibilities	√		√		Follow established procedures
	√			√	
		√	√		Establish new procedures
		√		√	Major intervention
Issues of community governance	√		√		Follow established procedures
	√			√	
		√	√		Establish new procedures
		√		√	Five parameters

Fig. 2
Five parameters for the governance of residential areas

to solve various problems reported by residents. At the same time, it is also necessary to bring in residents to improve governance efficiency and to tackle the persistent community problems.

Of course, problems related with "the tragedy of the commons" and "the tragedy of the anti-commons", still exist in primary-level governance. These problems have weakened the good use of community resources. Another fundamental challenge in community governance is the imbalance of revenues and expenditure in old residential areas. The healthy operation of such assets as residential compounds requires long-term and stable revenues. Currently, a community is usually funded by community maintenance fund, property management fees, donations and government subsidies. But substantial differences exist among communities. Some communities can make ends meet and keep their provision of facilities and services at a stable level, but the majority of communities, especially the old ones, often find it hard to do so, which in turns leads to their decline. Once a community begins to decline, they are very likely to enter a vicious cycle. In this case, I believe the residents must step in to take up the responsibility, but in reality, it is hard for the residents conventions to play a role. There are also problems in the decision-making process of property owners' committees.

The good thing is that we can take effective and specific measures based on the profile we have created for each community and reevaluate the effectiveness of these measures. So far, we have created public spaces to enhance the welfare of community residents, built a system for streamlined community services and implemented a pilot project that provides administrative services at people's doorsteps. More importantly, we have further improved the decision-making process by residents' committee, property management company and owners' committee under the leadership of the primary-level Party as an effort to establish a standardized model for community governance.

3. The future of primary-level governance

In the future, we hope to establish an effective system to evaluate the performance of community governance, to ensure a more transparent process, more structured contents, and more professionalized work in community governance. Primary-level democracy requires more specific rules that encourage residents to participate in community governance so as to guarantee the rule of law. Finally, we hope to inject sustained vitality into communities by providing residents easy and accessible public services, enhancing extensive participation in community governance, and allowing market-based activities.

FORUM

分论坛

Urban Culture and City Image
城市文化与形象

主持人·HOST

张伟民·Zhang Weimin

上海交大—南加州大学文化创意产业学院党总支书记兼院长

Dean of USC-SJTU Institute of Culture and Creative Industry

徐剑·Xu Jian

上海交通大学中国城市治理研究院副院长

Professor，Vice Dean，China Institute for Urban Governance，SJTU

艺术资源与城市形象

王廷信

中国传媒大学艺术研究院常务副院长

我要汇报的题目是"艺术资源与城市形象",我将从以下五个方面进行分析,艺术资源的界定、分类和特征,城市形象的定义,艺术资源和城市形象之间的关系,艺术资源的困境与机遇,如何去盘活艺术资源提升城市形象。

1. 艺术资源的界定及分类:有形与无形

艺术资源,泛指在人类艺术史上已经发生和正在发生的具有典型性的艺术事项,主要包括艺术家、艺术作品、艺术研究成果、艺术事件及其相关遗迹。如果这些在某个地区或者是某个城市已经发生,那这是一个历史性的资源。除了历史性的资源,还存在正在进行的艺术资源。比如在上海这样的城市中,正在进行的与艺术相关的事情,都可以叫做城市的艺术资源。整体来说,艺术资源是一种智性资源,因为它能够大致代表一个国家、一个民族、一座城市基本的智慧力量,包括它借助这种智慧所要表达的世界观。

艺术资源大致分成有形和无形这两种资源。有形资源具有显在性,是看得见摸得着的。比如名人、典籍、文物、机构等。无形资源具有隐秘性,是有形资源的基础,比如制度、政策、思想、技艺。因为有了这些无形资源,才会有口传、文字等形式的记录,所以无形资源是我们现存有形资源能够出现的根据。所有无形资源的核心是"人",我觉得"人"是一个最根本的东西,或者说每一个时代的环境下人的艺术智慧或艺术技能,是支撑一个城市或者一个地区艺术资源的最根本性的东西。

2. 何谓城市形象

城市形象不是一个严格的科学界定,而更多地基于人们对于某个城市的基本印象,比如说一个城市的地理位置、历史地位、气候环境、文化性格、经济活力、交通条件、社会影响等，这都是人们对某个城市产生整体印象的一些支配性的因素。比如我们把北京叫做"帝都"，是因为北京有大约 800 年的建都史，一直都是政治中心；我们把上海叫做"魔都"，是因为所有的想象得到或者想象不到的事情都可能在上海发生，上海是个奇幻之都。此外人们认为"上有天堂，下有苏杭"，认为南京是"江南佳丽地，金陵帝王州"，都是人们综合上述因素所得出的形象化的概括。所以说城市形象是一个综合性的印象，这种印象很难用科学去界定，它实际上是人们在一个城市物质文明和精神文明基础上对该城市性格的总体认知，潜移默化地影响着人们生活以及城市发展。

城市形象决定着该城市在人们心目中的地位和影响，是一个城市发展前景的重要决定因素之一。那么城市形象的价值可以从哪些方面来考量？

第一，城市形象决定着人的聚集度。为什么普通民众愿意去北上广深等一线城市，以及武汉、成都这样的中心城市旅游、生活、工作？都是因为这个城市的基础形象号召着人们，人们感觉得到这个城市是可以有好的生活，或者是可以找到好工作的，或者是可以见到美的景象的。

第二，城市形象决定着资金的聚集度。因为整个社会发展靠的是人，而精英人口一定是引导世界前进的重要人群，那么精英到上海、北京等这些大城市的同时自然会把非常重要的资金带到这个城市里。

第三，城市形象决定着创造力的聚集度。创造力也是和人直接相关的。我曾经发明过一个词，叫做"艺随人走"，意味着艺术是随着人走的。艺术是无形的，我们写出来的作品、画出来的画、或者弹出来的曲子，尽管这些载体看得见听得着，但实际上仍依靠无形资产而存在，因为它们是靠记忆支配的。身怀技艺的人走到哪里，艺术就可能在哪里诞生存在。历史上有很多艺术家云游四方，而每个地方都愿意纪念艺术家在本地流传的故事、留下的作品、或者是发生的各种艺术事件，因为这些艺术家的创造力对塑造城市形象发挥了重要作用。

3. 艺术资源是城市形象建构的基础之一

影响城市形象的因素非常之多，艺术资源只是考量城市形象的一个重要基础。我认为艺术资源应该是每一个城市特殊的文化资本。为什么上海现在有这么多艺术演出、有这么多艺术家定居？可以说没有近代的西方资本、西方文化聚集在上海这样一个码头，上海就不会有今天。恰恰是因为这段历史是其他城市无法复制的，上海才能拥有我们可以看到的文化资本。所以说艺术资源的特殊性主要体现在其以感性的形式表述着一座城市的智慧和情怀。艺术资源对城市而言具有如下特殊价值：

第一，一座城市拥有的艺术家数量和类型，决定着这个城市性格的宽度和厚度。每一个艺术家其实都是独特的，艺术家的艺术个性各不相同，一个城市如果能够拥有众多数量的艺术家和终端类型的艺术，这个城市一定有足够的宽度和厚度。

第二，艺术的独特性，一个城市可能有很多种类的艺术，而其中某一种艺术比较突出。比如"瓷都"景德镇，"陶都"宜兴，"音乐之都"哈尔滨——因为哈尔滨从历史上到现在积累了大量的音乐学家、表演艺术家、歌唱家、演奏家，直到今天哈尔滨的音乐节都办得非常好。

第三，一个城市艺术遗迹的多寡意味着该城市发展的潜力。

第四，一个城市艺术事件的多寡意味着该城市结构的复杂度。比如说鲁迅在上海和北京与其他人进行了一系列的论战，这就造成了一个艺术事件；扬州八怪在扬州创作出很多有价值的画作，这也是一个艺术事件，都会被艺术史所记载。

第五，一个城市艺术机构的多寡意味着该城市发展的活力。小城市的艺术机构是单一的，比如说从宣传部到文化局到各个文化馆就是非常单一的条线。但大城市或者是艺术资源比较多的城市，艺术机构相对密集，各种艺术机构渗透到一个城市里边，互相碰撞从而迸发出更多的活力和创造力。

第六，一个城市艺术机制的灵活度意味着该城市智慧的丰富性。

4. 艺术资源的困境和机遇

中国拥有五千年的历史，如今我们怎么去看待艺术资源？实际上艺术资源是存在很多困境的。比如说在很多情况下人们意识不到保护、利用和开发，尤其是在保护这方面，我觉得做得非常不到位；还有种情况是没有财力保护利用和开发；再有是只保护，但不注意利用和开发，或者缺乏保护而过度利用与开发，这些现象都是存在的。

与困境相对的是艺术资源面临的机遇。如今艺术资源面临的机遇很多，大致上我觉得可分为四点。

第一是国家对文化建设的空前重视。中国改革开放40多年来，尽管前30年间中央政策对文化重要性的表述很多，但真正让我们感觉到国家对文化建设空前重视的是十七届六中全会，这是党的历史上第一次在全会上集全党之力来讨论文化问题。十八大以后，国家对文化的重视远远超过了学者的想象，国家对于文化的思考更加深刻更加透彻。从中共中央办公厅和各个部委的文件可以看出，国家的文化政策都是带着资金和指向性的，如此丰富的文化政策在改革开放前30年是没有过的。

第二就是国家艺术人才培养的空前规模和多样化。目前中国有2 800多所大学，90%以上的大学都有艺术系或者是艺术专业，这个数据不可小看。以前艺术是一个非常小的专业，但到了今天艺术是全国最大的专业之一，没有任何一个专业比艺术的考生更多。那么从90年代末期到今天，我们培养出大量的艺术人才，都在支撑着艺术的发展，也是重要的艺术资源。

第三是时代给艺术提供的技术条件空前充裕。比如智能手机、计算机、互联网等催生出了新的艺术形式，如果没有这样的技术条件，艺术普及不到今天这样的程度。社交网络本来是用来社交的，但是如今可以看到大量的艺术作品和艺术家都渗透到社交网络里，成为艺术传播链中非常关键的一条。

第四是民众对艺术需求的增加，这和人们生活条件的富足程度息息相关。

5. 艺术资源与城市形象举例

首先是联合国教科文组织给中国的一些城市赋予的名称。比如北京、上海、深圳、武汉为"设计之都"，南京为"文学之都"，苏州、杭州和景德镇为"手工艺与民间艺术之都"，哈尔滨为"音乐之都"，青岛为"电影之都"，长沙为"媒体艺术之都"，这代表的是联合国对中国的认知。还有一种情况是城市本身对自己的定位，比如说北京自称为"东方演艺之都"，上海自称为"亚洲演艺之都"；杭州要打造成为"中国演艺之都"。此外大众对每个城市也是会有印象的，比如人们称北京、上海为"电影之都""戏剧之都""美术之都""音乐之都"等，因为北京和上海艺术资源特别集中。

表1
艺术资源与城市形象举例

城　市	称　　号	自　　称	大众印象
北京	设计之都（联合国2012）	东方演艺之都	电影之都、戏剧之都、美术之都、音乐之都
上海	设计之都（联合国2010）	亚洲演艺之都	电影之都、戏剧之都、美术之都、音乐之都
深圳	设计之都（联合国2008）		
武汉	设计之都（联合国2017）		
南京	文学之都（联合国2017）		
杭州	手工艺与民间艺术之都（联合国2012）	中国演艺之都	
苏州	手工艺与民间艺术之都（联合国2014）		
哈尔滨	音乐之都（联合国2010）		
青岛	电影之都（联合国2017）		
长沙	媒体艺术之都（联合国2017）		
景德镇	手工艺与民间艺术之都（联合国2014）		瓷都

6. 激活艺术资源，提升城市形象

那么我们的城市要怎么去定位城市形象？从三个角度来看，一是官方定位，二是机构定位，三是大众定位。所以整体上来讲，我觉得要提升好树立好城市形象，关键还要盘活艺术资源。

第一，要重视共生理念，特别要重视艺术和政治、经济、文化、科技、教育等之间的关系，注意到支撑国民经济和社会发展最重要的是五大领域之间的一种共生性。以前我们以为经济和艺术是没有关系的，但如今文化产业当中有相当一部分是艺术产业，其在经济社会中创造了强大的GDP。所以这种共生关系值得在理论上去探讨，在实践上去摸索。

第二，要树立良好的城市形象，还要创设优良机制，包括政策机制、生产机制、评价机制、传播机制和教育机制等五大机制。有了这五大机制的良性运转，一个城市的艺术形象才能很好地塑造。以传播机制为例，京剧是中国的国粹之一，从清末到新中国成立之前，很多北京、天津的知名京剧演员如果没有来过上海就不算在全国有影响力。上海最早接触到西方的文化运转系统，媒体多、报纸多、剧院多、商人多，民间对艺术需求的力量大，因此它的传播机制非常好，所以说像梅兰芳这样有名的京剧演员都会定期在上海演出。这实际上就是艺术机制对于艺术形象的影响。

第三，要高度重视人才，尊重人才，用好人才。第四，要注意资源关联，处理好抢救、保护、传承、发展之间的关系。第五，要注意资源定位，突出特色，避免雷同。

行为空间的设计与城市文化形象

范圣玺

同济大学设计创意学院党委书记

我是做设计行为认知这方面研究的，每次讲课汇报时都会先引用庄子的这句话："道行之而成，物谓之而然"。"道行之而成"讲的是行为，"物谓之而然"讲的是认知。鲁迅曾说过，其实地上本没有路，走的人多了，也就成了路。一个城市或一个局部空间很多时候都有此类现象，所以我们往往会从各种角度来批评践踏草坪这件事情。但是从我的角度来看，走出来的路一定有它的合理性，而"经济性法则"左右人的所有行为，于是就有了"行之而成"的"道"。

1. 人的行为空间

我关注的是如何在城市里做设计，主要的试点都集中在人上。这是我拍摄的新冠肺炎疫

图1

2020 年上海，冰冻空间

情暴发期间上海的照片。这座城市成了一个灯光还在闪耀但是没有人的冰冻空间，完全没有任何生机。由此可见城市的硬件和人只有有机结合了才能焕发出生机。人类生活的空间不是物理性的或者地理性的，它是一个体验和行为的空间。

那么从"affordance（功能的可见性）"这个角度讲，决定我们行为的不是物理的世界，而是一个知觉的实践。我们感受到的环境，是我们自己创造出来的。比如我老家附近有一个湖，夏天我们在湖面划船，小的时候还可以游泳，到冬天它就完全变成了一个溜冰场，所以湖还是湖，但是因为人的行为不同，所以行为和物理性的空间不是一个概念。我一直在拿上海的国家会展中心作为一个典型例子在讲。尽管会展中心外观非常漂亮，完全是对称的，但是在里边很难识别方位，只要你走错一处，就要用30—45分钟时间才能够修正回来。这个设计没有做到行为的"行"，而去一味追求形态的"形"。

图2
上海国家会展中心外观图和内部图

图3
横条和纵条公共座椅

有时候我也研究产品，一把小剪刀为什么能获国际大奖？其实它只是做了一点变化，把剪刀的手柄"弓"起来了，拿剪刀的时候就完全对应了一个动作一个行为。很多大学校园里边铺了石路，但是行人是不会在那走的，这种石路走一步一个石阶的话，会走出很滑稽的步伐，要是两步一个石阶走，步子就迈得太大，这就没有考虑到人的行为。再比如公园里的长椅，一般都认为人坐得越多越好，但是人的行为有个心理和文化的问题，每个人都对个人空间有一定的需求。将椅子设计成如图3所示的竖条状，其背后的心理机制是，如果椅子是横条状，具有放射性，坐在上面感觉是没有边界的，所以三人座的椅子可能只能坐两个人；但是变成纵条以后，只要隔了一两个板条，人们就可以心安理得地坐下，这就利用了人类"行为正当化"的心理。

2. 人的行为和城市形象的关系

所以这种"场"的概念就非常重要，同样还是这把椅子，放在我曾经读书的校园里就会经常坏掉。其实不是椅子设计得不好，而是椅子放在这个场所不对。人的需求是多样的，所以大家会把椅子变换成不同的组合形状，搬来搬去就坏了，所以它还是一个行为的问题。人和环境的函数关系是 $B = F(P, E)$，其中 B 代表行为，P 代表个人内在心理因素，E 代表环境，包括外界自然、社会环境的影响。这张照片（图4）是很多年前就有的北京天安门广场旁边的一个椅子。我们发现不同的人、不同的关系、不同的心理，都会产生不同的使用方式。

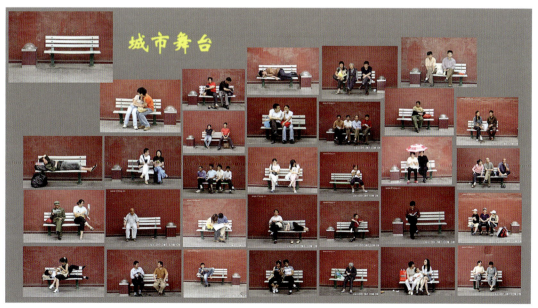

图4
城市舞台

所以说城市是一个非常生动的舞台，每个人都是演员。

我之前到米兰，印象最深的是我经常看到当地的女士坐在那里，整个人的姿态就好像别人在给她拍照一样，即使旁边没有人。城市里每个人都好像把这个城市当作舞台一样，显得意气风发。在北欧，当地居民即使是在很冷的天排队，人与人的间隔也会很大，而不是天越冷人靠得应该越紧。人在等着过斑马线的时候，不同的人种、不同的时段人际距离都不一样的，这背后折射的是不同民族不同的文化心理。我们所说的国民性，往往是一个地区或者一个国家一个民族的人们表现出来的一种普遍的行为方式。以罗马西班牙阶梯为例。西班牙大阶梯是罗马的地标之一，大家坐在西班牙阶梯上的风景我也非常喜欢。但是从 2019 年开始，罗马实行"禁坐令"，禁止行人坐在西班牙阶梯上面，违者将会被罚款。一方面罗马政府是从保护和维持景区秩序的角度出发，但另一方面罗马政府没有意识到的是，其实西班牙阶梯风景是人坐在阶梯上构成风景，而不是这个阶梯本身。另外一个例子是上海人比较熟悉的松江泰晤士小镇。泰晤士小镇刚建好的时候，我想了解小镇真实的生活状态是怎样的，于是我特意去那边找了个宾馆住了一夜。其实早晨起来你闻不到跟小镇空间形象相对应的味道，比如咖啡、烤面包的味道，人们还是拿着包子、豆浆当早餐，还是在跳广场舞锻炼。所以空间是空间，人并不是因为空间改变就完全改变了。如今我们发现全世界无论哪里城市尺度都非常像，这种"均质"的尺度对应的却是"异质"的生活。无锡拈花湾在各种小镇中被认为是做得比较好的，拈花湾建筑的形式很像日本岐阜的合掌村。屋顶上的草尽管花费很高做了上去，但是因为草毕竟是有机自然的东西，还是会慢慢脱落，就完全不是当初的风景。拈花湾和合掌村的差别在于，合掌村最好的风景不是传统技艺和文化，而是社区的概念、命运共同体的概念。每年全村的人一起来给屋顶换草形成了一个盛大的节日，人跟人之间的交流沟通，才是当地最好的风景。

今天的主题是城市，其实也是社区的概念。如果没有生活只是单纯照搬形式，就会出现问题。美学其实是生活的美学，少了生活的关注，国际化大城市建设就会带来均质化的问题。中国传统文化的根在农村，那么如何在城市的文脉中来讲述一个乡村的故事呢？上海的"三大文化"——红色文化、江南文化、海派文化的形象怎么来构建呢？按照传承与创新，民族与世界的概念，从我设计创意的角度看，其实一直是一对矛盾体，一个是生活文脉，一个是设计创新；一个是聚合，一个是发散；一个是日常性，一个非日常性；一个追求价值，一个追求新奇；一个是可能的设计，一个是设计的可能。简单说就是情理之中和意料之外的关系，所以就存在着均质如何异化，异质如何同化的问题，我把这两个关系的交集统称为"生活行为"。我提出"城市形象系统设计"的概念，在文化资源和生活方式之间去找到一种联结，然后找到一个文化载体，把它从行为设计的方式全部落实到一个人的生活行为上来，由此变成可操作的系统。这个系统的建立是非常好的，它是活色生香的、可持续的、多元多样的。

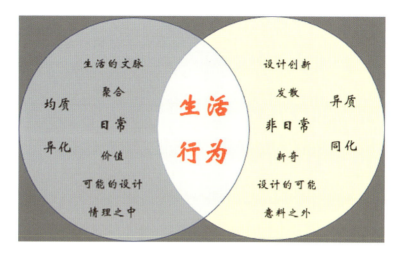

图 5
生活行为：均质异化
与异质同化

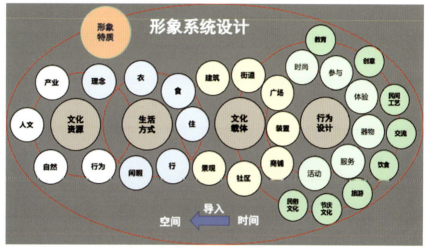

图 6
形象系统设计

　　我最近比较关注的就是"五感"，一个城市的形象一定是活的，就像一堆木材在燃烧，我们的皮肤能感受到它的热度，我们的眼睛能看到火苗的颜色，我们能听到木材燃烧发出的啪啪啪的声音，我们会嗅到木材燃烧的味道，它是一个通感的东西。而"共感"塑造的城市文化形象也会变得有滋有味。我最近在写一本书，主题就是"设计即生活"，生活是设计的出发点，也是设计的终极目标，城市文化形象实际上是一个生活的样相。

文化场景与城市发展

陈 波

武汉大学国家文化发展研究院常务副院长

我报告的主题是"文化场景与城市发展"，将分为两个方面，第一个是城市发展过程与问题，第二个是文化场景如何影响城市发展，包括维度设计和相关评价。

1. 城市发展过程与问题

首先我谈一下对于城市发展过程的理解。实际上人类绝大部分历史事件中是没有城市这个概念的，城市出现在人类历史上的时间非常短暂，几乎可以忽略不计。但恰恰就是因为城市的出现，人类社会驶入快车道，至今仍以加速度发展。因此城市建立的初心是为了文明能够延续，或者说以最小的资源获得最大化的发展。正如吴良镛先生所说："在远古时代，人类从茫茫荒野之中走进城市，这是人类社会的最伟大的进步之一，正是人类从蒙昧到野蛮再到文明——走进城市，使城市文明成为划时代的界标"。

文化可以理解为人与自然的关系。据科学家考证，原始人类穴居野处、构木为巢，持续相当长时间，并无实质性变化。这种长期实践的成本非常高，例如需要采集植物性食物、捕捉动物性食物以及防止野兽侵袭。此外，突发事件等外部因素促使家庭之间结合，例如邻居夜间受到侵袭，本能争斗，引发外部性，相邻家庭受益，于是不同家庭开始聚集结合，出现原始城市的雏形。

随着市中心的壮大，出现了传统的采集和狩猎场所，随之交叉重合，并产生所谓"边界"的问题。边界问题属于物理空间问题，文化空间包括物理空间和精神空间，空间感知是维系一个民族个体再生产的重要基础资源，并且是核心战略资源。物理空间之所以会出现问题，以及如今的功能城市之所以能集聚资源，都是为了保障资源区域内的所有个体能够顺利地再生产。生产分工是文明的表征，城市中生产的分工越来越细，表明城市仍在不断发展。

图 1
野蛮社会到文明社会

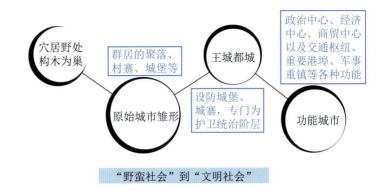

在图 1 中，原始城市雏形主要是群居的聚落、村寨和城堡等；王城和都城主要为设防的城堡和城寨，专门用于护卫统治阶层；功能城市主要为政治中心、经济中心、商贸中心以及交通枢纽、重要港埠、军事重镇等。

一直到今天，城市的最大功能就在于以更快的速度和更密集的方式聚集各种人才、技术、资金以及信息，使城市成为一个地区、一个国家的政治、经济、文化的中心。城市是人类创造的一种环境，人类必然还将根据社会经济的进步，对城市进行持续建设，以达到持续发展的目的。

但城市发展到现在也出现了很多问题，比如拥挤、贫穷、社会分化、污染、住房紧张、犯罪、交通堵塞、教育不平衡、失业、公用设施超负荷等。这些问题要如何解决呢？"文化治理"的概念应运而生。在西方国家，城市开始植入区域文化，在城市中建设一个区域，区域中的个体及其所处的自然空间、物理空间和精神空间共同构成文化空间，由此形成完备的空间整合体。得益于这种完备且稳定的空间架构体系，即使区域出现什么问题，人们的生活未受太大影响。因此，我们提出了将文化植入城市发展的概念。

2. 文化场景如何影响城市发展

（1）文化提供城市场景。

城市场景既是城市发展的基础，也是城市发展的结果。每座城市因其独特的文化而产生不同的城市场景，城市场景是人感知的最直接的物理结果，对个体的认知和感知有直接的贡献。在城市，个体将感官接收的物理刺激形成特定的信号，在脑海里加工并形成特定认知，从而产生对这座城市的认知，这种认知经过和个体知识的互动，就会形成对这个城市的特定符号化的东西，也就是城市场景。

那么如何衡量城市场景呢？这不仅是中国的难题，也是西方国家的难题。芝加哥大学的社会学派为此组建了一个国际团队，长时间研究如何解构城市场景，即城市场景到底由哪些维度构成，以及如何衡量或度量这些维度。我们有幸也参与了相关的研究，研究结果出版成

表 1
城市发展理论模式的演变

发展模式	主要内容	核心要素	生产阶段
经典模式	公司驱动，更多工厂带来更多就业与收入，吸引聚集人口	土地、资本、劳动力和管理等	工业时代
人力资本模式	教育学习驱动，通过教育、培训与保健等劳动力供给	人力资本、人力资源的多少与质量高低	工业时代向后工业转变
社会资本模式	社会组织驱动，更多参与与自治传统	社会资本，如社会信任、公众参与网络与互惠规范等	工业时代向后工业转变
创意阶层模式	创意阶层驱动，3T 理论，即技术、人才和宽容度	创意资本，创意创新并非专业人士特权，鼓励大众创新	后工业时代
场景模式	文化场景驱动，市民文化艺术参与对城市发展的作用	文化资本，居住社区层面、便利设施、多样人群等集合场景，及场景中价值观、生活方式与生活质量等	后工业时代（新时代）

书《场景理论》。城市发展模式从最基础的经典模式，到人力资本模式、社会资本模式、创意阶层模式，再到现在西方学者普遍支持的场景模式。场景模式强调文化场景驱动和市民对文化艺术的参与对于整个城市的推动作用，通过文化资本、居住社区、便利设施等核心要素，激发整个区域的创新活力，也就是文化创新。

场景理论则是芝加哥大学终身教授特里·尼克尔斯·克拉克（Terry Nichols Clark）领衔的研究团队提出的城市研究新范式。研究团队通过对一些国际大都市的研究发现，都市娱乐休闲设施和各种市民组织的不同组合，会形成不同的都市"场景"，从而形成特定的文化价值取向，这种文化价值取向吸引着不同的群体前来进行文化实践，从而促进区域经济社会的发展。

经过多次探讨，基于场景理论我们提出了"文化舒适物"的概念，这个概念现在已经被中国学者普遍接受。之前国内将公益系统化设计、非公文化设施等都称为文化设施，而文化舒适物大大地提升了文化设施的广度，不仅包括酒吧、书店、医院、邮局等设施，也包括文化输出的密度、布局以及空间架构，这对个体的感知度产生了深刻的影响。

场景理论的主要内容包括客观结构和主观认识。客观结构是指城市便利设施，即物理空间维度。主观认识即精神空间，指其蕴含的文化价值观，包含着真实性、戏剧性和合法性的内容。

在此基础上我们加入了机制空间。现有的个体及其所在空间架构并非严格分为物理的和精神的，其中一定有特定的内在关联，这种关联我们暂时称之为机制空间。这种机制如何解构，其维度如何设定，我们和许多学者仍在研究探索中。

表 2
场景价值量表

主维度	次维度	主维度	次维度	主维度	次维度
真实性（authenticity）	理性的	戏剧性（theatricality）	亲善的	合法性（legitimacy）	传统主义
	本地的		正式的		自我表现
	国家的		展示的		实用主义
	合作的		时尚魅力		超凡魅力
	少数群体的		挑衅的		平等主义

场景理论的主观认识体系包括 3 个主维度和 15 个次维度，是根据消费者对周边设施和环境所可能产生的情感体验设定的这 15 个次维度基本可以判定一个消费娱乐设施的价值取向，比如教堂的相对保守性、酒吧的开放性以及图书馆与博物馆的实用性，但是要对场景价值取向进行判断，必须对综合场景内不同生活娱乐设施进行量化分析。场景理论不仅提供了一个新的视角，从都市生活娱乐设施中所蕴含的文化价值取向来考察城市发展，还构建了一个衡量场景文化价值观的分析框架。

《场景理论》一书翻译成中文并加以中国化后，推动了相关的课题研究，同时深圳等一线城市开始将理论运用于实践，现在成都市政府也准备在全市推行场景理论实践。

结合中国文化政策转型头践，中国学者将文化场景理论逐步中国化，吴迪（2013）提出了基于场景理论的物理建筑效用衡量，吴军（2017）提出把空间看作是汇集各种文化消费行为的聚合体。它试图把形而上的、充斥着学术语言的文化议题转变为可被普通人知晓以及政策上容易被操作化的场景，并具体运用到城市经济社会发展。而我认为文化场景理论实际上是由特定的文化空间构成，这一空间架构包含物理空间、精神空间和机制空间，以此将场景理论与中国实际相结合，即基于场景理论的文化空间理论。近些年，国内一直都在研究中国的文化场景理论实践。场景理论与中国实际的结合丰富了文化空间相关的基础架构体系的内涵，比如文化遗产空间架构。

（2）文化提供城市公共空间。

物理空间是城市居民参与公共文化生活的好去处，精神空间是城市居民的精神慰藉与心灵安放之处。然而随着城镇化加速推进，原有空间体系受到挑战，新型文化空间建设需要引起足够重视。我们在很多地方经常提出文化空间这一概念，因为个体的喜怒哀乐实际上都是由它的文化空间决定的。中国历史虽然历经唐宋元明清的王朝更替，但在一定程度上，文化空间基本是复制下来了，所以大部分情况下，老百姓的心理倾向或者基础价值倾向相对稳定。而在新型城镇化的背景下，原有基于传统文化圈层架构的文化空间体系发生剧烈变化，新的文化空间体系尚未完全建立，个体出现明显的空间丧失感，变得焦虑且缺乏安全感。通过文化特色、文化产业打造新型文化空间，能明显缓解个体情绪，促进社会和谐，产业本身也会带来丰厚的回报。

（3）文化场景提供城市发展动力。

城市的文化特征、文化内核是城市的诚信度和综合素质。文化场景能够真正展示城市的价值品位和可贵的风尚，文化场景能够成为一座城市的凝聚力和自信心的源泉。同时，城市的魅力和吸引力，主要来自文化，文化决定城市发展的本质特征，是城市内在的美。

（4）文化场景的模式选择。

文化场景模式包括文化符号植入模式、设计与生活融合模式、工业区复兴模式、城市运营模式、历史名城发展模式、文化休闲街区模式、文化与区域融合模式。

第一是文化符号植入模式，即在一个区域内植入文化符号。提到贵州、山东等地，大多人都悉数列举当地旅游资源，但其实真正缺乏的是文化符号，游客在贵州游历三至五天，或许自己也不知道感知到了什么符号。现在许多地方热衷于历史名城发展模式，通过文旅结合打造复古气息，这就是物理空间的复制。相比物理空间，更重要的是文化符号的植入。

第二是设计与生活融合模式。个体与生活融合，慢，静、合。大家可以想象一下这个场景，白天上班很累很忙，晚上加班之后需要有个地方安静一下，喝一杯咖啡，略作修整，如果一个城市有很多这样的文化空间，这个城市就是有温度的，是贴合人们生活的。

第三种是工业区复兴模式。我们也将其称为文化空间的唤醒机制。对于一个人来说，由于外在空间的挤压，比如说生活工作上的压力，原来的初心难免会被部分封存，那么什么情况下把初心重新唤醒呢，就要通过文化空间。比如说来到某个地方，能让人想到以前的生活场景，以前的点点滴滴，这个唤醒过程让人感到非常温暖，从而回归自己的初心，这就是文化空间的魅力所在。

第四种是以西安曲江为代表的城市运营模式，考虑内生发展动力机制，推动城市发展转型；第五种是以开封宋城古都为代表的历史名城发展模式；第六种是以成都为例的文化休闲街区模式；第七种是以各种特色小镇为例的文化与区域融合模式。

（5）城市复兴的文化产业悖论。

从目前中国文化产业的发展情况来看，比起其他国家，国内文化产业园区寿命不太长。我认为这种现象的原因在于艺术家往往会定居在各大城市的旧城区，这样一来就算城区再破只要有艺术家进驻，它就成为一个文化空间。问题在于，随之而来的文化博弈往往会向小资化和贵族化演变，进而导致资本驱逐；一旦商业需求被驱动就出现了空心化现象，最后造成平庸化、同质化以及原真性的丧失，这个地方就不再是原来的文化空间，而是变成了商业地产。

图2
城市复兴中的文化产业悖论

旧城区　　小资化　贵族化　资本驱逐　　商业化

良好的区位　文化创意　地价升高　商业需求　空心化　平庸化
便利的交通　产业进入　　　　　　　　　　　　　同质化
低廉的租金　　　　　　　　　　　　　　　　　　原真性丧失

（6）以苏荷区为代表的空间营造模式。

原有物理空间保留，在个体记忆与时代变迁中形成强烈的符号空间，形成强烈的空间唤醒机制。苏荷区原是纽约19世纪最集中的工厂与工业仓库区。20世纪中叶，美国率先进入后工业时代，旧厂倒闭，商业萧条，仓库空间闲置废弃。美国艺术新锐群起后，各地艺术家以低廉租金入住该区，眼光敏锐的画商在该区先后设立画廊，原在上城高级街区的不少老字号画廊也相继移来。世界现代艺术史的大师级人物沃霍、李奇斯坦、劳森柏格、约翰斯等都是那里的第一代居民。六七十年代之交，纽约市长作出具有高度文化远见的决定：全部保留苏荷区旧建筑景观，通过立法，以联邦政府的立场确认苏荷为文化艺术区。

现在我们也面临着新时代的发展，就是人民对美好生活的追求，文化空间存在感是美好生活需求的重要表征和重要保证。2020年6月我在人民论坛发了一篇文章，题目是"'文化空间获得感'及其发展向度"，论证了这个观点。文化是一座城市的灵魂，构成了城市的精神空间基础，它与物理空间结合构成了"城市场景"，为城市居民提供了满足文化需求的公共空间，同时也为城市发展提供了源源不断的动力。文化场景是城市基础空间体系。文化空间是居民生存的基础空间，文化改变一座城，文化成就一座城。

抓住"数字文旅"发展机遇，推动长三角文旅一体化

冯学钢

华东师范大学商学院院长

1. 研究背景

2020 年 9 月 21 日，国务院办公厅印发《关于以新业态新模式引领新型消费加快发展的意见》，提出文旅部将进一步贯彻落实党中央、国务院相关工作部署：一是要加快文化和旅游资源的数字化；二是要促进文化产业和旅游产业"上云、用数、赋值"；三是要发挥互联网平台的赋能和效益提升作用；四是要构建数字文旅的产业生态。

而早在 2019 年 12 月，《长江三角洲区域一体化发展规划纲要》中就明确提出了促进文化和旅游融合，深化旅游合作，统筹利用旅游资源，推动旅游市场和服务一体化发展，共建世界知名旅游目的地，"一体化""融合发展""高质量"是国家对长三角发展寄予的厚望和要求。

长三角文旅一体化发展至今，区域文旅产品丰富，创新能力全国领先；文旅市场高度发达，双向与多向互动活跃；创新政策不断出台，政策效应持续释放。但与此同时，长三角文旅一体化存在着议而不决、悬而不决等问题，一体化资源整合利用不足、创新策源能力不够、落地产品缺乏，共同项目相互掣肘，未能催生新消费市场。一体化始于协作机制对话，联盟数量多，但存在一些浅层次合作甚至是形式大于内容的合作。因此，长三角文旅一体化发展必须强化创新策源动力，挖掘市场潜力，释放数字化对产业的放大、叠加、倍增作用。

我今天报告四个方面的内容：第一个是文旅资源数字化"活起来"，第二个是在线文旅新业态"热起来"，第三个是文旅新平台拓展"多起来"，最后一个就是长三角文旅一体化"融起来"。

2. 文旅资源数字化"活起来"

（1）长三角文博资源开放开发现状。

整个长三角的文旅资源富集，文物藏品数约占全国的 10% 以上，但与故宫博物院、敦煌

博物馆近年来发展相比，长三角博物馆资源盘活、创意点睛、市场运作等方面都未能彰显突出优势，原因在于：一是文化部门对于文博资源活化与文创创新发展的理解与认识不到位；二是文化单位存在市场经验不足、内控机制不健全等问题，不可避免地出现市场授权相关的纠纷与失误；三是文化单位项目申请周期长，面向消费端的市场、技术迭代更新的频率快，长期存在滞后效应；四是文化单位存在人才储备缺陷，难以有效实现互联网技术运用、虚拟现实新技术操作以及设备管理。

（2）强化技术支撑：共性关键技术手段。

加强智能技术、生产技术、分发技术、服务技术和管理技术等手段应用。从文旅产业与新技术融合发展来看，2019 年 8 月 13 日，为促进文化和科技深度融合，全面提升文化科技创新能力，国家六部委共同研究制定了《关于促进文化和科技深度融合的指导意见》，指出：科技对文化建设支撑作用的潜力还没有充分释放，对文化和科技融合的重要性和紧迫性的认识尚需进一步提高。目前青少年人群对虚拟文化空间还是有较强的依赖性，他们在很多情况下是通过虚拟世界来感受文化的，而美国在文化空间上有领先优势，现在已经围绕虚拟博物馆形成了一套相对成熟的商业模式。

（3）开放开发：授权激活与创新转化。

长期以来，博物馆、剧院等事业单位的基本定位是进行文物等的保护、管理和科学研究工作，在既定属性之上，事业单位的市场逻辑以及消费者面向确实出现了不同程度的问题。从长三角发展现状来看，近期上海文博会、上海书展等文化活动在面向消费端时，文化活动策划思路和市场需求确实存在较大错位。如何盘活资源，实现文化资源良性发展，亟待文化资源的对外开放开发，向互联网企业开放文创资源，彻底革新文化资源的运行机制、模式，打造面向长三角的一体化博物馆联盟文创平台。以故宫博物院为例，依靠丰富的文创资源，已授权几百家 IP，进行文创产品的联名开发、销售，建立了良好的市场化竞争机制。

3. 在线文旅新业态"热起来"

最近上海刚刚出台了《上海在线新文旅三年行动方案》，提出要拓展智慧互联的文旅价值链，培育文旅流通的平台服务链，推进科技研发链迭代更新，构建跨界融合的产业链。

（1）在线新文旅全新领域。

纵观在线文旅产业的发展，共经历了三个阶段：文旅在线——在线文旅——在线新文旅，新冠肺炎疫情之后中国在线文旅产业已快速推进到第三阶段。第一阶段"文旅在线"的主要功能是信息展示和网络预订；第二阶段"在线文旅"的主要功能是网络营销和提升体验；第三阶段是虚拟现实技术在文旅场景中的应用，以及通过人机交换方式获取实时、动态的文旅服务信息。

（2）文旅直播经济生态圈。

依托直播技术，"文旅＋直播电商"模式涌现，成为全行业布局的创新型业务，线上OTA、线下文化场馆、旅游景区、行业门店等不断积累线上资产，"文旅直播经济生态圈"已初现雏形。促进文化产业和旅游产业"上云、用数、赋智"，进一步完善文旅直播经济生态圈，鼓励有条件的企业开拓直播电商销售渠道，与直播平台跨界合作、搭建自有直播平台、创办文旅MCN机构、孵化文旅直播带货达人等。在中国重要的在线旅游OTA企业中，上海携程成立MCN机构，打通不同平台端口进行直播带货，线上效益显著；驴妈妈开发新的驴客严选App，成为多方政府"直播带货计划"的指定直播平台。

图1
2019年中国在线旅游厂商交易规模指数

其他，45.4
驴妈妈，4.19
途牛，9.15
美团，14.26
同程艺龙，20.25
飞猪，41.15
携程系，145.13

（3）线上文旅虚拟式到达体验。

从消费形式来看，借助门户网站、移动客户端、微信小程序等技术，"云游"成为常态化活动，但多为公共文化服务项目。从国内在线新文旅付费体系来看，主要包括以演艺活动为主的直播付费观看产品；面向消费者或企业的文化旅游付费知识课程；直播推广目的地的同时进行酒旅套餐和旅游特产销售。国外线上文旅的盈利模式与国内有所不同，主要是付费直播的虚拟旅行体验模式，有丰富的云旅游消费产品，包括目的地艺术、文化、烹饪、运动等直播虚拟式到达体验。一个比较典型的案例是Amazon Explore服务，这是疫情期间亚马逊科技公司推出的全新平台，该平台通过线上视频，为导游、讲师和消费者提供一对一的会话机会，消费者可以预订由旅游目的地专家组织的实时虚拟体验，体验内容包括学习DIY技能，对海外旅游景点、景区或文化地标进行虚拟游览。

（4）线下VR（虚拟现实）沉浸体验。

虚拟现实技术应用于文旅项目开发，能够从内容、模式等方面不断创新，推动文旅业态创新和产业结构优化。国内VR技术多由科技公司提供技术应用方案，应用于景区、博物馆、剧场等，丰富提升游客体验。国外则是打造了众多独立的线下门店体验项目，如航空公司推出了VR航空旅行服务，使旅客不用离开本土就能乘坐虚拟航班前往古罗马竞技场、纽约时代广场、新西兰峡湾国家公园等全球知名旅游景点。日本First Airlines是有"世界上第一个虚拟航空设备"的客机模拟虚拟体验公司，旨在打造等同于现实商业航班的虚拟乘机体验，乘客在购买虚拟机票后即能获得打印登机牌、候机登机、空乘服务等逼真的航空旅行体验。Fly

View 是一家为游客提供巴黎虚拟旅行体验的科技公司，场馆提供独一无二的虚拟实境体验，游客在体验店带上喷射背包，利用高科技 VR 技术，身临其境，仿佛飞到巴黎上空，360 度全景游览巴黎真实的名胜古迹。其提供的 VR 体验内容包括巴黎圣母院、埃菲尔铁塔以及凯旋门等地标建筑，以技术手段实现文化遗产的创新传承。

4. 文旅新平台拓展"多起来"

（1）互联网平台企业：流量引领。

上海在培育文旅领域的互联网平台企业"新方阵"方面取得了较大成绩。从表 1 可以看出，互联网平台企业采用流量引领的方法，成为文旅新平台的排头兵。其中 bilibili 月活用户1.3 亿，成为国内最大的年轻人文化社区，并已推出 bilibili yoo 社区旅游品牌；小红书打造文旅"种草"原生内容，成为新的出游决策平台；喜马拉雅开展"有声城市""建筑可阅读"等项目，用科技手段打造文旅新场景。

参考市场化程度较高的在线影视、线上数字资源、网络游戏等数字文化产业的开发模式，文旅企事业单位可借力互联网平台企业的流量力量，文博机构、旅游景区等与平台型互联网企业联合扩展"会员模式""流量转化模式""体验付费模式"等。

表1

上海涉文旅互联网平台企业用户规模（2019—2020 年）

	日活用户（万）	月活用户（万）	注册用户（万）
bilibili	3 800	13 000	/
小红书	2 500	10 000	30 000
喜马拉雅	10 000	6 800	60 000
蜻蜓 FM	/	4 300	45 000
抖音（上海）	40 000	51 800	/

（2）互联网平台企业：内容出海。

长三角三省一市地脉相连、文脉相亲、水脉相济、史脉同源，具有"最东方、最江南、最诗意"的文化共性，破解现有区域一体化国际旅游形象不鲜明、不突出的问题，应发挥区域内文化内容出海运营平台的力量，创新数字文旅内容海外市场运营的商业模式，破解跨文化语境下的文化隔膜，共同策划推出长三角高品质文旅在线内容，提振长三角数字文旅内容全球力量。现已入驻上海的 WebTVAsia 葡萄子被 YouTube 扶持成为亚洲第一家官方认证MCN 合作伙伴。从 MCN 到 MPN，再到内容公司，葡萄子打造"全亚洲网络内容生态链"，运营管理韩国、中国、日本和马来西亚的顶级内容创作者。

5. 长三角文旅一体化"融起来"

（1）强化科技和一体化资源充分对接。

文旅和科技深度融合，不但要求科技公司与文旅机构、从业者合作，实现技术手段和文旅资源的充分对接，还要共同进行技术场景的概念打造、内容制作等。上海正成为具有全球影响力的科技创新中心，不断放大人才"虹吸效应"，汇集大批人工智能、大数据、虚拟现实工程等高新技术人才，拥有冠勇科技、叠境数字、亮风台、魔珐科技、视辰科技等为文旅行业提供新技术应用解决方案的优势企业，具备文旅产业和新技术齐头并进、助力长三角文旅融合一体化发展的先发优势。

（2）促成一体化新业态消费合力。

抓住时下直播、短视频风口，发挥科技企业之力盘活长三角"江南""红色"同源文化旅游资源，应加强利用"三大力量"。第一，OTA 龙头企业力量，以"文旅＋直播电商""文旅＋短视频电商"模式促成一体化新消费合力；第二，互联网平台企业力量，以 PGC（专家生产内容）＋UGC（用户生产内容）双轮驱动，生产传播长三角"江南""红色"文旅数字内容，提升线上数字内容吸引要素；第三，主攻网络内容海外运营的企业力量，通过内容出海，打造长三角文旅内容聚合、生产、分发的底层价值，树立长三角世界著名旅游目的地国际形象。

（3）共建文旅技术创新共同体。

促进长三角一体化科技与文旅深度融合，应构建起文旅技术创新共同体，成立长三角文旅技术创新合作中心，促进长三角文旅科技创新成果全要素对接转化和协同创新，促进长三角科技企业与文旅机构建立合作伙伴关系。

文化品质与城市休闲产业提升战略研究

顾 江

南京大学长三角文化产业发展研究院院长、南京大学经济学院教授

我今天报告的题目是"文化品质与城市休闲产业提升战略研究"，但听完之前嘉宾的报告，我认为有个问题值得思考，即行为范式和场景范式的交汇。如果追溯过去历史的行为范式，它如果不能与当代的意识和当代人的偏好结合，可能就会盲目地对现代性进行否定，并对过去的东西丝毫不动地保留，这种方式值得商榷。而场景范式认为环境造物能够形成一种消费习惯和审美偏好和行为。但是如果是纯粹地照搬，就像西安曲江新城，并不是曲江新城的文化吸引人，而是协商经营的地产卖得好，是大雁塔带来的效果。所以提升文化品质是不能采取绝对主义的方式来肯定和否定。特别是面临历史文化和现代当代结合的问题时，更重要的是要考虑为当代人提供服务的产品能够发挥多大的功效。

1. 文化品质对于提升休闲产业发展的作用

（1）文化品质的提升对于休闲产业的发展能够产生规模经济效应。

规模经济效应既包括消费方面的利益，表现为随着规模的扩大，单位消费品或消耗品的平均支出下降（文化品质作为休闲产业发展的一种投入要素，具有不可分割性和专业化因素）；也包括生产方面的利益，表现为当生产的平均成本下降而产出上升时，规模经济便产生。当文化品质投入到休闲产业中时，在生产出同样多的休闲产值时，由于文化品质的成本分摊在产出增加时，随着休闲产业产值的增加，平均生产成本会下降。

文化资本对城市文化建设非常重要。而文化资本怎么定义？我认为文化资本不仅仅包括实物资本，还需要抽象归纳出本质的东西。在现当代城市的发展过程中，有一些可以与城市共生的投入要素，这些要素可以把文化资源转化为文化资本。值得一提的是，并不是所有文化资源都能转换为文化产业，有的仅仅是一个符号，比如说孔府和孔庙。所以从这层意义上讲，我们对文化资本的思考不能简单地认为越是和历史文化相关，越能变成当代人所期望的东西。

以乌镇为例，首先，我觉得"我在乌镇等你"这个符号非常好，看到这个概念我就会联想到，为什么等我？在乌镇能看到什么景象？乌镇戏剧节从 2013 年第一届开始一直到第六届，每一期的主题、时间以及戏剧节的内容特征都是移步换景，把场景行为艺术有机地结合起来，而不是昆曲、越剧这种传统戏曲的表达方式。其次，乌镇戏剧节从 2017 年就开始举办了青年专场的主题活动，虽然也是戏曲，但不仅仅局限于长三角，还邀请了国外剧团参演。每年戏剧节期间，游客主要来自全国艺术机构、高等院校及其他戏剧艺术爱好者，达到了一种我既是观众、也是参与者的效果，体验感自然而然地融入其中了。最后，乌镇把它的历史老舞台全部集中起来，变成一个"衣食住行游购娱"完整的产业链。除举办"世界互联网大会"之外，乌镇还开发高级商务住所，提供养生、休闲、娱乐等服务，满足不同层次人群需求；保护非物质文化遗产，设立博物馆、体验馆；举办"童玩节"，宣传传统手工艺；利用名人故居发展教育基地，促进文化发展。

（2）文化品质的提升增加休闲产业的竞争力。

第二点就要讲到一个非常重要的概念——唯一性战略。我们知道心理学当中有个概念叫做第一印象，在文化产业领域也是如此。以唯一性的角度去看故宫，为什么游客愿意反复参观游览？因为人们认为故宫是中国艺术和历史的代表。而近些年故宫的"走红"并不是其旅游业的发展，而是故宫文创。仅 2016 年一年就为故宫带来了 10 亿元左右的收入。截至 2016 年底，故宫博物馆的文创产品已达到 9 170 种。这就是 IP 战略的唯一性，将文化资源变成 IP，就成为可延伸性的产品。以中国优秀文化 IP 资源，外加中国传统美学元素的糅合，高品质的文化内涵造就了故宫文创持续的吸引力和消费热点。故宫文创将这种文化 IP 与时下最流行、火爆的载体进行合作，延续故宫文创的核心竞争力。

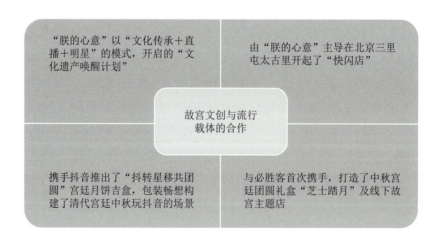

（3）文化品质的提升优化休闲产业结构。

动态角度看，产业结构的主要表现是哪些产业会逐步衰退，哪些部门会优先。从静态视角看，运用投入产出法可以反映产业间的最终需求与最终产品去向的多部门关系。中国行业发展的现状是一、二、三产业当中第三产业已成为第一大产业，特别是信息传输、软件和信息技术服务业，租赁和商务服务业增长较快，远高于国民经济平均增速。而旅游、文化、体育、健康、养老服务业稳定健康发展，幸福产业在国民经济中比重也在不断提升，休闲产业作为服务业的重要组成部分，以及作为幸福产业的基础，将在产业结构的优化升级中起到重要作用。

以德国的鲁尔区产业结构转型为例，鲁尔区号称"德国工业的心脏"，曾是世界上最大的传统工业区，经济结构以重工业为主，是德国重要的重型机械制造基地、钢铁基地和能源基地。1989年，鲁尔区将独立运作的购物旅游、景观公园、休闲、博物馆等零星景点进行区域统一开发，连接12个典型工业城镇、6个国家级博物馆和19个工业旅游景点，使工业旅游成为鲁尔区的新经济增长点。此外，鲁尔区又吸引高新技术企业入驻该区域，成为区域新引擎，建设相配套的现代化的商业、住宅和服务基础设施，形成工业旅游复合式体验区。德国鲁尔区之所以能够成功转型，从重工业污染的产业结构，成功转型走向休闲产业为主导的全球工业化旅游的标杆城市，就是因为基于鲁尔区深厚的工业文化，在这一文化品质的内核下，推动经济增长从工业空间向文化空间拓展，建造出了一个连接休闲、消费和生活方式的"工业文化空间"，从而由工业经济向休闲文化体验经济转型。

（4）文化品质的提升促进人才的聚集。

文化品质是一个区域文化氛围、人文精神、城市软实力的集中体现。一个城市所具有的文化氛围、人文精神、城市软实力均会吸引到创意人才的入驻，营造城市创新创意氛围，从而形成休闲产业的人才聚集。休闲产业的创新创意，需要优秀的人才支撑，人才是重要生产要素之一。休闲产业的多样性，很大程度上是靠人才的多样性带来的，创意人才的集聚，有利于休闲产业的创造力和创新性的形成，从而形成"大众创业，万众创新"的环境。休闲资源的丰富性和内容属性，需要优秀的创新创意人才的加入。

2. 文化品质助推休闲产业发展的战略路径

（1）深度挖掘文化内涵，促进休闲产业的高品质发展。

文化品质是休闲产业的核心元素，是城市休闲产业的核心资源。文化资源是休闲产业最重要的"原材料"。发展休闲产业要把休闲与文化的融合作为发展休闲产业的着力点，主打文化牌、打好文化牌。做好文化促休闲，围绕休闲做文化。加大休闲产品与服务的融合力度、文化推介、文化解读和文化发掘，提升休闲产品和休闲服务的文化内涵、文化品位以及城市的整体文化形象。

（2）促进文化产业与休闲产业的深度融合，完善高端休闲产品价值链。

文化产业与休闲产业的融合，通过"文化""休闲"两大元素的注入，实现区域资源有机整合。在文化产业与休闲产业融合过程中产生的新服务、新产品、新技术取代了某些传统的技术、产品或服务，提高了消费者的需求层次，同时产业融合催生出的新技术吸纳更多的传统产业部门，促使其产品与服务结构的升级，改变着传统产业的生产与服务方式，由此完善休闲产品的价值链。而影响当今人才选择的，除薪资及政策外，还有很多的"非物质"因素左右着人才对城市的喜好。我们通常所说的"幸福感"，在经济学上就是消费所带来的效用。而这种幸福感则始于对所在城市的文化品质的认同。

（3）将文化品质与高科技进行嫁接，丰富休闲产业业态。

文化品质转化为休闲产品需要一个文化物态化、活态化和业态化的过程。文化就是文化，没有非凡的文化创意和量身定制的产品转化方式，成不了休闲产品。基于互联网和移动互联网等新技术，实现休闲消费产品的极致化、个性化、审美化需求，从而满足人类消费产品的体验化、交互性、场景化需求已经成为未来休闲产业发展的新方向。因此，将文化品质与高科技进行嫁接，通过科技革命催生新兴的产业业态，如互联网相关的泛娱乐产业、流媒体音乐等相关文化产业、数字内容产业，以及 VR、大数据、云计算、人工智能等新技术在休闲产业的应用，丰富休闲产业业态，提高休闲产业附加值。

（4）制定有利于休闲产业发展的人才战略，提高复合型人才占有率。

创意能力是休闲经济的核心竞争力。文化品质的本质是文化内容，内容来自文化创意，"内容决定一切"。人才是这个产业中最活跃、最重要的因素，休闲产业的多样性，很大程度上是靠人才的多样性带来的。如何将文化品质中的精品内容，演绎成休闲产业热点，需要拥有一批把素材变成"内容"、具有故事演绎能力的人才。提高具有创意创新思想的复合型人才的占有率，是休闲产业发展的重点任务之一。

可沟通的人文城市建设

朱春阳

复旦大学新闻学院教授

中共十九届五中全会公报确立了 2035 年成为文化强国的政策目标。目前中国已经是当之无愧的政治大国、经济大国，但是还不足以被称为文化大国。文化大国的一个典型特点是强大的文化辐射力。以影视产业国际贸易来看，美国占据了全球 70% 的市场份额，而中国的市场份额不足 5%。

另外一个研究文化强国的重要基点就是一个国家的文化产品，这与它的国内市场规模和文化折扣有关。中国的显著优势是拥有无与伦比的超大国内市场规模，但是这一优势并没有充分得到发挥，因为我们是以省市为单位参与国际竞争，省际流动非常少，造成了市场的分割。

1. 文化与城市

谈到城市，文化是必不可少的因素。引用刘易斯·芒福德的观点来解释文化和城市的关系，即城市是文化容器，城市的功能是贮存文化、流转文化、创造文化。我一直以来有一个观点，就是我们更多的时候不是纯粹地在谈文化，而是在经济的基础上谈文化，文化是为了经济服务，所谓"文化搭台，经济唱戏"。因此我提倡"文化搭台，文化唱戏"，这样我们的文化才能够真正地强大起来。

但是，当我们谈论文化和城市时，不可避免地会谈及经济因素，那么从经济的视角看文化和城市又是什么关系呢？芒福德认为，城市最好的经济模式是关心人和陶冶人，城市应当具有保留文化差异的人文区域，才能让城市发展具有稳定性与个性，而不是滑向只有建筑物的城市。我曾经做过一个实验：我在国内出差到一个城市，就发几张这个城市的照片，请大家猜一猜这是哪个城市，遗憾的是几乎没有人能猜出来。大家都认为我拍的照片缺少特点，但关键问题是这些城市本身就没有特点。

诸大建教授也有一个观点，从全球城市的发展来看，普遍表现为从以经济为先导的传统发展模式，转向以提高生活质量为先导的现代化发展模式。

2. 人与城市

城市是人才的聚集地。现代城市发展的基本思路是提高城市的质量，吸引人才来推动城市的发展。上海 2035 年城市总体规划的核心就是"创新之城、人文之城、生态之城"，都是围绕着以人为本的核心理念。离开了人，创新就无法实现；生态友好实际上也是服务于"人"这一中心。上海世博会的宣传语"城市，让生活更美好"，也让我们看到了上海为改善人和城市关系所做出的努力。

讲到城市的时候，很多人会认为城市是一个反人性的冰冷的水泥钢铁的城市。在人生最欢愉的时刻，人们更多的时候所做的选择是逃离城市。例如春节时期的上海，大街小巷几乎是空荡荡的，人们并不把上海作为自己的家乡看待。人们为什么不能在最欢愉的时候呆在这个城市里？为什么上海作为一个移民城市平复不了我们的乡愁？在上海人们更多的感受是它是一个工业城市与现代化城市，人与人之间始终保持着距离，而在曾经生活的乡村里，人与人有着沟通的空间，大家保持着一种亲密的关系，这也是人类社会现代化带来的一个问题。

3. 可沟通的城市

上海的城市精神是"海纳百川，追求卓越、开明睿智、大气谦和"。尽管上海仍在努力实现，但它可以作为凝聚人心的精神气质。上海作为一个移民城市，它的文化传统实际上就是"海纳百川"，强调了各种文化的融合交流才造就了上海这样一座大都市。

如今我们可以看到上海社会关系的多元化、碎片化程度远高于之前的任何一个时代，各个群体之间的沟通交流状况并不特别理想。从新闻传播学的角度来讲，我们本以为新媒体的发展给我们带来了更多沟通交流的机会，使我们关系更加密切，使我们离真相更近，但实际却令我们陷入"信息茧房"的危机当中，我们这个时代又被称为"后真相时代"。

我认为一个理想化的全球城市应该立足于国际文化的交汇性，开放的态度、可沟通的城市治理理念、便捷的传播网络体系是全球城市的核心配置，否则大城市的"冷漠症"将会放大文化的冲突，使全球化成为一种灾难。全球文化冲突现象级灾难的代表就是纽约的世贸双子大厦。"9·11"事件始终警示着人类文化的建设也要考虑到文化之间的沟通交流。基于这样的考虑，我列出了一些可沟通的人文城市建设的面向，探讨未来文化产业、文化交流发展的方向：

如何实现城市社区内部沟通关系网络的相互联结与对话？

如何实现各产业集聚区内部企业间创新关系网络的优化？

如何实现各产业集聚区与周边社区之间的可沟通关系网络的优化？

如何实现上海与长三角城市群之间对话关系网络的优化？

如何实现上海与全球城市体系之间的可沟通关系网络的优化？

如何实现传统文化与创新文化之间的对话与融合？

如何实现政府与多元文化治理主体之间可沟通关系网络的优化？

如何实现城市与乡村的沟通与融合？

如何实现互联网线上与线下的互动与融合？

文化能量：新冠肺炎疫情与全球城市

托马斯·古德奈特

南加州大学安娜伯格传播与新闻学院

文化能量是活动、表演和场所等构成城市的要素的统称。面对新冠肺炎疫情，我们的一切文化活动都受到了冲击。接下来，我会简要概述疫情期间我们在交流方面以及研究领域所面临的压力，以及所做的工作。

1. 交流

交流为人类带来了诸多便利。在 20 世纪，越来越多的人迁入城市、改造城市，让城市变得越来越繁荣。到了 21 世纪，我们迎来了城市数量大幅增长的关键时期。这意味着原有的交流方式虽然好，但我们不能一成不变，我们必须变得更好。随着越来越多的人生活在一起，我们必须有沟通机制和实践活动，让人们充满活力，并且我们需要对这些活动进行统筹规划，让人们能够和谐高效地生活在一起，及时恢复意外事件或灾难所造成的破坏。

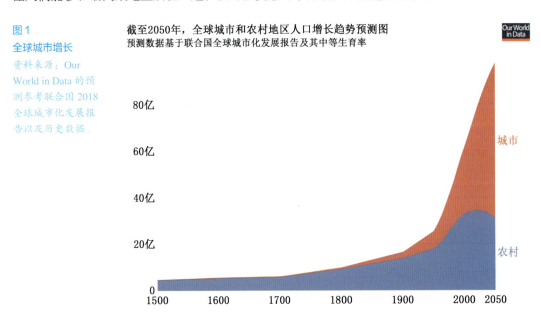

图 1
全球城市增长
资料来源：Our World in Data 的预测参考联合国 2018 全球城市化发展报告以及历史数据。

截至2050年，全球城市和农村地区人口增长趋势预测图
预测数据基于联合国全球城市化发展报告及其中等生育率

到了 2050 年，城市和农村的人口都会增加，但城市居民的数量将远远大于农村居民的数量。我认为，如今大城市的区域范围足够大，能够容纳较大人流，所以我们可以保留大面积的绿化空间以及其他建设农村的基本组成部分。我们可以让农村焕然一新，还可以建造美丽的国家公园。但是我们需要思考在个体层面、在群体之间以及邻里之间的交流是如何产生的。因此，我们的交流实践必须变得更好，城市之间要共享应对新冠肺炎疫情的相关措施。这样，即使疫情还在，我们也能够重启正常的生活。

2. 疫情和城市

流行病似乎是人类面临的众多自然灾害之一。这些灾难过去被看作是不可抗的自然活动，也或许是神的报复。但是到了 21 世纪，我们发现流行病是由我们的社会行为造成的。我们可以通过保持社交距离、戴口罩或封城的方式减少交流，降低这种灾难的破坏性。但是，我们也需要用科学手段来研制疫苗和治疗方法，找到人类和传染病共存的方法。我们不会通过大规模群体免疫的方式应对疫情，因为全球不同地区会有不同的药物，也会有不同类型的病毒。我们还不能完全消灭病毒。在疫情全球蔓延之际，全球各国仍在适应疫情，学习如何应对疫情。在美国，人们对美国的科学寄予厚望，但美国的政治体系却令人失望。最终我们能做到什么程度，还需要进一步的观察和等待。如果科学发展水平较弱，疫情带来的冲击会尤为剧烈，因此世界各国都在积极发展科学研究水平。科学领域各种数字编程技术的结合，开启了一个转型的时代。我们一直在研究科学的计算模型这一理论，但疫情这一突发状况，加速了科学实践和研究的步伐。

大流感是 20 世纪的一次大战役，大流感造成的死亡人数比在惨烈的堑壕战中死亡的人数还要多。大流感流行之际，美国的洛克菲勒基金会和约翰霍普金斯大学加速了美国的科学发展。美国疾病控制中心（Centers for Disease Control）和国家卫生研究院（National Institutes of Health）的成功并非偶然。这是与流感斗争后留下的伟大历史遗产，并且流感和流行病不仅仅影响了科学的发展。

美国国家博物馆记录了 1918 年的流感所带来的文化变革。我的曾祖父和他的几个孩子都死于那场流行病。所以，当我们想到文化的时候，我们可以从制度层面和国家层面来考虑它，或者从地方性和个人化角度看待它。疫情引导并储存文化能量，促进科学发展，增强城市的韧性。

众所周知，公共卫生不仅仅涉及科学。中国取得的进展给我留下了深刻印象。在中国做有关于禽流感和猪流感的研究时，我看到中国和亚洲进行了更广泛、更先进的干预措施。随着我们逐渐加深对于交流、合作和科学的理解，我认为，只要我们能够针对变化的领域进行交流和共享，我们就可以进行跨国家的合作。

3. 破坏

今天，我将引用《新冠肺炎病毒对城市和郊区的影响：针对多个行业的要点》一文中的内容。跨行业的要点意味着跨理论的实践或跨学科的研究。我认为，学习传播学的关键之一是借鉴清华大学的组合学思想。组合学着眼于理论和实践的多重关系。

我认为在城市中心，我们可以试着研究有关传播的问题，以了解文化能量的发展方向和未来转变的可能性，也有可能把我们从如今新冠肺炎病毒肆虐的世界变成一个更有活力的和可持续发展的城市世界。新冠肺炎疫情不仅让美国机构，也让全球机构明白了一点，那就是新自由主义导致了巨大的贫富差距。这一贫富差距表现在那些能在家工作的人和那些不能在家工作的人之间。从根本上来讲，那些在家工作的人能赚更多的钱。我的儿子和他的妻子都有工作，他们一边工作一边在家照顾刚出生的孩子。在美国，有一类人被称为"基本工种工人"。"基本工种工人"是指那些不能呆在家里，必须外出检查食品杂货、开卡车或送货的人。基本工种工人靠每天的基本工资生活，他们必须维持食品、药品和能源供应链的正常运转，这样社会才能正常运作。非基本工种工人则是那些需要工作，但失去了工作，并且要被房东赶出去的人。

因新冠疫情，人们开始重新设计公共街道、停车场和人行道，将其改造为人行道和自行车道、餐厅和超市。在新冠肺炎疫情期间，为了保持社交距离，人们对公园和开放空间的使用和需求有所增加。

疫情导致了交通中断。图2中的机场空无一人。机场是国际化城市的关键设施。公共交

图2
机场空无一人

通的使用量也大幅下降。单人交通工具的使用量增加了，尤其是自行车。因此，可能是因为出行费用有所减少。

新冠疫情还扰乱了社交—商业空间。其中严重的问题是如何接送家里上学的孩子，如何保护老人，以及如何采取临时管理体制来保护群居人群（如监狱）的安全。与此同时，我们也需要勇于承担一些风险。

最后一点是新冠肺炎疫情对大自然的影响。由于疫情，人们纷纷涌向国家公园，以缓解居家隔离的无聊。这也导致新冠肺炎病毒传播到了部落地区。印第安人采取了措施保卫家园。在没有污染的情况下，野生动物回到了洛杉矶。在美国西部，野火爆发，烧毁了400万英亩土地，人们不得不边灭火边抗击新冠肺炎疫情。自然灾害再也不是简单的一次性事件，而是相互作用。

4. 文化能量

文化能量随着城市生活的活动而发展。这种能量表现在日常的工作和娱乐生活中，以及构成日常生活的平时活动和紧急行动中。当灾难来临时，文化能量会被重新引导。我们迫切需要重新思考和重建城市，以应对新冠肺炎和未来潜在的大流行病，并建设更具复原力、更具包容性和可持续的城市。我们知道这是完全有可能的。

在全球性与地方性之间：基于上海抗疫的文化思考

叶祝弟

《探索与争鸣》主编

新冠肺炎疫情是一场席卷全球的公共卫生事件，控制疫情成为人类必须面对的一个棘手难题。上海由于大经济体量、超大规模人口和高流动性，在防疫前期很容易成为新冠肺炎疫情爆发的高风险地区，日常时刻的"超大规模优势"转换为紧急时刻的"超大规模劣势"。上海早在 1988 年应对甲型肝炎疫情以及 2003 年应对 SARS 疫情时就已对公共危机事件进行了充分的演练，也有了自己的一套"硬核"的应对体系。

作为中国最具全球地方性特征的城市，综合来看，上海的"硬核"一方面体现在制度和文化的相互交融上。上海充分挖掘城市文化，将非制度优势内化为抗疫的理念和精神支撑，快速达成了社会共识，确保抗疫成果长久维系。另一方面，上海的"硬核"体现为专家与民众的协力，尊重专业主义，构建规范基层社区社会关系网，普通市民与专家共同抗疫，真正实现了"群体免疫"。

1. 依法抗疫：疫情防治的基石与保障

（1）快速响应，紧急立法。

从行为主体角度看，全球治理视野下的区域路径既包括政府间制度，也包括非政府机制。区域通过在国家主义与全球主义之间的妥协与缓和，在一定程度上解决国家层次和全球层次难以解决的问题，在两者之间架起一座互通的桥梁，成为兴起中的全球治理的重要补充性层次。上海作为特大型城市，也是国际化、现代化的大都市，由于其特殊性成为连接中国与世界的重要环节。上海借鉴 2003 年抗击 SARS 和 2010 年世博会筹办期间的做法，主动回应当前疫情防控工作中急需的法治需求，在 10 天内完成了地方紧急立法。

（2）构建韧性的社会治理共同体。

法律的生命力在于实施，要充分考虑法律可落地的现实可能性。同时，中国以政党的全面领导为特色的举国模式不仅需要有立法支撑，更重要的在于构架不同社会主体之间的协同参与机制，使得各种社会力量可以在不同层面、以不同形式参与抗疫，形成自发秩序，构建社会治理共同体。上海疫情防控期间的立法充分考虑了中国制度体制的优势和现有的执法力量，还广泛动员社会力量参与，从而形成了良好的法治实施环境。除了行政体制主导的"自上而下"，"自下而上"的"参与式治理"同样关键。对上海抗疫网络信息的高频词抓取显示，"企业"（25176）在高频词中排名第二，频度上仅次于"疫情"（100882）；"物业"（8869）也在排名中占据第七名的位置，高于"病毒"（7981）、"志愿"（7860）和"肺炎"（6927），充分显示出上海抗疫对多元主体的重视程度。

2."全球本土化"语境中的上海社区抗疫

"社区作为具体化的社会，是社会的窗口和缩影。"良好的社区治理所形成的基层社会关系网以及与此相伴的行为规范，对疫情防控有着重要意义。上海城市社区在抗击新冠肺炎疫情过程中的经验，一方面受到全球化力量的深刻影响，另一方面基于上海独特的历史和人文背景而展现了自身的本土性，丰富了全球社区卫生治理的内涵。

（1）倒逼"和"转危为机"机制。

当代中国的社区治理实践是随着经济体制转型、为解决"单位人"转变为"社会人"过程中衍生的多重社会问题而展开的。正如李友梅所言："从某种程度看，改革开放中出现的棘手问题也会以一种倒逼方式，要求党和国家及时提供问题解决方案。""摸着石头过河"的渐进改革路线，不断对中国社会治理提出更高要求，迫使决策者提供新的解决方式。改革开放以来，上海打造了"两级政府、三级管理"的基层治理新框架，形成独特的"上海模式"。新冠肺炎疫情是中华人民共和国成立以来传播速度最快、感染范围最广、防控难度最大的重大突发公共卫生事件。公共卫生危机同样也推动上海完善社区治理体系、改善社区卫生服务条件。

（2）城市管理重心下移，推动政治势能下沉落地。

"政治势能"是中国公共政策执行中的重要学理概念，"科层组织一旦遇有政治势能强大的公共政策，各级执行主体可以突破惰性和部门割裂，具有高化的效能和执行力"。上海扩大街道管理权限，配套下放人、财、物，建立第三级管理的条块协调组织。这一体制确定了上海城市社区建设的基本框架，使街道办事处成为社区管理的实质主体。疫情期间，中国多数城市小区为加强防控，禁止各类送餐平台骑手进入小区，给居民和餐饮行业带来不便。上海普陀区长风街道为此联动阿里本地生活服务公司，在辖区内推行"饿了么骑手外卖绿色通行证"，由街道设计制作并发给阿里公司。上海街道积极作为，走在全国前列。尽管"两级政府、三级管理"体制在长期运行中也出现了一定矛盾和问题，但在行政力量积极介入社区管理、社会生活的情况下，"政治势能"更容易发挥和累积，对于处理紧迫的疫情防控任务起到积极作用。

正如王宁所指出的，所谓"单一现代性"仅仅是全球化时代的一个神话，由于不同国家的不同条件和发展模式，现代性也存在多种形态。近代以来形成的上海城市形态是"彼时彼地、国际与国内、中央与地方、内政与外交、政府与人民、现实与历史各种错综复杂的矛盾交互作用的结果"，这种不可复制性意味着，上海城市的地方性有着极为特殊的内涵。上海城市社区抗击新冠肺炎疫情的初步经验，为全球治理格局的完善提供了一种有价值的方案。在这些经验中，可以发现丰富的"全球化"与"中国化"标记。这启示人们，在城市社区治理中，应当基于各自的个性化特征，在建构性的全球互联互通中形成一种开放而共享的地方性传统，从而形成丰富的全球治理资源。

3. 非正式制度：全球地方化的重要文化根基

非正式制度是诸大建教授在比较上海与武汉抗疫模式后得出的同一个概念。他认为，文化因素在社区管理中发挥着重要作用。正式制度具有一定的稳固性，在一段时期内较少发生变动。而地域历史记忆、地方性传统作为居民日常生活的精神根基，凝聚了当地居民的世界观，指导其行为方式。传染病防控和公共健康维护取决于公众的知情、信任与合作，非正式制度因此发挥着重要作用。

新冠肺炎疫情防控在一定程度上折射出中西文化理念的差异。面对以"人传人"为主要传播方式的重大传染病，切断病毒携带人群的自由流动是非常有效的防控手段。中国和欧美国家都采取了交通管制、疫区封锁、要求居民减少外出等类似举措。但是西方民主政治中更强调"有限政府""公民自由"等理念，由此形成了"各负其责、优胜劣汰"的西方抗疫模式。欧美有自己的国情，个人主义、自由主义盛行，很多人愿意自行担责，不希望政府过多干涉。美国疫情管控初期，酒吧、沙滩、街道仍然人头攒动，即便在危急时刻，他们也可能会优先考虑个人自由和隐私，这会让抗疫更加困难。不少美国民众反对专家建议，抗议政府采取的居家法令和技术监控措施，要求重开经济和公共生活，高呼口号如"不要欺负我""让我自由，或者让我死"，以及"我们有权决定如何保护自己。让威权主义政府滚开"等。可见，在正式制度既定的情况下，以地方传统、文化心理为代表的非正式制度起到巨大作用。

（1）海纳百川的共同体意识。

上海是一座具有典型意义的移民城市，其居民来自中国各地。1949 年以前，上海居民中85% 来自全国各个省区。与此同时，上海自近代以来就是中国全球化程度最高的城市，全球与本土的互动在这里始终持续。海纳百川，实质就是吸收全中国、全世界文化中的先进因素。明代的徐光启就主动同西方传教士交往，学习先进科学，体现出非凡勇气和见识。民国时期，上海广泛学习西方物质文明、精神文明成果，已是众所周知。改革开放后，上海较早在污水治理、旧房改造、公共交通等领域，积极同其他国家开展技术合作，学习先进经验。在中国融入世界现代性的浩荡大潮中，上海长时期处于引领风气之先的地位。这一文化特征是上海城市精神的基底。

第一财经杂志原主编秦朔认为，从对这座城市的向心力、自豪感来说，上海意识的的确确是存在的，是"爱城主义"（civicism），是一种自然的融入、热爱与责任，上海尊重人民，敬畏人民，人民热爱上海，相信上海。"爱城主义"是清华大学贝淡宁教授在《城市的精神》一书中提出的一个理念：我们需要有独特的城市精神，来抵挡异化和遗忘，守望我们的历史和未来，城市精神应被视为一种"和而不同"的团结的力量，城市精神应该表现城市居民最有共鸣的情感。城市与人民之间，构成了一个韧性的共同体。这种共同体意识，来源于共同的利益、价值共识和长期互动形成的信任。

在中华人民共和国建立之初的 30 年中，"上海以大约全国 1/1 500 的土地，1/100 的人口，提供全国 1/6 的财政收入，1/10 的工业产值"。其他地区向上海提供的主要是原材料、能源、农产品，而"上海支援全国"的则多为高技术产品、高附加值产品。这样的历史推动催生了上海人独特的上海意识。21 世纪以来，上海人的城市文化认同日益清晰，本地媒介、方言、文艺创作的繁荣，诸如"海派清口"和小说《繁花》，推动了上海人对本土文化的认同。文化上"自己人"的划定，使得社会中的个体能够超越隔离和障碍，建立人与人之间的连接关系、信任关系和情感纽带。社会共同体的建设正是以这种社会自发的情感联系和社会自组织为本。而在巨大危机面前，共同体意识显然有助于促使社会力量更有效积聚，激发社会自救机制，政社协同，转危为安。

（2）尊重科学精神，崇尚专业主义。

上海自近代以来就是中国的科学技术重镇，科学主义和专业精神在这座城市有着悠久的传统。早在清末，上海就出现了圣约翰书院、南洋公学、东亚同文书院等一系列知名学府。中国第一家近代军工企业江南制造局于 1865 年在上海开办，许多高技术含量的工厂、发明都在上海诞生。上海在近代中国科学文化方面担当了"领跑者"的角色。这一文化传统也在市民阶层中传承，构成上海现代化国际大都市文明建设和发展的内在动力之一，影响着在公共卫生危机发生时上海的应对。

1988 年的甲肝大暴发，使上海市民在饮食习惯上吸取教训，一定程度上改变了不良卫生习惯。2003 年 SARS 疫情期间，作为常住、流动人口近 2 000 万的特大城市，上海的感染者仅有个位数，但其后上海即未雨绸缪，在金山建立了常设 500 张病床的上海公共卫生临床中心。人们调侃说，当武汉紧急上马"火神山""雷神山"，大秀基建能力时，上海默默掏出了16 年前准备好的上海版"小汤山"。上海人崇尚专业知识、尊重专业人士，讲究科学方法和态度，从垃圾分类到新冠肺炎疫情，这座城市培养起了足够的尊重科学、尊重专业的风气。

上海文化中的尊重科学精神，崇尚专业主义，突出体现上海市民对此次疫情中因敢讲真话，在全国引起广泛关注的上海医疗救治专家组组长张文宏教授的赞许上。疫情期间，张文宏教授因为及时向公众通报疫情情况、科普相关知识、准确预测疫情走势，并凭借自己精湛的专业技能、高尚的伦理精神、诙谐幽默的语言，赢得了市民的广泛尊敬，并在互联网上迅速走红，被人们亲切地称为硬核医生。

张文宏现象彰显了一个正常社会所必须存在的两个基石：一是敢于讲真话；二是专业主义精神。首先，张文宏身上体现了敢于担当、敢于讲真话的勇气，他把疫情中的真实情况及时告知公众，并实事求是告知市民真实的情况。在疫情刚开始，他提出医生中的共产党员先上，"不能欺负老实人"，一石激起千层浪。考虑中国特殊的政治文化环境，才能理解张文宏话语背后的巨大的社会意义。"共产党员先上"，在中国的日常生活中有着复杂的政治意味以及背后源远流长的文化记忆。"共产党员先上"本来是中共的一条纪律，以彰显共产党人的先进性、模范性，然而，在日常生活中，共产党员先上并不能得到有效贯彻。但是，在疫情面前，张文宏提出不能让老实人吃亏。在考验共产党人的时刻，隐藏在这句话背后的政治逻辑被摆在了台前，挑战了某种政治潜规则。总之，专家史无前例从幕后走向台前，一改以往"政治话语不爱听，专业话语不想听"的尴尬局面，政治势能与专业主义结合，重塑了社会信任。其次是专业主义，即必须坚持科学态度、务实精神，即使在外界质疑下，依然能够坚持己见，同时能够根据科学研究，尽早作出预测。比如他对疫情走势的判断，近期他对"全球第二波疫情正在发展，而且反弹力度已经超过第一波"的判断，显然是基于他和他的团队在尊重事实、讲究证据、实事求是基础上作出的慎重的判断。

（3）实用理性。

上海人有一句俗语为"拎得清"，即在政治理性之外，上海人能够有自己的判断。新冠肺炎疫情期间，坊间流传着一句话：钱能捐，物能捐，张医生（张文宏）绝对不能捐！看似调侃的背后，彰显的正是上海市民文化中流行的实用理性精神。本次疫情中，上海人展现出比其他地方更强的自律意识和规则意识。在"禁足令"发布之后，上海人说不出门就不出门，碰到事情绝对有自律，这在当年抗击 SARS 的过程中也有所体现。上海人是"守规矩"的，不会轻易和决策者"唱反调"，比如疫情期间各地频繁出现拒不配合疫情检查、辱骂殴打工作人员、擅自设卡等行为，上海却鲜少发生。并且上海市民自觉当起"猎人"，监督和举报违法或不道德行为，自发维护疫情防控秩序。上海人讲实惠，讲理性，尤其是涉及切己利益的时候，上海文化中所谓的精明意识更加显现。上海的文化理念培养的不是那种口是心非的精致的利己主义者，也不是毫不利己的可敬的利他主义者，而是拎得清大河有水小河满、利他利己可以兼得的实用理性主义者。

一个地区的地方性传统何以形成，必须到历史脉络中探寻。上海曾经是民国时期的全国经济、金融中心，工商业发达，市民较早形成了个体本位意识、契约意识和尊重专业人士的精神，此外，上海市民的自治意识传统也可溯源到近代的历史记忆。租界文化本身具有某种自治性特征，治理上呈现西方"小政府、大社会"的特点。由此，"中外一体、全力共享、责任共担的近代市民自治意识"在上海居民中留下种子，影响其摆脱传统遗留的危机面前依附行政当局的心理，推动社区自主抗疫。西方文明因素的较早渗透，在上海文化中形成了亦中亦西、宽容开放的文化积淀。历史文化方面的非制度因素，以复杂而隐蔽的方式潜藏在上海居民心态的深处，对新冠肺炎疫情防控工作起到积极作用。上海所孕育的海派文化向以创新、开放、多元示人，海派文化是传统儒家为基础的江南文化与西方现代文明所碰撞、融合、化生的新的文明形态。这是一种双轮驱动的文明形态，一方面，它接受了西方先进文明的熏陶，西方启蒙运动以来的文化遗产比如法治、理性、包容等现代文明形态在这座城市得到很好继承，同时也小心翼翼避免了西方文化中极端个人主义的弊病；另一方面，对于普通上海市民来说，中国传统文化中的儒释道文化融合而形成的江南文化，同样构成了上海文化的内核。传统文明的现代性转化以及西方文明的"洋为中用"，使得这两种文明形态在上海文化中都有非常好的融合和张力。

疫情社会治理本质上应是一种经由双向对象化过程的双向主体化实践。一方是以"政府主导、社会参与"为基本构架的治理主体，另一方是作为治理活动目的和效用归宿的人民主体。二者都以应对和战胜疫情、保障人民的生命健康为实践目的。为了实现这一共同目标，治理主体和人民主体之间必然发生着双向对象化活动，而这种双向对象化过程，又内在地要求社会治理中人民主体发挥中心作用。应对新冠肺炎疫情，需要更日常的城市精细化管理，上海形成了决策者、专业人士、社会群众三合一的系统性联动机制，其中"海派"作为上海的城市文化基因，它的"遗传密码"对于上海的疫情防控具有重要意义。非正式制度决定了城市的治理效能，上海城市治理的"硬核"，其深层意义就蕴含于上海人的文化层面。

上海抗击新冠肺炎疫情的举措特点，一个层面是站在国家的视角，逐渐将社会组织逻辑纳入国家的权力体系，追求"国家能力在基层社会的实现"；而在另一层面上，则体现了上海兼具世界主义特征和本土特点的独特现代性，高风险、大流动已经成为全球化背景下社会的重要特征，局部疫病、地域性事件很容易演化为全球性公共卫生事件。新冠肺炎疫情的全球大流行再次证明了这一点，全球公共卫生治理已经产生迫切的现实需要。要实现良好的全球公共卫生治理，必须推动全球与地方在思想资源上的良性互动。正如里贾纳·杜阿尔特（Regina Duarte）所说，"普遍的"科学知识本来就是"混血儿的、杂糅的和跨国性的"。全球卫生防疫既要关注全球性的科学技术和医学知识的进展，又要能够充分调用"地方性知识"的灵活性和能动性。本土化与全球化的势力相伴而行，相互借鉴，从而形成一种"全球本土化"（glocalized）的理论经验。这正是我们关注全球抗疫中上海城市经验的意旨所在。

全球著名体育城市建设的国际比较与上海实证

郑国华

上海体育学院教授

改革开放以来，北京、上海、南京、广州等城市在城市文化建设中取得了巨大成就，城市文化的国际影响力不断攀升，城市文化的国际排位和声望与日俱增。特别是在近十年来，各大城市在发展规划中明确提出了建设体育城市的目标，并将其作为城市文化品牌建设的重要任务。

上海早在"十五"计划中就提出了"亚洲体育中心城市"的目标，后在"十二五"体育发展规划中改为"国际知名体育城市"，"十三五"规划提出要打造"全球著名体育城市"。近日召开的上海市政府常务会议原则同意《上海全球著名体育城市建设纲要》，指出要加快完善公共服务体系，让全民健身更智慧、更便利、更普及。要加快发展体育产业，着力扩大体育消费，繁荣体育文化。要合力推进体育事业发展，有序开放各类体育场地设施，让人民群众共享体育发展成果。

结合中共上海十一届市委九次全会通过的《中共上海市委关于深入贯彻落实"人民城市人民建，人民城市为人民"重要理念谱写新时代人民城市新篇章的意见》来看，城市治理要打造"人性化城市、人文化气息、人情味生活"，在凸显特色、打造个性、塑造气质的过程中，体育日渐成为紧扣城市脉搏、点燃城市激情的助推器，成为打造活力之城的重要组成部分和提高人民获得感、幸福感的重要民生事业。上海要以全民体育促进全民健康，同时带动体育产业，用体育激发城市活力，努力建设全球著名体育城市，让"体育"成为人民城市不可或缺的关键要素和重要品牌。

如何抓住国际体育名城建设的重要契机，充分发挥体育的正面影响，为助力提升城市文化的国际影响，改善城市形象，而追求最大效益，是我们思考的一项重要任务，也是中国城市文化品牌建设所追求的重要目标。

表1
中国部分城市体育助力城市文化品牌定位情况

城　　市	体育助力城市文化品牌定位	时间	来　　源
北京	国际化体育中心城市	2003	《关于加强新时期体育工作建设国际化体育中心城市的意见》
	国际体育中心城市	2006	北京市"十二五"体育发展规划
上海	亚洲体育中心城市	2001	上海市"十五"体育发展规划
	国际知名体育城市	2007	上海市"十二五"体育发展规划
	全球体育著名城市	2017	上海市"十三五"体育发展规划
广州	国际体育强市	2006	广州市体育发展"十一五"规划
	国际体育名城	2011	广州市体育发展"十二五"规划
南京	亚洲体育中心城市	2011	南京市第十三次党代会
	世界体育名城	2012	《关于建设亚洲体育中心城市和世界体育名城的意见》
晋江	国家体育城市	2007	晋江市"十二五"发展规划
	体育城市	2016	《关于印发2016年晋江市体育城市建设行动方案的通知》
深圳	现代化国际化创新型体育强市	2016	深圳市体育发展"十三五"规划
武汉	国际体育名城	2017	武汉市体育设施空间布局规划（2016—2030）
厦门	国际滨海运动休闲之城	2017	厦门市体育发展"十三五"规划
重庆	中西部地区体育强市	2016	重庆市体育发展"十三五"规划
杭州	世界体育名城	2016	杭州市体育发展"十三五"规划
南宁	东盟国际体育中心城市	2017	南宁市体育发展"十三五"规划
黄石	宜居运动新城	2017	黄石市体育发展"十三五"规划
三亚	国际文体服务示范城	2018	三亚市文化广电出版体育服务体系"十三五"发展规划
大连	国际体育名城	2016	大连市体育发展"十三五"规划

1. 纽约体育名城建设的实践与成效

　　纽约多次上榜英国专业体育咨询机构 ArkSports 的"世界顶级体育城市"评选和美国"最佳体育城市"的评选，属于名副其实的国际体育名城，享有世界"体育之都"的美誉。根据洛杉矶、东京、纽约和上海四个全球特大城市的比较，纽约体育全球影响力指数位列第一，这与纽约采取的一系列措施是分不开的。首先，纽约打造了一套城市体育公园智能系统，方便市民选择自己喜爱的运动项目，寻找运动场地和运动伙伴。此外，纽约形成了"世界性体育赛事—自主品牌赛事—职业体育赛事—学校体育赛—社区体育赛事"的赛事体系，培养了深厚的群众基础。最后，依据本土体育文化特色，通过政府免税政策和资金扶持，培育了66支职业体育球队，其中有13支是世界著名的职业体育球队，并且大部分球队俱乐部建立了自己的电视和电台网络传播平台。据统计，纽约市政府2020年财政预算中在健康领域的投入是730亿美元。近十年来，政府在公园体育健身场地建设和维护的投入每年都在12亿美元以上。

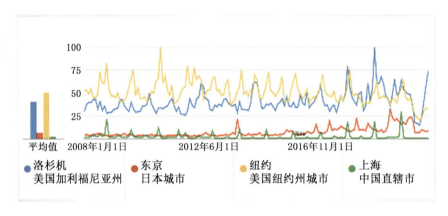

图1
洛杉矶、东京、纽约和上海城市体育全球影响力指数的对比

从纽约的案例中，可以得出以下四点启示：

第一，纽约市政府致力于公园体育的发展，为纽约城市体育、大众体育的发展提供平台。政府投入资金在全市各地免费提供健康健身计划，翻修校园的体育场所，并要求学校体育场馆不运行的时间内向校外开放，打造"口袋公园"即打造居民身边尽可能利用的小场地。

第二，公园体育系统降低体育参与成本，提高体育参与人口。政府打造无边界公园、增加公园用地，使社区居民10分钟内必达体育公园、增加公园体育设施基础建设，为纽约人免费锻炼提供便利。

第三，在政府政策的支持和推动下，职业体育获得了进一步发展，纽约成为世界职业体育之都，以及美国职业联盟总部数量和球队数量最多的城市。所有职业球队都由政府实施免税政策扶持发展，甚至政府出巨资为职业俱乐部修建球场。如洋基球馆（Yankee Stadium）的翻修，政府出资了1.67亿美元，使其为洋基职业俱乐部主场。

第四，本土体育赛事助力城市文化品牌建设。纽约体育赛事由社区赛事—学校赛事—职业赛事—自主品牌赛事—世界性赛事形成了"金字塔"式的层级递进推动力，使赛事具有深厚的群众基础。根据NYC & Company的官网提供的数据，对2018年纽约体育赛事进行统计分析，结果呈现以下几个特点：一是赛事整体总量不多，2018年纽约举行了和即将举行的各类体育比赛128次，其中国际体育赛事仅6次，122次为本土体育赛事；二是职业体育赛事贯穿全年；三是大学体育赛事火爆；四是赛事时间、地点固定，水平高；五是赛事组织娱乐化；六是赛事内容的多元性；七是赛事组织规范。

2. 伦敦体育名城建设的实践与成效

依据全球体育城市指数排行榜（Global Sports Cities Index），近十年来，伦敦在评估的600多个城市中长期蝉联第一的位置，被称为"世界最运动之城"。伦敦打造全球著名体育城市，政府的顶层设计和整体性治理发挥了重要的作用。特别是伦敦市政府实施的《运动伦敦计划》更是助推了城市文化品牌的复兴。

伦敦案例主要给我们带来以下几点启示：

第一，积极承办有顶级影响力的赛事，即奥运会和顶级足球赛事。伦敦对一般性的国际大赛承办比较保守，在近十年中伦敦仅承办了世界田径锦标赛，欧洲足球锦标赛半决赛和决赛，欧洲游泳锦标赛，UCI世界田径自行车锦标赛，以及女子曲棍球和板球世界杯等为数不多的十几项赛事。伦敦承办的大型赛事虽不多，但是由于承办比赛的巨大影响力，依然在以赛事为评估核心的排行榜上长期蝉联榜首。

第二，降低了市民参与体育的成本。从"运动伦敦计划"可以看出其具体战略是大幅度的政府资金投入和立足于市民居住小区的体育运动就近免费参与原则，着力降低市民的经济成本和交通成本。特别值得一提的是，"运动伦敦计划"非常重视对弱势人群的关注，通过对残障和经济困难的市民的优先支持，鼓励了特殊人群的运动参与，并使体育参与可负担化。

第三，伦敦的全球著名体育城市建设是长期分阶段实施的过程。如2015年提出的"运动伦敦计划"，阶段性实施的结果就是在全英国体育人口锐减22.6万的情况下，实现伦敦全市体育人口100万的增量。

第四，通过重点资金扶持基层俱乐部来扩大运动参与，建立更好的城市体育文化。伦敦市的政府资金投入重点在扶持基层私营的小俱乐部，2018年政府投入是280万英镑。

3. 洛杉矶体育名城建设的实践与成效

近一个世纪以来，"洛杉矶"几乎成了"卓越运动"的代名词。洛杉矶也将成为继伦敦和巴黎之后，又一个举办三次奥运会的城市。除此之外，洛杉矶还举办了一系列国际锦标赛和冠军联赛，打造了洛杉矶职业体育之城的名誉。

洛杉矶拥有上千个丰富完备的体育场馆设施，可以同时满足体育组织者和体育爱好者的多重需求，人均场地面积也达到38.1平。此外，洛杉矶拥有顶尖的职业团队和赛事成绩，其物质保障源于其高标准的体育场馆。洛杉矶有一批著名体育馆，如洛杉矶纪念体育场、玫瑰碗体育场等，不仅是大型体育赛事的举办地，作为著名职业球队的主场，同时也是体育旅游的重要打卡点,每一个场馆都得到了多方面的应用。2028 年洛杉矶奥运会场馆充分利用现有的体育场馆资源,将体育赛事活动分散在四个主要的体育公园中进行,并鼓励非营利组织的参与。大赛之后,这些投入都将直接授惠于民。

经过对洛杉矶案例的分析我们发现:一是洛杉矶重视非营利组织的参与,本土体育文化民治民享。二是洛杉矶积极提升职业体育竞技能力,打造城市标志性体育运动与团队文化。三是承办国际影响力大的赛事,创新办赛模式、营造赛事文化。四是提升体育场馆的综合利用率,注重体育场馆文化遗产保护。五是关注青少年体育,推动体育可持续发展。

4. 东京体育名城建设的实践与成效

东京与伦敦、纽约并列三大顶级世界城市,在"全球顶级体育城市排行榜"中,东京两次入选"全球顶级体育城市"。东京是典型的通过举办国际大赛带动公共体育服务设施完善的城市。东京曾在 1964 年作为第 18 届夏季奥运会承办城市,以及 2002 年世界杯的承办城市。自承办完国际大赛后,东京的社区体育人口、社区体育经费、社区体育场地等都得到了极大的提高和完善,享有"世界公共体育服务之城"的盛名。

东京的经验主要有四点:

第一,东京市通过举办国际重大体育赛事如奥运会和世界杯足球赛等来完善城市体育场馆设施和体育服务软环境,以世界公共体育服务名城建设助推东京城市文化品牌建设。

第二,政府采取措施,有效利用体育设施,发挥体育场馆"事后回溯效应",积极开放大型场馆使其得到充分利用,充分体现可持续发展的理念。

第三,东京市打造体育城市名片,也是从建设本土体育文化和体育配套服务入手。例如标志性的体育文化景观,包括标志性体育馆、体育博物馆、体育名人堂及体育主题公园等。

第四,有自己的体育文化传统,如东京每个俱乐部都有自己忠实的球迷和俱乐部文化。注重积极强化城市运动文化特色,积极宣传和引导市民的体育观赏,培养运动情节和运动习惯。

5. 上海体育名城建设的实践与成效

上海在体育助力城市文化品牌建设中已经走过了十多年,成效如何?国际体育名城的城市文化品牌建设目标是否实现了?

如表 2,从 2016 年到 2018 年上海全球体育影响力城市排名都落后于南京。南京 2016 和 2017 年全球排名都是第 19,2018 年和 2019 年分别是第 10 和第 11。上海 2016—2019 年间各年的排名分别是 36、36、33、37。

表 2
全球体育影响力城市排名比较

城　市	2016 年			2017 年（排名）	2018 年			2019 年		
	排名	得分	有影响力赛事数量		排名	得分	有影响力赛事数量	排名	得分	有影响力赛事数量
伦敦	1	18 694.87	13	1	2	16 494	12	6	10 747	12
东京	3	16 163.21	11	3	1	16 494	12	1	19 867	13
里约热内卢	2	16 632.13	7	2	3	15 713	8	4	13 801	8
巴黎	6	10 934.64	13	6	4	15 342	14	2	16 048	15
多哈	5	12 067.82	10	5	5	12 460	10	5	13 679	10
莫斯科	4	13 123.34	14	4	9	12 053	12	7	10 241	11
北京	9	7 134.91	7	9	9	7 315	6	8	8 388	7
南京	19	4 939.18	5	19	10	6 740	6	11	6 615	6
上海	36	3 405.98	5	36	33	3 590	6	37	3 446	5
广州	81	2 185.36	3	81	90	1 961	3	112	1 825	3

资料来源：Sportal Global Sports Impact（GSI）Cities Index（数据覆盖 14 年，即过去 7 年和未来 7 年）。

从榜单排名来看，十多年来上海的国际体育名城建设并没有取得预想的效果。2019 年全球城市体育赛事影响力排名，上海不仅落后于伦敦、北京等国际大都市，也不如南京、成都等国内大城市。

从财政拨款来看，2017 年上海在体育事业财政拨款中比以往多出近 40 亿，2018 年支出

表 3
2019 年全球城市体育赛事影响力排名

排名	城市	国家	得　分
6	伦敦	英国	10 717
8	北京	中国	8 388
11	南京	中国	6 615
28	成都	中国	4 087
37	上海	中国	3 446
113	中国香港	中国	1 825

资料来源：https://www.sportcal.com/GSI/GSICitiesIndex.

平均值　2008年1月1日　　　2012年6月1日　　　2016年11月1日

● 南京　　　● 深圳　　　　天津　　　　● 成都　　　　● 武汉
　中国城市　　　中国城市　　　中国直辖市　　　中国城市　　　中国城市

更是达到 66 亿元，超过之前三年的总和。整个体育产业，增长势头迅猛，但结构相对单一，体育服务业产值占总产值的一半。从国际赛事的数量来看，十几年来，上海举办的国际赛事数量迅速增长，由 2001 年的每年 11 项，增长到 2017 年的 61 项。从基础设施建设来看，近三年上海人均体育场地有了较大突破，2020 年达到了 2.4，但与上述体育名城仍有较大差距。近十年来，上海在社区公共运动场数量、社区健身场地面积、社区公共运动场面积等方面变化不大。

对标国际，国内大部分城市在体育助力城市文化品牌建设中存在的主要问题如下：

第一，追求国际赛事数量，而不注重质量，赛事文化的影响力未显现。究其原因，国际赛事文化资源深耕不足、影响力不大，专业化运作团队欠缺、综合实力不强，赛事举办尚未整合有序形成合力，赛事综合体系构建市场化运作空间不足，文化品牌塑造差异化、特色化不明显，赛事传播理念和营销路径局限。根据百度和谷歌搜索指数，尽管上海每年举办 70 场左右国际体育赛事，但绝大多数国际体育赛事国际关注度较少。Sportcal 的体育赛事影响力排名指标也显示，上海近十几年被认可的有影响力的赛事只有 5 到 6 场。

第二，政府对大众体育投入不足，市民参与体育成本过高。究其原因，一是城市体育场馆营利性突出，二是城市体育场馆惠民性缺失。纽约针对不同年龄段市民划定体育场地收费标准，例如纽约公园灯光球场对 18 岁以下市民免费开放；纽约公园网球场、室内娱乐健身中心的票价则根据年龄段和有无市民卡进行了划分，对青少年和老年人实施优惠政策，且优惠力度极为可观。而上海的体育场馆在收费上并无年龄区分，青少年、成年人、老年人皆为同一收费标准，且费用昂贵，未能体现出惠民政策。

第三，体育城市独特文化内涵及识别体系构建不足。究其原因为本土特色体育文化建设不足，地标性体育文化景观较少，节庆类体育文娱活动不足。

第四，体育文化原创性资源深度挖掘、评估与整合力度不够。究其原因为本土体育文化品牌建设不足，体育自然资源、人文资源和地方特色资源三类资源协调发展不够，体育资源整合转化潜力不足。

第五，体育、旅游、娱乐等文化要素整合嵌入品牌市场化开发程度不足。究其原因为产业项目开发及优惠政策不足，招商引资范围不全面，区域协同有待加强，公共设施与服务体系还需完善。

第六，集体育文化创意与市场营销于一体的复合型人才短缺。打造著名体育城市，需要扩大引进、大力培养体育赛事、营销运营、运动健康人才队伍，培育市场主体、健全健身组织体系、赛事体系、节庆活动等，体育产业复合型人才短缺是普遍存在的问题。

第七，促进体育文化消费与贸易的动力结构及体育文化生态不健全。究其原因为多元化市场主体不足，市民参与体育成本太高，时尚体育消费场域及模式构建不足，投融资结构政策不完善，品牌运营综合实力不够，体育旅游综合体建设不足。

第八，体育发展速度、产业结构、产品附加值及规模与国际化标准匹配不足。究其原因为体育人口与全球著名体育城市不匹配，体育产业结构不合理，产业园区未形成规模，运动健康市政服务体系不完善。

世界名城与策略传播

黄懿慧

香港城市大学媒体传播系讲座教授

1. 世界名城的定义和标准

世界名城，即所谓的全球城市（global city）或世界城市（world city）。其概念来自地理学和城市研究。世界名城在全球经济和贸易体系中处于重要节点的位置，并且对全球社会具有直接影响。世界名城的主要标准，包括是否拥有一系列国际化的金融服务、在周边区域的经济贸易中处于主导地位、是跨国公司跟金融机构的总部所在、在国际事务上具有一定的话语权或者拥有独特性的特质——比如商业、经济、文化、政治或者是创新中心等。总的来讲，世界名城的标准涵盖了经济、文化、宜居、环境、交通、基础设施和旅游等范畴。我们也可以看到在全球不同的机构采用不同的指标来定义世界名城，包括全球城市实力指数（GPCI）、GaWC（Globalization and World Cities Research Network）、最具经济实力的城市、全球化城市指数、全球城市竞争力指数等。

2. 世界名城形成过程中的策略传播

（1）CPC 理论模型。

CPC 是我在研究策略传播过程中所建构出来的理论模型。第一个 C 代表 "communication"，即沟通传播，它既可以发生在大众媒体（mass communication）上，也可以发生在人际传播（Interpersonal communication）上。第二个 P 代表两个 "promotion" 或者 "prevention"，即传播的目的是倾向于去推广或促销，抑或是去做负面消息的防治，也就是所谓的议题管理或者危机管理。第三个 C 是 "context"，指传播的场景是在线、线下或者两者共融。简而言之，CPC 模型是对策略传播进行策略性或纲要性的探讨。

（2）城市品牌营销与城市公关：城市形象的培养。

培养理论（cultivation theory），也称涵化理论，由格伯纳（Gerbner）等人提出。其研究

图 1
CPC 模型图解

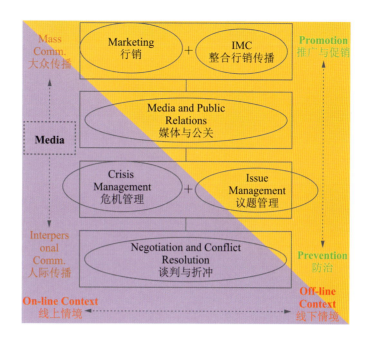

团队在 20 世纪 70 年代针对黄金时间的电视内容进行了一系列分析，发现看电视越多的受众，对于社会上实际发生暴力的预估比例就越高。这其中原因就在于大众传播媒体提示的"象征性现实"，对于人们认识理解现实社会发挥着巨大影响。因为大众传播媒体有一定的倾向性，所以人们在自己的"主观现实"认知上，跟实际存在的"客观现实"之间就呈现很大的偏离，而且这种影响不是短期的，它是一个长期的、潜移默化的、"培养"的一个过程。通过对象征性事物的选择、加工、记录和传达，电视等大众传媒使人们共享相当同质的社会真实。

涵化理论学派还提出了"主流效果"和"回响效果"理论。"主流效果"是指观看电视的不同的群体中，立场和行为之间的差异会缩小。这种主流化的过程，经历了模糊、混合和屈服的过程，即电视会模糊由于文化、政治、经济、地区和阶层所产生的不同，使人们的态度混同于电视中的主流意识形态，从而屈服于电视所展示的政治和经济体制，因此在媒介上塑造良好的城市形象就显得相当重要。而"回响效果"是指一旦受众从电视或者大众传播媒体得到的某一印象，在现实中得到印证，那么受众就会对这个印象深信不疑，使得电视对受众的涵化效果也会增强。反之，如果个人的经历跟媒体的描绘不相符合，那么受众也会不再相信媒介所呈现的内容。"回响效果"给打造世界名城带来的启发是必须为城市人提供相应的经历，也就是说议题管理和危机管理，在城市品牌营销或者是城市公关上也相当重要。

（3）城市品牌营销与城市公关：理论与模型。

引用徐德娅的观点，她认为城市公关可分成三个类型，即引导的、自主的或是有机的。其中"引导的"是指政府或相关部门的公关从业人员通过广告、宣传片等方式组织或赞助城市形象推广的相关活动；"自主的"则是指独立制片，通过新闻、电影、电视剧等自发提供与城市形象相关内容的传播途径；"有机的"是一般公众通过个人的亲身经历、人际传播或者社交媒体平台所获得的与城市形象相关的信息和交流。其中，城市公关的重点，一是"引导的"类型中的隐秘引导，即观众不能轻易判断有关城市的信息来源是相关部门或旅游公司；二是刚才提到的"自主的"；三是"有机的"类型中"主动的"和"被动的"，即主动地或者被动地从他人口中获取与城市有关的信息。

另外，在当前社交媒体十分普遍的情况下，"涉入和体验"是至关重要的。"涉入和体验"就是用看、听、用、参与的方式，充分刺激和调动受众的感官、情感、思考、行动、关联等感性和理性的因素，重新定义设计一种思考方式的营销方法。而将其结合社交媒体产生的UGC（用户生成内容），则会起到更好的传播效果。这种思考方式突破了传统意义上的理性人假设，强调受众或消费者在处理信息或者是消费的时候，是兼具理性和感性的，所以用户体验才是整个消费行为或者是品牌经营的关键。

3. 个案展示

第一个体验营销的案例是加拿大啤酒的"我是加拿大人"广告。在 2017 年 7 月 1 日，加拿大的国庆日，加拿大啤酒将放满啤酒的冰箱摆在街头，设定要用六种语言喊出"我是加拿大人"才能够解锁冰箱，获得免费的啤酒。这个广告在除了交互体验之外，更重要的是传达了加拿大作为一个移民国家所拥有的多元包容的价值观。

第二个案例是"凌晨四点发生在北京的故事"。2016 年 5 月，新世相向读者征集凌晨四点北京发生的故事，之后于 6 月 16 日在微信公众号来发布这些文章，内容为读者在后台发送的短故事，并在文末邀请读者观看直播讲述北京凌晨的故事，最后拍摄系列短片，获得了不错的反响。这一案例典型地运用了所谓的用户涉入"六步曲"方法：了解受众，用走心口号唤起行动，建立"价值观共同体"，寻找适合的赞助商共同执行，奖励用户勇于超越日常，协助用户成就自己。新世相提出的走心的口号包括"有预谋的集体熬夜""睡着的人拥有睡眠的时候，我们拥有整个城市"等，所建立的价值观体现了个人的存在感、集体的联结和参与以及共同的存在。关键的是，这次体验营销借由听众等受众的涉入，融合了认知、情感和行动，达到了在线和线下串联的效果。

城市文化产业对标体系：实践与思考

曾　原

上海市委宣传部印刷发行处处长

提出城市文化产业对标体系这个话题的初衷主要有四点，首先，对标国际最高标准、最好水平，这是对上海这座城市的要求，也是上海文化发展的要求。其次，"十三五"期末上海基本建成国际文化大都市，目标本身就包含了对标的意涵。再次，越过"十三五"这个关键时间点之后，进一步跻身全球一流文化城市行列依然任重道远。最后，对标体系既是事业发展的标杆，又是检验成果的标尺，然而文化发展需要测度，却又不容易测度。

1. 问题：从主观感性到客观理性

文化是从主观感性到客观理性，它既可以是群体的宏大叙事，也可以是个体的独特体验，所以要给文化下一个令人满意的定义非常困难。英国学者威廉斯曾提到，"英文中间有两三个比较复杂的词，文化（culture）是其中一个"。美国的两位人类学家阿尔弗雷德·克洛依伯和克莱德·克拉克洪曾经在《文化：概念和定义批判分析》中列举了 1871 年到 1951 年间文化的 164 个定义，所以不同的概念或者不同的人对文化的认知是千差万别的。

进一步从文化聚焦到文化产业，文化产业不是冰冷的工业体系，人才的作用越来越凸显，文化产业会有多个角色的人参与。我在这里提出一个概念叫做"人化产品"，舞台艺术是非常典型的人化产品，它既是人本身，是艺术家或者演职人员，又是作品，两者是不可分割的。另外文化产业领域有一个问题在于，话语权多掌握在从业者手中，特别是一些文化名家在本领域一言九鼎，而个人的感性判断往往会和执行之间形成自然的联通，这就决定了他们有时会用个体感受替代群体决策，所以我们需要一个从感性到理性的过程。

国际文化大都市不是独立的存在，它是在对标体系之下，通过科学的决策判断提出的较长一段时期的发展和建设目标。目标形成的过程，也是关注指标、使用指标进行水平测度进而形成决策的过程。在党政工作中，我们的决策需要听取业内的、学界的以及其他领域的意见建议，但决策的形成还是要回归理性。

文化产业发展指标体系有两个作用，一是纵向比较知晓自身发展状况，二是横向比较知晓相应范围内的发展地位。所谓知己知彼，上海做对标研究时不仅要对标纽约、巴黎、伦敦、东京以及北京等国际大都市，在城市群发展以及区域竞争日益重视的大背景下，也要同步关注广东、长三角地区以及相关省会城市的发展情况。

2. 现状：难度、持续动态性及趋好

目前的对标体系由三个维度构成，数量维度、时间维度和主体维度。数量维度就是结合产业发展自身规律形成多个可量化描述的数据群；时间维度是指形成一定度量周期的数据积累使得数据在时间轴上可追溯、可比较；主体维度是指在掌握考察对象自身指标体系基础上，横向获得其他主体的数据指标。

产业测度及决策维度也在不断变化进阶，使得文化产业指标体系又呈现出持续动态的特点。"十三五"时期之前，相关研究更多聚焦于文化本体，但到了"十三五"后期，在注重文化本体的同时，促进文体旅融合发展成为重要方向。不仅要在此前文化相关指标基础上引入旅游、体育的指标元素，更关键地，还要设计体现融合的指标并进行相应的数据采集。这种变化，在此前研究和决策过程中都没有明确涉及。

模式的提升和技术的发展又使得数据获取相对容易。将庞杂的文化产业类目简单分成传统产业和新兴产业两类。一方面，以媒体业、艺术业、休闲娱乐业等为代表的传统文化产业，近年来也迎接新技术、拥抱互联网，从注重自我展示到强化供需互动，从大众传播到精准抵达，这样"专业化、信息化"的过程使得数据的获取成为可能。另一方面，网络文化服务业、信息技术服务业等新兴文化产业本身就是建立在技术与内容融合基础之上的业态样式，数据不再需要专门去收集，而是成为行为的一部分。

3. 实践：不求一统江山但求可用管用

传统官方的做法是制定《文化及相关产业分类》，每年定期编制《上海文化统计概览》，形成官方数据统计口径，积累历年数据。随着对大数据的应用和重视，更多非结构化的数据在政府决策中发挥着重要作用。比如说城市数据团及其数据运用。我们也研究了很多指标体系，其中比较有代表性的是"上海城市文化发展指数"，它从公共文化、文化产业、文化市场、文化创新、社会环境五个方面列举了 21 个数据的指标，通过平均加权方式后形成每年的过程数据和最终数值。另外一个指标体系来自《世界城市文化报告》，该报告由伦敦市长办公室于 2007 年发起，英国 BOP 文化创意产业研究机构与英国伦敦国王学院、全球城市研究机构共同承担研究。该指标有以下几个方面的特点：一是它的整个数据体系相对稳定，从文化

基础设施、文化产出、文化消费与公共参与四个方面进行分析，有比较完整的构建思路和逻辑；二是可横向比较，从 2008 年至今，参与城市从最初的 5 个扩展到 27 个，全球主要文化城市均在其中；三是数据的时间持续，间隔 2—3 年发布，数据量较为客观。"十三五"期间，我们基于《世界城市文化报告》的统计指数，选择并重构了若干指标，分成基础指标、特色指标和重点指标三类，形成了"十三五"期间上海基本建设成为国际文化大都市的指标体系。

4. 小结：引进、消化吸收、再创新

最后做一个小结。经过多年的工作我发现，"没有一个指标体系能够直接应用"不是个案，而是大多数对标研究中都会遇到的普遍问题。这个问题的出现也体现了问题自身的价值。那么从现实可行性的角度来讲，应该就是基于"拿来主义"的"引进—消化吸收—再创新"。在梳理、分析并尊重已有研究结果的基础上，根据自身的需要，一方面要加强对已有数据的分析利用，另一方面也要及时补充尚未出现但又实际需要的数据，同时还要关注关联性数据的使用，重视大数据对未知行为的揭示，最终来形成一个共性和个性兼顾的"对标体系"。

Art Resources and City Image

Wang Tingxin

Executive Vice-President of Institute of Art, Communication University of China

My topic is "Art Resources and City Image". I'm going to address five related aspects, namely, the definition, classification and characteristics of art resources, the definition of a city's image, the relationship between art resources and a city's image, difficulties and opportunities of art resources, and finally, how to revitalize art resources so as to promote a city's image.

1. Definition and classification of art resources: the tangible and the intangible

Generally speaking, art resources comprise artistic phenomena that have taken place or are taking place at the moment. They may include artists, artistic works, achievements in artistic researches, artistic events and related relics. Historic art resources are artistic phenomena having happened in an area or city, whereas ongoing artistic resources describe all the ongoing affairs related to art, such as what we find in Shanghai today. In general, art resource is a type of intelligence resource. It represents basic intelligent capacity of a country, a nation and a city, as well as a world view.

Art resources include both tangible art resources and intangible art resources. Tangible art resources are visible, such as celebrities, classics, cultural relics, and institutions. Intangible art resources, such as systems, policies, ideas and skills, are often invisible and form the basis of tangible art resources. Intangible art resources are the very reason we need to pass down an art form through word-of-mouth or in written form. Therefore, intangible art resources are the basis of the existing tangible art resources. I believe "people" stand at the core of all intangible art resources. The artistic wisdom or skills of people in any given era serves as the foundation of a city's or a region's art resources.

2. City image

There is no a clear definition of city image. It mainly refers to people's general impression of a city, which is usually affected by its geographic location, historical status, climate, environment, culture character, economic vitality, transportation and social influence. For example, Beijing has been called the "Imperial Capital" by being the capital and the political center of China for 800 years. Shanghai is called "Magic City" because magic can happen here. In addition, we also have cities that "Paradise above, Suzhou and Hangzhou below" and "Beauties live in regions south of the Yangtze River, and capitals lie in Nanjing". Therefore, city image is a general impression, and cannot be scientifically defined. In fact, it reflects people's overall perception of the character of a city based on its material and spiritual civilization and affects people's life and the city's development.

The image of a city determines how people perceive of its status and influence. It is one of the important factors in the development of a city. So how do we measure the value of a city's image?

First, the image of a city determines the density of its population. Why people like to travel, live and work in big cities like Beijing, Shanghai, Guangzhou and Shenzhen? Because a city can draw people and make them believe that they can have better lives and jobs, or enjoy beautiful sceneries in these cities.

Second, the image of a city determines the concentration of capital. A society relies on its people for development, and the elite are no doubt the most important group of people to lead a city. When the elite move to Shanghai and Beijing, they will naturally bring their money with them.

Third, the image of a city determines the amount of creativity. Creativity is also closely related to people. I once coined a phrase, "Art Going with People", which means that art goes hand in hand with people. Art is intangible. Although art is presented through writings, paintings or songs, it is essentially an intangible asset and relies on people's creation. Art goes hand in hand with people. The stories, works and artistic events of artists in the history were well-recorded wherever they go. The creativity of these artists plays an important role in shaping a city's image.

3. Art resources as a foundation for the city image construction

The image of a city impinges on a variety of factors. Art resources are just one, albeit an important one, to measure a city's image. I think art resources are a special cultural property of a city. Why so many art performances and artists choose to settle in Shanghai? As a port city, Shanghai would not be what it is without the influence of modern western capital and culture. Shanghai possesses the cultural capital that we see today simply because it has a history that cannot be repeated by other cities. Therefore, art resources are unique because they appeal to our senses about the wisdom and spirit of a city. The value of art resources in a city is reflected in the following ways:

First, the number and types of artists a city has determine the diversity of its character. Every artist is unique and has different artistic personalities. If a city can attract numerous artists and various arts, it is bound to have a rich personality.

Second, the uniqueness of art determines a city's image. A city may have many kinds of art, but it must have one that is the most prominent. For example, people call Jingdezhen City "City of Porcelain" and Yixing "City of Pottery". Harbin is called "City of Music" because it has produced so many musicologists, performing artists, singers and performers in the history. Even today Harbin has continued to host so many successful music festivals.

Third, the abundance of artistic relics a city has affects its development potential.

Fourth, the number of artistic events a city has adds layers to its structure. For example, it is in Shanghai and Beijing that Lu Xun entered debates with others. And it is in Yangzhou that the Eight Eccentric Artists created many valuable paintings. These art events are well-recorded in the art history.

Fifth, the number of art institutions a city has reflects its vitality in development. Small cities tend to have simple art institutions, for example, they only have the cultural affairs bureaus and cultural centers. But in big cities or cities with multiple art resources, the concentration of art institutions means that they will penetrate every possible corner and they will interact with each other to generate more vitality and creativity.

Sixth, the flexibility of the artistic systems of a city adds richness to a city's smartness.

4. Difficulties and opportunities faced by art resources

How shall we perceive of China's art resources, given its five-thousand-year history? In fact, art resources are faced with many difficulties. Often people are not made aware of their utilization, development, and protection, particularly on the front of protection. Sometimes, there is little investment for the protection, or we focus on the protection alone and ignore the utilization and development. Sometimes, people over-exploit art resources without any protection.

Corresponding these challenges, art resources also face a lot of opportunities. I would like to point out four types of opportunities:

First, China attaches great importance to the development of culture. In the first three decades since the reform and opening up, although there was talk on the importance of culture, it was not until the Sixth Plenary Session of the Seventeenth Central Committee of the Communist Party of China that the biggest importance was attached to cultural construction. The Session also marks the first time that cultural issues were given priority in the plenary session. Since the 18th National Congress of the Communist Party of China, the importance China attaches to cultural development and the amount of reflection on the national level has gone far beyond our expectation. The guidelines issued by the General Office of the Central Committee of the Communist Party of China and by various ministries and commissions indicate that national cultural policies are favoring the development of culture. In fact, there have never be so many favorable cultural policies in the first 30 years since the reform and opening up.

Second, artistic talents are now cultivated on a large scale in multiple ways. China now has over 2 800 universities and colleges. More than 90 percent of them have set up art departments or majors. This is not a figure to be underestimated. Art used to be a small major, but today it is one of the largest majors in China and enrolls the biggest number of students. Since the late 1990s, we have cultivated a large number of artistic talents. They support the art development and are also important art resources.

Third, there has never been a time that offers so many technologies for art development. Smart phones, computers and the Internet have given rise to new forms of art. Without these technologies, art could never have been so popular. Social media was originally used for social communication, but now a large number of art works and artists can be accessed via social media. It has become key to the spread of art.

Fourth, people's demand for art is on the increase. This change is closely related to the improvement of people's living standards.

5. Examples on city images related to art resources

First, the United Nations Educational, Scientific and Cultural Organization (UNESCO) has named some of China's cities based on their art resources. For example, Beijing, Shanghai, Shenzhen and Wuhan are all named "City of Design"; Nanjing, "City of Literature"; Suzhou, Hangzhou and Jingdezhen City, "City of Handicraft and Folk Art"; Harbin, "City of Music"; Qingdao, "City of Film", and Changsha, "City of Media Art". These names reflect UN's impressions of China. Second, a city can also name itself based on the position it intends to project. For example, Beijing wants to be

"City of Performing Arts in the Orient", Shanghai, "City of Performing Arts in Asia", and Hangzhou wants to become the "City of Performing Arts in China". Third, the ordinary people can also give names to a city based on their general impressions. For example, thanks to the concentration of artistic resources in Beijing and Shanghai, people call these two cities "City of Film", "City of Drama", "City of Fine Arts" and "City of Music".

Table 1
Examples of city images related to art resources

City	Name	Self-positioning	Public Impression
Beijing	City of Design (UN 2012)	City of Performing Arts in the Orient	City of Film, City of Drama, City of Fine Arts, City of Music
Shanghai	City of Design (UN 2010)	City of Performing Arts in Asia	City of Film, City of Drama, City of Fine Arts, City of Music
Shenzhen	City of Design (UN 2008)		
Wuhan	City of Design (UN 2017)		
Nanjing	City of Literature (UN 2017)		
Hangzhou	City of Handicraft and Folk Art (UN 2012)	City of Performing Arts in China	
Suzhou	City of Handicraft and Folk Art (UN 2014)		
Harbin	City of Music (UN 2010)		
Qingdao	City of Film (UN 2017)		
Changsha	City of Media Art (UN 2017)		
Jingdezhen City	City of Handicraft and Folk Art (UN 2014)		City of Porcelain

6. Revitalizing art resources and improving a city's image

How can we position a city's image? It can be defined at the official, the institutions and the public levels. On the whole, the key to improving and establishing an excellent city image is to revitalize art resources.

First, we should attach importance to the synergy, and in particular the symbiotic relationship between art and politics, economy, culture, science and technology and education. This relationship will eventually support the national economy and society development. We used to believe that the economy is not related to art, but now the art industry forms as sizable part of the cultural industry and has made considerable contributions to the GDP. This kind of symbiosis is worth investigation both in theory and in practice.

Second, to build a good image, a city should also establish a good system that encompass policy, production, assessment, communication and education fronts. With these well-functioning systems, we can build up a better city image. Take the communication as an example. We all know that Beijing Opera is a quintessential Chinese culture. Starting from the late Qing Dynasty all the way to the founding of the People's Republic of China, many famous Beijing Opera actors from Beijing and Tianjin were not considered influential nationwide until they performed in Shanghai. As the first city in China to be exposed to the Western cultural systems, Shanghai is known for its media, newspapers, theaters, businessmen, and great demand for art from the public, which gives the city a well-functioning communication system. That is why famous Beijing Opera actors such as Mei Lanfang regularly performed in Shanghai. This is how the city image is influenced by the artistic system.

Third, we should value, respect and give talented people a place to make a difference. Fourth, we should pay attention to the links of art resources and take care of the relationship between the preservation, protection, inheritance and development of art resources. Fifth, the positioning of art resources is also a factor to consider. Each city must try to be distinctive to make an impression.

Urban Cultural Image and the Design of Behavior Spaces

Fan Shengxi

CPC Committee Secretary, College of Design and Innovation, Tongji University

Every time I give a lecture, I quote Zhuangzi's saying first: a path is made by people walking on it; things are so by their being named. The first sentence talks about behavior, while the second is about cognition. A quote from Lu Xun conveys the similar idea that, originally, there is nothing, but as people walk this way again and again, a path appears. Those who step on the grass are often criticized, for their behavior may lead to trampled grass. But from my point of view, the formed path can be justified, for human behaviors are shaped by the "law of economy".

1. The behavior spaces of human

I carry out design projects in cities and focus on people's reactions. This is a picture of Shanghai

Fig. 1

Shanghai in 2020, an empty space in COVID-19 lockdown

I took during the COVID-19 pandemic. The city became a frozen space where the lights were still shining, but no one was there. Thus, a city is full of vitality only when there are people in it. The space people live in is a space of experience and behavior, not just a physical or geographical space.

From the perspective of "affordance", or functional visibility, what determines our behavior is not the physical world, but the perceptual practice. The environment we feel is created by ourselves. For example, there is a lake in my hometown. We used to boat on the lake and swim there in summer, while in winter it became an ice rink. It's people's behavior that changes the lake. So, a behavior space and a physical space are two different concepts. I always take the National Convention and Exhibition Center (NCEC) in Shanghai as a typical example. NCEC is very beautiful and symmetrical outside, but people easily get lost inside. If you go in the wrong direction at one fork, you may need 30—45 minutes to find your way back. The design of NCEC doesn't take into consideration people's behavior but blindly pursues the external "shape".

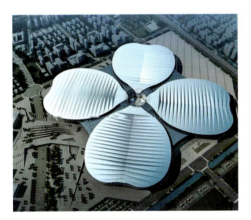 

Fig. 2
The exterior and interior of Shanghai National Convention and Exhibition Center

Consider this question. How come a simple pair of scissors win an international award? In fact, there is only a slight change: the handle of the scissors is designed in a "bow" shape, which perfectly matches the movement of your hand when using scissors. Here is another example. Many university campuses pave their roads with stones, but pedestrians rarely choose to walk there. Because the spacing of stones is awkward, being either too long or too short for one step. Another example is the benches in the park. We take it for granted that the more people sit on it, the better. But people's behaviors are related to their cultural and psychological preferences, and everyone has different needs for personal space. A bench with horizontal-stripes tricks people into sitting on it, thinking that there is boundary or room for privacy. So, a chair for three may only accommodate two people. But when people sit on a bench with vertical stripes, they feel at ease even when they are sitting close to each

other. This is because the human behavior in this context is justified by the design of the bench.

2. The relationship between human behavior and city image

The concept of "context" or "the right place" is very important. If you put the same kind of benches on the campus, it would easily break down. It's not that the benches are poorly designed, but the benches are in the wrong place. People have different needs, so they use benches for different purposes. Benches are moved around and sometimes damaged. Therefore, human behaviors need to be taken into consideration when deciding where to put the benches. The functional relationship between people and environment is B=F (P, E). B represents behavior, P represents internal psychological factors of individuals, and E represents the influence of both the physical and the social environment. This is a picture (Fig. 4) taken many years ago of a bench near Tian'anmen Square in Beijing. People use the same bench for different purposes which are affected by different individual psychological factors and the different types of relationships they have with those who sit with them. So, a city is like a stage where everyone is an actor.

When I was in Milan, what impressed me most was how often I saw ladies sitting somewhere and posing as if they were being photographed, even when no one was around. Everyone there seems to see the city as a stage where he or she is a high-spirited actor or actress. In Northern Europe, locals used to queue as far apart from each other as possible even on a cold day, instead of standing close to each other. When people are waiting to cross streets, this "queue etiquette" changes among

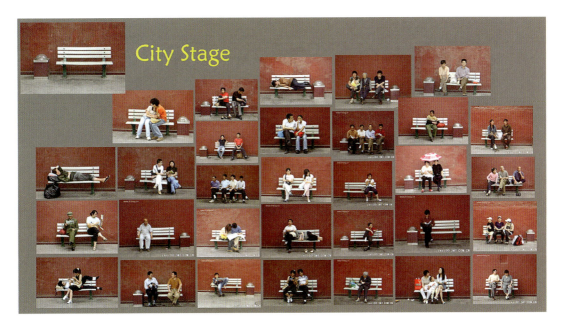

Fig. 4
City stage

different races and in different time periods, which reflects different cultural psychology of different nations. What we refer to as the national character is sometimes a general behavior pattern of people in a region, country or nation. Take the Spanish Steps in Rome, for example. The Spanish Steps is one of the landmarks of Rome. I enjoy seeing people sitting on it. However, since 2019, Rome has implemented a "No Sitting Law", prohibiting pedestrians from sitting on the Spanish Steps. Violators will be fined. The Roman government issued this ban to maintain the order of the scenic spot. But the beauty of the Spanish Steps actually lies in people sitting on the steps, rather than the steps themselves. Another example is Songjiang Thames Town, which is familiar to Shanghai people. When Thames Town was completed and open to the public, I went there and stayed in a hotel for a night, trying to learn about the life there. But when I got up in the morning, I didn't smell coffee and toast, which matched the town's image. Instead, people still ate steamed buns and soybean milk for breakfast, and did square dancing. So, people will not change just because the surrounding environment has been changed. Now we find that cities everywhere in the world are very similar in design, but people who live in those cities have different lifestyles. The architecture of Nianhua Bay in Wuxi, which is considered to be one of the best among towns with distinctive features, is very much like that of the village of Shirakawa-go in Gifu, Japan. In the Nianhua Bay in Wuxi, the expensive grasses on the roof gradually fell off, because they were, after all, natural things. As time goes by, it is no longer what it was before. The difference between Nianhua Bay and Shirakawa-go Village lies in that the best scenery in Shirakawa-go Village is not traditional craftsmanship or the culture, but the concept of community with a shared destiny. Every year, the whole village comes together to trim grasses on the roof, which becomes a grand festival, and the interaction among people is the most beautiful scenery.

A city is also a community. If there is no life style but a mere copy of the form, there will be a problem. Aesthetics is all about life. Without paying attention to life, the construction of big international cities will eventually lead to homogenization. Traditional Chinese culture is rooted in the countryside. Then, how can we tell the story of the countryside in the urban context? How can we build the image of Shanghai's "three major cultures", namely red culture, Jiangnan culture and Shanghai-style culture? From the perspective of design, the two pairs concepts — inheritance and innovation, the nation and the world, seem to contradict with each other. Inheritance values the context of life while innovation calls for innovative designs; the nation speaks for convergence, while the world embodies diversity and divergence; the first concept of each pair stands for the pursuit of

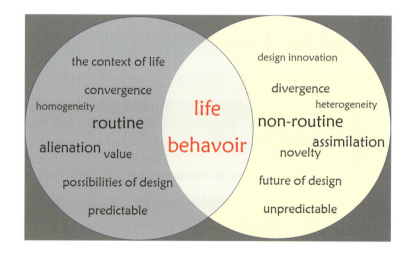

Fig. 5
Life behavior:
homogeneous
alienation and
heterogeneous
assimilation

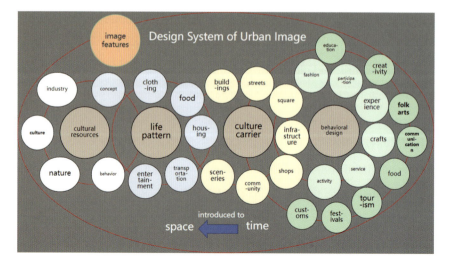

Fig. 6
Image system
design

提升社区和城市品质

value, while the other one is the pursuit of novelty. To put it simply, it is the relationship between what is reasonable and what is unexpected, so there is the problem of how to alienate homogeneity and how to assimilate heterogeneity. I refer to the intersection of these two relations as "life behavior". I put forward the concept of "urban image system design", to locate the connection between cultural resources and lifestyle. Based on a cultural entity, we can implement it from behavior design to a person's life behavior. Then the system could become operational. The well-established system will be vibrant, sustainable and diverse.

I'd like to talk about the "five senses". The image of a city must be vivid, just like a piece of burning wood. We can feel its heat, see the color of the flame, hear the sound, and smell it. It is a synaesthesia. An urban cultural image shaped by "synesthesia" will make a vivid impression on people. I am writing a book proposing that "to design is to reshape life". Life is the starting point and the ultimate goal of design, and a city's cultural image is a mirror of life.

Cultural Scenes and Urban Development

Chen Bo

Executive Vice Dean, National Institute of Cultural Development of Wuhan University

My presentation will be divided into two parts: one is about the urban development process and its problems; the other is how the cultural scene promotes urban development, including the dimension design and related evaluation.

1. The process and problems of urban development

Let me begin with the urban development process. It is generally believed that there is no such concept as a city for most of human history. The history of urban development has been so short as to be negligible compared with that of human beings. But it is the emergence of cities that accelerates social development ever after. The original purpose of establishing a city was to preserve human civilization, or to use as few resources as possible to gain maximum advantage. As the Chinese architect and urban planner, Wu Liangyong said, "Our ancestors' migration from the vast wilderness to urban areas could be one of the greatest advances of human society. Human beings went from being primitive to being barbaric and finally to being civilized, which makes urban civilization an epoch-making landmark in human history."

Culture can be interpreted as the relationship between humans and nature. Scientists found that primitive men had lived in caves or wooden shelters for a long time without substantial changes. The enduring practice was highly cost-consuming, since it involved plant collection and animal hunting for food while defending against beasts. Moreover, unexpected incidents and other external factors promoted the unity of families. For example, isolated households were more likely to suffer from attacks at night, while adjacent households benefited from staying together. That explains why neighbors began to gather and unite, thus forming the prototype of a primitive city. As urban centers grew, traditional plant collecting and hunting grounds emerged and overlapped, resulting in the issue of "boundaries". Here, "boundary" means the boundary of a physical space. A cultural space is made up of a physical space and a spiritual space. The spatial perception is a fundamental and essential resource to maintain a nation's reproduction. The emerging problems in the physical space and the increasing ability of today's functional cities to pool resources, are the results of the efforts to ensure the successful reproduction of all individuals in the selected resource area. As a symbol of civilization, the division of production in cities has been ever more specialized, which is an indicator of urban development.

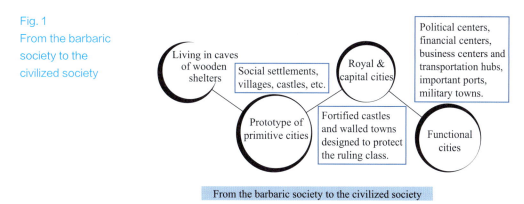

Fig. 1
From the barbaric society to the civilized society

From the barbaric society to the civilized society

As Fig. 1 shows, the prototype of primitive cities were clustered settlements, villages, castles and so forth. The royal or capital cities were fortified castles and walled towns designed to protect the ruling class. Functional cities mainly included political centers, financial centers, business centers, transportation hubs, important ports, and military towns.

The soundest function of a city has always been to gather various kinds of resources, such as talents, technologies, funds and information in a more efficient and intensive manner. This advantage shapes a city into the political, economic or cultural center of a country or a region. A city is a kind of man-made environment, and human beings will continue to keep the urban construction in line with social progress and economic growth to achieve sustainable development.

However, urban development now faces a range of challenges, such as overcrowding, poverty, social division, pollution, housing shortage, crime, traffic congestion, educational inequality, unemployment, and overloaded public facilities. To tackle these challenges, the concept of "cultural governance" was initiated. Western countries began to integrate culture into a selected area of a city. Individuals in the area, together with their surrounding natural space, physical space and spiritual space, constitute a cultural space which will grow into a complete spatial integration. This spatial structure is so complete and stable as to sustain people's daily life even when something goes out of function in the area. In this case, the concept of integrating culture into urban development was proposed.

2. The influences of cultural scene on urban development

(1) Culturally-supported urban scenes.

An urban scene is both the foundation and the result of urban development. Each city has a distinctive urban scene thanks to its unique culture. An urban scene, as the most perceptible physical space, directly contributes to individual cognition and perception. Individuals transform the physical stimuli of a city into specific signals to develop in them an understanding of the city. This understanding, after interacting with their background knowledge, grows into specific symbols of the city i.e., the urban scene.

The measurement of the urban scene is a challenge not only for China but also for the West. To this end, the Chicago school of sociology from the University of Chicago has assembled an international team to conduct a long-term study on how to deconstruct the urban scene. Specifically, they have been looking into what dimensions the urban scene consists of, how to measure those dimensions, how to calculate multi-combinations and how to turn them into something measurable. Our research team at Wuhan University participated in part of the research. At last, the research findings were published in a book entitled Scenescapes: How Qualities of Place Shape Social Life. Urban development models evolved from the traditional model, to the human capital model, to the social capital model, to the creative class model, and to the scene model that western scholars now generally support. The scene model emphasizes the importance of cultural scenes and highlights citizens' participation in arts and cultural activities as the driving force behind the progress of the whole city. The innovation vitality of the whole region is stimulated through core factors such as cultural capital, residential community and convenience facilities, which leads to cultural innovation.

The Theory of Scenes is a new paradigm of urban research proposed by a team led by Terry Nichols Clark, a tenured professor at the University of Chicago. Based on the study of some international metropolises, his research team found that urban recreational facilities and various civic organizations would together form different urban "scenes" that construct specific cultural value orientations, which appeal to different groups to conduct cultural practices and further promote the social and economic developments of the region.

As the result of many discussions based on the Theory of Scenes, the concept of "Cultural Amenities" has been widely recognized by Chinese scholars. Cultural amenities greatly extend the scope of cultural facilities that previously covered only the systematic design of public welfare and

Table 1
Evolution of urban development models

Development Models	Main Content	Core Elements	Phases of Production
Traditional Model	Driven by company: with increasing factories creating more employment and revenue, and attracting and gathering people	Land, capital, labour and management etc.	The industrial age
Human Capital Model	Driven by education or learning: labour supply through education, training and healthcare	Human capital: the quantity and quality of human resources	The shift from the industrial to post-industrial age
Social Capital Model	Driven by social organization: more participatory and autonomous traditions	Social capital: social trust, civic engagement network and norms of reciprocity	The shift from the industrial to post-industrial age
Creative Class Model	Driven by creative class: 3T theory, i.e. Technology, Talent and Tolerance	Creative capital: creativity and innovation are not privileged to professionals, and mass innovation is encouraged	The post-industrial age
Scene Model	Driven by cultural scene: the role of citizens' participation in arts and culture for urban development	The cultural capital: the residential community, the amenities, the scenes of diverse group gatherings, and the values, lifestyles and quality of life reflected in the scenes	The post-industrial age (A new era)

non-public cultural facilities in China. Cultural amenities include not only facilities such as bars, bookstores, hospitals and post offices, but also the density, layout and architecture of cultural output. All these have a profound effect on the individual's perception.

The Theory of Scenes mainly involves physical structures and subjective perception. The physical structures refer to the urban facilities, i.e., the dimension of physical spaces. Subjective perception refers to the spiritual space and its cultural values including authenticity, theatricality and legitimacy.

On top of that, the mechanism space should be added. The spatial structure in which all individuals live, is not strictly divided into a physical and a spiritual one, between which there must be a specific internal correlation. The correlation is temporarily called the mechanism space. How to deconstruct this mechanism and to set its dimensions are still being investigated by us and many other scholars.

The subjective perception system of the scene theory includes 3 dimensions and 15 sub-dimensions, which are set based on consumers' potential emotional experience stimulated by surrounding facilities and environments. These 15 sub-dimensions can be used to measure the value orientations of a consumer entertainment facility, such as the relative conservativeness of a church, the openness of a bar, and the utility of a library or a museum. But the measurement of a scene's value orientations requires a quantitative analysis of various living and entertainment facilities in comprehensive scenes. The Theory of Scenes examines urban development from a new perspective — taking into account the cultural value orientations embedded in urban living and entertainment facilities. It also helps to construct an analytical framework in measuring the cultural values of scenes.

Table 2
Values of scenes

Dimension	Sub-dimensions	Dimension	Sub-dimensions	Dimension	Sub-dimensions
	Rational		Amiable		Conventionalism
	Local		Formal		Self-expression
Authenticity	National	Theatricality	Exhibited	Legitimacy	Pragmatism
	Cooperative		Fashion		Charisma
	Minorities		Provocative		Egalitarianism

The translation of the book into Chinese and the theory-to-practice initiative welcomed by a group of cities in China have advanced the research on related subjects. The theory has been put into practice by first-tier cities such as Shenzhen. The Chengdu municipal government plans to do the same.

Chinese scholars are adding to the Theory what they have learned from the changes of China's cultural policies. For example, Wu Di (2013) proposed the theory-based measurement of buildings' utility systems; Wu Jun (2017) proposed to view space as a container of various cultural consumption behaviors. The Theory aims to transform the metaphysical expressions and academic phrases in previous studies on urban development into descriptions of scenes that can be well understood by ordinary people and easily turned into policies which can then implemented to boost the economic growth and social development of cities. From my perspective, a cultural scene is actually constituted by specific cultural spaces which are structured by physical, spiritual and mechanism spaces. The Theory of Cultural Spaces is created on the basis of the Theory of Scenes and aims to combine the latter with China's national setting. China has been working on the practices of cultural scene theory these years. The Theory of Cultural Spaces enriches findings on the infrastructure system of cultural spaces, such as the architecture of cultural heritages.

(2) Culturally-supported urban public spaces.

A physical space is a good place for citizens to participate in public cultural life, while a spiritual space allows them to seek psychological comfort and emotional security. The acceleration of urbanization, however, brings challenges to the existing spatial system and calls for more attention to the construction of a new cultural space. The cultural space is frequently mentioned for its defining role in individuals' emotional states, be it happiness or anger, sadness or joy. Chinese feudal society went through repeated dynasty changes from the Tang Dynasty, the Song Dynasty, the Yuan Dynasty, the Ming Dynasty to the Qing Dynasty, but the cultural spaces were basically preserved. This explains why psychological tendencies or basic values of people in these dynasties were relatively stable. Modern urbanization, however, triggered dramatic changes to the original cultural space system that is based on the structure of traditional culture. Yet the new cultural space system has not been well in place. As a result, individuals have a strong sense of space loss, anxiety and insecurity. The construction of a new cultural space through cultural industries with regional features will significantly promote individuals' emotional stability and a harmonious society, while the industries can be quite profitable.

(3) Culturally-boosted urban development.

The characteristics and core elements of a city's culture lie in its credibility and overall quality. Cultural scenes present the values and customs of a city as they are, and inspire the cohesion and confidence of the whole city. The charms and attraction of a city are largely defined by its culture, from which urban development and underlying beauty derive.

(4) Models of cultural scenes.

Cultural scene models include a model of implanting cultural symbols, a model of design-and-life integration, a model of revitalizing industrial districts, a model of urban operation, a model of developing historical cities, a model of developing culture and leisure blocks, and a model of culture-and-regional integration.

The first is the model of implanting cultural symbols, which features the implantation of cultural symbols into a region. Guizhou, Shandong and provinces alike always remind people of their rich tourism resources, but they are in lack of cultural symbols which tourists have no idea of even if they spend 3—5 days there. Although the model of developing historical cities is now popular in replicating a physical space and creating a vintage atmosphere, the implantation of cultural symbols outweighs the building of physical spaces.

The second is the model of design-and-life integration, which calls for the full engagement of individuals in their lives in a comfortable, peaceful and harmonious manner. Imagine that you are eager for a quiet place to enjoy a cup of coffee and have a refresh after working overtime till late at night. If the city you are living in provides you with many cultural spaces to satisfy those needs, you will be impressed by the city's hospitality and the attentiveness to its residents' daily life.

The third is the model of revitalizing industrial districts, which aims to bring cultural spaces back to life. An individual may be forced to suppress his or her original aspiration due to all kinds of pressure from external spaces, for example, work pressure. Cultural spaces can remind people of their original aspirations. For example, a visit to a place may stimulate the imagination of what life was like in the past, warm people's hearts and remind them of the original aspirations. This is the charm of cultural spaces.

The fourth is the model of urban operation and Qujiang in Xi'an is a good case in point. This model aims to promote the transformation of urban development through the internal impetus mechanism. The fifth is the model of developing historical cities. The development of Kaifeng, the ancient capital of the Song Dynasty, serves as a good example. The sixth is the model of developing cultural and leisure blocks. Cultural and leisure blocks in Chengdu is a case in point. The seventh is the model of culture-and-regional integration, of which various towns with distinctive local features are good examples.

(5) The cultural industry paradox in the process of urban revival.

In view of the current development of China's cultural industries, the life-cycle of cultural industry parks is shorter than those of other countries. This can be attributed to artists' habitual settle-down in old districts of cities. However shabby a district is, the arrival of artists turns it into a cultural space. The problem is that the cultural space will later be affected by petty bourgeoisie and gentrification, which will result in the dominance of capital. The emergence of commercial demands will immediately lead to deindustrialization and finally mediocritization, homogenization and loss of authenticity. Consequently, this cultural space will become commercial real estate.

(6) The space creation model: a SOHO case.

The retained physical spaces evolve according to individuals' memories as time goes by

Fig. 2
The cultural industry paradox in the process of urban revival

Old City Districts	Petty Bourgeoisie	Gentrification	Dominance of Capital	Commercialization
Good Location Convenient Transportation Low Rent	Entry of Creative and Cultural Industries	Rising Land Price	Commercial Demands	Deindustrialization	Mediocritization Homogenization Loss of Authenticity

resulting in impressive symbols and a powerful space awakening mechanism. SOHO was once the most concentrated area of factories and warehouses in New York in the 19th century. The middle of the 20th century witnessed the United States being the first country entering the post-industrial era when old factories were closed, business was slow and warehouses sat unused. A new generation of American artists rose up and flocked to the low-rent SOHO, where discerning art dealers set up galleries, and many established art galleries previously located in the upscale uptown also moved in. Among the first batch of residents in SOHO were influential figures in the modern art history, such as Warhol, Lichstein, Rauschenberg, and Johns. At the turn of the 1960s and 1970s, the mayor of New York City made the visionary decision of great cultural significance — preserving SOHO's old architectural landscape and passing laws recognizing SOHO as a cultural arts district by the Federal Government.

The development of the new era prioritizes people's pursuit for a better life, for which the existence of cultural spaces is an important representation and guarantee. This view was supported by one of my articles entitled "'Sense of Acquisition of Cultural Spaces' and Its Direction of Development", which was published in the People's Forum in June 2020. Culture is the soul of a city, supporting the city's spiritual spaces. A combination of the spiritual and physical spaces results in "urban scenes", which serve as public spaces attending to urban residents' cultural needs and the driving force for urban development. Cultural scenes are part of a city's basic spatial system. Cultural spaces represent one of the basic necessities for urban residents. Culture can both change a city and make a city attractive.

Seizing the Development Opportunity of "Digital Cultural Tourism" to Promote the Integrated Development of Cultural Tourism in the Yangtze River Delta

Feng Xuegang

Dean, Business School, East China Normal University

1. Research background

On September 21, 2020, General Office of the State Council issued "Opinions of the General Office of the State Council on Accelerating the Development of New Types of Consumption Driven by New Business Forms and Patterns". According to it, the Ministry of Culture and Tourism should further implement the work deployed by CPC Central Committee and the State Council. First, the Ministry will speed up the digitization of culture and tourism resources; second, the Ministry will promote the actions of "migrating to cloud, using digital tools and enabling intelligence" in the culture industry and the tourism industry; third, the Ministry will give full play to the empowerment and efficiency of Internet platforms; fourth, the Ministry will build the industrial ecology of digital cultural-tourism.

In December 2019, it was explicitly put forward in the "Outline of the Integrated Regional Development of the Yangtze River Delta" that in the Yangtze River Delta, we should promote the integration of culture and tourism, deepen cooperation in the tourism industry, consolidate tourism resources, boost the integrated development of the tourism market and service, and thus build world-famous tourist destinations. Yangtze River Delta is expected and required to be developed with three characteristics: "Integration", "integrated development" and "high quality".

With the steady progress of the integrated development of cultural tourism in the Yangtze River Delta, the region is rich in its cultural tourism products, recognized as the leading player in innovation, known for its highly-dynamic and highly-developed cultural tourism markets, and has benefited from well-developed policies; innovation policies are constantly introduced and take positive effect. At the same time, however, there are some tough problems in the integrated development of cultural tourism in this region, such as insufficient integration and utilization of resources, insufficient innovation curation capacity, problems in product landing, and mutual constraints of common projects, which leads to the failing of creating a new consumer market. The integration starts from the building of cooperation mechanisms and the forming of a large number of alliances, but there is insufficient cooperation that yields no results because the specific contents of cooperation are not carefully deliberated. Therefore, the integrated development of cultural tourism in the Yangtze River Delta must strengthen the driving force of innovation, tap the market potential, and make it possible for digitalization to boost the development of the whole industry.

Today, I would like share with you my idea regarding the following four aspects: the first is the digitalization of cultural tourism resources; the second is the promotion of the new business forms of online cultural tourism; the third is the expansion of new cultural tourism platforms; the fourth is the full integration of cultural tourism in the Yangtze River Delta.

2. The digitalization of cultural tourism resources

(1) The development of culture and museum resources in the Yangtze River Delta.

The Yangtze River Delta is rich in cultural tourism resources, and its cultural relics collections account for more than 10% of all such collections in China, but compared with the development of the Palace Museum and Dunhuang Museum in recent years, museums in the Yangtze River Delta have failed to show its outstanding advantages in terms of resources revitalization, creativity and market operation. There are four main reasons. First, local culture departments lack the understanding of the activation of cultural and museum resources and cultural innovation. Second, there are some problems in the operation of cultural organizations, such as insufficient market operation experience and deficient internal control mechanism, which inevitably lead to disputes and mistakes related to market authorization. Third, the application period of culture projects is too long, and there is a time lag effect because of the frequent update of technology and the changing consumer-oriented market. Fourth, cultural organizations are suffering from talent shortages, which makes it difficult to effectively apply Internet technologies, operate new virtual reality equipment and manage smart facilities.

(2) Strengthening technical support by applying shared key technologies.

The application of intelligent technology, production technology, distribution technology, service technology and management technology should be strengthened. On August 13, 2019, in order to promote the deep integration of culture and science and technology and comprehensively enhance the innovation ability of culture and science and technology, six ministries jointly formulated and released the "Guiding Opinions on Promoting the Deep Integration of Culture and Science and Technology", pointing out that the potential of science and technology in supporting culture building has not been fully released, and the understanding of the importance and urgency of the integration of culture and science and technology needs to be further improved. At present, teenagers still have a strong dependence on the virtual space where they are exposed to different cultures. The United States has a leading advantage in building cultural spaces, and has formed a relatively mature business model for running virtual museums.

(3) Developing resources by encouraging activation and innovation.

For a long time, the primary function of institutions such as museums and theatres is to carry out the protection, management and scientific research of cultural relics. On the basis of the established attributes, the market logic and consumer orientation of public institutions have been indeed faced with various problems. From the perspective of the current development status of the Yangtze River Delta, the recent cultural activities of the Shanghai Cultural Expo and Shanghai Book Fair are oriented towards the consumer end, but there is a significant mismatch between the planning ideas of cultural activities and the market demand. To revitalize resources and realize the sound development of cultural resources, it is urgent to open and develop cultural and creative resources to the outside world, enable Internet enterprises to have access to these resources, thoroughly renovate the operation mechanism and mode of cultural resources, and build a platform of cultural innovation for the alliance of museums in the Yangtze River Delta. Taking the Palace Museum as an example, based on its rich cultural and creative resources, the Palace Museum has become a successful producer of intellectual property for cultural and creative products, and a sound market competition mechanism has been established.

3. The promotion of new business forms of online cultural tourism

Recently, Shanghai has just issued "Online New Cultural Tourism Development Action Plan (2020—2022)", which proposes to expand the value chain of smart and interconnected cultural tourism, cultivate a platform service chain for cultural tourism circulation, promote the iterative and updated scientific research and development chain, and build an across-border integrated industrial chain.

(1) A brand-new field of online new cultural tourism.

The online cultural tourism industry has experienced three stages of development: launching online platforms of cultural tourism; promoting cultural tourism through online marketing; developing new online forms of cultural tourism. Affected by the COVID-19, China's online cultural tourism industry has rapidly advanced to the third stage. In the first stage, online platforms of cultural tourism are set up to display tourism information and provide the online booking service; in the second stage, online platforms are used for online marketing and customer experience improvement; in the third stage, virtual reality technologies are applied in cultural tourism scenes and real-time and dynamic cultural tourism service information can be acquired through human-machine interaction.

(2) An ecosystem of the live streaming economy in cultural tourism.

Relying on the live streaming technology, the mode of "cultural tourism plus live streaming e-commerce" has become an innovative business mode adopted by the entire cultural tourism industry. Not only Online travel agencies, but also offline cultural venues, tourist attractions, physical stores are developing their online businesses and accumulating online assets. An ecosystem of the live streaming economy in cultural tourism has taken initial shape. As mentioned before, the Ministry of Culture and Tourism will promote the actions of "migrating to cloud, using digital tools and enabling intelligence" in the culture industry and the tourism industry, To this end, the Ministry will further develop this ecosystem of the live streaming economy, encourage qualified enterprises to develop live streaming e-commerce sales channels and cooperate with enterprises specialized in providing live streaming platforms to build their own live streaming platforms, establish cultural tourism MCN organizations, and incubate live streaming e-commerce influencers in cultural tourism etc. For example, Shanghai Ctrip, a major online travel agency in China, has established a MCN organization that combines different channels to conduct live streaming e-commerce that generates high profits. Lvmama, another well-known OTA in China, has developed a new App called "Lvke strict selection", which has become the designated live streaming platform for the implementation of the "live streaming e-commerce plans" of many local governments in China.

Fig. 1
Index of the transaction size of China's online tourism providers in 2019

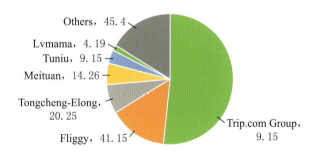

(3) Online virtual reality experience of cultural tourism.

Internet portals, mobile platforms, WeChat small programs have made it possible for more and more people to "travel online", which is mostly supported by the government. The online new cultural tourism in China consists of three parts. First, live streaming programs, mainly live entertainment programs; second, cultural tourism learning programs; third, live commerce targeting tourist attractions, which combines live streaming programs and online sales of flight and hotel packages and local specialties. The profit model of online travel in foreign countries is different from that in China. In some foreign countries, online virtual reality experience of travel is adopted to present consumers with various virtual products including those related to arts, culture, culinary and sports of the tourist sites. Take Amazon Explore as an example, it is a new platform unveiled by Amazon during the COVID-19 pandemic. The videoconferencing service of the platform enables tourist guides, lecturers and consumers to communicate with each other. The platform also provides not only interactive live-streaming services where customers can book live, virtual experiences led by local experts all over the world, but also various virtual experiences focused on DIY skills, virtual tours to cultural landmarks, etc.

(4) Offline virtual reality experience.

The application of virtual reality technology can help cultural tourism continue to innovate in terms of contents and modes to optimize its industrial structure. In China, VR technology and its application, provided mainly by technology companies, is adopted in tourist attractions, museums, theaters, etc., to enrich and improve the tourist experience. In foreign countries, many independent offline store projects aiming to improve customer experience have been created. For example, airlines have launched VR air travel service, enabling passengers to take virtual flights to world-famous tourist attractions such as the Colosseum in ancient Rome, Times Square in New York and Fiordland National Park in New Zealand without leaving their home country. For example, First Airlines, a Japanese airline company with "the world's first virtual aviation equipment", offers customers a virtual experience as if they were taking a real trip on a plane. The company is dedicated to providing customers with immersive and realistic flight experience. After purchasing a virtual ticket, passengers can get the whole package of air travel experience such as getting boarding passes, waiting for boarding and having flight attendants at their service. Fly View is a technology company that offers customers a virtual Paris travel experience. It provides them with a unique virtual reality experience. Customers put on a jet pack at its experience store and "fly in the sky" in Paris, enjoying a full view of all the landmarks in Paris including Notre-Dame de Paris, the Eiffel Tower and the Arc de Triomphe, etc.

4. The expansion of new cultural tourism platforms

(1) Internet platform enterprises: website traffic counts.

With the support of the Shanghai Municipal People's Government, Internet platform enterprises specialized in cultural tourism have enjoyed sound development. As shown in Table 1, Internet platform enterprises are taking the initiative to increase their network traffic. For example, Bilibili has 130 million monthly active users, making it the largest youth cultural community in China. Bilibili has launched its new travel brand Bilibili yoo; Xiaohongshu has become a new platform with attracting contents on tourist attractions helping viewers make their own decisions on where and how to take their next trips; Himalaya carries out projects such as "audio-visual cities (有声城市)" and "readable buildings (建筑可阅读)", using technology to create new scenes of cultural tourism.

Referring to the newly-developed forms in the digital culture industry, such as online film and television, digital resources and online games, enterprises specialized in cultural tourism should cooperate with Internet platform enterprises to tap into their website traffic; cultural and museum institutions, tourist attractions should also consider joining hands with them to bring in the "membership system", "traffic transformation mode" and "paid experience mode" into their business.

Table 1

The number of users of Internet platform enterprises in Shanghai (2019—2020)

	Daily Active Users (M)	Monthly Active Users (M)	Registered Users (M)
Bilibili	3 800	13 000	/
Xiaohongshu	2 500	10 000	30 000
Himalaya	10 000	6 800	60 000
Dragonfly FM	/	4 300	45 000
Tik Tok	40 000	51 800	/

(2) Internet platform enterprises: make Chinese culture globally known.

The three provinces of the Yangtze River Delta are connected by the similar cultural traditions and historical memories. To make the tourist attractions of the Yangtze River Delta more appealing globally, Internet platform enterprises should give full play to its communication power, innovate the business mode to fit the overseas market, create quality digital contents of cultural tourism that can be adapted to multi-cultural contexts, to strengthen their international reach. With the support of YouTube, WebTVAsia has become the first MCN(Multi-Channel Network) in Shanghai, China. Growing from MCN(Multi-Channel Network), to MPN(Multi-Platform Network) and to a content-oriented company, WebTVAsia has now established itself as an Internet platform where content creators from Korea, China, Japan and Malaysia can share their well-made short videos.

5. Full integration of cultural tourism in the Yangtze River Delta

(1) To fully apply science and technology into integrated resources.

The deep integration of cultural tourism and technology not only requires technology companies to cooperate with organizations and practitioners in cultural tourism to fully integrate technological applications into cultural tourism resources, but also to jointly create technology-enabled scenes and contents. Shanghai is becoming a science and technology innovation center with global influence, constantly expanding its talent pool in AI, big data, virtual reality engineering and other high-tech fields. Enterprises such as FIRSTBRAVE, Dgene, HiAR, Xmov, Sight Plus have been playing a leading role in providing technological applications and solutions for cultural tourism, facilitating the integrated development of the Yangtze River Delta.

(2) To promote the integration of new forms of consumption.

As the industry of live streaming and short video grows, science and technology companies should utilize the featured cultural tourism resources of the Yangtze River Delta in China. First, online travel agencies promote the integration of new consumption forms by giving full paly to the "cultural tourism+livestreaming" mode or "cultural tourism + short video e-commerce" mode. Second, Internet platform enterprises should produce more appealing digital contents. Third, enterprises aiming at spreading Chinese culture overseas should cooperate in promoting the integration, production and distribution of contents of cultural tourism so as to transform tourist sites in the Yangtze River Delta into world-known attractions.

(3) To jointly build a community of technological innovation for cultural tourism.

To promote the in-depth integration of technology and cultural tourism in the Yangtze River Delta, we should build a community of technology innovation, establish a cooperation center for technology innovation, promote collaboration on the transformation of scientific and technological achievements, and establish a partnership between scientific and technological enterprises and cultural tourism institutions in the Yangtze River Delta.

Study on Cultural Quality and Promotion Strategies for the Urban Leisure Industry

Gu Jiang

Professor, Head of Yangtze Delta Region Industry Development Institute, Nanjing University

Today my topic is "Study on Cultural Quality and Promotion Strategies for the Urban Leisure Industry". After listening to the previous speeches, I think there is a question worthy thinking about — how can the behavioral paradigm and scene paradigm in our field of study be balanced? If the behavioral paradigm of the past is not in tune with contemporary human consciousness and preferences, it may induce us to blindly deny modernity and complete inheritance of the past, which is a questionable way to promote cultural quality. From the perspective of scene paradigm, the environment stimulates consumption habits and aesthetic preferences and behaviors. But if the theory is applied without further thinking, it doesn't work. Qujiang New Town in Xi'an City is a case in point. It is not the culture of Qujiang New Town that attracts people, but the success of the real estate project and the neighboring tourist attraction—Giant Wild Goose Pagoda. Therefore, regarding the promotion of cultural quality, we cannot simply focus on the culture itself. Especially in the case when the historical part of the culture and modernity is combined, it is more important to consider how much this combination will contribute to serving people.

1. The role of cultural quality in promoting the development of the leisure industry

(1) The improvement of cultural quality can lead to economies of scale for the leisure industry.

Economies of scale affects consumption. That is, the average spending per unit of consumer goods decreases as the production scale expands. As an input factor of the development of the leisure industry, cultural quality is an inseparable and irreplaceable part. It also brings production benefits, because when the average cost of production falls and output rises, economies of scale are achieved. When the cultural quality is put into the leisure industry, the average production cost will decrease as the profit increases, compared with the production without this input factor.

Cultural capital is essential to urban cultural development. In my opinion, cultural capital is composed of both the physical capital and abstract values. In the urban development in contemporary times, there are some input factors that can co-exist with cities, and these factors can transform cultural resources into cultural capital. It is worth mentioning that not all cultural resources can be converted into cultural industries, because some resources are just symbols, such as the Temple and Mansion of Confucius. Therefore, in this sense, even if the cultural capital is of historical significance, it would not necessarily become what people expect it to be.

Take Wuzhen as an example. First, I think the slogan "I'm waiting for you in Wuzhen" is very good. It leaves me wondering that why "you are waiting for me". What can we expect to see in Wuzhen? From the first Wuzhen Theatre Festival in 2013 to the sixth in 2018, the theme, event time and content of the Festival are all different. The organizer integrated the scene and performance art in the Festival, rather than adopt a traditional way to showcase opera such as Kunqu Opera and Yue Opera. The Festival started to hold thematic activities for youth from 2017. Although they were also based on opera performance, troupes from the Yangtze River Delta and abroad were invited to participate in these activities. Every year during the Wuzhen Theatre Festival, visitors from China's national art institutions, colleges and universities as well as other opera lovers visit Wuzhen. They are not only there to enjoy the annual performance, but also participate in the performance, so that they can have an unforgettable experience in the Festival. Besides, Wuzhen organized all its historic stages together and converted them into an industrial chain where clothing, food, housing, transportation, shopping and recreational services are provided. The World Internet Conference has been held in Wuzhen annually since 2014. Wuzhen has built high-end business apartments, and provided health care, leisure and entertainment services to meet the needs of visitors of different groups. Attaching great importance to the protection of intangible cultural heritage, it has set up museums and experience centers, organized "Children's Fun Festival" to promote traditional handicrafts, and opened the former residences of historic figures to the public for educational purposes, all of which have contributed to the local cultural development.

(2) The improvement of cultural quality increases the competitiveness of the leisure industry.

Also, I would like to put forward a very important concept which is called "uniqueness strategy". There is a psychological concept called First Impression which is also applicable in the field of cultural industry. From the perspective of uniqueness strategy, why are tourists willing to visit the Forbidden City more than once? Because people believe the Forbidden City is the representative symbol of Chinese art and history. But the Forbidden City's popularity in recent years is not attributed to the development of tourism, but the cultural creation of the Palace Museum, which generated profits of 1 billion yuan in 2016 alone. By the end of 2016, the Palace Museum has launched 9 170 kinds of cultural and creative products. The creation of unique IP (intellectual property) is also part of the uniqueness strategy. Cultural resources are turned into IP resources, and then they become extensible products. With the combination of China's excellent cultural IP resources and Chinese traditional aesthetic elements, the cultural and creative products of the Palace Museum have been endowed with lasting attraction and unique selling points. The combination of cultural IP resources and the most trending carriers helps maintain the core competitiveness of the Palace Museum's cultural and creative products.

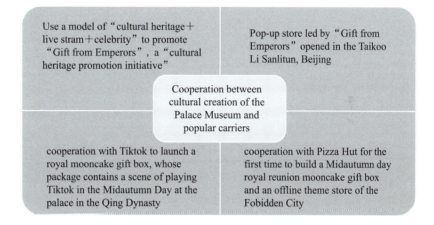

Fig. 1 Cooperation between cultural creation of the Palace Museum and popular carriers

(3) The improvement of cultural quality optimizes the leisure industry structure.

From a dynamic perspective, what matters to the industrial structure is which industries will gradually decline and which sectors will decline first. From a static perspective, the input-output method can reflect the multi-sector relationship between the final demand and the destination of final products among industries. The current situation of China's industrial development is that the tertiary industry has accounted for the largest market share among different industries. The tertiary sector covers a wide range of activities, among which the information transmission, software and information technology, rental and business services are enjoying a growth rate that is much faster than the national average. Tourism, culture, sports, health and elderly care services are growing in a stable and healthy way. The proportion of the happiness industry in the national economy is also increasing. As an important part of the service industry and the foundation of the happiness industry, the leisure industry will play an important role in optimizing and upgrading the industrial structure.

Take the transformation of the industrial structure of Ruhr area in Germany as an example. known as the "heart of German industry", Ruhr area used to be the largest traditional industrial area in the world. With its economic structure dominated by the heavy industry, it was once the important heavy machinery manufacturing base, steel base and energy base in Germany. In 1989, the unified development was carried out in the Ruhr area. Shopping sites, landscape parks, leisure facilities, museums and other scattered scenic spots which were originally operated independently were connected to 12 typical industrial towns, 6 national museums and 19 industrial tourist attractions, making industrial tourism a new driver of Ruhr area's economic growth. In addition, Ruhr area has also attracted high-tech enterprises to settle here, and these enterprises have become a new engine of the regional development. In addition, modern commercial, residential and service infrastructure have been constructed to form a complex for industrial tourism. Because of its profound industrial culture, Ruhr has successfully transformed itself from an industrial area of heavy pollution to a remarkable city with the leisure industry as the main industry and a globally-known industrial tourism. Thanks to this culture, Rhur has shifted its focus from growth in the industrial sector to growth in the cultural industry. An "industrial culture space" combined with leisure, consumption and lifestyle was built to help Rhur establish itself as both a leisure economy and a cultural economy.

(4) The improvement of cultural quality attracts talents.

Cultural quality is a reflection of cultural atmosphere, humanistic spirit and soft power of a city. Creative talents are likely to be drawn by them to a city, which will stimulate innovation and creativity in the city and in the end turn it into a magnet for talents in the leisure industry. Talent plays a significant role in promoting the innovation and creativity of the leisure industry. The diversity of the leisure industry largely depends on a diverse talent pool enabled by the gathering of creative talents A growing number of creative talents in a city is conducive to the creativity and innovation in its leisure industry and helps the city to build an environment of "mass entrepreneurship and innovation". To enrich the leisure resources requires the participation of outstanding creative talents.

2. A strategy of utilizing cultural quality to boost the development of the leisure industry

(1) Digging deep into culture and promoting high-quality development of the leisure industry.

Cultural quality is the core element of the leisure industry, serving as a core resource of the urban leisure industry. Cultural resources are the most important "raw materials" of the leisure industry. The efforts of developing the leisure industry should focus on the integration of leisure and culture while at the same time making full use of the progress in the cultural industry. The development of the cultural industry facilitates the leisure industry, and vice versa. We should strengthen the integration of leisure products and services, facilitate the cultural promotion, cultural interpretation and cultural exploration, and improve the cultural connotation, cultural taste of leisure products and services as well as the overall cultural image of the city.

(2) Promoting the deep integration of the cultural industry and the leisure industry, and improving the value chain of high-end leisure products.

The integration of the cultural industry and the leisure industry enables regional resources to be organically connected. The new services, products and technologies generated during the integration of the two industries have replaced some traditional technologies, products and services, helping consumers to move onto higher pursuits. New technologies have been applied to more traditional sectors, leading to the upgrading of products and service structures. This has also transformed the traditional way of industrial production and service, thus improving the value chain of leisure products. In addition to salaries and policies, there are many nonphysical factors that influence talent's preference for cities today. What we usually call "happiness" is the benefits of consumption in economics. The kind of happiness people gain from living in a city emerges from the identification of the cultural quality of the city.

(3) Combining cultural quality with high technologies to enrich forms of business in the leisure industry.

To transform cultural quality into leisure products, a city's culture needs to be turned into physical products and business. Without extraordinary cultural creativity and customized ways of turning creative ideas into products, the cultural quality would not be transformed into leisure products. We need to make full use of internet technologies to meet consumers' growing aesthetic needs as well as their needs for personalized leisure products, so that their needs for experience, interaction and scenario-orientation can be also attended to which is a new direction for the development of the leisure industry in the future Therefore, we should combine cultural quality and high technologies to stimulate new forms of business, such as the Internet-related recreation, music streaming, digital content, VR, big data, cloud computing and AI businesses. The application of new technologies will enrich the forms of business and enhance the added value of the leisure industry.

(4) Developing talent strategies conducive to the development of the leisure industry and increasing the number of versatile talents with a comprehensive skillset.

Creativity is the core factor of leisure economy. Cultural contents derive from cultural creativity and decide the cultural quality. In other words, "the content decides everything". Talents plays an active and important role in this industry. The diversity of the leisure industry, to a large extent, is attributed to a diverse pool of talents. The translation of the high-quality content of cultural quality into the biggest attraction of the leisure industry requires a group of talented people who specialize in turning the materials into "quality contents" and are effective story tellers. To increase the number of versatile talents with a comprehensive skillset and numerous creative and innovative ideas is one of the key tasks we must accomplish in developing the leisure industry.

Humanistic Urban Development Boosted by Communication

Zhu Chunyang

Professor, School of Journalism, Fudan University

The fifth plenary session of the 19th Central Committee of the CPC set the goal of turning China into a country with great cultural influence by 2035. At present, China is indeed a political and economic power, but it does not qualify as a country with great cultural influence. A typical characteristic of a country with great cultural influence is that its cultural products are absorbed by other cultures. In terms of the global film and television industry, the United States accounts for 70% of the market share, while China's market share is less than 5%.

Another important basis for studying a country with great cultural influence is its cultural products, which are related to its domestic market size and cultural discount. China's unrivaled domestic market size, one of its significant advantages, has not been fully exploited because we participate in the international competition on the basis of provinces and cities, so there is very little inter-provincial mobility, resulting in market fragmentation.

1. City and its culture

Culture is an essential part of a city. Lewis Mumford's point of view can be cited to explain the relationship between a city and its culture, that is, a city is a cultural container and its function is to store, transfer, and create culture. Most of the time, we do not talk about culture itself but talk about its role in the economic development. In other words, we tend to think that cultural development serves economic development. But I believe that culture should be developed for culture's sake. Only in this way can we build a country with great cultural influence.

However, when we talk about a city and its culture, we will inevitably mention the city's economy. So, what is the relationship between a city and its culture from an economic perspective? Mumford believes that the best economy of a city is the "care and culture" of human beings. A city should preserve cultural differences, so that it can develop in a stable and distinctive way, instead of becoming a container for buildings. I once did an experiment: when I was on a business trip to a city in China, I sent several photos of the city and ask others to guess which city it was. Unfortunately, almost no one made a right guess They all thought my photos failed to include distinctive features of the city, but the point was that the city itself was featureless.

Professor Zhu Dajian believes that the development of global cities has changed from the traditional model which takes economy as the priority to the modern model which takes quality of life as the priority.

2. City and its people

A city is a hub for talents. The basic idea underpinning the development of a modern city is to improve the quality of life in the city to attract talents. The core of Shanghai 2035 urban master plan is to turn Shanghai into "a more dynamic innovation city, a more attractive humanistic city and a more sustainable eco-city", highlighting the people-centered development. Without people, innovation cannot be realized. Also, eco-friendliness centers around people. "Better City, Better Life", the slogan of the Expo 2010 Shanghai China, also reminds us of Shanghai's efforts to improve the relationship between people and the city.

Many people think that cities are made of cold concrete and steel that are contrary to humanity. Most people flee the city at the happiest time of their lives. During Spring Festival, for example, the streets of Shanghai are almost empty. People don't regard Shanghai as their hometown. Why wouldn't people stay in Shanghai during the happiest days of their life? Why can't Shanghai, a city of immigrants, soothe their homesickness? Shanghai usually gives people an impression that it is a modern industrial city, where people always keep others at a distance. But in the countryside where they used to live, people communicated with each other and maintained an intimate relationship. Therefore, it is also a problem brought about by the modernization of human society.

3. Communicable city

Shanghai is renowned for its city spirit, that champions inclusiveness, encourages the pursuit of excellence, embraces cultural diversity, and advocates magnificent modesty. Although this spirit has not been fully concretized, it still plays a significant role in uniting people together. As a city of immigrants, the core of Shanghai's cultural tradition lies in its inclusiveness, which emphasizes that the integration and communication of various cultures make Shanghai such a metropolis.

Now we can find that the social relations in Shanghai are more diversified and fragmented than those in any previous era, and the communication between different groups has not achieved ideal results. From the perspective of journalism and communication sciences, we thought that the development of new media would bring us more opportunities for communication and keep us closer to the truth. However, we have fallen into the "Information Cocoons" crisis. That's why the era we live in is called the post-truth era.

In my opinion, an idealized global city should be based on the convergence of international cultures. An open attitude, communicable urban governance philosophy and convenient communication networks are essential elements for a global city. Otherwise, the "apathy" of big cities will magnify cultural conflicts and turn globalization into a disaster. What happened to the Twin Towers in New York epitomizes the global disaster of cultural conflict. The 9/11 attack has warned people that human beings should take the communication between cultures into consideration in cultural development. Therefore, I've listed some questions that we can discuss when considering how to improve communication. They are all questions regarding the direction of the development of cultural industry and cultural interaction in the future:

How can the interconnection and dialogue of communication networks within urban communities be achieved?

How can the innovation relationship network among enterprises in each industrial cluster be optimized?

How can communication networks between the industrial clusters and their surrounding communities be optimized?

How can the dialogue network between Shanghai and the city cluster within the Yangtze River Delta be improved?

How can the communicable network between Shanghai and the global urban system be enhanced?

How can the dialogue and integration between the traditional culture and the innovative culture be realized?

How can communication networks between the government and the multicultural governance agents be optimized?

How can the communication and integration between urban and rural areas be achieved?

How can the online and offline interaction and integration be realized?

Cultural Energy: COVID-19 and the Global City

G. Thomas Goodnight

Annenberg School of Communication & Journalism, University of Southern California

Cultural energy is a general term referring to activities, performances and sites that make up the city. With COVID-19, all of our cultural practices are under stress. I'd like to outline the stresses on communication these days and areas of study and things we're doing.

1. Communication

Communication has done well for human beings. The city has thrived as more people have moved into it and revised it throughout the 20th century. In the 21st century, we've reached a take-off point where cities are going to grow into very large numbers. This means that the old communication is a good space to build from, but we can't stay the same. We've got to get better. As more people live

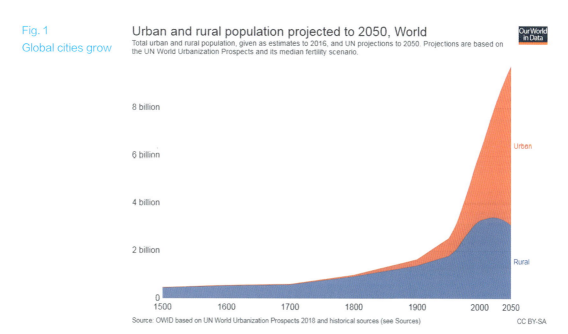

Fig. 1
Global cities grow

Urban and rural population projected to 2050, World
Total urban and rural population, given as estimates to 2016, and UN projections to 2050. Projections are based on the UN World Urbanization Prospects and its median fertility scenario.

Source: OWID based on UN World Urbanization Prospects 2018 and historical sources (see Sources)

CC BY-SA

together, we have to have communication structures and practices that energize us and put together activities where we can live together peacefully and productively, and repair the damage that's been done by unexpected events or catastrophe.

By 2050, the urban and rural world will both be greater, but the proportion of people living in cities will be substantially more significant than those living in rural areas. In my view, the great regional metropolitan area is broad enough to incorporate flows of people, so we can preserve lots of green space and lots of elements that make rural areas successful. We can renew the village beautiful and have access to beautiful national parks. But we need to think about how communication occurs at the individual level of agency as well as within groups and neighborhood. So, our communication practices have to get better. By sharing responses to the COVID-19 among cities, we can restart the world even as the pandemic is with us.

2. Pandemics and the city

Pandemics seemed to be a subset of catastrophes that nature visits on human beings. These catastrophes used to be viewed as immutable acts of nature, perhaps revenge of the gods. But in the 21st century, we understand pandemics as to be facilitated by our social behaviors. We can make them more or less devastating by the kinds of relationships, and communication we have with one another at a social distance or masking or in lockdown. But we also need science to come up with vaccines and remedies to help make the pandemic a livable way. We won't essentially resist the pandemic through a giant herd immunity in the same way, because different parts of the globe will have different mixes of medicines as well as different types of the virus. We don't count the virus out yet. All of us are still adapting and learning across the globe as it spreads to its disruptions. In the United States, there were such great expectations of US science while its political system was such abject failure. We'll have to wait and see how well we ultimately do. If your science is short, the pandemic is especially brutal, so scientific research is at a fever pitch today. The combination of digital programming technologies in science has ushering in an era of transition. Computational models of science have been a theoretical space that we've worked in. But what you see is an urgency that's really accelerating scientific practice and research these days.

The Great Influenza is about the first great war in the 20th century and it killed more people after the war than during the horrible, catastrophic trench warfare of the battles. The great influenza epidemic is a story of how science was constructed in the United States with the help of the Rockefeller Foundation and Johns Hopkins University. The success of the US's Centers for Disease

Control and National Institutes of Health was no accident. It was rather a legacy of this historical battle with influenza, by the way, influenza and pandemics not only live in science.

The US's National Museum had a history of cultural changes brought about by influenza in 1918. My great grandmother lost her husband and children to that epidemic. So, when we think of culture, we can think of it at the institutional level and national or we can think of it as local and very personal. Pandemics direct and preserve cultural energy, and they fuel science to lend resilience to a city.

As we all know public health is not a matter of science alone. One of the things I have been very impressed with is the progress China has made. When I did research in China during the bird flu and the swine flu, What I saw in China and Asia more broadly are very advanced interventions. With the pace of learning about communication and coordination and science, I think as long as we share sites or areas of change, we can coordinate and cooperate across nations.

3. Disruptions

Today, I'll be quoting exactly from "COVID-19-Impacts on Cities and Suburbs: Key Takeaways across Multiple Sectors". Takeaway across sectors means practices across theories or research across disciplines. One of my guides for studying communication is the idea of combinatorics, which I borrow from Tsinghua university. Combinatorics looks at multiple relations of theories and practices.

I think the urban center is a guide where we can start studying communication problems to get the direction of cultural energy and future possibilities of transition and take us from the virus to an even more vibrant and sustainable urban world. One of the things that the COVID-19 has made clear to not only US institutions, but global institutions as well, is a growing disparity left over from neoliberalism between the very wealthy and the very poor, which is manifested in the disparity of those who can work at home and those who can't. Those who can work at home essentially are doing more business. My son and his wife both have jobs and they take care of their new baby at the house while doing jobs. There is a category in the United States called the "essential workers". "Essential workers" are those who can't stay at home and have to check out groceries or drive trucks or deliver goods. Essential workers live on day-to-day paychecks, and they essentially have to keep the supply chains of food and medicine and energy going, so that society continues. Non-essential workers, on the other hand, are people who need work, but lost their jobs, and are facing eviction.

Because of the COVID-19, cities are beginning to redesign to convert public streets, parking spaces, and sidewalks into spaces for walking and biking, restaurant diners, and retail. To keep a social distance, the use and demand for parks and open space has increased during the COVID-19 crisis.

The COVID-19 caused disruptions in transportation. The airport in Fig. 2 is empty. Airports were key to the global city. Public transport has significantly declined. Single transport has increased, particularly bicycles. So it may be that travel is less more expensive.

Fig. 2
An empty airport

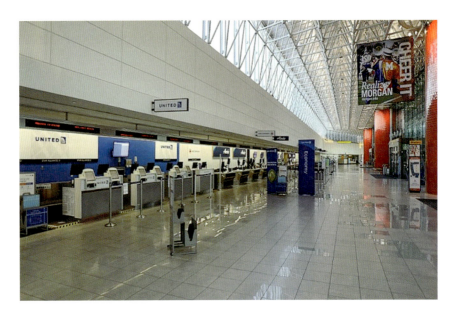

The disruption includes social-commercial spaces. One of the big questions is how to send family kids to schools, how to protect older residences, our conglomerate living, such as prisons. We should take testing regimes to make sure that they're safe. At the same time, we need to take some risks.

The final thing is nature impacts. Due to the pandemic, people flock to national parks to escape home self-quarantine. Therefore, COVID-19 spread to tribal lands. Indians take measures to guard. Wild-life returns to Los Angeles during absence of pollution. In the West, Wildfires break out with 4 million acres burned, and people are having to fight wildfires and deal with COVID-19. Catastrophes are not just one-off any more, but rather are interactive.

4. Cultural energy

Cultural energy pulses with the activities of life within the city. The energy is expressed in the routines of work and play, routine and emergency actions that constitute everyday life. Cultural energies are redirected when catastrophe threatens and unfolds. There is an urgent need to rethink and transform cities to respond to the reality of COVID-19 and potential future pandemics, and to recover better, by building more resilient, inclusive and sustainable cities. We know that this is possible.

Between Localization and Globalization: Cultural Reflections on Shanghai's Fight Against COVID-19

Ye Zhudi

Editor-in-Chief, Exploration and Free Views

COVID-19 pandemic is a global public health crisis. How to control the pandemic has become a thorny problem that human beings must face. Due to its large economic size, super large population and high mobility, Shanghai would easily become a high-risk area for COVID-19 in the early stage of prevention and its advantage of being a "large-scale" city may become a disadvantage in an emergency. Shanghai responded well to the Hepatitis A epidemic in 1988 and the SARS epidemic in 2003 and gained a lot of experience. It has formed its own "hardcore" way to manage public health crises.

As the most globalized city in China, Shanghai's "hardcore" is, on the one hand, reflected in the integration of its institutions and cultures. By fully exploring the urban culture and using the non-institutional advantages to spiritually support the fight against COVID-19, Shanghai quickly reached a social consensus and ensured the sustainability of the anti-epidemic achievements. On the other hand, Shanghai's "hardcore" control measures are embodied in the cooperation between experts and the public and the respect for professionalism. In order to fight the pandemic, Shanghai built a standardized network of grassroots communities for citizens and experts to work together, and finally realized "herd immunity".

1. Fighting COVID-19 in accordance with the law: the cornerstone of pandemic prevention and control

(1) Quick response and legislation.

From the perspective of actors, the regional paths of global governance include both intergovernmental systems and non-governmental mechanisms. The regional paths can compromise and mitigate the gap between nationalism and globalism, so as to solve the intractable problems at the national and global levels to a certain extent and build a bridge of communication between them, which are important supplementary elements of the emerging global governance. Shanghai, as a megalopolis, is also an international and modern city, which makes it an important link connecting China with the world. To meet the urgent need of preventing and controlling COVID-19 in accordance with the law, Shanghai completed the local emergency legislation within 10 days by drawing on the practices of fighting against SARS in 2003 and preparing for the World Expo.

(2) Building a resilient social governance community.

The vitality of laws lies in their implementation. We should fully consider the possibility of fully implementing the law. Besides, China's governing model, characterized by the overall leadership of the Communist Party, needs not only the support of legislation, but also collaborative participation among different social agents. In this way, various social agents can be gathered at different levels and in different forms in the fight against the pandemic, so that a spontaneous order and a social governance community will be built. Shanghai's legislation on COVID-19 prevention ion and control fully took the institutional advantages of the Chinese system and the existing law enforcement forces into account. Shanghai also mobilized the participation of various social agents, thus forming a favorable environment for the implementation of the rule of law. In addition to the "top down" form dominated by the administrative system, the "participatory governance" in the form of "bottom-up" is also critical. Statistics of words about Shanghai's COVID-19 fight on the internet show that "epidemic" (100 882) and, "enterprise" (25 176) are the two most frequently used words; "property management" (8 869) ranks the seventh, higher than "virus" (7 981), "volunteer" (7 860) and "pneumonia" (6 927), which fully shows the importance Shanghai attaches to the diversity of social agents in the fight against the pandemic.

2. Community-based COVID-19 fight in the context of "glocalization"

"A community is the window and epitome of a society." The basic social networks and behavioral norms formed by good community governance are of great significance to the prevention and control of the pandemic. On the one hand, Shanghai communities' fight against COVID-19 is deeply influenced by globalization. On the other hand, it also demonstrates its own indigenous nature based on Shanghai's unique historical and cultural background, which enriches the connotation of global community health governance.

(1) The mechanism of "forcing" and "turning crisis into opportunity".

During the economic system transition, the current community governance in China aims to solve the multiple social problems derived from the shift from the "life tenure system" to the "employment system". As Youmei LI said: "To some extent, the thorny problems arising from the reform and opening up also force the Party and the country to provide timely solutions." The gradual reform path of "moving forward step by step" has constantly raised higher demands on China's social governance, forcing policymakers to work out new solutions. Since the reform and opening up, Shanghai has created a new framework for primary-level governance with "two levels of government and three levels of management". Namely, on the basis of the municipal and district governments, Shanghai has formed a three-level vertical management system of municipal, district and sub-district offices, which is a unique "Shanghai Model". Since the founding of the People's Republic of China, COVID-19 has been a major public health emergency with the fastest transmission rate, the widest infection range and the greatest difficulty in prevention and control. The public health crisis also pushed Shanghai to improve its community governance system and the conditions of community health services.

(2) The shift of focus in urban management activates the political potential energy.

"Political potential energy" is an important theoretical concept in the implementation of public policy in China. "Once bureaucracy encounters a public policy with strong political potential energy, the executive agents at all levels can break through the inertia and division of departments, and gain high efficiency and executive power." Shanghai has expanded the administration authority of sub-district offices, delegated human resources, financial resources and materials, and established a coordinated organization managed by the third level. This system determines the basic framework of Shanghai community building and makes the sub-district offices the essential agent of community management. During the pandemic, to strengthen prevention and control, most urban communities in China prohibited deliverymen from entering the residential compounds, which brought inconvenience to residents and the catering industry. To overcome this inconvenience, the Changfeng sub-district office of Putuo District, Shanghai, cooperated with Alibaba's local life service company, implemented the "Green Pass for Ele. me deliveryman" within its jurisdiction. The pass was designed and made by the sub-district office and issued to Alibaba. Shanghai's sub-district offices took active actions, taking the lead in the whole country. Although there have been some problems in the long-term operation of the "two levels of government and three levels of management" system, when administrations actively manage community affairs and people's life, "political potential energy" is easier to be activated and accumulated, which plays a positive role in the prevention and control of the pandemic.

As Ning WANG pointed out, the so-called "single modernity" is just a myth in the era of globalization. Due to different conditions and development models in different countries, there are many forms of modernity. The urbanization of Shanghai in modern times is "the result of the interaction of various complicated contradictions between the world and China, the central government and the local offices, internal affairs and foreign affairs, the government and people, reality and history". This unique nature means that the locality of Shanghai has a very special connotation. The experience of Shanghai communities in fighting against COVID-19 provides a valuable solution for improving global governance. It also shows evidence of "globalization" and "sinicization". This suggests that in the governance of urban communities, an open and shared local tradition should be formed in the constructive global interconnection based on their individual characteristics to accumulate rich resources for global governance.

3. Informal institutions: an important cultural foundation for glocalization

An informal institution is a concept that Professor Zhu Dajian came up with after comparing the anti-epidemic models of Shanghai and Wuhan. He believes that cultural factors play an important role in community management. Formal institutions are stable and seldom change over a period. As the spiritual foundation of local residents' daily life, the regional history and local traditions consolidate their world outlook and guide their behavior. The epidemic prevention and control and the maintenance of public health depend on public knowledge, trust and cooperation, so informal institutions play an important role.

To some extent, the ways to prevent and control COVID-19 reflect the differences between Chinese and Western cultural beliefs. COVID-19 spread mainly from person to person, so isolating the people infected is a very effective measure. China, the U. S. and European countries, have imposed similar measures such as traffic control, lockdowns and travel restrictions However, western democratic politics put more emphasis on the concepts of "limited government" and "civil liberties". The western anti-epidemic model shows the idea of "each taking his own responsibility" and "survival of the fittest". Europe and the United States, where individualism and liberalism are prevalent, have their own national conditions. Many people are willing to shoulder their own responsibilities and do not want the government to interfere too much. In the early days of the pandemic control in the United States, bars, beaches and streets were still crowded. Even in times of crisis, they may prioritize personal freedom and privacy, making it even more difficult to control the pandemic. Many Americans opposed the advice of experts, protested against the government's home quarantine order and technological surveillance measures, and demanded the restart of the economy and public life. They shouted slogans such as "Don't bully me", "Let me be free or let me die", "We have the right to decide how to protect ourselves", "Get the authoritarian government out of my way" and so on. Therefore, when the formal institution is established, the informal institution represented by local traditions and cultural psychology plays a significant role.

(1) Embracing diversity.

Shanghai is a typical immigrant city whose residents come from all over China. Before 1949, 85% of Shanghai's residents came from all over the country. Shanghai has been the most globalized city in China since modern times. The interaction between the global and the local characteristics has always been ongoing here. The essence of embracing diversity is to absorb the advanced elements of both Chinese and global cultures. For example, in Ming Dynasty, Xu Guangqi took the initiative to communicate with Western missionaries and learn advanced science, showing extraordinary courage and insight. In the period of the Republic of China, it is well known that Shanghai extensively took in the achievements of Western material and spiritual civilization. Since the reform and opening up, Shanghai has actively learned from foreign countries and carried out technical cooperation in sewage treatment, renovation of old housing and public transport. As China pursues global modernity with the whole world, Shanghai has long taken the lead. This cultural feature is the basis of Shanghai's spirit.

Qin Shuo, the former chief editor of YiMagazine, believes that in terms of the cohesiveness and pride of the city, Shanghai consciousness does exist. It is "Civicism", a kind of natural integration, love and responsibility. Shanghai respects and revers its people, and its people also love and trust the city. Civicism is an idea put forward by Tsinghua University professor Daniel A. Bell in his book The Spirit of Cities: We need to have a unique city spirit, to resist the alienation and oblivion and protect our history and future. The spirit of cities should be regarded as a force of unity, showing harmony in diversity. He believes that the spirit of cities should reflect the most emotional resonance of the urban citizens. Between the city and its people, there is a resilient community. This sense of community comes from shared interests, value consensus and trust from long-term interaction.

In the first 30 years after the founding of the People's Republic of China, "Shanghai, with about 1/1 500 of the country's land and 1/100 of the country's population, provided 1/6 of the country's fiscal revenue and 1/10 of its industrial output". Other regions mainly provided Shanghai with raw materials, energy and agricultural products, while "Shanghai supported the whole country" mostly with high-tech products and high value-added products. Such history gave birth to a distinctive Shanghainese identity. Since the beginning of the 21st century, the cultural identity of Shanghainese has become increasingly clear. The prosperous development of local media, dialects, and literary creation, such as "Stand-up comedy (Shanghai version)" and the novel "Blossoms", have contributed to Shanghainese's identification with their local culture. The delineation of "One of Us" based on culture enables individuals in the society to overcome isolation and barriers and establish connections, trust and emotional ties. The construction of social communities is based on such spontaneous emotional connection and social self-organization. However, in the face of great crises, the sense of community does help to promote the effective use of social forces, stimulate the self-help mechanism of the society, and coordinate the political and social organizations to tide over crises.

(2) Respecting science and advocating professionalism.

Since modern times, Shanghai has been a tech hub in China and known for its long history of scientism and professionalism. As early as the late Qing Dynasty, many famous universities were established in Shanghai, such as Saint John's College, Nanyang Public School and Toa Dobunshoin University. The General Bureau of Machine Manufacture of Jiangnan, the first modern military enterprise in China, was established in Shanghai in 1865. After that, many high-tech factories and inventions were born in Shanghai. Shanghai played a leading role in modern Chinese science and culture. This has affected the commons and served as one of the internal driving forces for the civilization construction and development of Shanghai as a modern international metropolis, all of which has been influencing its response to the public health crisis.

In 1988, the outbreak of hepatitis A made Shanghai residents learn from the consequences of bad eating habits and to some extent encouraged people to pay more attention to hygiene. During the SARS epidemic in 2003, Shanghai, a megacity with a permanent and floating population of nearly 20 million, had only less than 10 confirmed cases. However, Shanghai still set up the Shanghai Public Health Clinical Center (SPHCC) with 500 beds in Jinshan District to take precautions. People joked that when Wuhan rushed to build "Huoshenshan Hospital" and "Leishenshan Hospital" and showed its infrastructure construction ability, Shanghai just sent patients to its own emergency hospital, SPHCC, which was completed 16 years ago. Shanghainese people value professional knowledge, respect professionals, and appreciate scientific methods and attitudes. From garbage sorting to COVID-19, the city has laid a solid base for respecting science and professionalism.

People's respect for science and professionalism is highlighted by their praise for Professor Zhang Wenhong, the head of the Shanghai medical expert team for the treatment of coronavirus patients. Zhang has attracted widespread attention nationwide for his courage to tell the truth during this pandemic. During the pandemic, with his exquisite professional skills, remarkable spirit and humorous language, Professor Zhang timely informed the public of the situation of the pandemic, spread knowledge of COVID-19, and accurately predicted the spreading trend, which made him popular online. Zhang won wide respect from the public and was dubbed a "hardcore doctor" by some netizens. China's medical workers, including those in Shanghai, have played a pivotal role in response to COVID-19. Professor Zhang's witty and professional interpretation of COVID-19 demonstrates the city's achievements in advocating science and professionalism. Because of his unique personal charisma, Zhang won respect from the public and became popular on the Internet.

From Wenhong ZHANG, we can find two cornerstones that must exist in a normal society: one is the courage to tell the truth; the other is professionalism. Zhang has the courage to bear responsibility and tell the truth. He kept the public informed of the fact about the pandemic. At the beginning of the pandemic, he proposed that CPC members fill frontline medical positions to fight COVID-19, as "one cannot bully the obedient". His words sparked heated discussion in China. To understand the enormous social significance behind Zhang's words, you need to take China's special political and cultural environment into consideration. "CPC members first" contains complicated political implications and is deeply rooted in the cultural memory in China. "CPC members first" was originally a discipline of the CPC to highlight the advancement and modularity of Communists. However, in daily life, CPC members don't always live up to that promise. However, faced with the pandemic, Zhang's remarks that "Don't bully the obedient. This is a time to test the Communists" made clear the hidden political logic and to some extent challenged the political hidden rules. In short, this is the first time that experts have gone from backstage to the front, helping people get out of the embarrassing dilemma of "being fed up with political discourse and failing to understand professional discourse". The combination of politics and professionalism has reshaped social trust. The second is professionalism, which means experts must adhere to science and pragmatism. Even if challenged by the outside world, they should stick to their own views. They should also be able to make early predictions based on scientific research. Take Zhang's judgment on the trend of the pandemic as an example. His statement that "the second wave of the pandemic is coming, and there are signs that the rebound has even exceeded the first wave" is obviously a prudent judgment made by his team based on facts, evidence and truth.

(3) Being practical and rational.

In the Shanghai dialect, there is a phrase called "lingdeqing", which means "dealing with people and things appropriately". Apart from political rationality, Shanghainese people rely on their own judgment. During the pandemic, there was a saying going around: We can donate money; we can donate supplies, but definitely not Doctor Zhang (Zhang Wenhong)! What seems to be behind the joke is the pragmatic reasoning and the spirit of being practical and rational rooted in Shanghai's civil society. In this pandemic, people in Shanghai are more self-disciplined and more aware of the rules than anywhere else. After the "stay-at-home order" was issued, Shanghainese people lived up to their words, staying at home as required. Their self-discipline was also reflected in the fight against SARS. Shanghainese people are "disciplined" and do not easily go against the decision-makers. For example, during the pandemic, there were frequent cases of people refusing to take a diagnostic test, insulting and beating staff members, and setting up unauthorized checkpoints. But these cases rarely happened in Shanghai, where citizens willingly played the role of "hunters", reporting illegal or unethical behaviors, and spontaneously maintaining the order of prevention and control. Shanghai people are clever and rational, especially when it comes to their own interests, showing the so-called shrewdness in their culture. Shanghai cultivates neither the self-serving elites nor the selfless altruists, but the practical rationalists who believe that when shared interests are protected, all will be benefited.

To know how local traditions are formed, we must look into the history of that place. Shanghai was once a national economic and financial center in the Republic of China. With advanced commerce and industry, its citizens developed a sense of individuality, honoring contracts and respecting professionals. In addition, the tradition of self-governance can also be traced back to the beginning of modern China, when international settlements were established in Shanghai. International settlements were autonomous concessions that were administered concurrently by several foreign countries; their governance was based on the idea of "small government, big society". As a result, Shanghai citizens have grown a modern sense of civic self-governance that comes from home and abroad with shared responsibility. They changed their traditional mindset of relying on the government in the face of crises. This change has driven the community-based COVID-19 fight. The early infiltration of western civilization has encouraged Shanghainese to be open to both Chinese and western cultures. Non-institutional factors related to history and culture are affecting in their minds in a complex and covert way, playing a positive role in COVID-19 prevention and control. Shanghai-style culture is innovative, open and diverse. It is a new form of civilization, a mix and match of the Jiangnan culture that values traditional Confucianism, and modern western civilization. It is driven by two wheels. On the one hand, it has been nurtured by advanced Western civilization. The cultural heritage of the West since the Enlightenment has been inherited in Shanghai, such as the rule of law, rationality and inclusiveness. At the same time, it avoids extreme individualism in Western culture. On the other hand, for Shanghai citizens, the Jiangnan culture embodying the traditional Chinese Confucianism, Buddhism and Taoism is also the core of Shanghai culture. The modernization of the traditional Chinese culture and the domestication of western culture makes Shanghai culture a good mix of the two civilizations.

In essence, the government and its people influence each other in social governance during the pandemic. The government is the main body of governance with the basic "government-led and society-participated" structure, while the purpose and utility of governance activities are people oriented. The practical purpose of both is to respond and defeat COVID-19 and protect people's lives and health. In order to achieve this goal, the governance must generate reciprocally beneficial relations. This process inherently requires that the people play a central role in social governance. The response to COVID-19 requires an increase in meticulous urban management on a daily basis. Therefore, Shanghai has formed a systematic mechanism engaging decision-makers, professionals and the community. Shanghai-style culture is of great importance in implementing prevention and control measures. An informal system determines the effectiveness of urban governance, and the secret of success is embedded in the local culture.

Shanghai's fight against COVID-19 has the following features. First, it is from a national perspective that gradually integrates the logic of social organization into the power system of the state, pursuing the "realization of state capacity in the grassroots". Second, it reflects Shanghai's unique modernity, which is both cosmopolitan and local. High risk and high mobility have become important features of society in a globalized world. Local infectious diseases and regional events can easily evolve into a global public health crisis. The COVID-19 pandemic has once again proved that we are in urgent need global public health governance. In order to achieve sound global public health governance, it is necessary to promote the positive interaction among countries to exchange ideas and experience, especially those gained in community-level practices. As Regina Duarte puts it, "universal" scientific knowledge was inherently "mestizo, hybrid, and transnational". Global pandemic prevention should not only focus on the progress of global science, technology and medicine, but also tap into the flexible and self-motivated "local knowledge". By combining localization with globalization, we can form a theory known as "glocalization". That is why we should learn from Shanghai in this global fight against the pandemic.

The International Comparison of the Development of Global Sports Cities and a Case Study of Shanghai

Zheng Guohua

Professor, Shanghai University of Sport

Since the implementation of the Reform and Opening-up policy in 1978, Chinese cities such as Beijing, Shanghai, Nanjing, Guangzhou, have made great achievements in promoting their urban cultures. Their urban cultures have gained a bigger international presence and reputation. Over the past ten years, major cities have put forward a clear goal of building sports cities in their development plans and made it an important task in building city cultures.

In as early as 2001, Shanghai included the goal of building itself into a city as the center of sports in Asia in its 10th Five-year Plan. Later, the goal was changed to building Shanghai into a "World-renowned Sports City" in the 12th Five-year Plan. In the 13th Five-year Plan, Shanghai proposed to become a "Global Sports City". A recent executive meeting of the Shanghai municipal government adopted "Guidelines for Building Shanghai into a Global Sports City". To achieve the goal proposed by the document, it was necessary to improve the public service system, enable more people to exercise in more convenient way, build smart sports facilities, provide universal access to sports venues and facilities. Meanwhile, to boost the sports industry, sports-related consumption should be expanded and sports culture should be enriched. We should make the fruits of sports development, such as sports venues and facilities, accessible to a wider public in an orderly way.

According to a previously adopted government document of guidelines on building a people-oriented city, it is important to turn Shanghai into a city with cultural vitality and a city whose humanized urban planning and development helps its citizens feel more closely connected. In this process, sport plays a growing role, as it has the power of unifying people, stimulating their enthusiasm, and bringing them joy and satisfaction as well as a sense of achievement. More people engaging in sport contributes to a healthier population, a more energetic city, and a more prosperous sports industry. Joint efforts should be made to build Shanghai into a Global Sports City, and make sport an indispensable part of daily life and an important feature of Shanghai.

Table 1

Different kinds of sports cities that some Chinese cities position themselves as in their development plans

City	Sports cities that Chinese cities position themselves as	Year	Source
Beijing	International Sports City	2003	On Building an International Sports City
	World Sports City	2006	The 12th Five-year Plan of Sports Development of Beijing
Shanghai	Asian Sports Center	2001	The 10th Five-year Plan of Sports Development of Shanghai
	World-renowned Sports City	2007	The 12th Five-year Plan of Sports Development of Shanghai
	Global Sports City	2017	The 13th Five-year Plan of Sports Development of Shanghai
Guangzhou	International Sports City	2006	The 11th Five-year Plan of Sports Development of Guangzhou
	World-renowend Sports City	2011	The 12th Five-year Plan of Sports Development of Guangzhou
Nanjing	Asian Sports Center	2011	The 13th Party Congress of Nanjing
	World-renowned Sports City	2012	On Building Nanjing into A City as the Center of Sports in Asia and World-renowned Sports City
Jinjiang	National Sports City	2007	The 12th Five-year Plan of Jinjiang
	Sports City	2016	On Building Jinjiang into A Leading Sports City 2016
Shenzhen	Modern, International, and Innovative Sports City	2016	The 13th Five-year Plan of Sports Development of Shenzhen
Wuhan	World-renowned Sports City	2017	The Plan of Sports Facilities of Wuhan 2016—230
Xiamen	International Coastal Sports City	2017	The 13th Five-year Plan of Sports Development of Xiamen
Chongqing	Leading Sports City in Central and Western China	2016	The 13th Five-year Plan of Sports Development of Chongqing
Hangzhou	World-renowned Sports City	2016	The 13th Five-year Plan of Sports Development of Hangzhou
Nanning	ASEAN Sports City	2017	The 13th Five-year Plan of Sports Development of Nanning
Huangshi	Livable Sports City	2017	The 13th Five-year Plan of Sports Development of Huangshi
Sanya	International Sports Service City	2018	The 13th Five-year Plan of Cutural and Sports Service of Sanya
Dalian	World-renowned Sports City	2016	The 13th Five-year Plan of Sports Development of Dalian

Building a Global Sports City is a significant opportunity for cities to reshape their images and gain bigger international influence in terms of culture. How to make full use of this opportunity is a key topic of this study, and an important goal of urban cultural branding in China.

1. Sports city development in New York

New York has repeatedly been listed as "Global Top Sports Cities" by British sports consulting agency Arksports and "Best Sports Cities" in the United States. It is truly a global sports city and enjoys the reputation of "the professional sporting capital of the world". Among four international megacities, namely Los Angeles, Tokyo, New York, and Shanghai, New York ranks first in the terms of the Global Sports Impact (GSI) Cities Index, which is attributed to a series of measures taken by its government. First of all, New York has built a smart platform of city sports parks to make it easier for citizens to choose the sport they favor, find sports venues of that particular sport and exercise partners whom they can play the sport with. In addition, New York has formed a pyramid-like system of sports events, covering community events, school events, professional events, self-owned brand events and global events, which aims to encourage more people to participate in sports events. Also, the New York government provides tax exemption and financial support to 66 professional sports teams, among which 13 are world-famous professional teams. Most of them have their own TV and online radio platforms. According to statistics, New York plans to spend $73 billion on the health and sports sectors in 2020. In the past 10 years, the government has invested more than $1.2 billion annually in the construction and maintenance of sports parks.

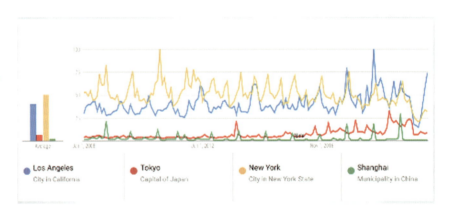

Fig. 1
The performance of Los Angeles, Tokyo, New York, and Shanghai in the GSI Cities Index

There are four takeaways from the case study of New York.

First, the New York government focuses on developing sports parks to enable more citizens to exercise. The government has invested money to provide free fitness programs throughout the city, renovate sports venues in schools and require them to be opened to the public when not in use. The government has also turned smaller spaces around residential areas into pocket parks.

Second, the sports parks system makes sports activities affordable and encourages more people to exercise. The government builds parks without borders to ensure that its citizens can reach nearby sports parks within 10 minutes. More sports facilities are placed in the parks so that New Yorkers can enjoy convenient sports activities free of charge.

Third, with the policy support of the government, New York has become the professional sporting capital of the world. It has become the city with the largest number of professional sports league headquarters and teams in the United States. All professional teams are eligible for the government's tax exemption, and even enjoy stadiums built by the government. For example, the government paid $167 million for the renovation of Yankee Stadium, the home field for the New York Yankees.

Fourth, local sports events have contributed to the cultural branding of the city. New York sports events range from community events, school events, professional events, self-owned brand events, and world events, forming a "pyramid" system to encourage more people to participate in sports. Based on data provided by NYC & Company, a statistical analysis is conducted on the 2018 New York sports events, showing the following characteristics. First, the overall number of sports events held in 2018 is not large. All together, there were 128 events including 8 international ones and 122 domestic ones. Second, professional sports events were organized throughout the year. Third, college sports events gained great popularity. Fourth, the time and place of events were fixed, and events were often of high levels. Last, events were becoming more entertaining, diverse, and well-organized.

2. Sports city development in London

For the past decade, London has ranked the first among over 600 cities in the GSI Cities Index, and has been renowned as "World's Top Sports City". The top-down design and overall management of the government have played an important role in building London into a global sports city. In particular, the Sports London Plan implemented by the London government has promoted the city and its culture.

The practices in London provide the following experience:

First, London has been active in hosting influential sports events, including the Olympics and top-level soccer tournaments. London is relatively conservative in hosting international competitions. Over the last 10 years, only about a dozen sports events were held in London, including the World

Athletics Championships, the Semi-finals and finals of the European Football Championships, the European Aquatics Championships, the UCI World Championships, Women's FIH Hockey World Cup and ICC Cricket World Cup. Although London hosted only a few international events, the great influence of these events still brought London to the top of the GSI Cities Index a ranking that uses sports events as its core evaluation criteria.

Second, London has made sports activities more affordable for its citizens. According to the Sports London Plan, the London government has increased its investment in sports development and built free facilities that are close to residential areas so as to reduce the costs for citizens to participate in sports. It is worth mentioning that vulnerable groups are one of the priorities of the Sports London Plan. It provides help for people with disabilities and economically challenged citizens, and encourages them to take up sports, making sports activities affordable and accessible.

Third, building London into a Global Sports City requires a long-term strategy with specific stages. For example, one of the specific stage goals in the Sports London Plan in 2015 is to increase the sports population in London. London has claimed success in achieving this goal for its sports population has gone up by one million, while sports participants in the UK decreased by 226 000.

Fourthly, the London government has channeled special funding to grassroots sports clubs to promote sports participation and develop a better sports culture. In terms of funding, London prioritizes private sports clubs, which received £2.8 m from the government in 2018.

3. Sports city development in Los Angeles

For nearly a century, Los Angeles has been a synonym for elite sports. It will be the third city to have ever hosted the Olympics three times. In addition, Los Angeles has hosted a series of international championships and champion league, and is renowned as the city of professional sports.

In Los Angeles, there are over 1 000 well-equipped stadiums that can meet the various needs of sports event organizers and sports lovers, and the sports site per capita has reached 38.1 square meters. They are also home stadiums of professional sports teams and the cultural heritage of major sports events. Moreover, these high-standard stadiums in Los Angeles have ensured the development of the top-ranking professional sports teams that have achieved great competition results. Los Angeles has made full use of its well-known stadiums, including the LA Memorial Coliseum and the Rose Bowl Stadium. They are not only the venues for major sports events and the home stadium of famous professional sports teams, but also important tourist attractions. The 2028 Los Angeles Olympic will make full use of existing stadiums, and competitions will be held in four major sports parks. Los

Angeles also encourages non-profit organizations to participate in the preparation work. After the Olympics, these facilities will continue benefiting the citizens.

The features of sports development in Los Angeles are specified as follows:

First, Los Angeles has attached importance to the participation of non-profit organizations, so that its citizens can promote and enjoy their own sports culture. Second, Los Angeles has strived to improve the performance of its professional sports teams, developing its characteristic sports and team culture. Third, LA has hosted events with great international influence, during which the city has innovated its approach in organizing sports games and developed sports event culture. Fourth, LA has improved the usage rate of stadiums and preserved important sports stadiums as cultural heritages. Finally, Los Angeles has encouraged teenagers to participate in sports activities, promoting sustainable development of sports culture.

4. Sports city development in Tokyo

Tokyo, London and New York are the top three global cities. In the ranking of sports cities, Tokyo has twice been crowned as "the World's Top Sports City". International sports events can promote the development of public sports service facilities, which is proved by the case of Tokyo. Tokyo hosted the 18th Summer Olympic Games in 1964 and the FIFA World Cup in 2002. Since these international events, sports population and funding in Tokyo communities have significantly increased, and sports stadiums have also been improved. As a result, Tokyo has been renowned as "the City of Public Sports Services".

Through the case study of Tokyo, the characteristics of its sports development can be summarized as follows:

First, Tokyo has held major international sports events, including the Olympic Games and the FIFA World Cup, to improve the city's sports facilities and the non-physical environment for sports services. Tokyo has also promoted its city culture through the development of public sports services.

Second, the Tokyo government has taken measures to make full use of sports facilities after the events and opened stadiums to the public to ensure the sustainable development of stadiums.

Third, in building itself into a sports city, Tokyo starts from the development of local sports culture and sports services. Tokyo has also promoted its sports culture landmarks, including stadiums, museums, Hall of Fame, and sports theme parks.

Fourth, Tokyo has its own sports culture tradition. For example, every Tokyo sports club has its own well-known stars, loyal fan bases, and club culture. Tokyo emphasize the role sports play in their culture and actively encourage citizens to not only watch games but also participate in sports activities themselves, so as to develop sporting habits and love for exercise.

5. Sports city development in Shanghai

Shanghai has been promoting sports culture for over a decade. What achievements has the city made? Has it accomplished the goal of becoming a well-known international sports city?

As shown in Table 2, Shanghai lagged behind Nanjing in the ranking of the GSI Cities Index from 2016 to 2018. Nanjing ranked the 19th in both 2016 and 2017, the 10th in 2018, and the 11th in 2019. From 2016 to 2019, Shanghai ranked the 36th, 36th, 33rd and 37th respectively.

The rankings indicate that Shanghai fails to achieve its expected goal. In the GSI Events Index, Shanghai falls behind not only international metropolises such as London and Beijing, but also other Chinese cities such as Nanjing and Chengdu.

Shanghai has invested a great deal in sports development. For example, in 2017, the appropriation in the sports industry was nearly RMB 4 billion more than before, and the government

Table 2
The GSI Cities Index

City	2016			2017 Rank	2018			2019		
	Rank	Score	Influential Event		Rank	Score	Influential Event	Rank	Score	Influential Event
London	1	18 694.87	13	1	2	16 494	12	6	10 747	12
Tokyo	3	16 163.21	11	3	1	16 494	12	1	19 867	13
Rio de Janeiro	2	16 632.13	7	2	3	15 713	8	4	13 801	8
Pairs	6	10 934.64	13	6	4	15 342	14	2	16 048	15
Doha	5	12 067.82	10	5	5	12 460	10	5	13 679	10
Mosco	4	13 123.34	14	4	9	12 053	12	7	10 241	11
Beijing	9	7 134.91	7	9	9	7 315	6	8	8 388	7
Nanjing	19	4 939.18	5	19	10	6 740	6	11	6 615	6
Shanghai	36	3 405.98	5	36	33	3 590	6	37	3 446	5
Guangzhou	81	2 185.36	3	81	90	1 961	3	112	1 825	3

Source: Sportal Global Sports Impact (GSI) Cities Index.

Table 3
The 2019 GSI Cities Index

Rank	City	Nation	Score
6	London	United Kingdom	10 717
8	Beijing	China	8 388
11	Nanjing	China	6 615
28	Chengdu	China	4 087
37	Shanghai	China	3 446
113	Kong Kong	China	1 825

Source: https://www.sportcal.com/GSI/GSICitiesIndex.

spending in sports in 2018 was RMB 6.6 billion, which surpassed the total spending in the previous three years. Although the entire sports industry is developing rapidly, its structure is relatively simple, with sports services accounting for half of the industry value. For over a decade, the number of international events held in Shanghai has grown rapidly from 11 in 2001 to 61 in 2017. Sports infrastructure in Shanghai has also developed. The per capita sports site in Shanghai has significantly increased in the past three years, reaching 2.4 in 2020, but there is still a great gap between Shanghai and other sports cities in terms of sports infrastructure. In the last ten years, the number and the floor area of public sports grounds in Shanghai's residential areas have not changed much.

Compared with sports cities in other countries, most of Chinese cities have the following shortcomings in their sports development:

First, although a great number of international events have been held in Chinese cities, the cultural benefits of those events are undervalued. Specifically speaking, Chinese cities have not made full use of the cultural influences of international sports events, and failed to organize events systematically. In addition, the diversified features of different sports cultures in different cities

Fig. 2
The performance of Nanjing, Shenzhen, Tianjin, Chengdu, and Wuhan in the GSI Cities Index(January 1, 2008-October 28, 2020)

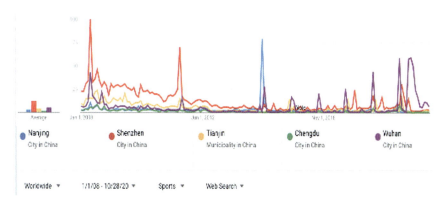

have not been highlighted, and the marketing of sports events have been constrained by limited approaches. According to search results from Google and Baidu, although Shanghai hosts about 70 international sports events every year, most of them attract little international attention. Sportcal's GSI Events Index also shows that in the past decade, only five or six events held in Shanghai have been recognized as influential.

Second, governments did not invest enough in public sports, and the cost for citizens to exercise is too high. This is because, many sports venues are money-oriented and tools to make profits, instead of being people-oriented and making their facilities and events accessible to the public at reasonable prices. In New York, ticket prices for sports venues are set according to age. For example, football fields in New York are free for citizens under 18. Tennis courts and indoor recreation and fitness centers charge customers according to their age, and offer generous discounts for IDNYC holders, teenagers, and seniors. However, sports venues in Shanghai charge the same high price for all age groups, showing little intention to benefit the public.

Third, cities in China have not done enough in building distinctive sports cultures. To become global sports cities, they need to develop their own sports cultures with local characteristics, build sports culture landmarks, and organize more festive sports events.

Fourth, original sports culture resources in China have not been fully studied and utilized. This is because the sports culture hasn't contributed enough to the cities' development. In addition, various factors, including nature, culture, and characteristics of cities, haven't been integrated into the sports culture.

Fifth, sports, tourism, and entertainment haven't worked together very well to build a bigger market for sports. Chinese cities need to launch more projects for sports development, implement more favorable policies, attract various investments, enhance regional coordination, and improve public facilities and service systems.

Sixth, more talents who specialize in both marketing and creative culture are needed. These cities should attract talents to organize sports events, marketing products, and operating the sports industry. They should also encourage more entities to get into the sports market, improve the system of events and sports activities, and hold more festive sports events.

Seventh, the momentum for the consumption and trade of sports culture needs to be improved, and a systematic sports culture should be developed. More entities should enter the Chinese sports market, and sports activities need to be more affordable. Chinese cities need to develop sports fashion consumption field, improve the structure and policy of investment and financing. Moreover, these cities should enhance their capacity for brand operation and further develop sports tourism.

Eighth, development speed, industrial structure, added value and the scale of the sporting goods industry have not met the international standard. In Chinese cities, the sports population is smaller than that of global sports cities, and the structure of the sports industry is not well-balanced. These cities should expand their sports industry parks and upgrade their municipal service system for sports health.

Global Cities and Strategic Communication

Huang Yihui

Chair Professor, Department of Media and Communication, City University of Hong Kong

1. Global city: definition and criteria

The concept of global city comes from geography and urban studies. A global city is a critical node in the global economic network and hasa direct impact on the global community. The main criteria for a global city include: whether it has a range of international financial services; whether it is a dominant player in the trade and economy within the region; whether it is where the headquarters of multinationals and financial institutions are located; whether it has a voice in international affairs or whether it has unique characteristics, such as being a commercial, economic, cultural, political or innovation center. Generally speaking, the criteria for a global city cover many aspects such as economy, culture, livability, environment, transportation, infrastructure and tourism etc. To define a global city, different organizations around the globe use different indicators, including the Global Power City Index (GPCI), Globalization and World Cities Research Network (GaWC), Most Economically Powerful City, Global Cities Index, Global City Competitiveness Index etc.

2. Strategic communication during the formation of a global city

(1) The CPC Theoretical Model.

CPC is a theoretical model I constructed while studying strategic communication. The first C stands for Communication. It can be Mass Communication or Interpersonal Communication. The P has two meanings: Promotion and Prevention. The purpose of communication is either to promote or to prevent, which could be in the form of issue management or crisis management. The last C stands for Context or communication scenarios, which could be online, offline, or a combination of the two.

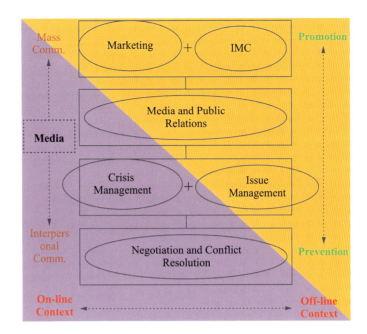

Fig. 1
Diagram of the
CPC model

In short, the CPC model is a model that illustrates how strategic communication is carried out and presents its schematic structure.

(2) City branding and city public relations: the cultivation of a city's image.

The cultivation theory, also known as the engagement theory, was proposed by Gerbner and others. Gerbner's research team conducted a series of analyses of prime-time television content in the 1970s. They found that people who spend more time watching television are more likely to give an overestimation of the level of violence within society. The reason is that the "symbolic reality" conveyed by the mass media has a huge influence on how people perceive reality. Due to a certain tendency of the mass media, the "subjective reality" people perceive deviates from the actual "objective reality". Moreover, media effects are long term, cumulative, and known as the cultivation effects. Through selecting, processing, recording and transmitting symbolic things, the mass media, such as television, allows people to share a social reality that is homogeneous.

Cultivation theory also puts forward two concepts: mainstream effects and resonance effects. Mainstream effects refer to the narrowing differences in positions and behaviors of various groups of TV viewers. This process of mainstreaming includes blurring, blending, and submission. Television blurs the differences generated by culture, politics, economy, region, and class. Hence, people's attitudes are blended with the dominant ideology in television, thereby submitting themselves to the political and economic systems presented in television. This underlines the importance of portraying a good city image in the media. Resonance effects mean that once an impression that viewers get from

TV or other types of mass media is confirmed in reality, they will be fully convinced of it. Thus, the cultivation effect is also enhanced. On the contrary, if viewers' personal experience does not conform to what the media describes, then they would no longer believe whatever the media presents. What we learn from the concept of resonance effects is that to build a global city, it is necessary to provide citizens with actual lived experiences that are congruent with the things viewed on television. It also indicates that issue management and crisis management are fairly important in city branding and city public relations.

(3) City branding and city public relations: theory and model.

According to Xu Deya, there are three types of city public relations: guided, independent and organic ones. The "guided" one refers to the activities for city image promotion through advertisements, videos, etc., which are organized or sponsored by public relations practitioners from government departments and related organizations. The "independent" one refers to the actions of independent producers to promote a city through news, movies, TV series, etc. The "organic" one means that the general public obtains information related to city image from personal experiences, interpersonal communication or social media platforms. Among them, the key points of urban public relations are: first, the covert guidance in the "guided" PR, that is, the audience cannot easily tell whether the information about the city comes from government departments or travel agencies; second, the "independent" type mentioned earlier; third, regarding the "organic" PR, whether the general public actively seeks or passively obtains information related to the city from others.

Also, "engagement and experience" is crucial in PR when social media has become a pervasive instrument of communication. The market strategy focusing on "engagement and experience" redefines our way of thinking. Engagement or experiential marketing intends to fully stimulate and mobilize the audience's senses, emotions, thinking, actions, etc., by offering them something they can view, listen to, touch and feel, so that the audience can be actively involved and develop a relationship with the brand or product promoted. Combining this marketing strategy with UGC (user-generated content) on social media delivers better results for communication. This way of thinking, breaking away from the hypothesis of rational person in the traditional sense, emphasizes that the audience or consumers are both rational and emotional when processing information or buying things. Therefore, the user experience is the key to influencing consumer behavior and brand management.

3. Two cases of experiential marketing

The first case of experiential marketing is the "I AM Canadian" campaign launched by a

Canadian brewing company. On July 1, 2017 the National Day of Canada, a refrigerator full of beer was placed on the street and it challenges people to say "I am Canadian" in six different languages to open the refrigerator and enjoy free beer. In addition to the interactive experience, this campaign conveyed the values of diversity and inclusiveness of Canada as a country of immigrants.

The second case is "Beijing at Four in the Morning". In May 2016, Xinshixiang, a media content provider, collected stories which happened at 4 am in Beijing from its users and posted these stories on its WeChat Official Account on June 16. Xinshixiang also invited users to watch live streams of people sharing their stories at 4 am. Finally, Xinshixiang shot a series of short films that were well received. In this case, Xinshixiang uses the so-called "six-step" approach to user engagement: getting to know your audience, evoking their actions with well-designed and heart-touching slogans, building a "community of shared values", finding the right sponsors to work with, rewarding audience for stepping out of their comfort zone, and helping them reach their full potential. The slogans put forward by Xinshixiang include "There will be a prearranged collective action of staying up late", "We own the whole city when others are asleep" and so on. These slogans advocate for the support for one's personal presence, collective connectedness and participation, as well as coexistence. Most importantly, because of the user engagement, this campaign integrates users' cognition, emotions and actions into marketing, successfully providing users with positive and satisfying experiences both online and offline.

Benchmarking Systems of the Cultural Industry in a City: Practices and Reflections

Zeng Yuan

Head of the Printing and Distribution Office, Publicity Department,

CPC Shanghai Municipal Committee

I will talk about benchmarking systems of the cultural industry in a city. Four main reasons for bringing up this topic are as follows. First of all, it is a requirement for Shanghai and its cultural development to meet the highest international standards. Secondly, the goal of building Shanghai into an international cultural metropolis by the end of the 13th Five-Year Plan is benchmarking Shanghai against other cities. Thirdly, the 13th Five-Year Plan is a critical point for Shanghai, after which there is still a long way to go to build Shanghai into a world-class cultural metropolis. Finally, the benchmarking system is a benchmark to measure the development of cultural industries and test achievements. Cultural development needs to be measured, but it is not easy.

1. Problems: from being subjective to being objective

Culture can be both subjective and objective. Culture can be either a grand narrative of a group or a unique experience of an individual, so it is very difficult to give it a definition. Raymond Williams, a British scholar, once said, "Culture is one of the two or three most complicated words in the English language". In *Culture; a Critical Review of Concepts and Definitions*, two American anthropologists, Alfred L. Kroeber and Clyde Kluckhohn, compiled a list of 164 definitions of "culture" from1871 to 1951, suggesting that different people have different understandings of "culture".

Human resources are playing an increasingly important role in the cultural industry, where talents often are involved in multiple roles. Here I put forward a concept called "humanized products", of which stage performance is a very typical example. On one hand, their value lies on practitioners such as artists or cast members; on the other hand, they are also artworks. That is to say, people who create the products and the products themselves are inseparable. One problem is that practitioners, especially those famous ones, have more say in the cultural industry. Words of well-known practitioners are influential and their practices are easily affected by their subjective view, which means that the decision which ought to be made by the group is affected by their personal feelings. Therefore, the transition from being subjective to objectiveis necessary.

The goal of building an international cultural metropolis is not an isolated one. Instead, it is connected to a long-term development target based on science-based decisions under the benchmarking system. The process of setting goals is also a process of consulting and using indicators to make lateral comparisons and final decisions. When making decisions within the Party and governments, we need to hear opinions and suggestions from insiders, academia, and other fields while maintaining rational thinking.

The indicator system of cultural industry development is used in two ways: evaluating self-development by vertical comparison and knowing relative positions by horizontal comparison. As the saying goes, "know yourself and know your enemy", and in our context, it is "know yourself and know your counterparts". Considering the fast development of city clusters and more fierce regional competition, Shanghai should not only benchmark itself against international metropolises such as New York, Paris, London, Tokyo and Beijing, but also pay close attention to the development of cities in Guangdong and the Yangtze River Delta region as well as a group of provincial capitals.

2. The current situation: difficulties, continuous changes and a better future

The current benchmarking system is composed of three dimensions: quantity, time and subject. In the quantity dimension, quantifiable data clusters are made according to the development norms of an industry. In the time dimension, data within a specific cycle are accumulated so that data can be compared and traced on the time shaft. In the subject dimension, on the basis of consulting indicators concerning the studied subject, indicators of other benchmarking subjects are also included.

The measurement and decision-making concerning the cultural industry are changing, so the indicator system of the industry is also changing continuously. Before the 13th Five-Year Plan, relevant studies focused more on culture itself. However, during the of the 13th Five-Year Plan period, scholars not only paid attention to the culture itself, but also discussed how to promote the integrated development of culture, sports and tourism. In addition to culture-related indicators, tourism indicators and the sports industry indicators should be included. More importantly, indicators reflecting integration should be designed and data collection should be covered accordingly. The previous research and decision-making process did not reflect the aforementioned points.

The upgrading of models and the development of relevant technologies have made data relatively easy to be obtained. Massive cultural subdivisions can be categorized into traditional and emerging ones. The traditional cultural sector, made up of media, art, leisure and entertainment industries, has embraced new technologies and the Internet in recent years. The sector has shifted its focus from self-display to strengthening the interaction between supply and demand, from mass communication to targeted communication. It has become more specialized and information-oriented, making data more widely available. On the other hand, newly emerging industries, including the internet-based cultural service industry and information technology service industry, are the result of the integration of technologies and contents. Data in these industries no longer need to be collected but have become an integral part of the industry.

3. Practices: not seeking a unified solution, but a feasible and effective one

The traditional official practice is to formulate the "Classification of Culture and Related Industries" and compile the "Shanghai Statistical Abstract of Culture" every year so as to set the official statistical method and accumulate data over the years. With the application of and emphasis on big data, unstructured data are playing important roles in government decision-making. For example, Urban Data Group and its usage of data. We studied many other indicator systems, of which the informative "Shanghai Urban Culture Development Index" is very impressive. It uses 21 indicators from five perspectives, including public culture, the cultural industry, the cultural market, cultural innovation and social environment. The annual process data are obtained and final values are calculated through the weighted average of the 21 indicators. We also studied the "World Cities Culture Report". It was a research project first initiated by the Mayor of London in 2007. The research was jointly carried by BOP Consulting, King's College London and Global Cities Institute. This report has several features. First, it proposes a relatively stable data system. The comprehensive analysis of data is carried out from four perspectives, namely, cultural infrastructure, cultural output, cultural consumption and public participation. Second, horizontal comparisons are involved. Since 2008, the number of cities involved has expanded from 5 to 27, covering all major cultural cities in the world. Third, the Report is released every 2—3 years and well-recognized for its reliable and massive data. During the 13th Five-Year Plan period, we selected and reconstructed several indicators based on the World Cities Culture Report, which could be divided into three categories: basic indicators, special indicators and key indicators, forming an indicator system for assessing Shanghai's performance in turning itself into an International Cultural Metropolis.

4. Conclusion: introducing ideas of others, applying them and innovate

Here is my final conclusion. After years of work, I found that "no indicator system can be directly applied" is not an individual case, but a common problem encountered in most benchmarking studies. This problem is worth solving, and solutions to it will be of great value. From the perspective of practical feasibility, we should introduce the ideas of others into our research, apply these ideas while attending to the context of our research and innovate so as to make our research findings more meaningful. Existing research results should be respected, categorized and analyzed. We should, according to our own needs, on the one hand, further analyze the existing data. On the other hand, we should add new data in a timely manner. Meanwhile, we should pay attention to other relevant data, for big data often reveal unknown behavior after being carefully analyzed. Hopefully in the end, we will create a benchmarking system covering both common characters and individual features.

POSTSCRIPT

后记

世界城市日是联合国大会设立的国际日，源自上海世博会的精神遗产。作为"世界城市日"的主题活动之一，2020 全球城市论坛以"提升社区和城市品质"为主题，重点围绕新兴技术与协同治理、宜居城市、未来社区、城市应急管理、城市文化与形象等领域，以及长三角公园城市等主题，展开了为期两天的交流和讨论。

本届论坛共邀请了来自联合国人居署、世界银行、中国房地产业协会、中国城市建设研究院、中国城市和小城镇改革发展中心、上海市委宣传部、上海市住房和城乡建设管理委员会、上海市应急管理局、上海市绿化和市容管理局、上海市奉贤区政府、杭州市下城区政府、上海市浦东新区三林镇政府、上海市徐汇区虹梅街道、深圳市南山区桃园街道办事处、成都市双流区黄水镇政府、上海市大数据中心、上海城市树木生态应用工程技术中心、《探索与争鸣》编辑部、上海市世界城市日事务协调中心等机构的领导，美国哈佛大学、美国南加州大学、美国乔治·华盛顿大学、伦敦大学学院、英国谢菲尔德大学、英国布拉德福大学、英国诺丁汉大学、法国路桥学校、俄罗斯公共管理和行政服务学院、新加坡国立大学、澳大利亚新南威尔士大学、澳大利亚昆士兰科技大学、日本明治大学、日本金泽大学、日本熊本大学、韩国高丽大学和国内的香港大学、香港城市大学、清华大学、浙江大学、上海交通大学、复旦大学、中国人民大学、南京大学、武汉大学、西安交通大学、同济大学、华东师范大学、吉林大学、东南大学、中国传媒大学、中国社科院、华中师范大学、河海大学、上海体育学院、湖南工商大学、浙江农林大学、安徽农业大学等高校的学者，以及丹麦哥本哈根城市规划设计事务所、上海大众、商汤科技、Urban Space 等企业的专家，共商全球城市社区品质提升的相关话题。中外嘉宾在开幕式、主旨演讲、平行分论坛、主题论坛和闭幕式等环节，先后发表了致辞、主旨演讲、主题演讲、特邀报告和互动讨论。论坛形成了一系列富有启示性和前瞻性的观点和研究成果，为此我们特编辑此书，将本次论坛的观点和宝贵研究成果与读者分享。

本届全球城市论坛在上海交通大学徐汇校区举行，得到了上海交通大学党委办公室、宣传部、学生指导委员会、文科科研处、国际合作与交流处、发展联络处、中国城市治理研究院、国际与公共事务学院、网络信息中心等部门和单位领导的大力支持。

本书由上海市人民政府发展研究中心城市研究处负责全书编辑工作。本书的出版得到了上海交通大学、世界银行、上海外国语大学、上海世纪出版集团格致出版社的大力支持。上海交通大学中国城市治理研究院常务副院长吴建南教授、上海交通大学国际与公共事务学院党委副书记李振全教授、上海交通大学国际与公共事务学院副院长张录法教授、上海交通大学中国城市治理研究院办公室主任徐柳青老师、国内合作与研究部副主任李超老师等，在论坛会议资料、现场录音、摄影图片收集和文字审校方面给予了鼎力帮助。上海外国语大学赵美娟教授、黄协安教授及其学生志愿者团队等在文稿整理和翻译方面做了大量的工作。格致出版社副总编辑忻雁翔女士为本书的编辑出版付出了辛勤劳动。上海市人民政府发展研究中心科研处、信息处、秘书处的同仁也给予了大力支持，在此一并表示感谢！

World Cities Day is an international day established by the United Nations General Assembly, and derives from the spiritual legacy of the Shanghai World Expo. As one of the theme events of World Cities Day, the Global Urban Forum 2020, with the theme of "Valuing our Communities and Cities", focused on the areas of collaborative governance, liveable cities, future communities, emergency management, urban culture, as well as the themes of garden city development in Yangtze River Delta.

Leaders from UN-Habitat, the World Bank, China Real Estate Association, China Urban Construction Design and Research Institute Co., the China Center for Urban Development, Publicity Department of CPC Shanghai Committee, the Shanghai Municipal Commission of Housing and Urban-Rural Development, Shanghai Emergency Management Bureau, Shanghai Municipal Landscaping Management and Supervision Office, Fengxian District, Xiacheng District, Sanlin Township in Pudong New Area, Hongmei Subdistrict in Xuhui District, Taoyuan Subdistrict in Nanshan District, Huangshui Township in Shuangliu District, Shanghai Big Data Center, Shanghai Center for Urban Trees Ecological Applied, *Exploration and Free Views*, the Shanghai World Cities Day Coordination Centre, and other organizations were invited to this year's Forum. Centre, and leaders and experts from Harvard University, University of South California, George Washington University, University College London, University of Sheffield, University of Bradford, University of Nottingham, Ecole Nationale des Ponts et Chaussées, The Russian Presidential Academy of National Economy and Public Administration, National University of Singapore, University of New South Wales, Queensland

University of Technology, Meiji University, Kanazawa University, Kumamoto University, Korea University, University of Hong Kong, City University of Hong Kong, Tsinghua University, Zhejiang University, Shanghai Jiao Tong University, Fudan University, Renmin University of China, Nanjing University, Wuhan University, Xi'an Jiao Tong University, Tongji University, East China Normal University, Jilin University, Southeast University, Communication University of China, the Chinese Academy of Social Sciences, Central China Normal University, Hohai University, Shanghai University of Sport, Hunan University of Technology and Business, Zhejiang Agriculture and Forestry University, Anhui Agricultural University and other universities, the manager of Gehl Architects Finance & Communication ApS, SAIC Volkswagen, SenseTimes, Urban Space, to discuss topics related to valuing the communities and cities. Chinese and foreign guests delivered speeches, keynote addresses, keynote speeches, invited presentations and interactive discussions during the opening ceremony, keynote speeches, parallel sub-forums, thematic forums and closing ceremony. A series of insightful and forward-looking perspectives and research results have emerged from the Forum, for which we have compiled this book to share with readers the perspectives and valuable research results of the Forum.

This year's Global City Forum was held at the Xuhui Campus of Shanghai Jiao Tong University with the support of the leaders of the Party Committee Office, the Propaganda Department, the Student Guidance Committee, the Office of Liberal Arts and Research, the Office of International Cooperation and Exchange, the Development Liaison Office, the China Institute of Urban Governance, the School of International and Public Affairs and the Network Information Centre of Shanghai Jiao Tong University.

The City Research Division of the Development Research Centre of the Shanghai Municipal People's Government were responsible for the editing job of this book. For the publication of the book, we're indebted to Shanghai Jiao Tong University, the World Bank, Shanghai Foreign Studies University, Truth & Wisdom Press of Shanghai Century Publishing Group for their kind support. Jiannan Wu, Zhenquan Li, Lufa Zhang, Liuqing Xu, Chao Li and other leaders and experts from the School of International and Public Affairs and the China Institute of Urban Governance of Shanghai Jiao Tong University,have given us valuable assistance in collecting procedural materials, meeting records, photographs and text-proofing. Meijuan Zhao, Xie'an Huang and the student volunteers from Shanghai International Studies University have made great contributions in text editing and translation, and Yanxiang Xin has made great contributions in publication. The colleagues from the Scientific Research Division, the Information Division and the Secretariat of the Development Research Center of the Shanghai Municipal People's Government, have made support to make the book a reality. We're grateful to them all!

图书在版编目(CIP)数据

提升社区和城市品质:联合国第七届世界城市日全
球城市论坛实录/上海市人民政府发展研究中心编.—
上海:格致出版社:上海人民出版社,2022.9
ISBN 978 - 7 - 5432 - 3346 - 1

Ⅰ.①提…　Ⅱ.①上…　Ⅲ.①城市管理-研究-上海
Ⅳ.①F299.275.1

中国版本图书馆 CIP 数据核字(2022)第 045054 号

责任编辑　　忻雁翔
装帧设计　　人马艺术设计·储平

提升社区和城市品质
——联合国第七届世界城市日全球城市论坛实录
上海市人民政府发展研究中心　编

山	版	格致山版社
		上海人民出版社
		(201101　上海市闵行区号景路 159 弄 C 座)
发	行	上海人民出版社发行中心
印	刷	上海商务联西印刷有限公司
开	本	787×1092　1/16
印	张	36.75
字	数	764,000
版	次	2022 年 9 月第 1 版
印	次	2022 年 9 月第 1 次印刷

ISBN 978 - 7 - 5432 - 3346 - 1/F · 1437
定　　价　　268.00 元